MICROSOFT® CERTIFIED SYSTEMS ENGINEER
& MICROSOFT® CERTIFIED SYSTEMS ADMINISTRATOR

MCSE/MCSA Managing and Maintaining a Windows® Server 2003 Environment Study Guide

(Exam 70-290)

Anil Desai

McGraw-Hill/Osborne

New York   Chicago   San Francisco   Lisbon   London   Madrid
Mexico City   Milan   New Delhi   San Juan   Seoul   Singapore   Sydney   Toronto

McGraw-Hill/Osborne
2100 Powell Street, 10th Floor
Emeryville, California 94608
U.S.A.

To arrange bulk purchase discounts for sales promotions, premiums, or fund-raisers, please contact **McGraw-Hill**/Osborne at the above address. For information on translations or book distributors outside the U.S.A., please see the International Contact Information page immediately following the index of this book.

MCSE/MCSA Managing and Maintaining a Windows® Server 2003 Environment Study Guide (Exam 70-290)

34567890 DOC DOC 019876

Book p/n 0-07-222323-5 and CD p/n 0-07-222324-3
parts of
ISBN 0-07-222322-7

Publisher Brandon A. Nordin	**Acquisitions Coordinator** Jessica Wilson	**Composition** Tabitha M. Cagan, George Charbak
Vice President & **Associate Publisher** Scott Rogers	**Technical Editor** Larry Passo	**Illustrators** Kathleen Edwards, Melinda Lytle, Lyssa Wald
Acquisitions Editor Timothy Green	**Copy Editor** Bob Campbell	**Series Design** Roberta Steele
Project Editors Betsy Manini, Jenn Tust	**Proofreader** Mike McGee	**Cover Series Design** Peter Grame
	Indexer Valerie Perry	

This book was composed with Corel VENTURA™ Publisher.

DEDICATION

To Monica

ABOUT THE AUTHOR

Anil Desai, MCSA, MCSE, MCSD, MCDBA, is an independent consultant based in Austin, TX. He specializes in evaluating, developing, implementing, and managing solutions based on Microsoft technologies. He has worked extensively with Microsoft's server products and .NET platform.

Anil is the author of several other technical books, including *Windows 2000 Directory Services Administration Study Guide* (Sybex, 2001), *Windows NT Network Management: Reducing Total Cost of Ownership* (New Riders, 1999), and *SQL Server 2000 Backup and Recovery* (McGraw-Hill/Osborne, 2000). He has made dozens of conference presentations at national events and is also a contributor to magazines. When he's not busy doing techie-type things, Anil enjoys cycling in and around Austin, playing electric guitar and drums, and playing video games. For more information, please contact him at anil@austin.rr.com.

About the Technical Editor

Larry Passo has over 20 years experience in the computer industry as a developer, design engineer, trainer, and consultant. He holds certifications as a Microsoft Certified Systems Engineer (MCSE) and as a Microsoft Certified Systems Administrator (MCSA). He lives in Irvine, California, with his wife, Debra, and son, Hank. In his free time, he develops custom network administrative applications that are available through his web site, www.AdminPowerTools.com.

CONTENTS

PREFACE

In This Book

This book is organized to serve as an in-depth review for the Microsoft's Exam 70-290, "Managing and Maintaining a Microsoft Windows Server 2003 Environment." This exam is designed to test candidates' experience in performing important systems administration tasks using the Windows Server 2003 product in a network environment. The skills that are tested are all important ones in the real world, and you'll have to have a solid understanding of how Microsoft's latest server operating system works in order to pass the exam.

This book is designed to help you toward that goal. Each chapter covers a major aspect of the exam. The technical information begins with important background information that will help you understand the underlying concepts that are related to a particular tools, feature, or procedure that's included with Windows Server 2003. You'll learn about why you should care about these topics, and how understanding them can benefit you and your organization. Then, drawing on this information, you'll read details about how you can perform important Windows Server 2003 systems administration tasks. Finally, each chapter ends with a review of the information presented and, of course, practice questions that will help you test your understanding. All of this information will help prepare you to tackle Microsoft's Exam 70-290, and to work with Windows Server 2003 in the real world!

On the CD-ROM

For information about the CD-ROM, please see the Appendix.

Exam Readiness Checklist

At the end of the Introduction, you will find an Exam Readiness Checklist. This table has been constructed to allow you to cross-reference the official exam objectives with the objectives as they are presented and covered in this book. The checklist also allows you to gauge your level of expertise on each objective at the outset of your studies. This should allow you to check your progress and make sure you spend the time you need on more difficult or unfamiliar sections. References have been provided for the objective exactly as the vendor presents it, along with the section of the study guide that covers that objective and a chapter and page reference.

In Every Chapter

We've created a set of chapter components that call your attention to important items, reinforce important points, and provide helpful exam-taking hints. Take a look at what you'll find in every chapter:

- Every chapter begins with the **Certification Objectives**—what you need to know in order to pass the section on the exam dealing with the chapter topic. The Objective headings identify the objectives within the chapter, so you'll always know an objective when you see it!

- **Exam Watch** notes call attention to information about, and potential pitfalls in, the exam. These helpful hints are written by authors who have taken the exams and received their certification—who better to tell you what to worry? They know what you're about to go through!

- **Practice Exercises** are interspersed throughout the chapters. These are step-by-step exercises that enable you to get the hands-on experience you need in order to pass the exams. They help you master skills that are likely to be an area of focus on the exam. Don't just read through the exercises; they are hands-on practice that you should be comfortable completing. Learning by doing is an effective way to increase your competence with a product. You will find that these exercises are a great way to get familiar with the many features of Windows Server 2003, and they'll help prepare you for any simulation questions that you'll see on the Managing and Maintaining a Windows Server 2003 Environment exam.

- **On the Job** notes describe the issues that come up most often in real-world settings. They provide a valuable perspective on certification- and product-related topics. They point out common mistakes and address questions that have arisen from on-the-job discussions and experience.

- **Inside the Exam** sidebars highlight some of the most common and confusing problems that students encounter when taking a live exam. Designed to anticipate what the exam will emphasize, getting inside the exam will help ensure you know what you need to know to pass the exam. You can get a leg up on how to respond to those difficult-to-understand questions by focusing extra attention on these sidebars.

■ **Scenario and Solution** sections lay out potential problems and solutions in a quick-to-read format.

■ The **Certification Summary** is a succinct review of the chapter and a restatement of salient points regarding the exam.

■ The **Two-Minute Drill** at the end of every chapter is a checklist of the main points of the chapter. It can be used for last-minute review.

■ The **Self Test** offers questions similar to those found on the certification exams. The answers to these questions, as well as explanations of the answers, can be found at the end of each chapter. By taking the Self Test after completing each chapter, you'll reinforce what you've learned from that chapter while becoming familiar with the structure of the exam questions.

■ The **Lab Question** at the end of the Self Test section offers a unique and challenging question format that requires the reader to understand multiple chapter concepts to answer correctly. These questions are more complex and more comprehensive than the other questions, as they test your ability to take all the knowledge you have gained from reading the chapter and apply it to complicated, real-world situations. These questions are aimed to be more difficult than what you will find on the exam. If you can answer these questions, you have proven that you know the subject!

Some Pointers

Once you've finished reading this book, set aside some time to do a thorough review. You might want to return to the book several times and make use of all the methods it offers for reviewing the material:

1. *Reread all the Two-Minute Drills*, or have someone quiz you. You also can use the drills as a way to do a quick cram before the exam. You might want to make some flash cards out of 3 × 5 index cards that have the Two-Minute Drill material on them.

2. *Reread all the Exam Watch notes*. Remember that these notes are written by authors who have taken the exam and passed. They know what you should expect—and what you should be on the lookout for.

3. *Review all the Scenario & Solution sections* for quick problem solving.

4. *Retake the Self Tests*. Taking the tests right after you've read the chapter is a good idea, because the questions help reinforce what you've just learned.

However, it's an even better idea to go back later and do all the questions in the book in one sitting. Pretend that you're taking the live exam. (When you go through the questions the first time, you should mark your answers on a separate piece of paper. That way, you can run through the questions as many times as you need to until you feel comfortable with the material.)

5. *Complete the Exercises.* Did you do the exercises when you read through each chapter? If not, do them! These exercises are designed to cover exam topics, and there's no better way to get to know this material than by practicing. Be sure you understand why you are performing each step in each exercise. If there is something you are not clear on, reread that section in the chapter.

ACKNOWLEDGMENTS

Writing a book (especially one as large as this one) involves a lot of work. Of course, the author is only one part of the overall process. Therefore, I'd like to take thank many different people that have helped bring you the polished product you're looking at right now.

Many people at McGraw-Hill/Osborne worked hard on the creation of this book, and deserve recognition. I would like to thank: Elizabeth Campbell, Robert Campbell, Tim Green, Gareth Hancock, Betsy Manini, Brandon Nordin, Scott Rogers, and Jessica Wilson. Their hard work and experience have launched a great series of books that I'm sure readers will find to be very valuable in their certification studies.

Although I'd like to take credit for writing every technical fact, procedure, exercise, and practice exam question correctly on the first try, that's rarely the case when writing a book manuscript. That's why I'd like to thank Larry Passo for doing an excellent job of verifying the technical details in this book, and for adding useful technical (and some nontechnical) comments.

Also, I'd like to thank VMWare, Inc. (www.vmware.com) for the donation of the use of their VMWare Workstation product. Through the use of this virtual machine software, I was able to quickly and easily simulate the many different server configurations that you'll find throughout this book.

Finally, I'd like to thank the many IT professionals that I've worked with over the years. Although their names are far too numerous to mention here, much of the knowledge that I've gained has been through interactions with other IT professionals and from learning about their experiences.

All of these people have helped ensure that the book that you're reading is of the highest quality and value!

INTRODUCTION

As you already know, this book is designed to prepare you for Microsoft Exam 70-290, "Managing and Maintaining a Windows Server 2003 Environment." In this section, we'll take a look at some important information about the exam, and what you need to do to successfully prepare for the test.

Preparing for Exam 70-290

There are several important steps that you should take before you attempt to take Microsoft's 70-290 certification exam. If you've taken many Microsoft exams in the past, chances are, you're familiar with the basic format and requirements for these tests. In this section, you'll see some basic information that will help you prepare specifically for Exam 70-290.

About the Exam Objectives

It's just as important to fully understand a technical topic as it is to know how to implement it. Therefore, the approach I've used in this book is to first provide a thorough discussion of the theory and concepts related to some technology. Then, through the use of demonstrations and descriptions, I outline the processes that you must carry out in order to implement the technology. Don't be tempted to skip to the procedural stuff only—remember, almost anyone can click through a series of screens in a Windows wizard. "Real" IT professionals will understand all of the options that they're offered and will be able to make recommendations and informed decisions.

The focus of the Microsoft exam (and, consequently, this book) is on the tasks that systems administrators will need to perform in order to manage a network environment that supports Windows Server 2003. Specifically, the major objectives for Exam 70-290 include the following:

- Managing and Maintaining Physical and Logical Devices
- Managing Users, Computers, and Groups
- Managing and Maintaining Access to Resources
- Managing and Maintaining a Server Environment
- Managing and Implementing Disaster Recovery

You'll notice that the keywords "managing" and/or "maintaining" appear in all of the objectives. The purpose of this exam is to test your ability to work with Windows Server 2003 in a networked environment. Specifically, you'll need to know various ways in which you can perform common tasks such as setting up new users and groups, managing security settings, implementing backup and recovery, and performing other general Windows Server 2003 tasks. Each of these objective areas includes many different areas of detail. For more information on those items, see the "Exam Readiness Checklist." Of course, we'll also be covering all of these topics in detail throughout this book.

Finally, if you've taken Microsoft's Windows 2000 Server Administration Exam (Exam 70-215), you may have noticed that this list seems considerably more focused than that exam. For example, there are several content areas that were covered previously but that are no longer covered on Exam 70-290, including the installation of the operating system, and automated installation methods. You'll also find that the Exam Preparation Guide lacks coverage of basic networking features, including DHCP, DNS, and other services.

Don't let this fool you—understanding these concepts will be helpful (both as you take this exam and in the real world). In order to get the most out of preparing for these certification exams, you should avoid trying to learn just the bare minimum to pass the exam. And if you plan to pursue further certifications (perhaps on the way to gaining an MCSA or MCSE credential), it's likely that these items will be covered on one or more of those exams.

e x a m

ⓦ a t c h *Although this is not commonly done, Microsoft does reserve the right to change exam objectives. Before you take the exam, be sure to take a look at the* *Exam Preparation Guide for Exam 70-290 at www.microsoft.com/traincert. The Guide will include information about when it was last updated.*

Prerequisites: Experience Counts

I often get questions asking about the value of certification vs. the value of experience in the IT industry: What's more important to employers? Which should I get first? How do I get one without the other? These are all excellent questions. The answers, unfortunately, are not always all that easy. The best (and easiest) answer is that both certifications and experience are important. Since you're reading this book, you probably already understand the value of certification.

The Exam Preparation Guide for Exam 70-290 mentions that the ideal candidates for this test will have 6–12 months of experience administering client and network operating systems in "the typically complex computing environment of medium to large companies." Although this level of experience will definitely help you on the exam, in my opinion, it's not absolutely necessary. If you've had a reasonable amount of exposure to working with Microsoft's network operating systems, you'll likely have enough knowledge to begin preparing for the exam.

Many IT professionals are faced with a dilemma: certification requires experience, but many organizations want employees to be certified before they're placed in positions that will provide them with that experience. Although this can be a frustrating situation, keep in mind that you can learn about Windows Server 2003 in many different ways. For example, you might be able to volunteer some time working in a community computer lab (perhaps at a local library). Or, you might be able to set up a test environment that provides some basic experience with the product. And, you can definitely benefit from the technical content and many exercises that are included in this book. In any case, it's definitely possible to study for and pass Exam 70-290, even if you don't fit into the category of an "ideal candidate."

You should always remember that the ultimate goal of learning about any technology is to apply it to improve some business situation. When dealing with network operating systems, this generally means that you should be able to identify which features will be able to help your organization and the users that you support. Although you might be able to memorize a collection of facts before you take the exam, Microsoft will challenge you by forcing you to apply the information that you've learned. This is for good reason: In the real world, your employer and your coworkers will expect you to know how to perform real-world administrative tasks. Few will be impressed with your ability to memorize Windows Server 2003 trivia. Keep this in mind as you read through the technical information and perform the exercises in this book.

Setting Up a Test Environment

In an ideal world, you'd have an entire system of computers (including servers, clients, and network devices) at your disposal. Whenever you wanted to test something for your real environment, you could use a test environment that very closely mirrors your production environment. You would even have enough hardware and software resources to set up dozens of extra machines in order to performance load-testing and monitor performance before you go "live" with whatever you're implementing.

However, we all live in the real world, where things (at least for most of us) are quite different. First and foremost, few of us have the budget to purchase an entire test environment and set it up just to test some configuration settings. Second, even if we could purchase the hardware and software required, managing that environment could be a full-time job. And, often changes have to be made quickly and efficiently. That means that, when you're preparing for Exam 70-290, you need to make the best of the resources that you have available.

So what should you have available for testing configuration settings and for learning about how to use Windows Server 2003? Well, at a bare minimum, you can get through many of the exercises in this book by using just a single Windows Server 2003 computer. You'll be able to walk through configuration steps and work with the user interface to accomplish important tasks. In fact, I used only a single computer to write most of the exercises in this book. Keep in mind that the "server" that you use should not be relied upon by other users in your environment. Also, you might want to take advantage of Microsoft trial version of the Windows Server 2003 operating system (see www.microsoft.com/servers for more details). If you're going to be preparing for the exam primarily from home, you may be able to set up a dual-boot configuration on one of your current machines (see the Windows Server 2003 Help and Support Center for more information on multiple-boot configurations). Of course, if the company you are working for has a test environment or a training lab, you can probably take advantage of those resources as well.

In order to truly test your configuration in a client/server environment, it would be helpful to have at least one client in addition to the server. This can be helpful for learning and testing various features of Windows Server 2003. For example, in Chapter 4, you'll see how to set permissions on resources that are accessed over the network. And in Chapter 7, you'll learn several methods for managing Windows Server 2003 from a remote computer. Although you could perform these operations on a single machine, you'll learn more by using separate client and server systems.

Of course, you could go even further. If you want to test advanced networking features and multiple-server configurations, you could implement routers, switches, and even WAN connections. The cost to do this would be far higher, so it may not be all that valuable. However, in general, setting up new network environments can lead to great learning opportunities. As many systems administrators can attest, it's rare for any two environments to have the exact same problems and solutions.

On Exam 70-290, you can expect pretty much all of the questions to focus on various tools, technologies, and techniques related to the Windows Server 2003 product. That's the obvious part. Although the focus on this exam is not related to managing the Active Directory, you'll find that many scenarios include environments that are running in Active Directory environments. That means that you'll need a basic understanding of the Active Directory Users and Computers administrative tool, as well as some familiarity with the purpose and function of Active Directory domains. You'll read some additional information about setting up the Active Directory in Chapter 1.

Additionally, you can expect many of the questions on Exam 70-290 to present some basic business and technical information about an organization. Given that information, it will be your job to determine the best solution. These goals may range from implementing a new server to troubleshooting file system permissions. In all cases, however, you should be sure to read through all of the information that's provided. Although some of it may not be relevant, the parts that are important could easily make the difference between answering a question correctly and getting it wrong.

Other Learning Resources

In addition to all of the technical content that you'll find in this book, there are various other resources that can provide you with useful information. Although this is by no means a complete list, I can point you to some resources that I've found to be very helpful as I've looked for technical information or details about certification. This list of resources includes:

- **Coworkers**   An often-overlooked source of technical information can be people you work with. For example, if you're a systems administrator, you might be able to learn a lot from some people in your organization's network administration group. Or, you could learn about the "black arts" practiced by the mystics that manage your SQL Server or Exchange Server installations. Sometimes, offering a coworker a free lunch can be the cheapest and most cost-effective training method!

- **Consultants**   If your organization uses consultants from time to time, ask your management about whether you can get a little of their time (or, better yet, just shadow them for a little while), to learn something new. Of course, be sure that you're not getting in the way and that it's okay with the consultant for you to hound them around. I've learned a lot about specific topics by talking with individuals that specialize in certain technical areas, just by working with them for just a few hours. That was definitely time well spent for myself (and the organization that I was working for).

■ **Web sites** One of my favorite quotes is, "Freedom of the press belongs to those who own presses." For hundreds of years, this was definitely true. You may have the best ideas in the world (and the freedom to express them), but how would you get this information out to the people who might want it? Well, the Internet has changed a lot of that. Now, in most parts of the world, you can create a web site with a negligible amount of money. The result is that there's a lot of information available on the Internet that simply wasn't available a decade ago. When it comes to IT, there's no shortage of technical information online, and you can find huge volumes of valuable information (often for free) by simply performing a web search. Start with a search engine such as Google (www.google.com) or Yahoo! (www.yahoo.com). You'll probably find more information that you can read in a lifetime (which presents a different challenge—having too much information at your disposal). I have a few words of advice regarding Internet resources, however: Be sure to consider the source of the information that you're reading (for example, you don't want to hear vendors performing an "objective comparison" between their product and that of another company). And, you should know that a lot of the information that you'll encounter hasn't been peer-reviewed or verified for the accuracy of information. Still, if you're careful, you can find lots of valuable information.

■ **Newsgroups** An often-overlooked (but extremely useful) Internet protocol is the Network News Transport Protocol (NNTP). NNTP was designed to allow users to collaborate, sharing information and ideas, over the Internet. Microsoft has a public news server that is accessible to everyone. In order to access it, you'll have to have a newsreader application (Microsoft's Outlook Express includes newsreading functionality, as do many other freeware, shareware, and commercial news reader applications). Microsoft's news server is accessible at the address of msnews.microsoft.com (this is the server address that you'll need to specify in your news server application), and you can just log on anonymously. For more information, see http://support.microsoft.com. As shown in the following illustration, you can access any of thousands of discussion groups (many of which have thousands of messages in them). If you have a specific question, or if you just want opinions and feedback from your peers, be sure to take advantage of the newsgroups.

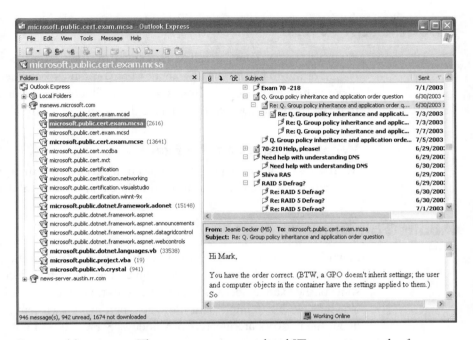

■ **Print publications** There are many specialized IT magazines and, of course, other books that can help you fill in gaps in your knowledge or to keep you on top of improvements and changes in the products you use and support. One magazine that I often read (and contribute to) is *Microsoft Certified Professional Magazine*, which you can find more information about at www.mcpmag.com. You can find out about other print publications at a newsstand, or by just doing a web search.

My point in mentioning all of this is that the current IT landscape has evolved to provide you with *many* opportunities to learn and increase your skill set. I am pleased that you've decided to make this book one of the resources that will help you achieve certification in Windows Server 2003, and I (along with the editing team at McGraw-Hill/Osborne) have gone to great lengths to ensure the value of this book.

Before you take the exam, be sure to brush up on any information that you're not completely comfortable with. Although this book is designed to be a complete resource that covers all of the topics that you will encounter on Microsoft's Exam, it can be helpful to take the time to take advantage of other resources. Sometimes, just hearing the information in another context can be the key.

About Exam 70-290

Whether you've taken a dozen Microsoft certification exams, or this will be your first, it's important to have some idea about what you can expect when you ultimately sit down to take Exam 70-290. In this section, we'll look at some important information that you should know before you tackle the exam.

What to Expect on the Exam

Microsoft's certification program has been in existence for many years, and the company has worked hard to ensure that its exams remain valid and challenging.

About This Book

A writer faces numerous challenges in writing technical certification books, and although I've written several, each new one involves some important decisions. For example, some of the exam objectives refer to concepts that pretty much stand on their own. You may be able to implement file system permissions without really knowing much about the network architecture of Windows Server 2003 or understanding the details of the Active Directory. Other exam objectives cover many different topic areas and rely on a basic understanding of many concepts. So, the challenge is to provide as much technical information as possible without straying too far from the exam objectives. In writing this book, I've tried to err on the side of including too much information instead of not enough. In some cases, you might not see a specific exam question that focuses on some background knowledge, but in almost all cases, I think the additional information will help you out, overall—both on the exam and in the real world.

About the Exercises

One of the best ways to learn is by actually doing something. Of course, you must first have some basic knowledge. But when you actually walk through the process of implementing a new feature of Windows Server 2003, you should be able to get a very good feel for how things work. In my opinion, a lot of exercises in various technical books seem to focus on the simplest of operations. For example, an exercise will walk through a two-step procedure for creating a new group. Fortunately for all of us, Microsoft has gone to great lengths to make all versions of its Windows operating systems as easy to set up, configure, and maintain as possible. Most systems administrators (and users, for that matter) would have little difficulty using the Active Directory Users and Computers tool to create a new group.

However, the real challenge lies in understanding the purpose and function of groups, and, drawing on this understanding, to implement them in a way that makes the most sense for a specific organization. You'll find all of these types of information covered within the content of every chapter in this book. And, I hope you'll find that many of the exercises walk you through more than just the basics of working with Windows Server 2003's many tools and features.

Some Final Words

Judging by the physical weight of this book, you're probably already aware that there's a great deal of information that you must learn about Windows Server 2003, prior to taking Exam 70-290. I highly recommend that you pace yourself as you walk through the content of this book. That's especially true if you have not worked extensively with previous versions of Microsoft's server operating systems. The content has been logically organized so that you can work at your own rate. Still, there's a lot of information you must process.

However, with enough patience and hard work, I believe, you'll be well prepared to tackle Microsoft's Exam 70-290 (and any further exams you plan to take). Finally, if you have any questions, comments, or feedback about the book, please feel free to send me an e-mail message at anil@austin.rr.com. I'll try to respond as quickly as possible. With all of this said, it's time to dive into the technical content. Let's get started!

Exam Readiness Checklist

Official Objective	Study Guide Coverage	Ch #	Pg #	Beginner	Intermediate	Expert
Managing and Maintaining Physical and Logical Devices		2, 5, 8				
Manage basic disks and dynamic disks	Configure, manage, and troubleshoot server disks using the Disk Management tool	5				
Monitor server hardware.	Configure, manage, and monitor server hardware	2				
Optimize server disk performance	Monitor and optimize server hardware performance	8				
Troubleshoot server hardware devices	Troubleshooting Hardware Devices	2				

Exam Readiness Checklist

Official Objective	Study Guide Coverage	Ch #	Pg #	Beginner	Intermediate	Expert
Install and configure server hardware devices	Installing & Configuring Software	2				
Managing Users, Computers, and Groups		3				
Manage local, roaming, and mandatory user profiles	Manage local, roaming, and mandatory user profiles	3				
Create and manage computer accounts in an Active Directory environment	Create and manage groups	3				
Create and manage user accounts	Create, manage, and troubleshoot user accounts	3				
Troubleshoot computer account	Create and manage computer accounts	3				
Troubleshoot user accounts	Create, manage, and troubleshoot user accounts	3				
Troubleshoot user authentication issues	Create, manage, and troubleshoot user accounts	3				
Managing and Maintaining Access to Resources						
Configure access to shared folders	Create and manage shared folders	4				
Troubleshoot Terminal Services	Manage and troubleshoot Terminal Services	4				
Configure file system permissions	Manage file system security	4				
Troubleshooting Access to Files and Shared Folders	Create and manage shared folders	4				

Exam Readiness Checklist

Official Objective	Study Guide Coverage	Ch #	Pg #	Beginner	Intermediate	Expert
Managing and Maintaining a Server Environment		4, 7, 8				
Monitor and analyze events	Track performance using Performance Logs and Alerts, Event Viewer, and other tools	8				
Manage software update infrastructure	Manage Windows operating system updates	7				
Manage software site licensing	Understand and manage software licensing	7				
Manage servers remotely	Manage servers remotely	7				
Troubleshoot print queues	Configure, manage, and troubleshoot printers and print queues	4				
Monitor system performance	Monitor system performance using System Monitor; Monitor and optimize server hardware performance	8				
Monitor file and print servers	Monitor system performance using System Monitor	8				
Monitor and optimize a server environment for application performance	Monitor system performance using System Monitor; Monitor and optimize server hardware performance	8				
Manage a web server	Configure and manage an IIS web server	6				

Exam Readiness Checklist

Official Objective	Study Guide Coverage	Ch #	Pg #	Beginner	Intermediate	Expert
Managing and Implementing Disaster Recovery						
Perform system recovery for a server	Perform system recovery for a server	6				
Manage backup procedures	Understand backup concepts, procedures, and operations; Restore data and manage backup media using Windows Backup	6				
Recover from server hardware failure	Perform system recovery for a server	6				
Restore backup data	Restore data and manage backup media using Windows Backup	6				
Schedule backup jobs	Create and schedule backups using Windows Backup	6				

MICROSOFT® CERTIFIED SYSTEMS ENGINEER
& MICROSOFT® CERTIFIED SYSTEMS ADMINISTRATOR

1

An Introduction to Windows Server 2003

CHAPTER OBJECTIVES

1.01   Understand the Windows Server 2003

1.02   Install Windows Server 2003

1.03   Understand the Active Directory

    Two-Minute Drill

Taking Exam 70-290 may be your first step toward becoming an MCSA and/or an MCSE. And, preparing for that exam will be your first in-depth look at the many features of Microsoft's server-side network operating system. If you're new to working with the Windows Server 2003 product, you should know some basic information before you dive into the technical details that are presented throughout this book.

Therefore, in this chapter, we'll look at several different areas that are not included in Microsoft's Exam 70-290. Specifically, you'll receive an overview of the Windows Server 2003 operating system platform, including the various editions that are available. Then, we'll look at the process of installing a new server with this operating system. Finally, we'll look at one of the most important features in Microsoft's server operating systems: the Active Directory.

Even though the Exam Preparation Guide doesn't include specific bullet points that cover these areas, the information should be very useful, both on the exam and in the real world. Let's get started by looking at some basic information about Windows Server 2003.

If you've been using Windows Server 2003 for quite some time and you want to cover only the topics that are required for the exam, you can skip this chapter. Note, however, that you'll be missing out on some basic information that might be helpful to know when taking the exam.

CERTIFICATION OBJECTIVE 1.01

Understanding Windows Server 2003

One of the most important aspects of the job of an IT professional is to match technical solutions to business problems. It's not enough that you understand how to perform technical procedures; you must be able to figure out the best way to apply technology to meet certain goals. When it comes to working with network operating systems, it can be helpful to know the key features of the product, and how they fit with the environment that you're working in.

In this section, we'll take a look at the history of Microsoft's Windows operating systems. Then, I'll try to answer what's likely to be one of the most burning questions in your mind: "What's new in Windows Server 2003?" Finally, we'll look at the various editions of Microsoft's newest server platform. Let's start with the past and then move forward.

A Brief History of Windows

Microsoft has had a long and successful history with its Windows line of operating systems. With more than a dozen editions of various client and server versions of the Windows platform, it can be very difficult to keep track of these. Since many systems administrators will need to support a wide range of operating systems, we'll take a brief look at a history of Windows in this section. This information will be particularly useful if you are new to supporting Microsoft technologies, but if you are a veteran, you might like to remember just how far this software platform has come.

Unfortunately, Microsoft's marketing group has come up with some very nonintuitive names for the versions of their operating systems. The end result seems to be a lot of confusion over the various OSes and how they interrelate. Let's take a very brief look at the various operating systems that have been developed by Microsoft.

Chronologically, the major server-side network operating systems are:

- Windows NT Advanced Server 3.1
- Windows NT Server 3.5
- Windows NT Server 3.51
- Windows NT Server 4.0
- Windows NT Server 4.0 Enterprise Edition
- Windows NT Server 4.0 Terminal Server Edition
- Windows 2000 Server Platform (multiple editions)
- Windows Server 2003 Platform (multiple editions)

The client operating systems can be divided into two groups. The first group includes the Windows operating systems that are based on the Windows NT platform:

- Windows NT
- Windows NT Workstation 4.0
- Windows 2000 Professional
- Windows XP (Home and Professional)

The client operating systems that are based on MS-DOS and earlier versions of Windows include:

- Windows 3.x
- Windows 95

■ Windows 98

■ Windows Millennium Edition (Me)

Many of these operating systems had several revisions and updates. For example, Microsoft made limited releases of its Windows 98 Second Edition (SE) operating system, and Service Packs and "Option Packs" have added significant functionality to older products such as Windows NT 4.0.

For more information about the history of windows, you can see the illustrated Windows timeline at http://www.microsoft.com/windows/WinHistoryIntro.mspx.

An Overview of What's New in Windows Server 2003

From some fairly humble beginnings, Microsoft has made its Windows platform a powerful force in the network operating system marketplace. With a huge market share for client operating systems and a growing share of the server marketplace, the Windows platform is the default operating system for many organizations throughout the world, ranging in size from "Mom & Pop" shops to global enterprises. Of course, it's likely that you already know this, since you're pursuing a career involving Microsoft's products!

The purpose of this book is to describe tools, techniques, and features related to Windows Server 2003. Note, however, that a great deal of the information that is covered in this book is also applicable to other versions of Windows (including client-side operating systems and the Windows NT 4.0 and Windows 2000 platforms). There's a good chance that the majority of information will also apply to future Windows operating systems. Keep this in mind as you work with Microsoft's products in the real world.

In this section, you'll be provided with a high-level overview of some of the many new features in Windows Server 2003. Although we can't cover all of these features in detail here (that's what the rest of the book is for!), we can take a high-level look at important features and what Microsoft's goals for Windows Server 2003 are.

New Features in Windows Server 2003

Many software vendors work hard to constantly improve their products, and Microsoft is no exception. Without keeping up with the latest technological advances, most software products will eventually fall into obscurity. Although I'm not a Microsoft "insider," I can offer some educated guesses into what Microsoft's Product Managers were thinking as they decided what would be done to make Windows Server 2003 a compelling upgrade. Let's take a look at how Windows Server 2003 fits in.

First, Microsoft is trying to follow up on an already successful product line—the Windows 2000 Server platform. In some ways, this can be a more difficult task than fixing an older operating system or application that didn't meet most of its customers needs. Many organizations have migrated to Windows 2000 Server and are quite happy with that operating system. In fact, many of Microsoft's customers (especially many large organizations) are happy running Windows NT 4.0 Server. So, the challenge for Microsoft is to provide compelling reasons for customers to upgrade their server operating systems.

In general, Windows Server 2003 is an incremental improvement over its predecessor, Windows 2000 Server. Those that are deploying the operating system will find that it's not as large a shift as was moving from Windows NT 4.0 to the Windows 2000 platform. For example, the architecture of the Active Directory remains largely unchanged, although there have been several improvements in performance, reliability, and management features. In fact, Microsoft's marketing efforts are strongly focused on providing compelling reasons for Windows NT 4.0 users to upgrade to Windows Server 2003. Of course, that's not to say that organizations won't find it worthwhile to upgrade from Windows 2000 Server.

So, the question remains, what are the major enhancements in Windows Server 2003? In this section, we'll look at improvements in Windows Server 2003, when compared to Windows 2000 Server.

on the **Job**

For more details about the new features and technologies in the Windows Server 2003 product, see Microsoft's Windows Server 2003 home page at http://www.microsoft.com/WindowsServer2003/. You'll also be able to find a comparison between Windows NT 4.0 Server and Windows Server 2003 on this site.

Active Directory Enhancements   One of the most valuable features of Microsoft's current Windows server operating system platform is its ability to support the Active Directory. You'll see some basic technical information about this technology later in this chapter. Regarding the administration of the Active Directory, Microsoft has made several improvements. First, the much-requested feature of drag-and-drop support in the Active Directory administrative tools has been added. You can also select multiple objects and easily change related properties all at once.

Windows Server 2003 supports another much-requested Active Directory feature: the ability to rename domains. Since mergers and acquisitions are common in the current business environment, this feature enables systems administrators to adapt their domain names and structures to organizational changes. Note, however, that renaming a domain is not as simple as renaming an object such as a file; there's a fairly lengthy sequence of steps that must be carried out in order for the process to occur successfully.

In terms of security, resources can now be easily shared between separate Active Directory forests through the use of trust relationships between forests (instead of just trusts between domains in different forests, as was supported in the Windows 2000 version of Active Directory). This allows for sharing network resources between organizations, and between independent business units or sections of a single organization.

Although not all of these features are revolutionary, they can simplify administration in many environments.

on the
Job

As IT professionals, many of us really love to live on the cutting edge. As soon as new software is released, we want to try it out. And, we're always looking for ways to get our hands on the latest versions of products. This is great for learning, but from a business point of view, you should always keep in mind the real benefits of upgrading to a new application. If a new version of an application features only better-designed icons and superficial changes, it's probably not worth the cost and effort of upgrading. If, on the other hand, there are significant new enhancements and features for users, it might be worth the costs of upgrading to increase overall productivity. Always focus on the overall value of an upgrade to a new product or version.

Group Policy Enhancements   Through the use of Group Policy settings, systems administrators are able to exert more control over their Windows-based client and server operating systems than ever before. The effective application of Group Policy Objects (GPOs) can result in well-managed client computer configurations. This, in turn, can reduce administration costs and can improve the end-user experience.

One of the challenges of working with Group Policy in Windows 2000 Server was the sheer number of options and the many ways in which they could be applied. This often made it difficult to troubleshoot specific policy-related problems. Group Policy–related enhancements in Windows Server 2003 include the Group Policy Management Console. This administrative tool (which must be downloaded from Microsoft's Windows Server 2003 web site) provides the ability to view GPO-related information throughout the environment using a single console. It's no longer necessary to open multiple Active Directory administration tools to hunt down the right settings or the cause of a problem. Figure 1-1 shows the main screen of the Group Policy Management console. This powerful tool includes additional wizards, such as the Group Policy Modeling Wizard (which allows you to plan for the application of GPOs) and the Group Policy Results Wizard (which calculated overall effective GPO settings).

Another new feature related to managing Group Policy is the Resultant Set of Policies tool. As its name implies, this tool can be used to determine the actual policy settings that apply to a specific Active Directory user or computer. The tool goes further by allowing systems administrators to choose a logging mode (which calculates existing policy settings) and a planning mode (which allows for the testing of Group Policy settings, before they're applied). The Resultant Set of Policies console can be used to identify and plan for the proper application of GPOs (see Figure 1-2).

FIGURE 1-1   Using the Group Policy Management console

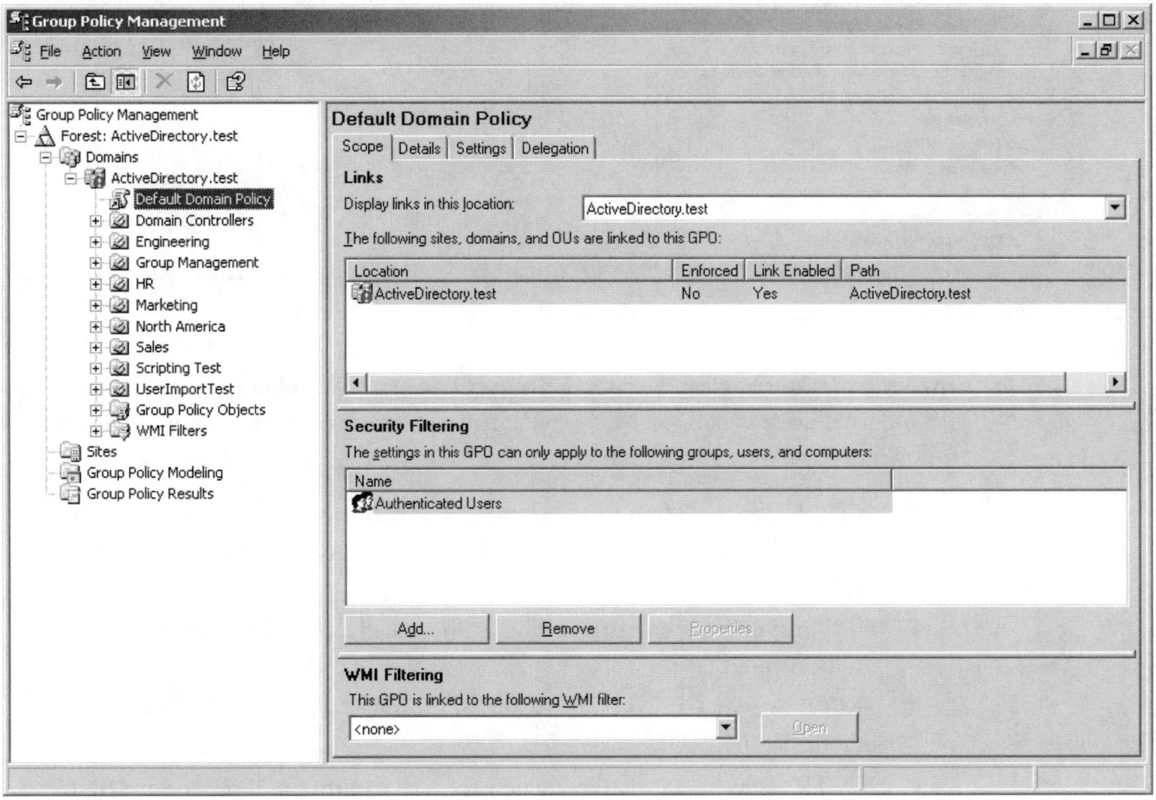

FIGURE 1-2   Using the Resultant Set of Policies administrative tool

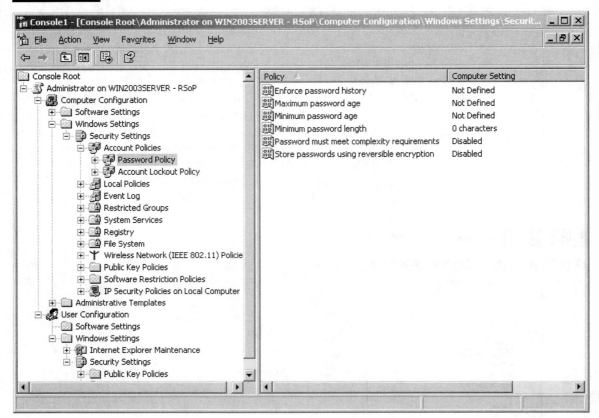

Internet Information Server Enhancements   Windows Server 2003 includes IIS 6.0, the latest version of Microsoft's Internet server platform. IIS includes the following server-side functionality:

- ■ **HTTP Server**   Used to serve static web content, as well as process dynamic server-side requests for "active" web sites (such as those that are written in ASP, ASP.NET, or other supported languages).

- ■ **FTP Server**   Provides the ability to host and share files over the Internet or an intranet.

- ■ **SMTP Server**   Used to relay e-mail messages within and outside an organization.

- ■ **NNTP Server**   Used to provide access to Internet and private newsgroups.

Many organizations rely on their Internet servers to provide for communications throughout their organization. IIS 6.0 is a completely rewritten version of this platform. Its major new feature is improved process isolation through the use of application pools. This allows administrators to separate different areas of web applications from each other, thereby adding protection against application crashes.

The Windows Server 2003 version of IIS also provides additional features that should be of value to organizations that depend on it. Overall performance has been improved through the implementation of new kernel-level routines that reduce performance overhead. Also, administration has been simplified through, for example, configuration settings that are stored in XML files. We'll cover IIS administration in detail in Chapter 7.

Windows Server 2003 also ships with built-in support for Microsoft's .NET Framework. This feature allows web and standard application developers to easily take advantage of Microsoft's new programming architecture. Although Microsoft states that this is a major benefit of Windows Server 2003, it's important to note that the .NET Framework can be quickly and easily installed on Windows 2000–based computers through a free download.

Other Enhancements   In addition to the major feature areas that you've seen thus far, Windows Server 2003 includes many other enhancements over Windows 2000 Server. Here are a few of those improvements:

- **Effective Permissions**   One of the challenges related to managing security in a network environment is in dealing with file system permissions (a topic that we'll cover in Chapter 4). Windows Server 2003 now includes a new tab in the properties of files and folders called Effective Permissions. This tab can be used to calculate a user's overall permissions on an object. It takes into account group membership and security settings on the object—something that administrators had to do manually in previous versions.

- **Command-line utilities**   One of the primary strengths of the Windows operating system platform is its wealth of graphical administration and configuration tools. However, in some cases, systems administrators might want to perform tasks from a command line (or through a batch file). Windows Server 2003 includes dozens of new command-line utilities that can be used to perform common tasks without launching a graphical user interface. Systems administrators that are familiar with using other operating systems (such as Unix or Linux) will find these tools to be welcome additions. Throughout this book, we'll look at command-line methods of Windows Server 2003 tools.

- **Support for "Previous Versions" functionality**   Windows Server 2003 provides systems administrators with the capability of storing previous versions of files on shared folders. This can greatly reduce common systems administration tasks related to restoring files that were accidentally deleted or modified. We'll look at this feature in Chapters 5 and 6.

- **Improve clustering scalability**   For organizations that require the highest levels of reliability and scalability, clustering can be a useful option. The Enterprise and Datacenter Editions of Windows Server 2003 now provide support for eight-node clusters (compared to a maximum of four nodes in the previous Datacenter version of Windows).

- **Support for wireless networks**   Windows Server 2003 now includes enhanced administration tools that enable monitoring wireless networks according to the 802.1x specifications. Additionally, the operating system can now improve security for wireless connections through enhanced authentication and encryption methods.

Of course, there are many more enhancements that can make life easier for all users in your organization. It's important to determine which of these features will provide real enhancements to your organization's users when you're evaluating whether or not to implement Microsoft's newest server operating system. Now that you have a good overview of the new features of Windows Server 2003, let's take a look at the various available editions of the product.

Choosing an Edition of Windows Server 2003

Microsoft has aimed the Windows Server 2003 product at many different market segments, ranging from small businesses to the largest distributed network environments in the world. Like previous editions of the Windows NT 4.0 and Windows 2000 platforms, Windows Server 2003 comes in various "editions." Each edition has a different price and offers different features. The editions include the following:

- **Web Edition**   This edition of Windows Server 2003 is designed to function as a web server and a web application server. The Web Edition is the lowest-cost version of Windows Server 2003 and is available only with the purchase of a new server computer. It does have limitations related to the maximum hardware configuration that is supported. The Web Edition also cannot function as an Active Directory domain controller and cannot run Microsoft's SQL Server.

- **Standard Edition**   The Standard Edition of Windows Server 2003 is aimed at small businesses and was created for use as a server in workgroups or small departments. Its main limitations are in the area of hardware support.
- **Enterprise Edition**   The Enterprise Edition of Windows Server 2003 is designed to provide support for larger applications and higher-end server hardware than the Standard Edition. The main benefits are support for up to eight CPUs and up to 32GB of memory (64GB on 64-bit versions). This edition also supports eight-node clustering configurations.
- **Datacenter Edition**   The Datacenter Edition of Windows Server 2003 is designed to provide the ultimate level of hardware scalability. This edition is available only when shipped with new systems that are designed by hardware manufacturers.

Both the Enterprise Edition and the Datacenter Editions support 64-bit Intel Itanium systems, providing support for high-end server configurations. Table 1-1 lists the types of hardware that are supported by each of the editions of Windows Server 2003.

For more information about the details of each edition (and for pricing and licensing information), see www.microsoft.com/WindowsServer2003.

TABLE 1-1	Edition	Max RAM	Max # of CPUs
Maximum System Specifications for Various Editions of Windows Server 2003	Web Edition	2GB	2
	Standard Edition	4GB	4
	Enterprise Edition	32GB (32-bit) 64GB (64-bit)	8
	Datacenter Edition	64GB (32-bit) 512GB (64-bit)	8–64

CERTIFICATION OBJECTIVE 1.02

Installing Windows Server 2003

A Chinese philosopher named Laozi is credited with saying "A journey of a thousand miles must begin with a single step." Well, here you are—at the first step toward learning about Windows Server 2003. It probably comes as no surprise to you that we'll start by walking through the information and concepts that are related to installing Microsoft's newest server-side operating system.

In some ways, the path is well paved. That is, Microsoft has gone to great lengths to make the setup process as quick and painless as possible. Drawing on experience and feedback based on over a decade of GUI-based operating systems, the setup process has been streamlined. For example, you'll be asked a lot of the important questions early on during the installation so that you can take a lunch break or get some much-needed coffee while the setup process does its work.

And, there's more good news to keep in mind: If you make a misstep during the installation process, it's generally not a huge problem. Most configuration options and settings can be changed quickly and easily after you install Windows Server 2003. In fact, some settings (such as networking options) can be *easier* to set after the installation is complete. Of course, that's not to say that you should dismiss the questions that setup asks you as a mere annoyance. Some choices (such as disk partitioning details) are important and cannot easily be changed after setup has completed.

Don't let the simplicity of the installation process fool you, though. Windows Server 2003 is a very powerful operating system. And, the configuration options are very important. In this chapter, I'll start by presenting information about the various decisions you'll need to make during the setup process. The focus of the initial sections in this chapter is on concepts. Then, drawing on this information, we'll walk through the process of installing Windows Server 2003 using the choices we've made.

Understanding Windows Server 2003 Setup Options

Since Microsoft has gone to great lengths to make the installation process as quick and painless as possible, I'll provide a discussion of the various installation options that are available in this section. Then, using this information, we'll walk through the exact setup process for Windows Server 2003.

This approach is also a good practice in the real world. Before you begin setting up a new server, be sure you understand the details of what the server will be doing and how it should be configured. For example, before you get to the Licensing selection screen, you should have decided which licensing mode you plan to use. And, before you get to the Network Settings options, you should understand how your server is supposed to be configured to communicate on the network. Having this information ahead of time will ensure that your selections during setup are exactly what you want.

Determining Compatibility

Before you begin installing Windows Server 2003, you should do a little bit of homework to ensure that your current configuration is compatible with Windows Server 2003. Although this is a recommended practice for any operating system installation, it's especially true for servers (where reliability, uptime, and performance are critical).

You can save a lot of time and prevent serious headaches by taking the time to consult the Hardware Compatibility List (HCL) before you begin the setup process. There are few things worse than getting two-thirds of the way through the setup process and then finding that some critical hardware is not supported. For more information about checking for hardware and software compatibility, see Chapter 2.

One of the first decisions you'll have to make is how you want to install Windows Server 2003. So, let's take a look at the two installation options that are available.

Understanding Upgrade Installations

If you are using a supported Microsoft operating system, you may be able to perform an *upgrade* installation of Windows Server 2003 on the same machine. An upgrade installation will keep many of the configuration settings in the previous operating system intact, but the entire operating system will be upgraded. You can upgrade to Windows Server 2003 from the following products:

- Windows NT Server version 4.0 with Service Pack 5 or later
- Windows NT Server version 4.0, Terminal Server Edition, with Service Pack 5 or later
- Windows NT Server version 4.0, Enterprise Edition, with Service Pack 5 or later
- Windows 2000 Server
- Windows 2000 Advanced Server

An upgrade installation is one that is performed over an existing installation of the Windows operating system. When you choose to perform an upgrade installation of Windows Server 2003, you should keep the following points in mind:

- *You will not need to reinstall applications.* Most of your applications will keep their settings and configuration after the upgrade is complete.

- *Some applications may not be compatible.* In some cases, some of the applications, utilities, or services that are installed on your machine may not be compatible with Windows Server 2003. In this case, you'll be given details regarding the potential problems.

- *Most configuration settings will be retained.* For example, if you configured shared folders, users, groups, and other settings for your server, these settings will be retained after the upgrade process is complete. Note, however, that some types of settings cannot be automatically upgraded due to changes in newer operating systems. If your server is running any critical processes, be sure to consult Microsoft's support resources before you perform the upgrade.

on the job

The process of installing and configuring a Windows-based server is generally a fairly easy one in many environments. In the real world, you might often choose to perform a new installation instead of performing an upgrade, even when you're starting with a compatible operating system. Who knows—you might even find several areas for improvement in the configuration!

Keep in mind that, even though you're performing an upgrade installation, it's highly recommended that you create a backup of all of the data on your system (for more information on performing backups, see Chapter 6). If it's not possible to perform an upgrade installation, or if you would like to start with a "clean slate," you can perform a new installation of Windows Server 2003. Let's look at that process, next.

Understanding New Installations

A *new* installation of Windows Server 2003 configures the product with its default options. This is the only choice you'll have if you're setting up a new server that does not yet have an installed operating system. Or if you're trying to upgrade from an earlier version of a Microsoft operating system (for example, Windows NT 3.51 Server), or one that does not support upgrading to Windows 2003 Server (such as Windows 2000 Professional), you will have to perform an installation "from scratch" (that is a new installation that requires you to reconfigure all of your settings and reinstall software).

Before you perform a new installation, keep the following in mind:

■ *You can easily reconfigure disk storage settings.* When you perform a new installation, you can change the sizes and types of partitions (if you don't mind losing the data stored on those partitions). This can help make more efficient use of storage.

■ *Document your current configuration.* In many cases, you'll need to reconfigure the new server in accordance with the configuration guidelines of your IT environment. Before you perform a new installation, be sure that you make notes related to the purpose of the server, along with any important settings. For example, if the machine is a DHCP server, be sure to document which IP addresses are available in its DHCP scopes.

■ *Back up important files.* Although the setup process will not destroy any data unless you tell it to do so, you should always back up any critical files that are stored on the server before you perform an upgrade.

■ *You can minimize risk and the potential impact to your production environment.* When you perform a new installation, you can set up a brand new server while the current one remains in production. This will give you time to learn the new features of Windows Server 2003, and it will give you the opportunity to perform adequate testing before the machine is released into the production environment.

■ *You have an opportunity to fix past configuration issues.* As systems administrators, we often have pet peeves about such things as the naming of folders or files on the system. Perhaps your IT department has created standards for naming shared folders, users, and groups. If you are willing to perform a new installation, this would be an excellent opportunity to correct some of the problems in the existing configuration, since you'll be forced to start from scratch.

There are some special considerations for upgrading Windows NT 4.0 Server computers.

Upgrading Windows NT 4.0 Domain Controllers   In Windows NT 4.0, domains used a very different architecture from that of the Active Directory (the domain model supported by both Windows 2000 Server and Windows Server 2003). We'll cover some information about the Active Directory later in this chapter. For now, however, let's look at some important information about upgrading from Windows NT 4.0 Server computers.

Windows NT 4.0 Server computers can assume one of several roles:

■ **Primary Domain Controller (PDC)**   Windows NT 4.0 domains use a "single master" architecture, and the PDC is the only domain controller on which security-related changes can be made. There must be exactly one PDC per Windows NT 4.0 domain.

■ **Backup Domain Controller (BDC)**   Every Windows NT 4.0 domain can contain zero or more BDCs. These servers are domain controllers that store copies of the domain security database. BDCs are used to authenticate users and to perform other security-related functions.

■ **Member Server**   A Windows NT 4.0 Server computer can be configured as a member of a domain. Member servers belong to a domain but do not contain any domain security information.

■ **Stand-Alone (Workgroup) Server**   When Windows NT 4.0 is configured to work in a stand-alone configuration, it does not participate in a domain at all. Instead, the server contains its own security database that must be administered separately from the security on other machines.

The role that a Windows NT 4.0 Server will play in a domain environment must be determined when the server is installed. Once the operating system is installed, a server cannot be promoted to a domain controller (or cease to be a domain controller if it was installed as one originally) without reinstalling the operating system from scratch. A complete upgrade strategy will include a determination of which types of servers will be upgraded first and how the domain will be migrated to the Active Directory. For example, you might choose to upgrade your domain controllers first. Or, you could choose to upgrade particular member servers before the domain itself is upgraded.

on the **job**

The task of migrating a domain from Windows NT 4.0 to the Active Directory can be a considerable undertaking for all but the smallest environments. Be sure to allocate plenty of time for planning the migration.

The details related to upgrading a Windows NT 4.0 domain to an Active Directory environment are beyond the scope of this book. However, you should know that there are special considerations when you plan to upgrade Windows NT 4.0 domain environments to the Active Directory. For more information, see the Windows Server 2003 Help and Support Center.

Multiboot Configurations

In some cases, you might want to install multiple operating systems on a single physical computer. It is possible to install Windows Server 2003 and another operating system on the same computer. This is often done on test computers (to support, for example, software developers who must ensure that their products work on a variety of systems), and in training labs.

The best way to support multiple operating systems on one machine is to configure multiple disk partitions—one for each of the operating systems you plan to install. If you are installing an MS-DOS-based version of Windows (such as Windows 95, Windows 98, or Windows ME), you should start by installing that operating system first. Then, you should install Windows Server 2003. The setup process should be able to detect the other operating system installation and will add it as an option on the boot menu. It's also important to note that MS-DOS-based versions of Windows support only the FAT and FAT32 file systems and that they will be unable to read information stored on NTFS partitions.

Note that other operating systems, such as Linux, will require special types of disk partitions and may modify the boot process. For more information on multiple boot configurations with these systems, see the documentation that comes with the software.

Choosing a Licensing Mode

Microsoft requires that users of its server operating systems purchase sufficient Client Access Licenses (CALs) for the number of users or devices the server will be supporting. During the setup process, you'll be prompted to choose which licensing mode you want to implement for your server. The two options are

- **Per Server** This method allows you to configure CALs for the local server, and it will limit the number of concurrent connections that are supported on the computer.
- **Per Device or Per User** In this method, you will need to purchase licenses for each of the users or devices that will be accessing any Windows Server 2003 installation.

Figure 1-3 shows the options that you'll see during the setup process. If you are unsure about which licensing mode you will use, it's best to choose "per server," as you can later switch this to the other mode. Note, however, that the opposite conversion is not allowed. For more details about choosing licensing methods, see Chapter 7. Also, note that even if you have Windows 2000 Server (or earlier) CALs, you must upgrade to Windows Server 2003 CALs.

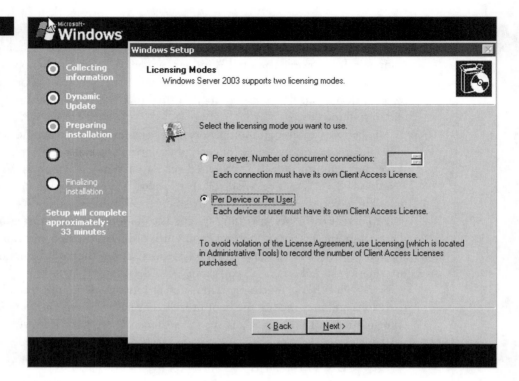

FIGURE 1-3

Choosing a
licensing mode
during setup

Choosing Network Settings

Windows Server 2003 is designed as a network operating system, and most
implementations of the product will involve its use on a LAN. When you install
Windows Server 2003, you'll be prompted to specify network configuration options
(see Figure 1-4). You have two main options:

- **Typical Settings** This is the default option that you'll be presented with.
  When you select this option, setup will attempt to get network information
  from a DHCP server, if one is available. If a DHCP server cannot be contacted,
  then the network configuration settings will be automatically assigned in
  accordance with algorithms, used by the setup process. Generally, systems
  administrators will want their server computers to keep the same IP address.
  This can be accomplished through the use of DHCP (using address reservations),
  or by choosing the Custom Settings option.

- **Custom Settings** If you know how you want to configure various network
  settings, you can choose to manually provide them during setup. You'll need

to know which protocol(s) you want to install, along with configuration settings (such as an IP address, a default gateway, and information about name resolution servers).

If you're in doubt about these settings, it's best to just choose the typical settings option. Even if this isn't the "correct" choice, you can easily make changes after setup is complete. Note, however, that you may not be able to access any other computers on the network until you fix the network configuration.

Joining a Domain vs. a Workgroup

Networked Windows Server 2003 computers can participate in a workgroup or a domain. A *workgroup* is simply a collection of computers that define themselves by belonging to a single logical grouping. Each computer within a workgroup maintains its own security database and other settings.

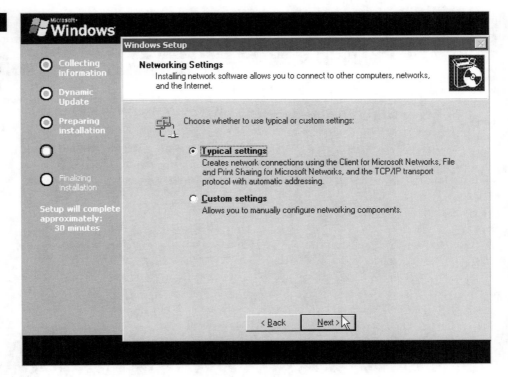

FIGURE 1-4

Choosing network settings during Windows Server 2003 setup

A *domain* works as a single, centralized security database that stores information about user accounts, computer accounts, and other resources that are available on the network. Windows Server 2003 can function as a member of a domain, if you have one in your environment (see Figure 1-5). In order to add a computer to the domain, you must have already created an account for the computer, or you must be able to provide authentication information for a user that has permissions to add a user to the domain.

A Windows Server 2003 computer can participate as a member of a Windows NT 4.0 domain or as a member of an Active Directory domain. If you want to make your computer a domain controller for an Active Directory domain, you'll be able to do this after the setup process completes (we'll cover the details later in this chapter).

Like several other options that you'll specify during setup, the choice of whether to join a workgroup or a domain is not a critical one, as it can easily be changed after setup completes. If you're in doubt, just install the server as a workgroup server.

FIGURE 1-5

Choosing whether to join a workgroup or a domain

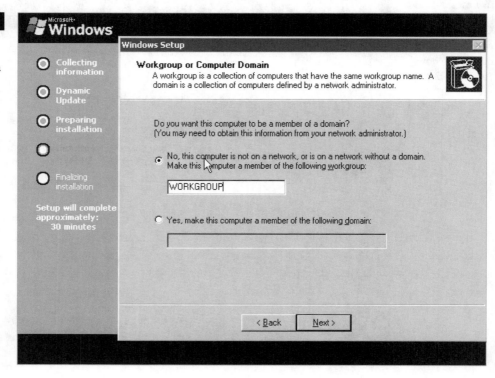

Choosing a File System and Disk Partition Settings

When you're installing Windows Server 2003, you'll need to choose how you want to configure physical hard disks on your server. The simplest configuration will consist of only a single partition that will store the boot files, the operating system, applications, and all data (shown next). In order to simplify some systems administration operations, however, you might want to configure multiple partitions. For example, you might choose one partition to store the operating system files and program files, another to store user data, and another for special applications such as Microsoft's SQL Server or Exchange Server product.

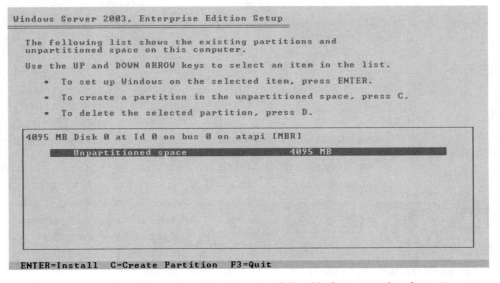

```
Windows Server 2003, Enterprise Edition Setup

    The following list shows the existing partitions and
    unpartitioned space on this computer.

    Use the UP and DOWN ARROW keys to select an item in the list.

        • To set up Windows on the selected item, press ENTER.

        • To create a partition in the unpartitioned space, press C.

        • To delete the selected partition, press D.

    ┌──────────────────────────────────────────────────────────────┐
    │ 4095 MB Disk 0 at Id 0 on bus 0 on atapi [MBR]                │
    │    Unpartitioned space                        4095 MB         │
    │                                                                │
    └──────────────────────────────────────────────────────────────┘

    ENTER=Install   C=Create Partition   F3=Quit
```

on the job

Choose your partition arrangement carefully. Unfortunately, there is no easy way to change the size and location of the operating system and program files partitions. Although third-party utilities are available for performing some tasks, they often require downtime and additional effort. Therefore, you should take the time up-front to ensure that the partitions you create are large enough to accommodate growth.

In addition to determining the disk partitioning options, you'll need to specify the file system to use for each partition (shown next). The default (and recommended) file system supported by Windows Server 2003 is NTFS. NTFS provides increased performance, efficient usage of disk space, and file system security options. Since it has so many advantages, you generally will want to choose NTFS as your file system.

```
Windows Server 2003, Enterprise Edition Setup

    The partition you selected is not formatted. Setup will now
    format the partition.

    Use the UP and DOWN ARROW keys to select the file system
    you want, and then press ENTER.

    If you want to select a different partition for Windows,
    press ESC.

        Format the partition using the NTFS file system (Quick)
        Format the partition using the FAT file system (Quick)
        Format the partition using the NTFS file system
        Format the partition using the FAT file system
```

```
ENTER=Continue   ESC=Cancel
```

You have the option of installing Windows Server 2003 to a FAT or FAT32 partition; however, FAT and FAT32 file system choices are included mainly to support older operating systems on the same machine in a multiboot configuration. We'll cover the details of working with these different file systems in Chapter 5.

e x a m

ⓦ a t c h *A good rule of thumb is to use NTFS wherever you can, and FAT/FAT32 wherever you must! That is, choose FAT/FAT32 only if it's necessary to support a specific configuration. This is generally required only if you want to support a multiboot system.*

Starting the Windows Server 2003 Setup Process

So far, you've looked at a lot of different information that's required before you begin the setup process. Once you have made these decisions, the good news is that the setup process is fairly quick and easy to perform.

If you are planning to upgrade an existing installation of the Windows operating system, you should boot into that operating system and simply insert the Windows Server 2003 CD-ROM. This will launch a setup menu that allows you to choose from among various options. From here, you should just follow the prompts that walk you through the installation process. Once a basic system check is performed, you'll be given the option to specify whether you want to perform a new installation or (if it's supported) to perform an upgrade. Once the necessary setup files are copied to your local file system, you will need to reboot the computer to begin the text-mode portion of the setup process.

The other way to install Windows Server 2003 is to start the setup process directly from the installation media. This is the best method available if you are installing the operating system on a new computer. Note that you may need to configure the computer's BIOS to include the CD-ROM as a boot option (consult your hardware documentation if you need to know how to do this). Since the Windows Server 2003 CD-ROM is bootable, this will automatically start the text-mode portion of the setup process.

Regardless of which way you originally launch the setup process, you'll be shown the first screen of the text mode of setup (shown next). Here, you'll be able to choose from various options (all of which were described earlier in this section) for how to configure the operating system.

```
Windows Server 2003, Enterprise Edition Setup

  Welcome to Setup.

  This portion of the Setup program prepares Microsoft(R)
  Windows(R) to run on your computer.

     •  To set up Windows now, press ENTER.

     •  To repair a Windows installation using
        Recovery Console, press R.

     •  To quit Setup without installing Windows, press F3.











  ENTER=Continue   R=Repair   F3=Quit
```

Next, let's take a look at some ways in which you can troubleshoot setup problems.

Troubleshooting the Setup Process

In general, problems during the setup process are fairly rare with Windows Server 2003. The most common problems that will occur are due to hardware configuration or hardware incompatibility. Hopefully, you can avoid these by performing compatibility checks before the setup process. However, when problems do occur, it's important to be able to troubleshoot the setup process. In this section, you'll see several ways in which you can troubleshoot the installation.

Troubleshooting Setup Failures

If you run into problems that prevent the setup process from successfully completing, there are some steps that you can take. In some cases, the best thing to do might be nothing at all. That is, the Windows Server 2003 setup process has been designed to be fault-tolerant. If a critical error occurs, setup will start where it left off (actually, just past the point where it left off to avoid creating the same problem again). Therefore, you should just reboot the computer and try to continue the setup process.

If the setup process fails during the hardware detection phase, then the problem is likely to be related to a hardware incompatibility. If that's the case, you'll probably need to use another computer to see if it's a known issue. Another useful option is to search the Microsoft knowledge base (available at http://support.microsoft.com), for specific articles that document the problem you're having.

Checking the Event Logs

After the Windows Server 2003 setup process has completed, it's still possible that some errors or problems occurred. It's always a good idea to check the System event log to find any problems that may have occurred. You can do this by clicking the Event Viewer item in the Administrative Tools program group. Specifically, you should search for any warnings or errors that might indicate problems. For more information about viewing the event logs using Event Viewer, see Chapter 8.

Post-Installation Steps

Generally, once you've installed the Windows Server 2003 operating system, your job is just beginning. Before you can place the server in use, you'll need to perform various tasks in order to configure the server to meet the needs of your environment. As Windows Server 2003 includes many different types of functionality, the product can work in many different roles. Primarily for reasons of security, Microsoft has made a conscious decision to disable all but the most critical components of the Windows Server 2003 operating system, by default. This ensures that systems administrators will enable only the tasks that are required for a specific machine, and will reduce the chances that unneeded services and features will cause security or reliability problems.

Fortunately, Microsoft has included several tools that can help you enable and configure the many different features in Windows Server 2003. In this section, you'll take a high-level look at some of these methods.

Using the Configure Your Server Wizard

As mentioned earlier, one of the changes that Microsoft has included in Windows Server 2003 is that the operating system runs only a minimal set of services and features after the installation process is complete. Therefore, it's up to systems administrators to determine which features they want to enable and implement. Fortunately, the Configure Your Server Wizard has been designed to provide the basic steps that are required in order to set up Windows Server 2003 to perform various common tasks.

Accessing the Configure Your Server Wizard is fairly easy. When you first log in to Windows Server 2003, after installation, you'll be presented with this wizard (verify this). You can also launch this wizard by choosing Start | Programs | Administrative Tools | Configure Your Server. The following illustration shows the various options that are available after you click Next to begin using the wizard.

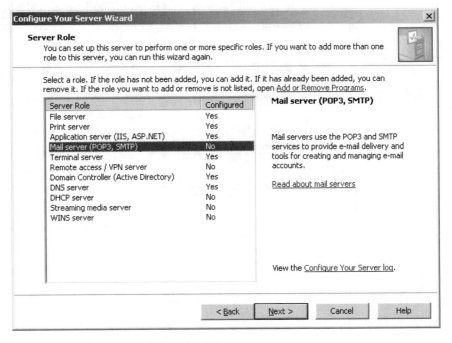

The list of server roles includes the following:

- File Server
- Print Server

- Application Server (IIS, ASP.NET)
- Mail Server (POP3, SMTP)
- Terminal Server
- Remote Access / VPN Server
- Domain Controller (Active Directory)
- DNS Server
- DHCP Server
- Streaming Media Server
- WINS Server

Note that these are the options that are available within the Enterprise Edition of Windows Server 2003—other editions may not have all of these features available for use. Selecting a role to enable couldn't be much simpler—you will basically highlight one of the available options and then click Next. If the role has already been configured, you'll be prompted for any details that might be required to remove this role. If the role has not yet been configured, you'll need to provide any required information in order to set up that role, as shown here:

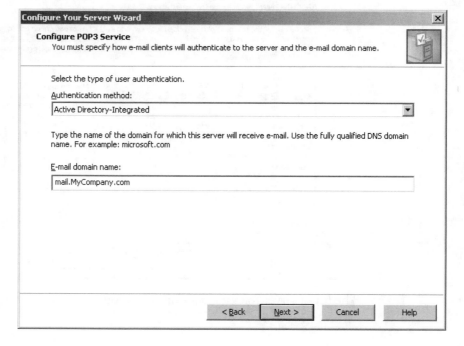

You'll see the Configure Your Server Wizard in action throughout the remaining chapters of this book. For now, however, you should keep in mind that this wizard should be your first step when you want to implement new functionality.

Using the Manage Your Server Wizard

Configuring a new server role is generally just the first step in making that role ready for your users to access. Generally, further configuration is necessary. For example, if you choose to configure a file server, you must still select which files should be shared, and who should have access to those files. Or if you're setting up a new application server, you'll need to configure specific sites and services. You'll look at the technical details related to most of these server roles in later chapters.

All of the features of the Windows Server 2003 operating system can be configured using the standard administrative tools that are included with the server. However, the new Manage Your Server Wizard is designed to provide a single central place from which you can launch the most common administrative tools and options.

This Manage Your Server Wizard is automatically launched after you add a new role using the Configure Your Server Wizard. You can also launch the tool by choosing Start | Programs | Administrative Tools | Manage Your Server. The following illustration shows the main screen of this wizard.

A section for each of the configured server roles on the local machine is displayed. Within each section, you'll see hyperlinks for performing common operations. For example, if you're configuring a print server, you'll see options for adding a printer, adding a printer driver, and opening the Printers and Faxes administrative tool. Some of these links will launch an administrative tool (such as the "Active Directory Users and Computers" MMC console), and others will launch wizards or help information that can walk you through common setup processes, as shown here:

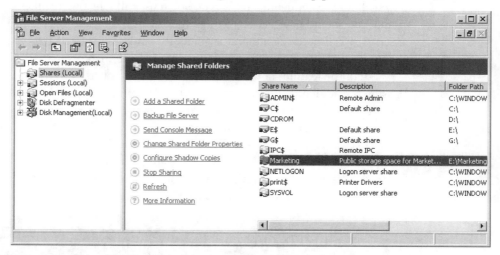

Installing the Windows Server 2003 Support Tools

In addition to all of the files, tools, and utilities that are installed with Windows Server 2003, Microsoft has made the Windows Support Tools available for systems administrators. This set of tools is included on the standard Windows Server 2003 setup CD-ROM, and it's located within the \Support\Tools\ folder. To install the tools, simply double-click on the SupTools.msi file from within a current Windows operating system. This will launch the Windows Support Tools Setup Wizard. When prompted for the installation type, choose Complete to ensure that the deployment tools are installed.

When the installation is complete, you'll have a new Windows Support Tools program group in your Start menu. In addition to providing the tools that you'll use in the following sections of this chapter, the Support Tools include several command-line utilities. Table 1-2 provides some examples of a few of the utilities, along with their purposes.

TABLE 1-2		Examples of Windows Server 2003 Support Tools and Their Purposes	
Tool Name	**Command**	**Purpose**	**Notes**
ACL Diagnostics	Acldiag.exe	Provides information about the access control list (ACL) on various objects	Useful for calculating effective permissions on an object and for troubleshooting security problems
Directory Usage	Diruse.exe	Provides a breakdown of the amount of storage space used by specific directories	This tool is very useful for determining how much space specific users or applications are using on a file server
Disk Manager Diagnostics	Dmdiag.exe	Displays information about the configuration of disks and other storage devices	
DHCP Server Locator Utility	Dhcploc.exe	Finds active DHCP servers	Useful for troubleshooting DHCP address assignment problems.
File Version	Filever.exe	Displays details about the exact version of a file	Can be useful in troubleshooting application installation and compatibility issues
Get Security ID	GetSID.exe	Gets the Security Identifier (SID) for an operating system object such as a file or folder	Can be useful for troubleshooting security issues.
Pool Byte Monitor	Poolmon.exe	Displays detailed statistics related to memory usage on the local machine	
Process and Thread Status	Pstat.exe	Displays detailed information about processes and threads that are running on the local machine	This detailed information can sometimes be useful for detailed crash analysis
XCacls	Xcalcs.exe	Command-line utility for changing the permissions on file system objects	Useful for scripting and automating the application of permissions; also useful when moving files or folders to different volumes

For more information about these tools (including a complete list of commands and their syntax), be sure to check out the online help that is installed with the Support Tools (shown in Figure 1-6).

Using the Help and Support Center

Many online help systems are notorious for being difficult to use and not detailed enough to be truly useful. If you're like me, you get annoyed by help files that state only something like "To convert the file system, click Convert." Almost anyone can figure that out, and without further details about choosing a file system and how the conversion process works, this information is really a waste of time.

As a result, many users and systems administrators will resort to using online help only when all other efforts (including random trial and error) fail. Fortunately, the Windows Help and Support Center (HSC) is far superior to most types of online

FIGURE 1-6   Viewing the Online Help for the Windows Server 2003 Support Tools

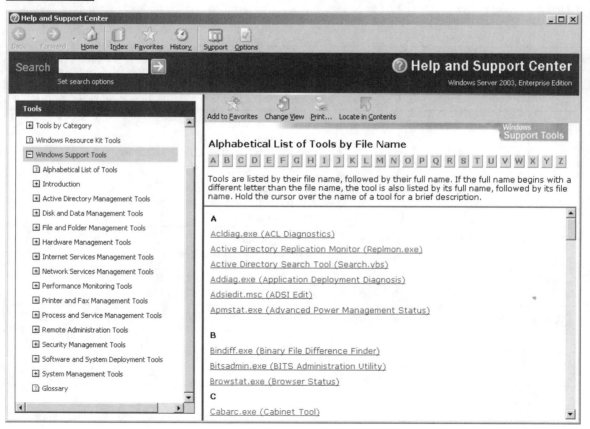

help, and it can be an invaluable resource! To access the HSC, simply choose Start | Help and Support. You'll see the introduction screen shown in Figure 1-7. As you can see, this help system provides primary topics for many of the most important tasks that systems administrators need to perform.

When you perform a search for a specific topic, this new Windows Help tool will not only search its internal database for information, but it will also automatically search the Microsoft Knowledge Base for articles related to your search. This ensures that you'll have easy access to the latest information about a specific problem. That is, there's no more need to search multiple resources just to get the answers that you're looking for!

FIGURE 1-7   Accessing the Windows Help and Support Center

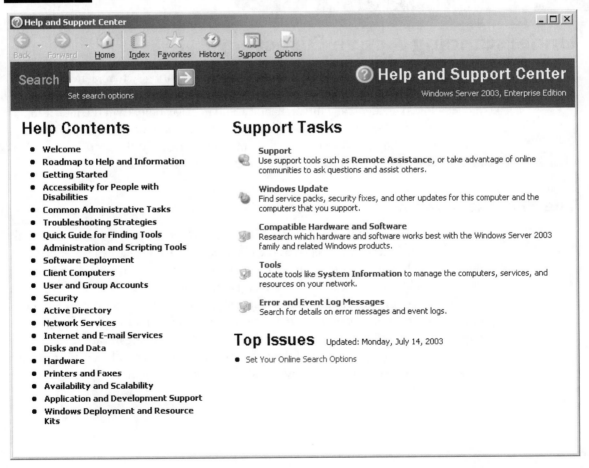

In various portions of this book, I'll direct you to consult the HSC if you need more information about a specific topic. Generally, I'll do this when something isn't necessarily included in the scope of Microsoft's 70-290 exam, but it's valuable to learn about, anyway. You should do the same—if you run into a problem or just want some more in-depth information about a topic, be sure to consult Windows Server 2003's help system.

Now that you have a good idea of some of the ways in which you can start to configure Windows Server 2003 after the operating system is installed, let's move on to looking at one important server role in particular.

CERTIFICATION OBJECTIVE 1.03

Understanding Active Directory

When Microsoft released its Windows 2000 Server operating system platform, one of the most important features was its support for Active Directory. This new domain model allowed greater scalability, reliability, and manageability than the model that it replaced. Windows Server 2003 adds some important enhancements to Active Directory, but the overall architecture is largely unchanged. In this section, you'll look at some basic information related to how Active Directory works.

The Purpose of Active Directory

Before you start looking at the details of how Active Directory works, let's take a look at why Active Directory is needed in the first place. Active Directory is intended to serve as a replacement for the domain model that was supported in server-side editions of Windows NT 4.0 and earlier Microsoft server operating systems.

A fundamental purpose for modern server-based operating systems is to provide a unified, central storage point for important organizational information. The generic term for this functionality is "directory services." Almost all organizations will have valuable network resources located throughout their environment. IT staff are generally responsible for making these resources available in an efficient and easy-to-use manner to the users that need them.

A network directory can contain information about objects, such as users, computers, groups, and contact information. Many directory service systems provide methods for logically organizing these objects, in a way that reflects an organization's structure. The goal of a directory services mechanism is to provide for simplified, efficient systems administration, while still providing strong administrative capabilities that ensure security and reliability. That might seem like a tall order, but it's something that many of us take for granted in the modern networking world.

Prior to the introduction of Active Directory, Microsoft's directory services architecture was based on a flat domain model. Although users and resources in one domain could be given permissions in other domains, there was no clearly defined domain organization. There were several major limitations to this domain model.

First, a limitation on the size of domains has some very real practical limitations. The number of objects (such as users and groups) would have to remain fairly small in order for replication to occur efficiently. Furthermore, domains were not related to each other in a hierarchical fashion. Instead of creating a logical domain structure that maps to a company's organizational needs, systems administrators had to create multiple, independent domains. Resources could be shared between domains through the use of trusts, but this method could quickly get out of hand as the number of domains grew. For example, many organizations would have literally hundreds of Windows NT 4.0 domain trusts. All of this led to fairly complex systems administration, especially for medium- to larger-sized organizations that supported many thousands of users.

on the **Job**   *If you're planning to migrate from Windows NT 4.0 (or earlier) domains to Active Directory domains, it's important to take the time to fully plan for, and design, your new domain environment. Only by ensuring that you fully understand the business and technical needs of your organization can you ensure that your new Active Directory structure will meet your needs.*

As you may have already guessed, Active Directory was introduced to provide a way to get around many of these problems. Let's look at the logical and physical structures of Active Directory in more depth.

The Logical Structure of Active Directory

Active Directory is based on a structure of domains. Domains can be created and configured in a hierarchical fashion, reflecting the business and technical needs of an organization. In this section, we'll take a brief overview of how Active Directory domains work, along with some features that can help systems administrators manage environments with many different types of requirements.

Understanding Domain Structure

In the simplest Active Directory configuration, a single domain can exist by itself. For example, you might create a domain called "ACMETools .com" to support all of the users within your business. For various reasons (including security and administrative goals), you might also want to configure additional Active Directory domains within the environment. For example, you might choose to create domains named "US.ACMETools.com" and "Corporate.US.ACMETools.com." Figure 1-8 shows an example of a hierarchical arrangement of Active Directory domains.

Active Directory domains can be configured in a variety of arrangements that are called trees and forests. A *tree* is an arrangement of Active Directory domains that share a contiguous namespace. For example, the following domains would all be part of a single Active Directory tree:

- Sales.NetworkProducts.com
- Consulting.NetworkProducts.com
- US.Sales.NetworkProducts.com

Note that all of these domain names are part of the "NetworkProducts.com" domain. In some cases, you will want to create associations between noncontiguous domains within the same environment. That's where Active Directory *forests* come in. Each forest has its own, independent domain namespace. These domains are in separate forests:

- Company1.com
- Company2.com
- MyOrganization.org

FIGURE 1-8

An example of an
Active Directory
domain
environment

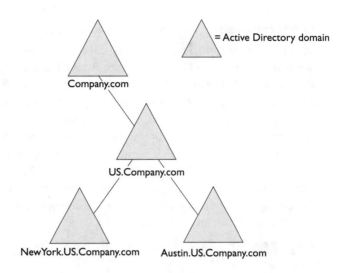

Figure 1-9 provides another example of the various arrangements that are possible
using Active Directory domains, trees, and forests.

FIGURE 1-9

An example of
Active Directory
trees and forests

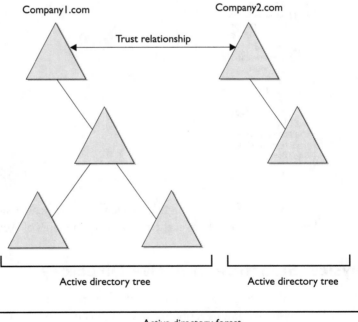

Understanding Organizational Units

Systems administrators can create logical hierarchies within a domain through the use of *Organizational Units (OUs)*. OUs are Active Directory objects that serve as containers for other objects. For example, you might create separate OUs named "Sales," "Marketing," and "Engineering" within your organization's domain. You can then place other Active Directory objects (such as users, computers, and groups) within OUs. Figure 1-10 shows an example of an OU structure within a single Active Directory domain.

The benefit of using OUs is that they allow systems administrators to easily organize and manage Active Directory objects. Once a domain has been created, systems administrators can use Active Directory Users and Computers tool to manage OUs and the objects that are contained within them. The following illustration shows an example.

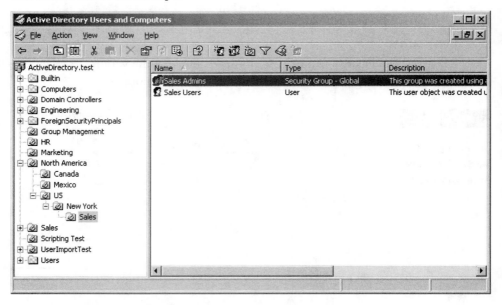

Now that you have a high-level view of the logical organization of Active Directory, let's move on to looking at the physical components of Active Directory.

The Physical Structure of Active Directory

One of the major benefits of Active Directory is its ability to adapt to the business and systems administration needs of an organization. You saw how hierarchical domain arrangements and OU structures can be used to add organization. Another important

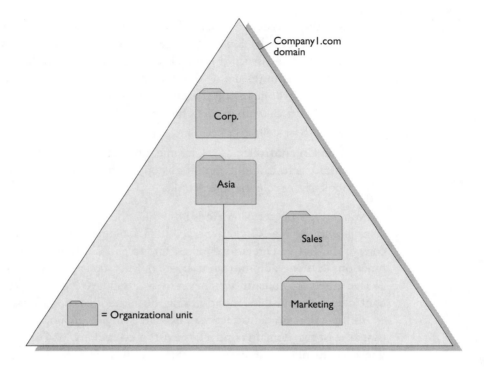

aspect of configuring and maintaining directory services is to adapt to the physical structure of a network environment. This refers to concerns such as network bandwidth limitations and network design considerations. In short, Active Directory must be able to accommodate an organization's technical limitations. In this section, you'll look at how Active Directory does this.

Domain Controllers and Active Directory

Related to domains, a Windows Server 2003 computer can assume one of three roles:

- **Stand-alone server** In this configuration, a Windows Server 2003 computer is configured to function as a member of a workgroup. All computers that are configured as stand-alone servers contain their own security database. They do not participate with Active Directory in any way. This option is sometimes used for publicly accessible servers (such as an organization's Internet web server), and for single-task situations in which participation in an organization's directory services environment is not necessary or desired.

- **Member server**   A *member server* is a Windows Server 2003 computer that has joined a domain but does not contain a copy of the domain security database. In this role, the server will be accessible by members of the domain (assuming that they have the appropriate permissions), but changes to domain objects cannot be made on these computers. Member servers typically function as file/print servers, web servers, database servers, or e-mail servers.

- **Domain controller**   A domain controller is a part of the Active Directory infrastructure, and it contains a copy of the Active Directory database. Let's look at this role in more detail.

An Active Directory domain is hosted by one or more domain controllers. A *domain controller* is a Windows Server 2003 computer that is configured to host a copy of the Active Directory database and to participate in other Active Directory functions. Systems administrators create objects such as users and groups within an Active Directory domain. Whenever users attempt to log on to a domain, a domain controller is responsible for performing the authentication process.

Multiple domain controllers can exist in a single domain, and it is recommended that at least two domain controllers exist in every domain. This is because each domain controller contains a copy of the Active Directory database. In the event of the failure of one of these domain controllers, the remaining domain controllers will still be able to carry on the necessary functions for the domain. Later in this section, you'll see how a Windows Server 2003 computer can become a domain controller.

Sites and Site Links

One important concern for systems and network administrators is in managing the replication traffic between domain controllers. Every time a change is made on a domain controller (for example, when a new user object is created or group membership is modified), this change must be replicated to other domain controllers in the environment. In many organizations, the amount of traffic that these actions generate can be considerable.

That's where the concept of Active Directory sites comes in. Sites are designed to allow systems administrators to define and control how replication traffic occurs in their environment. Sites correspond to locations that are generally well connected (usually by a local area network [LAN] that has links of at least 10 Mbps). Each site is defined by one or more subnet objects—a range of network Internet Protocol (IP) addresses that defines the network.

For example, an organization that has a central Corporate office and three remote branch locations could configure a total of four sites (one for each location). Domain controllers in each site would be placed within these. The Active Directory's replication engine can automatically determine how and when to connect to the various sites. Additionally, site information can be used to determine to which domain controller clients will log on. Figure 1-11 provides an example of a site organization.

Administrators can use the Active Directory Sites and Services tool to manage sites. Once sites have been configured, there are further options, such as site links that can further control how and when replication occurs. For example, in environments that have very busy wide area network (WAN) connections, sites can be configured to communicate replication data only during nonbusiness hours.

It is important to keep in mind that site structure is completely independent of domain structure. That is, a single domain can span many sites, and a single site can have multiple domains. Put another way, sites correspond to the physical design of your network environment, and domains relate to its logical design.

Implementing the Domain Controller Server Role

Now that you've looked at a lot of the background information that is related to the Active Directory, it's time to see how you can set up a new domain environment using Windows Server 2003. This is done by promoting a Windows Server 2003 computer

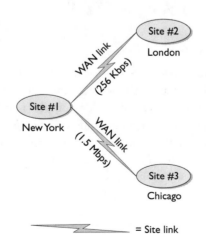

FIGURE 1-11

How Active Directory sites can be used to manage replication traffic within a domain

to a domain controller by configuring the "Domain Controller (Active Directory)" server role. The Active Directory Installation Wizard is the tool that will walk you through that process. In this section, we'll take a high-level look at some of the important options that are related to creating a new domain.

There are two ways in which you can launch the Active Directory Installation Wizard. The first is through the Configure Your Server administrative tool. Simply select the "Domain Controller (Active Directory)" server role to continue. The other method is to choose Start | Run and then type the **dcpromo** command. Both methods will start the Active Directory Installation Wizard. To begin the process of promoting the domain controller, click Next.

In order to learn about the domain controller promotion process, let's walk through the various steps of the wizard. You should note that, depending on the configuration of your Windows Server 2003 computer and the choices that you make during this process, you will encounter different steps and options within the wizard. The following steps assume that you are setting up the first Active Directory domain in a new network environment. The steps are:

■ **Operating System Compatibility** On this step of the wizard, you're provided with an important warning. Unlike the default authentication system supported by Windows 2000 Server, Windows Server 2003 domain controllers use an updated, more secure method for communicating between client computers and servers. As the message states, computers that are running Windows 95 or Windows NT 4.0 with SP3 or earlier will be unable to log on to a Windows Server 2003 domain controller. This is an important consideration if you're supporting a mixed environment that includes earlier versions of Windows.

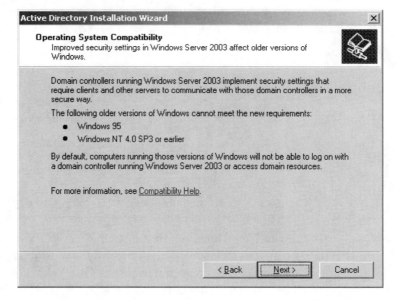

■ **Domain Controller Type** The first decision that you'll need to make when promoting a server is to specify whether you want to create a new domain or you want the new domain controller to be part of an existing domain. In general, you will want to have at least two domain controllers for each domain in your environment (although there are many reasons to have more). Note the warning regarding adding a domain controller to an existing domain. You must take special care to ensure that you do not have any encrypted files, since these files will no longer be accessible after the promotion process is complete. For the sake of this walkthrough, I will assume that you're setting up a domain controller for a new domain.

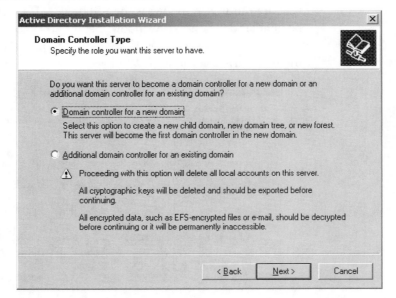

- **Create New Domain** In this step, you'll be able to specify at which level in an Active Directory environment you want to create a new domain. The first option is to create a new forest. This is the only option that you can choose if you do not currently have any Active Directory domains in your environment. The next option is to create a child domain in an existing tree. This will allow you to create a domain such as "marketing.MyCompany.com" below your "MyCompany.com" domain. The third option is to create a new domain tree in an existing forest. This will create a new top-level Active Directory domain that is not a child of any current domain. Since you are setting up the first domain in a new environment, choose the first option and then click Next.

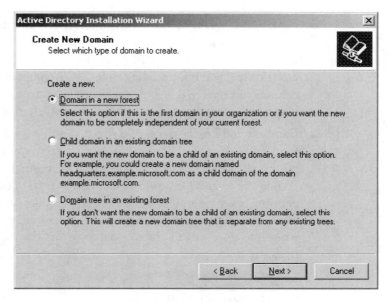

- **New Domain Name** On this step, you'll need to specify the fully qualified name of the domain that you wish to create. The name generally consists of multiple parts and may be the same as a DNS domain name used for an organization. For example, you might specify that the new domain should be called "Corporate.MyCompany.com." Note that the name that you provide is case-insensitive, but it is case-preserving. Therefore, using mixed case can improve readability (especially in very long domain names).

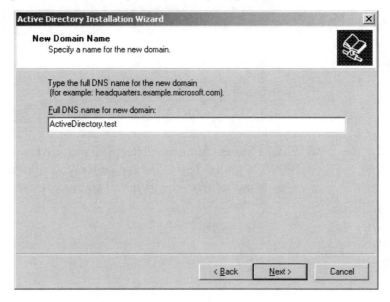

- **NetBIOS Domain Name** Versions of the Windows operating system (both clients and servers) that were released before the Active Directory will be unable to refer to the domain name that you specified in the preceding step. On this step, you must provide a NetBIOS-compatible name by which the domain will be referred. This name can be up to 15 characters in length and may not contain any special characters other than an underscore.

- **Database and Log Folders** On this step, you'll need to specify the file system location of the actual Active Directory database and the log file. By default, both paths will be specified as the "NTDS" subfolder of the folder into which Windows Server 2003 was installed. As specified in the note, you can improve performance by storing the database and log files on separate physical hard disks. The performance improvement comes from the fact that data can be written to the Active Directory database and the Active Directory log file at the same time.

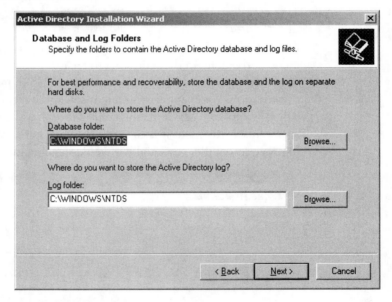

- **Shared System Volume** Here, you will need to specify the location of the SYSVOL folder. This folder is used for replicating information between domain controllers. The path that you specify must reside on a local NTFS file system. By default, the path is specified as a subfolder named SYSVOL within the Windows Server 2003 operating system folder.

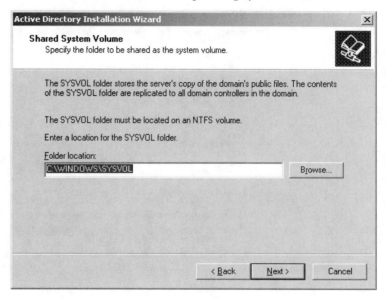

■ **DNS Registration Diagnostics**   The Active Directory is dependent upon the Domain Name System (DNS) network standard in order to resolve names and communicate with other computers. On this step of the Active Directory Installation Wizard, an automatic analysis of the current DNS configuration will be performed. If a valid DNS server has been found (either on the local server or within the network environment) and it is properly configured, you will be able to continue. Otherwise, you will receive a message similar to the one shown in the illustration. Here you will have several options. First, you can choose to correct the problem manually (perhaps by setting up another DNS server) and then choose to rerun the diagnostics. Or, you can choose to have the Active Directory Installation Wizard perform the necessary DNS configuration by setting up the local computer as a DNS server. This is the best option if you are setting up a new Active Directory environment, since it performs the DNS configuration (which can sometimes be fairly complicated) automatically. The final option, which is listed as Advanced, specifies that the wizard should not correct the problem and that you wish to continue, anyway. For the sake of this walkthrough, you'll select the second option and continue.

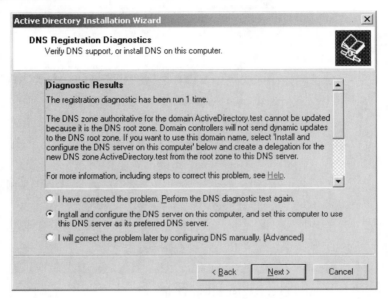

- **Permissions** Here, you'll need to specify the level of permissions that you want to implement within the new Active Directory domain that you're creating. The first option is to support pre–Windows Server 2000 operating systems (that is, the non–Active Directory domains supported in Windows NT 4.0 or earlier). Note that this option is less secure and should be chosen only if necessary. For example, some older hardware-based virtual private network (VPN) devices require the weaker permission in order to function properly. The other option, to use permissions compatible only with Active Directory domains, is more secure and should be chosen if possible.

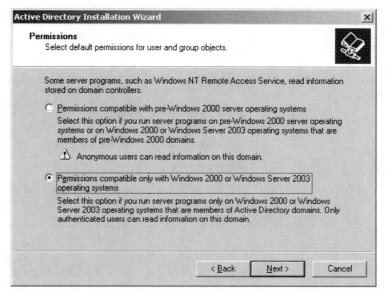

- **Directory Services Restore Mode Administrator Password** Although the primary purpose of this server (after it is promoted) will be to function as an Active Directory domain controller, there may be times when you will need to boot the machine in Directory Services Restore Mode. For example, if the Active Directory database becomes corrupt, or you accidentally delete some required domain objects, you will need to perform a restore operation. In this special boot mode, Active Directory will not be running. Therefore, you'll need to specify the Administrator account as the login credentials, along with the password that you specify here. Be sure that you record this password in a safe place, because it can be very important in an emergency.

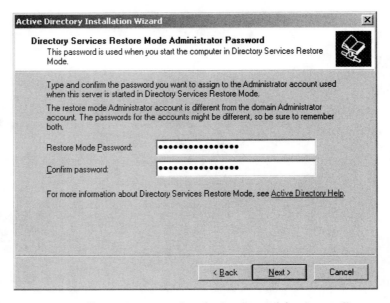

- **Summary** Finally, you've arrived at the last step of the Active Directory Installation Wizard. In this step, you'll be able to review a text summary of the options that you've selected. Since the process of creating an Active Directory domain is an important one, you should take the time to review the information that's presented. You might even want to copy and paste the text into a file to keep a log of your selections. Once you have confirmed that the options are correct, you can click Next to begin the implementation of the Active Directory.

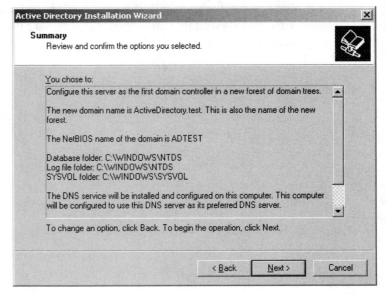

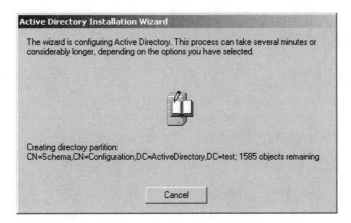

Once you have finished the Active Directory Installation Wizard, you will need to reboot your computer to start the services that will set up your new Active Directory domain. You can then use the Manage Your Server Wizard to determine which other steps you might need to take.

CERTIFICATION SUMMARY

In this chapter, you looked at a lot of basic information and concepts related to working with the Windows Server 2003 operating system. You began by looking at an overview of the new features in Windows Server 2003. There are many significant improvements in Microsoft's latest server-side operating system, and users of Windows 2000 Server (and, especially, earlier versions of Windows) will find worthwhile reasons to upgrade. Of course, on the server side, one size doesn't fit all. So, you then looked at the various editions of Windows Server 2003 and their capabilities.

Next, you looked at the process of installing the Windows Server 2003 operating system. Overall, the steps required to set up a basic server are very simple. However, it's important that you take the time to collect the required information and make some decisions before you begin the setup process. You also looked at some of the ways in which you can configure Windows Server 2003 after the operating system is installed.

Last (but certainly not least), you were given a high-level overview of Microsoft's Active Directory technology. Specifically, you looked at logical components (including domains and Organizational Units), and physical components (including domain controllers and sites). For most organizations, implementing Active Directory will provide significant value.

Armed with all of this information, you should be well prepared to begin covering the information that you'll need in order to prepare for Microsoft's 70-290 Exam.

TWO-MINUTE DRILL

Understand the Windows Server 2003 Platform

❑ Windows Server 2003 is available in four editions: Web Server, Standard, Enterprise, and Datacenter.

❑ Windows Server 2003 provides major enhancements in the areas of Active Directory, Group Policy Management, and Internet Information Services.

Install Windows Server 2003

❑ It's important to decide on the basic configuration of a new Windows Server 2003 computer before beginning the setup process.

❑ An upgrade installation of Windows Server 2003 allows you to retain your operating system configuration and settings, but this process can be performed only from specific operating system versions.

❑ A new installation of Windows Server 2003 installs the server using the default options and settings.

❑ After Windows Server 2003 is installed, you can use the Configure Your Server Wizard and Manage Your Server Wizard to enable and configure various server roles.

Understand Active Directory

❑ Active Directory provides a directory services infrastructure that can help organizations manage resources throughout the network.

❑ The logical structure of Active Directory is based on a system of domains that can be arranged in trees and forests.

❑ Organizational Units (OUs) are used to provide hierarchical structure within domains.

❑ Through the use of domain controllers and sites, Active Directory can be configured to work within the constraints of an organization's physical network design.

MCSE/MCSA

MICROSOFT® CERTIFIED SYSTEMS ENGINEER
& MICROSOFT® CERTIFIED SYSTEMS ADMINISTRATOR

2

Implementing and Managing Hardware

CERTIFICATION OBJECTIVES

2.01	Install and configure server hardware	2.03	Troubleshoot server hardware
2.02	Configure, manage, and monitor server hardware	✓	Two-Minute Drill
		Q&A	Self Test

I n many ways, a server is only as good as its components. The hardware resources that you have installed in your machine form the foundation for the capabilities, performance, and reliability of the machine itself. If you get everything right, your servers will be running reliably and efficiently. If not, however, you could be faced with troubleshooting some difficult intermittent issues (or, worse, with a sudden need to update your resume!).

Modern computer hardware involves a lot of complexity. There are many subsystems that must communicate with each other, and there are resources that must be properly managed to prevent conflicts. One of the fundamental purposes of any operating system is to abstract this underlying complexity and to make it all look simple. Windows Server 2003 is no exception. From the time of installation of the operating system through to the time of upgrades and other changes, much of the installation and configuration of hardware happens behind the scenes.

That's not an excuse for failing to understand Windows Server 2003's hardware architecture, however! Through the many tools included with Microsoft's server platform, you can view and manage device drivers and hardware settings. On the exam, Microsoft wants to be sure that you understand how to work with hardware. You need to know how to install and configure new hardware, how to monitor the hardware configuration of your server, and how to troubleshoot hardware-related problems.

In this chapter, you'll look at many different topics that are related to installing and configuring hardware devices on Windows Server 2003. Specifically, you'll look at how device drivers work, and what you, the systems administrator, can do to resolve problems when they occur. Drawing on this knowledge, you'll be well prepared to deal with the wide array of hardware that's available for modern servers. And, you'll be well prepared for hardware-related questions on the exam!

Understanding Server Hardware Architecture

I already mentioned that one of the fundamental functions of an operating system is to serve as a bridge between software and the underlying hardware. Often, when it comes to server management, systems administrators focus on applications and features such as the Active Directory. However, in order for those types of services to operate properly, you must be sure that the hardware platform is properly configured.

Like most modern operating systems, Windows Server 2003 supports a vast array of different types of devices. Many of these devices are pieces of hardware that are critical to the proper operation of your server. For example, storage and networking functionality is vital to the proper operation of almost any server. Other types of hardware devices (such as a scanner or a digital camera), might be less likely to be found on the server side.

Here's a listing of some of the types of hardware that are supported on Windows Server 2003:

- **FireWire (IEEE 1394) Bus**   This high-speed external bus is used to connect various types of devices that range from digital video cameras to external storage.

- **Hard disk controllers**   The two most common specifications for hard disk controllers are IDE and SCSI. Windows Server 2003 supports both types of disk controllers.

- **Hard disks**   Fixed storage devices of many different types are supported in Windows Server 2003. For more information on configuring storage resources, see Chapter 5.

- **Input devices**   Input devices are the main ways in which users and systems administrators interact with their computers. Many different types of input devices are available, but the most common are the keyboard and the mouse.

- **Modems**   These devices are used to allow computers to communicate over analog phone lines. On the server side, remote access servers might be connected to one or more modems to allow users to create a "dial-up" connection to their networks.

- **Monitors**   Monitors provide graphical output of information for users and systems administrators. On the server side, systems administrators can use a keyboard-video-mouse (KVM) switch to connect one monitor, one keyboard, and one mouse to many different servers. Some environments have switched to a "headless" server configuration (also referred to as "lights out" server management). This configuration involves only remote management of servers over the network or through other devices (such as a serial port).

- **Motherboard components**   Modern system motherboards contain a great deal of functionality, including disk controllers and I/O connectors (such as serial, parallel, and USB ports). The motherboard provides support for expansion cards through PCI and AGP slots. Additionally, lower-level features, such as power-saving modes, are also provided by components of the server's motherboard.

- **Network adapters** One of the fundamental uses of a server is to provide access to resources over a network. Network adapters allow communications over Ethernet networks (at speeds of 10, 100, or 1000 megabits per second), or through wireless networks.

- **Printers** These devices are used to generate paper-based output, and they can be shared with users over the network. Printers may be physically connected to a server, or they may be located on the network. More information on configuring and managing printing is presented in Chapter 4.

- **Removable storage devices** This broad category includes all types of removable media, such as floppy disks, CDs, and DVDs. Generally, these storage devices are used to install new software or to transfer data between machines that are not connected by a network.

- **Universal Serial Bus (USB)** An external connection mechanism that allows the connection of many different types of devices to a machine. Generally, modern servers will have several USB connectors.

- **Video adapters** The basic purpose of a video adapter is to provide server output to a monitor. Modern video adapters provide 3-D acceleration support (primarily for entertainment software), as well as many options for optimizing output.

All of these types of devices are supported on Windows Server 2003. Now, let's look at how the operating system communicates with hardware.

Understanding Device Drivers

Windows Server 2003 uses device drivers to form a bridge between the operating system and the hardware that it's running on. Device drivers are pieces of software that specify how the operating system can communicate with hardware, and which features the hardware supports. For example, a device driver for a network adapter would specify the features of the network card (maximum speed, duplexing modes, power-saving options, and so on). Figure 2-1 provides a high-level view of the purpose of device drivers.

When device drivers are properly implemented, users, systems administrators, and software can all depend on the ability to use hardware with minimal effort and management. For example, once a device driver for a network adapter is loaded, administrators can focus on tasks such as setting network addresses and configuring routing options.

Since Microsoft has designed Windows Server 2003 to support the vast majority of devices that are available on its supported hardware platforms, drivers for literally thousands of hardware devices are provided as part of the operating system. For

FIGURE 2-1 A conceptual view of how device drivers create a bridge between the operating system and hardware devices

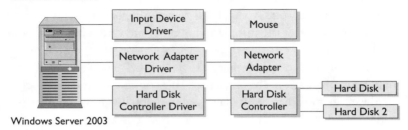

Windows Server 2003

example, if you decide to add a new IDE hard disk to your computer, Windows Server 2003 will generally detect it automatically and load the appropriate drivers without any user interaction. However, because new hardware devices are constantly being introduced into the market, built-in operating system drivers may not always be available for the hardware that you're trying to install. It's also important to keep in mind that, like any other type of software, device drivers are often upgraded to fix problems and to introduce new features.

Although device drivers are provided with the Windows Server 2003 operating system platform, it is ultimately the responsibility of hardware manufacturers to provide these drivers for their products. Often, device drivers are included on removable media (such as floppy disks or CDs) and are shipped with new hardware. A good method for getting the latest drivers for your system is to download them from your hardware manufacturer's web site. Generally, manufacturers will make the latest drivers for their devices (including any patches or fixes that might have been made) on their web sites.

on the job

With many different types of modern hardware, overall performance and features are often dependent on the quality of device drivers. For example, well-optimized video drivers can provide large performance increases, without any hardware changes. On the other hand, poorly designed drivers can lead to compatibility problems and system reliability issues. When choosing hardware for your server, be sure to select devices from companies that have a reputation for providing solid device drivers and support for their devices.

Later in this chapter, you'll look at how you can install various types of hardware and related device drivers.

Understanding Plug and Play

The plug and play (sometimes abbreviated "PnP") specification was developed by Intel Corporation as a method for enabling the automatic detection, installation, and configuration of hardware devices on the PC platform. Windows Server 2003 can automatically detect and install devices that conform to the PnP standard. In the modern hardware world, virtually all devices support PnP, and your servers will automatically detect the installation of new hardware (either immediately or after a reboot).

Non-PnP devices (also referred to as "legacy" hardware) might require special manual configuration. In some cases, this configuration can be performed only in hardware. For example, you may need to manually move jumpers on an old sound card to specify which resources the card should use. Fortunately, the PnP specification allows for interoperability with non-PnP hardware.

If your servers are still supporting non-PnP hardware, it's probably time to replace these devices. The cost of replacing older hardware devices with newer ones will likely be offset by a reduction in administrative effort, and increased reliability of your servers. If alternatives are available, it's probably not worth the effort to support legacy hardware on modern computing platforms.

Understanding Hardware Resources

Devices that function within a modern computer require access to several types of resources in order to communicate. For example, certain operations that a network adapter can perform might require the attention of the CPU, or access to specific memory addresses. In order to prevent conflicts between the many components of modern server hardware, it's important that resources are properly managed.

There are four main types of resources that hardware devices may require in order to function properly. These are

- **Direct memory access (DMA) channels**   In older PC-based architectures, system components were required to communicate with the CPU in order to access memory. This often caused a significant performance bottleneck. Through the use of DMA, system devices can directly access system memory, thereby improving performance. As with other resources, in general, each device should use its own DMA channel.

- **Input/output (I/O) ports**   I/O ports are logical addresses through which the computer's CPU can communicate with hardware devices. Hardware devices must use nonoverlapping I/O port addresses.

- **Interrupt request (IRQ) line numbers**   Interrupt requests are generated by hardware when they need the attention of the system's CPU. In general, each hardware device must have its own IRQ (and some devices might require multiple IRQs). However, the PCI specification for hardware devices allows for the sharing of IRQs.

■ **Memory address ranges**   Hardware devices often require access to areas of system memory in order to function properly. These memory address ranges are assigned to specific hardware devices, and their ranges should not overlap.

If two devices are assigned the same resources, a device conflict may occur. When this happens, you may find that the hardware devices that are conflicting don't function properly. For example, if two different network adapters are assigned the same I/O ports, it's possible that neither card will function. Or, you may see intermittent errors when using these network adapters.

If this sounds like a lot of minor details to manage, you can relax: For the most part, Windows Server 2003 (as well as all current Microsoft operating system platforms) handles the allocation and management of these resources behind the scenes. In fact, it's generally recommended that users and systems administrators not try to second-guess the operating system by manually changing and reassigning settings.

Fortunately, thanks to PnP and other hardware-related standards, resource conflicts are rarely encountered on modern computing platforms. We'll see how resources are managed, should the need arise, later in this chapter.

on the **job**

If you're like me, you might be tempted to build your own servers for your environment. Though there may be some potential benefits to taking that approach, you'd be hard-pressed to out-engineer modern hardware manufacturers. There are several important reasons for this. First, reputable hardware manufacturers spend considerable time and money in making sure that what they ship will work as expected. That means that they iron out the potential compatibility kinks before the server ships. Second, when you run into problems, you'll be able to turn to a single vendor for support. These benefits are significant in most environments, and they generally far outweigh any potential benefits of assembling your own servers.

Determining Hardware Compatibility

If you run into problems during the installation of Windows Server 2003, it's very likely that the cause of the problem is related to hardware (for more information on installing Windows Server 2003, see Chapter 1). Poorly written drivers can cause all kinds of problems, ranging from intermittent system lockups to extended periods of server downtime. Therefore, it's definitely worth the time and effort to ensure that your hardware platform supports Windows Server 2003 before you migrate to this platform.

Before you install Windows Server 2003, you can perform a preinstallation hardware check from the main screen that is automatically displayed when the installation media is inserted into a computer. All you need to do is select Check System Compatibility from the main page. Note that this option is available only

FIGURE 2-2 Selecting "Check System Compatibility" functionality

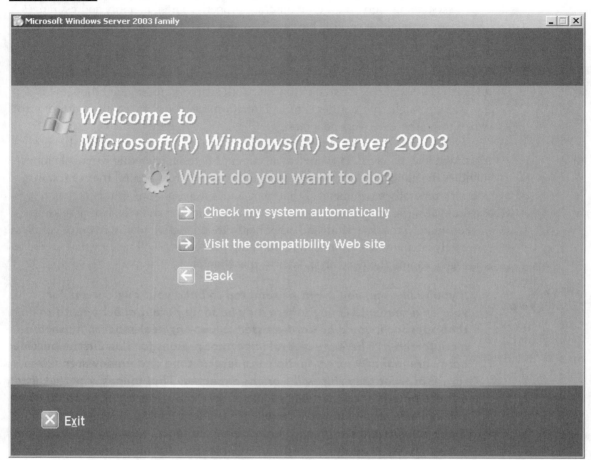

if you're already running a supported version of Windows. You'll be presented with two different options (see Figure 2-2).

The first option, Check My System Automatically, will launch the Microsoft Windows Upgrade Advisor. After searching through your hardware configuration, the wizard will return the results of the system check. You'll be presented with a report that includes any errors or warnings that might affect the installation of Windows Server 2003).

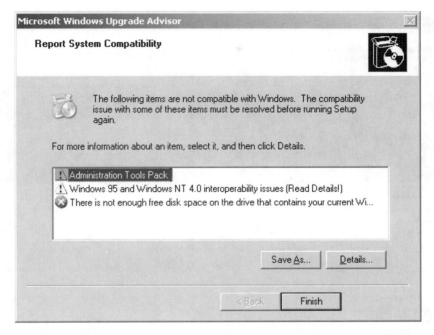

For more information about any of the items that appears in the list, click Details. Or, you can save this information to a file by using the Save As command. It's important to take all of the reported issues seriously: Microsoft has gone to significant lengths to test many different system configurations and to identify potential issues. Often, a little time spent up-front can save hours of troubleshooting effort during and after the installation process.

You can also run the compatibility test by executing the following command from within the I386 folder of the Windows Server 2003 installation media:

```
winnt32 /checkupgradeonly
```

The second option that's available when you select Check System Compatibility from the Windows Server 2003 installation menu is entitled Visit The Compatibility Web Site. This option will launch your default web browser and take you to the online "Windows Server Catalog" site. The URL for this site is http://www.microsoft.com/windows/catalog/server/, and you can access it from any system that has a current web browser. The Windows Server Catalog includes a wealth of information about which hardware devices have been tested for use with Windows Server 2003 (see Figure 2-3). It includes details about hardware devices that are supported on Microsoft's Server platforms, and about any known issues with specific hardware. You can search

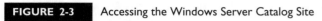

FIGURE 2-3   Accessing the Windows Server Catalog Site

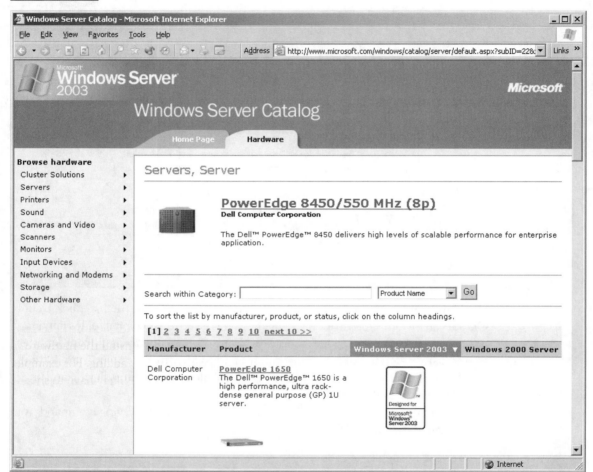

the entire catalog for a specific hardware device, or else you can browse through the various categories of hardware devices. If you have questions about your critical hardware, or if you're planning to purchase new hardware, it's a good idea to consult the Catalog before you make a decision.

Overall, it's very important to do whatever you can to ensure that your hardware and software will properly support Windows Server 2003, before you begin the installation process. With all of this in mind, let's move on to looking at how you can configure and manage server hardware.

CERTIFICATION OBJECTIVE 2.01

Installing and Configuring Server Hardware

Before hardware devices can be used in Windows Server 2003, they must be properly installed and configured by the operating system. The first time that hardware detection and configuration is performed is during the installation of the operating system. The Setup process will automatically take an inventory of all of the hardware devices that are present on the system, and if possible, it will install and configure these devices. The entire process requires little user interaction.

However, there are many cases in which you will want to install and configure hardware after the operating system has been installed. The most obvious scenario is one in which you are introducing a new hardware device into your server system. Let's look at how this is done.

Installing a New Hardware Device

When you purchase new hardware for your computers, you'll likely receive instructions within the product packaging. If Windows Server 2003 already includes the necessary device drivers for the hardware, you'll probably be instructed to install the hardware first. How you do this will depend on the type of hardware you're adding. For example, if you're adding a new network adapter to the computer, you will likely have to shut down the server, open the case and add the hardware to an available expansion slot, and then boot the computer. After you log on to the server, you'll be presented with information that either specifies that the hardware was installed or else informs you that you'll need to provide additional information.

For other types of devices, you may be able to just plug them into the system while it is running. For example, you can connect new USB devices without first shutting down the computer. Generally, these will automatically be detected by the operating system. Certain types of devices might be installed automatically, and without any user interaction. With this in mind, let's look at various ways in which you can install new hardware on your servers.

Using the Add Hardware Wizard

For most plug and play–compatible devices, Windows Server 2003 automatically launches the Add Hardware Wizard whenever a new hardware device is connected to the system and additional interaction is required. However, your new hardware may come with instructions that specify that you should use the Add Hardware Wizard to install the device. Or, you may be installing legacy hardware that is not automatically detected by Windows Server 2003. In these cases, you'll need to manually install the hardware device.

You can launch the Add Hardware Wizard manually by clicking the Add Hardware icon in the Control Panel. The introduction screen of the wizard looks like this:

When you click Next, the wizard will automatically start searching for any new hardware that you have installed in the system. The process can take up to several minutes, depending on the server hardware. During the process, Windows Server 2003 searches for any hardware that is connected to the computer but for which no device drivers have been loaded.

If new hardware has been found, you will be prompted to provide additional information about how it should be installed (you'll learn the details later in this chapter). Otherwise, you'll be asked whether the hardware that you selected has already been installed in, or connected to, the computer. If you select the No option, the wizard will kindly inform you that you should shut down the computer and add the new hardware.

If you select Yes and click Next, you'll be prompted to provide information about the category of the new hardware device that you wish to install. The list of device types will include all of the hardware that has already been configured on the computer. If you select an existing hardware item, Windows Server 2003 will perform a quick check to determine whether or not the device is properly installed. If the device is properly installed, the wizard will inform you of that fact and will not perform any further configuration.

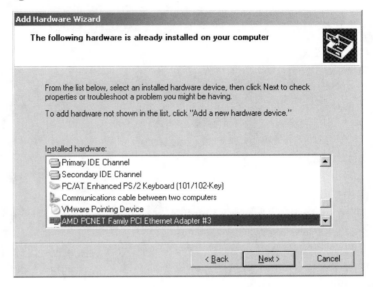

If the device is not properly installed, or if you select Add A New Hardware Device (the last option in the list), you'll be prompted to provide information about how the drivers should be installed).

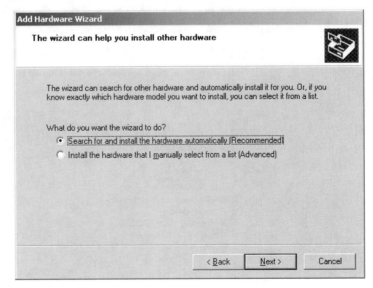

The first (and recommended) option is to automatically search for and install the hardware. When you choose this option, Windows Server 2003 will perform a thorough search for any unconfigured hardware that may be present on the system.

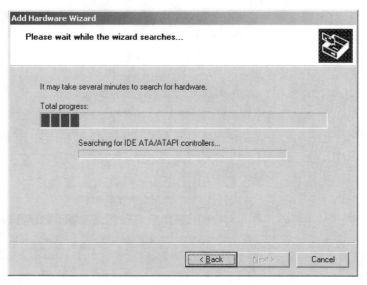

If a hardware device was found, you'll be prompted to walk through the process of configuring it. If one was not found, or if you chose the Install The Hardware That I Manually Select From A List (Advanced) option, you'll be presented with a list of hardware device types. The options include the many different categories of common hardware types that are supported by the Windows Server 2003 operating system.

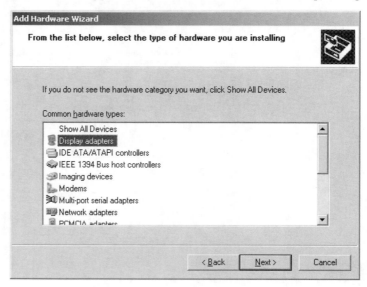

This list includes

- Display adapters
- IDE ATA/ATAPI controllers
- IEEE 1394 bus host controllers
- Imaging devices
- Modems
- Multiport serial adapters
- Network adapters
- PCMCIA adapters

- PCMCIA and flash memory devices
- Ports (COM and LPT)
- Printers
- SCSI and RAID controllers
- Sound, video, and game controllers
- System devices
- Tape drives

Generally, you'll have a good idea of what type of hardware you're planning to install. If not, however, you can choose the first option, Show All Devices. Once you make a selection and click Next, the Add Hardware Wizard will provide you with a list of all of the available drivers that are installed on the system. As shown next, the list of available drivers is grouped by manufacturer, and then by the model of the hardware. Notice that this step of the wizard will also tell you whether or not a particular driver is digitally signed (you'll read the details of digital signing later in this chapter).

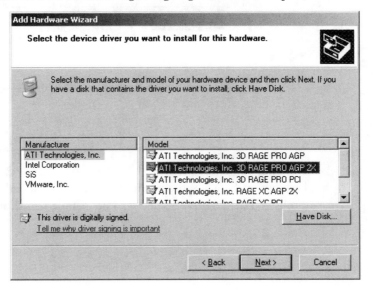

If the manufacturer and model of the hardware that you want to install are shown in the list, you should select the appropriate items and click Next.

In some cases, you will not be able to find the hardware that you want to install in the list. To install hardware in this situation, you must have access to Windows Server 2003 drivers that support the hardware. To provide your own drivers, click Have Disk. As shown next, you'll be prompted to provide the location of the drivers. This location can be a location in the file system (such as "C:\Drivers"), a location on removable storage media (such as floppy disks or CD-ROMs), or it can be a network location (assuming your network is properly functioning). Specifically, the Add Hardware Wizard will search for *.inf files in the location that you specify. These files provide details about the driver and how it should be installed.

As shown next, you'll be provided with a list of the driver or drivers that are described in the *.inf file. You should select the appropriate driver for the hardware that you are planning to install and then click Next.

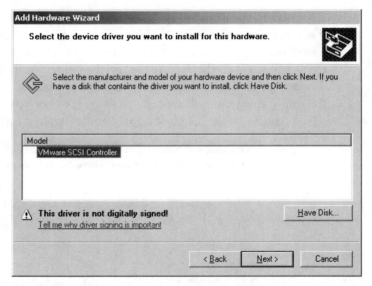

Whether you choose to install a driver from the list of available manufacturers and models or if you choose to supply the driver manually, you'll see a confirmation that tells you which driver is about to be installed and configured.

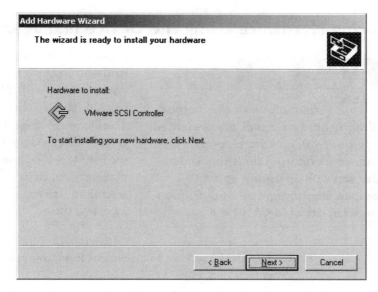

When you click Next, the Add Hardware Wizard will start to load the specified drivers. During the installation process, you may receive a warning if the driver has not been digitally signed (you'll read the details later in this chapter). Finally, once the wizard has completed, you will see information that the device is ready for use. If, for some reason, the driver was not properly installed, you will need to perform additional hardware troubleshooting (a topic treated later in this chapter).

Now that you've walked through the process of installing new server hardware, let's look at how you can monitor what's installed on your system.

CERTIFICATION OBJECTIVE 2.02

Configuring, Managing, and Monitoring Server Hardware

Once you have performed the initial installation of your hardware devices, you may occasionally want to check on the status of your hardware and the device drivers that are installed in the system. Windows Server 2003 provides several different ways in which you can monitor your server hardware. Let's start by looking at the most familiar and powerful tool: the Device Manager.

Monitoring Hardware Using the Device Manager

If you've had experience with configuring hardware on any Microsoft operating system starting with Windows 95, you're probably familiar with the Device Manager. The Device Manager is designed to provide a graphical method for viewing and configuring the hardware (and associated device drivers) that are installed in your system. There are several ways to access the Device Manager, including these:

exam
watch
In addition to the methods of monitoring hardware that are presented in this chapter, you can use several performance monitoring tools to ensure that your server is operating optimally. Performance monitoring and optimization are covered in detail in Chapter 8.

- Launch the Computer Management item from the Administrative Tools program group. Click Device Manager.
- Right-click the My Computer desktop icon and choose Manage. Click Device Manager.
- Launch the System Control Panel applet and select the Hardware tab. Click the Device Manager button.

Figure 2-4 shows an example of the default screen of the Device Manager's user interface. The default interface displays information about all of the hardware that is connected to the system, grouped by the type of the device. To view a list of devices in any category, simply expand the appropriate branch.

The Device Manager has several different view options. You can view a list of these by right-clicking the top node of the Device Manager and selecting the View menu, or by choosing the appropriate option from the View menu of the MMC console. The options include

exam
watch
Since configuring and managing hardware is a very important aspect of server management, only users that have Administrator permissions on the local computer will have access to perform many of the functions listed in this section.

- **Devices by type**   This is the default view that most users and systems administrators are used to seeing in the Device Manager. All of the hardware in the computer is grouped by type. For example, all fixed storage devices are listed under the "disk drives" grouping, and all standard network adapters are listed under the "network adapters" grouping. This view is best for getting an overall snapshot of the hardware installed in your system, if you know which device(s) you want to configure.

■ **Device by connection** This option allows you to view all of the devices that are attached to the computer, grouped by their type of connection (see Figure 2-5). For example, you may be able to navigate the following branch: Standard PC | PCI Bus. This will provide you with information about all of the PCI devices that are currently connected to the computer. Similarly, you could drill down to view the device or devices that are attached to specified USB ports.

■ **Resources by type** When you're troubleshooting issues related to resource access, you can choose this option to view resources grouped by type. As shown in Figure 2-6, the groups include DMA, IRQ, I/O, and Memory (all of which you read about earlier in this chapter). By expanding a branch, you can view all of the devices that are using that type of resource. For example, to view details about IRQ usage, simply expand the IRQ branch. All of the IRQs will be listed in order, along with the device(s) that are using each resource. This view provides a quick and easy way to isolate any resource conflicts or to simply get a quick snapshot of resource usage.

FIGURE 2-4 The default view of the Device Manager

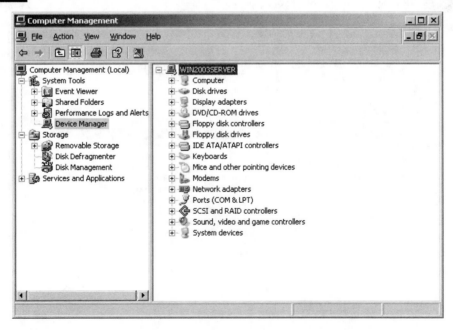

FIGURE 2-5   Viewing device information, grouped by connection

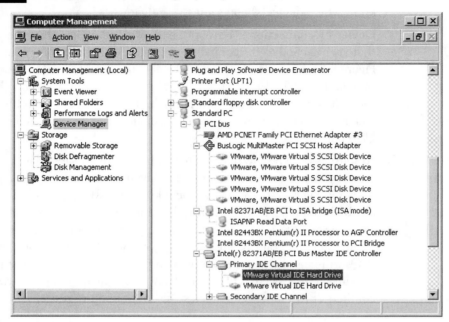

FIGURE 2-6   Viewing resource information, grouped by type

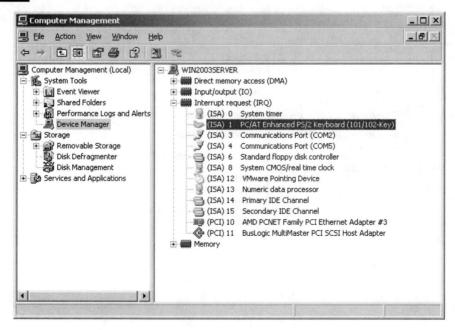

- **Resources by connection**   This view is similar to the "resources by type" option, but it allows you to view device information grouped by connections. Again, the top-level groupings will include the various resource types that are in use. By expanding a branch, you can drill down into the various connections that are using resources (see Figure 2-7).

- **Show hidden devices**   When hardware has been removed from the system, or if certain types of legacy hardware are present, the default display of the Device Manager might hide these items. By checking the Show Hidden Devices option, you can be sure that you're viewing information for all of the hardware that has been connected to the machine.

Many times in the past (when consulting or working with other IT staff), I've run into systems administrators that claim that the Windows platform is unstable or that they have to regularly reboot their servers in order for the servers to work properly. Microsoft Windows Server 2003 is the evolution of many versions of the Windows platform, and regular system crashes should not occur. If they are occurring, you should look into your hardware configuration to find possible compatibility issues. A poorly written driver can cause problems with overall system stability. Of course, there could be other causes of instability, including application memory leaks. However, you should always start by assuming that the problem is not Windows itself, but instead your configuration!

FIGURE 2-7   Viewing resource information, grouped by connection

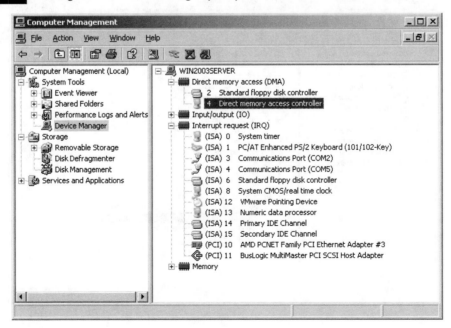

Generally, the Device Manager will include a list of all of the hardware that is currently installed and configured on your computer. If all is well, the default view will have all of the device types collapsed. However, if there is a problem (such as an incorrectly installed driver or a disabled driver), the Device Manager will automatically expand the appropriate device type node. You will see either a yellow exclamation mark (which specifies that a device driver is not properly installed for this hardware device), or a red X if a device driver is disabled. Figure 2-8 provides an example. Later in this chapter, you'll see how you can troubleshoot these types of problems.

If you have recently added new hardware to the system, it may not automatically show up in the Device Manager view. To force a refresh of the information shown in the display, you can click the Scan For Hardware Changes button, or you can select Action | Scan for Hardware Changes. This operation will scan for new hardware devices that are connected to the computer. If new hardware is detected, the Add New Hardware Wizard may be automatically launched.

One additional useful feature is that you can also use the Device Manager to view resource information about remote computers. To do this, simply right-click the Computer Management (Local) icon (from within the Computer Management administrative tool), and select Connect to another computer. You'll see a dialog box that allows you to specify to which computer you want to connect. As long as

| FIGURE 2-8 | Viewing information about an incorrectly installed SCSI controller in the Device Manager |

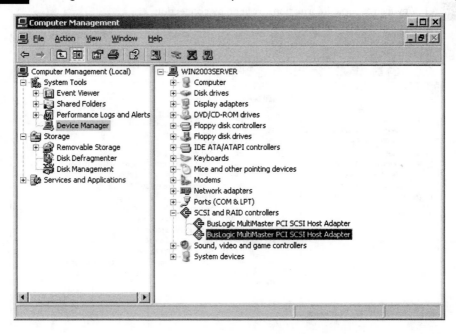

you have the necessary permissions on the remote computer, you'll be able to view the Device Manager's information for that machine. There is one limit to this feature, however: The information that you see is read-only. That is, you can't make driver or resource configuration changes on remote computers.

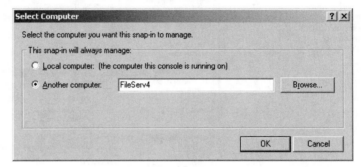

Now that you have a good overview of the Device Manager, let's look at some other ways in which you can monitor server hardware.

Using the System Information Tool

Often, when you're working with an installation of Windows Server 2003, you want to get a quick snapshot of the server's configuration. Although you could open the Device Manager and expand various branches to find details about particular devices, this may not provide the information you're looking for. Fortunately, there's a better way to get a system summary.

The System Information tool is somewhat buried within the Start menu. To launch it, choose Start | Programs | Accessories | System Tools | System Information. After a few seconds, you'll see a quick, high-level summary of the status of your system (see Figure 2-9).

on the *job*

In the real world, you'll often want to get a quick snapshot of the hardware installed on a server. This can most easily be done by choosing Start | Run and typing msinfo32*. The process will launch the System Information tool. This will also work on Windows 2000 and Windows XP computers.*

There are several very useful features in the System Information tool. Related to monitoring server hardware, the "Hardware Resources" section can provide a great deal of information. Within this branch you can view details grouped by resource usage (see Figure 2-10). If you suspect that your computer is experiencing a hardware resource conflict, this is a good place to get details.

FIGURE 2-9   Viewing system summary information in the System Information tool

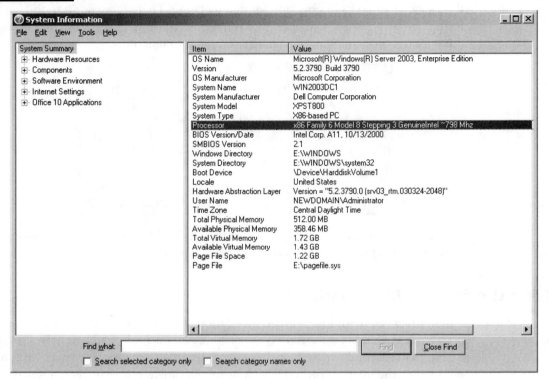

The System Information tool provides several useful features for tracking information. The first is the ability to save (and later open) *.nfo files. Both of these options are available from the File menu. When you choose to save the current information to a file, the System Information tool will collect all of the data that it needs and then create a new file with the name that you provide. This is a simple (and almost effortless) way to create basic server documentation! It's also a good way to keep track of configuration changes over time. By comparing system information from various points in time, you can see when changes have occurred. Note that, on most systems, it can take up to several minutes for the System Information tool to collect all of the data that it needs.

The *.nfo file that's created with the Save command is generated in a special format that can be viewed only using the System Information tool. In some cases, you might want to dump all of the data to a single text file. The Export command (available on the File menu) does exactly that. Note that, unlike the Save command,

FIGURE 2-10   Viewing hardware resource information, based on IRQ usage

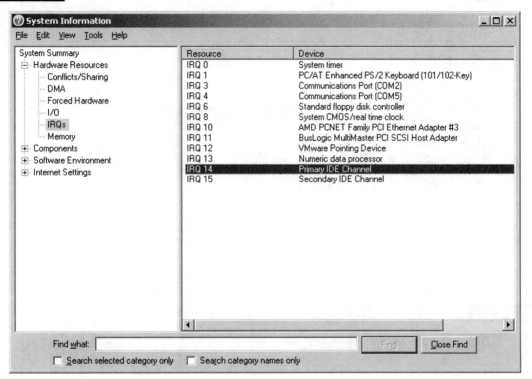

the Export command will save only the information that is contained within the selected portion of the System Information display. So, for example, if you want to save only IRQ-related hardware resource information, you can click the appropriate branch in the tree and then use the Export command. You can view the resulting text in any text editor (such as Notepad), or you can create scripts or applications that can parse the output for useful data. Figure 2-11 shows an excerpt of the data collected from my desktop computer.

In terms of monitoring hardware, there's one particularly useful section of the Hardware Resources node: Conflicts/Sharing. This node, shown in Figure 2-12, can provide information about any hardware devices that are sharing the same resources. This is a good first place to look when you suspect that your server might be experiencing problems related to resource assignments. However, note that just the presence of items in this display does not necessarily mean that something is

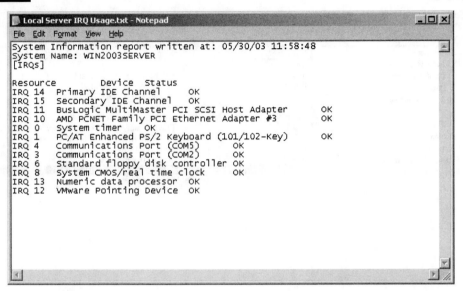

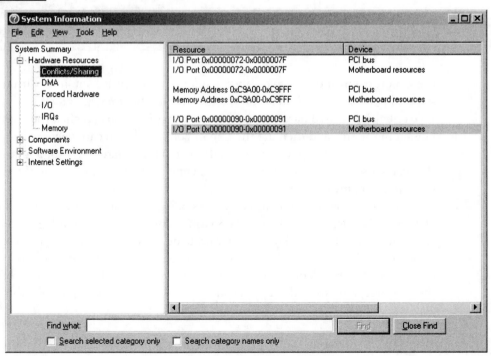

SCENARIO & SOLUTION

You want to get a quick inventory of the complete hardware configuration of the local machine. You also want to save this information to a text file.	Use the System Information tool to view the information. The Export command will allow you to save the content to a text file (or to a *.nfo file).
You suspect that some hardware in your system is experiencing a resource conflict. You want to determine which device(s) might have conflicts.	Use the Device Manager or the System Information tool. In the Device Manager, you can change the display to view information based on resource usage. And in the System Information tool, you can access the Hardware Resources	Conflicts	Sharing node.
You want to view hardware-related information for a remote computer.	Both the Device Manager and System Information tools enable you to view information from a remote computer.

wrong with your configuration. For example, in modern systems, multiple devices may be sharing the same IRQs, and this may not cause any problems.

Another useful feature is the Search option at the bottom of the System Information tool. If you know the name of a device or driver that you want further details about, you can enter the name of the item and have the tool search through the configuration information for it.

Finally, the System Information tool isn't limited to just viewing information about the local machine: You can also view information about another computer on the network using the View | Remote Computer option. As you can see, the System Information tool can provide a great deal of useful information about a system in a single place!

Now that you have a good idea of how you can view information about server hardware resources, let's look at how resources can be managed.

Configuring and Managing Server Hardware

After your server has been set up and is running properly, you might want to make some changes to the hardware configuration. Common tasks include updating device drivers (to fix bugs, add features, or improve performance) and changing device settings (perhaps due to changing requirements for the server). As you might have expected, Windows Server 2003 provides many different tools that allow you to configure your hardware. In this section, you'll look at the features that can help you optimize and better manage your server's hardware platform.

on the
job

Although this isn't always easy for technical people, it's important to resist the urge to make hardware-related changes just to see what will happen. In general, if your server is functioning properly, you should avoid making changes, unless you have a clear reason to do so. For more details on taking an organized approach to improving system performance, see Chapter 8.

Configuring Device Properties and Settings Using the Device Manager

Many types of hardware devices can have settings. For example, you might be able to specify the transfer rate data transfer mode that should be used on an IDE disk controller, or a network adapter may allow you to set various transmission options. The Device Manager is the main tool that you'll use to configure your hardware settings. To access detailed settings for a device, simply right-click a device in the Device Manager and select Properties. Depending on the type of hardware that you choose (and the specific device driver that is installed), you may see some or all of the following configuration tabs:

- **General** The General tab (shown in the following illustration) is available for all types of device drivers, and as its name suggests, it provides you with a high-level overview of the status of the device driver. The information presented includes the device type and the name of the manufacturer of the device. The Device Status box describes the current status of the hardware, in text form. There are two functions that you can perform from the General tab. The first is to click Troubleshoot to launch a Hardware Troubleshooter from the Windows Server 2003 Support and Help Center. The troubleshooter that is launched may be a generic one, or it may be specific to the type of hardware you are viewing. The other option is to specify whether the device is enabled or disabled.

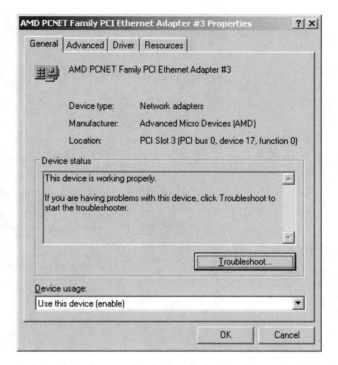

■ **Driver** This tab is also available for all device drivers that are installed on the system. Important information includes the provider of the driver (generally either "Microsoft" or the name of the manufacturer of the hardware device), the date of the driver, and the version of the driver. This information is extremely useful when you want to check which driver you're using. For more information about the specific files that are included in the device driver (along with their versions), you can click the Driver Details tab. You'll learn about the other three options later in this section.

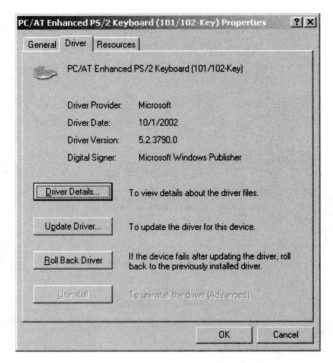

■ **Resources** On the Resources tab, shown next, you'll see which resources are being used by the specified hardware device. This tab will be available only if the hardware that you select is actually using resources. For example, hard disk controllers will use resources (such as memory addresses and IRQs), but hard disk devices will not (since they use the same resources as the controller to which they're attached). For many types of devices, you will be unable to configure hardware resource settings manually. This is because the settings are managed by the computer's BIOS and/or the Windows Server 2003 operating system. For legacy devices, however, you may be able to change resource settings, if necessary.

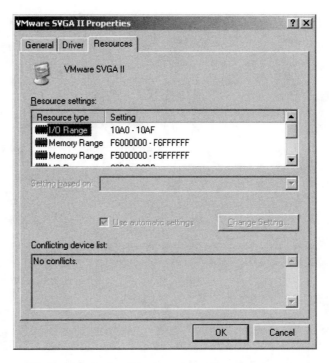

on the **Job**

In the not-so-distant past, having to manually manage resource settings for hardware was a common task. However, on current hardware platforms, this is rarely necessary. You should generally think of the manual management of hardware resources as a last resort to troubleshooting hardware-related issues.

In addition to these properties tabs, there are several others that can provide device-specific configuration information. For example, a mouse device might include an Advanced Settings tab that allows you to fine-tune the performance of the mouse.

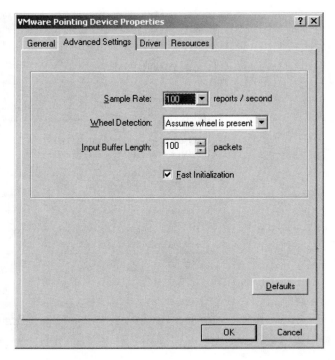

Storage devices, in particular, have several other options. For example, you can configure write caching for hard disks on the Policies tab. Also, you can view additional details about the logical volumes that are contained on a physical hard disk by selecting the Volumes tab and clicking Populate. For more information on configuring storage resources, see Chapter 5.

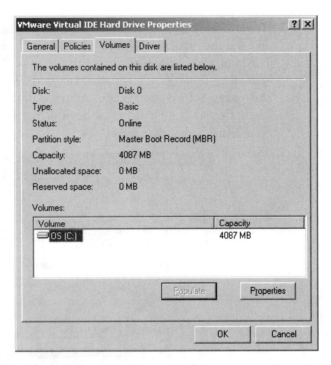

Exercise 2-1 walks you through the process of viewing configuration options for various types of devices.

EXERCISE 2-1

CertCam & MasterSim 2-1 ON THE CD

Configuring Hardware Using the Device Manager

Note that in this exercise, you will walk through configuration options for several different types of hardware. You will not be making any configuration changes, to prevent any hardware-related problems. In some cases, your server may not have all of these devices installed, so you may have to skip a step. You should also be able to perform all of these steps on a client computer that is running Windows 2000 or Windows XP.

1. Log on to the computer as an Administrator and open the Device Manager by selecting the Computer Management administrative tool and clicking Device Manager.

2. Your first step will be to view configuration options for an IDE disk controller. Expand the branch for IDE ATA/ATAPI Controllers. You will likely see a hardware device listed as the controller, as well as two IDE channels. Right-click the primary IDE channel device and click Properties. Then, select the Advanced Settings tab. As shown in the illustration, you will see information about the transfer mode for the devices that are attached to this IDE channel. When finished, click Cancel.

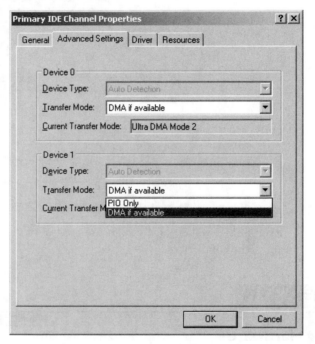

3. Next, let's look at the properties for a hard disk drive device. In the Device Manager, expand the Disk Drives node, right-click a hard disk, and select Properties. Select the Policies tab to view write caching options for this hard disk. Depending on your specific system configuration, some of the options may be disabled (see illustration). For example, if the hard disk is not removable, the option to Optimize For Performance will be selected, by default. Note that you can choose whether you want to enable write caching and, if so,

if you want to use the Advanced Performance option. This latter option could lead to the loss or corruption of data in the case of a power failure or improper server hardware, but it can improve disk write performance through the use of caching. When finished, click Cancel.

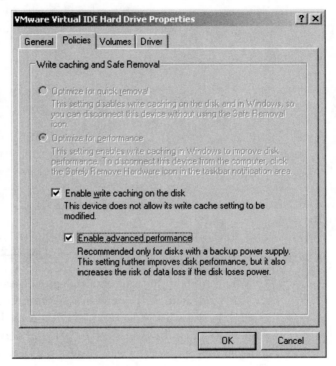

4. Now, take a look at some configuration options for common external hardware connections. In the Device Manager, expand the Ports (COM & LPT) node. Right-click any Communications Port device and select Properties. Select the Port Settings tab. Note that you can specify various options related to the data transfer rate and method for the serial port. These options are useful for troubleshooting issues that might occur when you try to use devices that are connected to the serial port. When finished, click Cancel.

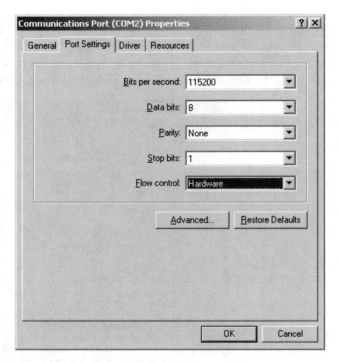

5. Your final stop on this tour of device properties is the Advanced properties
   for a network adapter. To access these properties, in the Device Manager,
   expand the Network Adapters node. Right-click a network adapter and select
   Properties. Click the Advanced tab. If your network adapter driver provides
   configuration options, you will see a list similar to that shown in the illustration.
   These settings can be used to optimize network performance, or to troubleshoot
   specific network-related issues. For example, you may be able to specify whether
   the network adapter is operating in half- or full-duplex mode. When finished
   viewing the properties, click Cancel. Close the Device Manager.

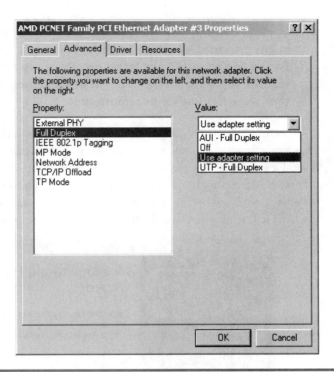

We left a couple of loose ends in covering the operations that you can perform using the Device Manager. Let's look at those, next.

Updating Drivers Using the Device Manager

After a server is up and running properly, one of the most commonly performed tasks for systems administrators is to update device drivers. There are several reasons to stay up-to-date with the latest device drivers. First and foremost, newer device drivers can fix bugs that resolve potential issues. Since the failure of critical device drivers can lead to downtime, this reason alone is probably enough to warrant the updates! There are other reasons to update drivers, however. The overall performance and feature set of many types of modern hardware are often based largely on the quality of their drivers. For example, in the area of video performance, updated drivers can provide significant performance enhancements in demanding applications (especially games). The same can be true for network adapter drivers, disk storage controllers, and practically any other device that you can install on your server.

In some cases, if you want to live on the cutting edge of technology, you might get cut! On critical systems, you might want to hold off on being the first in line to install the latest drivers or system patches. By letting others test the software first, you might avoid some potential problems or issues that were not known at release time.

Fortunately, the process of updating drivers is a fairly simple one. If you want to update a driver for a device that is already configured on your system, start by opening the Device Manager, right-clicking the appropriate device, and selecting Update Driver. Alternatively, you can click the Update Driver button on the Driver tab in the properties of the hardware device. This will launch the Hardware Update Wizard, which will walk you through the steps that are required to update a device driver.

Much of the process of updating a driver is similar to the process of adding new hardware to the system (a topic covered earlier in this chapter). The first decision you'll have to make is whether you want the wizard to automatically search your system for an updated driver. This option is useful if you have recently installed new driver versions on your system and you want those drivers to be automatically chosen.

The other option that you have with the Hardware Update Wizard is to manually choose the driver that you want to install (the option reads, Install From A List Or Specific Location (Advanced)). As shown next, you have several options. The default is to have Windows Server 2003 automatically search removable media devices. This is useful if you have a CD-ROM or floppy disk that contains updated drivers. Just insert the media into the appropriate device, and the wizard will search it for updated drivers. You can also choose to specify a location in which the wizard should search for new drivers (for example "C:\Download\Drivers"). Click Next to begin the search process. If the wizard finds appropriate updated drivers, they will be installed automatically. If not, you'll be informed that no changes were made.

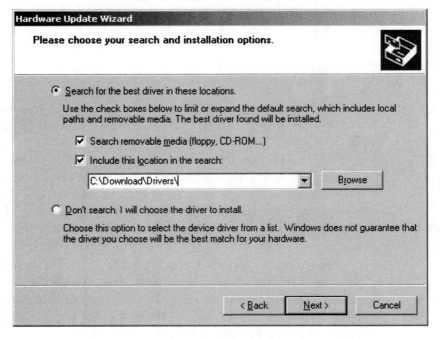

The other advanced option in the Hardware Updated Wizard is labeled, "Don't search. I will choose the driver to install." When you select this option, you will be presented with a list of compatible hardware device drivers that Windows Server 2003 is aware of. The list will include the currently installed driver, along with any newer and older versions of the driver that are available.

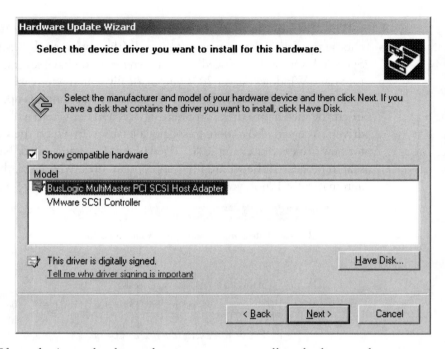

If you don't see the driver that you want to install in the list, you have two options: The first is to uncheck the Show Compatible Hardware box. This will present you with a list of hardware manufacturers and models from which you can choose the driver to install. The other option is to click Have Disk and to specify the file system or network location that contains the driver files that you want to install.

Once you have completed selecting drivers in the Hardware Update Wizard, the wizard will attempt to install the drivers. If the installation is successful, you'll see the message shown next (you'll read about troubleshooting later in this chapter). Note that the installation of some types of drivers might require you to reboot the computer before they go into effect.

Uninstalling a Hardware Device

Most internal components of modern PCs can be removed only when the server hardware is powered off. For such devices, it's often possible to remove the device without informing the Windows Server 2003 operating system. For example, if you want to remove a network adapter, you must first power off the server. Then, you can open the server and physically remove the adapter card (assuming, of course, that it is a removable expansion card). Then, when you reboot the computer, Windows Server 2003 will automatically detect that the device has been removed.

In some cases, you might want to remove or uninstall an item using the Device Manager before you physically remove the hardware. To do this, you can simply find the appropriate hardware device in the Device Manager. Right-click the device that you want to remove and click Uninstall to remove that device from the system's configuration.

Disabling Hardware Devices

Windows Server 2003 allows you to disable devices that may otherwise be properly installed and running on the system. Although it's not common to want to disable a hardware device, you can do this to troubleshoot potential conflicts between hardware components, or to prevent the use of some functionality on the server. For example, you may have multiple physical network adapters installed and configured on a server. If you move the server to another network, you may not want all of these network adapters to be functional (perhaps for security purposes). Although you could physically remove the network adapter from the computer (assuming that it is a removable card), it's easier to just tell Windows Server 2003 to disable it.

The process is simple and can be performed in one of two ways. To disable a device, you can right-click it in the Device Manager and select Disable. Or, you can select the General tab of the properties for the device and use the drop-down list for Device Status to specify whether the device should be enabled or disabled.

Once a device has been disabled, it will still appear in the Device Manager, but the item itself will have a red X on it. When you view the properties of this device, the General tab will show further details (see the following illustration). Generally, the device will be unavailable for use by the system. For example, if you disable a specific hard disk, it may appear as "offline" or may not be available in the Disk Management utility.

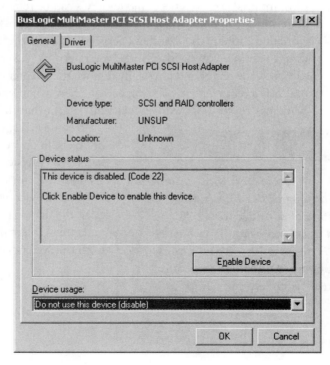

To reenable the device, you can simply click the Enable Device button, or you can choose Use This Device (Enable) from the Device Usage drop-down menu.

Configuring Hardware Using the Control Panel

The Device Manager can be used to view and modify various details about hardware devices that are installed on your system. For some types of hardware, however, the Device Manager is limited. Certain types of hardware have additional settings that you may want to configure. A common operation is to adjust the display resolution, color depth, and refresh rate for your monitor and display adapter. To handle these kinds of details, you can use various applets that are located within the Control Panel. In relation to hardware configuration and monitoring, here are some useful Control Panel items:

- **Add Hardware** This icon launches the Add Hardware Wizard, covered earlier in this chapter.

- **Display** You can configure various display settings by accessing the Display Properties dialog box. These properties allow you to set various options that control how Windows Server 2003 looks. You can change desktop settings on the Themes, Desktop, and Appearance tabs, and you can change the screen saver settings on the Screen Saver tab. Specifically, related to hardware, the Settings tab includes options related to the resolution and color depth of the display.

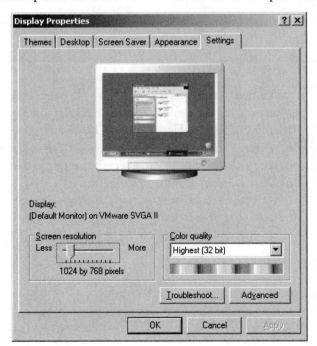

FIGURE 2-13 Using the Video Display Troubleshooter

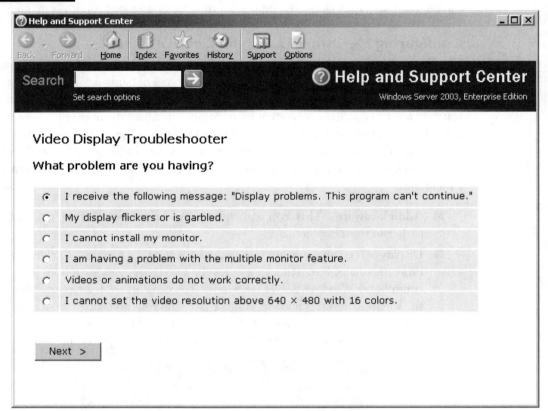

The two buttons on this page provide even more options. If you are experiencing problems with the display, you can click Troubleshoot to launch the Video Display Troubleshooter (see Figure 2-13). The Troubleshooter will walk you through a series of questions and will make recommendations to fix the most common problems. By clicking Advanced, you can access more properties of the display settings, including any device driver–specific options.

Note that you can also access the Display properties by right-clicking the desktop and choosing Properties.

- **Game Controllers** Although you're probably not going to use this option often on your production servers, you can configure game controllers (such as game pads, joysticks, and steering wheels) using this applet.

- **Keyboard** This tab provides options for fine-tuning keyboard performance. You can specify the key repeat rate and delay, as well as the cursor blink rate. Many third-party keyboard drivers provide various extensions that allow the configuration of additional buttons, the mouse wheel, and other hardware-specific options.

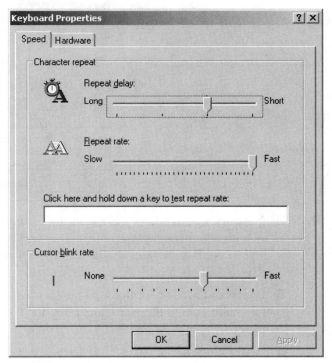

- **Mouse** This applet allows you to configure settings for the mouse that is attached to the computer. Options include setting mouse cursor types and mouse performance. Often, third-party input drivers provide additional tabs and functionality via this applet.

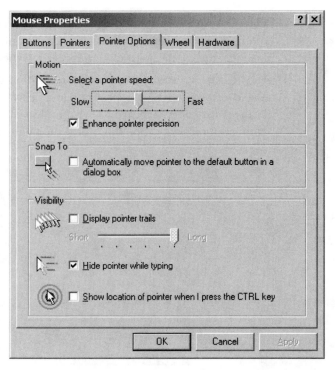

- **Network Connections** These settings are primarily intended to allow systems administrators to configure network options (such as TCP/IP addresses), but they can also be used to view and modify network adapter device configuration.

- **Phone and Modem Options** These settings enable you to specify settings for analog communications, including any dialing prefix that may be required to access an outside line.

- **Power Options** In an effort to decrease power that is wasted by idle computers, modern machines provide the ability to automatically enter various power savings modes. On most production server systems, the Always On option is the most appropriate. For details regarding other options, see the Windows Server 2003 Help and Support Center.

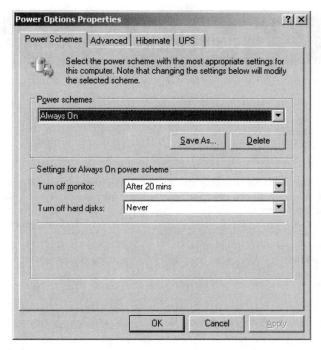

- **Printers and Faxes** As its name implies, this applet allows you to configure print devices and fax devices. For more information, see Chapter 4.

- **Scanners and Cameras** Digital cameras and scanner devices are common on desktop computers. Using this Control Panel applet, you can add, remove, and configure scanners and cameras.

- **Sounds and Audio Devices** In addition to the basic hardware settings that are available for audio hardware, these settings allow you to further fine-tune sound output. For example, on the Volume tab, you can indicate what types of speakers are connected to the computer.

- **System** Through the use of this Control Panel applet, you can monitor and manage various areas of the system configuration. In relation to hardware resources, you can access the Device Manager (covered in detail throughout this chapter), the Performance Logs and Alerts functionality (see Chapter 8), and the Disk Management utility (see Chapter 5).

All of these Control Panel applets provide additional configuration methods for managing and troubleshooting all of the many hardware devices that might be present on computers that you support. Although not all of them will be used frequently on

SCENARIO & SOLUTION

You want to change resource settings for a legacy sound card.	Access the Resources tab of the properties of the sound card in the Device Manager.
Recently, you have moved your multihomed computer to a different subnet. You want to disable one of the network adapters on the machine without physically removing it.	In the Device Manager, right-click the appropriate network adapter item and disable it. This will prevent the hardware from being usable in Windows Server 2003.
A vendor has recommended that you update drivers for a SCSI controller to improve performance and fix some minor bugs.	Use the Update Driver feature in the Device Manager. You can either right-click the SCSI device and choose Update Driver or click the Update Driver button on the Driver tab of the properties dialog box of the device.
You want to configure some advanced driver-related settings for a network adapter that you recently installed in a server.	Use the Device Manager and access the Advanced tab for the properties of the device.

your server machines, be sure that you know where to go to configure details for a specific type of hardware device.

CERTIFICATION OBJECTIVE 2.03

Troubleshooting Server Hardware

When managing the servers in your environment, it may become necessary to troubleshoot hardware problems. Issues can arise from improper driver installation, from poorly written drivers, or from a variety of other types of problems. You should always treat hardware-related issues seriously, since they can result in unscheduled downtime or intermittent errors. Remember, just about everything your server does is dependent on the hardware it's running on! In this section, you'll look at many different ways in which you can troubleshoot hardware problems using the tools provided with Windows Server 2003.

General Hardware Device Troubleshooting

Throughout this chapter, you've looked at various features in Windows Server 2003 that can be used for managing hardware. Some of these tools and techniques can also be used for troubleshooting. Here are some general hardware troubleshooting guidelines that can be used to isolate and resolve common issues:

■ **Keep your systems up-to-date**   I've already mentioned several times in this chapter that the proper functioning of hardware devices often depends on the quality of their drivers. As you perform routine maintenance on your servers, be sure to remember to check for updated device drivers. One quick and easy way to find the latest drivers is to use the Windows Update functionality (see Figure 2-14, and Chapter 8 for more information).

Keeping up-to-date with the latest drivers can sometimes offer benefits to system performance and reliability. However, in some cases, the latest drivers may not be the "greatest." If your systems are working properly, you might want to consider leaving them running with their current drivers. Of course, be sure to keep your eyes open for updates that resolve potential problems and look for significant enhancements.

FIGURE 2-14   Updating device drivers in Windows XP using Windows Update

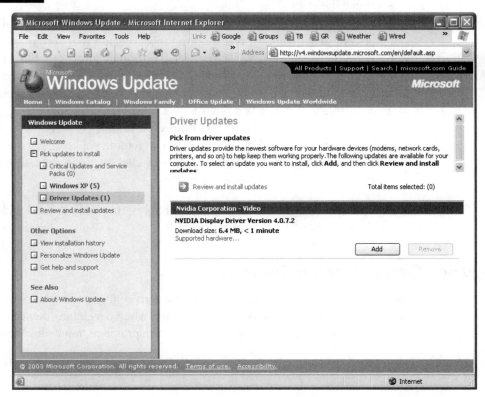

■ **Create a test environment**   If you are considering updating drivers on a critical production server, it is very helpful to verify the proper functioning of the drivers in a test environment. In the real world, this can be particularly difficult, since test hardware may not be identical to high-performance production machines. However, if you can detect problems before you modify your most important systems, the potential time and cost savings can be great!

■ **Maintain a log of hardware changes**   Troubleshooting hardware issues can be difficult, especially when problems are intermittent. Particularly in environments in which multiple systems administrators might be able to modify server hardware configurations, it's important to keep track of all changes. This might be done simply through the use of a text file or a Word document in which the date and time of a change, along with the purpose and details of the change, are documented. Then, whenever issues arise, you can look through the change log to find a potential correlation between a change and the problems that you're experiencing. As with many other areas of systems administration, there aren't any good alternatives to using good management techniques.

■ **Use Hardware Troubleshooters**   Many systems administrators totally ignore online help and troubleshooting tools because these often focus on only the simplest of issues. For example, I personally don't feel like I need a help file to tell me to verify whether a network cable is plugged in. In some cases, help files may be annoying, at best. However, the Troubleshooters that are available within the Windows Server 2003 Help and Support Center can be very helpful. Generally, it takes only a few minutes to walk through one of the troubleshooters, and the information can remind you to check the obvious. You can access Hardware Troubleshooters by clicking the Troubleshoot button on the General properties of a device.

Now that you have a good idea of basic troubleshooting techniques, let's look at some specific features in Windows Server 2003.

Configuring Driver Signing Options

A disappointing aspect of working with many modern computers and hardware devices is that vendors and manufacturers often cut corners when developing device drivers. Unfortunately, these drivers can cause serious system problems, many of which are difficult to troubleshoot. Microsoft has found that a significant portion of server reliability issues are caused by poorly written device drivers. In an attempt to alleviate these problems, the company has created a program for testing and verifying device drivers to ensure that they meet the guidelines and requirements for properly running on various versions of the Windows platform.

In order to meet these standards, hardware manufacturers must submit their device drivers to Microsoft for testing. Drivers that have passed Microsoft's review process are granted the use of a "Designed for Microsoft Windows Server 2003" certification, which assures systems administrators that the device drivers have been reviewed by Microsoft. Note, however, that this cannot provide a 100-percent guarantee that you won't have problems; it just provides some added reassurance. In order to prove that drivers have been properly tested, Microsoft provides digital signing features in Windows Server 2003.

By default, whenever you attempt to install a driver that has not been digitally signed, you will receive a warning message. You can still choose to continue the installation of the driver, or you can choose to abort it.

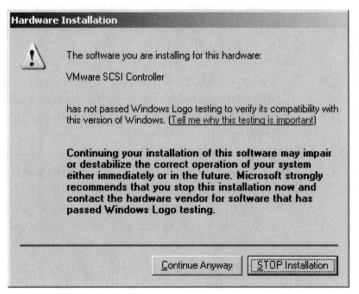

To configure driver signing, you should launch the System Control Panel applet. Click the Hardware tab and then select Driver Signing. As shown next, there are three options for driver signing configuration.

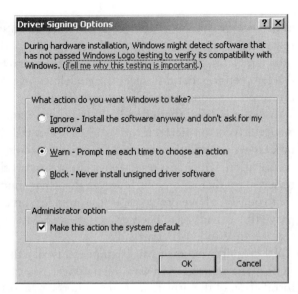

- **Ignore** This setting effectively disables any warnings associated with the lack of a digital signature. Drivers, whether they are signed or unsigned, will be automatically installed without any warning. This is the least restrictive (and most dangerous) option.

- **Warn** This setting, which is the default for new installations of Windows Server 2003, provides a warning whenever an unsigned driver is being installed. Users will be able to specify whether or not they want to continue the installation.

- **Block** This setting specifies that the system will not allow installation of unsigned device drivers. This is the most restrictive (and safest) option available. The rules are simple: If the driver is not signed, it cannot be installed into the operating system. Here is the error message that you'll receive when you attempt to install an unsigned driver:

There is also an option to make these settings the defaults for all users on the system. Ideally, you would install only drivers that are certified by Microsoft (particularly on important production systems). However, some hardware vendors do not want to go through the time and cost of getting their drivers certified. A good general rule of thumb is to be especially wary of drivers that have not been digitally signed.

Using File Signature Verification

Software installation routines can make many different types of changes to your system configuration. Sometimes, products may automatically install updated drivers or replace critical system files with other versions. The end result can be numerous problems, especially if other applications and operating system features are depending on the replaced files.

To help get around these potential problems, Microsoft has digitally signed all of the files that are included with the operating system. By checking for a digital signature for critical system file and drivers, systems administrators can ensure that they are using safe versions. If a file is lacking a digital signature, it is likely that it was replaced through the installation of another product or device driver. This is a good way to track down issues that might have been caused by the installation of unsigned drivers.

The File Signature Verification tool can be used to perform an automated search of all of the files located within the Windows Server 2003 system root directory. It can then return a report of any files that are not digitally signed. To launch this tool, click Start | Run and type **sigverif**.

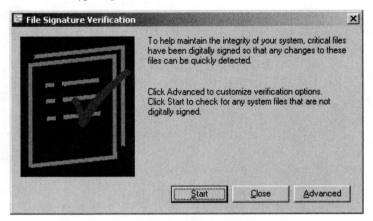

When you click Advanced, you can specify which files will be scanned. Also, the default option is to store the signature verification results in a text file called SigVerif.txt. You can change the logging options to specify if and how the log file should be written. To begin the signature verification process, click Start. The verification process may take several minutes, because several thousands of files must be scanned.

When the process is complete, you'll see an onscreen report of any files that are not digitally signed. You can use this information to identify driver files or system files that have been overwritten or that have not passed Microsoft's verification testing.

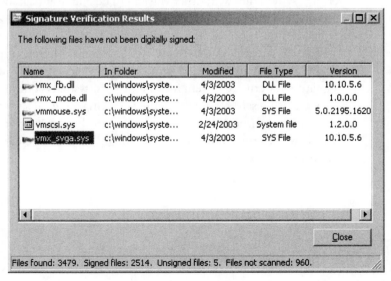

Exercise 2-2 walks you through the process of configuring driver signing options, and of using the File Signature Verification tool.

EXERCISE 2-2

Configuring Driver Signing Options

1. Log on to the computer as an Administrator and open the System Control Panel applet. Click the Hardware tab.

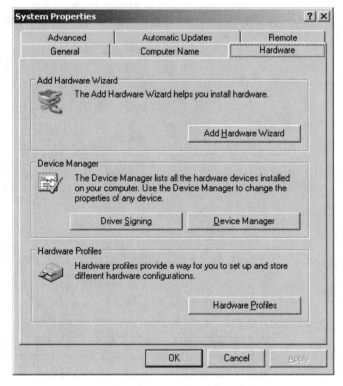

2. Examine the driver signing options for the local Windows Server 2003 machine. Click the Driver Signing button to access the driver signing device settings. There are three main options for the device driver configuration settings (see the earlier section "Configuring Driver Signing Options"): Ignore, Warn, and Block. The default option, Warn, allows the installation of unsigned drivers after a warning is displayed. If you want to ensure that

only signed drivers are installed, you can select the Block option. For the sake of this Exercise, make no changes. Then, click OK twice to exit the driver signing properties.

3. Open the File Signature Verification tool by choosing Start | Run and typing **sigverif**.

4. Before you start the file signature verification process, make some configuration changes that affect how the utility will be run. Click Advanced to access these options. On the Search tab, leave the settings at their defaults. Note that, in addition to searching system files, you can choose to search any local file system directory. You can also restrict the search to examining only certain file types (*.dll files, for example).

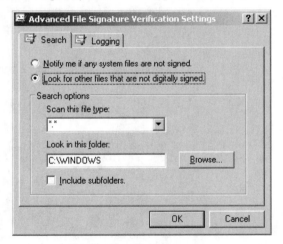

5. Click the Logging tab. The default options are to save the file signature verification log to a file. By default, this information will be stored to a text file called SigVerif.txt, and it will be located within the user's \Windows folder (for example, "C:\Documents and Settings\User1\Windows"). Ensure that the first option is checked, and that you have chosen to overwrite the log file. Change the name of the log file to **SigVerif-Test.txt**. Note that you can also provide a fully qualified local path, such as "C:\Data\SigVerif-Test.txt." Then, click OK.

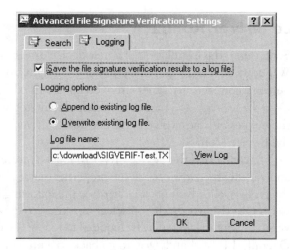

6. To begin the file signature verification process, click Start. Since you have chosen the default option of analyzing all system files, the process could take up to several minutes to complete.

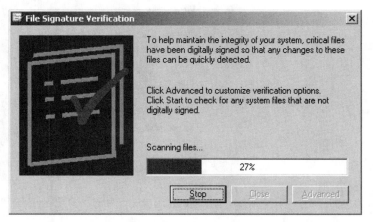

7. When the tool is finished scanning your system files, you'll see a new window that lists any files that were not digitally signed. You'll also see statistics related to how many files were scanned. When finished, click Close twice to exit the File Signature Verification Tool.

8. Optionally, load the file that you specified in step 5 in a text editor (such as Notepad) and view the details about which files were scanned.

Using Device Driver Rollback

Sometimes, the installation of a new device driver might introduce problems in Windows Server 2003. For example, you might start experiencing intermittent network connectivity issues after you update the device drivers for a network adapter. Or, a device such as a mouse or keyboard may stop working when updated. To resolve these types of issues, you can use the device driver rollback functionality from within the Device Manager.

You can access the device driver rollback feature by opening the Device Manager and viewing the Driver tab of the properties dialog box of a hardware device. To begin the process, click Roll Back Driver (see the following illustration). You will be prompted to confirm this action. If you select Yes, the driver will be reverted to its earlier version. Note that you may be required to reboot the computer for some driver changes. Overall, this is a handy way to go back to a known good configuration if an updated driver is causing problems.

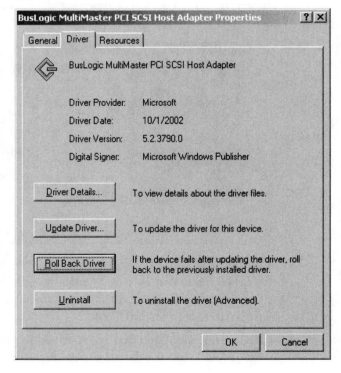

Using the "Last Known Good" Configuration

Windows Server 2003 depends on the successful functioning of many different types of hardware devices and device drivers in order to boot properly. If an incorrect or poorly written device driver is loaded for a critical system component (such as hard disk controller), the operating system may fail to start. Fortunately, there's a quick and easy way to try to solve this problem.

One of the boot options that's available on the Windows Server 2003 startup menu is to choose the "Last Known Good" configuration. You can access this menu by pressing the F8 key just before Windows Server 2003 begins booting, or by selecting special options from the boot menu. This feature relies on the fact that, after every successful system interactive logon, the operating system saves its configuration information. This information includes driver versions, hardware settings, and other details. When you choose the Last Known Good option from the boot menu, Windows Server 2003 will start up with older configuration information. Generally, this will allow you to access the operating system and to make any necessary configuration changes to restore the server to working order. Note, however, that there is a major limitation to using the Last Known Good boot option. Since the configuration information does not include copies of actual driver files, if your new driver installation overwrote or deleted some of the older files, this process may not work. In that case, your best bet would be to try to use the device driver rollback functionality (assuming, of course, that your server boots properly).

on the **Job**   *If you have just rebooted your server after making configuration changes and it appears to be acting erratically, don't log onto the computer. Just power it off and try to reboot using the Last Known Good configuration. This will prevent Windows Server 2003 from thinking that the boot process was successful and overwriting the previous Last Known Good configuration data.*

exam
ⓦatch   *There are several other options for troubleshooting boot issues. See Chapter 6 for more information on   other boot options and details about using the Recovery Console.*

Command-Line Hardware Troubleshooting Utilities

In addition to all of the hardware troubleshooting tools and features that you have considered thus far, Windows Server 2003 includes some additional utilities that can be used for diagnosing and resolving hardware issues.

One such utility is the DriverQuery command. As its name implies, the purpose of this tool is to build a list of information about all of the drivers that are installed on a computer. The DriverQuery command can be used to return information about the local computer, or to get information from a remote computer. Output can be provided in several formats, including table (the default), list, and comma-separated values. This makes it easy to use the DriverQuery command to document your server configuration from a basic script file. Figure 2-15 shows an example of running this command on a Windows Server 2003 machine.

Another useful command-line utility is the Device Console Utility. This utility can be run from a command line using the command DevCon. Though you might think that it would join your server to a Top Secret Military project, its purpose is

---

FIGURE 2-15   Getting driver details with the DriverQuery command

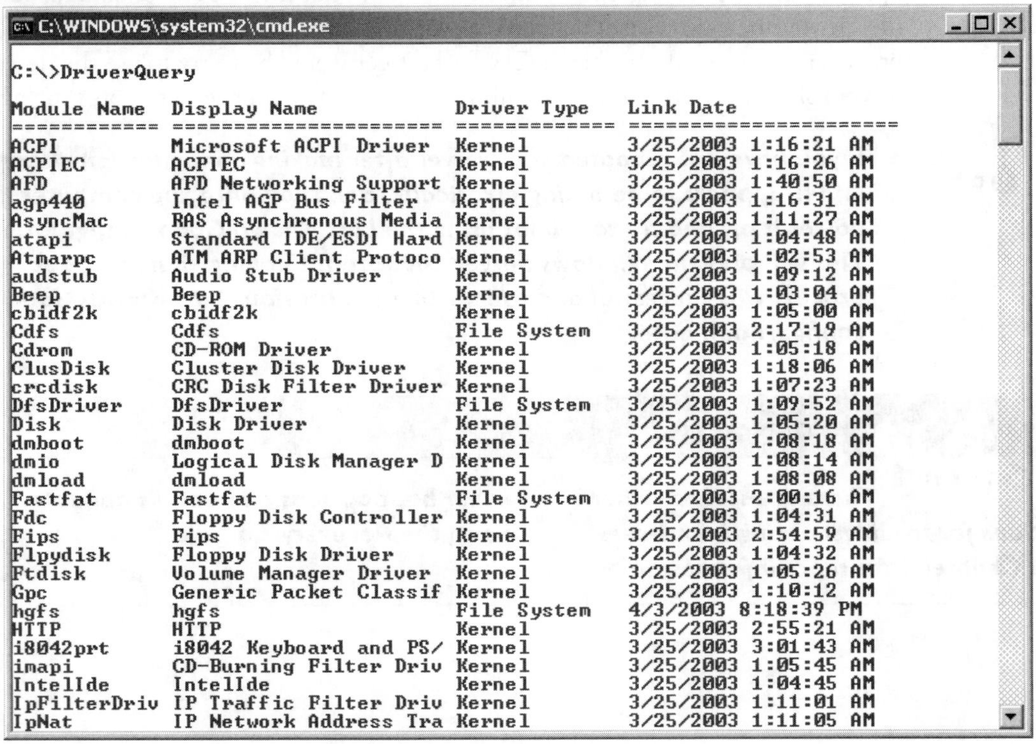

```
C:\>DriverQuery

Module Name   Display Name          Driver Type    Link Date
===========   ====================  ============   =====================
ACPI          Microsoft ACPI Driver Kernel         3/25/2003 1:16:21 AM
ACPIEC        ACPIEC                Kernel         3/25/2003 1:16:26 AM
AFD           AFD Networking Support Kernel        3/25/2003 1:40:50 AM
agp440        Intel AGP Bus Filter  Kernel         3/25/2003 1:16:31 AM
AsyncMac      RAS Asynchronous Media Kernel        3/25/2003 1:11:27 AM
atapi         Standard IDE/ESDI Hard Kernel        3/25/2003 1:04:48 AM
Atmarpc       ATM ARP Client Protoco Kernel        3/25/2003 1:02:53 AM
audstub       Audio Stub Driver     Kernel         3/25/2003 1:09:12 AM
Beep          Beep                  Kernel         3/25/2003 1:03:04 AM
cbidf2k       cbidf2k               Kernel         3/25/2003 1:05:00 AM
Cdfs          Cdfs                  File System    3/25/2003 2:17:19 AM
Cdrom         CD-ROM Driver         Kernel         3/25/2003 1:05:18 AM
ClusDisk      Cluster Disk Driver   Kernel         3/25/2003 1:18:06 AM
crcdisk       CRC Disk Filter Driver Kernel        3/25/2003 1:07:23 AM
DfsDriver     DfsDriver             File System    3/25/2003 1:09:52 AM
Disk          Disk Driver           Kernel         3/25/2003 1:05:20 AM
dmboot        dmboot                Kernel         3/25/2003 1:08:18 AM
dmio          Logical Disk Manager D Kernel        3/25/2003 1:08:14 AM
dmload        dmload                Kernel         3/25/2003 1:08:08 AM
Fastfat       Fastfat               File System    3/25/2003 2:00:16 AM
Fdc           Floppy Disk Controller Kernel        3/25/2003 1:04:31 AM
Fips          Fips                  Kernel         3/25/2003 2:54:59 AM
Flpydisk      Floppy Disk Driver    Kernel         3/25/2003 1:04:32 AM
Ftdisk        Volume Manager Driver Kernel         3/25/2003 1:05:26 AM
Gpc           Generic Packet Classif Kernel        3/25/2003 1:10:12 AM
hgfs          hgfs                  File System    4/3/2003 8:18:39 PM
HTTP          HTTP                  Kernel         3/25/2003 2:55:21 AM
i8042prt      i8042 Keyboard and PS/ Kernel        3/25/2003 3:01:43 AM
imapi         CD-Burning Filter Driv Kernel        3/25/2003 1:05:45 AM
IntelIde      IntelIde              Kernel         3/25/2003 1:04:45 AM
IpFilterDriv  IP Traffic Filter Driv Kernel        3/25/2003 1:11:01 AM
IpNat         IP Network Address Tra Kernel        3/25/2003 1:11:05 AM
```

to provide command-line access to the types of functionality that are available from the graphical Device Manager tool. For example, you can use DevCon to view a list of devices that are installed on the system, to scan for new hardware, to reconfigure driver settings and options, and to disable device drivers. Figure 2-16 provides an example of running the following command:

```
DevCon Status *
```

For further details about these command-line utilities, see the Windows Server 2003 Help and Support Center.

SCENARIO & SOLUTION

After updating a device driver for a SCSI controller, the vendor notifies you that the driver might cause stability problems in certain configurations. You want to revert to using the older driver for the controller.	Use the Rollback command within the properties of the SCSI controller. This will load the previous driver that was installed for that device.
You want to obtain hardware driver–related information from the command line.	The DriverQuery command-line utility can be used to obtain a list of device drivers, or to return details about specific drivers.
You recently installed a new device driver on your computer. However, when you reboot the system, the Windows Server 2003 screens fails to appear. You want to troubleshoot this issue with the least effort.	A good first step in trying to resolve this problem is to try to boot the computer using the "Last Known Good" configuration. This doesn't require significant effort, and it could immediately solve the problem.
You suspect that another systems administrator has installed nonsigned drivers on a Windows Server 2003 machine. You want to search for any nonsigned files.	Use the File Signature Verification tool to search for nonsigned files.

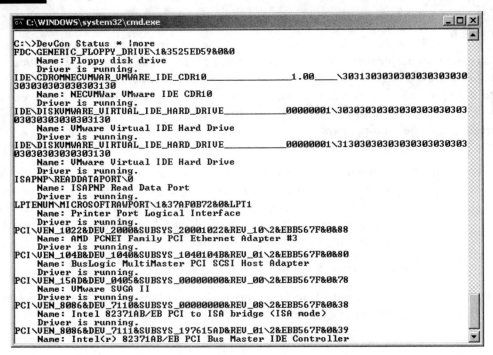

CERTIFICATION SUMMARY

The importance of proper hardware configuration on production servers cannot be overstated: Simply put, the hardware platform forms the basis for everything your server does. Throughout this chapter, you looked at many different server hardware–related tools and techniques. You began by taking a look at Windows Server 2003's hardware architecture, including the concepts of device drivers and plug and play.

Then, you looked at how you can install new hardware on your servers. The process is actually very simple, but it requires a basic understanding of hardware types. Next, you looked at ways in which you can monitor your server hardware, after it has been installed and configured. Windows Server 2003 also provides several different ways in which you can configure your hardware device, ranging from the Device Manager to device-specific Control Panel applets.

Finally, you looked at methods to perform the important task of troubleshooting server hardware problems. Fortunately, there are many methods for resolving these potentially serious issues. Drawing on the information presented in this chapter, you should be well prepared to tackle hardware-related issues—both on the exam and in the real world!

✓ TWO-MINUTE DRILL

Install and Configure Server Hardware

❑ Most types of hardware devices require the use of one or more resources, including IRQs, DMA addresses, memory addresses, and I/O ports.

❑ Windows Server 2003 relies on the use of device drivers to interact with hardware devices.

❑ During the setup process, Windows Server 2003 automatically detects and installs as much hardware as possible.

❑ The Add Hardware Wizard can be used to install new device drivers.

Configure, Manage, and Monitor Server Hardware

❑ The Device Manager provides several views through which you can monitor your hardware devices.

❑ If a device appears in the Device Manager with a yellow icon, this means that the driver for this device is not properly installed, or the hardware is not working properly.

❑ The System Information tool can provide a great deal of information relating to hardware resource usage and hardware-related conflicts.

Troubleshoot Server Hardware

❑ Driver signing is designed to allow only fully tested device drivers to be installed on a Windows Server 2003 computer. Systems administrators can configure options that specify whether device drivers must be signed.

❑ You can use the device driver rollback functionality in the Device Manager to revert to the previous driver for a piece of hardware.

❑ The DriverQuery and DevCon command-line utilities can be used for obtaining hardware-related information from a command prompt.

❑ The Last Known Good boot option can resolve common driver-related issues that may prevent Windows Server 2003 from booting properly.

SELF TEST

The following questions will help you measure your understanding of the material presented in this chapter. Read all the choices carefully because there might be more than one correct answer. Choose all correct answers for each question.

Install and Configure Server Hardware

1. Rajesh is planning to install an old legacy hardware device into a computer that is running Windows Server 2003. He shuts down the server, installs the hardware, and then boots the operating system. After logging in to the server, he does not receive any messages. However, the device does not appear in the Device Manager. Which of the following tools should he run to most easily install the hardware?

   A. The System Control Panel applet

   B. Hardware Troubleshooter

   C. The Update Driver Wizard

   D. The Add Hardware Control Panel applet

   E. System Information

2. You are planning to install Windows Server 2003 on a two-year-old server that is currently running Windows 2000 Server. Before you begin the installation process, you want to make sure that the hardware platform is supported for this operating system. Which of the following methods can you use to verify compatibility before installing Windows Server 2003? (Choose all that apply.)

   A. The Windows Server Catalog web site

   B. The Add Hardware Wizard

   C. The Device Manager

   D. The Check System Compatibility feature of the Windows Server 2003 setup media

   E. The System Control Panel applet

   F. The File Signature Verification Wizard

3. Luis is installing a new plug-and-play network adapter into a server that does not currently have any network adapters. He physically installs the hardware and then boots into Windows Server 2003. After he logs on, he sees the Add Hardware Wizard. He follows the prompts to attempt to automatically find drivers for the new device, but the wizard informs him that a suitable driver cannot be found. In which of the following ways can Luis directly provide the driver to the wizard? (Choose all that apply.)

A. From a local directory

B. From a network share

C. From a floppy disk

D. From a CD-ROM

E. From the vendor's web site

4. In general, which of the following types of resources should not be shared between multiple physical hardware devices? (Choose all that apply.)

A. Virtual memory

B. Physical memory

C. Storage resources

D. Direct memory access (DMA) addresses

Configure, Manage, and Monitor Server Hardware

5. You are hired as a consultant to assist in managing a server farm that includes 53 web servers. The servers were purchased at different times and therefore have different hardware configurations. In order to track server configurations, you decide that you want to take an inventory of all of the hardware and software installed on these machines. You want this information to be stored to a file that can later be used to view server configuration information. Which of the following tools/methods will allow you to most easily do this? (Choose all that apply.)

A. System Information | Export

B. Device Manager | Print

C. The System Control Panel applet | Export

D. System Information | Save As

E. The Add Hardware Wizard

6. You want to change hardware device settings for this device, which is installed on ten different Windows Server 2003 machines in your environment. Which of the following can you use to change hardware resources? (Choose one.)

A. A single instance of the Device Manager, running on one of the Windows Server 2003 machines

B. An instance of the Device Manager running locally on each of the servers

C. An instance of the System Information tool, running locally on each of the servers

D. Both A and B

E. Both B and C

F. None of the above

7. You suspect that more than one hardware device in your computer is using a specific IRQ, and that this is the reason a serial port device is not working. Which of the following views in the Device Manager will provide you with a sorted list of IRQs, along with the devices that are using them? (Choose all that apply.)

A. Devices by type

B. Devices by connection

C. Resources by type

D. Resources by connection

8. Rekha is experiencing problems using a mouse connected to a computer that is running Windows Server 2003. The problem seems to be that the mouse pointer is moving erratically across the screen, making it difficult to administer the computer. Which of the following can she use to view and/or change mouse-related options and settings? (Choose all that apply.)

A. The Resources tab of the properties of the mouse in the Device Manager.

B. The Driver tab of the properties of the mouse in the Device Manager.

C. The Mouse Control Panel Applet

D. The Advanced Settings tab of the properties of the mouse in the Device Manager

9. Following the installation of a second network adapter in your Windows Server 2003 machine, the server has automatically rebooted three times. Previously, you never had any problems with this server, so you suspect that the addition of the new hardware has caused the problems. Specifically, you believe that there may be a hardware resource conflict between two or more devices in the server. Which of the following tools will help you isolate or rule out any hardware resource conflicts most quickly?

A. The File Signature Verification Wizard

B. The System Information Tool | Hardware | Conflicts / Sharing

C. The Add Hardware Wizard

D. The Networking Control Panel applet

Troubleshoot Server Hardware

10. Following the installation of an updated SCSI controller device driver, your Windows Server 2003 computer fails to reboot. Before the logon screen is displayed, the server spontaneously restarts the boot process. Which of the following methods can you use to troubleshoot the issue with the least amount of effort?

A. Use the Device Manager to disable the SCSI controller.

B. Use the Rollback function in the Driver tab of the properties of the SCSI controller.

    C. Use the Windows Server Recovery Console.

    D. Use the Safe Mode boot option.

    E. Use the Last Known Good Configuration boot option.

11. Which of the following command-line utilities will allow you to change the configuration of a device driver?

    A. DeviceManager.exe

    B. DriverQuery.exe

    C. DevMgr.exe

    D. DevCon.exe

    E. HWConfig.exe

    F. None of the above

12. In order to troubleshoot a network routing issue, Paul has decided that he wants to prevent Windows Server 2003 from using two of the three network adapters that are installed in a Windows Server 2003 computer. As a first troubleshooting step, he wants this option to be easily reversible. Which of the following methods will allow Paul to most easily accomplish these goals?

    A. Delete the driver files for the device.

    B. Disable the hardware device using the Device Manager.

    C. Reconfigure the network connection and assign it a static IP address.

    D. Use the Update Driver Wizard to install "loopback" drivers for the device.

    E. Use the Device Manager to uninstall the drivers for the network devices.

13. You are attempting to install a vendor-provided driver update for a display adapter that is installed on your computer. However, when you attempt to install the driver, you receive an error message stating that it cannot be installed. Based on this information, which of the following Driver Signing options is the server currently using?

    A. Prevent

    B. Warn

    C. Deny

    D. Ignore

    E. None of the above

14. Previously, another systems administrator was responsible for managing a specific Windows Server 2003 computer that seems to be experiencing intermittent lockups. You have been asked to troubleshoot the problem. You find that the Driver Signing option is set to Ignore, and you suspect that unsigned drivers have been installed. Which of the following methods can you use to most quickly find out which unsigned drivers have been installed on the computer?

A.   Access the Drivers tab in the properties sheet for all of the drivers that have been installed on the computer.

B.   Access the General tab in the properties sheet for all of the drivers that have been installed on the computer.

C.   Use the File Signature Verification Wizard.

D.   Use the System Information tool.

LAB QUESTION

You are a systems administrator for an environment that supports 25 production servers. Recently, you upgraded all of the machines to run Windows Server 2003. These computers were purchased at different times, and with differing configurations. Many of the servers were originally implemented over two years ago, and they are beginning to show their age. Your organization has grown by 30 percent, and new applications and a greater reliance on network resources are putting significant strain on your servers.

You have been tasked with evaluating each server to determine whether hardware should be upgraded or entirely replaced. To make things more challenging, you have a limited budget. Since all of these servers are currently in production, your primary goal is to minimize the disruption of service when the hardware or software is upgraded.

Based on performance monitoring results for all of your servers, you make the determination to upgrade some servers and to completely replace others. Following the upgrades, you find that overall server performance is significantly improved (especially for the computers that were completely replaced).

However, you now find that four of the servers are experiencing intermittent issues, ranging from spontaneous system reboots to periodic application errors. None of these problems were experienced before, and other than the hardware upgrades or replacements, no other changes have been made. What are some steps you can take to monitor and troubleshoot these issues?

SELF TEST ANSWERS

Install and Configure Server Hardware

1. ☑ **D.** Through the use of the Add Hardware Wizard, Rajesh can force Windows Server 2003 to search for the legacy hardware device. He will then have the option of either installing or providing the appropriate drivers for the device.

   ☒ **A, B, and E** are incorrect because they do not allow for the installation of new drivers. **C** is incorrect because a hardware device must be visible in the Device Manager before the Update Driver Wizard can be used.

2. ☑ **A and D.** Both of these methods will allow you to verify the current hardware platform before you perform the installation.

   ☒ **B, C, E, and F** are incorrect because, although they may provide hardware-related information, they cannot provide you with details about whether the devices in your computer have passed Microsoft's compatibility tests.

3. ☑ **A, C, and D.** Luis can specify that the driver files should be loaded from a removable media device (such as a CD-ROM or floppy disk), or from a folder that is located on the local file system.

   ☒ **B** is incorrect because, although a network path could normally be specified, the question clearly states that the server does not have any other network adapters. Therefore, until this device is configured, the drivers cannot be loaded from a network share. **E** is incorrect because Luis must first download the appropriate drivers from the vendor's web site before they can be used by the Add Hardware Wizard.

4. ☑ **D.** Hardware devices require their own unique DMA addresses in order to function properly. Generally, this is handled automatically by the operating system. However, if you're using older hardware, you should keep this in mind when troubleshooting hardware-related problems. Also, since modern hardware allows for the sharing of IRQs between multiple devices, just the fact that multiple devices are sharing the same resource does not necessarily indicate a problem.

   ☒ **A and B** are incorrect because physical and virtual memory resources do not apply directly to hardware devices.

Configure, Manage, and Monitor Server Hardware

5. ☑ **A and D.** The System Information tool allows you to export data to a text file (option **A**), and to save information to a binary *.nfo file (option **D**). Both methods can be used to later view server configuration information for each of the machines.

⊠ **B, C,** and **E** are incorrect because they are not functions that allow you to save configuration information to a file.

6. ☑ **B.** Although you can use the Device Manager to view information on remote computers, you can modify hardware resource settings only from a locally running copy of this utility.
⊠ A is incorrect because the Device Manager cannot be used to modify hardware resources on a remote machine. C is incorrect because the System Information tool does not allow for modifying hardware resources.

7. ☑ **C** and **D.** Both of these Device Manager views will return a list of IRQs and the hardware devices that are using each.
⊠ A and B are incorrect because they do not provide information in the required format.

8. ☑ **A, B, C,** and **D.** All of these methods can be used to either view or change settings for the mouse. The Driver, Resources, and Advanced Settings tabs all provide methods for viewing details about the device driver that is installed. And through the use of the Mouse Control Panel applet, Rekha can modify settings that might affect mouse movement.

9. ☑ **B.** The quickest and easiest way to return a list of any hardware resources that are in conflict is to use the Conflicts / Sharing view in the System Information tool. Although you could obtain the same information via other tools and troubleshooting steps, this view will provide the information that you need in one place. Also, note that if resources are listed as "shared," this does not necessarily mean that there is a problem, since modern computers allow multiple devices to share IRQs.
⊠ A and C are incorrect because these methods will not provide information about hardware resource usage and conflicts. D is incorrect because there is no such Control Panel applet.

Troubleshoot Server Hardware

10. ☑ **E.** The purpose of the Last Known Good option is to revert the system configuration to its state following the last successful logon. Since the problem is likely due to the installation of the updated driver, this is the quickest and easiest way to boot the server so that further troubleshooting can be performed. However, keep in mind that, if the installation of the new driver deleted the older driver, the Last Known Good boot option will not fix the problem, since the older driver is no longer accessible.
⊠ A and B are incorrect because, since the server is not booting at all, these methods cannot be used to configure or troubleshoot the driver. C and D are possible methods by which this problem could be resolved, but both require more effort than option E.

11. ☑ **D.** The purpose of the DevCon.exe command-line is to provide the functions that are possible through the Device Manager in a command-line format.

☒   A, C, and E are incorrect because these are not Windows Server 2003 command-line utilities. B is incorrect because the main purpose of the DriverQuery command is to return information about the drivers that are installed in the system.

12. ☑ **B.** The easiest and safest method of preventing the use of these network adapters is to disable them using the Device Manager. This function will leave the device drivers in place but will not allow the operating system to access the hardware. Paul can easily reenable the devices, if necessary, using the Device Manager utility.
☒   A is incorrect because this is not a valid method for disabling a device. C is incorrect because this would not prevent the use of the network adapter. D is not supported in Windows Server 2003. Finally, E is a possibility, but it's not the easiest method to prevent the use of the device.

13. ☑ **E.** It is likely that you are trying to install unsigned device drivers. The only option that would automatically prevent the installation of unsigned device drivers is the Block setting.
☒   A and C are incorrect because these are not options for the Driver Signing configuration. B and D are incorrect because these options would not prevent the installation of an unsigned driver.

14. ☑ **C.** By running the File Signature Wizard, you will be able to quickly find the names of any unsigned driver files that have been installed on the computer.
☒   A is incorrect because it is not the quickest method for finding driver signing information. B and D are incorrect because they do not provide driver signing information, at all.

LAB ANSWER

It's fairly obvious that the problems that you are seeing are due to hardware changes. Since the only changes to the environment involved hardware modifications (either complete server replacements or component upgrades), this is the first area that you should suspect. In many environments, this issue can be very common. Unfortunately, you've experienced pretty poor results based on your hardware upgrades—since four out of the 25 servers are experiencing problems. Fortunately, there are ways to either avoid these problems or to troubleshoot them once they occur.

The first step that you should take when deciding to perform upgrades is to verify compatibility with Microsoft's Hardware Compatibility web site. On that site, you can easily find out if the server computers that you plan to purchase fully support Windows Server 2003. If the computers that you are purchasing are listed on the site, this means that they have been certified by Microsoft to support this server operating system. Additionally, should you encounter problems with using the server, the vendor should be able to provide you with support.

The case is a little more complicated for performing upgrades of servers. You should still begin by ensuring that the device(s) that you plan to purchase have been tested for compatibility. Next, you should verify with the original hardware manufacturer that the upgrade is supported. Many hardware platforms place limitations on memory type, supported CPUs, and other hardware components. Finally, you should be sure that you select and install only digitally signed drivers. As you saw from the results of the upgrades, hardware device driver issues can cause significant problems.

In this scenario, most of this is in hindsight. So, what can you do to isolate the issues that you're experiencing now? First, you can start by using the Device Manager and System Information tools to identify any resource conflicts or device driver problems. Either of these can point you toward the device(s) that might be causing the problem. When you isolate a problem area, you should try to update the current driver with a digitally signed one (if one exists). You may be able to use Windows Server 2003's Hardware Troubleshooting Wizards to resolve common issues. Or, you can choose to either disable or uninstall the device. Unfortunately, you might find that the quality of some hardware (and the accompanying drivers) is so low that you'll have to simply replace the product with something more reliable.

Finally, you can use the File Signature Verification tool to identify any drivers or other system files that have not been digitally signed. This can help you quickly identify which components might be causing problems.

By using all of these methods together, you can avoid many common hardware-related issues, and you can resolve the ones that do come up!

3

Managing Users, Groups, and Computers

CERTIFICATION OBJECTIVES

O ne of the fundamental features of network operating systems is to provide for the ability to securely share information between users and computers. As organizations increase their reliance on electronic communications and tools, the importance of implementing and administering security increases as well. If you look at a ranked list of the tasks that are commonly performed by systems administrators in organizations of almost any size, you're likely to find user and group management to be at (or at least close to) the top of the list.

In this chapter, you'll look at some of the core tools and features that are included in Windows Server 2003. Specifically, you'll look at ways in which you can manage users, computer, and group objects that map to the organizational needs of your business. The chapter focuses on the tools and methods used to administer security in an Active Directory environment. The goal is to provide in-depth details about security-related features that many of us take for granted.

In this chapter, we'll begin with a topic that can greatly simplify the task of managing Windows configuration settings through the use of user profiles. There's a lot to cover, so let's get started!

CERTIFICATION OBJECTIVE 3.01

Managing Local, Roaming, and Mandatory User Profiles

Modern Windows client and server operating systems offer a great number of configuration options and settings. These range from the aesthetic (such as screen saver and desktop settings) to the functional (including operating system and application-specific configurations). Often, it can take quite a while to get all of these settings "just right" (if that ever happens). So, naturally, users and systems administrators would like their settings to be available every time they log on to a computer. Additionally, I might have many different files that I want to have available, regardless of which computer I log on to.

However, there can be challenges to doing this in a networked environment. For example, as a systems administrator, I may log on to over a dozen different systems in a single morning! Users might share computers, or their systems might be replaced during an upgrade. That's where user profiles come in.

Windows NT–based operating systems (including Windows NT 4.0, Windows 2000, Windows XP, and Windows Server 2003) all allow multiple users to access a

e x a m

w a t c h   *Non–Windows NT–based operating systems (such as Windows 3.1 and Windows 95/98/ME) also store configuration information. However, these operating systems use a different method for doing this. The focus in this chapter is on Microsoft Windows NT–based network operating systems. For more information on user profile configuration in other operating systems, see the help file that accompanies the product.*

single installation of the operating system. Each user can create and maintain separate configuration settings. When the user next logs on to the same system, by default, all of her settings will be automatically reapplied. Let's look at how this process works.

How User Profiles Work

In order to provide a consistent user experience, whenever a new user logs on, the operating system creates a new user profile using the "Default User" profile that is found on each system. The user profile is stored in the Documents and Settings folder, which is created on the same volume on which the operating system has been installed. Within this folder, you'll see subfolders for each of the users that have logged on to the operating system.

User profiles contain many different kinds of information, including the following:

- ■ **Operating system settings**   Options such as desktop background, screen saver options, user interface selections, and Start menu options are all stored as part of a user profile. Additionally, many user-specific Control Panel settings are also stored so that they can be reapplied when the user logs in again.

- ■ **Windows Explorer settings**   The taskbar and view options that users select when using Windows Explorer will be automatically reapplied after subsequent logons.

- ■ **User data files**   Contents of the My Documents folder, the My Pictures folder, the Desktop, Start Menu items, and related files and folders will be stored as part of the profile.

- ■ **Internet Favorites**   Many of us depend on the shortcuts that we have created in order to easily access our favorite web sites. And, we often use cookies to simplify the process of visiting web sites. These bookmark links and cookie files are stored as part of the user profile so that they can be made available on subsequent logins.

- ■ **Application-specific settings**   Most modern applications store their configuration information in the Registry. Furthermore, most well-designed applications allow users to individually configure various options to their liking. For example, in Microsoft Word, I might define a specific toolbar configuration, while other users of my system might prefer to use another configuration. These settings are stored in user-specific portions of the Windows Registry, and this information is stored as part of the user profile.

■ **Registry settings** In addition to the many different types of settings and options that we've already discussed, there are additional user-specific settings that can be stored in the Registry. These are also included as part of the user profile. Specifically, the name of the file that is stored is NTUSER.DAT. This file contains the contents of the HKEY_CURRENT_USER Registry hive.

Figure 3-1 shows the directory structure for a user profile stored on a Windows Server 2003 computer. Note that many of the folders that are located here are hidden, by default. Therefore, you'll have to enable the option to show hidden files and folders (which can by found by choosing Tools | Folder Options in Windows Explorer) to see them all. In general, it is not a good idea to manually modify any of the files or settings that are stored in these folders.

FIGURE 3-1 Viewing the contents of a user profile folder via Windows Explorer

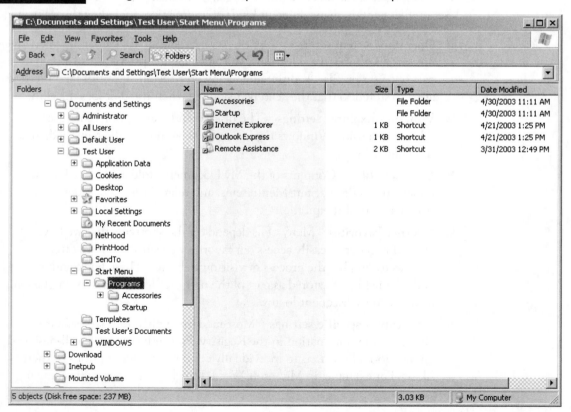

Two special user profiles are available, by default, in the Documents and Settings folder. The first is Default User. The contents of this folder will be copied whenever the operating system needs to create a new user profile. Whenever new programs must be installed with specific application settings, or if you want to configure defaults for new user profiles, those settings are stored here.

The other special folder is called All Users. Settings stored within this folder apply to all users of the system. This folder is used to store the program groups and program icons that appear on the Start menu. There are two types of program groups that can be created. The first is specific to only the user that created the program group. For example, as a SQL Server database administrator, I might create a new program group including shortcuts to my commonly used tools. The other type of program group, called "common program groups," are available to all users on the system. These are generally created when you install a new application on the computer and you want to make its program group and shortcuts available to all users of the system. These common program groups are stored in the All Users folder.

I already mentioned that user profiles are created the first time that a user logs on to a computer. In order to retain any of the changes that are made by a user during his session, the operating system will update the local user profile when the user logs off. Then, as you might expect, whenever the user logs into the same system again, these settings are read from the user profile folder and are reapplied.

By default, user profiles are stored on the local computer. However, there are several different ways in which they can be configured to work in a networked environment. With this in mind, let's take a look at some different types of user profiles.

User Profile Types

User profiles are helpful for working on a local system. After all, who wants to go through all of the hassle of configuring desktop and application settings after every login? Fortunately, you can also create other types of user profiles that are useful when working in networked environments.

There are four different types of user profiles. They are

- **Local user profiles**   As their name implies, local user profiles are created, stored, and updated on the local computer. This is the default setting for client operating systems that are not configured with other policies. The major drawback to local user profiles is that they are stored only on the local computer. If the same user logs on to another machine, she will not be able to automatically access these settings upon login.

- **Roaming user profiles**   A roaming user profile is created and stored on a network server. The purpose of roaming user profiles is to allow for centralized storage of configuration settings and files. Instead of looking for a local copy of a user profile during the login process, a remote profile is copied over the network. The major benefit of roaming user profiles is that they can be made available to users, regardless of which computer they log on to. For example, I might log on to Workstation1 and make several configuration settings. When I log off a computer on which this profile is used, the roaming profile on the server is automatically updated. Then, I can later log on to Workstation2 and have the same settings automatically applied during the logon process.

■ **Mandatory user profiles** In some types of environments, systems administrators may want to enforce consistency for all types of user settings. For example, you might want to apply a certain set of configuration options for all members of the Accounting Clerks group. Furthermore, you would want to prevent any of the members of this group from making changes to the profile. That's exactly the purpose of a special type of roaming user profiles called mandatory user profiles. Unlike other profile types, mandatory user profiles are generally created by systems administrators (not the end users that will be using them). If the mandatory user profile is not available, the user will not be allowed to log onto their computer. When the user logs off the system, the mandatory profile is not updated. Therefore, whenever users log on again, they'll have the same system configuration that they had after their previous logon. In addition to the scenario I already mentioned, mandatory user profiles can be useful for training environments and single-use computers (for example, an Internet kiosk terminal).

■ **Temporary user profiles** In networked environments, it is possible that user's profiles cannot be loaded due to connection failures. Or, due to other problems (such as security permissions issues or the accidental deletion of the profile folder), the operating system may not be able to load the user's profile upon login. In these circumstances, the system can automatically create a temporary user profile for just that session. The user will not have her settings applied after the login process completes, and the user profile will not be automatically updated after log off. Although this situation is not ideal, it does allow users to log in whenever a roaming profile cannot be loaded.

e x a m
ⓦ a t c h **Be careful not to confuse
hardware profiles with user profiles—
they are completely different features of
Windows Server 2003! Hardware profiles
store information that is specific to the
configuration of a computer, while user
profiles store details related to operating
system and application configurations.
For more information on hardware profiles,
see Chapter 2.**

Now that you know the different types of profiles that are available, let's look at how these profiles can be created and managed.

Creating and Managing User Profiles

The main method for administering user profiles on a Windows Server 2003 computer is by accessing the Advanced properties tab in the System Control Panel icon. Alternatively, you can access this tab by right-clicking the My Computer desktop icon and selecting Properties. The User Profiles dialog box, shown next, can be accessed by clicking the Settings button in the User Profiles section of the Advanced tab.

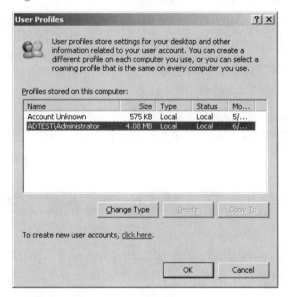

The list includes all of the user profiles that are currently being used on the local computer. There are three operations that can be performed when you select one of the user profiles. These options are

■ **Change Type** When you select a user profile and click the Change Type button, you will be able to specify whether the profile is a local or roaming profile (see the following illustration). Note that you will not be able to change the profile type for the user that is currently logged on to the system.

- **Delete** This option is as straightforward as it seems: When you click Delete, the selected user profile (along with all user configuration information and settings) will be completely deleted from the system. As you might expect, it is not possible for the currently logged-in user to delete his or her own user profile. However, other users (assuming they have sufficient permissions) can use this function when they know that the user profile is no longer needed on the local computer.

- **Copy To** For various reasons, you may want to copy the contents of a user profile to another location (either on the same computer, or on a network server). You can perform this operation by using the Copy To command. The following illustration shows the available options. You can specify the local or network location to which the profile will be copied. This will cause all of the contents of the selected user profile to be copied to the specified destination folder. You can also specify security permissions related to the copied profile by clicking the Change button in the Permitted To Use section. This operation will allow you to specify which user(s) and/or group(s) will be able to access the copied profile.

Primarily, these commands are used to administer local user profiles. Now, let's look at the details of creating roaming and mandatory user profiles.

Creating a Roaming User Profile

As I mentioned earlier, the primary feature of roaming user profiles is that they are stored on a server (instead of on the local computer). The process to set up a roaming user profile is fairly simple, involving only a few steps. The first step is to create a shared folder for the remote user profile on your server. (For more information on creating and managing shared folders, see Chapter 4.) The shared folder in which the roaming user profile will be stored can be located on any Windows Server 2003 computer that is a member of the domain. This includes domain controllers and member server computers.

Once you have created the new shared folder, it's time to assign the path to this folder to the appropriate user account. The Active Directory Users and Computers tool is used to configure and manage users' profile paths. To find the setting, start by right-clicking a user account and selecting Properties. Then, select the Profile tab. In the User Profile section of this dialog box (shown next), you can specify a shared folder location for the "User profile path setting."

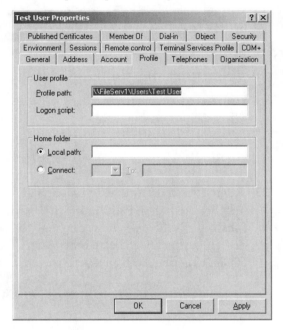

If you want to make this a roaming user profile, you must provide a Universal Naming Convention (UNC) network path to the folder. For example, you might enter **\\Server1\Users\JManager** for the user profile path for a user account. This specifies that the roaming user profile will be created and stored in the JManager folder, which is located within the Users share on Server1.

EXERCISE 3-1

Configuring a Roaming User Profile

1. Log on to the computer as an Administrator. Using Windows Explorer, create a new shared folder called "TestUserProfile." For the purpose of this exercise, the location of this shared folder is not important. For more information about creating and sharing a folder, see Chapter 4.

2. Open the Active Directory Users and Computers tool. Create a new OU named "Profile Test." Within this OU, create a new user that has a logon name of "TestUser1" (use the defaults for all other settings). More information about creating new user accounts is presented later in this chapter.

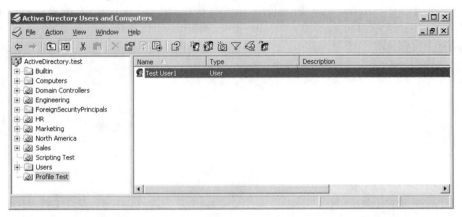

3. Right-click the TestUser1 account and select Properties. Select the Profile tab. For the Profile Path setting, type a UNC name such as **\\Server1\ TestUserProfile** (you'll need to replace "Server1" with the name of the server on which you created the folder). Click OK to save the settings. Then, close the Active Directory Users and Computers tool.

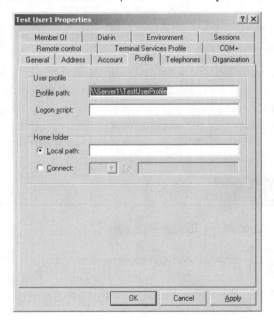

4. To test the new roaming profile, log on to another computer using the TestUser1 account. Make changes to the desktop settings (such as the background and screen saver). Then log off that computer. Repeat this process on another computer. Note that, regardless of which computer you use, the TestUser1 account will always have access to the last-saved user configuration information.

As you can see, the process of setting a shared folder for a single user account is fairly simple. But, what if you want to assign roaming user profiles for several dozen users? One method of doing this would be to access each of the users' account properties individually and make the user profile setting changes manually. If you're like me, you'd probably like a better way (that's an awful lot of clicking, which provides a lot of room for error). Fortunately, the Active Directory Users and Computers tool allows you to select multiple user accounts (by using the CTRL-click operation) and then select Properties. This will allow you to change the profile path for multiple users, shown next.

This dialog box offers you the option to configure user profiles in two different ways. First, you can enter in the path to a single user profile (for example "\\Server1\Users\Engineering"). If you configure the profile path in this way, all of the users will be using the exact same profile folder. And by default, changes made by any of the users will be automatically seen by other users when they next log on to the system.

The other option is to use an environment variable setting so that all of the selected users will have separate profile folders. This can be done through the use of the "%UserName%" system environment variable. For example, you can set a user profile path of "\\Server1\Users\%UserName%." This specifies that each user will have a user profile path based on their logon username. For example, if you specify this user profile path for the user accounts User1 and User2, the user profile path for User1 will be "\\Server1\Users\User1," and the user profile path for User2 will be "\\Server1\Users\User2." Of course, you must have created the root shared folder into which the profiles will be stored (the individual profile folders will be automatically created). However, it does offer you an easy way to set user profile path settings for dozens of users at the same time!

Creating a Mandatory User Profile

As you might expect, the process for creating and assigning a mandatory user profile is similar to that of configuring roaming user profiles. After all, mandatory user profiles are simply roaming profiles that must be applied upon login and that are not updated when a user logs off.

The first step in the assignment of a mandatory user profile is to create the user profile itself. To create a new profile, simply log on to a computer using any user account. Then, make the changes that you want and log off. This will save all of the settings that you have made. For example, you might create a special user account called "Sales User." Any changes that you make after you log on the computer using this account will be saved in a new user profile. The next step is to configure the new user profile as mandatory. This is simply done by renaming the NTUSER.DAT file to NTUSER.MAN. Notice that only the extension of the file is being changed. The .MAN extension will specify that this profile is meant to be mandatory and that it will not be updated when a user logs off his or her computer.

Once you have created the profile that you want to make mandatory for one or more users, you should copy the profile information to a network shared folder that will be accessible to all of the users to which this profile should apply. The best way to do this is to use the User Profiles dialog box (which was covered earlier in this section). Just select the Copy To command, and then specify the network location to which the profile should be copied. Also, be sure to set the appropriate permissions for the user(s) or group(s) that will need access to the profile.

Now that the mandatory user profile is ready for use, the last step is to assign the mandatory user profile to the user(s) that require it. To do this, simply follow the same procedure that you walked through to configure a roaming user profile. All of the settings will be similar (even when modifying multiple user accounts at the same time).

For users that have been assigned a mandatory user profile, the profile will be automatically downloaded and applied upon login (in the same way that a local or roaming user profile is used). The only major difference is that any changes that users make to the profiles will not be saved to the profile. Therefore, users will always have a consistent starting point every time they log on to their computers. Should the need arise to make changes to the profile, an Administrator can make the changes to the common user profile by using the same process that was used to create the profile.

Next, let's take a look at some more methods by which you can modify user profile settings.

Configuring User Profiles Settings Using Group Policy

You can use several Group Policy settings to configure user profiles. The relevant Group Policy settings can be found in the following path: User Configuration (or Computer Configuration) | Administrative Templates | System | User Profiles. As shown in the following illustration, there are many different options that can be configured to fine-tune the behavior of local and roaming user profiles.

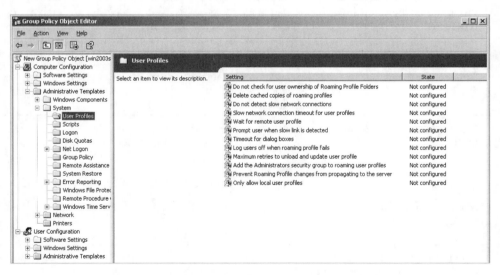

Table 3-1 lists the available options, along with their purposes.

TABLE 3-1   User Profile Group Policy Settings, and Their Purposes

Group Policy Setting	Purpose
Do not check for user ownership of Roaming Profiles folders	Specifies that ownership information will not be checked for the Roaming Profiles folder when a user attempts to log on. In order for this setting to take effect, it should be configured on the client computers that will be using roaming profiles.
Delete cached copies of roaming profiles	By default, for performance reasons, a copy of a user's roaming profile is stored locally on the client computer. If you enable this setting, you will prevent the profile from being stored on the client computer. This can increase security, but it can decrease performance, especially across slow links.
Do not detect slow network connections	When enabled, this setting specifies that the client and server should not use slow link detection during the logon process. If enabled, all settings related to slow link detection will not apply.
Slow network connection timeout for user profiles	This setting specifies the threshold for when a connection between a client and server will be considered a "slow connection." If enabled, administrators can specify the connection speed (in Kbps), and the round-trip communications time (specified in milliseconds).
Wait for remote user profile	Specifies that the client computer should wait for a remote profile to load, even if it is taking a long amount of time.
Prompt user when slow link is detected	If enabled, users will be presented with a dialog box whenever a slow link is detected during login (assuming slow link detection is enabled). Users will be given a choice of whether they want to load a local copy of the policy or whether they want to wait to download the remote copy.
Timeout for dialog boxes	Specifies the amount of time (in seconds) that the system will wait when dialog box prompts are displayed during login (for example, the slow link detection prompt).
Log users off when roaming profile fails	When enabled, if the user's roaming profile cannot be located or transferred to the client computer, the user will automatically be logged off. This is a useful setting if you want to ensure that a user can access his or her roaming profile, but it can prevent users from accessing their systems if the user profile server is unavailable.
Maximum retries to unload and update user profile	This setting specifies how many times the client will retry to update a user profile if an application currently has Registry keys open. The default for this setting is 60 retries.
Add the Administrators security group to the roaming user profiles	If enabled for computers, when a new roaming user profile is created on that machine, members of the Administrators group will automatically be granted permissions on it.

TABLE 3-1	User Profile Group Policy Settings, and Their Purposes *(continued)*	
Group Policy Setting	**Purpose**	
Prevent Roaming Profile changes from propagating to the server	Generally, when a user logs off her client computer, the server copy of the roaming profile is updated. If this setting is enabled, the server copy will not be updated with any changes that were made to the local copy of the profile.	
Only allow local user profiles	Specifies whether roaming user profiles will be available on specific computers. When enabled, users will only be able to create local user profiles on their computers.	

All of these Group Policy settings can be enabled or disabled. Many settings also allow you to further configure how profiles will behave. For example, the following illustration shows the available options for setting limits on what defines a slow network link.

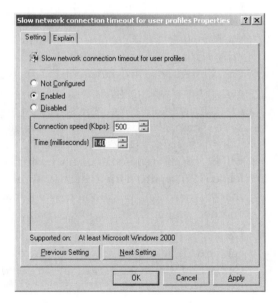

User Profile Best Practices

So far, we've covered a lot of information related to working with user profiles. Let's wrap up this discussion by looking at some suggestions and recommendations that are related to implementing and managing user profiles on Windows Server 2003:

■ *Configure user profile shared folders with the minimum required permissions.* Since user profiles can contain sensitive information—user data files, Internet settings, and so on—it's important that systems administrators implement proper security for the shared network folders that contain user profile data. In general, this means that the profiles should be stored on a volume that is configured with the NTFS file system and that only the user(s) for whom the profile should apply and members of the Administrators group should have access to these folders. For more information on configuring and securing shared folders, see Chapter 4.

■ *Beware of hardware-specific settings that might affect shared profiles.* Since user profiles contain information about display settings (such as screen resolution and color depth), it is possible to run into problems when certain settings are applied to machines with different hardware configurations. For example, if a user has configured his desktop computer to use a resolution of 1600 × 1200 pixels and 24-bit color depth, these settings may be incompatible with older computers.

■ *When logging on to multiple machines, remember that profiles are updated during the logoff process.* Some types of users may log on to multiple machines using their roaming user profiles. Since profiles are updated when the user logs off the computer, some changes that are made in one of the sessions may be lost. As an example, suppose I log on to both Workstation1 and Workstation2. On Workstation1, I decide to make some desktop configuration changes and install a new application. On Workstation2, I decide to make some desktop configuration changes. I log off Workstation1 first, and then log off Workstation2. In this case, only the changes that were made on Workstation2 will be effectively saved to the roaming user profile, and the other changes will be lost. You should also remember that, since user profiles are only loaded and applied during the logon process, changes to a roaming profile that you make on one computer will not affect your use of that profile on another computer (until you log off and then log on to the system again).

■ *Do not use the Encrypting File System (EFS) with user profiles.* Although EFS can provide additional security for the data stored in user profiles, EFS is not supported for roaming user profiles. For more information about EFS, see Chapter 4.

■ *Provide adequate disk space for roaming user profiles.* Keep in mind that user profiles can grow significantly in size, depending on the volume of data that users are storing. Be sure that the servers on which roaming profiles are stored have adequate disk space. Also, if you configure disk quotas for the server volume that contains the roaming profiles, be sure to provide a reasonable limit that allows for the storage of Registry and configuration settings in addition to user documents and files. For more information about implementing and configuring disk quotas, see Chapter 5.

SCENARIO & SOLUTION

You want specific users in the Accounting department to all use the same user profile whenever they log on to the system.	Create a new mandatory profile for these users and then assign the same profile path for all of the users using the Active Directory Users and Computers tool.
John has a laptop computer that is rarely connected to a network. He wants to make sure that his user settings and configuration are retained whenever he logs off the computer.	The ideal solution for John is to use local user profiles. Since this type of profile is created automatically, you don't need to take any special actions. Settings changes will automatically be stored to John's local user profile.
Several users in your environment may use multiple computers throughout the day, depending on their work tasks. You want to ensure that users' profile information is available, regardless of which computer they're using.	Configure individual roaming user profiles for each of these users. To avoid the loss of user configuration settings, instruct the users to be sure to log off a computer before they log on to another one.
You want Monica's user profile to be accessible to a new employee named Jason.	Use the User Profiles dialog box to select Monica's user profile, and specify either a local or network location for the destination of the operation. Specify that Jason should have permissions to use the profile.

■ *If you run into problems, be sure you have the appropriate permissions.* In order to perform tasks such as assigning a user profile directory for a user account, you must be a member of the Domain Administrators, Enterprise Administrators, or Account Operators group.

By keeping these best practices in mind, you should be well prepared to manage user profiles.

CERTIFICATION OBJECTIVE 3.02

Creating, Managing, and Troubleshooting User Accounts

Since the fundamental purpose of most network environments is to provide computer resources to authorized employees, it should come as no surprise that creating and administering user accounts is a very important task. In this section, you'll start by taking a look at some basic information related to the security architecture of Windows Server 2003. Then, you'll look at some common administrative tasks and how you can perform them using standard operating system features.

Understanding Basic Security Concepts

A common administrative task for systems administrators is the management of basic network objects. Daily tasks might include creating new user accounts, disabling unneeded accounts, and modifying group membership. Therefore, it should come as no surprise that Microsoft expects you to be able to show that you understand how to perform these important tasks on the exam. Windows Server 2003 includes several different tools and many features related to handling common systems administration tasks.

Before we dive into the technical details of working with users, groups, and computers, it's important to understand some basic security concepts. In this section, you'll take a look at concepts related to security principals, as well as different types of accounts.

Understanding Security Principals

In order to ensure that security is maintained in modern operating systems, certain types of objects must be uniquely identified. This is especially true in networked environments where there may be many thousands of users and related network objects. In Windows Server 2003, a security principal is an object to which security-related permissions can be applied. User principal types include users, computers, and groups. If you've performed any routine systems administration in the Windows world, you're probably familiar with setting basic permissions and user rights. These operations are performed on security principals.

In Chapter 4, you'll look at further details related to setting and managing permissions at the level of the file system. The concepts are the same, but the procedures might be slightly different.

Every security principal is identified by a unique security identifier (SID). Internally, Windows Server 2003 uses SID information to keep track of users, groups, and computers. For the most part, the operating system deals with SIDs and security principals behind the scenes. However, it's important to keep in mind that SIDs are created when a new security principal is created and that SIDs do not change. For example, if you create a new group called Managers, the new group has a unique SID. Whenever you assign permissions to the Managers group, the settings are really made for the group's security identifier. This is important to note because, even if you rename the group, the security identifier will remain unchanged.

In this section, you'll look at some details related to security mechanisms that most of us take for granted when we're working with a network operating system. Let's start with discussing local security.

Local Security

In the world of Microsoft's network operating systems, there are two main types of security systems. The first is security that is designed for a single machine or for small groups of computers. In this type of security, called "workgroup security," all security principals and information are stored separately on each computer. That is, each computer in such an environment will have its own security accounts database (which includes all security principals, along with their SID information). Figure 3-2 provides an overview of how local security works.

An important aspect of local security is that local user accounts are designed to allow permissions only on the computer on which the account was created. Local accounts pertain to the following Windows computer configurations:

■ **Client computers** Whether or not they belong to a domain, client computers have local user accounts that can be configured. This applies primarily to computers that are running a client-side version of Windows, such as Windows

FIGURE 3-2

Understanding local (or "workgroup") security

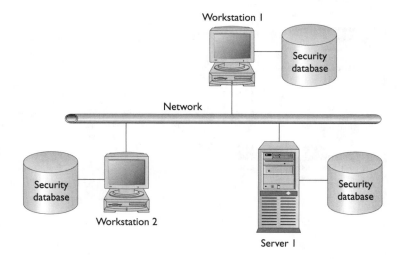

2000 Professional or Windows XP (Home or Professional Edition). Client computers have their own local accounts database, regardless of whether or not they are members of a domain.

■ **Stand-alone servers** This server configuration is not a member of a domain. Instead, it either does not participate on a network at all (which in the real world, is fairly rare) or is configured to function in a workgroup. Stand-alone servers have their own accounts database that is specific to that computer. All user accounts are created on the local computer, and permissions can be assigned only to resources that exist on that machine.

■ **Member servers** Member servers are server computers that are joined to a domain, but that are not domain controllers. That is, they participate in domain-based security, but they do not hold a copy of the Active Directory database. Member servers have a local accounts database, as well as access to the domain database.

To administer local user accounts, you can use the Computer Management administrative tool. By clicking the Local Users And Groups item and then on Users, you'll be able to see a list of all of the user accounts that are defined on the local system. To administer the settings for local users, you can simply right-click a user object and select Properties. Figure 3-3 shows a list of the users that are configured on a Windows XP computer.

FIGURE 3-3   Using the Computer Management tool to administer local users and groups

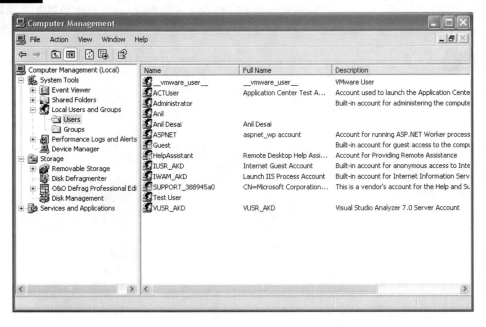

There is a significant drawback to using local user accounts: You must set them up on each of the computers on which they exist. It doesn't take much imagination to see that this method can quickly get out of hand. For example, whenever a new employee is added to your organization, you might have to create a new account for that user on dozens of different computers. And, worse yet, if you need to remove a user account, you'll have to go through the same trouble. If you forget to disable or delete the account on even one machine in the environment, you have created a potential security risk!

Clearly, there's a better way to centrally manage user accounts and information in a networked environment. Let's look at that, next.

Domain Security

Domain user accounts can be created on computers that are functioning as domain controllers. In the world of Active Directory, this means that it only pertains to computers that are members of the Windows 2000 Server and Windows Server 2003 platforms. Specifically, related to Windows Server 2003, any edition except for the Web Server Edition can function as a domain controller (see Chapter 1 for details on the various editions of Windows Server 2003).

Domain-based security uses a centralized security database in which all security information is stored. Users, computers, and groups are all included within a domain database. Figure 3-4 provides an example of how domain-based security works. Other computers (including client computers and other servers) can choose to join a domain to participate in this security model. Such computers are referred to as "members" of the domain, and they will automatically have access to the domain's security database.

There are many benefits of working in a domain-based environment. Most significantly, since all security information is stored and managed centrally, each user in the environment will generally have only one user account. Since all of the computers that are part of the domain have access to the central user database, systems administrators can provide permissions for these accounts on any of the computers in the domain. When a new user account needs to be created, it only has to be done in one place. And whenever changes to computer accounts or groups are required, they also can be done quickly and easily.

FIGURE 3-4

Understanding
domain-based
security

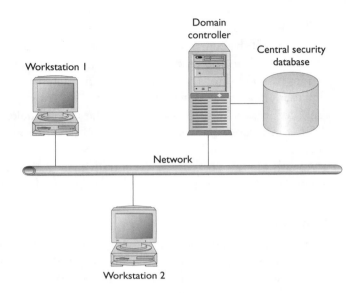

Let's look at a very high level overview of how you can set up and administer a domain-based environment.

Administering Domain Security   You can create a new Active Directory domain environment by promoting a Windows 2000 Server or Windows Server 2003 computer to a domain controller. This process walks you through the steps that are required either to create a new domain or to join an existing one. Basic information about Active Directory domains is covered in Chapter 1.

Once you promote a computer that is running Windows Server 2003 to an Active Directory domain controller, you will no longer be able to access the local accounts database. When you launch the Computer Management tool, you'll no longer see the Local Users and Groups branch. This is because you generally do not use or

exam
watch   *It is beyond the scope of this book (and the 70-290 exam) to cover the details of implementing Active Directory in depth. This chapter focuses on concepts and tasks related to monitoring users, groups, and computers. More information about* *working with the Active Directory is covered in MCSE Windows Server 2003 Active Directory Infrastructure Exam 70-294 (McGraw-Hill / Osborne, 2003) and on Microsoft's 70-294 exam.*

administer local security principals on domain controllers. Instead, you create and manage domain users, computers, and groups.

The primary tool that is used to create, configure, and manage domain accounts is the Active Directory Users and Computers administrative tool. The following illustration shows the types of information that can be viewed using this tool.

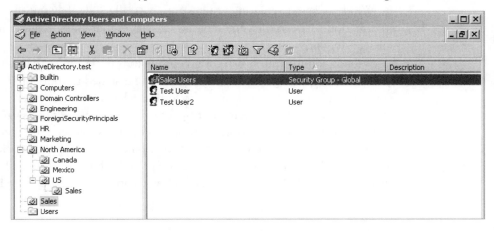

Although you can run Active Directory Users and Computers on many different versions of Windows, you can administer domain user accounts only by connecting to a domain controller. For more information on remotely administering domain controllers, see Chapter 7.

Since the Microsoft exam objectives specifically state that you should be able to modify and manage user accounts using the Active Directory Users and Computers tool, most of the remainder of this chapter (including the exercises) will be performed on a Windows Server 2003 domain controller. Note, however, that much of the information presented here will also apply to configuring and managing local user accounts.

With all of this in mind, let's start looking at how you can create and manage user accounts.

Understanding User Accounts

User accounts are most often assigned to individual employees within an organization. Most users will have only a single account, but all users that require network access will have one. These accounts (and their passwords) should not be shared between members of your organization. User accounts can also be used for special purposes, such as applications that are configured as services.

A user account is an object that can be given access to network resources. Most commonly, users connect to various resources (either locally or over the network) using a combination of their user account name and their password. Other methods, such as the use of smart cards or biometric devices, are also becoming increasingly popular replacements for standard authentication methods. Once users are logged in, Windows-based operating systems automatically and safely transfer authentication information between the computers and resources that might require this information for security purposes.

Systems administrators can assign permissions to resources that define which users can access them. In general, user accounts are assigned to individual employees in your organization. User accounts also form the basis for other types of security. For example, you can implement auditing for some or all of your users, in order to track certain actions that are performed on your client and server computers. You can also grant permissions to user accounts on Shared Folders and operating system files and folders. Details about these topics are presented in Chapter 4. Throughout this section, you'll look at ways in which you can create, manage, and troubleshoot user accounts.

Creating New User Accounts

In an Active Directory environment, the primary tool that is used to create and manage user accounts is the Active Directory Users and Computers administrative tool. Using this console, you can view a list of the structure of an Active Directory domain (which is mainly defined through the use of Organizational Units [OUs]), as well as any objects that reside within the domain.

To create a new user account, you can simply right-click the folder or OU in which you want to create the new user object and select New | User. This will display the New Object – User dialog box.

When you start creating a new user account, you'll need to specify information about the user's first, last, and full name (see the following illustration). This information will be available to other users and administrators that might need to identify to which employee a user account belongs. You will also need to specify a user logon name. This value is what the employee for whom you're creating the account will use to log on to his or her computer. Often, systems administrators will use a naming convention to determine the user logon name. For example, a common method is to use the employee's first initial, following by his or her full last name.

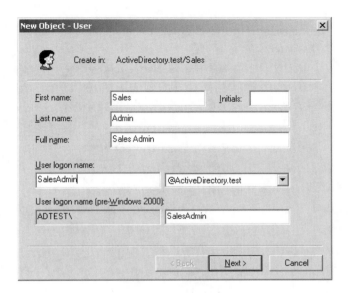

The complete user logon name actually consists of two parts. In addition to the user logon name, you must also specify the User Principal Name (UPN) suffix for the user. This value is set using the drop-down menu. The default setting for the UPN suffix is the DNS name of the domain on which the account is being created (for example, "mycompany.com"). When combined together, the user logon name and UPN suffix form the entire unique username. An example might be jdoe@mycompany.com. Most commonly, the default UPN name will be adequate. In large, distributed, multidomain environments, however, systems administrators may need to change the UPN suffix.

The final piece of information that's required on the first step of creating a new user object is a pre–Windows 2000 user logon name. Windows NT 4.0 and earlier versions of the Windows platform used names that were specified using a combination of the NetBIOS name of the domain, followed by a backslash and the name of the user account (for example "MyDomain\User1"). The default logon name will be the same as the one entered in the User Logon Name text box.

When you click Next, you'll see the second step of the process of creating a new user account (see the following illustration). On this step, you must provide (and confirm) the password that the employee will use to log on to the system. The password that you assign must meet any settings that govern the length and complexity of the password. If it doesn't, you'll see an error message when you attempt to create the user process. We'll cover more information about password policies later in this chapter. There are also several other options available on this screen:

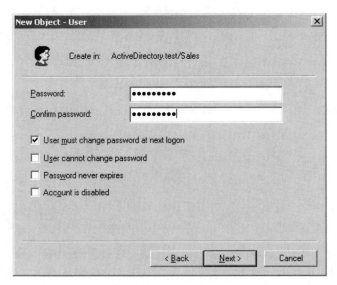

- **User Must Change Password At Next Logon**   Since the default password for the user account will be created by a systems administrator, this is an important option. If it is enabled, the user will be prompted to change his or her password upon the first login to the domain.

- **User Cannot Change Password**   In some cases, you might want to prevent users from changing the password for an account. For example, if you are supporting a test environment in which many different users share a simple user account, you wouldn't want anyone to change the password setting. As you might expect, you cannot specify both this and the preceding option.

- **Password Never Expires**   For security purposes, it is a recommended practice to force users to change their passwords after a certain period of time. When a password expires, users will be prompted to enter a new password before they can log on to the system. This is done to prevent compromised passwords from being used indefinitely, and to create a "moving target" for unauthorized users who might be trying to guess passwords. Generally, you will want to disable this option. However, in some cases (for example, if you're creating a new account for use by an application or an automated service), you may want to specify that the password should never expire.

■ **Account Is Disabled**   Often, systems administrators will need to create accounts for incoming employees before they arrive for their first day of work. In such cases, it can be helpful to disable the account during creation. Disabling an account is a safe operation, since it only prevents the use of the account that you are creating for logon purposes. You can still assign permissions and configuration settings for a disabled user account. Therefore, it's often a good idea to disable an account for a period of time before you permanently delete it.

After you provide the logon information and click Next, you'll see a summary of the options that you have chosen (see the following illustration). When you click Finish, the new user account will be created and will appear in the Active Directory Users and Computers interface.

The process of creating a new user account is fairly straightforward, but it includes only some of the many possible settings that can be assigned to a User object. Let's take a look at some of those next.

Configuring User Properties

Once a user account has been created, you can perform the most common configuration tasks for the User object through the Active Directory Users and Computers administrative tool, shown in the following illustration. By right-clicking an existing User object, you'll see many of the most common operations. The list of options includes

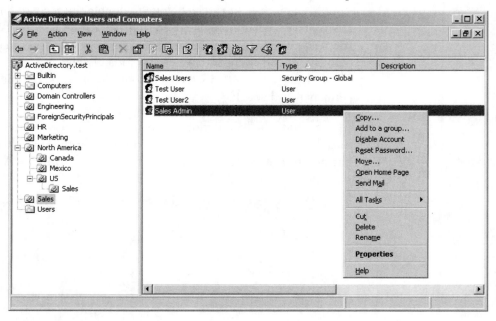

- ■ **Copy** The Copy command allows you to take many of the settings for an existing user account and create a new account with those same settings. This option is very useful when you want to quickly create multiple users that have similar properties. In larger network environments, systems administrators will often create "template" users for this purpose. The template user account is generally disabled, but it contains the most common settings that are used for new user objects.

- ■ **Add To A Group** Security permissions are most often managed by placing users in groups. By using this command, you can quickly add a user account to a group. We'll cover the details of managing group membership later in this chapter.

- ■ **Disable Account** If you need to temporarily make an account unusable for logon purposes, this is a quick way to do that. Accounts are often disabled after employees leave an organization, or when employees are away on vacation. Disabled user accounts can easily be identified in the various administrative tools (such as Active Directory Users and Computers and the Computer Management tool) with a red icon.

■ **Reset Password**   Perhaps one of the most common (and annoying) tasks that many systems administrators perform is to reset passwords for users that have forgotten them. Using this option, you can quickly provide a new password for the user account:

■ **Move**   Another common operation is to move a user account between folders or OUs that show up in the Active Directory Users and Computers interface. You can right-click one or more objects by choosing the Move command. You'll be presented with a dialog box that asks you to specify to where the accounts should be moved. You can also move Active Directory objects by using simple drag-and-drop operations (much as you would do with files in Windows Explorer).

■ **Open Home Page**   If you have defined a URL for an employee's home web page, selecting this option will launch your default browser and open that page.

■ **Send Mail**   If you have provided information about the user's e-mail address, you can quickly send him or her an e-mail message using your default mail client. Note that you must have an e-mail program configured on your system before you can send a message.

So far, we've discussed only the most common operations that can be accessed by right-clicking user objects. The complete set of user properties options can be accessed by right-clicking a user object and selecting Properties. When you first access these properties, the list of potential tabs and user settings can be overwhelming! Fortunately, the dozens of available settings are grouped onto various tabs, and you'll often want to modify settings for only a few of them. Here is some information about some important user properties:

■ **General**   On the General tab (shown in the following illustration), you can provide full name information and a description for the user account. Although it may take a few extra seconds up-front, it's worthwhile to add description information about the purpose and function of the account. This will prevent accidental deletions, and it will allow you to quickly understand what the account is used for.

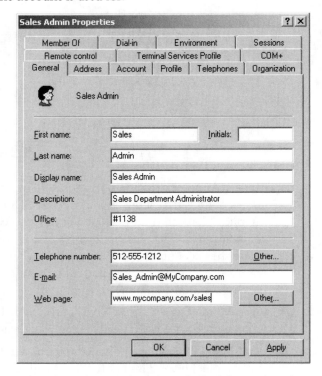

- **Member Of** This tab provides a list of all of the groups this user is a member of. You can easily add and remove group membership here.

- **Profile** These settings determine how and where a user's profile resides (a topic that was covered earlier in this chapter). Additionally, you can choose to map a network drive to a specific path, and you can assign a default home directory for the user.

- **Environment** This tab allows you two options for the user's environment, including the running of any program on startup and whether network resources will be connected to automatically whenever the user logs in.

- **Sessions** On this tab (shown in the following illustration), you can control how the user's session is managed by the operating system. Options for determining the amount of time the user must be idle in order for a connection to automatically time out are available.

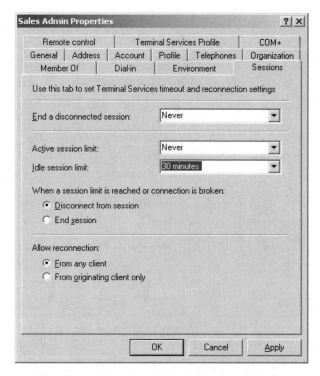

In addition to the basic tabs that are available for all Active Directory users, new applications and operating system features can provide additional options. For example, if you have configured Windows Server 2003 as a Terminal Service (a topic that's covered in Chapter 7), you will see various settings related to remote connections. Similarly, if you install Microsoft's Exchange Server 2000 (or later), you'll find additional settings related to messaging configuration.

A good method of discovering all of the available options is to simply click the various tabs. You can also use the What's This? help icon to obtain details about various settings. Further details are also available in the Windows Server 2003 Help and Support Center.

Another very useful feature that's available through the Active Directory Users and Computers tool is the ability to select and modify settings for multiple user accounts at the same time. To do this, simply select multiple user objects and then right-click one of the selected objects and choose Properties. This will show you a common dialog box that can used to create settings for all of the selected objects. As shown in the following illustration, however, there are limitations: Only certain types of settings can be modified for multiple users at the same time. For example, on the General, Address, and Profile tabs, you can specify the same location, contact information, and organizational information for all of the selected objects. This is a great way to save a lot of typing, and to ensure consistency in data entry.

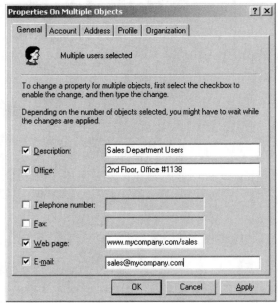

When you select multiple user objects, several useful options are available on the Account tab (shown in the following illustration). Using this dialog box, you can quickly make changes to settings such as the available logon hours for the user account.

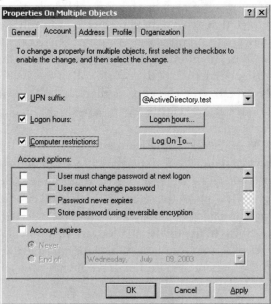

Now that you've seen how to create and configure user accounts using Active Directory Users and Computers, let's take a look at some other methods of working with user accounts.

Importing User Accounts

If you're working in a very small organization that consists of only a few users and groups, you'll probably find the graphical user interface of the Active Directory Users and Computers tool to be sufficient for most purposes. But, what if you're tasked with creating 14,000 new user accounts as part of a new Active Directory implementation? You might wish you were a consultant that was being paid by the click, or that you had a robot to handle this incredibly tedious task. Fortunately, Windows Server 2003 includes a couple of utilities that can be used to import user accounts.

A common task for some systems administrators (and many database administrators and application developers) is to transfer information between systems. In many cases, organizations might have information in one format (such as a text file or a relational database system) and want to import the information into another format. Microsoft realized that many organizations would want to take, for example, a list of users from a database export and automatically create those users within the Active Directory. There are two command-line utilities that can be used to perform this task. In this section, you'll look at details related to using both.

Using CSVDE

The first utility that can be used for importing and exporting Active Directory information is called the CSV Directory Exchange, csvde. The syntax of this command is

```
csvde [-i] [-f FileName] [-s ServerName] [-c String1 String2]
      [-v] [-j Path] [-t PortNumber] [-d BaseDN] [-r LDAPFilter]
      [-p Scope] [-l LDAPAttributeList] [-o LDAPAttributeList]
      [-g] [-m] [-n] [-k] [-a UserDistinguishedName Password]
      [-b UserName Domain Password]
```

By running the command "csvde (that is, the command without any arguments) from a command prompt, you will see the following help and reference information for the command:

```
CSV Directory Exchange
General Parameters
-i              Turn on Import Mode (The default is Export)
-f filename     Input or Output filename
```

```
-s servername   The server to bind to (Default to DC of computer's domain)
-v              Turn on Verbose Mode
-c FromDN ToDN  Replace occurences of FromDN to ToDN
-j path         Log File Location
-t port         Port Number (default = 389)
-u              Use Unicode format
-?              Help
Export Specific
-d RootDN       The root of the LDAP search (Default to Naming Context)
-r Filter       LDAP search filter (Default to "(objectClass=*)")
-p SearchScope  Search Scope (Base/OneLevel/Subtree)
-l list         List of attributes (comma separated) to look for in an
                LDAP search
-o list         List of attributes (comma separated) to omit from input.
-g              Disable Paged Search.
-m              Enable the SAM logic on export.
-n              Do not export binary values
Import
-k              The import will go on ignoring 'Constraint Violation' and
                'Object Already Exists' errors
Credentials Establishment
Note that if no credentials is specified, CSVDE will bind as the currently
logged on user, using SSPI.
-a UserDN [Password | *]          Simple authentication
-b UserName Domain [Password | *]   SSPI bind method
Example: Simple import of current domain
    csvde -i -f INPUT.CSV
Example: Simple export of current domain
    csvde -f OUTPUT.CSV
Example: Export of specific domain with credentials
    csvde -m -f OUTPUT.CSV
        -b USERNAME DOMAINNAME *
        -s SERVERNAME
        -d "cn=users,DC=DOMAINNAME,DC=Microsoft,DC=Com"
        -r "(objectClass=user)"
No log files were written. In order to generate a log file, please
specify the log file path via the -j option.
```

If you don't often use command-line utilities, you'll likely find the examples particularly useful. One important limitation of the CSVDE utility is that it cannot be used to import or export password information. This is done by design to prevent potential security problems of viewing passwords (remember, not even Administrators can view password information). Therefore, when user accounts are imported, they will automatically be set to disabled.

The CSVDE utility is used to import and export Active Directory information to and from comma-separated values (CSV) files. CSV files are simple text files that contain information that is separated by commas. After an export operation, the resulting text file can be viewed in Notepad.

```
export.csv - Notepad                                                    _ □ ×
File  Edit  Format  View  Help
DN,objectClass,cn,sn,givenName,distinguishedName,instanceType,whenCreated,whenChanged,disp
"CN=Test User1,OU=Sales,DC=ActiveDirectory,DC=test",user,Test User1,User1,Test,"CN=Test Us
"CN=Test User2,OU=Sales,DC=ActiveDirectory,DC=test",user,Test User2,User2,Test,"CN=Test Us
"CN=Test User3,OU=Sales,DC=ActiveDirectory,DC=test",user,Test User3,User3,Test,"CN=Test Us
"CN=Test User,OU=Sales,DC=ActiveDirectory,DC=test",user,Test User,User,Test,"CN=Test User,
"CN=Engineering User1,OU=Sales,DC=ActiveDirectory,DC=test",user,Engineering User1,User1,En
```

Performing an export is also a good way to learn the format and available fields that can be provided in a CSV file that you want to use for importing users.

on the job

A very handy way to deal with CSV files is to use Microsoft Excel to open them. In most cases, Excel will automatically organize the contents of the CSV file into rows and columns that you can easily edit. When you are done making your changes, be sure that you save the file in the CSV format so that it can be used with tools such as CSVDE.

The CSVDE command can also be used to modify user account information through simple text file manipulation. For example, if you want to change some information for hundreds of different users, you could simply export the relevant information, make the changes in the text file, and then reimport that data. Next, let's look at a similar Active Directory import/export utility.

Using LDIFDE

Another command-line utility is available for importing and exporting Active Directory information to and from specially formatted files that store LDAP information. The name of the command is LDIFDE, and its syntax is:

```
ldifde [-i] [-f FileName] [-s ServerName] [-c String1 String2]
       [-v] [-j Path] [-t PortNumber] [-d BaseDN] [-r LDAPFilter]
       [-p Scope] [-l LDAPAttributeList] [-o LDAPAttributeList]
       [-g] [-m] [-n] [-k] [-a UserDistinguishedName Password]
       [-b UserName Domain Password] [-?]
```

You'll notice that, for the most part, the LDIFDE command is quite similar to the CSVDE command. The major difference between the two is that the formats of the files that can be used for import and export are different. As an example, the following is a single user record that has been exported using LDIFDE:

```
dn: CN=Test User1,OU=UserImportTest,DC=ActiveDirectory,DC=test
changetype: add
accountExpires: 9223372036854775807
cn: Test User1
codePage: 0
countryCode: 0
displayName: Test User1
distinguishedName: CN=Test
User1,OU=UserImportTest,DC=ActiveDirectory,DC=test
givenName: Test
instanceType: 4
name: Test User1
objectCategory:
 CN=Person,CN=Schema,CN=Configuration,DC=ActiveDirectory,DC=test
objectClass: top
objectClass: person
objectClass: organizationalPerson
objectClass: user
sAMAccountName: TestUser1
sn: User1
userAccountControl: 512
userPrincipalName: TestUser1@ActiveDirectory.test
uSNChanged: 70340
uSNCreated: 70335
whenChanged: 20030611192752.0Z
whenCreated: 20030611192751.0Z
```

For more syntax information about this command, just type **ldifde** (the command without any arguments) to display the command-line help. As is the case with CSVDE, LDIFDE also does not import or export passwords. Therefore, all imported accounts will be disabled, by default.

Exercise 3-2 walks you through the process of performing an export and an import using the LDIFDE command.

EXERCISE 3-2

Importing User Data Using LDIFDE

Note that in order to complete this exercise, the domain into which you will be importing user accounts must allow blank passwords to be assigned to new users. If this is not allowed, you will see a password-related failure when you try to import the new user accounts. Information on changing this policy is presented later in this chapter.

1. Log on to a Windows Server 2003 domain controller as a member of the Domain Administrators group and then open the Active Directory Users and Computers tool.

2. For the purpose of this exercise, you will begin by creating a new top-level OU. Within the default Active Directory domain, right-click the name of the domain and select New | Organizational Unit. For the name of the OU, type **UserImportTest** and click OK.

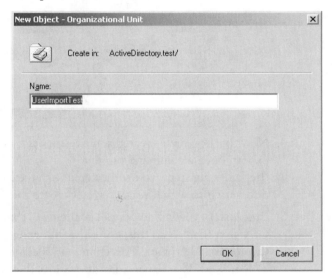

3. Next, you will create several new user accounts within the UserImportTest OU. Select the OU by clicking it in the Active Directory Users and Computers tool. Then, by right-clicking the name of the OU and choosing New | User, create all of the user accounts shown in the following table. For the purpose of this exercise, you will need to provide passwords for each of these accounts. Feel free to make up any password that meets your domain's password requirements. Leave all other options at their defaults. When finished, leave the Active Directory Users and Computers tool open (you'll be returning to it in a later step).

First Name	Last Name	Logon Name
Test	User1	TestUser1
Test	User2	TestUser2
Test	User3	TestUser3

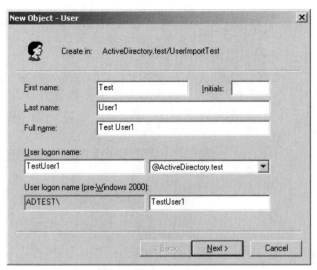

4. Now that you have created some test users that you can use for performing an export, open a command prompt by choosing Start | Run and typing **cmd**. In the following steps, you will be creating an export file, so change to a local directory into which you can safely create this file (for example, "C:\Temp").

5. In this step, you will export all of the users that you created in step 3 to a CSV text file. To do this, enter the following command on a single line at the command prompt. This command specifies that you want to export to a file named "UserExport.ldif." It specifies that the output should be verbose, and that you only want to export user object types from the UserImportTest OU. Note that you will need to replace the italicized parameters with the correct values for your Active Directory domain.

```
ldifde -f UserExport.ldif -v -r "(objectclass=user)" -d
"OU=UserImportTest,DC=DomainName,DC=com" -m
```

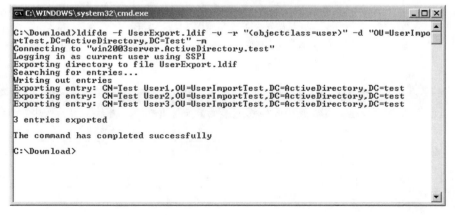

6. Return to the Active Directory Users and Computers tool and delete the user accounts that you created earlier in step 3. Leave the tool open, and then return to the command prompt.

7. Next, to examine the contents of the text file that was created in the preceding step, type the following command at the command prompt: **notepad UserExport.ldif**. This will open the Notepad application, and you should be able to see several rows of information. Before continuing to the next step, be sure that word wrap is turned off by clicking the Format menu in Notepad. When finished, close Notepad.

```
UserExport.ldif - Notepad                                      _ □ ×
File  Edit  Format  View  Help
dn: CN=Test User1,OU=UserImportTest,DC=ActiveDirectory,DC=test
changetype: add
accountExpires: 9223372036854775807
cn: Test User1
codePage: 0
countryCode: 0
displayName: Test User1
distinguishedName: CN=Test User1,OU=UserImportTest,DC=ActiveDirectory,DC=test
givenName: Test
instanceType: 4
name: Test User1
objectCategory:
 CN=Person,CN=Schema,CN=Configuration,DC=ActiveDirectory,DC=test
objectClass: top
objectClass: person
objectClass: organizationalPerson
objectClass: user
sAMAccountName: TestUser1
sn: User1
userAccountControl: 512
userPrincipalName: TestUser1@ActiveDirectory.test
uSNChanged: 70465
uSNCreated: 70459
whenChanged: 20030611195325.0Z
whenCreated: 20030611195325.0Z

dn: CN=Test User2,OU=UserImportTest,DC=ActiveDirectory,DC=test
changetype: add
accountExpires: 9223372036854775807
cn: Test User2
codePage: 0
countryCode: 0
displayName: Test User2
distinguishedName: CN=Test User2,OU=UserImportTest,DC=ActiveDirectory,DC=test
givenName: Test
instanceType: 4
name: Test User2
```

8. Finally, you'll get to the main point of this exercise: importing user accounts. To do this, simply return to the command prompt, type the following command, and press ENTER. When the command completes, you will see results similar to those shown in the illustration. Close the command prompt window.

```
ldifde -i -f UserImport.ldif -v
```

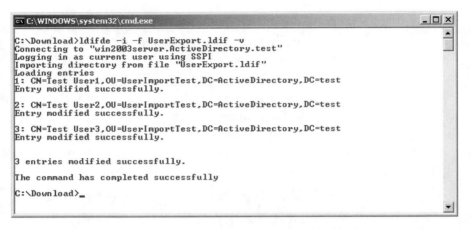

9. The final step of this exercise involves verifying that the users were properly imported. To do this, return the Active Directory Users and Computers tool. If it is not currently selected, click the UserImportTest OU. You should now see five user accounts listed in the display. If you do not see the users, press the F5 key to refresh the display. Note that all of the users have been imported and that all of them have the same last name of "User." When finished, close the Active Directory Users and Computers tool.

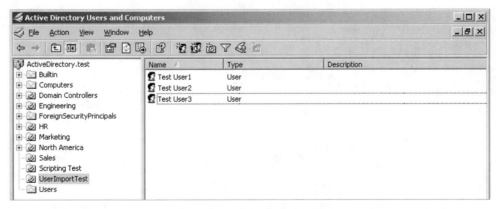

For complete details about the available options for the CSVDE and LDIFDE commands, see the Windows Server 2003 Help and Support Center.

Windows Server 2003 also includes methods that can be used to programmatically create and modify user accounts. You'll look at those methods later in this chapter.

Don't worry too much about memorizing all of the command-line options for the CSVDE and LDIFDE commands. Instead, spend your time *understanding how these utilities can be used. Ideally, you'll be able to perform a simple test import of user accounts to get a feel for the process.*

Creating and Modifying Users and Groups Through Automation

Windows Server 2003 provides methods for creating and modifying user objects programmatically through a technology known as automation. Automation simply refers to the ability to programmatically access the functions and features of other tools and applications. Although there are many details related to how this works, to create and modify user accounts, you really only need to understand the basics. That's what we'll cover in this section.

on the
Ⓙob

I've found that systems administrators often shy away from trying to learn how to "program" using scripting. In the not-too-distant past, it was a needlessly complicated task to write a simple script to perform an operation. However, in newer Microsoft operating systems, the methods of creating and running scripts can be extremely useful, powerful, and (best of all) easy! It's likely that any time that you spend learning how to create new automation scripts will pay for itself quickly in overall time savings.

Automation can be implemented through the use of many different types of languages and technologies. For example, you can create a script file using Microsoft's Visual Basic Scripting Edition (VBScript) language. You can also implement automation through many different languages, including Microsoft's .NET languages (including Visual Basic .NET and C Sharp) and many other programming tools from Microsoft and other vendors.

For the purpose of preparing for the exam, it's best (and easiest) to learn how to administer user accounts through automation using VBScript. VBScript files are simply text files that can be created with any text editor (such as Notepad). By convention, VBScript files are created with the .vbs file extension. When you double-click a .vbs file, Windows Server 2003 will automatically launch the Windows Scripting Host (WSH), which will execute the VBScript file.

In this section, you'll look at some ways in which you can create simple VBScript files to automate the creation and modification of user accounts. While an in-depth discussion of programming concepts is far beyond the scope of this book, this information should provide you with enough details to script some basic administrative tasks.

on the **Job**

It's very easy to create a lot of damage to your network environment by running malicious scripts. Before you attempt to execute a script file, be sure that it has come from a trusted sender and that you have reviewed the contents of the script. This is one area in which an ounce of prevention is definitely better than a pound of cure!

Walking Through an Automation Script

To begin creating a new script, you can create a new text file in a utility such as Notepad. The following code listing provides an example of some VBScript automation code that can be used to create Active Directory objects using automation:

```
'Connect to the default Active Directory Domain
Set oRoot   = GetObject("LDAP://rootDSE")
Set oDomain = GetObject("LDAP://" &  oRoot.Get("defaultNamingContext"))
'Create a new Organizational Unit
Set oOU=oDomain.Create("organizationalUnit","ou=Scripting Test")
oOU.Put "Description", "Scripting Test OU"
oOU.SetInfo
'Create a new Group object
Set oGroup = oOU.Create("Group", "cn=Scripting Test Group")
oGroup.Put "sAMAccountName", "EngineeringUsers"
oGroup.Put "Description", "This group was created using automation."
oGroup.SetInfo
'Create a new User object
Set oUser = oOU.Create("User", "cn=Scripting Test User")
oUser.Put "sAMAccountName", "Scripting Test User"
oUser.Put "Description", "This user object was created using automation."
oUser.SetInfo
'Set additional Properties for the new user object
oUser.SetPassword "TestPassword123"
oUser.AccountDisabled = False
oUser.SetInfo
'Add the new user to the group that we created previously
oGroup.Add oUser.ADSPath
```

If you're new to scripting, this code might look a little intimidating. Once you understand what's going on, however, it will likely become second nature! Let's walk through this code, line by line. Before we walk through the actual code, let's note some important things about this script file. First, the VBScript programming language itself is not case-sensitive. However, the actual arguments that are used by functions may be either case-preserving or case-sensitive. For example, the password itself is case-sensitive and may need to use mixed-case to meet the password policies of your environment. Therefore, if you're new to scripting, be sure to enter the scripts with the same case as shown in the code listings. Also, it is recommended that you use some kind of naming convention in order to distinguish objects and variables that might be used throughout the script.

Second, all of the lines that begin with an apostrophe character are treated as comments and are completely ignored by the Windows Scripting Host. Finally, the numbers that precede each line of code were added for the sake of referencing the code in the script file. For an executable version of the script, see Exercise 3-3. Specifically, this VBScript file performs the following operations:

- Creating a new Organizational Unit named "Scripting Test"
- Creating a new Active Directory Group object named "Scripting Test Group"
- Creating a new Active Directory User object named "Scripting Test User"
- Setting various properties for the newly created user, including the password and enabling the user account
- Adding the "Scripting Test User" to the "Scripting Test Group"

Okay, with all of this basic information out of the way, let's start examining the actual script code, line by line.

The first step in creating an automation script is to create new objects that reference a connection to an Active Directory domain. Lines 2–3 do exactly that. The Set command is used to create a new object, and the GetObject function defines the namespace for the domain to which you want to connect. In this case, you are connecting to the "default naming context," which will be the domain of the local domain controller. Note, however, that the script could be modified to connect to any domain within an Active Directory forest.

The next step is to create a new OU object. Again, this is done using the Set command in line 5. This line references the "Create" operation of the oDomain object that you created earlier in the script. Since many different types of objects may be created within a domain, the two arguments that you must pass to the Create method are the type of "organizationalUnit" (notice the capitalization) and the name of the OU that you want to create. Now that you have a new OU object (called "oOU"), you can assign properties for the OU. To demonstrate this, in line 6, you're adding a description for the OU object. Finally, you will use the oOU object's SetInfo method (see line 7) to assign the new properties to the OU.

Now that you've created a new OU, the next step is to create a new group and a new user within that OU. You'll notice that you're using a set of steps that is similar to the one that you used for creating the new OU. In line 9, you're using the Create method of the oOU object. This time, you're creating a new group. Lines 10 and 11 set properties for the group object. Finally, line 12 updates the Group object with the properties that you have set.

Lines 14–17 walk through the process of creating a new user account. Note that the syntax and method calls are similar to the ones used to create a group. Next, in lines 19–21, you use some special methods of the oUser object. Specifically, you're setting the password property, and you're specifying that the account should be enabled.

The final executable line in this script is line 23. Here, you're using the Add method of the oGroup object to add the new user that you created to the group. Since this Add method requires a particular path for the object, you must use the ADSPath property of the oUser object.

Okay, with all of that out of the way, let's actually walk through the process of creating and executing an automation script file.

EXERCISE 3-3

CertCam 3-3 ON THE CD

Creating Users and Groups
Through Automation

1. Log on to a Windows Server 2003 domain controller as a member of the Domain Administrators group.

2. Open Notepad by clicking Start | Run and typing **Notepad**. Type the following text into the new, blank document that has been created. Note that this code is the same as the script that you examined within the text, except for the fact that all comments and line numbers have been deleted.

```
Set oRoot   = GetObject("LDAP://rootDSE")
Set oDomain = GetObject("LDAP://" & oRoot.Get("defaultNamingContext"))
Set oOU=oDomain.Create("organizationalUnit","ou=Scripting Test")
oOU.Put "Description", "Scripting Test OU"
oOU.SetInfo
Set oGroup = oOU.Create("Group", "cn=Scripting Test Group")
oGroup.Put "sAMAccountName", "EngineeringUsers"
oGroup.Put "Description", "This group was created using automation."
oGroup.SetInfo
Set oUser = oOU.Create("User", "cn=Scripting Test User")
oUser.Put "sAMAccountName", "Scripting Test User"
oUser.Put "Description", "This user object was created using automation."
oUser.SetInfo
oUser.SetPassword "TestPassword123"
oUser.AccountDisabled = False
oUser.SetInfo
oGroup.Add oUser.ADSPath
```

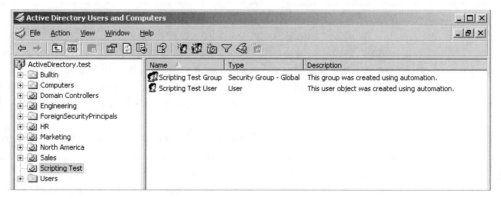

```
ScriptingTest - Notepad                                          _|□|x|
File  Edit  Format  View  Help
Set  oRoot    = GetObject("LDAP://rootDSE")
Set  oDomain  = GetObject("LDAP://" &  oRoot.Get("defaultNamingContext"))

Set  oOU=oDomain.Create("organizationalunit","ou=Scripting Test")
oOU.Put "Description", "Scripting Test OU"
oOU.SetInfo

Set  oGroup = oOU.Create("Group", "cn=Scripting Test Group")
oGroup.Put "sAMAccountName", "EngineeringUsers"
oGroup.Put "Description", "This group was created using automation."
oGroup.SetInfo

Set  oUser = oOU.Create("User", "cn=Scripting Test User")
oUser.Put "sAMAccountName", "Scripting Test User"
oUser.Put "Description", "This user object was created using automation."
oUser.SetInfo

oUser.SetPassword "TestPassword123"
oUser.AccountDisabled = False
oUser.SetInfo

oGroup.Add oUser.ADSPath
```

3. When you're finished typing in the script, choose File | Save As in Notepad. Save the file as "ScriptingTest.vbs" to a location on the local file system of the domain controller. Make a note of the location.

4. Using Windows Explorer, browse to the folder to which you saved the script file and double-click the file. You may notice that a command prompt running the CScript utility will open momentarily while the script runs.

5. After the script has completed, it's time to see the results of your work! Open the Active Directory Users and Computers administrative tool. Within the local domain, you should see an OU called "Scripting Test." Click this OU and verify that there are two objects (a User and Group) within it.

```
Active Directory Users and Computers                              _|□|x|
File  Action  View  Window  Help                                  _|♂|x|
←  →  |±||⌐|   |     |⌐|⌐|⌐|  |⌐|  |⌐|⌐|⌐|▽|⌐|⌐|

ActiveDirectory.test       | Name ▲              | Type                    | Description
  Builtin                  | Scripting Test Group| Security Group - Global | This group was created using automation.
  Computers                | Scripting Test User | User                    | This user object was created using automation.
  Domain Controllers
  Engineering
  ForeignSecurityPrincipals
  HR
  Marketing
  North America
  Sales
  Scripting Test
  Users
```

6. View the properties of the user and group that you created to verify that the description information that you set was properly updated.

7. Finally, to verify that the "Scripting Test User" account that you created is a member of the group "Scripting Test Group," right-click the group and select the Members tab. You should see the user as a member of the group.

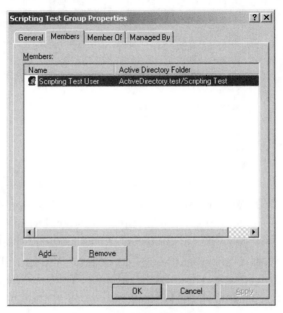

8. Once you're finished, delete the Scripting Test OU, including all of the objects located within it. Then, close the Active Directory Users and Computers tool.

At first, it might seem like a lot of work to create and execute a script for the simple purpose of creating an OU, a user, and a group object. However, through the use of some additional basic programming techniques, you should be able to easily create many users and groups with just a few lines of code. For example, if you need to create 100 test accounts for your company's lab, you can easily do that with a simple loop.

Once you've walked through the basics of creating objects through automation, it's a good idea to make changes to the script to create and manage additional users and groups. Especially if you start a new script from scratch, you'll have some valuable knowledge of how to easily perform common tasks through basic programming.

For more information and examples related to creating scripts and using automation, see the following resources:

- Windows Server 2003 Help and Support Center
- The Microsoft Software Developer Network (MSDN) Scripting Technologies web site: http://www.microsoft.com/scripting
- The Microsoft TechNet Web Site: http://www.microsoft.com/technet. Using this site, you can search for articles about scripting.

Implementing Security Policy Settings

So far you've looked at many different ways in which you can administer user accounts. But wait, that's not all! For some server installations, the default security settings that are implemented when Windows Server 2003 is installed (or when you create your first Active Directory domain) will be optimal. However, most systems administrators will want to modify the configuration on their production machines, to increase security and to meet various requirements for their organization.

In addition to the many options that are available for user accounts, Windows Server 2003 provides methods to control some important security settings that are related to logons and user accounts.

In order to change policies that apply to a Windows Server 2003 computer, you can use the administrative tools that are included with the operating system. For example, to configure settings for the entire domain, you can create or modify Group Policy Objects through the Active Directory Users and Computers tool. You can

INSIDE THE EXAM

Administration the Easy Way

One of the most important tasks for systems administrators is to find the *best* solution for a given problem. Often, the best solution isn't necessarily the easiest, nor is it the most familiar. This can definitely be seen in the many different ways in which users objects can be created using Windows Server 2003 and the Active Directory. By now, you're probably quite familiar with the Active Directory Users and Computers tool. When it comes to creating a few user or group objects, it really couldn't get much easier than using this tool.

But, what if your job is a little bit more complicated? For example, suppose you have to create a *thousand* user accounts. Sure, you could do this with standard graphical tools, but after you start typing a few user names and passwords, you'll undoubtedly begin to think, "there must be a better way!" Fortunately, there is. In this case, you have several options. First, you're typing in the information for user accounts from somewhere. If this is from an electronic document of some sort (for example, an Excel spreadsheet), then you should try to change the data into a format that will be usable by the CSVDE utility. By taking a few

hours to "massage" the data into a usable form, you'll probably save many hours of typing. And, that's not to mention the many errors that you would probably make in typing in a list of thousands of names.

But, what should you do if the data is not in a format that can be easily converted into a comma-separated values file? Another excellent solution is scripting. Using modern programming tools and automation, it can be fairly simple to read in the contents of a file (perhaps line by line), and to parse out the information that you need. Sure, it will take you a little while to set up a program to do this. But in the long run, it could save a lot of time and effort. For example, suppose that the HR Administrator finds out that he sent you the wrong list of users! In this case, you could surprise everyone by saying, "no problem!"

Best of all, when you start to use technologies such as scripting, you will learn some new skills that can really help make routine tasks much simpler. Remember, you should resist the urge to always do things using the most familiar method. This type of thinking will help you on the exam and in the real world!

also change domain options using the Domain Security Policy administrative tool. The settings that you make for domain security will apply to all of the user accounts in the entire domain. Therefore, it's important to take the time to get the settings "right" for your environment.

You can also configure policy settings at levels other than the domain level. If you want to configure security settings on domain controllers, the Domain Controller Security administrative tool is the right tool for the job. Or, you can configure security settings for the local computer through the use of the Local Security Policy administrative tool.

In this section, you'll walk through many security-related options that are available in Windows Server 2003. The goal is to provide you with a quick tour of important security-related policy options. The first stop on our tour is probably a popular one with systems administrators: password policies.

Password Policies

A fundamental aspect of security for all operating systems is in the area of authentication. Although newer technologies are available, authentication is still most often performed through the use of a login name and a password. From a systems administration standpoint, it's important to ensure that users are complying with password policies. It may be a scary thought, but if someone correctly determines that an Accounting clerk's password is her dog's name, your entire organization could be in for a lot of trouble!

You could rely on company policies that state that users must implement strong passwords and that they should change their passwords regularly. But, most us know that such a method would not be very effective. Fortunately, through the use of password policies, you can enforce authentication-related best practices. To access these policies, simply open a policy editing tool (such as the Domain Security Policy administrative tool shown in the following illustration) and click Security Settings | Account Policies | Password Policy.

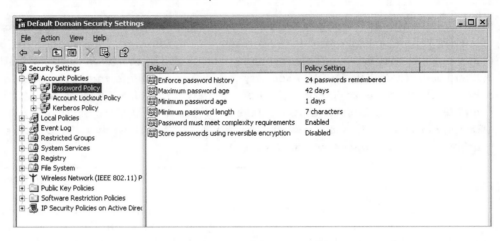

Table 3-2 provides a list of the available Password Policy options, along with their default settings and their purposes.

As you can see from the many settings in Table 3-2, systems administrators can increase or decrease security in accordance with the needs of the environment. If you're used to working with earlier versions of Windows server operating systems (such as Windows NT 4.0 Server or Windows Server 2000), you should make a note of the new default settings. These settings, in general, are more restrictive than the defaults that were provided with earlier versions of Windows server products.

on the job

The key to effective systems administration lies in finding a balance between security and usability. If you think that your organization would benefit from having all accounts use 30-character passwords, it might be time to think again. First, you'd be effectively forcing your users to record their password in some way (such as on the ever-popular and not-so-elusive sticky note affixed to the bottom of the keyboard). Second, users might find the process of logging on to network resources to be such a pain that they'd avoid it altogether. In the real world, remember that security is not everything, and your main job is to find a happy medium between security and usability.

TABLE 3-2   Password Policy Options, along with Their Default Settings and Purposes

Policy Setting	Purpose	Default Value (for Domain Controllers)	Notes
Enforce Password History	Prevents users from reusing a former password, once the password has been changed	24 passwords remembered	The default setting allows users to change passwords to the same password (for example, if the password has expired).
Maximum Password Age	Specifies the number of days before a user is forced to change their password	42 days	Users will be given warnings as this time limit approaches and will eventually be forced to change their passwords before they can log on.
Minimum Password Age	Specifies how old a password must be before it can be changed	1 day	Can be used to prevent users from immediately changing a password back to its original value after it has been changed.
Minimum Password Length	Specifies the minimum number of characters that must be provided for a valid password	7 characters	The default setting will only accept passwords that are at least seven characters in length.
Password Must Meet Complexity Requirements	Forces users to choose strong passwords	Enabled	When enabled, users will be required to use at least three of the following types of characters in their passwords: lowercase letters, uppercase letters, numbers, and symbols.
Store Password Using Reversible Encryption For All Users In The Domain	Uses weaker encryption for passwords	Disabled	This option is generally only necessary for troubleshooting and for supporting older applications; this option should only be enabled when you're sure it's required (one such case is when you need to support Digest Authentication in IIS).

Account Lockout Policies

In addition to the password options, there are several account lockout features that can be enabled to increase security. Implementing lockout functionality can provide a significant increase to overall security in important ways. For example, it can help prevent the success of password-guessing (both from casual users and from malicious unauthorized users). Later in this chapter, you'll see how account lockouts can help you detect other potential problems.

Of course, you want to strike a balance between security and administrative effort with account lockouts. For example, you don't want to indefinitely lock out a user's account after a single bad password entry. You can probably imagine the volume of help desk calls (and irate users) that would generate! It's fairly easy to implement more realistic settings. The following illustration shows the policy settings that are available by clicking Security Settings | Account Policies | Account Lockout Policy in the Domain Security Policy administrative tool.

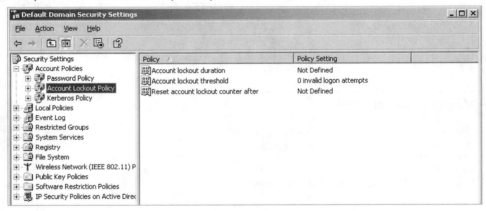

And, the next illustration shows the timeout setting for the Account Lockout Duration setting.

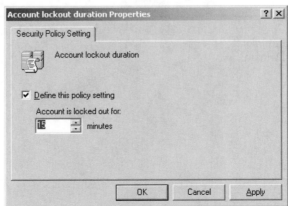

Table 3-3 lists details related to the Account Lockout Policy settings.

Managing User Rights

In addition to the account lockout and password policy settings that you can enable, Windows Server 2003 includes a fairly long list of available user rights. User rights are used to control which types of actions users can perform within your network environment. User rights are similar to permissions in that system administrations can assign them to users (effectively selecting which users or groups have a specific right). However, rights differ from permissions in that rights are not assigned to objects. Instead, each right controls a specific type of action that a user can perform on a system. Some of these are for actions that users or systems administrators may need to perform. Others are security-related rights that allow applications, services, or other processes to perform necessary tasks.

To manage user rights, you can access the Security Settings | Local Policies | User Rights Assignments node of a security policy editing tool. Figure 3-5 shows the available options in the Domain Security Policy tool.

TABLE 3-3   Account Lockout Policy Settings, along with Their Purposes and Default Settings

Policy Setting	Purpose	Default Value	Notes
Account lockout duration	Determines how long an account will be unavailable; automatically unlocks the account without requiring a systems administrator to unlock the account	Not defined	Available only if account lockout threshold is enabled
Account lockout threshold	Number of invalid password attempts before an account is locked out; prevents "brute force" password-guessing attempts	0 invalid attempts	Default setting allows an unlimited number of password guesses
Reset account lockout counter after	Specifies when the count of failed logon attempts is reset	Not defined	Available only if account lockout threshold is enabled

FIGURE 3-5   Viewing User Rights Assignments information in the Domain Security Policy administrative tool

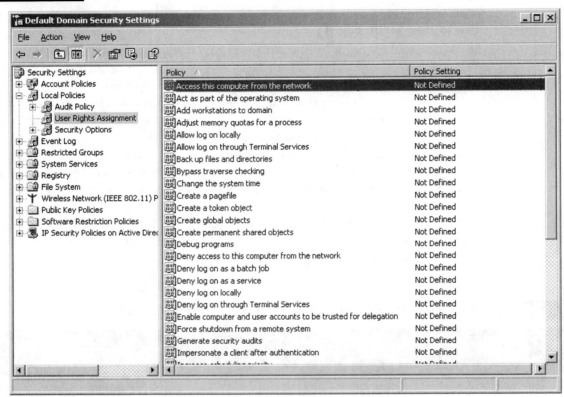

There are many different user rights that can be granted. Here's a (relatively) small list:

- Access this computer from the network
- Act as part of the operating system
- Add workstations to domain
- Allow logon through Terminal Services
- Back up files and directories
- Bypass traverse checking
- Change the system time
- Deny logon as a batch job
- Deny logon as a service

- Deny logon locally
- Deny logon through Terminal Services
- Force shutdown from a remote system
- Generate security audits
- Log on as a batch job
- Log on as a service
- Log on locally
- Manage auditing and security log
- Shut down the system
- Take ownership of files or other objects

By double-clicking any of the rights, you'll be able to add or remove users and groups from the list of accounts that have that right. The following illustration shows how to set User Rights Assignments for the "Profile system performance," and the list of users to which it applies.

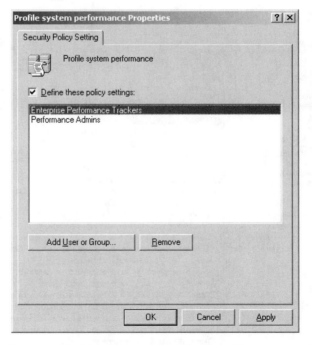

More details about each of these options can be found by viewing the help file: Just right-click the User Rights Assignments item and select Help.

Configuring Security Options

By now, I'll bet that you've seen enough security options to make your head spin. Well, hang on for just a little longer—there's just one more set of security settings that we're going to cover (in this section, at least)! By clicking Security Settings | Local Policies | Security Options, you will be able to modify numerous security settings (see Figure 3-6).

The list of options includes many different ways in which you can increase security. For example, you can configure an option that allows you to rename the Administrator account, and another to rename the Guest account. The options are somewhat grouped through the use of a uniform name at the beginning of related options. These "categories" include

- Accounts
- Audit
- Devices
- Domain Controller
- Domain Member

FIGURE 3-6   Viewing Security Options settings

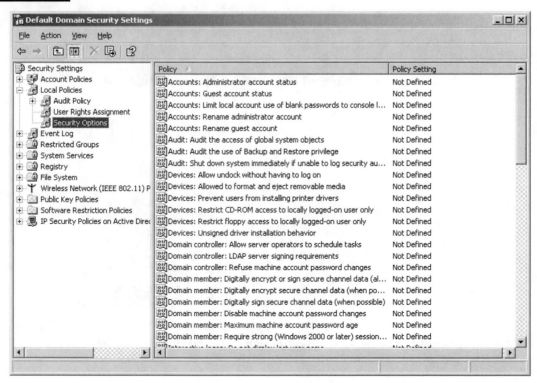

- Interactive logon
- Microsoft network client
- Microsoft network server
- Network Access
- Network Security
- Recovery Console
- Shutdown
- System Cryptography
- System objects
- System settings

For more details on all of the options, to which users they apply, and how they work, see the Windows Server 2003 Help and Support Center.

SCENARIO & SOLUTION

Recently, you have received many help desk calls from users that have incorrectly typed their passwords. You are fairly certain that these issues are caused by user error, and you want to reduce the frequency of these problems.	There are two good ways to handle this problem (without enrolling your users in a typing class). Both involve account lockout policy settings. First, you could increase the Account Lockout Threshold setting. Second, you could configure a minimal Account Lockout Duration.
You want to ensure that your users are using strong passwords that include special characters and mixed-case.	Enable the Password Must Meet Complexity Requirements Password Policy setting. To provide for additional security, you can modify other settings, such as the minimum password length.
Users have complained that the ten-character minimum password length has made it difficult for them to create and remember effective passwords. Management has agreed that the minimum password length should be decreased to six characters.	Set the minimum password length Password Policy setting option to six characters.
You have assigned a variety of permissions to the Jennie1 user account. Now, you want to make sure that this employee is not able to log on to a particular computer; however, you do not want to modify any of her user or group properties.	This is a situation in which user rights can come in very handy: Use the local security on the computer that you don't want this user to log on to. Add the Jennie1 account to the Deny Logon Locally user rights assignment setting.

Okay, as promised, this concludes our tour through many of the available security policy settings. Let's move on to the topic of troubleshooting problems that might occur with user accounts.

Troubleshooting User Account Issues

In general, once you have configured your Active Directory domain environment, operations such as user logons, password changes, and access network resources should be done without much assistance from systems administrators. However, when things go wrong, there are several ways in which you can troubleshoot user account issues. In this section, you'll take a look at a few of these ways.

Detecting and Resolving Account Lockouts

Earlier in this chapter, you looked at how systems administrators can configure automatic account lockout settings. In some cases, you might choose to specify that accounts should be automatically unlocked after a certain period of time. If you don't choose to use this option (or if you set it to a high value), you should be prepared to unlock user accounts that have been disabled.

Fortunately, this is easy enough to do through the use of the Active Directory Users and Computers tool. If you know which user account has been locked out, you can simply locate it by browsing through the domain structure (or by searching for the user account name). If you don't, you can easily identify locked-out accounts by the red X symbol on the account. Simply right-click the appropriate user account and choose Enable Account to allow users to log in again.

There's one important security-related benefit of using account lockouts: It can help notify you of possible password-hacking attempts. For example, a user might call in fairly frequently requesting his account to be unlocked, but he may state that he does not recall entering a bad password. That should set off some alarms in your head! It's likely that another user is trying to guess the password for the account.

on the
()ob

Remember that, while you can prevent some types of security breaches by implementing strict account lockout policies, you can also prevent authorized users from accessing their computers. Many organizations will find that the costs of the latter are much greater than the risk of what might occur with less stringent account lockout policies.

Troubleshooting User Account Issues with Auditing

A large part of security is accountability. In many cases, it may not be all that difficult for someone to commit a crime. For example, breaking into a car and stealing it is generally not prohibitively difficult (especially for "experts"). But, getting away with the crime can be a whole different story! In this example, there's a chance that somebody can identify the thief, or police officers may catch the individual as he or she tries to drive away. If they do avoid detection long enough, they may have the time to chop up the car and use it for parts. Still, many of the parts will be stamped with a vehicle identification number, which may enable authorities to trace the car to its origin.

Auditing provides an interesting level of security. Although it is not designed to prevent people from breaching security, it can be a powerful deterrent. That is, unauthorized users (especially those that might be a member of your organization) might be aware that you're tracking their actions. You may become aware, for example, of a user that is attempting to guess a password. Auditing also provides another powerful weapon: the ability to determine what happened after a security issue occurred. This can help identify the offender.

The main purpose of auditing is to record specific user actions. Auditing settings can be quite granular—for example, you can specify that you want to record an event whenever Samantha attempts to access files in the Accounts Receivable folder on a particular file server.

Even if you haven't used it before, it will probably come as no surprise that Windows Server 2003 includes robust auditing functionality. You can implement auditing through the use of several steps. These steps include the following:

- *Configure the size and storage settings for the audit logs*. These settings will control how much auditing information is recorded on your computers. The larger the log file, the more information you'll retain for later analysis. You can configure these settings by launching the Event Viewer application, right-clicking a log file, and selecting Properties, as shown in the following illustration. You can have separate settings for each type of log that is available on the computer.

■ *Enable auditing.* Before you can find useful information in the audit logs, you'll need to determine which actions you want to record. For example, you may audit when someone logs on to a computer, or you may want to know who has been trying to access files in the \\Server1\FinancialInfo share. You can configure auditing settings by using a security policy settings tool or Group Policy Object (as described in the preceding section). The relevant settings are located within Security Settings | Local Policies | Audit Policy. The following illustration shows the types of actions that can be audited.

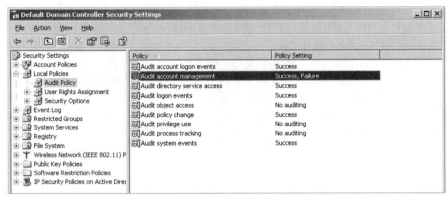

■ *Select which actions to audit.* For some of the auditing options, you'll need to specify exactly which objects and options you want to audit. This allows you to fine-tune exactly what information you want to record. For example, you can configure auditing settings for files and folders by accessing the Auditing tab in the advanced security configuration options (shown in the following illustration). In addition to controlling which user(s) will be audited, you can specify which actions will be audited.

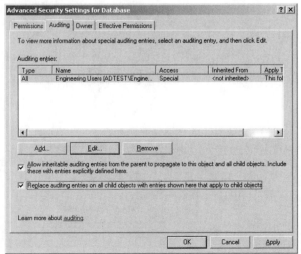

■ *Regularly review the audit logs.* Here's where a lot of systems administrators fall short. Often, they'll enable auditing of many different actions that occur on the system, but they'll fail to actually review the captured information to identify trends or security issues. For more information about working with the Event Viewer, see Chapter 6.

Note that there are trade-offs to implementing auditing. First and foremost, recording auditing information can consume system resources. This can decrease overall system performance and use up valuable disk space. Second, auditing many events can make the audit log impractical to view. If too much detail is provided, systems administrators are unlikely to scrutinize all of the recorded events. For these reasons, you should always be sure to find a balance between the level of auditing details provided and the performance management implications of these settings.

Overall, however, through the use of auditing of events related to logons and logoffs, you can isolate and troubleshoot common user account issues.

Understanding and Troubleshooting User Authentication

When it comes to managing security, one of the most important concepts to understand is that of authentication. Simply put, in the network world, authentication is the process of identifying a user. Currently, the most common method of authentication is through the use of a username and a password. For example, if I want to log on to one of my organization's database servers, I could input a username and password in order to gain access.

Although password-based authentication is convenient in many scenarios, it's almost certainly not the most secure. For example, users can quite easily share passwords (even after they're warned about the dangers of doing so). Or, they can forget the passwords and need to call a systems administrator to reset them.

Recently, "smart cards" have been developed for resolving some of these issues. The idea behind a smart card is that the user must be in physical possession of this card in order to authenticate on a computer system. The cards themselves might store information (including encryption keys and other personal data), and they will provide the information that is required to log on to a computer. For example, one type of smart card displays a number that changes every 30 seconds. This number must be used by the user to log on to a computer resource, so the user must be in possession of the card when they are logging in. Alternatively, you could equip your computers with smart card readers. Instead of having to remember and type in authentication information, all a user would need to do is enter his or her smart card into the reader (much as you might do to enter secure rooms with a pass card). If the card is lost or stolen, a new one can be issued and the old one can be deactivated immediately. There are other methods of increasing logon security, including biometric devices (which use fingerprints, handwriting recognition, or other methods for authentication purposes).

on the !ob

Keep in mind that authentication is one area in which policies are just as important as technical concerns. For example, the users that you support must understand the importance of creating strong passwords and best practices for ensuring the passwords are not misused. It's only when everyone in the organization truly understands the importance of security that your computer systems will be reasonably safe!

Since authentication is such an important part of network security, it will probably come as no surprise that Windows Server 2003 includes several methods for authenticating users. In this section, you'll take a look at the details of authentication in Windows Server 2003.

Authentication Mechanisms

Authentication can be performed in several different ways. The simplest scenario is one in which I want to log on to a computer. The process is very straightforward: At the logon prompt, I provide my username and password. If the information is correct, I will be permitted to access the system. Of course, authentication responsibilities in a networked environment can be considerably more complicated. For example, what should happen when I want to access resources on remote computers? The simplest solution might be for me to log on to that computer. Of course, this process would be very tedious (I may have to log on to a dozen different machines, just to get to the files that I need) and error-prone (I would have to maintain different passwords or synchronize passwords for all of these resources). Fortunately, in modern networked environments, there are better ways.

Let's begin by taking a look at the first step: user authentication. Windows Server 2003 can use several different methods for authenticating a user. These methods include

- **Kerberos v5**   Kerberos is the default method for processing authentication requests in current versions of Windows operating systems (including Windows 2000 Server and Windows Server 2003). Kerberos security is based on a fairly complicated system involving "tickets" that give users permissions to log on to a system. Kerberos is a very secure method for authenticating users and is therefore used by all clients that support Kerberos authentication. Although the concepts and foundation upon which Kerberos is based are complex, much of the hard work is performed by the operating system, and systems administrators do not need to perform much administration. You can further configure advanced Kerberos settings by accessing Security Settings | Account Policies | Kerberos Policy. The following illustration shows these settings for the Domain Security Policy.

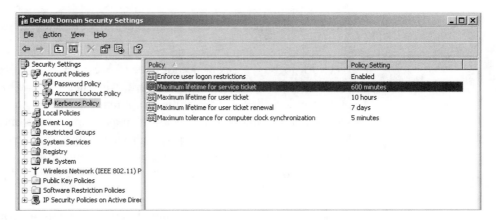

- **NTLM** NTLM authentication is primarily supported for backward compatibility with operating systems that do not support Kerberos-based authentication. In the Windows world, this includes Windows NT 4.0 operating systems. When this is the case, NTLM authentication will be performed automatically.

- **Secure Sockets Layer (SSL) / Transport Layer Security (TLS)** SSL/TLS security is based on a system of "certificates" that are used to authenticate users. The primary concept behind certificates is that a trusted issuer can provide information that certifies that a user or computer is what it claims to be. In the real world (and in Windows Server 2003), SSL and TLS are often used for web servers. For example, if I want to purchase something from an e-commerce web site, I might need to securely submit my credit card information. Through the use of SSL and/or TLS, the information that I am sending between my client and the web server is secured through encryption. Furthermore, these protocols ensure that it is me that is sending the information. We'll cover more details about the use of SSL and TLS in Chapter 7.

Each of these authentication methods provides a reasonable level of security in ensuring that a user is who he or she claims to be. Now that you have an idea about how authentications are performed, let's look at three different types of logons:

- **Interactive logons** As mentioned previously, an interactive logon is a simple process. Basically, a user or systems administrator can log on to a computer by providing username and password information. This information is then verified by a domain controller (if the machine is a member of a domain) or by the local machine (if the user is logging onto the local machine or if the machine is in a workgroup). Once the authentication process is completed, the user will have access to the machine and, optionally, to various network resources.

- **Network logons** Logons do not have to occur on a local machine. They can also be performed over the network. Although the user may be unaware of it, Windows Server 2003 will perform many authentications behind the scenes. For example, if you're working in a domain environment, and you logged onto Server1, Windows will automatically attempt to authenticate you with the same information on Server2. If your authentication doesn't allow you to access the machine, you still have the option of providing other credentials.

- **Terminal Services logons** Terminal Services sessions are somewhat of a hybrid between interactive and network logons. When you create a new Terminal Services session, you're working over the network, but you have really logged on to a process that's running locally on the server. Details related to working with Terminal Services can be found in Chapter 7.

Stored Usernames and Passwords

In an ideal world, we'd be able to use a single secure login to connect to all of the resources that we needed. Although there are several initiatives that are designed to do just that, it's still going to be a long time before a true "single sign-on" experience is a reality. In the real world, I might need one username and password to log on to a computer or domain. This username and password will then be used as the default combination for accessing any resources on the network. For example, if I log on to Workstation1 and need to access resources on Workstation2, Windows will first try to access the computer using my logon information. If that doesn't work, it may prompt me for an alternate username and password.

Similarly, if you're connecting to an Internet web site that requires authentication, you'll likely have another username and password to enter. All of this can be a huge hassle, especially when you're just trying to access the resources that you have been authorized to use. That's where the "stored user names and passwords" feature in Windows Server 2003 comes in. You can access this feature by using the Stored User Names And Passwords option in the Control Panel. To view details about any of the items in the list, just click Properties:

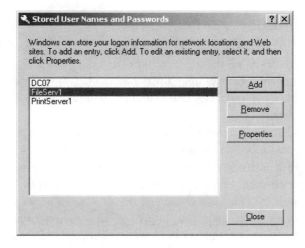

You can manually add stored usernames and passwords by using the Add button:

Whenever you connect to a network resource that forces you to enter in another username and password, this feature will automatically record the new information and store it securely. The next time you attempt to connect to the same resources, Windows Server 2003 will automatically send the authentication information, without requiring any user interaction.

Passport Authentication

The need to maintain different credentials on different servers is just one of the current hassles that's related to working in a distributed network environment such as the Internet. For example, I may have to log on to my company's intranet site, and I may have a different username and password stored for accessing my stock broker's online system.

In an attempt to solve the multiple password problem, Microsoft has recently introduced a new way of performing authentication. It's called Passport. The idea is that, when you set up a Passport account, you provide some additional information about yourself. This information can then be passed, with your permission, to other sites. So, for example, if you need to create a new username and password on an Internet site, you can simply sign in using your Passport account. Additionally, the Passport account could contain additional information such as your address and phone contact information. Of course, all of this works securely, and none of your information will be used without your consent (for all of the legalese details, see www.passport.com). Windows Server 2003 supports Passport authentication through IIS.

Troubleshooting Authentication with NLTest

If you run into problems with user authentication, there are methods for obtaining more information about the servers in your environment. One tool, the NLTest command-line utility, is designed to provide information about Windows NT 4.0–based authentication. Therefore, it is useful for testing replication status, trust relationships, and domain controller information in environments that still rely upon Windows NT 4.0–based authentication.

In order to use the NLTest utility, you must be running either Windows Server 2003 or Windows XP. The utility is included as part of the Windows Server 2003 Support Tools (which can be found on the operating system installation media).

The following illustration shows the command-line help for the NLTest command. You can access this by typing **NLTest -?** at the command prompt. Note that this has many different types of operations that can be used to diagnose problems related to Windows NT 4.0 authentication.

```
C:\>nltest /?
Usage: nltest [/OPTIONS]

       /SERVER:<ServerName> - Specify <ServerName>

       /QUERY - Query <ServerName> netlogon service
       /REPL - Force partial sync on <ServerName> BDC
       /SYNC - Force full sync on <ServerName> BDC
       /PDC_REPL - Force UAS change message from <ServerName> PDC

       /SC_QUERY:<DomainName> - Query secure channel for <Domain> on <ServerName>
       /SC_RESET:<DomainName>[\<DcName>] - Reset secure channel for <Domain> on <Se
rverName> to <DcName>
       /SC_VERIFY:<DomainName> - Verify secure channel for <Domain> on <ServerName>

       /SC_CHANGE_PWD:<DomainName> - Change a secure channel  password for <Domain>
 on <ServerName>
       /DCLIST:<DomainName> - Get list of DC's for <DomainName>
       /DCNAME:<DomainName> - Get the PDC name for <DomainName>
       /DSGETDC:<DomainName> - Call DsGetDcName /PDC /DS /DSP /GC /KDC
              /TIMESERV /GTIMESERV /NETBIOS /DNS /IP /FORCE /WRITABLE /AVOIDSELF /LDA
PONLY /BACKG
              /SITE:<SiteName> /ACCOUNT:<AccountName> /RET_DNS /RET_NETBIOS
       /DNSGETDC:<DomainName> - Call DsGetDcOpen/Next/Close /PDC /GC
              /KDC /WRITABLE /LDAPONLY /FORCE /SITESPEC
       /DSGETFTI:<DomainName> - Call DsGetForestTrustInformation
              /UPDATE_TDO
       /DSGETSITE - Call DsGetSiteName
       /DSGETSITECOV - Call DsGetDcSiteCoverage
       /PARENTDOMAIN - Get the name of the parent domain of this machine
       /WHOWILL:<Domain>* <User> [<Iteration>] - See if <Domain> will log on <User>

       /FINDUSER:<User> - See which trusted domain will log on <User>
       /TRANSPORT_NOTIFY - Notify netlogon of new transport

       /DBFLAG:<HexFlags> - New debug flag

       /USER:<UserName> - Query User info on <ServerName>

       /TIME:<Hex LSL> <Hex MSL> - Convert NT GMT time to ascii
       /LOGON_QUERY - Query number of cumulative logon attempts
```

For example, the following command will return detailed information about a specific user account named "User1":

```
nltest /user:"User1"
```

The following illustration shows the type of information that's returned for the local Guest account on a Windows Server 2003 domain controller.

```
C:\>nltest /user:"Guest"
User: Guest
Rid: 0x1f5
Version: 0x10002
AccountExpires: ffffffff 7fffffff = 9/13/30828 21:48:05
PrimaryGroupId: 0x201
UserAccountControl: 0x215
CountryCode: 0x0
CodePage: 0x0
BadPasswordCount: 0x0
LogonCount: 0x0
AdminCount: 0x0
SecurityDescriptor: 80140001 00000090 000000a0 00000014 00000044 00300002 000000
02 0014c002 01050044 00000101 01000000 00000000 0014c002 001fffff 00000101 05000
000 00000007 004c0002 00000003 00140000 0002031b 00000101 01000000 00000000 0018
0000 000f07ff 00000201 05000000 00000020 00000220 00180000 000f07ff 00000201 050
00000 00000020 00000224 00000201 05000000 00000020 00000220 00000201 05000000 00
000020 00000220
AccountName: Guest
AdminComment: Built-in account for guest access to the computer/domain
Groups: 00000201 00000007
LmOwfPassword: a7ed1643 6b4c3950 c3380412 19187f0f
NtOwfPassword: a7ed1643 6b4c3950 eeb5c493 1c265c46
NtPasswordHistory: 00010001
LmPasswordHistory: 00010001
The command completed successfully

C:\>
```

And, you can get a list of all of the domain controllers in the "MyCompany" domain by executing the following command:

```
nltest /dclist:MyCompany
```

For more information about how to use the many options of the NLTest command, see the Windows Server 2003 Help and Support Center.

CERTIFICATION OBJECTIVE 3.03

Creating, Managing, and Troubleshooting Computer Accounts

In order to maintain a secure network environment, authentication and the checking of permissions should occur at several different levels. Earlier, we discussed the importance of user accounts, which are attached to employees. Another type of security principal is a *computer account*. Computer accounts, like user accounts, are used to manage permissions on resources and actions that can be performed within a network environment. A computer account is related to a single computer that is located on the network. Systems administrators can use computer account objects to increase overall network security.

Servers and workstations are all given unique security identifiers (SIDs) whenever they're added to an Active Directory domain. Computer accounts have the same name as the name of the computer, and no two computers can have the same name within the same domain. Using computer account information, you can increase the security of your environment by specifying which computers will have access to communicate with the Active Directory. This provides an added level of security, since not only will a user have to provide a valid username and password in order to log on, but he or she would also have to log on from a computer that is a member of the domain.

Automatically Creating Computer Accounts

There are two main ways in which computer accounts can be created. The first is an automatic process that can occur when a computer is added to a domain. In order to add a computer to a domain, you must have the appropriate permissions. By default, this means that the user that is adding the computer to the domain must be a member of the Account Operators, Domain Admins, or Enterprise Admins groups. Also, all authenticated users are automatically given the "Add workstations to a domain" user right.

Adding a computer to a domain is a fairly simple process. You can start by accessing the System Control Panel applet and clicking the Network Identification (or, in Windows XP, "Computer Name") tab. As shown in the following illustration, you'll see information about the local computer's network settings. If the computer is part of a workgroup, you'll see that information displayed.

To add the computer to a domain, click Change. On this page (see the following illustration), you'll be able to specify the name of the domain to which you want to add the computer. You also have the opportunity to change the name of the computer. When you click OK, the local computer will attempt to locate a domain controller for the domain that you specified. It will then try to automatically create a new computer account for this machine in the Active Directory database.

The process of adding various versions of Windows computers to a domain will vary slightly in different operating system versions. For more information, see each operating system's help file.

Manually Creating Computer Accounts

The second method by which a computer account can be created is manually, through the use of the Active Directory Users and Computers tool. When a new domain is created, a folder named "Computers" is automatically created. By default, this folder does not include any computer-related information. As you add computers to the domain, entries are added to this folder.

However, you can create a new computer account before you add a computer to a domain. By pre-creating computer accounts within the Active Directory database, you can increase overall security by preventing users and administrators from adding just any computer to your network. To create a new computer account, simply open the Active Directory Users and Computers administrative tool, right-click the Computers folder, and select New | Computer. This will launch the New Object – Computer dialog box:

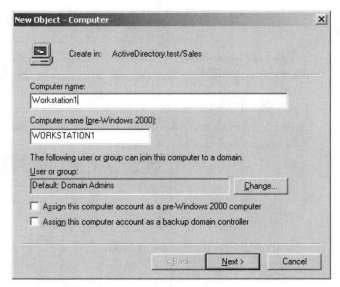

This dialog box contains several options that will control the creation of the computer account. The first piece of required information is the name of the computer. In the first text box, type in the name of the computer that will be added to the domain. The second text box provides a place for you to specify the pre–Windows

2000 name for the computer. This name will default to the Active Directory computer name, up to the 15-character limit.

Next, you'll need to decide which users or groups will have access to this domain. The default setting is to provide this permission only to members of the Domain Admins group. You can modify the setting by clicking Change. There are two other options at the bottom of the screen. First, you can specify whether the computer is running a version of Windows that is pre–Windows 2000 (for example, Windows NT 4.0). Next, you can specify whether this computer is intended to serve as a backup domain controller. This option is relevant only in environments that are using Windows NT 4.0 security.

When you click Next, you'll be able to specify whether or not you want this computer account to be for a "Managed" computer:

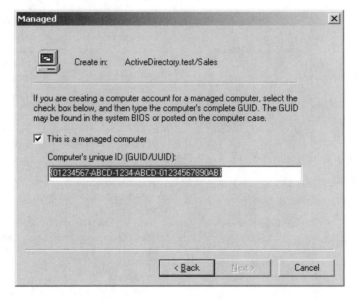

The idea behind this option is that it allows you to ensure that only a specific computer can be added to the domain. If you do not enable this option, unauthorized users might be able to rename a computer to match the name of the computer account, and add it to the domain (assuming, of course, that the account that they use has the appropriate permissions). This computer will be defined by its globally unique identifier (GUID) or its universally unique identifier (UUID). To find a GUID or UUID, you can access the computer's BIOS (assuming that the BIOS includes this type of information). Some hardware manufacturers may provide this information with the documentation that accompanies the PC.

When you click Next, you'll see a summary of the options that you specified for the new Computer account. To create the object, click Finish.

Adding Computers to a Domain from the Command Line

You can also add computers to a domain using the "dsadd "computer command-line utility. To obtain the help for this command, just type **dsadd computer -?** at a command prompt. Following are the syntax and options for the command:

```
Description: Adds a computer to the directory.
Syntax:  dsadd computer <ComputerDN> [-samid <SAMName>] [-desc
Description>]
        [-loc <Location>] [-memberof <Group ...>]
        [{-s <Server> | -d <Domain>}] [-u <UserName>]
        [-p {<Password> | *}] [-q] [{-uc | -uco | -uci}]
Parameters:
Value                      Description
<ComputerDN>               Required. Specifies the distinguished name (DN) of
                           the computer you want to add.
                           If the target object is omitted, it will be taken
                           from standard input (stdin).
-samid <SAMName>           Sets the computer SAM account name to <SAMName>.
                           If this parameter is not specified, then a
                           SAM account name is derived from the value of
                           the common name (CN) attribute used in <ComputerDN>.
-desc <Description>         Sets the computer description to <Description>.
-loc <Location>            Sets the computer location to <Location>.
-memberof <Group ...>      Makes the computer a member of one or more groups
                           given by the space-separated list of DNs
{-s <Server> | -d <Domain>}
                           -s <Server> connects to the domain controller (DC)
                           with name <Server>.
                           -d <Domain> connects to a DC in domain <Domain>.
                           Default: a DC in the logon domain.
-u <UserName>              Connect as <UserName>. Default: the logged in user.
                           User name can be: user name, domain\user name,
                           or user principal name (UPN).
-p {<Password> | *}
                           Password for the user <UserName>. If * is entered
                           then you are prompted for a password.
-q                         Quiet mode: suppress all output to standard output.
{-uc | -uco | -uci}        -uc Specifies that input from or output to pipe is
                           formatted in Unicode.
                           -uco Specifies that output to pipe or file is
                           formatted in Unicode.
                           -uci Specifies that input from pipe or file is
                           formatted in Unicode.
```

For example, you can add a new computer named "Workstation1" to the Active Directory domain through the following command:

```
dsadd computer "CN=Workstation1, OU=Sales, DC=MyCompany, DC=com"
```

This command will add a new computer account named "Workstation1" to the Sales OU within the Active Directory domain "MyCompany.com." For further details on the "dsadd command (which provides many different types of functionality), see the Windows Server 2003 Help and Support Center.

Now that you understand the process of creating computer accounts, let's see how Computer objects can be managed.

Managing and Troubleshooting Computer Accounts

So far, we have talked about several ways in which you can create computer accounts within an Active Directory domain. In this section, you'll look at ways in which you can manage computer accounts, once they've been created or added to a domain. The primary tool that is used to administer computer accounts is the Active Directory Users and Computers tool. By using this administrative tool, you can perform several different types of operations.

Like user accounts, computer accounts can be located within any of the OUs in your Active Directory domain. Using a drag-and-drop operation, or by right-clicking a computer object and selecting the Move command, you can "relocate" a computer to another OU. There are a few reasons to do this. First, the OU structure in which the computer account resides will determine which Policy settings will apply to the computer. Additionally, you can better keep track of the various workstations and other client computers that are part of your domain by organizing them according to your organization's logical structure.

When you create a new computer account, you provide only some very basic information about the machine. You can access additional properties for the computer object by right-clicking it and selecting Properties. This will display various tabs, including location information and security settings. You will also be able to configure relevant properties that apply to the computer. For example, the following illustration shows you can control settings that will be applied when this computer makes a remote connection to your network.

One other handy feature is the ability to right-click a computer name and select the Manage option. This will automatically open the Computer Management administrative tool and connect to the selected computer. This is a convenient method for obtaining many different kinds of information about the remote computer.

Let's look at some other operations that can be performed using the Active Directory Users and Computers tool.

Resetting Computer Accounts

Periodically, you might run into issues in which certain computers are unable to log on to an Active Directory domain. This can occur for a variety of reasons that are involved with the secure communications channels that are created between Windows 2000/XP computers and the domain controllers to which they authenticate. A common error message that might be seen on the client is the following:

```
The session setup from the computer DOMAINMEMBER failed to
authenticate. The name of the account referenced in the security
database is DOMAINMEMBER$. The following error occurred: Access
is denied.
```

In this case, users of the client computer (regardless of their user account permissions) will be unable to log on to the domain or access domain resources. Fortunately, there's a simple solution to this problem: resetting the computer account. The quickest and easiest method for resetting a computer account is to locate the relevant computer object using the Active Directory Users and Computers tool. Then, right-click the computer account and select Reset Account. This operation will allow computer-based authentication information to be reestablished the next time a user attempts to connect to the domain using the affected computer.

You can also reset computer accounts through the use of either the NLTest command-line utility (which was covered earlier in this chapter), or the NetDom.exe command-line utility. Since these commands can be run from any computer that is a member of a domain, you will be able to reset the computer account from another machine. For example, to reset a computer account for a machine named "SalesLaptop" (which is a member of the MyCompany domain), you can run the following command:

```
netdom reset SalesLaptop /domain:MyCompany
```

Disabling and Enabling Computer Accounts

Occasionally, you might want to prevent users from logging in to your domain using a particular computer. For example, suppose you have several "loaner" notebook computers that you provide to members of your Sales team, as needed. Whenever these computers are not being used by an authorized employee, you want to ensure that no one can log on to the domain from that machine.

You can easily meet these requirements by disabling an existing computer account. Using the Active Directory Users and Computers tool, simply right-click a computer account and choose Disable Account. This command will prevent users from logging on to the domain using this computer, regardless of their user account permissions. Disabled computer accounts, as shown in the following illustration, will be displayed with a red X above the computer icon.

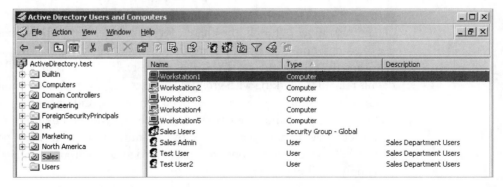

You can also enable or disable computer accounts using the "dsmod "computer command. For further details on the syntax of this command, type **dsmod computer /?** at a command prompt.

When you disable a computer object, no information is actually deleted. Therefore, you can quickly and easily reenable the account by right-clicking it and selecting the Enable Account option. Users of this computer will again be able to log on to the domain.

Deleting Computer Accounts

As you might have expected, once a computer account has been created, you can delete it using the Active Directory Users and Computers tool. After you right-click the computer account and select Delete, no users will be able to log on to the domain from that computer.

Since computer accounts are security principals, you should keep in mind the effects of deleting the computer account. Although you can easily re-create a new computer account with the same name, the new computer account will not automatically inherit any permissions or other settings that the old computer of the same name might have had. For this reason, you should delete a computer account only if you are fairly certain that users of that machine will never need to log on to the domain again.

CERTIFICATION OBJECTIVE 3.04

Creating and Managing Groups

Windows Server 2003 has been designed to support environments that range in size from a few users to thousands of users. Although you could administer security permissions and settings for these objects separately, that would require a large number of administrative staff. Plus, the chance for errors would be high. Through the proper use of groups, however, systems administrators can quickly and easily make changes that can affect thousands of users simultaneously. In this section, you'll look at the details related to working with groups in an Active Directory environment.

Groups are simply collections of users, computers, and/or other groups. Groups are security principals, and a new SID is generated whenever a new group is created. As with user and computer accounts, systems administrators can assign permissions to groups. Whenever permissions are granted or denied on group objects, the permissions will apply to all members of these groups.

User and computer accounts can belong to multiple groups, and this is quite common in most environments. For example, the RPatel user account might belong to the Accounting group, the Managers group, and the Corporate Users group.

Whenever this user attempts to access resources, she will effectively have a combination of all of the permissions that are assigned to her user account, as well as any permissions that are assigned to any groups of which she is a member.

Groups can be extremely helpful in managing environments of all sizes. Whenever a new employee joins the organization's accounting department (or when one leaves), a simple change to the group membership is all that's required to maintain the appropriate security. Therefore, a recommended practice is to place users in groups, and then to always assign permissions to groups instead of directly to users. In some cases, groups can contain other groups, further simplifying the task of dealing with varying user requirements. You'll look at details related to different types of groups later in this chapter. First, let's look at some basic information about types of groups.

<table>
<tr><td>

exam

watch *It's important to understand how group-related permissions interact. For more information about determining effective permissions for a user, see Chapter 4.*

</td></tr>
</table>

Understanding Group Types

The Active Directory supports two main types of groups. Although both are known as "groups," their purposes are very different. The first type is a *distribution group*. These groups are designed primarily for the purpose of messaging (and, specifically, e-mail communications). Distribution groups are *not* security principals. That is, they cannot be assigned permissions or user rights.

The second type of group is a *security group*. These groups are security principals and can be used for the assignment of permissions and user rights. Security groups form the basis of security administration in Windows Server 2003 and the Active Directory. Throughout the remainder of this chapter, we will be focusing only on security groups.

Systems administrators can convert security groups to and from distribution groups using the Active Directory Users and Computers tool. To do this, simply right-click a group and select Properties. As shown in the illustration, you will see the group scope information on the General tab.

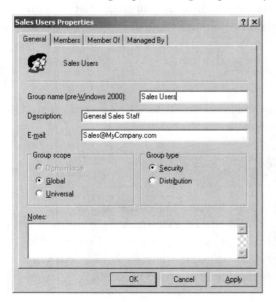

Understanding Group Scope

In order to support many different types of domain configurations, the Active Directory allows systems administrators to define the scope of a group when it is created. Both security and distribution groups must be assigned group scope. There are three types of group scopes. They are

- **Domain local groups** Domain local groups can be assigned permissions only within the domain in which they were created. Therefore, systems administrators usually create these groups to control access to resources within a single domain. Domain local groups can contain members from Windows NT 4.0, Windows 2000 Server, and Windows Server 2003 computers' domains.

- **Global groups** Like domain local groups, global groups can only contain members from a single domain. However, global groups can be assigned permissions to resources located in any domain within an Active Directory forest. Generally, global groups are used when a group of users that all reside in a single domain require access to other resources throughout the environment.

- **Universal groups** Universal groups are the most inclusive of all of the group scopes available in an Active Directory environment. Unlike domain local and global groups, universal groups can contain members from multiple domains. For example, you can create a single universal group that contains users and groups from the us.mycompany.com domain, as well as users and groups from the asia.mycompany.com domain. Additionally, universal groups can be granted permissions to resources that are located in any domain of an Active Directory forest.

Now that you understand group types and group scope, let's look at some of the default groups that are available in Active Directory domains.

exam

⚑atch *When working in an Active Directory environment, the types of groups that you can create will be based on the domain's functional level. Additionally, certain types of group scope conversions are allowed, and others are not. These topics are beyond the scope of this book (and the 70-290 exam). For more information, see the Windows Server 2003 Help and Support Center (you can start by searching for "group scope").*

Built-in Groups

When you first implement an Active Directory domain, several built-in groups are automatically created. These groups are included in the Builtin folder. To view the groups that are automatically created, you can use the Active Directory Users and Computers tool. As shown in the following illustration, you can click the Builtin folder to retrieve a list of the default groups.

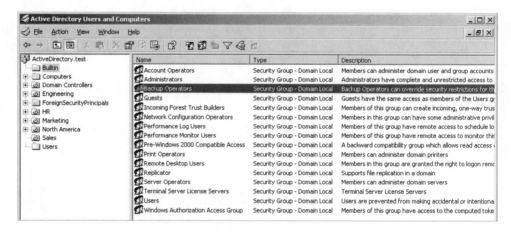

All of these groups are security groups, and they have the group scope of "Domain Local." The default groups work much like other security groups, since systems administrators can manage their membership by adding or removing users. However, the built-in groups include special permissions and user rights that have been predefined for common security situations. Since their purposes are predefined,

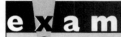

In general, remember that the default groups have plural names (although you can certainly choose any naming convention that you want for new groups that you create). Although there are some exceptions, this can be particularly useful when you're trying to determine whether permissions are assigned to Administrators (the group) or Administrator (the account).

you cannot modify the scope or type of a security group. When you access the properties of the group, you'll see that these options are disabled:

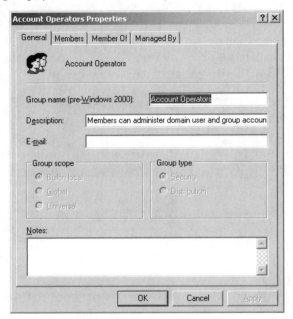

Table 3-4 shows the default groups and includes the default descriptions provided for the groups. As is the case with users, the exact list of groups that you have on your machine will be based on which applications and services are installed on the machine.

TABLE 3-4   Default Built-In Domain Local Groups that Are Installed with Windows Server 2003

Group Name	Description
Account Operators	Members can administer domain user and group accounts.
Administrators	Administrators have complete and unrestricted access to the computer/domain.
Backup Operators	Backup Operators can override security restrictions for the sole purpose of backing up or restoring files.
DHCP Administrators	These members have administrative access to DHCP service.
DHCP Users	These members have view-only access to the DHCP service.
Guests	Guests have the same access as members of the Users group by default, except for the Guest account, which is further restricted.

TABLE 3-4   Default Built-In Domain Local Groups that Are Installed with Windows Server 2003 *(continued)*

Group Name	Description
Incoming Forest Trust Builders	Members of this group can create incoming, one-way trusts to this forest.
Network Configuration Operators	Members in this group can have some administrative privileges to manage configuration of networking features.
Performance Log Users	Members of this group have remote access to schedule logging of performance counters on this computer.
Performance Monitor Users	Members of this group have remote access to monitor this computer.
Power Users	Power Users possess most administrative powers with some restrictions. Thus, Power Users can run legacy applications in addition to certified applications.
Pre–Windows 2000 Compatible Access	A backward-compatibility group that allows read access on all users and groups in the domain.
Print Operators	Members can administer domain printers.
Remote Desktop Users	Members in this group are granted the right to log on remotely.
Replicator	Supports file replication in a domain.
Server Operators	Members can administer domain servers.
Terminal Server License Servers	Computers that are members of this group are serving as License Servers for Terminal Server functionality.
Users	Users are prevented from making accidental or intentional systemwide changes. Thus, users can run certified applications, but not most legacy applications.
Windows Authorization Access Group	Members of this group have access to the computed tokenGroupsGlobalAndUniversal attribute on User objects.
WINS Users	Members have view-only access to the WINS server.

By default, the Everyone group no longer includes the "Anonymous Logon" in Windows Server 2003. You can **change this behavior by using security policy settings (described earlier in this chapter).**

In addition to the default domain local groups that can be found in the Builtin folder, additional default groups can be found in the Users container of every Active Directory domain. The following illustration shows these groups, and their scopes.

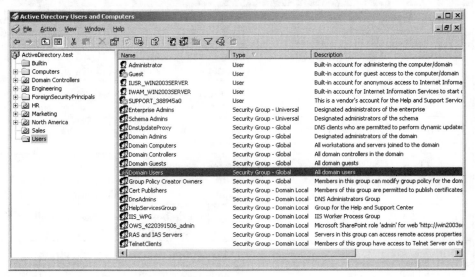

Now that you have an idea of some of the built-in groups that are available in Active Directory domains, let's see how you can create new groups.

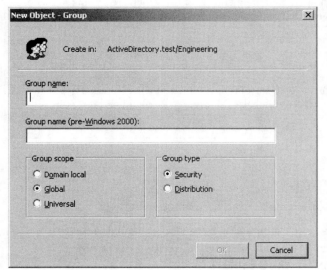

Creating New Groups

The process of creating new groups is a straightforward one. The most common method is to use the Active Directory Users and Computers tool. Right-click the container in which you want to create the new group and then select the New | Group command. You'll see the New Object – Group dialog box, as shown in the illustration. Groups can be created within any of the folders or OUs in your Active Directory environment.

The only information that's required for the new group is its name. You will need to provide the name by which Active

Directory users will access the group, as well as a pre–Windows 2000–compatible group name. Then, you must specify the group type and group scope. When you click OK, the new group will be created.

Managing Group Membership

When a new group is initially created, it does not contain any members. Therefore, one of the first tasks that you will perform is to add members to the group. To do this using the Active Directory Users and Computers tool, simply right-click the group whose membership you want to modify and choose Properties. Several tabs in these properties will be of interest:

- **General** On the General tab of the properties of a group, you will be able to change the name of the group, add a description for the group, and configure an e-mail address for the group. Additionally, you can modify the group scope and group type (according to the rules presented earlier in this section).

- **Members** On this tab, you can view and modify the list of members of the group (see the following illustration). By clicking Add, you'll have the ability to add other users or groups to the selected group object. You can also remove members of the group by clicking Remove.

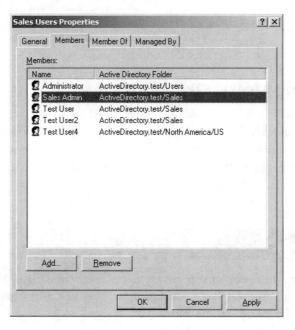

■ **Member Of** On this tab, you will see a list of the groups that this group is a member of. In other words, the list includes all other groups that include this group as a member (see the following illustration). If you want to add the selected group to another group, you can click Add.

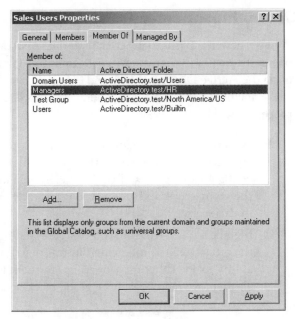

Now that you know how to determine group membership from the standpoint of a group, let's look at another way in which you can view group membership.

Determining Users' Group Membership

Often, when administering security for your Active Directory domain, you'll want to quickly determine which groups a particular user belongs to. You might do this to troubleshoot permissions issues. For example, if a user is unable to access specific files or folders, this might be because the appropriate permissions are denied for one of the groups of which the user is a member. Or, the user may not have been added to the necessary groups.

In order to effectively manage Active Directory users and groups, you must have a good understanding of *calculating effective permissions. We'll cover that topic in Chapter 4.*

Fortunately, you can easily determine to which groups a user belongs by using the Active Directory Users and Computers tool. Simply right-click a user account and select Properties. As with group objects, user objects also have a Member Of tab (see the following illustration). You can click Add to add the user to groups, and you can click Remove to remove the user from groups. This is a very simple way to isolate and troubleshoot problems that might be due to group membership.

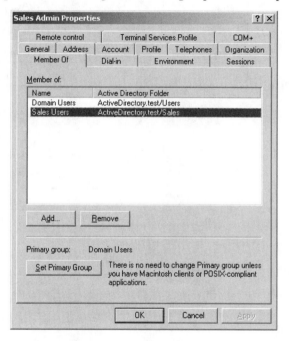

Exercise 3-4 walks you through the process of creating and managing groups.

EXERCISE 3-4

MasterSim 3-4 ON THE CD

Creating and Managing Groups

1. Log on to a Windows Server 2003 domain controller as a member of the Domain Admins group and open the Active Directory Users and Computers tool.

2. To begin this exercise, you will create several users accounts. You will then add these users to various groups and verify the group membership. Begin

by creating a new OU called "Group Management." Within the Group Management OU, create the following user accounts (use the defaults for all other user account options):

First Name	Initials	Last Name	Logon Name
James	D.	Admin	JAdmin
Clara	J.	User	CUser
Mary	A.	Manager	MManager
Jeff	J.	Manager	JManager

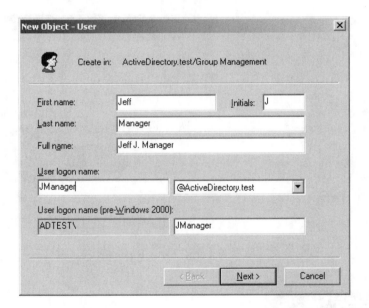

3. Now, you'll create some groups for testing purposes. Next, still within the "Group Management" OU, create the following global security groups (use the defaults for all other settings): "Accounting Managers," "Engineers," and "All Users."

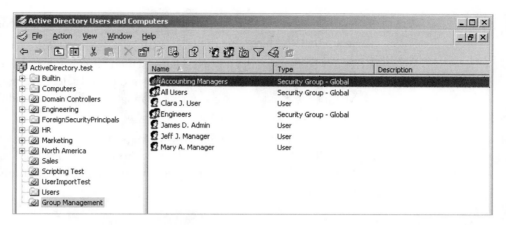

4. Next, add some users to the groups that you created. Right-click the "Accounting Managers" group and select Properties. Click the Members tab, and then click Add. Enter the names **JManager** and **MManager**. Click OK to save the Properties of the group.

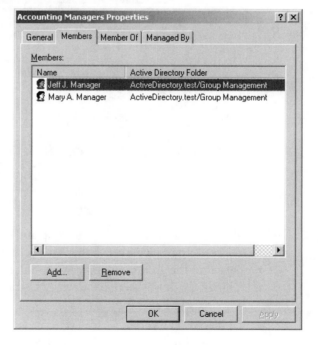

5. Right-click the Engineers group and add the Clara J. User account to the group (use the same procedure as in the preceding step).

6. In this step, you will add two groups (which already contain users) to the All Users group. Right-click the All Users group and select Properties. On the Members tab, add the Accounting Managers and Engineers global groups. Click OK to save the changes.

7. Now, let's check the membership settings for a group and a user. Right-click the "Clara J. User" account and select Properties. Click the Member Of tab. Note that this user appears as a member of the Engineers group. Click OK when done.

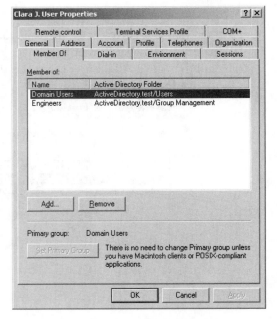

8. Finally, right-click the Engineers group and select the Member Of tab. Note that this group is a member of the All Users group. When finished, close the properties of the group. You may want to delete the "Group Management" OU. Finally, exit the Active Directory Users and Computers tool.

As you can see, Windows Server 2003 provides many different ways in which you can create and manage groups and group membership.

Best Practices for Managing Users and Groups

Managing security for production computers can be a difficult task for even experienced systems administrators. For one thing, the job is never really "done": As other technical and nontechnical changes occur in the environment, systems administrators must keep up with new requirements. Other organizational and technical changes can require significant administrative effort.

Throughout this chapter, you've looked at several methods by which you can manage users, computers, and groups. In this section, we'll conclude by providing some "best practices" that can be used to improve the management of these objects in an Active Directory environment. Some recommendations are

■ *Create (and enforce) naming conventions.* In order to keep your user accounts, computer accounts, and groups organized, it's very helpful to have an established naming convention. For example, many environments choose to use the first initial and full last name of an employee as his or her default username. Similarly, you might specify that all groups that are created for temporary employees begin with a specific set of characters (for example, "Temp-Marketing," "Temp-Sales," and "Temp-Engineering"). Often, taking a little bit of time to plan out naming conventions can save a lot of headaches and guesswork in the future.

■ *Rename the Administrator account.* Anyone who has worked with Microsoft's Windows server operating systems is probably aware that the default all-powerful user account is named "Administrator." Since it's such an important user account, many people who try to compromise security by guessing a password will try to log on using this account. One way to avoid that problem is to simply rename the account. In fact, you could create another account named "Administrator" as a decoy!

■ Assign users to groups and then assign permissions to groups: The proper use of groups can help to dramatically reduce the amount of effort required to grant permissions to resources. A good practice is to place users in groups and then to assign permissions to groups. This reduces administration (since group membership can be easily changed when employees are added and removed), and it makes it easier to assign permissions on files, folders, and other objects.

■ *Design your group structure and, wherever possible, assign permissions to groups (instead of directly to users):* Your ability to effectively manage security with minimal headaches will be based on the design of your groups. Be sure to create groups that reflect your business organization. For example, it might be a good idea to create groups called "Accounting Users," "Accounting Managers," "Marketing," and so on. Now, whenever department memberships change, you can easily add and remove users from these groups.

■ *Use the "Find" feature of the Active Directory Users and Computers tool.* By right-clicking an object (such as a domain or an OU) and selecting the Find operation, you'll be able to quickly and easily search the Active Directory database for certain types of objects. For example, you might want to perform a search of all user accounts that have not been used to log on within the last 30 days (see the following illustration). By identifying these accounts, you can find user objects that you may have forgotten to delete. And through the use of effective search criteria, you can find relevant information in even the largest of Active Directory domains.

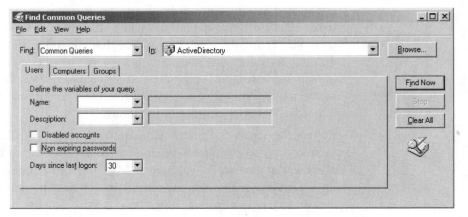

■ *Take the time to understand the needs of your users.* Often, IT staff will work in a vacuum, making what seem like good decisions in the area of security. However, the best solutions can often be found by explaining the value of security to end users, and in getting information about their needs. The ideal security implementation will take all of this into account.

SCENARIO & SOLUTION

Your organization has decided to replace three laptops with newer models. You want to make sure that no one is able to log on to the domain from these computers. However, you do want to keep the computers available for use.	Disable or delete the computer accounts so that they cannot be used to log in to the domain.
You are the administrator for a large Active Directory domain. You want to find a list of all of the disabled user accounts within the domain.	Use the Find feature in the Active Directory Users and Computers tool. Specifically, by choosing the Common Queries option, you'll be able to easily search for disabled accounts throughout the domain.
Recently, your department ordered 200 new computers that will be used to replace old computers. The new computers will be added to your Active Directory domain. You want to create these computer accounts from a command prompt.	Use the "dsadd" computer command to script the creation of the computer accounts.

CERTIFICATION SUMMARY

In this chapter, we covered a lot of important information that's related to managing a real-world Active Directory environment. We began with a look at how user profiles can enable users to maintain their computer configuration settings, regardless of which computer they use. Through the use of profiles, administrators can also enforce a consistent user experience.

Next, we looked at the important topic of managing user accounts. We started with a discussion of what security principals are, and how workgroup security and domain security differ. We then looked at the process of creating user accounts, both manually (using the Active Directory Users and Computers tool) and automatically (using CSVDE, LDIFDE, and scripting). We also covered the many different security policies, including password and account lockout configuration, that systems administrators can use to improve security in their environments. In relation to users, we also looked at how you can troubleshoot user authentication issues.

The next security-related topic that we covered was related to computer accounts. These accounts can be created to improve security by specifying which machines can connect to your domain. Finally, we walked through the process of creating groups for the purpose of simplifying systems administration. Through the use of various types of groups, you can efficiently apply consistent security settings throughout your environment.

TWO-MINUTE DRILL

Manage Local, Roaming, and Mandatory User Profiles

❑ User profiles contain user-specific information such as operating system settings, application data, user files, and Registry settings.

❑ By default, whenever a user logs on to a Windows computer, a local profile is automatically created.

❑ Roaming user profiles stored on a central server allow users to access and save their settings, regardless of the computer they're using.

❑ Mandatory user profiles are stored on a server, but they are not updated when a user logs off.

Create, Manage, and Troubleshoot User Accounts

❑ User accounts are security principals that map to your organization's employees. Through permissions placed on various objects, administrators can implement user-based security.

❑ The Active Directory Users and Computers administrative tool is the main method for creating and managing user accounts.

❑ The CSVDE and LDIFDE utilities can be used to import and export user account information.

❑ Password policies, account lockout policies, security options, and user rights assignments can all be used to increase security in an Active Directory environment.

Create, Manage, and Troubleshoot Computer Accounts

❑ Computer accounts can be created automatically when an authorized user adds a computer to a domain.

❑ To increase security, systems administrators can create computer accounts manually within an Active Directory domain. They can optionally identify computers through unique identifiers.

❑ Computer accounts can be reset, disabled, enabled, and deleted using the Active Directory Users and Computers tool.

Create and Manage Groups

- ❑ Group types include security groups and distribution groups.
- ❑ Group scopes include domain local, global, and universal.
- ❑ Active Directory domains contain many special groups that can be used to assign permissions to perform specific tasks.
- ❑ Information about the members of a group can be found in the Members tab of the properties of the group.

SELF TEST

The following questions will help you measure your understanding of the material presented in this chapter. Read all the choices carefully because there might be more than one correct answer. Choose all correct answers for each question, unless stated otherwise.

Manage Local, Roaming, and Mandatory User Profiles

1. You are a systems administrator at the Corporate office of a large multinational organization. Recently, the management of the Corporate office decided that it would be useful to provide visitors to the building with free Internet access. They would like you to set up several new computers that will be placed in the office lobby. You have created a new Active Directory domain user account named "InternetUser" and have placed instructions near each of these computers that explain that visitors must log in to the computer in order to access the Internet. You want to ensure that users will always receive the same, default operating system and application configuration whenever they log on to any of the computers. How can you do this with the least administrative effort?

   A. Create a roaming user profile for the InternetUser account on each computer.

   B. Create a mandatory user profile for the InternetUser account on each computer.

   C. Create a single roaming user profile for the InternetUser account.

   D. Create a single mandatory user profile for the InternetUser account.

   E. Create individual local user profiles for the InternetUser account on each computer.

2. Which of the following types of settings is/are *not* stored as part of a user profile? (Choose all that apply.)

   A. Application settings

   B. Device driver settings

   C. The HKEY_CURRENT_USER hive of the Registry

   D. The HKEY_LOCAL_MACHINE hive of the Registry

   E. Desktop configuration, including background and screen saver options

3. Recently, you installed a software application for use on the local computer. During the installation process, you chose to make the application available to all users. You now want to add a new shortcut to the program group that was created, and you want this shortcut to be available to all users on the computer (including those that have not yet logged on to the computer). Which of the following should you modify to do this with the least administrative effort?

   A. "\Documents and Settings\Default User"

   B. "\Documents and Settings\Default"

C. "\Documents and Settings\Program Groups"

D. "\Documents and Settings\All Users"

E. The local profile of all users that have logged on to the computer

4. Which of the following tools can you use to most easily copy a user profile from the local computer to a share located on a network server? (Choose one.)

A. Control Panel | System

B. Computer Management

C. Control Panel | User Settings

D. Control Panel | Taskbar and Start Menu

E. Control Panel | Stored User Names and Passwords

5. Anita is planning to implement roaming user profiles for several desktop computers in her organization's branch office. She wants to make sure that profiles remain secure and that the data contained in these profiles is stored only on the server. Which of the following Group Policy settings should she use to meet this objective?

A. Only allow local user profiles.

B. Set maximum retries to unload and update a user profile.

C. Delete cached copies of roaming profiles.

D. Do not detect slow network connections.

E. Wait for remote user profile.

Create, Manage, and Troubleshoot User Accounts

6. Which of the following Active Directory objects is/are considered a security principal? (Choose all that apply.)

A. Security groups

B. Distribution groups

C. Organizational Units

D. Computers

E. Users

7. You are the only systems administrator for a medium-sized environment. Your organization has implemented a single Active Directory domain that contains over 150 users. Recently, you have noticed that a few user accounts have been disabled. However, you're sure that you did not manually disable these accounts. Which of the following settings should you examine to find a potential cause of the problem?

A. Active Directory Users and Computers – Properties of the disabled user accounts

B. Active Directory Users and Computers – Properties of the domain

    C. Password policy

    D. Account lockout policy

    E. None of the above

8. Maria wants to make some security-related changes that affect all of the users in her organization's single Active Directory domain. She has logged on to a domain controller. Which of the following administrative tools should she use to change the settings, using the least amount of administrative effort?

    A. Active Directory Users and Computers

    B. Active Directory Domains and Trusts

    C. Computer Management

    D. Local Security Policy

    E. Domain Security Policy

    F. Domain Controller Security Policy

9. You are troubleshooting a problem in which three different users at a remote branch office cannot log on to your domain. Users in other locations, including yourself, seem to be able to log on without any problems. Which of the following utilities can you use to test for netlogon connectivity between the clients and the Active Directory domain controllers?

    A. NET TEST

    B. NET VERIFY

    C. DCStatus

    D. NLTest

    E. LDP

10. Bill is tasked with creating over 200 new computer accounts for a new department in his organization. The Human Resources department has provided him with a standard text file that contains user information (including usernames and unique account names) in a format that is delimited by commas. Which of the following tools/methods should Bill use to attempt to import the user accounts with the least administrative effort?

    A. CSVDE

    B. LDIFDE

    C. Active Directory Services Interface (ADSI)

    D. Windows Scripting Host (WSH)

    E. Automation

Create, Manage, and Troubleshoot Computer Accounts

11. Jose is a systems administer for his organization's Sales department. His department has purchased three different laptop computers for use by traveling members of the Sales team.

Recently, Jose has been asked to look at ways to increase the security of these laptops. Particularly, when the laptops aren't loaned to a member of the Sales team, users should not be able to use the machines to log on to the company's Active Directory domain. How can he do this, using the least amount of administrative effort?

A. Reset computer accounts after Sales employees return from traveling.

B. Reset computer accounts before Sales employees borrow one of the laptop computers.

C. Change the computer password before the laptops are loaned out.

D. Delete the computer accounts for the laptops when they are not in use.

E. Disable the computer accounts for the laptops when they are not in use.

12. Your IT department has recently purchase 20 new desktop computers for use in a branch office. All of these computers came with documentation that includes a universally unique identifier (UUID) and a default computer name for each computer. How can you make sure that only these computers are added to your Active Directory domain?

A. Create a managed computer account using the Active Directory Users and Computers tool.

B. Automatically create computer accounts for these machines by joining them to the domain.

C. Create an unmanaged computer object using the Active Directory Users and Computers tool.

D. Use the Computer Management tool on a domain controller to specify which computers may join the domain.

E. Use the Computer Management tool on each new desktop computer to authorize each to join the domain.

13. Scott is trying to add a new Windows XP computer, named Workstation7, to his organization's single Active Directory domain. When he tries to add the computer to the domain, he is prompted for a username and password. He enters his own credentials, but he then receives an error stating that he does not have sufficient permissions. To which of the following groups must Scott be added in order to be able to add computers to the domain? (Choose the answer that provides the minimal required permissions.)

A. The Administrator account on the local computer

B. The Administrators group on the local computer

C. The Domain Admins group on the local computer

D. The Domain Admins group in the domain

E. The Enterprise Admins group in the domain

14. Which of the following computer configurations can become a member of a Windows Server 2003 Active Directory domain? (Choose all that apply.)

A. A computer running Windows XP Professional

B. A computer running Windows Server 2003

C. A computer running Windows 2000 Server

    D.   A computer running Windows NT 4.0 Server, with Service Pack 6

    E.   A computer running Windows Me

Create and Manage Groups

15. You want to allow several different systems administrators to create and modify user accounts within your single Active Directory domain. To which of the following groups should you add these users? (Choose the option that provides minimal permissions.)

    A.   The domain local Administrators group

    B.   The domain local Domain Admins group

    C.   The domain local Account Operators group

    D.   The global Account Operators group

    E.   The universal Account Operators group

16. Which of the following scopes of groups can only contain members from a single domain but can be used to grant permissions to resources in other domains within an Active Directory environment? (Choose one.)

    A.   Domain local groups

    B.   Local groups

    C.   Global groups

    D.   Universal groups

    E.   None of the above

17. You want to determine which groups in your Active Directory environment have the "Engineering – Development" group as one of their members. You right-click this group and select Properties. On which of the following tabs can you find the required information?

    A.   Security

    B.   General

    C.   Members

    D.   Users

    E.   None of the above

LAB QUESTION

Recently, your organization, AD Consulting, has acquired another fairly large company, System Solutions, Inc. All employees of the new combined organization are hoping for a smooth transition. Related to network operations, your CIO has put you in charge of handling the migration of user accounts and setting up their environment so that employees of the acquired company are able to properly access resources within your organization's single Active Directory domain.

From an IT standpoint, System Solutions' network structure couldn't be much more different from that of AD Consulting's environment. For example, they use a Unix-based directory services infrastructure, although the majority of their client computers are running on Windows 2000 Professional or Windows XP Professional.

Based on the overall goals of the acquisition, you have been assigned several goals. These include

- Creating new user accounts in your Active Directory domain for the 450 new employees

- Configuring roaming user profiles for all of the new employee user accounts

- Allowing for securely adding the new users' computers to the Active Directory domain

- Providing methods for easily administering security permissions for the new users

Since the majority of your IT staff is already committed to other projects, you want to ensure that you can do all of this work with the least amount of administrative effort. Your primary goal, however, is to meet all of these requirements. Describe how you can most easily meet these objectives.

SELF TEST ANSWERS

Manage Local, Roaming, and Mandatory User profiles

1. ☑ **D.** Since you want to ensure that users of these computers cannot save any settings or changes they made, you must use a mandatory user profile. You should assign the mandatory user profile to the single domain account.

 ☒ A and C are incorrect because roaming profiles would be updated by users during the logoff process. B and E are incorrect because it is not necessary to create multiple profiles.

2. ☑ **B and D.** User profiles do not store machine-specific information, including device driver settings and contents of the Local Machine key of the Registry.

 ☒ A, C, and E are incorrect because these are all settings that are stored as part of a user profile.

3. ☑ **D.** When you specified the installation program should make the application available to all users, the program group was created in the All Users profile folder. By changing the program group shortcuts here, you give all other local users (including ones that have not yet logged on) access to the shortcut.

 ☒ A is incorrect because creating a shortcut within this folder would only affect users that have not yet logged on to the local computer. B and C are incorrect because these are not user profile folders that are created by default. Finally, E is incorrect because it would not affect users that have not yet logged on to the computer.

4. ☑ **A.** By using the Advanced | User Profiles settings within the System Control Panel applet, you can easily copy a user profile to another computer.

 ☒ B, D, and E are incorrect because they do not provide a method for copying the user profile. C is incorrect because this is not a valid Control Panel applet.

5. ☑ **C.** The Delete Cached Copies Of Roaming Profiles option can be used to ensure that a local copy of a roaming user profile is automatically removed from the local machine whenever a user logs off.

 ☒ A, B, D, and E are incorrect because, although they are valid Group Policy settings, they will not prevent the creation of a local copy of user profile data.

Create, Manage, and Troubleshoot User Accounts

6. ☑ **A, D,** and **E.** Users, computers, and security groups are all security principals. Systems administrators can assign permissions on resources to these object types.

 ☒ B and D are both incorrect because they are not security principals and cannot be granted permissions on other objects.

7. ☑ **D.** It is likely that the user accounts are being disabled due to an automatic account lockout policy. You should examine these settings to verify this and/or to determine if the settings are appropriate for your environment.

☒ A and B are incorrect because these items would not provide information about why an account might be automatically locked out. C is incorrect because password policy will not result in the automatic disabling of an account.

8. ☑ **E.** Maria can use the Domain Security Policy administrative tool to set various security options at the domain level.

☒ A, B, and C are incorrect because these tools are not used to directly make changes to domain policy settings. D and F are incorrect because these policy settings would only affect the local domain controller.

9. ☑ **D.** You can use the NLTest command-line utility to verify network connectivity between the netlogon process on the client computer and the services on domain controllers. This is a good way to troubleshoot user logon and authentication failure issues.

☒ A, B, and C are incorrect because these are not available Windows Server 2003 utilities. E is incorrect because LDP is used to directly query an Active Directory database, but not to troubleshoot connectivity issues.

10. ☑ **A.** Since the data was provided in a comma-separated values (CSV) text file, the CSVDE tool would be the best method to use to import the new user accounts. Of course, Bill would first have to verify that the information is in the correct format.

☒ B is incorrect because this tool does not use CSV files. C, D, and E are all possible options for performing the import, but they are not as easy to use as the CSVDE utility.

Create, Manage, and Troubleshoot Computer Accounts

11. ☑ **E.** By disabling the computer accounts, Jose can prevent users from logging on to the domain using the laptop computers. This will work regardless of the users' permissions.

☒ A and B are incorrect because they would not increase security. C is incorrect because computer accounts do not have passwords. D is incorrect because this would require significant administrative effort.

12. ☑ **A.** Since you have the UUID information for the new computers, the most secure method for adding them to the domain is to create managed computer accounts.

☒ B and C would work, but those options do not provide the desired security. D and E are incorrect because the Computer Management tool cannot be used to join a computer to a domain.

13. ☑ **D.** Of the choices, being a member of the Domain Administrators group would provide Scott with the minimal permissions required.

☒ A and B are incorrect because local computer permissions would not allow Scott to add computers to the domain. C is incorrect because there is no Domain Admins group on the local computer. E is incorrect because it does not provide the minimal permissions of the options listed.

14. ☑ **A, B, C,** and **D.** Computers running any of these operating systems can become a member of an Active Directory domain.

 ☒ E is incorrect because Windows Me computers cannot join a domain (although they can be granted access to domain resources).

Create and Manage Groups

15. ☑ **C.** The purpose of the domain local Account Operators group is to provide systems administrators with sufficient permissions to administer objects within an Active Directory domain.

 ☒ A, B, D, and E are incorrect because these types of groups would not provide the minimal permissions that Scott requires.

16. ☑ **C.** The purpose of a global group is to create a collection of members from a single domain and to then grant them permissions within another domain.

 ☒ A, B, and D are incorrect because they do not meet the definition.

17. ☑ **E.** The easiest way to retrieve the desired information is through the use of the Member Of tab.

 ☒ A, B, and C are incorrect because they would not provide the appropriate information. D is incorrect because this is not a tab that is available in the properties of a security group.

LAB ANSWER

The scenario that's described in this lab question is probably a familiar one for many systems administrators. In the real world, due to business, technical, and political issues, mergers and acquisitions can take many months to complete. Fortunately, the IT-related goals mentioned here can be fairly easily accomplished through the use of many tools and features in Windows Server 2003. Let's look at some potential solutions for each of the goals.

The first objective requires the creation of new user accounts in your organization's Active Directory domain. Had System Solutions been using Active Directory, you might have been able to simply create a trust relationship between the two domains. Since they're using a different system, you'll need to use a different approach of creating new user accounts. The most obvious method for performing this task involves the manual creation of the accounts, using the Active Directory Users and Computers tool. However, this approach would leave much to be desired. Apart from the amount of time that it would take (and the tediousness of the task), this method would leave a lot of potential room for error.

It's likely that System Solutions' IT staff can provide a list of employees in some format. A better way to create the new accounts would be to use either the CSVDE or LDIFDE utility to import the new user accounts into the Active Directory. For example, if their Unix-based directory services are using an LDAP-compatible architecture, it might be fairly easily to obtain data in the format that is required for the LDIFDE utility. Another alternative is to use automation to create the new user account. Although it would require some experience in scripting, you could fairly easily put together some code that creates new user accounts and that establishes some default properties (name, address, and location information, for example). Regardless of how you create them, the new users will be subjected to your organization's security policies (including password and account lockout settings).

Let's look at the second requirement: Setting up roaming user profiles. Once you have the new user accounts created, the process is fairly straightforward. First, you'll need to create server-based shared folders for each of the users. You can do this by using a simple batch file that combines a list of the user accounts that you created with the md command. Then, you can use the feature in Active Directory Users and Computers that allows you to view and modify profile properties for multiple user objects at the same time. By using environment variables, you can assign the "same" path for all user accounts (for example, \\FileServer3\Users\%UserName%).

Next comes the requirement of adding the new computers to the domain. The most secure way to do this would be to manually create computer accounts using Active Directory Users and Computers. Ideally, you'd be able to determine the unique identifier for each of the computers that are to be added. If not, you can still restrict the permissions related to who can add a new computer to the domain. And, you can leave the computer accounts as "Disabled" until you are ready to add the computers to the domain. Since you are adding a large number of computers, scripting or using the "dsadd" computer command can be very helpful.

So far, so good. Now, let's look at the final requirement: providing for simplified security administration. This should be a goal of every IT department, regardless of whether or not you're creating new user accounts. The simple answer to the question is to use groups. In many cases, you'll find that the new employees should belong to existing groups within your Active Directory domain. This is ideal, because it won't require you to set or change any permissions on resources such as files, folders, and printers. In other cases, you might need to create new security groups to accommodate a new business unit. Either way, you should be sure to verify the security settings that are provided for all of these groups.

As you can see, Windows Server 2003 includes many different methods for creating and managing users, computers, and groups. Keep these in mind when you're asked about performing systems administration tasks on the exam (and in the real world!).

4

Managing
Resource Access

W hen you think about servers running in organizations of almost any size, one of the primary functions that comes to mind is that of providing secure access to resources such as files and printers. By storing data centrally (instead of on client computers), systems administrators can more easily manage the information their organizations run on. Furthermore, users can rest assured that their files are being properly backed up and that only authorized users will have access to data.

One of the fundamental purposes of modern network operating systems is to secure resources. As a systems administrator, it's your job to ensure that only authorized people can gain access to sensitive information. Security should be a major concern for environments of any size, especially as companies increasingly depend on computer systems for critical line-of-business functions. However, it's also important to ensure that your information is accessible. Windows Server 2003 provides several different ways for you to secure your organization's data. Furthermore, it provides ways for systems administrators to easily control access to resources and to manage large groups of users.

Implementing security in the real world is far from being a one-click operation. Rather, security can be configured and implemented at many different levels, including the network infrastructure, the operating system, and applications. A flaw or misconfiguration in any of those layers can leave your critical systems open to attack. Even the best-designed network security systems can be compromised by a user who chooses his first name for a password. Therefore, it's important to know all of the many ways of securing modern network operating systems that help in keeping unauthorized users away from your sensitive information.

On the exam, Microsoft wants to make sure that you are able to carry out duties related to making server resources available to end users. You should be able to determine appropriate security settings, and you should have a solid understanding of the many features of Windows Server 2003 that make information sharing (and securing) easier for everyone. If you've worked with earlier versions of the Windows server-side platform, you'll see that there are several useful enhancements that can save time and reduce the chance for errors.

The focus of this chapter is on managing access to resources. This includes making resources (such as files and printers) available to network users, and ensuring that the appropriate permissions are set on those resources. Specifically, we'll start with a discussion of how file system permissions can be configured. These settings form the basis for controlling who can access which information in a networked environment. Then, you'll look at making resources available over the network using shared folders. Finally, you'll look at how you can share and manage printers. Let's get started by looking at some general security ideas and concepts that are very important to keep in mind as you manage your servers.

watch *The concepts and procedures presented in this chapter assume that you have a solid understanding of managing users, computers, and groups.*

Therefore, if you haven't already, be sure you're familiar with the content of Chapter 3 before continuing.

Understanding General Security Concepts

Network and computer security is a topic that receives much attention in the IT industry. Most organizations understand the importance of securing their information, as well as the potential disasters that can occur if they don't. There are several important points to keep in mind when working in networked environments. Let's start by describing some general "best practices":

- **Provide users with minimal permissions** When configuring and assigning security-related settings, you should generally default to giving your users the minimum set of permissions that they require to do their jobs. Often, systems administrators will want to give users full permissions on their machines because it is easier to set up and administer. However, providing minimal permissions can offer several benefits. First, users will be able to perform only the types of tasks that they should be doing. Therefore, you can worry less about users making improper Registry modifications, installing unauthorized software, or accidentally deleting critical files. Perhaps more important is the fact that, should a user account be compromised, you can limit the amount of potential damage by ensuring that the account has limited privileges.

- **Implement physical security** An often-overlooked aspect of overall computer and network security deals with the physical aspects of computing. Regardless of the levels of other types of security, it is vital that your organization limits access to its network and hardware. Physical security might start with controlled access to the building (monitoring by security guards and physical or electronic pass cards). Next, it's important to ensure that access to servers and other critical hardware is limited. Most environments will require some sort of key in order for systems administrators to access the server room. This security measure can help prevent unauthorized individuals from entering the room and simply removing (or physically damaging) critical systems. Finally, it's important to keep in mind the security of wireless networks, notebook computers, PDAs, and other electronic devices that may contain sensitive information.

- **Take advantage of network directory services**   The most secure and easy-to-administer method of providing for security is through the use of centralized directory services. In the Windows world, this means that it's highly recommended that you implement the Active Directory in your environment. By storing important information (including user logons and passwords) in a central system, you can easily keep track of resources and security principals. More information about implementing and managing the Active Directory can be found in Laura Robinson's, MCSE *Windows Server 2003 Active Directory Infrastructure Study Guide (Exam 70-294)* (McGraw-Hill/ Osborne, 2003), ISBN, 0-07-222319-7, and details are also covered in Microsoft's Exam 70-294, "Planning, Implementing, and Maintaining a Microsoft Windows Server 2003 Active Directory Infrastructure."

- **Make security a part of your organization's culture**   It's important that every employee in your organization understands the importance of securing sensitive resources. In general, users will better follow security guidelines when they understand the importance of those rules. Often, a little end-user education can dramatically improve overall system security.

on the
Job

To put things in perspective, many security experts state that 20 percent of real-world network security is a technical issue and that 80 percent of it is a process and policy in one. Don't make the mistake of trying to solve all security problems through the implementation of technology. You also need to establish and enforce system usage policies, physically secure your resources, and ensure that users are aware of any restrictions.

- **Find a balance between security and usability**   Security often involves a trade-off between the safety of a system and its usability. For example, if security was my only concern, I might decide to remove my server machine from the network and bury it in six feet of concrete. Surely, this would be secure, but it's not very useful to my users who might want to obtain resources from that machine! The same might be true for a network environment that requires users to log on multiple times or to use very complicated passwords. Users will often be forced to find a way around these measures (by writing down passwords, for example). Always try to strike a balance between the overall security and the usability of your systems.

With these general security practices in mind, let's move on to looking at specific ways in which Windows Server 2003 manages security.

Understanding Permissions

The central idea behind security is that users must have permissions in order to access resources. For example, before I can print to a color printer on the third floor of my office, I must be given permissions to do so. In Windows Server 2003, permissions work through a system of objects. There are many different kinds of "objects" that can be secured on the Windows Server platform. Object types include files, folders, shares, printers, Registry keys, and Active Directory objects.

Permissions are rules that govern which users and groups can access specific objects. Often, such sets of permissions are referred to as *access control lists (ACLs)*, and the specific rules themselves as *access control entries (ACEs)*. Each object contains an ACL that contains ACEs. Each ACE is made up of the *security identifier (SID)* of a security principal and a listing of which specific actions are allowed or disallowed. Security principals can be users, security groups, or machine accounts. For more information about security principals, see Chapter 3.

As a simple (but very important) example of how this system works, let's assume that you are a systems administrator and are configuring access to a file called AccountingData.dat. As long as the file is stored on the NTFS file system, the file itself will have an ACL. Within the ACL for that file, you can configure permissions such that members of the Accounting group will be able to modify it, and that other users will not have any access at all. Later in this chapter, you'll look at various details related to how permissions work in Windows Server 2003.

Understanding User Rights

User rights specify what types of functions users can perform. Unlike permissions, user rights are not based on ACLs. Instead, the rights are assigned to user objects (either directly or through group membership). There are two types of user rights:

- **Privileges**   These settings specify certain actions that users are allowed to perform in a networked environment. For example, a user may be able to bypass file system security in order to create backups (a topic that you'll look at in Chapter 6). Or, a user may have the right to add new computers to the network.

- **Logon rights**   As the name implies, logon rights control when and how users can access computing resources. For example, systems administrators can define to which computer(s) a user may log on over the network.

Users' effective rights are based on their group membership in a cumulative fashion. Users will have all of the rights that are assigned to all of the groups of which they are a member.

Domain vs. Workgroup Security

In a stand-alone configuration, Windows Server 2003 functions as a workgroup server. In this mode, each computer that is a member of a workgroup is a separate security entity. That is, each workstation and server manages its own list of users, groups, and permissions. This type of decentralized security can present many problems. First, since security information is stored in many different places, it can be difficult to configure. When a new user requires access to resources, her account may need to be added to many different machines. And, if the password for each account isn't the same, she may be forced to authenticate multiple times. If, for some reason, her account needed to be removed, it would again have to be removed on several different systems. If you accidentally forget about one, you could be introducing serious security problems! Fortunately, there's a better way to manage security.

Domains are designed to function as a single repository of security-related information for all of the users, groups, and computers that are members of the domain. Although it is beyond the scope of this book to discuss the Active Directory in detail, you should know that a large portion of security in a domain-based environment is configured through the Active Directory. Many of these settings will control the permissions that apply to an installation of Windows Server 2003 that is a member of a domain. A member of a domain obtains its primary security information from centralized domain controllers. Therefore, the local accounts database is used only for specialized purposes (to perform server recovery or troubleshooting, for example). As you saw in Chapter 1, Windows Server 2003 computers can function as domain controllers, each of which hosts a copy of the Active Directory information.

In some cases, you might choose to configure some of your Windows Server 2003 installations in a stand-alone server configuration. For example, suppose you have configured a public web server that is accessible via the Internet. For security purposes, you may not want Active Directory–related information to be stored on this machine, and you may want to manage permissions and other settings for this machine alone. In that case, making the server a stand-alone server might be a good choice. In many other cases, however, you'll want to take advantage of the centralized security and administrative benefits of making your servers members of a domain.

Now that you have a good overview of general security concepts, let's drill down into the important topic of understanding file system security.

Managing File System Security

One of the many benefits of networked systems is the ability to quickly and easily share data across systems. However, this benefit comes at the price of security. The file system is an extremely important part of modern computers. A large amount of most organizations' sensitive information is stored in the file system in the form of documents, images, and other pieces of data. As a systems administrator, it's your job to ensure that these files stay secure and that only authorized users can access them. That's where the important topic of file system security comes in.

Let's start with the most important point: If you want to implement security at the file system level, you must choose to use NTFS. The FAT and FAT32 partition types do not provide any security at all, and there's little to stop someone from booting off a floppy and accessing all of the information on your computers. Furthermore, the only level of network security provided by FAT-based partitions is at the level of shared folders (a topic that you'll encounter later in this chapter).

With that in mind, let's take a look at the file system security architecture of Windows Server 2003.

Understanding NTFS Permissions

Earlier, I mentioned that permissions are placed on objects through the use of ACLs that contain ACEs. Folders and files that are stored on an NTFS partition are treated as objects, each of which has its own unique identifier. You can protect files at the level of the file system using NTFS permissions. In Windows Server 2003, file system permissions can be applied to files and folders through the Security tab of the properties of the object. For example, to set properties on a file, you can right-click the file, select Properties, and then click the Security tab (see Figure 4-1).

on the
iob

It's important to keep in mind that file system security is only one part of an overall security strategy. Although NTFS permissions provide security while the operating system is running, it is possible to access this data without authorization, using a boot floppy disk and special utilities. To prevent this, it's important to provide for the physical security of your server computers!

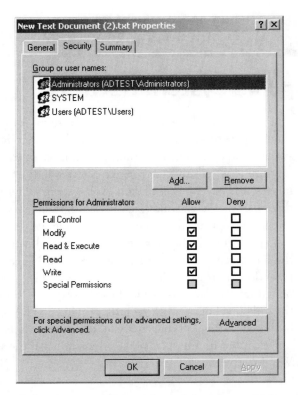

In the Security dialog box, you'll see a list of the users and groups for which permissions are configured. By clicking one of these items, you can view the permissions that are assigned. For each permission setting, you will see two columns: Allow and Deny. Actually, there are three possible states for each setting: You can choose to allow the permission, to deny it, or to leave it as unspecified (neither box will be checked). If the security permissions were inherited from a higher level (a topic that you'll consider in the next section), you will see that the boxes are grayed out and cannot be changed.

The permissions that are available for a file include the following:

- **Full Control**   This option provides full permissions on the object, including the ability to take ownership of files and to change security permissions.

- **Modify**   This permission specifies that users can open files and change their contents or delete them.

- **Read**   This permission allows users to read or open the specified file.

- **Read and Execute**   This permission allows users to read or open the files and to run executable programs.

- **Write**   This permission allows users to change the contents of existing files and to create new ones.

■ **Special Permissions (available for some objects)**   Through the use of the
Advanced button, you can specify much more detailed permissions on specific
objects (see Figure 4-2). In general, systems administrators will not need to
apply permissions at this level. The Windows Help and Support Center
provides details about the actual file and folder permissions that are assigned
when you choose from the standard permissions.

Certain combinations of permissions are not allowed for a single permission line
item. For example, you cannot deny Modify permissions and, at the same time, allow
Read and Execute. When you work with setting permissions using the Security tab,
you'll notice that the user interface will automatically check and uncheck boxes as
appropriate. Therefore, it's important to take the time to review your final selections
before you apply them.

The exact list of permissions that are available for various objects depends on the type
of object and the actions it supports. For example, folders also have a permission setting for
List Folder Contents. Or if you're setting permissions on a Registry key, you will see a
permission called "Create subkey" (see Figure 4-3). Later in this chapter, you'll look at
the steps that are required to assign permissions to files and folders. But first, you need to
understand a few additional concepts regarding file system permissions.

FIGURE 4-2

Viewing File and
Folder Special
Permissions
settings

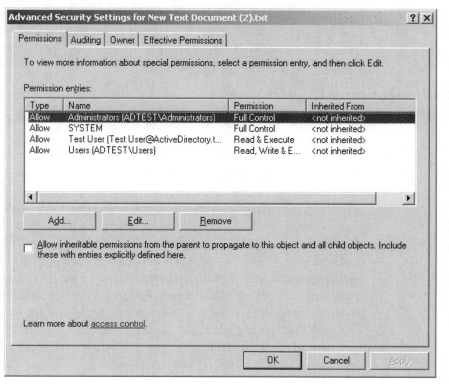

FIGURE 4-3

Setting advanced
permissions on a
Registry key

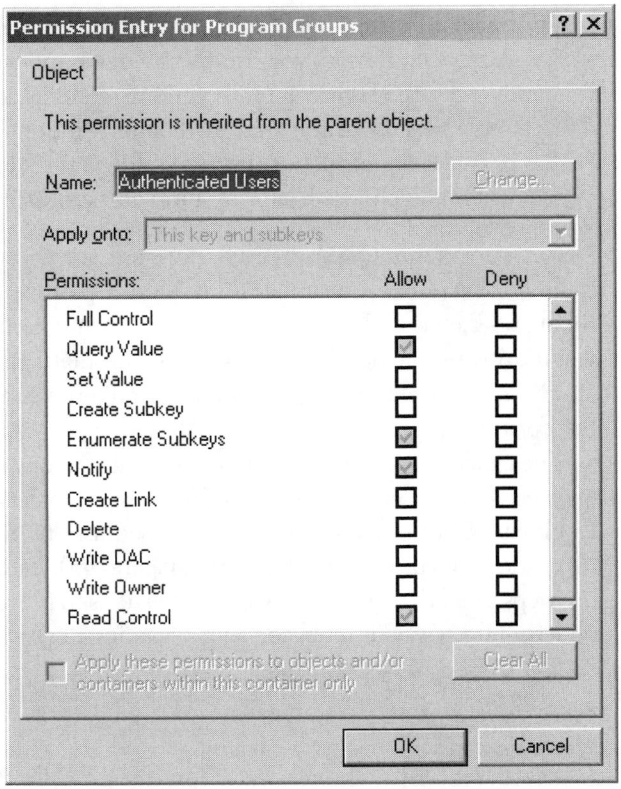

Understanding Inheritance

In modern networked environments, file systems tend to have many thousands of files
and folders. For systems administrators, this can pose a daunting challenge: How can
you possibly ensure that all of these objects have the right security settings? Even harder
would be setting the appropriate permissions for objects that have not yet been created
(such as new files or folders).

That's where inheritance comes in. The basic rule for inheritance is that permissions
that are assigned at a higher-level folder will propagate to child files and folders. This is
the default behavior for files and folders in Windows Server 2003.

There are two main types of permissions that can apply to objects. The first is
explicit permissions. These permissions are the access control rules that are directly
applied to an object. Implicit permissions, on the other hand, are access rules that
are defined for parent objects and that are propagated down to the object itself
(Figure 4-4 compares explicit and implicit permissions). Note that explicit permissions
automatically override implicit permissions. This is even true for the Deny permissions
on a parent level (an explicit allow permission will override an implicit deny).

FIGURE 4-4   Explicit vs. implicit permissions

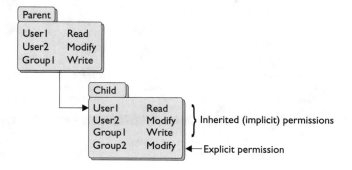

For example, if you grant Change permissions on a folder to members of the Engineering group, by default, all new files and folders created within that folder will have the same permissions.

As another example, suppose you have a folder called Sales that's used by your organization's salespeople. All of the data in the Sales folder and its subfolders should be made available to the entire sales team. In this case, you would assign the necessary permissions at the level of the Sales folder and choose to propagate the changes to all child objects.

By default, files and folders will inherit permissions from their parent objects. This is designed to make the administration of file system permissions simpler. So, if you create a new file called SalesData.xls in the Sales folder, the new file will automatically have the permissions that were applied to the Sales folder. If you attempt to remove a permissions entry on this page, you will see a warning message.

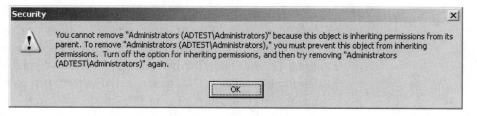

When you change permissions at any level (for example a parent folder), the permission changes will, by default, apply only to that object. That is, the permissions on subfolders and files will not be modified.

So, what if you really do want to set individual permissions on the SalesData.xls file, or you want to propagate the new security settings to all child objects? This is where the Advanced button on the Security tab comes in. When you click the Advanced button, you'll see two options (shown in Figure 4-5). The check boxes at the bottom determine the inheritance behavior for this object.

FIGURE 4-5

Selecting
inheritance of
permissions

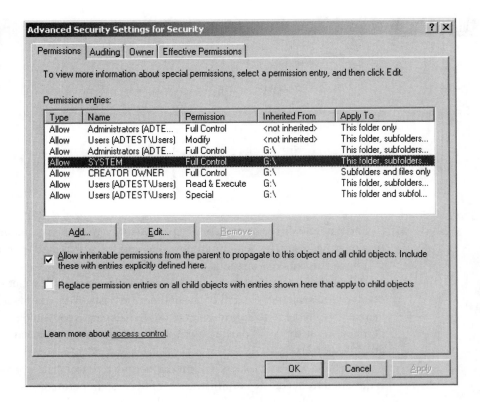

The two options are

- *Allow inheritable permissions from the parent to propagate to this object and all child objects. Include these with entries explicitly defined here.* When enabled, this option specifies that permissions assigned at higher-level objects (for example, a parent folder) will be inherited by this file or folder. By default, this option is enabled, and it specifies that inheritance is enabled. Therefore, certain actions (such as removing a permissions setting) are not allowed. If you uncheck the box, you will be given the opportunity to specify whether you want to Copy or Remove the inherited permissions (shown next). The Copy option will take all of the settings from the parent object and copy them to this object. Although they are not inherited, these permissions will be the same as those on the parent object. The other option, Remove, specifies that you want to start with a clean slate and that inherited permissions should not be copied to this object.

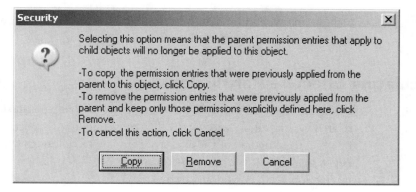

■ *Replace permission entries on all child objects with entries shown here that apply to child objects*. This setting applies only to folders (since files cannot contain child objects). When you select this option, you will be choosing to replace the permissions on any child files or folders with the permissions that you set for this folder. As the confirmation warning states, only the inheritable permissions will be propagated. For example, if a child object is a file, certain permissions may not apply. You should be careful with this option, since it can replace permissions on thousands of files and folders, and it can override other, more specific permissions. However, it is useful if you decide that you want to make permissions changes to an entire tree of folders and files.

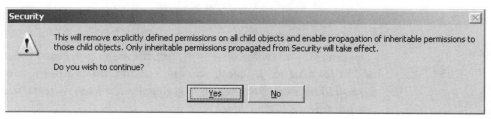

Now that you know how inheritance works, let's move on to looking at the topic of discovering the "bottom line" for security settings.

Calculating Effective Permissions

So far, you've looked at basic information about NTFS permissions, as well as details related to how inheritance works. The most important aspect of setting permissions, however, is to figure out the effective permissions that users will have on objects. The key to figuring out the overall permissions that a user has is in understanding the interaction between various permissions.

In general, the rule is that file and folder permissions are cumulative. That is, if John is a member of the Engineering and Research groups, he will have all of the permissions that are allowed for both groups. The one exception to this rule is the deny setting. A deny permission will always override corresponding allow permissions. When you specify the deny permission, you'll see a warning dialog box that asks if you are sure you want to make the change.

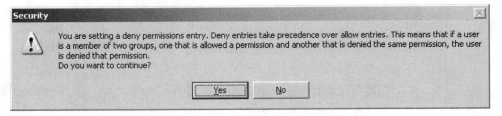

In general, you will not need to use the deny permission when controlling ACLs for objects. Instead, you can usually remove permissions for a user or group. The deny permission is generally used to override settings that may apply from a higher level.

When determining effective permissions, there are two main aspects of security to take into account. The first is the actual permissions that are placed on a specific file or folder. This includes considering the file system hierarchy to take into account any inherited permissions. You looked at this in the previous section on inheritance.

The second consideration is group membership. Permissions that are set for groups of which the user is a member will determine which permissions are applied to the user. For example, assume Susan is a member of the Sales group, the Marketing group, and the Corporate group. Four different sets of permissions can apply to her:

- Permissions set on the Sales group
- Permissions set on the Marketing group

- Permissions set on the Corporate group
- Permissions set directly on Susan's user account

The overall effective permissions are determined by combining the permissions applied to Susan's account, as well as the permissions applied to any groups of which she is a member. Again, there are three possibilities for permissions: allow, deny, and unspecified. Remembering that permissions are additive, with the exception of the deny permission, let's look at a quick example:

- Susan's account has been allowed Read permissions on the Documents folder.
- Members of the Sales group have been allowed "List Folder Contents" permissions on the Documents folder.
- Members of the Marketing group have been denied Write permissions for the Documents folder.

In this example, Susan's effective permissions will be Read and List Folder Contents for the Documents folder and she will be prohibited from writing to the Documents folder.

As you can see, determining effective permissions can be a fairly tedious and time-consuming process. Let's look at an easier way.

Using the Effective Permissions Tool

In larger network environments, users can belong to dozens of groups. Fortunately, Windows Server 2003 includes a method for you to determine the effective permissions for a user or group. You can find the Effective Permissions tab by clicking Advanced within the Security tab of a folder's properties. As seen in Figure 4-6, you can choose a user or group to view the effective permissions that this user has on the selected object.

To access the Effective Permissions property sheet, right-click a file or folder, select Properties, select the Security tab, and then click Advanced. This feature can be used to calculate and view the effective permissions for a user or group.

FIGURE 4-6

Accessing the
Effective
Permissions
feature

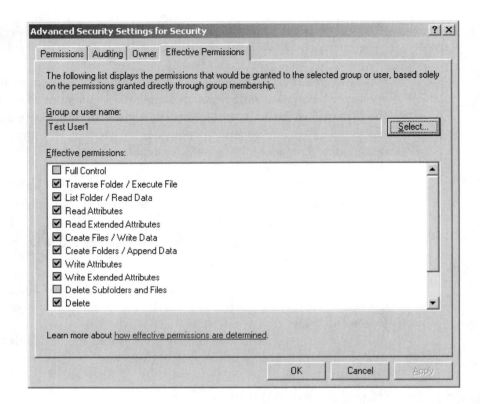

To calculate Effective Permissions for a user or a group, you must first click Select to find an object for which you want to determine permissions. Once you do this, the tool will automatically calculate and display the results. Note that you cannot make any changes to permissions on this screen. Also, you can view permissions information for only one user at a time. Using this GUI can save a lot of time when you're troubleshooting security issues. For example, if a user reports that he cannot access a specific file or folder over the network, you can start troubleshooting by determining the effective permissions on the folder. This is much easier and safer than the old practice of giving the user "Full Control" permissions as a temporary troubleshooting step.

There are some potential issues with determining effective permissions: First, the Effective Permissions tool does not take into account any logon-based restrictions that might affect the overall permissions a user might have on an object. The most likely example of this is in the difference in permissions between when a user logs on to a system and attempts to access files locally and when that user accesses those files over the network. One other limitation of the Effective Permissions feature is that it does not take into account share-level permissions. This is logically important because a single folder can be made available under multiple shares, and the shares may have more restrictive permissions than the files or folders themselves.

One other consideration to keep in mind is that, in order to view effective permissions for users, you must have access to read group membership information. By default, a domain administrator will have the permissions necessary to enumerate the members of all local and domain groups. Local administrator members will be able to determine members of local groups, but not domain groups. Also, if your Active Directory environment is running in pre–Windows 2000 domain mode, all authenticated users will be able to read group membership information.

Overall, the Effective Permissions tab can be a very useful method for verifying file permissions and to find potential errors in configuration.

EXERCISE 4-1

MasterSim 4-1 ON THE CD

Implementing and Verifying File System Permissions

In this exercise, you will create several local files and folders, and set permissions on those folders to view the interactions of inheritance and propagation.

1. Log on to the computer as an Administrator and create the following folder structure on your file system (the exact location is not important).

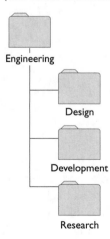

2. Next, create a blank text file in each of the four folders that you created in the previous step. The name of these files is not important—you will be using them only to test effective permissions settings.

3. Create a new user account called "Engineering User1." Make sure that the user is a member of only the Users group (the group may be a domain or a local group). You will use this account for assigning and testing effective permissions in this exercise.

4. To begin setting permissions, you will first assign permissions to the top-level Engineering folder. Open the properties of the Engineering folder and click the Security tab. Click Add and add the "Engineering User1" account. Leave the permissions settings as their defaults. Note that the user will be given the following three permissions: Read & Execute, List Folder Contents, and Read.

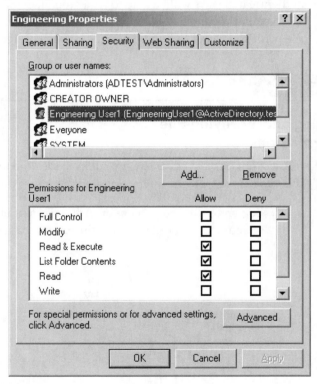

5. Next, you will want to propagate the new permissions that you have set to all of the files and folders located within the Engineering folder. Click Advanced and place a check mark in the option labeled "Replace permission entries on all child objects with entries shown here that apply to child objects." Leave other settings at their defaults and click OK. You will see a confirmation dialog box. Click Yes to continue. Note that this will override the permissions settings on all lower-level folders. Click OK to return to the Security tab, and finally OK, again, to exit the properties of the Engineering folder.

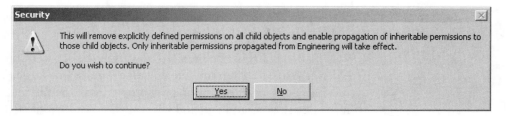

6. Now, let's set some specific permissions on the Development folder. Access the Security properties for the Development folder and select the entry for the Engineering User1 account. Click Remove. You will receive an error message that the entry cannot be removed because of inheritance. Click OK.

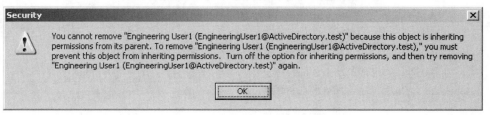

7. In order to remove the access control entry for Engineering User1, you need to disable inheritance. To do this, click Advanced and uncheck the option labeled "Allow inheritable permissions from the parent to propagate to this object and all child objects." You will be presented with a dialog box that asks whether you want to copy or remove the existing permissions. For the sake of this exercise, choose Copy.

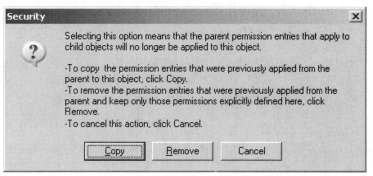

8. Note that the permissions now appear as they did earlier. However, since inheritance is disabled, you can now remove the entry for the Engineering User1 account. To do this, highlight the entry and click Remove. Also, remove any permission settings for members of the Users domain and/or local group and for the Everyone group. Since you want these permissions to affect child objects within the Development folder, enable propagation of

permissions. To make the changes effective, click OK. This will return you to the Security tab. Click OK again to exit the folder properties.

9. Now that you have set permissions on various objects within the Engineering folder, it's time to determine the effective permissions for the Engineering User1 account. Start by viewing the properties of the file that you created in the Development folder, and selecting the Security tab. Click Advanced and then choose the Effective Permissions tab. Click Select and select the Engineering User1 account. Click OK. Note that the Engineering User1 account does not have any permissions on this file.

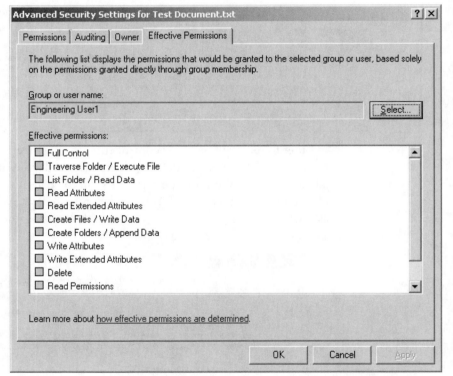

10. Once you are finished, close the properties of the Development folder. If you are done working with permissions, you may delete the Engineering folder.

Understanding Ownership

One potential problem that might occur when working with security is the possibility of an object becoming inaccessible. For example, you might accidentally deny access to an object to the Everyone group. Or, you might delete the only user account that had permissions on a file. Ordinarily, this object would be irretrievably lost, since no one would be able to access the file (or change permissions on it). The concept of ownership helps resolve this potential issue.

Every Windows Server 2003 object has an owner. This is true for files and folders residing on NTFS volumes, as well as for objects such as Registry keys or Active Directory objects. By default, the creator of an object is its owner. For example, when the user PetraK creates a new file, she will be automatically listed as the owner. In order to view file ownership information, you must click Advanced on the Security tab for the properties of a file or folder. When you click the Owner tab, you'll see who owns the object (see Figure 4-7).

exam
watch

There is a case in which an object can have more than one owner: If the owner is a member of the Administrators group, the object is owned by both the user account and the Administrators group. In all other cases, objects are owned only by an individual user account.

FIGURE 4-7

Viewing file ownership information

Advanced Security Settings for Security	? X

Permissions | Auditing | Owner | Effective Permissions

You can take or assign ownership of this object if you have the required permissions or privileges.

Current owner of this item:

Administrators (ADTEST\Administrators)

Change owner to:

Name
Administrator (ADTEST\Administrator)
Administrators (ADTEST\Administrators)

Other Users or Groups...

☐ Replace owner on subcontainers and objects

Learn more about ownership.

OK | Cancel | Apply

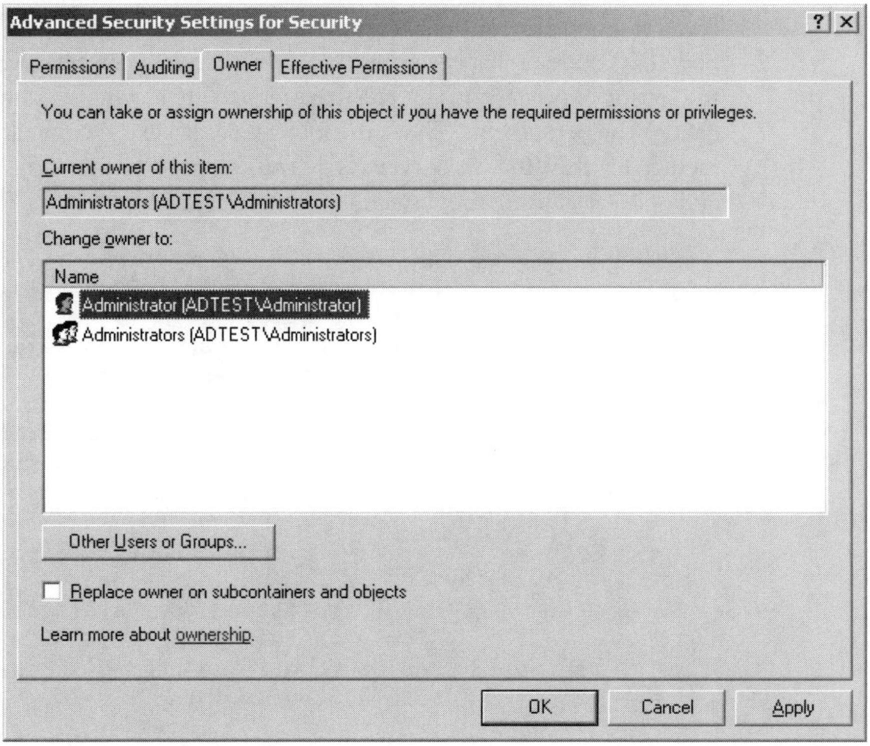

An owner of an object will always be able to access an object and change its permissions. This means that other users, regardless of their permissions, cannot lock that user out from accessing the file, as long as the user remains the owner of the file. Another feature of object ownership is that a member of the Administrators group can take ownership of a file or folder. This is useful in situations in which a file is not otherwise accessible (perhaps because the user(s) that had access to the file have been deleted, or the permissions exclude Administrator accounts from accessing the file). In such a case, the Administrator can take ownership of the files and can then replace the permissions, as required. Additionally, an object owner (or anyone with the "Change Permissions" permission) can grant "Take Ownership" permissions to another user or group in order to allow others to take ownership of files or folders.

w a t c h   *File ownership is also an important concept related to disk quotas, since it is used to determine how much disk space a user is using. For more information on disk quotas, see Chapter 5.*

Managing Permissions from the Command Line

If you're setting permissions on only a few objects, the GUI tools included in Windows Server 2003 are probably the best bet. However, in some cases, you may want to script the setting of permissions, or you may want to use a command-line utility to view and change the permissions. That's the job of CACLS.exe, a command-line utility that is included with Windows Server 2003. You can get a listing of the command's syntax and options by using the /? switch at the command line. Here's what you'll see:

```
CACLS filename [/T] [/E] [/C] [/G user:perm] [/R user [...]]
               [/P user:perm [...]] [/D user [...]]
   filename      Displays ACLs.
   /T            Changes ACLs of specified files in
                 the current directory and all subdirectories.
   /E            Edit ACL instead of replacing it.
   /C            Continue on access denied errors.
   /G user:perm  Grant specified user access rights.
                 Perm can be: R  Read
                              W  Write
                              C  Change (write)
                              F  Full control
   /R user       Revoke specified user's access rights
                 (only valid with /E).
   /P user:perm  Replace specified user's access rights.
                 Perm can be: N  None
```

```
                                              R   Read
                                              W   Write
                                              C   Change (write)
                                              F   Full control
            /D user        Deny specified user access.
Wildcards can be used to specify more than one file in a command.
You can specify more than one user in a command.
Abbreviations:
    CI - Container Inherit.
        The ACE will be inherited by directories.
    OI - Object Inherit.
        The ACE will be inherited by files.
    IO - Inherit Only.
        The ACE does not apply to the current file/directory.
```

Another utility that does the same job (but with slightly different syntax) is the XCACLS command. Figure 4-8 shows the syntax of this command.

FIGURE 4-8

Viewing help for the XCACLS command

```
C:\WINDOWS\system32\cmd.exe                                                    _ □ X
XCACLS filename [/T] [/E!/X] [/C] [/G user:perm;spec] [/R user [...]]
                [/P user:perm;spec [...]] [/D user [...]] [/Y]
Description:
     Displays or modifies access control lists (ACLs) of files.

Parameter List:
     filename                Displays ACLs.

     /T                      Changes ACLs of specified files in
                             the current directory and all subdirectories.

     /E                      Edits ACL instead of replacing it.

     /X                      Same as /E except it only affects the ACEs that
                             the specified users already own.

     /C                      Continues on access denied errors.

     /G user:perm;spec       Grants specified user access rights.

                             Perm can be:
                                 R   Read
                                 C   Change (write)
                                 F   Full control
                                 P   Change Permissions (Special access)
                                 O   Take Ownership (Special access)
                                 X   EXecute (Special access)
                                 E   REad (Special access)
                                 W   Write (Special access)
                                 D   Delete (Special access)

                             Spec can be the same as perm and will only be
                             applied to a directory. In this case, Perm
                             will be used for file inheritance in this
                             directory. By default, Spec=Perm.
                             Special values for Spec only:
                                 T   Valid for only for directories.
                                     At least one access right has to
                                     follow. Entries between ';' and T
                                     will be ignored.

     /R user                 Revokes specified user's access rights.

     /P user:perm;spec       Replaces specified user's access rights.
                             Access right specification as same as
                             /G option.

     /D user                 Denies specified user access.
```

They may involve a steeper learning curve than their graphical counterparts, but if you know what you want to do, the CACLS and XCACLS utilities can be a very effective way to view and modify file system permissions.

Best Practices for Managing Permissions

In this section, you have looked at many different aspects of file system security. Based on this information, here are some things to keep in mind when you design and implement file system security:

■ *Assign users to groups and then assign permissions to groups.* By logically grouping users according to their job functions, you can much more easily assign and administer security permissions. For example, you might place all of your developers in a group called "Developers." Then, whenever you need to assign permissions to these users, you'll just set the permissions for members of the Developers group. The benefit is that you can easily add to, or remove, members of this group without making security settings changes.

on the **Job**

By using the Active Directory, you can easily organize all of your departments, users, and groups into logical containers called Organizational Units (OUs). And, you can take advantage of several additional features, including Group Policy Objects, automated software deployment, and the creation of a hierarchical system of security and other settings that can apply to objects throughout the domain. Although it's beyond the scope of this book (and the exam it prepares you for), you should definitely look into the advantages that deploying the Active Directory can provide in your environment.

■ *Use understandable names for resources.* Since your users will be accessing files and folders by name, it's important that the names be intuitive and descriptive. Often, an abbreviation that makes sense to you might not make sense to others. Or, you might use different abbreviations from the ones that others are familiar with. Keep in mind that modern operating systems don't require you to adhere to very short names, and that users rarely type file or folder names. Therefore, it's probably better to name a folder "Marketing" than "mktg," "mrktg," or some other abbreviation.

■ *Create a logical hierarchy of folders based on your business requirements.* If you have sets of files that should be available to specific departments, you might want to create a top-level folder called "Departments." Then, within that folder, you could create separate folders for each of the departments. This structure will enable you to set permissions at various levels. For example, if your CEO and other executives require access to information in all departments' folders, you can set those permissions at the level of the Departments folders. Most other users and groups should be assigned access to the various subfolders of this one.

■ *Give users only the permissions that they require.* Many potential security problems can be caused by security permissions that are too lax. On the other hand, permissions that are too strict can prevent people from doing their jobs. Your goal should be to strike a balance between security and usability. That is, give your users the minimum permissions that they require to do their jobs. Sometimes, systems administrators will give some of their users full control permissions on files and folders. The logic is that those users should be able to perform all of the possible tasks on those objects. However, granting full control allows users to change permissions on the objects themselves—something that end-users rarely need to be able to do. A better choice would be to provide modify permissions, which still allow users to perform all of the other necessary options on the file.

■ *For greater control over security settings, use the Special Permissions options.* The most commonly used permissions settings are available in the main Security properties for most objects. You can easily choose options such as modify, read, and write for files and folders. Each of these options actually includes one or more lower-level permissions. In some cases, you might want more control over the specific security settings for a file or folder. That's where Special Permissions come in. You can access these settings by choosing the Advanced button on the security tab of many different objects. When you highlight an existing entry and choose the Edit button, you will be able to allow or deny additional permissions, such as Read Attributes, Write Attributes, Change Permissions, and Take Ownership. Additionally, other types of objects might include additional Special Permissions. For example, administrators can control who can create new Registry keys within specific Registry objects. This level of granularity provides a method for accommodating even the most complicated of permissions settings.

■ *Review permissions settings regularly.* Many businesses change quickly, and it's important that the IT department keep up with these changes. For example, a department reorganization might necessitate a change in your file system permissions. Often, these types of changes are overlooked. Plan to regularly review your security settings to make sure that you haven't forgotten about any changes that should be accounted for.

SCENARIO & SOLUTION

One member of the AccountingAdmins reports that he cannot access a specific folder on his local system. Other members of the group can access the server without any problems.	Check the permissions on the folder to ensure that there is no explicit Deny Permission for this user on the folder. You can also use the Effective Permissions tab to determine whether this is a permissions-related issue.
An employee recently left the company and you permanently deleted her user account. Now, members of her department report that they are unable to access certain important files. The employee was the only owner of the files.	Log in to the system as an Administrator and take ownership of the required files. Then, reset the necessary permissions on the files.
You want to replace permissions settings for a file, but a dialog box states that this cannot be done.	It is likely that the folder is inheriting permissions from a parent folder, and this is preventing the change. To disable inheritance, click Advanced and uncheck the appropriate option.

Now that you have a solid understanding of file system security features and tools, let's look at how network resources can be shared.

CERTIFICATION OBJECTIVE 4.02

Creating and Managing Shared Folders

NTFS permissions are designed to provide for security at the level of the file system. They determine which users have access to which files, and they specify the operations that can be carried out. But how do users actually access these files over the network? The answer is *shared folders*. Shared folders (which are often just called "shares") are designed to advertise to network users what resources are available on your Windows Server 2003 machines. Typical network environments will have *public* shared folders (which users can use to exchange files and information), as well as specific shared folders (for example, a folder that is accessible to only members of the Marketing department).

It is important to understand the relationship between file system folders and shared folders. The main concept is that a file system folder can be made available over the network through multiple shared folders. The name of the share itself can differ from the names of the underlying folders. Entire volumes can also be shared. Note that throughout this section, I'll refer to information about sharing folders. All of the same information applies to sharing volumes.

Users can find and connect to shares in many different ways. For example, they can browse for network resources using the My Network Places icon on their desktop. When they double-click the name of a computer, they'll see a list of all of the nonhidden shares that are available. They can then open the shares and, assuming they have the appropriate permissions, access the data contained in them.

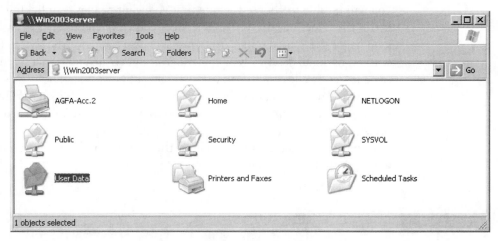

More experienced users might prefer to use the Universal Naming Convention (UNC) path to access the shared folder. This can be done most quickly by simply choosing Start | Run and then typing the full path to the share. A UNC path is made up of the name of the computer on which the share is located, followed by the name of the share that you want to connect to. Here are some valid UNC paths:

- \\Server1\Data
- \\FileServ02\Public
- \\FileServ11\Users

on the **Job**

You can better organize your shared folders through the use of the Distributed File System (DFS) feature in Windows Server 2003. More information about DFS is available later in this chapter.

Now that you've seen how shares work from a user's point of view, let's look at the details related to configuring shares.

Creating Shared Folders

As long as a user has the necessary permissions, a user or systems administrator can quickly create a new share for any folder on the system. The quickest way to create a new shared folder is by right-clicking a folder and choosing Sharing and Security. This will access the Sharing tab for the properties of the folder (see Figure 4-9).

Using this tab, you can choose whether or not the folder is to be shared over the network. If the folder that you have selected has already been shared, you will see information about the share. And if there are already multiple shares for this folder, you will be able to choose the one that you want to view by clicking the drop-down list. If the folder has not yet been shared, you will need to click New and provide a name for the shared folder. You must specify a name for the shared folder, along with an optional descriptive comment. You can create additional shares for the same folder by clicking the New Share button. Next, you must choose how many concurrent network connections you want to allow for this share. The default setting is "maximum allowed." This option will allow an unlimited number of users (up to the number that you are licensed to support) to connect to the share. Alternatively, you can choose to limit the number of concurrent connections that are supported for the share.

Viewing the Sharing properties for a folder

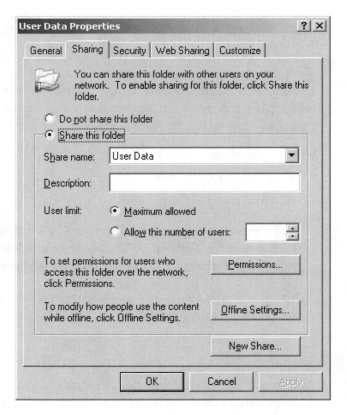

on the **Job**

A dollar sign ($) character placed at the end of a share name makes the share "invisible" to Microsoft's tools (such as the Windows Explorer). That is, the shared folder is accessible, but it will not show up when users are browsing through network resources. Therefore, users must know that it exists in order to access it. In general, "security through obscurity" is not the best way to secure systems, but it might help to hide shares that only a few users need to access. Keep in mind that this will not prevent knowledgeable users from finding these shares, especially through the use of third-party utilities.

Now that you've seen the basic steps that are required to create a share, let's look at how the security is configured.

Understanding Share-Level Permissions

As you may have guessed, shared folders have security permissions that control what permissions users have on the folder and its contents. An important step in understanding how shares work is to look at the interaction between file system permissions and shared folder permissions.

By clicking Permissions on the Sharing tab of a folder or volume, you'll be able to specify share-level permissions (see Figure 4-10).

FIGURE 4-10

Viewing share permissions for a folder

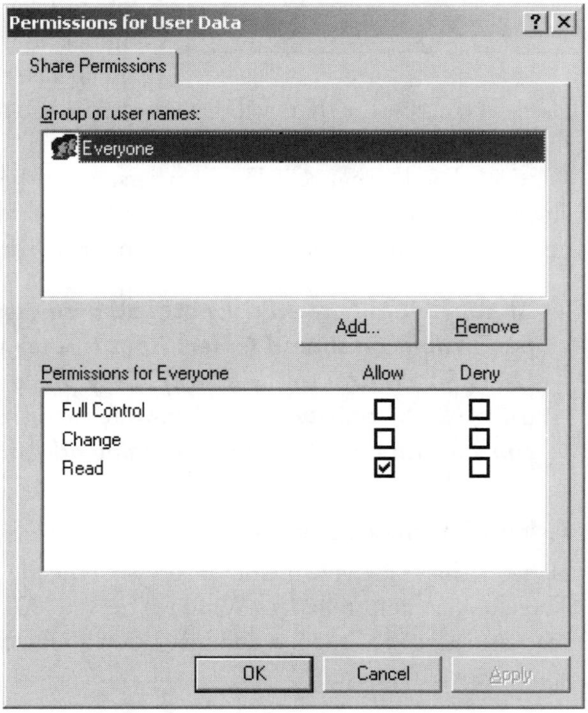

Permissions for User Data	? X

Share Permissions

Group or user names:

Everyone

Add...   Remove

Permissions for Everyone   Allow   Deny

Full Control	☐	☐
Change	☐	☐
Read	☑	☐

OK   Cancel   Apply

The list of share permissions is a short one and includes the following:

- **Full Control** This permission allows the user to perform any action on the contents of the shared folder. This includes the configuration of permissions for any folders located within the share.

- **Change** This setting allows users to read and write to the share. This means that they'll be able to access and modify current files and that they can create new files and folders.

- **Read** The most restrictive permission of the three, this setting affords users the ability to read the files that are stored in the share, but they cannot modify or create files.

exam

watch *Keep in mind that share permissions apply only when users are accessing a resource from over the network. Permissions set on shares have no effect on folders that are accessed locally on a computer.*

The default permission is to provide the Everyone built-in group read permissions on the contents of the share. It's very important to note that these permissions apply only to users who are accessing the share over the network. The settings have no effect for a user who is trying to access these files from the local file system.

Share-level permissions should be used in conjunction with NTFS permissions, not *instead* of them. The two levels of security work together. Users who access the share will have a combination of the more restrictive permissions that have been set. For example, if a user named "Carlos" has read permissions at the share level and "Change" NTFS permissions at the file system level, he will only be able to read the files. Similarly, if he has full control at the share level and only read permissions in the file system, he can only read the files.

on the

Job *Although it may seem risky at first, many systems administrators do not set permissions on shared folders (that is, they give Everyone, or Authenticated Users full control to the share). They place the appropriate permissions using NTFS security. This method reduces redundant administration and can save time while still maintaining adequate security.*

Administrative Shares

Network shares are very useful for accessing the file system on remote servers. Therefore, upon installation, Windows Server 2003 uses several built-in shares that are designed to support administration and network communications between applications. These are

- **ADMIN$** This hidden share points to the folder into which the operating system was installed (for example, C:\Windows).

- **FAX$** If your system is configured to support fax services, this share can be used to transfer and control jobs over the network. Generally, client and server operating systems will use this "behind-the-scenes" share.

- **IPC$** This share supports interprocess communications. Through the use of the IPC$ share, applications can communicate with each other over the network. IPC connections are also used by various administrative tools that are included with Windows Server 2003.

- *LogicalDriveLetter$* **(for example, "C$", "D$", and so on.)** One hidden administrative share is automatically created for each logical volume that is hosted by a server. These administrative shares point to the root directory of each logical drive. Only members of the Administrators or Backup Operators group can use these shares. When connecting using these shares, you'll be able to access and modify the full contents of the logical volume.

- **PRINT$** This share is used to support the remote management of print jobs. For example, if you want to cancel a print job on a network printer, the operating system will connect using this share. You'll learn additional details related to managing print queues later in this chapter.

- **NETLOGON** This share is used to store scripts and other data that might be requested by client computers during the logon process.

Systems administrators can use these shares for simplifying access to remote machines, and developers can take advantage of them for communicating between applications that are running on remote computers. Note, however, that the administrative shares provide a lot of power, and you should be especially careful to keep them secure from unauthorized users. In general, it is recommended that you not manually modify these shares. For example, if you reconfigure the PRINT$ administrative share, users may be unable to use this machine as a print server.

Viewing Shares and Open Files

Another method for creating and managing shared folders is through the Computer Management tool (accessible through the System icon in the Control Panel). As shown in Figure 4-11, when you click the Shared Folders item, you'll get a quick view of all of the shares on the local machine (see Figure 4-11).

By clicking Shares, you can quickly view a list of all of the shares on the local machine. Also provided is information about the physical path to the share and the

FIGURE 4-11

Administering
shared folders
from within
Computer
Management

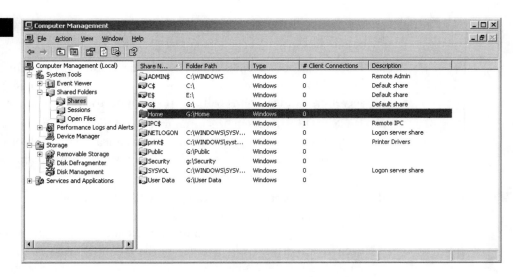

number of users that are currently connected. The Sessions item allows you to view
which users are currently connected to this machine over the network.

Finally, the Open Files item allows you to see exactly which files are being accessed
at the current time. Note that this display does not automatically refresh, so you
should do so manually using F5 or the Refresh option on the context-sensitive menu.
Using these administrative features, you can efficiently administer shared folders.

Note that, in order to view Shared Folders settings, you must have the appropriate
permissions. If you cannot view this information, make sure that you are logged
on to the specified computer as a member of the Administrators group, Server
Operators group, or Power Users group.

EXERCISE 4-2

CertCam & MasterSim 4-2 ON THE CD

Creating and Managing a Shared Folder

This exercise assumes that you have already configured your Windows Server 2003
computer with the "file server" role.

1. Log on to the computer as an Administrator and create a new folder named
   Marketing. The location of this folder is not important. Create or copy
   several files within the Marketing folder.

2. Right-click the Marketing folder and select Sharing. Select Share This
   Folder. For the name of the share, enter **Marketing Documents**. For the
   description of the folder, specify **Public storage space for Marketing staff
   members**. Leave the user limit as the default ("maximum allowed").

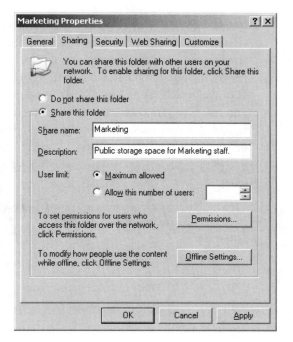

3. To set the permissions for this share, click Permissions. Note that the default permissions are to provide "Everyone" read permissions. Leave these settings as their defaults. Click OK to save the permissions settings, and then OK again to create the new shared folder.

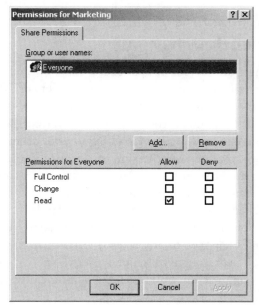

4. Next, from one or more other computers, access the files in the Marketing shared folder. To monitor the open files and activity in the shared folder, open the File Server Management console (located in the Administrative Tools program group). View the information in the "Shares (Local)," "Sessions (Local)," and "Open Files (Local)" sections. Note that you will see which users and machines are connected to the server, as well as any files that are currently in use. You may need to manually refresh the display to view any changes in activity. Once you are finished, close the File Server Management console.

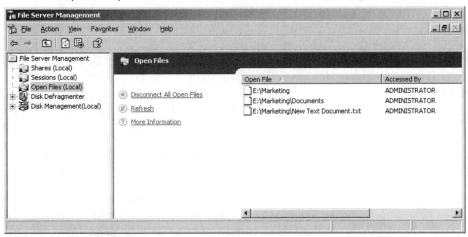

Mapping Network Drives

There are several ways to access shared resources in modern Windows systems. For example, users can start at their My Network Places desktop icon and navigate to the resources that they're looking for. Or, if your environment is running the Active Directory, they can find the various shared folders that you have made available by using Windows Explorer or other tools. Although these methods do work, you may want to simplify locating data as much as possible. For example, you might want to tell your users that information that they want to share should be stored on their P: "drive," and that private information that they want to have backed up should be stored on their H: drive.

You can easily accomplish this through the mapping of network drives. Drives can be mapped to any unused letter on your system, and they can point to any network resource to which a user has access. Network resources are specified through the use of Universal Naming Convention (UNC) paths. A basic UNC path includes the network name of the computer on which the shared resource is available, along with the name of the share itself. For example, you could use the shared folder path of \\Server1\Public to access the public shared folder on Server1. There are several ways to map network shares to drive letters. The following table provides some examples of how mapped drives and network resources are related.

Logical Drive Letter	Network Path
H:	\\FileServ1\Home\User1$
P:	\\Marketing3\Public
S:	\\AppServ3\Software

The first method for creating a mapped drive involves navigating to the share using the My Network Places (or Network Neighborhood in earlier versions of Windows) icon. Simply find the share that you wish to map to a network drive, right-click it, and choose Map Network Drive. You'll see the dialog box shown next. Just choose the letter to which the drive should be mapped. You can also choose whether this network connection should be reconnected at logon. If you or your users will frequently be accessing a specific mapped network drive, you might want it to be always available whenever they log on to their machines. On the other hand, if you only want to map the drive to run some commands for now and you don't want it to be available permanently, you can uncheck this option.

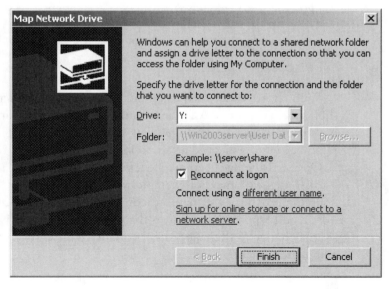

Another useful option is the ability to map a network drive using a different security account. This option provides users with the ability to provide different authentication information that will be used to determine the user's permissions on these folders. By default, the user's current name will be used when creating a new mapped network drive. In order to change this, simply click the Different User Name link. You will be able to provide a username and password for another account. Now, whenever this network drive is accessed, you will have the permissions that are granted to that account.

Mapping Network Drives Using the NET Command

You can also map network drives from the command line using the NET USE command. The syntax of the NET USE command (which you can get by typing **NET USE /?** at a command prompt) is as follows:

```
NET USE
[devicename | *] [\\computername\sharename[\volume] [password | *]]
        [/USER:[domainname\]username]
        [/USER:[dotted domain name\]username]
        [/USER:[username@dotted domain name]
        [/SMARTCARD]
        [/SAVECRED]
        [[/DELETE] | [/PERSISTENT:{YES | NO}]]
```

For example, you can use the following command to permanently map the X: drive to a network path:

```
NET USE P: \\Server1\PublicData\ /PERSISTENT:YES
```

To remove that network drive mapping, you can use the following command:

```
NET USE P: /DELETE
```

With regards to security, you should consider mapped network drives as just shortcuts to resources. All other security settings will still apply, and a user must have permissions to access a network resource before he or she can access that information via a mapped network drive.

Once a drive has been mapped, you can access it just as you would access a local storage volume. For example, you will see the new "drive" when you double-click the My Computer icon (see Figure 4-12). Or, you can choose Start | Run and type **X:** (where X: is the mapped network drive). Finally, you can simply change to the mapped network drive using the command "X:" from the command prompt.

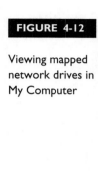

FIGURE 4-12

Viewing mapped
network drives in
My Computer

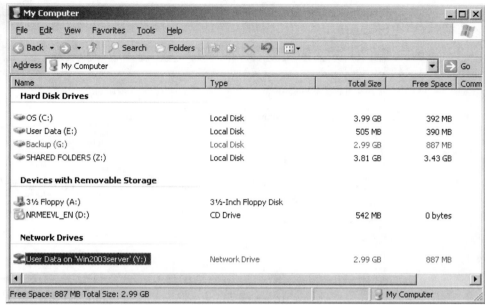

Managing Shared Folders Using the NET Command

The NET command can also be used to view, create, and manage shared folders.
To view a list of the available commands, simply type **net share /?** at a command
prompt. The syntax of the command is listed as follows:

```
NET SHARE
sharename
        sharename=drive:path [/GRANT:user,[READ | CHANGE | FULL]]
                             [/USERS:number | /UNLIMITED]
                             [/REMARK:"text"]
                             [/CACHE:Manual | Documents| Programs | None ]
        sharename [/USERS:number | /UNLIMITED]
                [/REMARK:"text"]
                [/CACHE:Manual | Documents | Programs | None]
        {sharename | devicename | drive:path} /DELETE
```

For example, to view a list of shares on the local computer, simply typing
the command NET SHARE at a command prompt. As shown next, this will

return the logical names and physical paths of all shared folders that are configured.

```
C:\WINDOWS\system32\cmd.exe                                          _ □ ×

C:\>NET SHARE

Share name     Resource                          Remark
-----------------------------------------------------------------------
print$         C:\WINDOWS\system32\spool\drivers
                                                 Printer Drivers
E$             E:\                               Default share
C$             C:\                               Default share
IPC$                                             Remote IPC
ADMIN$         C:\WINDOWS                        Remote Admin
G$             G:\                               Default share
Home           G:\Home
NETLOGON       C:\WINDOWS\SYSVOL\sysvol\ActiveDirectory.test\SCRIPTS
                                                 Logon server share
Public         G:\Public
Security       g:\Security
SYSVOL         C:\WINDOWS\SYSVOL\sysvol          Logon server share
User Data      G:\User Data
AGFA-Acc.2     LPT1:                    Spooled  AGFA-AccuSet v52.3
The command completed successfully.

C:\>
```

In order to create a new share, you can use a command such as the following:

```
NET SHARE "User Data"=D:\UserData /UNLIMITED
  /REMARK:"Storage space for user data."
```

This command will create a new share entitled "User Data." The share will point to a the physical location D:\UserData, and it will be configured to allow an unlimited number of connections. The NET SHARE command can be quite useful for scripting share creation and management across multiple servers.

Implementing a File Server

At the beginning of this chapter, I mentioned the importance of file services for a typical network server. As you might have guessed, Microsoft has included a server role entitled "File Server" that can be implemented using the Configure Your Server Wizard. This wizard will walk you through the process of setting up a new file server, including the most common options for setting up new shared folders.

To launch the Configure Your Server Wizard, simply choose Start | Programs | Administrative Tools | Configure Your Server. To begin the process, click Next twice. Then, select File Server from the list of available roles (see Figure 4-13), and click Next to continue.

FIGURE 4-13

Selecting the File
Server role in the
Configure Your
Server Wizard

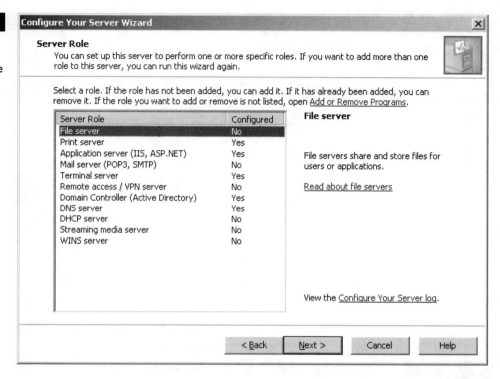

First, you'll have the option to specify disk quota settings (see Figure 4-14). These settings will specify the defaults for all volumes on the server. For more information about disk quotas, see Chapter 5.

Next, you will be prompted to specify indexing settings. By default, the Indexing Service is disabled. You'll learn more information about the Indexing Service later in this section.

Finally, you'll see a summary of the options you have chosen (see Figure 4-15). Note that, by default, the Share a Folder Wizard will be started as part of the implementation of the server role. Let's look at that next.

Using the Share a Folder Wizard

Earlier in this chapter, you looked at how you can create shared folders using the properties of a folder or volume. When you are enabling the file server role, the Share a Folder Wizard will automatically be launched. This wizard will perform the exact

FIGURE 4-14

Specifying disk quota settings when enabling the file server role

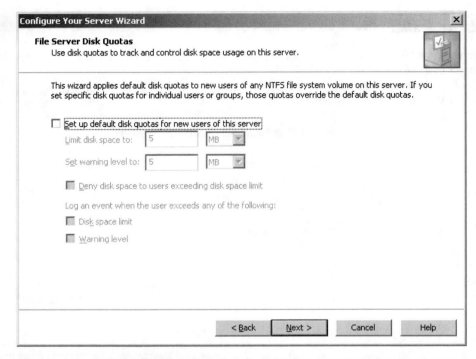

FIGURE 4-15

Viewing a summary of file server options

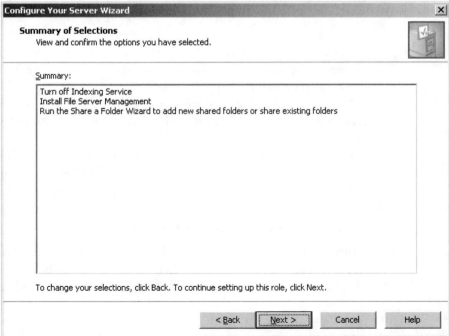

same steps that you can perform using the standard Sharing tab, but it will present the options in a stepwise fashion.

To begin the wizard, click Next to begin the process of creating a new share. The first piece of information that is required is the physical path to the folder that you wish to share. Here, you can type in the physical path, or click Browse to find the folder. To continue, click Next.

On the "Name, Description, and Settings" step, you can provide a name for the share. The name defaults to the name of the folder that you selected in the previous step. The Share Path window shows you the UNC name for the new share that you are about to create. Optionally, you can provide a description for the purpose and contents of the share. Finally, you can specify the configuration settings for offline files and folders (a topic covered later in this chapter). Click Next to continue.

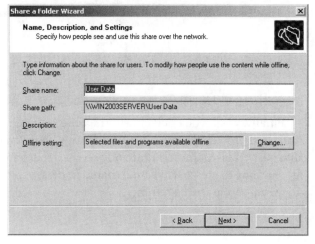

The Permissions tab of the Share a Folder Wizard allows you to choose from one of several common scenarios for new file shares. As shown in the next illustration, the options are as follows:

- All users have read-only access (this is the default setting).
- Administrators have full access; other users have read-only access.
- Administrators have full access; other users have read and write access.
- Use customer share and folder permissions: When you click this button, you'll be shown a dialog box that enables you to set the share-level permissions (on the Share Permissions tab), and the file system permissions for the folder (on the Security tab). Both of these tabs work exactly like their standard folder property sheets counterparts.

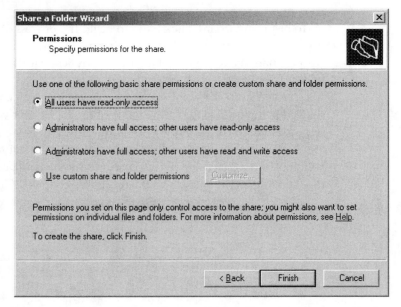

Finally, when you click Finish, the Share a Folder Wizard will create the share and then provide a summary of the settings that you chose. It might be useful to cut and paste this information into any server documentation that you are maintaining. If you want to create additional shared folders, you can use the check box to restart the wizard from the beginning.

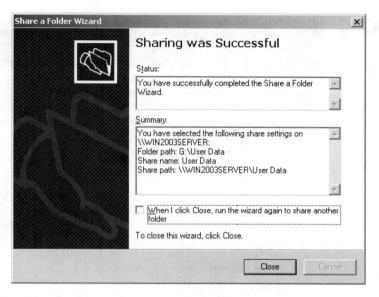

Using the File Server Management Console

Once you have configured an installation of Windows Server 2003 as a file server, you will be able to use the Manage Your Server Wizard to perform the most common tasks. You can access these features easily by choosing the Manage Your Server icon in the Administrative Tools program group. As shown in Figure 4-16, you'll see two options. The Add Shared Folder link will launch the Share a Folder Wizard.

The other option, Manage This File Server, will launch a new File Server Management console. This new console is also available through the File Server Management icon in the Administrative Tools program group. Note that you must have configured the file server role in order for this tool to be available. Figure 4-17 shows the File Server Management tool. Using this console, you can perform the most common tasks related to file servers, including viewing, creating, and modifying shared folders and viewing current sessions and open files. Other options include the Disk Defragmenter (covered in Chapter 8) and the Disk Management tool (covered in Chapter 5).

Removing the File Server Role

If, for some reason, you decide that you no longer want a specific machine to serve as a file server, you can use the Configure Your Server Wizard to remove this server role.

It is important to note that when you remove the file server role, all folders that were previously shared will become unavailable. The built-in administrative shares will continue to be available, however. Also, the File Server Management icon will be removed from the Administrative Tools folder and from the Manage Your Server tool.

FIGURE 4-16

Viewing Manage
Your Server
options for the
file server role

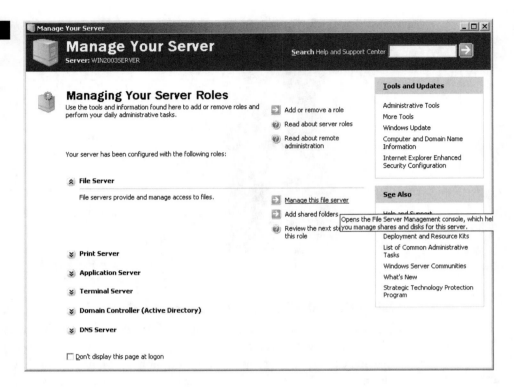

Understanding the Indexing Service

In most organizations, users have come to rely heavily on the documents stored on file servers. Often, there can be thousands of files that are stored on various shared folders and volumes. Ideally, the files would be logically organized, and users could simply navigate through the directory tree to find the resources that they need. In the real

FIGURE 4-17

Using the File
Server
Management tool

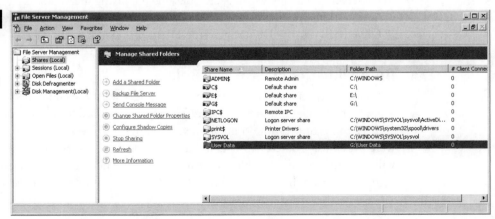

world, however, important files are often buried in illogically named folders or poorly defined folder hierarchies.

One way to find relevant files is to use the searching features in Windows Explorer. If you know the name of the file you are looking for, you can specify it (along with the search location), and hopefully it will be found. On current Windows operating systems, this feature can be accessed by choosing Search | For Files Or Folders.

The Search feature also allows users to search through the actual content of files. For example, if I'm looking for the phrase "Product XYZ specifications," I can have my client computer search on local and network resources for that phrase within files. As you can imagine, this can be a resource-intensive process. The contents of all of the files located in this location would need to be searched. On heavily used file servers, this can create significant load on the server and reduce overall performance.

That's where the Indexing Service comes in. To make quick searches through the contents of files possible, you can enable the indexing option for specific volumes. You already saw that one way this could be done was by configuring a file server role for a server. If you want to manually set up the Indexing Service, you can right-click any volume in Windows Explorer and select Properties. As shown in Figure 4-18, the last option on the page is "Allow Indexing Service to index this disk for fast file

FIGURE 4-18

Enabling the Index Service for a volume

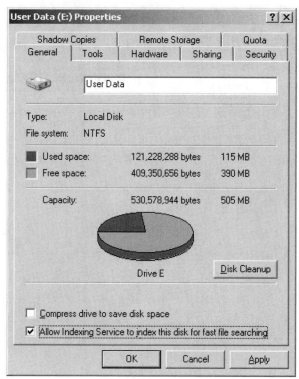

searching." When this option is enabled, the contents of the hard disk will automatically be indexed so that, when users perform a search, it will not be necessary to read through the contents of all of the files.

You can also manage the indexing process by using the Indexing Service MMC snap-in. Since there is no default administrative tool for this feature, you must manually create a new console by choosing Start | Run and typing **mmc**. Simply add the appropriate console, and you'll see an interface similar to the one that's shown in Figure 4-19. Using this interface, you can configure many different settings and features of the indexing service. For example, you can create and populate a new catalog, and you can view information about existing indexes. There's also an option to query an existing index to ensure that searching works properly.

The actual indexing of documents is done through the use of a Windows service, appropriately entitled the "Indexing Service." This service can be configured using the Services administrative tool. In order for indexes to be created and updated, this service must be running.

It's important to keep in mind that enabling the Indexing Service involves a trade-off. Instead of taking a performance hit whenever users attempt to search

FIGURE 4-19

Using the Indexing Service Manager tool

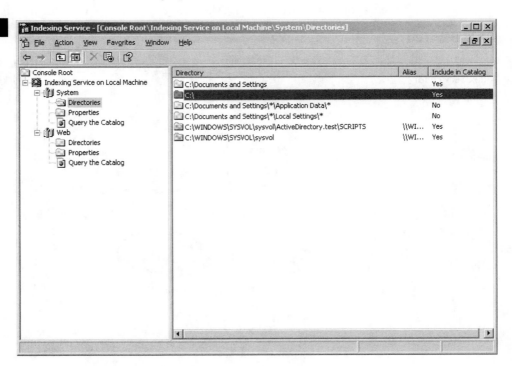

through the contents of various files, you will take the performance hit in creating the index. Additionally, the index itself will take up storage space on your hard disks. Therefore, it's best to enable indexing for volumes that users will frequently search.

Understanding Offline Files and Folders

A simple fact of working in modern organizations is that users will need access to their data, regardless of their locations. Even though technologies such as virtual private networks (VPNs) and wireless technologies are helping to ensure that people can connect to servers, there are still many situations in which users do not have physical connectivity to the resources that they need. For example, when I'm sitting on a three-hour flight, it sure would be nice if I had access to some of my frequently used files that are stored on a file server.

Also, in many network environments, it's common for file servers to be bogged down by many read and write requests. By default, many users might access files and folders (such as those stored on their H: "drive") to perform file updates and other operations. I'm a compulsive saver, and so far, I've saved a draft of this chapter 189 times! If I were working over a network connection, that could generate noticeable traffic. Lack of network reliability and bandwidth (such as is common for small remote branch offices) can add to the problem.

The simple solution would be for users to have copies of their files stored locally, but the problem with that is synchronizing the files—most users would simply forget. Another potential solution would be to create scripts or other methods for routinely copying files between the client and the server. But, the problem there would be that the user would be responsible for synchronizing files at the appropriate times, and users might be required to remember two different locations for those files.

That's where the Offline Files and Folders feature comes in. The idea behind offline files and folders is that users and systems administrators can choose to make network files available offline. Simply by modifying the properties of files and folders, a cached copy of those objects can be created on the local system. When users' computers are disconnected from the network, they'll still be able to access these files using familiar shortcuts (such as the H: drive mapping). The only difference will be that the files are actually being accessed locally. To complete the loop, once the user is again connected to the network, the files will automatically be synchronized with their network counterparts. If you've ever had to deal with the issue of keeping multiple computers and network locations in-sync, you'll know how great this feature can be!

Configuring Offline Settings

The process of configuring offline settings for a folder is very simple. You can start by accessing the Sharing tab of the properties of a folder or a volume. This image shows the options that you will see when you click Offline:

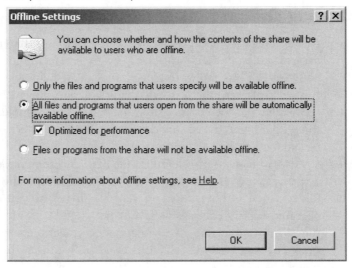

Here, you can specify whether you want users to be able to use the Offline Folders feature to copy the data to their local machine. The available options are

- *Only the files and programs that users specify will be available offline.* This setting (which is the default that is used when you create a new shared folder) specifies that when users access files on the server, they can choose which files should be made available offline. This is done by right-clicking a file or folder and selecting Make Available Offline. The benefit of this option is that it provides the user a choice of whether or not she wants the file to be made available offline. The drawback, however, is that users must select which content they want to take with them when they're disconnected from the network.

on the
ⓙo b

One important security-related issue to keep in mind is that the cached copies of files will be located on generally less-secure client machines. Therefore, users may have copies of sensitive information stored on company laptops, which are much more likely to be stolen than are your servers. Offline Files and Folders might still be a good solution, especially when used in conjunction with features like the Encrypting File System (covered later in this chapter), and strong password policies.

- *All files and programs that users open from the share will automatically be available offline.* This setting specifies that both data files and program files will be copied to the client machine automatically. This setting is useful when you want to make sure that the files users are accessing will be available if they're disconnected from the network. On modern client computers, there's usually ample disk space to enable this option. A suboption is Optimized For Performance. This setting automatically caches files and programs and runs the local copies to minimize network bandwidth usage. This is a good option for users that frequently access files, or for situations in which network bandwidth is either limited or unreliable.

■ *Files or programs from the share will not be available offline.* This setting prevents users from being able to take files, folders, and programs offline. This option is appropriate, for example, if you have sensitive data that resides on the server, and you don't want users to make offline copies of the files.

The benefits of caching include faster access to the data (since no trips over the network would be required), and the ability to access files when the client is disconnected from the network. Drawbacks include potential security risks— you may not want your end users to store copies of sensitive documents on their machines. Overall, the offline settings that are available for shared folders can make a very complicated task (keeping files synchronized) almost effortless!

Monitoring File Servers with System Monitor

Windows Server 2003 includes several different performance statistics that can be tracked using the System Monitor utility. Table 4-1 provides some useful counters and objects that can be used for monitoring and troubleshooting file server performance.

SCENARIO & SOLUTION	
Users are reporting errors that state that the server has exceeded the maximum number of connections.	Verify the settings for the maximum number of allowed users at the share level permissions. If this is currently set to "unlimited," you should also verify the license configuration for the server (see Chapter 7 for details about licensing).
Several shared folders on your network contain company files that are commonly searched. Recently, users have been reporting extremely slow performance in performing text searches.	Enable the Indexing Service for the volume(s) on which the frequently searched files reside.
You are experiencing problems with network reliability, and you want to make sure that users always have a local copy of their files from which to work.	Enable Offline Files and Folders for the shared folders and configure the offline settings to always store a copy of the network file on users' machines.

TABLE 4-1   Useful Performance Statistics for Monitoring File Servers

Object	Counter(s)	Purpose
Server	Bytes Received / sec Bytes Transmitted / sec Bytes Total / sec	These counters provide details relating to the overall data throughout for the server. Large values indicate that the server is sending a large amount of data to users. The "Total" value is the sum of the bytes received plus the bytes transmitted.
Server	Files Open	Indicates how many files are currently being accessed by network users. A large value indicates that many files are currently in use.
Server	Errors Access Permissions	Provides a count of the number of times users have tried to access an object and have been denied permissions. A high value might indicate that unauthorized users are frequently attempting to access files.
Indexing Service	Total # of queries	The total number of queries that have been handled by the Indexing Service. A high number indicates that the monitored index is often being used.
Indexing Service	Index Size (MB)	The size, in megabytes, of the selected Indexing Service index(es). If your file server is low on disk space, it might be worth checking the size of existing indexes.
Logical Disk	% Disk Time	The percentage of time that the monitored hard disks are busy. A high percentage indicates that the server is performing heavy I/O operations. Instances include the logical volumes on the system and a total value (an average percentage for all of the hard disks).
Logical Disk	% Free Space Free Megabytes	Indicates how much disk space is remaining on a volume, or on all volumes together. Monitoring this statistic is important to proactively prevent end-user issues that might occur when a volume is full.
Network Interface	Bytes Total / sec	The amount of data that is transferred over the selected network interface per second. High values might indicate that network throughput could be a bottleneck.

When used properly, all of these objects and counters can provide valuable information related to the functioning of your file servers. For more information on monitoring system performance, see Chapter 8.

INSIDE THE EXAM

Simplifying Resource Access: Selecting the "Right" Features

One of the goals for successful systems administrators is to find the best technical solutions for business problems. Although it's good to know how to implement solutions—such as shared folders or print servers—that's not always enough. Since server-based resources (such as folders and printers) are often depended upon by all users that are connected to a modern network, it should come as no surprise that Microsoft wants to make sure that you understand how to take advantage of the many different features in Windows Server 2003.

Often, on Microsoft exams, you'll see phrases that require you to perform a task "with the least administrative effort," or one that meets a number of different requirements. It is important to keep these phrases in mind as you consider possible solutions. Let's look at an example: Suppose you are implementing file servers for your organization's Sales department. You will probably start with the basics: setting up your storage resources, creating a folder structure, and sharing appropriate folders. You may choose to implement logon scripts that automatically map commonly used folders to drive letters.

Many systems administrators would stop there. After all, this meets the basic requirements of most users, since they can get to the resources they need. However, there are many other features that you can use to make this solution even better. For example, if some of your users will be traveling, offline files and folders might be a welcome feature. By implementing caching functionality, you can proactively avoid problems with synchronizing files. Another eventuality in most network environments is that disk space will be limited. Often, when left unmonitored, users can consume tremendous amounts of disk space. By implementing disk quotas, you can track and manage disk space usage.

When you're supporting all but the simplest of environments, you'll also need to ensure that you have set appropriate effective permissions on files and folders. The success of this often depends on implementing a well-planned system of groups and users. And to troubleshoot potential security issues or access violations, you might want to implement auditing. There are many other features in Windows Server 2003 that can help you implement better file services, including file system encryption, the use of fault-tolerant disk configurations, and the Distributed File System (DFS).

All of the concepts mentioned here are covered within this book (and many are covered in this chapter). However, it's up to you to figure out how to put them all to use, given a set of requirements. Remember, when you're preparing for Exam 70-290, keep in mind all of the different tools, techniques, and features that are at your disposal. Often, finding the best tool for the job (instead of just a "suitable" one) will make the difference that leads to answering a question correctly.

CERTIFICATION OBJECTIVE 4.03

Configuring, Managing, and Troubleshooting Printers and Print Queues

Despite the pace at which technology has improved many business processes, printing hard copies and transferring information on paper remains a necessary evil. In large network environments, entire teams of systems administrators may be responsible for managing printing devices and print configuration. Windows Server 2003 includes many features that make it excellent for providing print server functionality. In this section, you'll take a look at how these features can be enabled to make printers available over the network.

The exam objectives related to printing on Exam 70-290 are simply entitled "Monitor print queues" and "Troubleshoot print queues." Therefore,	that will be the focus in this and the next section of this chapter. If you want further details about how printing works in Windows Server 2003, see the Help and Support Center.

Understanding Printing Terminology

Before diving into the technical steps that are required to enable and manage printing in Windows Server 2003, it's important to understand some basic printing terminology. You should be familiar with the following terms:

- **Print device**   This is an actual physical device that is used to create hard-copy output. Print devices include laser printers, ink-jet printers, plotters, and many other devices.

- **Printer (logical)**   In Microsoft's printing terminology, the term printer refers to a logical printing device. A printer is what users send their documents to. The logical printer is responsible for managing print jobs through a print queue and for ultimately sending the print job to the physical printer. As you'll see later in this chapter, a logical printer can actually connect to many different physical printers.

- **Printer driver** Printer drivers are used to specify how the operating system should communicate to a printing device. They also include details about the print device's capabilities (such as color printing, duplexing, and other page formatting options). Because of the different capabilities of print devices, drivers are normally different for each brand and model of printer. Furthermore, different operating systems will require different printer drivers. For example, if you need to support both Windows 98 and Windows XP clients, you will need to make sure that you have separate drivers available for both operating systems.

- **Print servers** A computer running a server-side operating system (such as Windows Server 2003) can serve as a print server. The job of this machine is to manage print jobs and to send them to a print device.

- **Print queues** A print queue is a collection of the print jobs that are scheduled to be printed. As you'll see later in this chapter, printing administrators will be able to view and control the activity of specific printers, as needed.

With these terms in mind, let's look at some supported printer configurations.

Printer Configurations

There are many different ways in which printers can be configured in a standard computer environment. Let's start by taking a high-level look at the scenarios. Clients can print to any of the following locations:

- **Local printers** A local printer is one that is physically attached to a computer (generally through a parallel port, a USB port, an infrared port, or a serial port connection). The following illustration provides an example. The user or systems administrator installs print drivers locally and configures the system to print directly to the printer. Optionally, local printers can be shared for use by other computers.

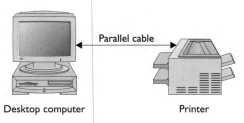

Desktop computer   Printer

Parallel cable

- **Network printers** Network printers are special devices that include a combination of a physical print device (such as a network interface card) and a print server engine embedded in the hardware. These devices have the ability to connect directly to a network. Users on the network can configure their systems to print directly to the printer, and systems administrators can usually use a web browser or special software to manage these printers.

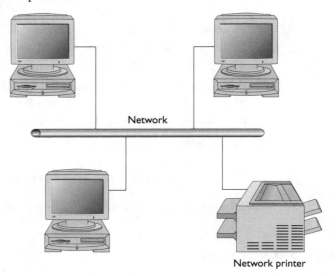

- **Print Servers**   Print servers are computers that process and manage jobs that are sent over the network (see Figure 4-20). Print servers provide access to one or more physical print devices and use a concept of a print queue to hold and organize jobs. The primary benefit of using a print server is that this machine can offload a lot of the processing overhead that's required to generate data in the format that printers can understand. Print servers can also provide many different security features. In the Windows world, Microsoft's client-side operating systems can function as print servers, but they have limited functionality. Server-side products such as Windows Server 2003 offer many features for configuring and managing printers.

The focus in this chapter will be on configuring Windows Server 2003 to function as a print server in a networked environment. With that in mind, let's look at the first steps.

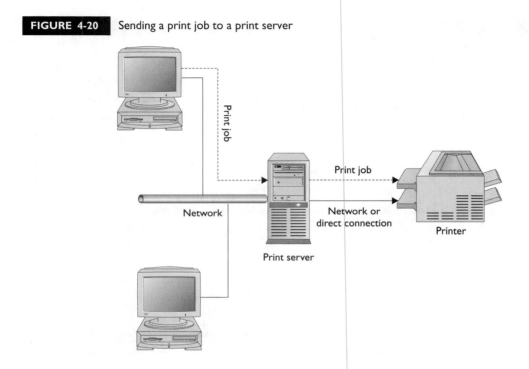

FIGURE 4-20   Sending a print job to a print server

Configuring the Print Server Role

In keeping with Windows Server 2003's tradition of disabling all but the most necessary services upon installation, you must first enable the print server role on your machines. This can be easily done through the use of the Configure Your Server administrative tool. Simply choose the Print Server role from the list of options and click Next. The only option that you'll have is to specify whether you will be supporting only Windows 2000 and Windows XP clients, or if you want to install printer drivers for other operating systems. If you're not sure about which clients you plan to support, rest assured that you can install additional printer drivers later.

When you click Next, you'll see a summary of the operations that will be performed. When you click Next again, this will launch the Add Printer Wizard. You'll look at that next.

You can also remove the print server role using the Configure Your Server Wizard (see Figure 4-21). You should keep in mind that this will automatically

FIGURE 4-21

Removing the
print server role
from a computer

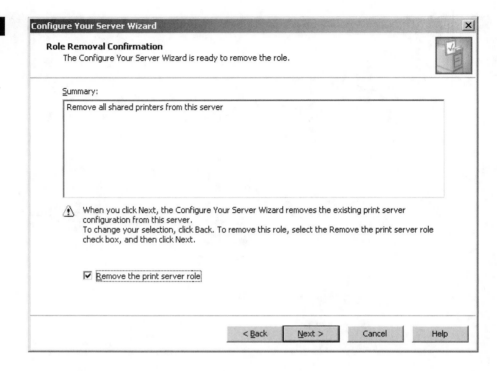

remove all shared printers from the machine, and network users will no longer be
able to submit print jobs.

Using the Add Printer Wizard

As you just saw, the Add Printer Wizard is automatically launched when you choose
to add the print server role to your Windows Server 2003 machine. You can also
launch the Add Printer Wizard by double-clicking the Add Printer icon within the
Printers and Faxes Control Panel applet. This wizard will walk you through the process
of installing a new printer for use on this machine.

Many different options are available. For example, you can choose to print to a local printer or to a printer that is located on the network. The next image shows the options for selecting a printer port.

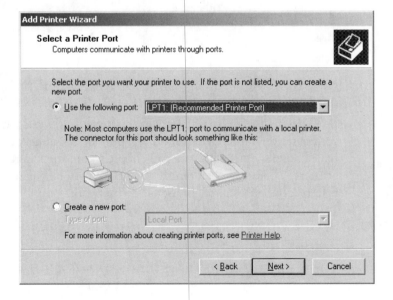

In relation to print servers, the most important step of the wizard is the option to specify printer sharing. You have two options. The first is to not share the printer. In this case, other users will not be able to send print jobs to this printer over the network. The other option is to provide a share name for the printer. This is the name that users will use to identify the printer over the network. Therefore, it is a good idea to provide a name that is descriptive of the location or purpose of the printer. When you click Next, you'll be able to provide more specific information about the location and add additional comments about the printer.

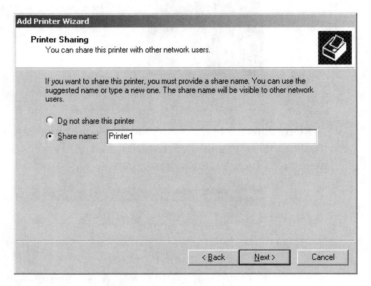

The wizard will also prompt you about printing a test page to verify the printer configuration. Finally, the wizard will provide a summary of the settings that you have chosen. Optionally, you can choose to run the wizard again to install additional printers. When you click Finish, the printer will be created and configured, and (if you so specified), shared for use on the network.

Sharing a Printer

Once you have enabled the print server role for a Windows Server 2003 machine, there are several ways in which you can administer shared printers. One way is to use the options in the Manage Your Server Wizard. Functions including adding additional printers and adding additional print drivers. You can also launch the Printers and Faxes tool (which is also available through the Control Panel). For most systems administrators, this tool will be the main point of administration for printers.

Much of the functionality in the Printers and Faxes tool is self-explanatory. For example, you can launch the Add Printer Wizard by double-clicking the Add Printer icon.

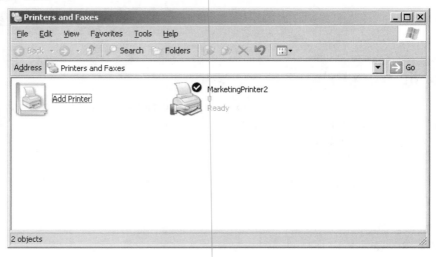

You can share a printer by right-clicking it in the list of current printers and selecting Sharing. This will open the Sharing tab of the properties of the printer. The List In The Directory option that is presented on this page controls whether or not the shared printer will be published in the Active Directory. In most cases, you'll want to stick with the default option (enabled) to make printers easier to find using directory services.

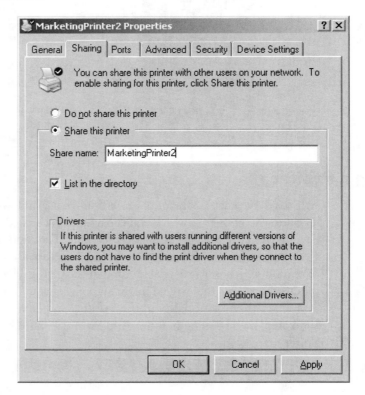

Configuring Printer Permissions

An important part of sharing any service or resource on the network is security. When it comes to sharing printers, this is easily managed by using the Security tab of the properties of a printer.

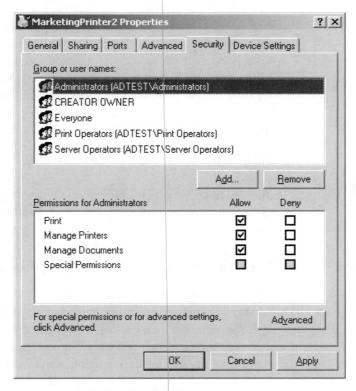

Here, you'll be able to specify which of the following permissions are assigned to users and groups on your network:

- **Print** This permission allows users to send new print jobs to the printer.
- **Manage Printers** This permission allows users to manage printer settings and properties.
- **Manage Documents** This permission allows users to control print jobs and documents in the print queue. For example, someone with this permission will be able to cancel a print job or change the priority of a job.
- **Special Permissions** In some cases, you may want to assign more specific permissions related to printing. The Special Permissions option allows you to exert more granular control over specific printing-related actions. By selecting an existing permissions setting and clicking Edit, you'll have several options.

The first allows you to specify whether the permissions that you are defining apply to this printer, to documents, or to both. Once you've decided on the scope of the permissions settings, you can set the actual allow or deny permissions. The list of options includes Print, Manage Printers, Manage Documents, Read Permissions, Change Permissions, and Take Ownership. Through the use of Special Permissions, you will have significant levels of control over who can do what with your printers.

The default print permissions that are assigned when a new printer is shared are shown in Table 4-2.

Now that you have a good idea of how printing works in Windows Server 2003, let's move on to looking at how you can monitor and manage print devices and print queues.

Monitoring and Troubleshooting Print Queues

Since printing is a fundamental service offered by many servers, Windows Server 2003 includes several different ways in which you can view and manage printers and print queues. In this section, you'll take a look at how you can administer local and remote print queues using the tools included with Windows Server 2003. As you're about to see, there are many different options, ranging from GUI tools to web browsers to command-line utilities!

TABLE 4-2   Default Print Permissions for Shared Print Devices

Group	Print	Manage Documents	Manage Printers
Administrators	X	X	X
Creator Owner	X		
Everyone	X		
Power Users	X	X	X
Print Operators	X	X	X
Server Operators	X	X	X

Viewing Print Queues

The easiest way to interactively monitor printers is through the use of the standard graphical tools that are provided with Windows Server 2003. The main method of administering and monitoring print queues is through the Printers and Faxes Control Panel applet. Using this tool, you can view a list of available printers, and you can add new ones. You can also configure the properties of the local print server by choosing File | Server options.

To view actual print queue information, simply double-click the name of a printer. As shown next, you will see a list of the print jobs that have been submitted to a printer, along with the status of the job. From the Printer menu, you can pause printing for this printer, or you can cancel all current jobs.

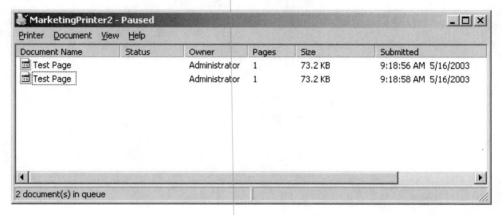

You can also click a specific document within the print queue and, using the Document menu, pause, resume, restart, and cancel a print job. To view additional details about a print job, select Properties from the Document menu. As shown in Figure 4-22, you'll be able to view important details, including the owner of the print job and when the job was submitted. You can also adjust the printing priority of a specific print job.

All of these options can be useful for looking at how much load your logical printers are under and for troubleshooting printer issues.

Sometimes you'd just like to get a list of the available shared printers in your network environment. There's a very easy way to do this, as well. One way to find the available printers in your environment is to use the Search | For Printers option

Viewing details about a document in the print queue

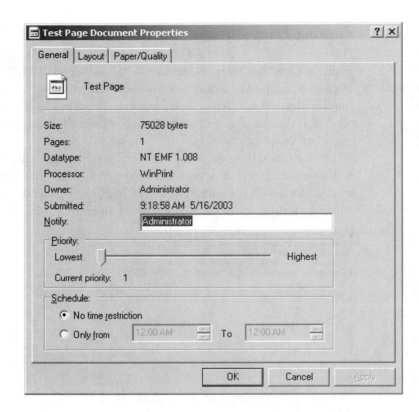

in the Start menu. As shown in Figure 4-23, this feature can be used to return a list of all of the available printers that are located on the network. You can also restrict the search so that you receive information only about printers that are located within a specific office or location.

Remotely Administering Printers

As you might have already guessed, it's almost as simple to remotely manage printers as it is to monitor them from the local machine. By using the My Network Places icon or the Windows Explorer, you can find printers located on remote machines. As long as you have the necessary permissions, you can simply click a remote printer to view the status of the print queue and the print device over the network.

FIGURE 4-23

Searching for
network printers

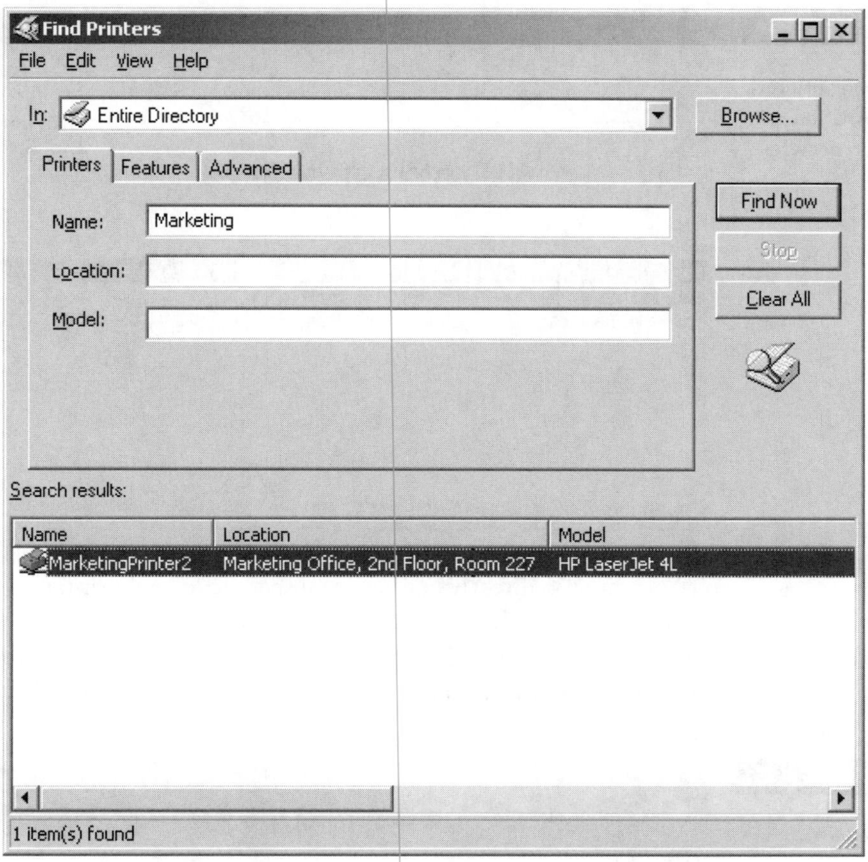

Monitoring Print Queues Using a Web Browser

In addition to using the standard Windows Server 2003 tools to administer printers, you can use a web browser to view and remotely administer print queues. Users can actually submit print jobs to a Windows Server 2003 print server using the Internet Printing Protocol (IPP). Since IPP functions over HTTP, this is a useful way for users to quickly and easily send a job to printers. With regards to managing print queues, systems administrators can navigate to a URL such as http://*PrintServerName*/printers (where *PrintServerName* is the name of the Windows Server 2003 machine that is hosting print services). Figure 4-24 shows an example of the list of printers on a remote computer.

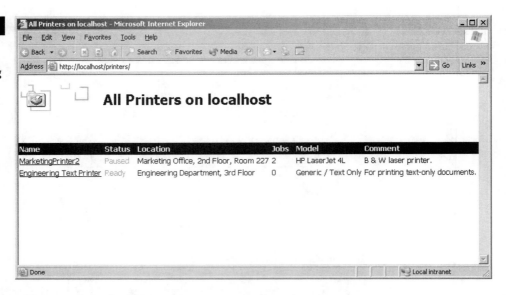

You can also directly connect to a specific logical printer by using a URL such as
http://*PrintServerName*/Printers/*PrinterName* (where the *PrinterName* is the logical
name assigned to the printer you want to monitor). Figure 4-25 shows the operations
that can be performed, and the types of information available.

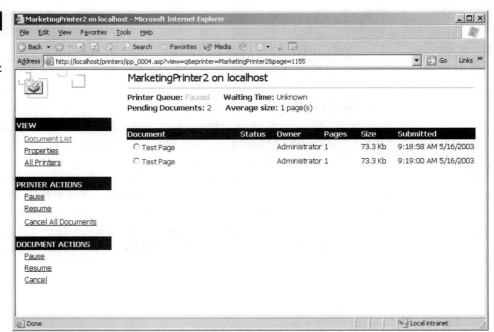

For security reasons, management of printers using a web browser is disabled in Windows Server 2003, by default, even after you enable the print server role. The first requirement in order to use the Internet Printing functionality is to enable Internet Information Services (IIS). For more information on implementing, configuring, and managing IIS, see Chapter 7.

In order to enable the Internet Printing functionality, you must use the Add/Remove Programs utility. When you selection Windows Components, you will be able to select Application Server | Internet Information Services (IIS) | Internet Printing. Once the Windows Component Wizard completes, you should be able to browse to the /Printers virtual directory on your server.

There are other ways in which you can manage print queues remotely, including the use of Remote Desktop for Administrator. For more information on these features, see Chapter 7.

Monitoring Print Queue Performance with System Monitor

Windows Server 2003 provides an object called Print Queue within the System Monitor utility. This object contains many different counters that can provide useful information about the performance and operations of your print queue. Table 4-3 lists the available counters. Note that most counters include multiple available instances that can be monitored.

Available instances include a "Total" (which is a sum for all print devices), and individual instances for each printer. The following illustration shows some of the available Print Queue counters, and their options. For complete details about using System Monitor to track performance, see Chapter 8.

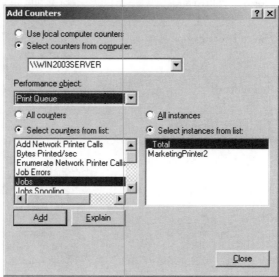

Print Queue Counter	Purpose
Add Network Printer Calls	A running total that lists the number of requests that have been made to add a printer since the server was restarted. This can be useful in determining how many users have chosen to print to this server.
Bytes Printed / sec	Specifies the amount of data throughput to printer devices.
Enumerate Network Printer Calls	Shows information about how many browse requests have been initiated from client computers.
Job Errors	The total number of print job errors that have occurred since the server was restarted.
Jobs	The current number of print jobs in the queue. This is a very useful statistics to track over time to determine when your print servers are busiest, and to isolate and troubleshoot complaints about slow printer performance.
Jobs Spooling	Specifies the current number of print jobs that are currently being spooled by the print server.
Max Jobs Spooling	The maximum number of print jobs that were spooling at any time since the server was restarted.
Max References	The highest number of open connections to a printer since the server was restarted.
Not Ready Errors	The total number of "printer not ready" errors that occurred since the server was restarted.
Out of Paper Errors	The total number of printing errors that occurred because a physical printing device reported that it was out of paper.
References	The current number of open connects to the current printer.
Total Jobs Printed	The total number of print jobs that have been processed by the printer. Note that jobs can vary greatly in size, and single-page printouts are treated the same as multipage printouts.
Total Pages Printed	Returns the total number of pages printed since the server was restarted. Tracking this value over time can be useful, since it can indicate which printers are overworked and can provide clues about how you can better allocate printers within your environment.

Managing Printing from the Command Line

There are several utilities that can be used to manage printing from the command line. Table 4-4 provides a list of these commands.

In addition to these command-line utilities, Windows Server 2003 includes several different Visual Basic Script (VBScript) files that can be used to administer printers. As shown in Table 4-5, these scripts can be very useful for performing common operations. Additionally, since you can easily view the source code of the scripts in any standard text editor, you can use these scripts as templates for building your own custom scripts and commands. The script files are located within the \System32 folder of your Windows Server 2003 system root. Since the contents of this folder are already in the path, you can run the commands from any folder at a command prompt.

For more information about these commands and scripts, you can simply type the name of the command followed by /?. Figure 4-26 shows an example of the help for

| TABLE 4-4 | Command-Line Utilities That Can Be Used for Managing Printing Functionality |

Command Name	Description	Notes
Print	Sends a file or document to the printer.	This command works only for local printers. If you want to print to a remote printer, you should use other client- and server-side features.
Net Print	Allows you to view and configure print jobs.	Examples of operations include holding or releasing a print job.
Net Start	Can be used to start and stop the spooler service.	Restarting the spooler service can help resolve many different types of printing issues.
Lpr	Used to send a print job to an LPD server.	The computer must be running the LPD Server service in order for this command to work. This command is useful for interoperability with Unix print servers.
Lpq	This command returns information about an LPD print queue.	The computer must be running the LPD Server service in order for this command to work. This command is useful for interoperability with Unix print servers.

	Script Name	Function
TABLE 4-5	PrnCnfg.vbs	Used to view and modify printer settings.
VBScript Files that Can Be Used for Managing Printing Functionality	PrnDrvr.vbs	Used to view, modify, and delete printer drivers.
	PrnJobs.vbs	Allows the management of print jobs, including listing, pausing, resuming, and canceling jobs.
	PrnqCtl.vbs	Used to manage print queues, including clearing the print queue and pausing a print queue. For testing purposes, this command can also be used to print a test page.
	PrnMngr.vbs	Used to control printer connections, including adding or deleting printer connections.
	PrnPort.vbs	Allows the management of TCP/IP printing ports.

the PrnCnfg.vbs script, and Figure 4-27 shows an example of the types of information that can be retrieved with the following command:

```
PrnCnfg -g -s localhost -p Printer1
```

FIGURE 4-26

Viewing help for the PrnCnfg.vbs script

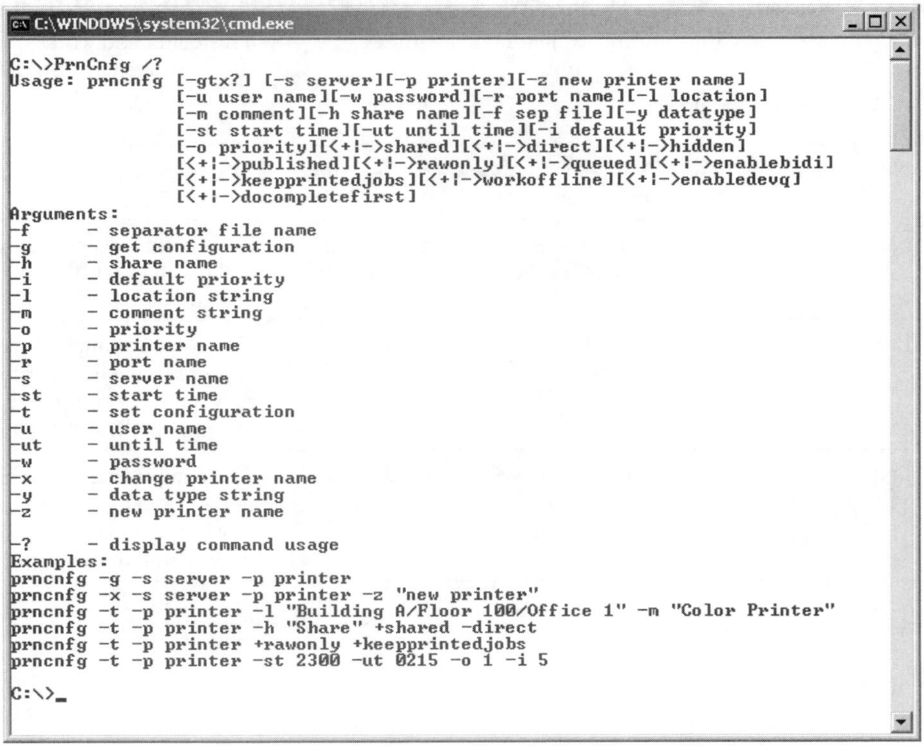

```
C:\>PrnCnfg /?
Usage: prncnfg [-gtx?] [-s server][-p printer][-z new printer name]
               [-u user name][-w password][-r port name][-l location]
               [-m comment][-h share name][-f sep file][-y datatype]
               [-st start time][-ut until time][-i default priority]
               [-o priority][<+!->shared][<+!->direct][<+!->hidden]
               [<+!->published][<+!->rawonly][<+!->queued][<+!->enablebidi]
               [<+!->keepprintedjobs][<+!->workoffline][<+!->enabledevq]
               [<+!->docompletefirst]
Arguments:
-f       - separator file name
-g       - get configuration
-h       - share name
-i       - default priority
-l       - location string
-m       - comment string
-o       - priority
-p       - printer name
-r       - port name
-s       - server name
-st      - start time
-t       - set configuration
-u       - user name
-ut      - until time
-w       - password
-x       - change printer name
-y       - data type string
-z       - new printer name

-?       - display command usage
Examples:
prncnfg -g -s server -p printer
prncnfg -x -s server -p printer -z "new printer"
prncnfg -t -p printer -l "Building A/Floor 100/Office 1" -m "Color Printer"
prncnfg -t -p printer -h "Share" +shared -direct
prncnfg -t -p printer +rawonly +keepprintedjobs
prncnfg -t -p printer -st 2300 -ut 0215 -o 1 -i 5

C:\>_
```

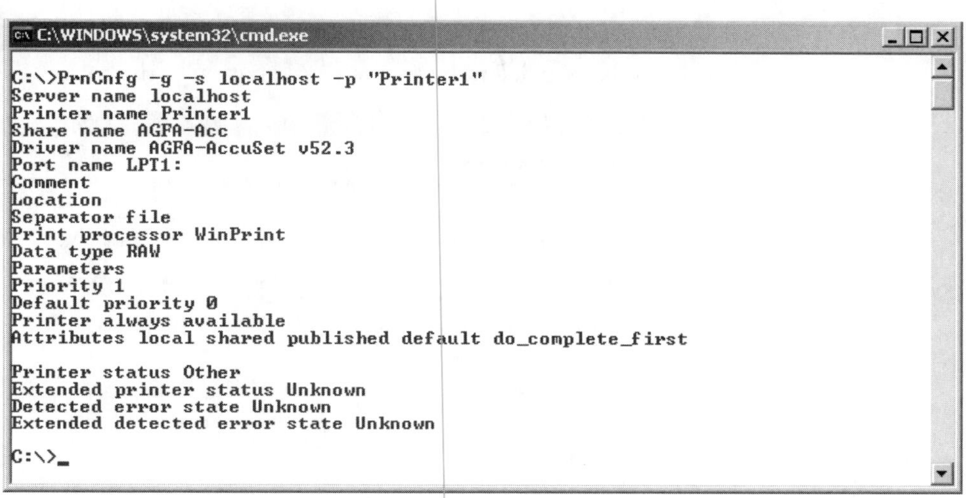

FIGURE 4-27

Getting printer information using the PrnCnfg.vbs script

```
C:\WINDOWS\system32\cmd.exe                                          _ □ ×
C:\>PrnCnfg -g -s localhost -p "Printer1"
Server name localhost
Printer name Printer1
Share name AGFA-Acc
Driver name AGFA-AccuSet v52.3
Port name LPT1:
Comment
Location
Separator file
Print processor WinPrint
Data type RAW
Parameters
Priority 1
Default priority 0
Printer always available
Attributes local shared published default do_complete_first

Printer status Other
Extended printer status Unknown
Detected error state Unknown
Extended detected error state Unknown

C:\>_
```

exam
watch

Don't try too hard to memorize the options for all of these commands. Microsoft is unlikely to ask you about a specific command-line *argument or switch on the exam. Instead, be aware of the names and types of command-line utilities that are provided with Windows Server 2003.*

Additional details about the purposes, functions, and options for these command-line utilities are available in the Windows Help and Support Center.

EXERCISE 4-3

CertCam 4-3 ON THE CD

Creating and Monitoring a Print Queue

In order to complete this exercise, it is not necessary for you to have an actual printer connected to your server. If you have a local printer connected to the LPT1: port, please power it off or take it offline. Finally, this exercise assumes that your server has not yet been configured with the print server role.

1. Log on to the server as an Administrator and open the Configure Your Server administrative tool. On the Server Roles step, select Print Server and click Next. On the Printers and Print Drivers step, leave the

default option of Windows 2000 And Windows XP Clients Only. Click Next twice to begin the configuration of the role.

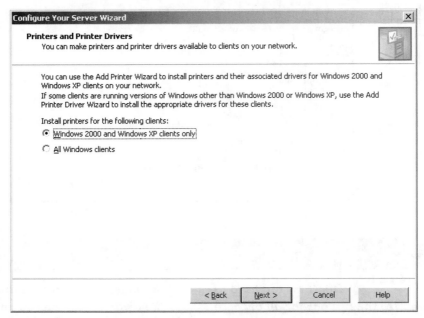

2. The Configure Your Server Wizard will automatically launch the Add Printer Wizard. Click Next to begin the setup of a new printer. On the local or network printer step, choose Local Printer Attached To This Computer, and uncheck the Automatically Detect And Install My Plug And Play Printer option. Click Next to continue.

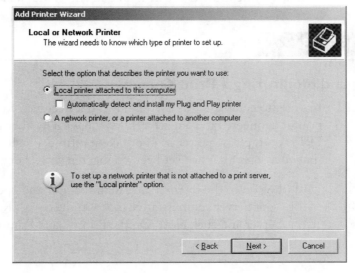

3. On the Select A Printer Port step, select the LPT1: port and click Next.

4. On the Install Printer Software step, select Generic for the Manufacturer of the printer. Then, select Generic / Text Only in the right column. Click Next to continue.

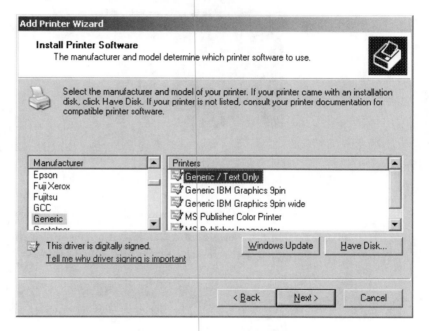

5. For the name of the printer, specify Test Printer and click Next.

6. On the Printer Sharing tab, share the printer under the name "Test Printer." Click Next.

7. Optionally, for the location and comment, enter some descriptive text about the printer. Click Next. When prompted, to print a test page, click Yes and click Next.

8. You will now see a summary of the choices you have made. To finish the addition of a new printer, uncheck the Restart The Wizard To Add Another Printer option and then click Finish.

9. You will see a Test Printer dialog box. Click OK to specify that the test page printed properly. Note that if you selected Troubleshoot, you would have been taken to the printer troubleshooting information.

10. You will now see a confirmation that tells you that the server is now configured with the print server role. Click Finish to complete the Configure Your Server Wizard.

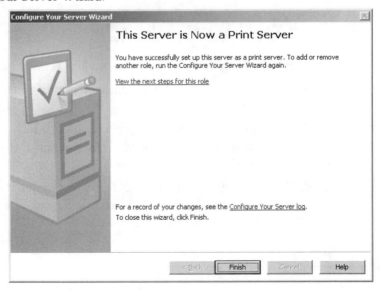

11. Now that you have finished the configuration of a new printer, it's time to monitor the print queue. Choose Start | Settings | Printers And Faxes to open

the Printers and Faxes tool. You will see the Test Printer icon that was created. Note that you can perform several tasks by right-clicking the printer icon.

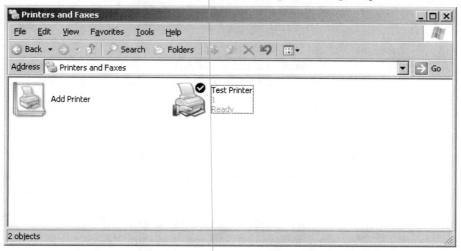

12. Double-click the Test Printer icon to see the current document that is located in the print queue. This document should be the test page that you attempted to print earlier. To view details about the document, double-click it. Note that you can change the priority of the document, and that you can view various pieces of information about it. Click OK when finished viewing the details.

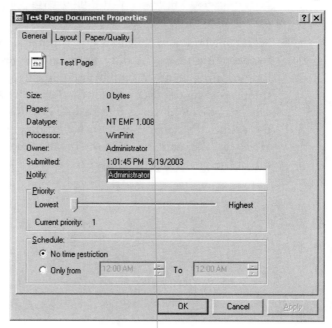

13. In the properties of the print queue, right-click the document in the queue and choose Cancel to remove it from the queue. Click Yes when prompted for confirmation. This will remove the document from the list of print jobs. Close the print queue properties and the Printers And Faxes icon.

14. Since you are now done with this exercise, you might want to rerun the Configure Your Server Wizard and remove the print server role.

Troubleshooting and Optimizing Printing Performance

In addition to the tools and techniques you've seen so far, several additional Windows Server 2003 features can help optimize printing performance. These include

- *Assign different priority levels for print jobs.* For many users, not all documents need to be printed immediately. One technique for allowing the prioritization of print jobs is to create multiple logical printers that send output to the same physical print device. One printer might specify "High Priority," and another might specify "Low Priority." Users could then choose to which logical printer each print job should be sent, depending on the importance of the job. Or if you want to allow only certain users to use each print queue, you can specify this through the use of share permissions.

- *Scheduling print jobs.* In many environments, printers might be used to their fullest capacity during regular business hours. In some cases, long-running print jobs might hold up the print queue and prevent the processing of other smaller (and possibly more important) documents. One way to avoid this is to schedule print jobs to occur outside of peak times. By default, printers are configured to always be available. However, the availability of the print queue can be set in the Advanced tab of the properties of a printer.

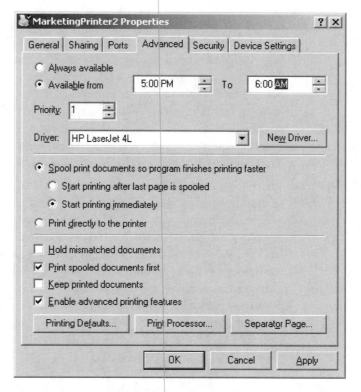

One sure-fire way to make the best use of your available printing resources is to encourage users to print less! In many organizations, a little end-user education might be able to help people understand alternatives to making hard-copies of their documents. I've often sat in meetings where over a dozen of the Engineering staff would print out 40-page documents. Rarely would they refer to even a few of the pages. A great way to avoid this waste was for users to bring their laptops to the conference room. That way, they could see all of their documents in full color, and all editing could be done within the document. Similarly, using duplexing options or printing multiple document pages per physical printed page can be helpful features. The end result will undoubtedly be better management of information and the savings of hundreds of pages of printouts per meeting.

■ *Set optimal print spooling options.* Also on the Advanced tab of the properties of a logical printer are several different options that can control how print jobs are spooled. The default setting is to enable spooling, which will generally result in a better end-user experience, since the print job will be submitted quickly to the print server. Generally, the Start Printing After The Last Page Is Spooled option is best for printers that are attached to print servers. The Start Printing Immediately option is best for users that have a printer connected directly to their computers. Another useful option is the Hold Mismatched Jobs setting, which keeps print jobs that mistakenly ask for envelopes or the wrong paper type from remaining in the output queue and delaying other print jobs. For more details on the other options, use the ToolTip help, or see the Windows Server 2003 Help and Support Center.

■ *Change the location of the print spool folder.* By default, print jobs are spooled to the \System32\Spool\Printers folder within the system root of your Windows Server 2003 installation. While this might be acceptable for some servers, on busy print servers, you might want to use a different location on another physical hard disk to spool print jobs. This can increase performance by reducing disk contention on the operating system hard disk, and it can provide much more available disk space for spooling print jobs. You can change the location of the print spool folder in the Advanced properties of the print server (which you can access by choosing File | Server Properties | Advanced in the Printers and Faxes Control Panel applet). The following illustration shows this dialog box.

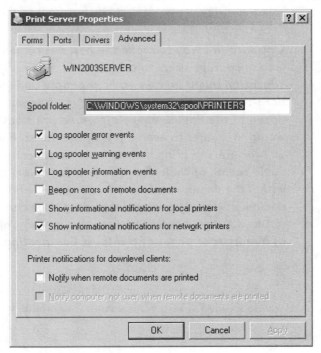

■ *Implement a printer pool.* In some situations, a single physical printer cannot meet the needs of the environment. Sometimes, the only solution is to add more printers. Although you can manually configure multiple logical print queues, each of which prints to a separate physical device, this can be difficult to manage. You would generally need to make the user choose a specific printer for output. A better way is to implement a printer pool. A *printing pool* consists of a single logical printer that can actually output to multiple physical print devices. Whenever a user submits a print job, the job will be automatically sent to one of the available printers. Since users will not know which physical printer generated their document, you should keep all of the printers located in a single area. You can enable printer pooling on the Ports tab of the Properties dialog of a logical printer.

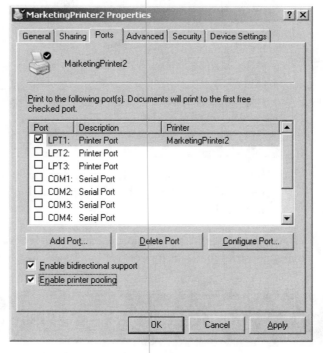

■ *Implement auditing of printer activity.* Sometimes, when you're troubleshooting printing problems, it can be helpful to retain detailed information about who is printing what, and when. That's where auditing comes in. You can configure auditing settings for a logical printer by accessing the printer's properties sheet. Click Advanced and then select the Auditing tab to view the settings (see Figure 4-28). By default, no auditing options are enabled,

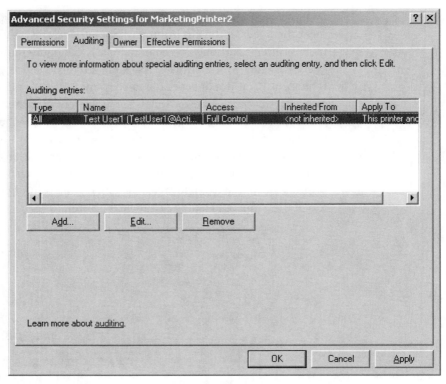

FIGURE 4-28

Configuring auditing settings for a printer

but you can specify which users and groups (and which actions) are being recorded by clicking Add. More information about auditing is covered later in this chapter.

As you can see from the information in this section, Windows Server 2003 offers many powerful methods for controlling, managing, and troubleshooting printers!

SCENARIO & SOLUTION

A user reports that she cannot print to "LaserPrinter1," but she can print to other printers.	Verify the permissions on the logical "LaserPrinter1" device to ensure that the user has Print permissions.
You want to allow department managers to reorder print jobs for printers in their department.	In the Security settings for the applicable logical printers, assign the Manage Documents permission.
You want to view the status of a print queue from a Linux computer.	Use a web browser to connect to the server's web-based printing URL. In order for this to work, you must have IIS properly configured, and the feature must be enabled on the server side.

SCENARIO & SOLUTION

Users report that, especially in the mornings, it can take up to an hour for print jobs to complete.	Use System Monitor counters to track the number of print jobs and the number of pages managed by various logical printers. Then, either reconfigure the logical printer settings or purchase additional hardware.
You want to allow users to specify whether their print jobs are "High Priority" or "Low Priority" when they submit jobs to the printer.	Create two logical printers, each of which connect to the same physical print device. Then, configure the appropriate priorities for each logical printer.

CERTIFICATION OBJECTIVE 4.04

Managing and Troubleshooting Terminal Services

Microsoft Windows NT 4.0 Server, Terminal Edition, Windows 2000 Server platform, and Windows Server 2003 platform all support multiple simultaneous logons to the same server. In Windows Server 2003, this function is referred to as Terminal Services. Terminal services is designed to allow remote computers to log on to a server over the network and to have an open, interactive Windows session on that server.

The primary client-side component is the Remote Desktop Connection application. Once a remote connection is made, all operations that the user carries out are actually executed on the Terminal Server. At a basic level, the Remote Desktop Connection software is responsible for receiving screen updates from the Terminal Server and for relaying keyboard and mouse signals to the Terminal Server. It also provides additional functionality, such as the mapping of local client resources, disk drives and printers, for instance, so that they're available from within the Terminal Services session.

Figure 4-29 illustrates the difference between applications being run using standard client computers and using Terminal Services functionality.

There are many potential benefits to using Terminal Services functionality. The first is centralized administration. Applications are installed in only one place, so application patches and updates can be quickly and easily applied without visiting client computers or investing in other software. Another major benefit is that Terminal Services functionality enables older computers to run the newest software. Since all that is required on the client is simple redirection of standard input and output, the client-side hardware requirements are low.

FIGURE 4-29 A logical overview of running applications using Terminal Services

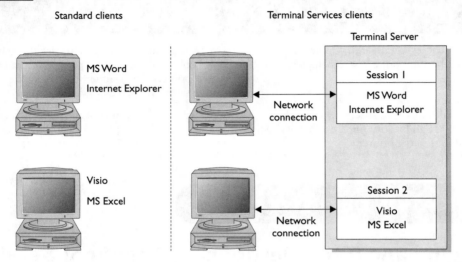

Of course, as with any technical solution, there are potential drawbacks to using Terminal Services functionality. First, Terminal Servers can introduce single points of failure to your network environment. That is, if a terminal server becomes unavailable (due to a hardware failure, server issue, or network problem, for example), many users could be affected. In the case of a network issue, many users could be prevented from working. There are, however, ways to mitigate these risks, including establishing multiple Terminal Servers and redundant network connections. Also, primarily because of the CPU and memory requirements of Terminal Servers, this functionality can place a large burden on even modern servers. Therefore, a terminal server can support only a limited number of connections (although this number is rapidly rising as hardware continues to improve). Still, Terminal Services is a useful option in many network environments.

In earlier versions of Windows, the term "Terminal Services" referred to using this functionality both for remote administration and for supporting end users. This terminology was confusing and has been changed with Windows Server 2003. The Terminal Services functionality that you will consider in this chapter refers to providing a method for end users to create remote connections over the network. More details regarding the use of a related feature, "Remote Desktop for Administration," for remote administration purposes is provided in Chapter 7.

In this section, you'll look at how you can manage and troubleshoot Terminal Services on Windows Server 2003.

Configuring the Terminal Server Role

The first step in the process of configuring Terminal Services is to use the Configure Your Server tool to enable the Terminal Server role. This process does not provide any options, and it works automatically. One important fact to note is that enabling this server role does require a reboot of the server. If you choose to continue, the reboot will happen automatically. So, be sure that you don't have any critical operations occurring at the time.

As with the other server roles, you can also remove the Terminal Server role using the Configure Your Server Wizard. Now that you have a quick overview of how Terminal Services can be enabled, let's look at the various configuration options that you'll need to understand in order to monitor and troubleshoot connections.

Configuring Security Settings for Terminal Services

The main utility that is used to configure Terminal Services options is called, appropriately, Terminal Services Configuration. This utility is available within the Administrative Tools program folder. There are two main functions that can be performed: The first is managing connections, and the other is configuring server settings for this service.

Every client connection must use a connection protocol in order to communicate with a terminal server. By default, Windows Server 2003 includes support for the Remote Desktop Protocol (RDP) version 5.2. By right-clicking the Connections object in the Terminal Services Configuration tool, you can choose to launch the Terminal Services Connection Wizard. This wizard will walk you through the steps that are required to support additional types of connections (if available). You will also be able to specify encryption settings and details about which network adapter(s) will support the protocol.

Microsoft originally licensed terminal services functionality from Citrix, Inc. (www.citrix.com). This company still provides add-on functionality that can improve the features and capabilities of Terminal Services.

You can also right-click an already-configured connection and choose Properties to view many different details related to how the protocol is configured. For example, the following illustration shows the Permissions tab, which allows you to specify which users will be able to connect to the Terminal Server using this protocol. By clicking Advanced, you can also enable auditing of the use of this connection. For more details on the other available options, see the help file.

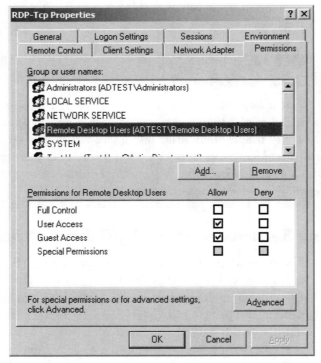

The other set of options that the Terminal Services configuration utility provides is a set of server settings. The available options allow you to specify temporary folder settings, security settings, and other related options.

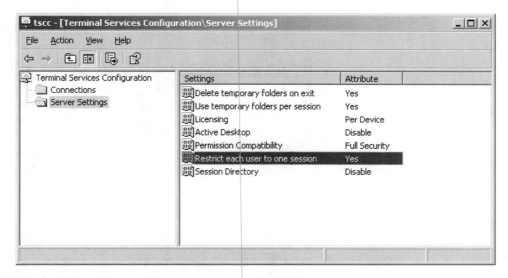

Configuring User Properties for Terminal Services

You can configure many different properties for a user once the Terminal Server role has been enabled. All of these options are available as part of the property information for users. If you're working on a stand-alone Windows Server 2003 computer, you can use the Computer Management tool to access these properties. If your Windows Server 2003 computer is a domain controller or a member of a domain, you can use the Active Directory Users and Computer tool. Let's take a look at the types of properties that can be important when working with Terminal Services:

- **Environment**   Using this tab (shown in the next illustration), you can specify a program that should be run automatically whenever the user logs in. For example, you might want to run some scripts that initialize the user environment. It's important that you ensure that the path and filename for the program are correct, because this could cause problems for users upon login. On this tab, you can also specify whether the client computer's resources (such as disk drives and printers) will be available from within the Terminal Services session. If they are enabled, users will be able to access local volumes and printers through special mappings that will appear when they use tools such as Windows Explorer.

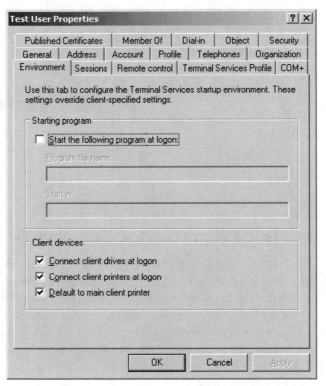

- **Sessions**   Whenever a user connects to a Terminal Server computer, he creates a new session on the server. Using the properties on this tab, you can control how connections are handled for this user (see the following illustration). The first option allows you to specify when a disconnected connection will be automatically terminated. The default setting is "Never," which means that, if a user disconnects from the system without logging off, his or her connection will remain active indefinitely. The active session limit setting determines how long a user can remain actively connected to a Terminal Server session. The idle session limit controls how long a user session will remain active without any end-user activity. You can also configure whether sessions should be automatically disconnected or ended when these limits are reached. All of these session limitations can be important, especially when you're trying to conserve server resources and Terminal Services licenses. Finally, you can specify whether, after users have disconnected from a session, they can reestablish the connection from any computer, or just from the one that created the connection.

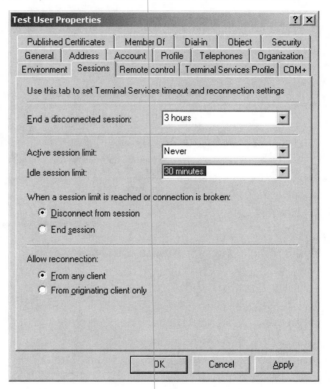

- **Remote Control** When using Terminal Services functionality, administrators have the ability to view users' sessions. This can be useful for assisting users with problems or for monitoring certain types of application usage. However, having this ability can also be a potential security problem, since users can see other users' data and files. The settings on the Remote Control tab (shown next) specify the settings for whether remote control of a Terminal

Services session is allowed. If so, you can specify whether the user's permission is required before remote control functionality can be used. Finally, you can choose whether you want to be able to control the user's session, or just to be able to view it. If the necessary settings have been made, you can view a Terminal Services session by using the Terminal Services Manager administrative tool.

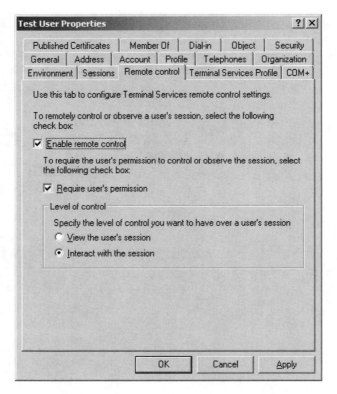

■ **Terminal Services Profile**   On this page, systems administrators can specify information about the profile that is assigned to a user when he or she is logging on to the Terminal Server. These settings are similar to those that appear in the Profile tab, but they allow systems administrators to create separate profiles that can be used only for remote connections. More information on user

exam

watch

If one or more users report that they cannot successfully log on to a Terminal Services server, you should

verify the Allow Logon To Terminal Server option on the Users' Remote Control Properties tab.

profiles is covered in Chapter 3. This page also includes an option that specifies whether or not the user is allowed to log on to a Terminal Server session.

■ **Member Of**   The groups to which a user belongs can also control whether or not she can log on to a Terminal Services session. For more information on configuring groups, see Chapter 3.

Now that you have a good idea of some of the types of user settings that can affect Terminal Services logons, let's look at how you can monitor remote server connections.

Monitoring Terminal Services Using Terminal Services Manager

Often, when administering a Windows Server 2003 terminal server machine, you'll want to see who's connected to the system. The primary tool included for monitoring Terminal Services usage is the Terminal Services Manager administrative tool. When you launch this tool from an interactive session (that is, when you're sitting at the server console), you'll receive a message telling you that the Remote Control and Connect options are available only when you are running the Terminal Services Manager from within a remote session. As shown in Figure 4-30, this administrative tool will include a list of all the known Terminal Servers on the network. You can click the name of a server and select the Session tab to list the current remote connections. This will also display the status of connections to the terminal server, along with the time that the connection was made and how long the session has been idle. All of these features are useful in tracking Terminal Services usage.

By expanding the branch for a terminal server in your environment and clicking a remote connection, you'll be able to perform several different types of operations.

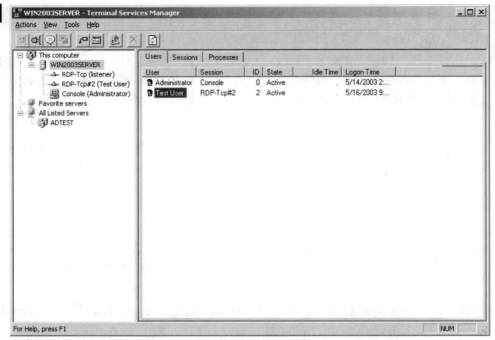

For example, by clicking one of the connections, you can see the processes that the session is running, as well as additional information about the connection (see Figure 4-31).

You can also right-click a connection and choose from several operations. Remember that most of these are available only if you're connecting from another remote session, and not if you're connecting from the console. The options include

- **Connect** This option will connect your session to an inactive Terminal Services connection.

- **Disconnect** With this command, you will disconnect a currently active Terminal Services session. Note that this will disconnect the user from the terminal server, but it will not end his or her session. You can disconnect users in order to troubleshoot client-side problems (for example, a "stuck" connection, in which users are not receiving screen updates).

- **Send Message** Periodically, you may need to reboot your server or perform other operations (such as software installation) that require users to be disconnected from the system. The Send Message command will cause a pop-up box to appear in the selected users' remote desktop connection.

FIGURE 4-31

Viewing client
information about
a Terminal
Services
connection

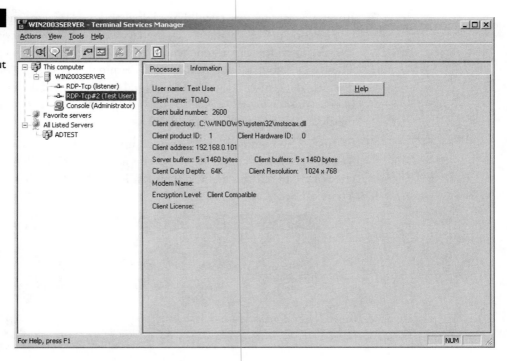

It's a good idea to notify users of any potential downtime or any other
changes that might affect them.

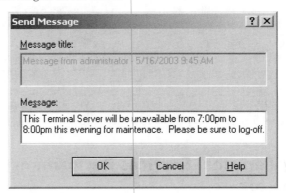

■ **Remote Control**   If a session is currently active and you have the appropriate
user properties set, you can use remote control to either view or control a
currently active remote connection.

■ **Reset** Sometimes users will have left abandoned sessions that have been idle for long period of time. Or, you may need to forcibly disconnect a session in order to perform maintenance or to resolve other resource usage issues. The Reset command will terminate a Terminal Services session and will disconnect the user. Note that this could cause a loss of data (if the user has any unsaved work open), so you should consider this step only if other methods (such as notifying the user) have failed.

■ **Status** This command will return additional status information about a Terminal Services connection. Systems administrators will likely want to check here first to get a quick overview if users are reporting problems using Terminal Services.

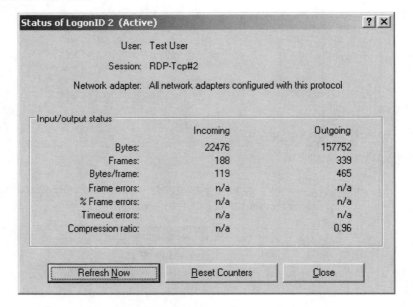

In addition to the Terminal Services Manager, there are other ways to monitor this functionality. Let's look at some more of these.

Monitoring Terminal Services Performance Using System Monitor

Windows Server 2003's System Monitor provides a great way to monitor the performance of Terminal Services functionality. Table 4-6 provides some useful objects and counters that can be used for managing and monitoring the overall usage of a machine that is configured as a terminal server.

For more information on configuring and using System Monitor, see Chapter 8.

| TABLE 4-6 | Useful System Monitor Objects and Counters that Are Related to Terminal Services |

Object	Counter	Purpose
Terminal Services	Total Sessions	Provides information about the total number of Terminal Services sessions. This number includes both active and inactive sessions.
Terminal Services	Active Sessions	Provides information about the total number of active Terminal Services sessions. Sessions are considered active when a user is currently logged on to the system.
Terminal Services	Inactive Sessions	Provides a count of the number of inactive Terminal Services sessions. Sessions are considered inactive if they have been disconnected but the user did not log off the Terminal Server.
Terminal Services Session	% Processor Time	Monitors the amount of CPU utilization that is caused by specific Terminal Services sessions. This information is useful in troubleshooting performance issues, since it allows for monitoring any of the current connections to the server individually.
Terminal Services Session	Total Bytes	This statistic provides information about the total number of bytes that are being transferred between a Terminal Services client and the server. If users are complaining about slow performance, a large amount of overall network traffic might be the cause.
Terminal Services Session	Total Errors	This counter measures the total number of any kind of errors that have occurred. Systems administrators can view information about errors for specific Terminal Services connections. If the number of errors is high, it's likely that there are problems with the underlying network connection.
Terminal Services Session	Page Faults / sec	Measures the number of pages that must be swapped to disk for specific Terminal Services sessions. If this number is high, it is likely that the server could benefit from additional physical memory.

Troubleshooting Terminal Services

So far, in this chapter, you've looked at several ways in which you can monitor and troubleshoot Terminal Services. In this section, I'll present a brief summary of things you should check when you're experiencing problems with Terminal Services. Troubleshooting steps for Terminal Services include the following:

- *Verify user and group security settings.* Users must have the necessary permissions to log on to a Terminal Services machine over the network. If some or all users are having trouble logging on to a Terminal Services session, you should check their User property settings and their group membership. For more information on these topics, see Chapter 3.

- *Ensure that you have the appropriate licenses for your terminal server.* Unlike other features of the Windows Server 2003 operating system, Terminal Services requires the purchase of special Terminal Services Client Access Licenses (TS CALs). You are given a 120-day period from the installation of the Terminal Server role before you must purchase and add licenses. If you do not add the licenses by then, this feature will be disabled. Every Terminal Services environment must have at least one server that is configured as a Terminal Services License Server. This can be administered through the use of the Terminal Services Licensing administrative tool. For more information on Terminal Services licensing, see the help file that is installed when you configure your server for Terminal Services functionality.

- *Verify protocol settings.* In order to make a connection to a Terminal Server, users must have permissions to use at least one remote desktop protocol. To verify the settings, you can view the properties of a connection in the Terminal Services Configuration utility. Specifically, the Security tab will include a list of users and groups that have permissions to connect.

- *Monitor overall server performance.* Terminal Services functionality often requires significant disk, memory, and CPU resources to work optimally. If you're troubleshooting performance-related problems with Terminal Services, you might have to make changes to get the level of performance your users expect. One possible method for doing this is to upgrade hardware (by, for example, adding physical memory or adding a faster disk subsystem). However, you might also be able to get a significant performance boost by lightening the load of other services that are running on the computer. For example, if the computer is a domain controller, the replication traffic for the Active Directory store might be causing significant load on the server. In that case, you might need to separate the Terminal Server and domain controller functionality onto different computers. As you'll see in Chapter 8, there are many different methods for determining what's causing your performance problems.

Overall, there are many different ways in which you can monitor and troubleshoot problems with Terminal Services. You should keep these tools and techniques in mind for the exam (and if you plan to implement this functionality in the real world)!

Other Resource Access Tools and Techniques

In addition to several areas of the functionality that were covered throughout this chapter, Windows Server 2003 includes many other features that can be used to help monitor and manage server resources. In this section, you'll take a look at features such as auditing, encryption, security configuration management tools, and the Distributed File System.

Enabling Auditing

By default, Windows Server 2003 is installed with auditing functionality disabled. That means it's up to you—the systems administrator—to turn the feature on. Fortunately, it's a fairly easy process: Open the Local Security Settings console (located in the Administrative Tools program group). To view and change the auditing options, go to the Local Policies | Audit Policies section. You'll see the settings for various auditing options, as shown in Figure 4-32.

The options include

■ **Audit account logon events**   When this is enabled, you can record all logon attempts (successes and/or failures) to a domain. Enabling auditing of logons can be very useful in determining who is using your machines and when. When failures are audited, systems administrators can find accounts that have many failed logons (a possible sign of someone trying to guess a password). Auditing logons is also helpful when you support remote access connections (through a dial-in modem bank or a VPN, for example).

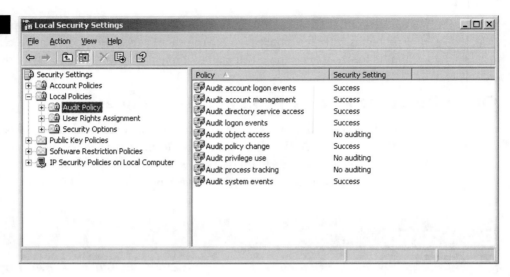

FIGURE 4-32

Viewing local
policy auditing
options

- **Audit account logon events**   This option is similar to the "audit logon events" option, but it pertains to logons that occur on the local machine.

- **Audit account management**   As discussed earlier in this chapter, properly managing users and groups is an important aspect of security, since it determines who can do what on your systems. This option will allow you to record when users or systems administrators are attempting to make changes to accounts.

- **Audit directory service access**   This option allows you to enable auditing for various actions that are taken on Active Directory objects. Once this option is enabled, you can use the Active Directory Users and Computers tool to fine-tune exactly what will be audited. You'll learn more about Active Directory in Part II of this book.

- **Audit object access**   There are many different types of security-related objects in the Windows Server 2003 platform. An object may be a file, a folder, a user account, or some other object. Enabling this option allows you to turn on auditing for any object supported by the operating system.

- **Audit policy change**   It's always a good idea to audit changes to the audit policy itself. A potentially embarrassing security breach would be one in which the intruder logged on and then changed the audit log settings so that his or her actions from that point would not be recorded.

- **Audit privilege use**   When enabled, this setting will record events that occur whenever an individual or process uses one of their access rights (for example, adding a workstation to a domain or rebooting a computer). You can view a complete list of user rights by clicking the User Rights Assignment item in the Local Policy security settings (see Figure 4-33).

- **Audit process tracking**   Auditing can be useful for troubleshooting and debugging in some cases. This option allows you to track actions taken by processes (such as applications or services) that are running on the machine. However, beware that, depending on the activity of your machine, enabling this option could generate a large amount of information in the audit logs.

- **Audit system events**   System events, such as startup and shutdown events, can be logged using this option. If you're having intermittent problems with a server, this might be a good option to enable.

To change the auditing settings for any of these options, simply double-click one of the items and select whether you want log success and/or failure events.

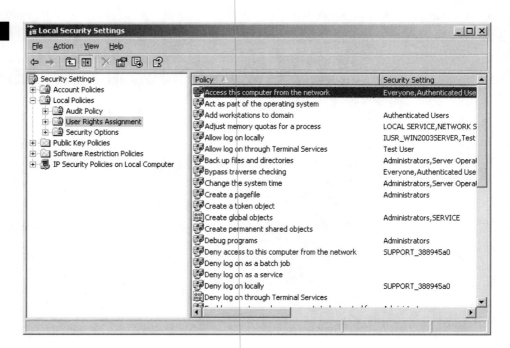

FIGURE 4-33

Viewing User Right Assignments in Local Policy settings

Selecting What to Audit In some cases, additional steps may be necessary in order to specify exactly what is being audited. Perhaps the best example is "Audit object access." If enabling this option did what its name might suggest—auditing all accesses to all objects—you might end up with volumes of information in just a few minutes! So, rather than turn on auditing for all of the objects and actions, Windows Server 2003 makes you specify which objects and actions you want to log. Let's take a quick look at how you could enable auditing for a single folder. View the properties of an existing folder and then click the Security tab. To access auditing settings, click Advanced and then choose the Auditing tab. You'll see a dialog box similar to one shown in Figure 4-34.

If you're used to setting NTFS permissions (a topic that was covered earlier in this chapter), you should have no problem understanding the user interface. To specify which users or groups will be audited, click Add. You'll then be given the opportunity

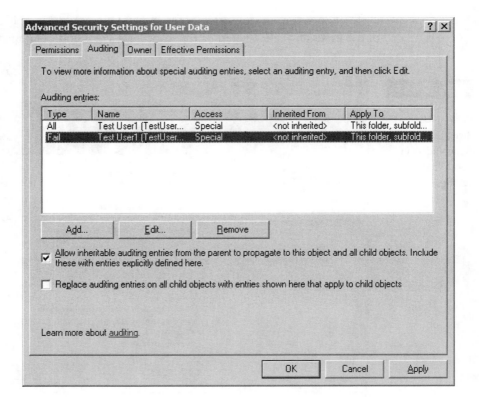

FIGURE 4-34

Configuring auditing settings for a folder

to select auditing of successes and/or failures for various actions that are possible for a folder. Notice that you have options related to inheritance in this dialog box.

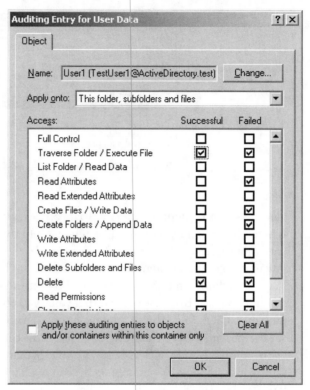

Once you've configured auditing, events will be written to various event logs. Figure 4-35 shows an example of an audited event. Be sure to regularly review this information to find anything suspicious. Although you have collected a lot of data, the filtering capabilities in Event Viewer can help you pinpoint the events that you really care about. Overall, auditing provides a very important and useful piece of the security puzzle.

Using the Security Configuration Manager

The power and flexibility of Windows-based operating systems is both a benefit and a liability. On the plus side, the many configuration options available allow users and systems administrators to modify and customize settings to their preference. On the negative side, however, it will be up to you—the systems administrator— to ensure that users have only the permissions that they require for doing their jobs.

FIGURE 4-35

Viewing the
Security event log
with Event
Viewer

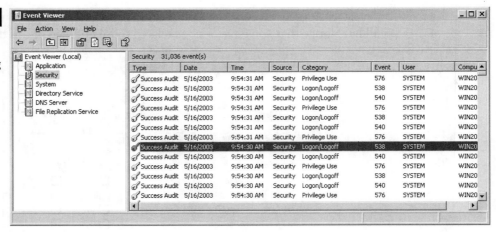

There are several potential problems that can be caused by providing novice users with too much functionality. For example, a user could try to delete critical system files in an attempt to free up disk space. Or, a user might inadvertently change the configuration of their system without regard to company policy.

Systems administrators can inadvertently introduce security issues, as well. One of the common issues that may occur is that you try to change permissions to troubleshoot a problem. Then, once the problem is resolved, you forget to return to that system to reset the permissions to their original state. This can be a significant security issue.

Fortunately, Windows Server 2003 provides many different methods for setting permissions and security parameters. In early versions of Windows operating systems, administering security was difficult. For certain settings to be made, you might have to physically visit client computers. And, many of the settings were far too restrictive. For example, in order to prevent certain types of undesirable actions, you might have to remove the permissions that are required for a user to install a new program. Furthermore, if you needed to make settings on many different computers, it could be a challenge to ensure that you have everything configured properly. As you might have guessed, there is a better way!

Security Templates   Although you could manage security settings manually through the use of Registry changes, this process can become quite tedious. Furthermore, manually modifying the Registry is a dangerous process and one that is bound to cause problems due to human error. In order to make the creation and application of security settings easier, Microsoft has included the Security Configuration and Analysis tool with Windows Server 2003. This tool can be used to create, modify, and apply security settings to computers using a uniform definition of settings that systems administrators can define according to their requirements. Through the use of security templates, systems administrators can define security settings once and then store this information in a file that can be applied to other computers. For example, you might create one security template for users in the Engineering department, one for users in the Sales department, and another one for your company's intranet servers.

Security template files provide a description of the settings that can be configured by systems administrators, along with information about the specific area(s) of the Registry that must be modified to make the settings take effect. For an example of the types of settings that are available, see Figure 4-36. Now that you know what security templates are, let's take a look at how you can use them to consistently administer security.

FIGURE 4-36

Viewing configuration options in a security template

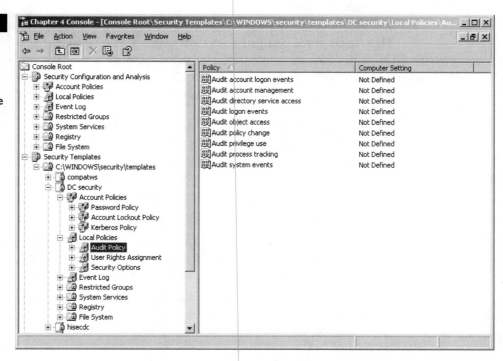

By default, these templates are stored in the *%SystemRoot%* \Security\Templates folder. The default templates include

- Compatws
- DC security
- Hisecdc
- Hisecws
- Iesacls
- Rootsec
- Securedc
- Securews
- Setup security

For more information on the purpose of these templates, see the Windows Help and Support Center.

The Security Configuration and Analysis Process   The Security Configuration and Analysis tool greatly simplifies the creation and applications of security-related settings on Windows-based computers. The overall process for working with the Security Configuration and Analysis tool is as follows:

1. Open or create a Security Database file. This file will be used to store information related to the security settings that you configure in later steps.

2. Import an existing Template file. The template file that you select will serve as a basis for security-related settings that you might want to apply to the local computer. For example, you might have a template file that is designed for "Server Security Level 2."

3. Analyze the local computer. The analysis process compares the security settings on the local computer with the settings that are defined in the template that you imported, and identifies any differences.

4. Make any setting changes. Based on the comparison of the local computer's settings with those in the template file, you can make changes to any of the security settings on the local computer.

5. Save any template changes.

6. Export the new template (optional). If you made any changes to the template file, you can store the new template for later use.

7. Apply the changes to the local computer (optional). So far, you have defined what changes you might want to make to the local computer's configuration, but you haven't actually applied the changes. If you want to make the changes effective, you can choose to apply them.

There is no default icon for the Security Configuration and Analysis utility. In order to access it, you must manually choose this snap-in from within the Microsoft Management Console (MMC) tool. This image shows the Security Configuration and Analysis tool at work:

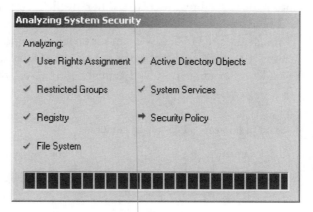

In addition to using the GUI interface, you can administer security using the secedit command-line utility. The available switches for the command (which can be obtained by typing **secedit /?**) are as follows:

```
secedit [/configure | /analyze | /import | /export
        |/validate | /generaterollback]
```

For more information about how to use the command-line options, see Help and Support, or type one of the switches without any arguments (for example, "secedit / analyze").

Understanding the Distributed File System

As a systems administrator, one of your most fundamental jobs is ensuring that your users have access to the resources that they need. By being able to quickly and easily connect to file shares and other shared storage areas, users can efficiently get to the data files and applications that they require. Although many of us take this for granted, keeping track of the location of various shares can be difficult for administrators and users alike.

One solution to this problem is to use mapped network drives (a technique that was covered earlier in this chapter). With these mappings, users can access specific storage points by remembering only a single letter. However, it's easy to see how this method isn't all that manageable or scalable. First, you're limited to only about 20 or so letters (assuming that several of the letters are already used by local storage devices). Second, although some mappings may be intuitive (like "P" for the Public storage area and "H" for a user's home directory), others may be just as hard to remember as the full pathnames themselves. Finally, you can't easily handle changes (for example, when a share is moved to a different server), or provide for fault-tolerance that will automatically redirect users to a different file server in case one is unavailable.

The Distributed File System (DFS) was designed to address many of these problems. Through the use of DFS, you can set up a hierarchical system of shared folders that your users can take advantage of to find the resources that they need. Figure 4-37 provides an example of how this might work. Note that, instead of remembering on

| **FIGURE 4-37** | A logical overview of a DFS implementation |

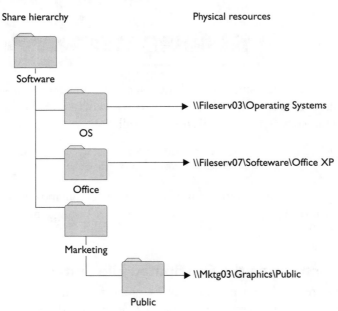

which server the "Microsoft Publisher" share is located, the user can simply navigate through the tree (from Software | Applications | Marketing | Microsoft Publisher). This functionality, by itself, can save a lot of time and administrative effort. But wait, there's more!

In addition to making resources easy to find, DFS can abstract the behind-the-scenes location of network resources. This greatly simplifies administration. For example, if I want to move the "Applications" share from Server1 to Server2, I could simply move the files and then make the corresponding change in the DFS configuration. Users would not even notice the change, since they still use the same navigation method to access their data. Furthermore, you can create a logical directory of applications independent of their physical location. For example, you could create an "Applications" share-point within both the Sales and Marketing shares and have them point to the same physical shared folder. This type of organization can make it much more intuitive for users to find the resources that they need.

on the
Job

Although DFS was first officially supported by Microsoft in Windows 2000 Server, limited but free implementations of DFS for Windows NT 4.0 Server are available as a free download from Microsoft. Note, however, that earlier implementations of DFS offer less functionality than those included with Windows Server 2003.

Through the use of this architecture, DFS can also be configured to provide for fault-tolerance and load balancing—two very important features for any network environment that relies on the data stored in shared folders. These goals are accomplished by DFS' ability to specify multiple physical shared folders for one logical one. For example, the "Applications" share-point could actually refer to three different shared folders (for example, \\Server1\Applications, \\Server2\Software\ Applications, and \\Server3\Apps). When users request access to the "Applications" share through a DFS share-point, they could be directed to the actual shared folder that is currently experiencing the least load. And, if one of the shared folders is unavailable, that one could be automatically removed from the list of available shares.

As you've seen so far, DFS offers many advantages that can be used to better manage file sharing. Another added bonus is that setting up, configuring, and managing the DFS is a simple, straightforward process that can be accomplished in just a few minutes! To create a new DFS root and to configure share points, you can launch the Distributed File System administrative tool.

Understanding DFS Architecture   In order to understand how to implement and support DFS, you should first understand the related concepts and terminology. The important components are

- **DFS Host Server**   This term refers to the server(s) on which DFS is configured.
- **DFS Root**   This location serves as the starting point for access into DFS. All shared resources on a server are logically organized under the DFS root node.
- **DFS Link**   A link is a pointer to a shared folder or to another DFS root. Links provide a method for organizing shares and point to the actual resources that are being shared.
- **Target**   A target is the actual shared resource destination to which a DFS link points.

Stand-Alone vs. Domain Configurations   You can choose to implement the DFS in a stand-alone configuration or in a domain-based configuration. In a stand-alone configuration, the basic functionality of DFS is available for use. That is, you can create new DFS links that point to targets on the local server or on remote servers. Users can connect to the stand-alone DFS root and view an organized system of shared folders. The information about the DFS configuration is stored within the Registry on the host server. Also, you can configure only a single level of folders within a stand-alone DFS configuration. Although this is useful functionality, it does leave some features to be desired.

Domain-based DFS configurations add support for the advanced features of DFS, including

- **Storage of DFS information in the Active Directory**   Since the Active Directory database is replicated between all of the domain controllers in a domain, storing DFS information there provides two major advantages. First, users can get information about the shared resources that are available through a DFS root from any domain controller. This is particular helpful in environments in which the DFS server may be very busy or may be located across a slow network link. Second, the storage of DFS information in the Active Directory provides for fault-tolerance. In the event of the failure of a DFS root server, users will still be able to get DFS information from other domain controllers.
- **Support for the File Replication Service (FRS)**   Earlier, I mentioned that systems administrators can use DFS to provide load balancing and fault-tolerance by having multiple targets for a single DFS link. The FRS is designed to keep multiple shared folders synchronized automatically.

■ **Support for multiple levels of shared folders** A stand-alone configuration of the DFS can support only one level of shared folders, but the domain configuration can support many levels. In fact, you're limited only by the fact that Windows systems allow only up to 260 characters for the entire pathname.

e x a m

ⓦ a t c h *Since the focus of this book (and the exam) is on Windows Server 2003, we'll look mainly at the features available in the stand-alone configuration. For more* *information about the domain-based configuration of DFS, see the Windows Server 2003 Help and Support Center.*

on the **ⓙ o b** *In the real world, the advantages of a domain-based DFS configuration could be enough justification for some environments to decide to deploy the Active Directory, if they haven't done so already.*

Table 4-7 provides a summary of the features of domain-based and stand-alone DFS configurations.

TABLE 4-7   Comparing Stand-Alone and Domain-Based DFS Configurations

Feature	Stand-Alone Configuration	Domain-Based Configuration	Notes
Supports multiple levels of shares	X	X	
Supports automatic replication		X	Administrators of stand-alone configurations must manually synchronize the contents of shared folders
Fault-tolerant configuration		X	In domain-based configurations, DFS information is stored in the Active Directory

DFS and Security It's important to understand that the primary purpose of DFS is to provide for ease of access to shared resources and to allow systems administrators to more easily manage these resources. DFS is *not* designed to be a security mechanism. Whether or not users can access specific resources is still dependent on the security permissions that they have on shared folders and NTFS permissions on the servers that host the targets.

DFS Client Support In order to take advantage of the DFS, clients must support DFS functionality. Newer versions of Microsoft's operating systems support DFS natively (that is, the necessary components are included with the operating systems). Others require the installation of software updates. Table 4-8 provides a

TABLE 4-8   Client-Side Support for the Distributed File System

Operating System	DFS Compatibility	Notes
Windows Server 2003	Built-in client-side and server-side support	Supports stand-alone and domain DFS server configurations
Windows 2000 Server	Built-in client-side and server-side support	Supports stand-alone and domain DFS server configurations
Windows NT 4.0 Server	Available for download from Microsoft	Requires SP3 or later to be installed; supports only the stand-alone server configuration
Windows NT 4 Workstation	Available for download from Microsoft	
Windows XP Professional and Home Edition	Built-in client-side support	
Windows 2000 Professional	Built-in client-side support	
Windows ME	Built-in client-side support	
Windows 98	Built-in basic support; update available for download from Microsoft	Basic support provides access to stand-alone DFS configurations only, but the update adds support for accessing domain-based DFS configurations
Windows 95	Available for download from Microsoft	
Windows 3.x	No support	
MS-DOS	No support	

summary of client support for DFS. All of Microsoft's Server operating systems that support DFS can function as DFS servers and DFS clients.

On the server side, in order to support automatic file replication between shares, the actual shared folders that are to be synchronized must reside on installations of Windows Server 2003 or Windows 2000 Server.

Using the Encrypting File System

Throughout this chapter, you've looked at many different ways that you can secure the file system to prevent unauthorized access to files over the network or through the operating system. But, there are potential workarounds. For example, someone could remove an NTFS-protected hard drive from your machine and place it in another machine to gain access to files. Or, they could reinstall the Windows Server 2003 operating system and give themselves full permissions over all files. Although this may sound like a huge security issue, it really underscores an important aspect of security: preventing physical access to machines that store sensitive data. Still, Microsoft has included the Encrypting File System (EFS) in Windows Server 2003 to prevent the usability of data in the case that it's stolen.

Implementing EFS is a fairly simple process, despite the complexity of everything that's going on behind the scenes. Encrypting a file or folder is a simple process: You can access the properties of the object that you want to encrypt. On the General tab, click Advanced. You will see the screen shown in the following illustration. Just select the Encrypt Contents To Secure Data option for the object. If there are child objects, you'll be prompted about whether or not you want to compress those, as well.

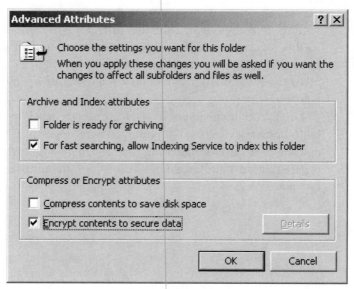

Note that NTFS compression and EFS are not compatible—that is, a file cannot be both compressed and encrypted (Microsoft should have made the two options that are listed radio buttons instead of check boxes). Although it adds security in one sense (by preventing the usability of stolen data), encryption has one major risk: If you lose the encryption key, the data will be forever useless. That's why Windows Server 2003 allows an Administrator or another designated recovery agent to restore encrypted files in the event that the original user cannot do so. You can also use the CIPHER command-line tool to administer encryption.

CERTIFICATION SUMMARY

The focus of this chapter was on one of the most important roles for servers in the real world: providing and managing access to resources. You began by looking at the basis for many of Windows Server 2003's most important security features: file system permissions. Since administering permissions is a common task for most systems administrators, features such as inheritance and the ability to propagate permissions changes can be very useful. You also learned how to determine effective permissions (both manually and using a new feature in Windows Server 2003).

Next, you looked at how shared folders can be used to provide easy access of files and folders to network users. When properly implemented, shared folders can make day-to-day activities for users and systems administrators much more efficient. You also looked at sharing another important network resource: printers. There are many ways in which systems administrators can manage and monitor printers in Windows Server 2003.

Terminal Services functionality provides systems administrators with a new method of centrally administering applications and for allowing older computers to be able to remotely run newer, more demanding applications. You looked at the many tools and methods that allow you to configure, monitor, and troubleshoot this powerful feature.

Finally, no discussion of managing resource access would be complete without including topics such as file system encryption, auditing, the Distributed File System, and the Security Configuration Manager. The purpose of all of these topics was to ensure that only authorized users can access the sensitive information that is housed on your servers!

✓ TWO-MINUTE DRILL

Manage File System Security

- ❏ File system permissions are available only on NTFS partitions.
- ❏ By default, file system permissions placed on folders are inherited by child files and folders.
- ❏ When changing permissions on folders, administrators can choose to propagate the new permissions to child objects.
- ❏ The recommended way to manage security is to assign users to groups and to provide groups with permissions on objects such as files and folders.
- ❏ When calculating effective permissions, you must take into account file system security and group membership. You can also use the Effective Permissions tab of the properties of files or folders to automatically calculate this information.

Create and Manage Shared Folders

- ❏ To enable the "file server" role, use the Configure Your Server Wizard.
- ❏ A folder that is located on the local file system can be shared for network use. A single folder can have multiple share names.
- ❏ Share permissions work in conjunction with NTFS permissions, and the most restrictive settings are what will apply to users.
- ❏ Windows Server 2003 includes many automatically created administrative shares.
- ❏ Offline folders can help make data available to users when they are not connected to the network.
- ❏ The Indexing Service can automatically index documents to increase the speed of file content searches.

Configure, Manage, and Troubleshoot Printers and Print Queues

- ❏ To enable the "print server" role, use the Configure Your Server Wizard.
- ❏ The Printers and Faxes tool is the best way to obtain information about local printers and to monitor print queues.

❑ You can remotely monitor and manage print queues using a web browser, or by navigating to the printer over the network.

❑ System Monitor includes the Print Queue object for monitoring various counters related to printing performance.

Manage and Troubleshoot Terminal Services

❑ Terminal Services protocol support can be configured using the Terminal Services Configuration tool.

❑ The Terminal Services Manager administrative tool allows systems administrators to view details related to current Terminal Services connections.

❑ Various System Monitor objects and counters can be used for monitoring and troubleshooting Terminal Services performance issues.

SELF TEST

The following questions will help you measure your understanding of the material presented in this chapter. Read all the choices carefully because there might be more than one correct answer. Choose all correct answers for each question.

Manage File System Security

1. Jennie is a member of three domain local groups: Sales Users, Sales Support, Sales Admins. You have assigned the following NTFS permissions on the Sales Leads file system folder:

   ■ **Sales Users**   Allow Read

   ■ **Sales Support**   Allow Write, Deny Read & Execute

   ■ **Sales Admins**   Allow Modify

   Which of the following options specifies Jennie's effective permissions on the Sales Leads folder? (Choose the best option.)

   A. Modify

   B. Write

   C. Read

   D. Read & Execute

   E. Cannot be determined (not enough information)

2. Paulo, a user in the Engineering department, reports that he is having problems accessing a specific folder on his local file system. Specifically, the C:\Design Documents folder appears to be empty. However, he seems to be able to copy files into that folder. Which of the following permissions will allow Paulo to see the files in this folder? (Assume that only permissions for Paulo's user account are assigned at the folder level, and choose all that apply.)

   A. Allow List Folder Contents

   B. Allow Read

   C. Allow Read & Execute

   D. Allow Modify

   E. Deny Read & Execute

3. You are attempting to remove a permission entry on a folder and you receive an error message. Which of the following is most likely to resolve the problem?

   A. Ensure that the server has network connectivity with a domain controller.

   B. Disable permissions inheritance.

    C. Enable permissions inheritance.

    D. Disable permissions propagation.

    E. Enable permissions propagation.

    F. None of the above.

4. Maria has recently called your organization's IT help desk and has reported that she is getting an "Access denied" error message when she attempts to access the C:\Data\2002 Expenses.xls file on her local computer. You verify the permissions on this folder and find that Maria's user account has explicitly been allowed Modify permissions on the file. Which of the following is a possible reason for the error message that Maria is receiving?

    A. You must propagate the permissions on the C:\Data\2002 Expenses.xls file to child objects.

    B. You must enable permissions inheritance in order for the permissions to take effect.

    C. You must disable permissions inheritance in order for the permissions to take effect.

    D. Maria's user account is a member of a group that has been denied Read permissions on the file.

    E. None of the above.

Create and Manage Shared Folders

5. You are attempting to troubleshoot a folder access problem for a user that reports she is unable to create new files when accessing a shared folder over the network. She can, however, read existing files in the shared folder. You use the Effective Permissions tab for the folder on the server, and you find that the user has an effective permission of modify. Which of the following is a likely explanation for why the user cannot access the folder?

    A. You must refresh the Effective Permissions feature with the information stored on a domain controller.

    B. Group Policy settings are preventing the necessary access to the folder.

    C. Shared folder permissions are preventing the necessary access to the folder.

    D. The user's account has been locked out.

    E. None of the above.

6. You have recently configured a new shared folder named "Invoices" on a machine named "Server1." The Invoices shared folder maps to the E:\Accounting\Invoices local folder on Server1. The share-level permissions for the Invoices shared are set to Read for all users. You have allowed Modify NTFS folder permissions on the shared folder for members of the Accounting group, and no other permissions have been set. Carl, a member of only the

Accounting group, logs on locally to Server1. What effective permissions will he have on the files stored in E:\Accounting\Invoices?

- **A.** Modify
- **B.** Read
- **C.** Full Control
- **D.** Change
- **E.** Cannot be determined (not enough information)

7. You have recently created a new shared folder on a Windows Server 2003 file server. Which of the following describes the correct default shared folder permissions?

- **A.** Administrators: Allow Full Control; Everyone: Allow Read
- **B.** Administrators: Allow Full Control; Everyone: Allow Change
- **C.** Users: Allow Change; Everyone: Allow Change
- **D.** Users: Allow Change
- **E.** Users: Allow Read
- **F.** None of the above

8. Which of the following tools or methods can you use to view how many files are currently being accessed on a Windows Server 2003 file server? (Choose all that apply.)

- **A.** Computer Management
- **B.** System Monitor
- **C.** The File Server Management Console
- **D.** The NET command-line utility

Configure, Manage, and Troubleshoot Printers and Print Queues

9. You have recently detected a problem with one of the laser printers that is managed by PrintServer1. How can you temporarily prevent jobs from being printed to the affected printer without losing the jobs in the queue? (Choose all that apply.)

- **A.** In the Printers and Faxes tool, right-click the printer and choose Use Printer Offline.
- **B.** In the properties of the affected print queue, highlight all of the current documents and select Document | Pause.
- **C.** In the properties of the affected print queue, select Printer | Cancel All Documents.
- **D.** In the Printers and Faxes tool, right-click the printer and choose Pause Printing.
- **E.** In the properties of the affected print queue, select Printer | Pause Printing.

10. You have recently configured your Windows Server 2003 machine as a print server for your department's only physical printer. In order to address complaints about some low-priority print jobs slowing down overall printing performance, you decide to implement a method by which users can specify whether their print jobs are high or low priority. You do not want to allow users to change the priority of a job after it has been submitted. In which of the following ways can you accomplish this? (Choose all that apply.)

    A. Instruct users to submit a print job and then to use the Printers and Faxes utility to change its priority.

    B. Create two logical print queues, each with a different priority, and configure each to use a different physical print device.

    C. Change the port configuration options for the logical printer.

    D. Create two logical print queues, each with a different priority, and configure both to use the same physical print device.

    E. None of the above.

11. You are a systems administrator for a large branch office that supports 35 physical printers. Recently, users have complained about having to wait for long periods of time before their print jobs are completed. The problem seems to be rare, apparently occuring only on certain printers during certain times of the week. Which of the following would be the best way to isolate which printers are causing the problem, and when the problems are occurring?

    A. Enable auditing of printer usage.

    B. Use the web-based Internet Printing functionality to view details about print queue statistics.

    C. Monitor the print queue object using System Monitor.

    D. Monitor the printer performance object using System Monitor.

    E. Use the Printers and Faxes tool to view details about print queue statistics.

Manage and Troubleshoot Terminal Services

12. Recently, you implemented a Windows Server 2003 terminal server to support your organization's Customer Support department. You currently have 35 users who connect to the server. To support those users, you have purchased and installed 35 licenses. Occasionally, however, users are receiving error messages that state the Terminal Server does not have enough licenses for them to log in. You are sure that there are never more than 30 active connections on the server at any time. Which of the following ways will allow you to avoid this problem with the least administrative effort?

    A. Change the idle session and automatic disconnection settings in the Session properties for all of the Terminal Services users.

    B. Manually monitor inactive connections using the Terminal Services Configuration tool, and disconnect inactive sessions.

    C. Manually monitor inactive connections using the Terminal Services Manager tool, and disconnect inactive sessions.

    D. Purchase and install several additional licenses on the Terminal Server.

    E. None of the above.

13. Which of the following tools will allow you to remotely control an active Terminal Services connection, assuming that the appropriate permissions have been set? (Choose all that apply.)

    A. Computer Management

    B. Terminal Services Licensing

    C. Terminal Services Configuration

    D. Terminal Services Manager

    E. Active Directory Users and Computers

    F. Manage Your Server

14. Anh wants to use System Monitor to track the CPU usage for a specific, currently active Terminal Services session. Specifically, she wants to track statistics over a period of several days and record them for later analysis. Which of the following System Monitor counters will allow her to monitor this information? (Choose one.)

    A. Terminal Services Session | % Processor Time

    B. Terminal Services Session | % Privileged Time

    C. Terminal Services | Active Sessions

    D. Terminal Services | Total Sessions

    E. None of the above

LAB QUESTION

You are a systems administrator for the Corporate office of a large multinational organization. Specifically, your job requirements include implementing and monitoring file services for this entire location. Over time, your users have demanded additional disk space and easier access to their documents. You have recently met with Corporate Management to determine the requirements for upgraded file services.

    Your business-related requirements include the following:

■ All users must store the master copies of all of their files on a file server, in order to facilitate backups and to provide for centralized security administration.

■ Each user must have her own "private" server storage space, plus access to both department-specific and company-wide shared folders for sharing files.

■ Members of the Sales and Marketing groups, as well as all Vice Presidents, must have the ability to easily take files offline when they leave the office.

■ You must log access to security-sensitive files and folders. For example, you want to log information about unauthorized access attempts to the Executive shared folder. The files stored within the folder must be stored securely.

■ Certain branch managers should also have access to some files stored on Corporate file servers.

■ The IT department will provide monthly reports of disk usage to all of the other departments. Funds for purchasing additional hardware (such as hard disks) will come from department budgets.

In addition to these business requirements, you have a developed a set of technical requirements. These include the following:

■ You want to be able to monitor file system performance for seven critical file servers from a single console. You want to view real-time information, and you want to track disk performance over time.

■ The solution must allow you to monitor disk space usage per user.

■ Your servers must be able to continue functioning, even in the event of the failure of a hard disk.

Considering these requirements, you have decided to implement several new Windows Server 2003 machines at the Corporate office. Which operating system features will allow you to best meet these requirements?

SELF TEST ANSWERS

Manage File System Security

1. ☑ **B.** Jennie's effective permissions on the folder will be Write. To determine the effective permissions, start by "adding" all of the allowed permissions. In this case, that would leave you with Allow Modify (which includes read and write permissions). Then, you should subtract all of the Deny permissions. Denying Read & Execute will leave only Write and Delete permissions on the folder.

☒ **A, C and D** are incorrect because of the additive nature of permissions and the overriding nature of the Deny permission.

2. ☑ **A, B, C,** and **D.** All of these settings will allow Paulo to view the contents of the folder.

☒ **E** is incorrect because this setting would not specifically allow Paulo to view the contents of the folder.

3. ☑ **B.** The most likely error message is one that states that the permissions cannot be removed since they are being inherited from a parent folder. In order to remove the permission, you must first disable inheritance by accessing the Advanced security properties.

☒ **A** is incorrect because the lack of network connectivity generally will not cause an error message to occur when setting permissions. C, D, and E are incorrect because they will not enable you to remove the permissions entry.

4. ☑ **D.** It is mostly likely that Maria is a member of a group that has been denied permissions to access the file. Since the question doesn't mention whether or not Maria is a member of any other groups, you should check this first. You can also use the Effective Permissions tab of the file to determine whether this is the cause of the problem.

☒ **A** is incorrect because propagation is available for files (since files cannot have child objects). B and C are incorrect because, by checking the existing permissions on the file, you have determined that inherited permissions are not the problem.

Create and Manage Shared Folders

5. ☑ **C.** Since the user is able to access current files in the shared folder, and the Effective Permissions feature reports sufficient permissions, the most likely cause of the problem is share-level permissions. Since the Effective Permissions functionality does not take into account share-level permissions, you must check these settings manually when troubleshooting problems that involve accessing the file over the network.

☒ **A** is incorrect because the Effective Permissions functionality does not specifically require synchronization with a domain controller. B is incorrect because the user can access the shared folder, but she cannot create new files. D is incorrect because the user must have been able to log on in order to access the shared folder at all.

6. ☑ **A.** Carl will effectively have Modify permissions on the files. In this case, the shared folder permissions do not have any bearing on the overall effective permissions, since Carl is logging on locally.

   ☒ **B, C,** and **D** are incorrect because the only permissions that will affect access to these files are the file system permissions.

7. ☑ **F.** When a new shared folder is created, the default permissions are to provide the Everyone group with Read shared-level permissions.

   ☒ None of the other options define the default permissions that are placed on a new shared folder.

8. ☑ **A, B, C,** and **D.** All of these tools provide a method for viewing information about the open files on a server computer.

Configure, Manage, and Troubleshoot Printers and Print Queues

9. ☑ **A, B, D,** and **E.** All of these options are available for temporarily disabling printing without losing any queued print jobs. When a printer is specified as being "offline" or the "pause printing" option is selected, users can still submit jobs to the printer. However, the jobs will not be physically printed until the printer is brought back online.

   ☒ **C** is incorrect because canceling the documents will cause them to disappear from the queue. Users will need to resubmit their print jobs in order for them to be printed after the problem is correct.

10. ☑ **D.** In Windows Server 2003, you can create multiple logical print queues for a single printing device. Since your department has only a single physical printer, you can create two queues with different priorities. Users can then specify to which print queue their jobs will be submitted, according to the priority of the job.

    ☒ **A** is incorrect because it will require users to manually modify print jobs after they are submitted. **B** is incorrect because the question states that you have only one physical print device. **C** is incorrect because changing port options will not affect printing priority.

11. ☑ **C.** The best method for tracking performance issues, especially when supporting many different print devices, is to use the System Monitor to monitor printing-related statistics over time. Specifically, the print queue object can return details related to the number of pages printed per unit of time and the number of jobs processed.

    ☒ **A** is incorrect because this method would not necessarily provide details related to how large specific print jobs were, and how long they took to process. It would also be difficult to track the many audit events that would be generated for your organization's 35 printers. B and E are incorrect because these methods would not provide a good way to track the performance of many printers over time. They are both designed to provide a quick snapshot of current printer activity. D is incorrect because this is not a System Monitor performance object.

Manage and Troubleshoot Terminal Services

12. ☑ **A.** The likely cause of this issue is that users are disconnecting from their Terminal Server sessions, instead of logging out. Even when their connections are inactive, server licenses are counted as in use. By setting automatic disconnection and idle time properties, you can automatically log off inactive users.

    ☒ B is incorrect because this tool does not provide detailed information about current sessions. C is incorrect because it would involve manually monitoring the Terminal Server. D is incorrect because this would only raise the threshold at which licenses are used up, and it will not prevent the problem from recurring in the future.

13. ☑ **D.** Only the Terminal Services Manager allows you to view current connections and to remotely connect to them.

    ☒ A, B, C, E, and F are incorrect because they do not allow you to remotely connect to a Terminal Services session.

14. ☑ **A.** The Terminal Services Session object will allow Anh to collect performance statistics that are related to a single Terminal Services connection. By using System Monitor, she can track performance over time and save the data for later analysis.

    ☒ B is incorrect because this will not track CPU usage. C and D are incorrect because they do not allow the monitoring of a single Terminal Services connection.

LAB ANSWER

If you've read through all of the sections of this chapter, it should be fairly easy to figure out which tools, features, and technologies will help you meet the requirements presented in this question. Let's look at some potential approaches.

First, let's start with the business requirements (all of which might seem familiar, if you've administered file servers in the past). The first requirements—that users store their files on servers—is technically a simple one. Once you configure the "file server" role for your Windows Server 2003 machines, you will be able to create shared folders. The second business requirement suggests that you might want to create many different shared folders. The first might be a "Home" folder, within which each user will have his or her own private folder. The permissions for these folders will be set such that only the Owner will have access to those files. Next, an office-wide "Public" folder might be created to accommodate the sharing of files between departments. Finally, department-specific shared folders (such as "Sales," "Engineering," "Research," and "Executive") would allow users and systems administrators to effectively manage their files. You can implement mapped network drives (ideally through logon scripts or other settings) to ensure that users can use familiar device letters for storing their files.

A good way to make files available to users that travel is the Offline Files and Folders feature. This is very easy to set up in Windows Server 2003, and it should be a good solution for all but the most sensitive files (which you may not allow to be taken offline for security reasons). One shared folder that will require additional consideration is the "Executive" folder. To meet the security requirements for this folder, you start by ensuring that you have the appropriate effective permissions set for users that should have access to these files. For additional protection, you should implement auditing (to track unauthorized access attempts), and file system encryption (to protect the files, themselves, from unauthorized access).

Another business requirement is to allow specific branch office managers to access files stored on Corporate file servers. Windows Server 2003 and the Active Directory are well designed to meet these requirements. Through the use of domain and local groups, as well as Organizational Units, you can easily administer access to these folders.

Let's look at a couple of the technical requirements that we haven't yet covered. You want to be able to track disk usage by user and (for budgeting purposes) by department. This can be accomplished through the use of disk quotas. You also want to implement fault-tolerance for your file servers' hard disks. That's a job for Windows Server 2003's mirrored or RAID-5 disk volumes. Both topics (disk quotas and advanced disk configurations) are covered in Chapter 5. Finally, you'll want to monitor your file servers for real-time performance information, and for data that you can collect over weeks and months. You can use System Monitor to easily perform both of these types of tasks (see Chapter 8 for details).

As you can see, the many file services features in Windows Server 2003 can be used to meet many different business and technical requirements. Keep these in mind as you prepare for the exam!

5

Managing Storage Resources

CERTIFICATION OBJECTIVES

O ne of the most important duties of a server is to store data and provide information to the users that need it. From database servers that house critical company information to file servers that store users' important documents, managing storage resources is an important aspect of server administration. As a Windows Server 2003 systems administrator, you'll need to know how to implement and manage fixed storage devices, in terms of your organization's requirements.

For decades, the hard disk drive has been the primary storage device for all kinds of data. As organizations' needs have evolved, so too have methods for implementing and managing storage solutions. By testing you on the exam objectives covered in this chapter, Microsoft wants to make sure that you not only understand the basics of how fixed storage works in Windows Server 2003, but also how to create optimal configurations given various requirements.

In this chapter, you'll take a detailed look at how hard disk–based storage is managed in Windows Server 2003. You'll start by taking an overview of disk architecture in general, including an overview of file system choices. Then, you'll move on to basic disks and dynamic disks. Of particular interest will be advanced configurations that allow for increased performance and fault tolerance. These are features that many environments can quickly and easily put to use for added peace of mind. You'll also look at many of the different methods in which storage resources can be managed— including familiar GUI tools, command-line utilities, and features such as disk quotas. Let's get started by looking at how Windows Server 2003 manages disk-based storage.

CERTIFICATION OBJECTIVE 5.01

Understanding and Selecting Server Disk Configurations

In many ways, the Windows platform has come a long way since the days of the popular Windows 3.1 operating system (which ran on top of MS-DOS). Since that time, some aspects of disk management have changed dramatically. Other concepts have remained fairly static. Microsoft has designed Windows Server 2003 to provide a reliable, high-performance, flexible disk architecture. In this section, you'll start by looking at the types of file systems and disk configurations that are available.

General Disk Concepts

If you're new to working on PC-based storage technologies, it's a good idea to take a few minutes to understand some basic disk concepts. You'll rely on a solid understanding of these concepts throughout this chapter as you learn of the ways in which Windows Server 2003 manages storage.

First, let's start with the basic hard disk drive. This device is the actual hardware that is responsible for recording data on magnetic platters. Hard disk drives are considered "fixed" media because they generally are not designed to be removed from servers. The operating system and required files must be stored on fixed storage devices, since they're always required. Additionally, user files, databases, program files, and other information will generally be stored on fixed storage devices.

In most servers, hard disks are attached to a hard disk controller that is located physically within the server itself. Each hard disk can be attached to only one controller at a time, and each controller can control multiple devices. The purpose of the hard disk controller is to manage communications between the operating system and the actual physical hard disk devices. Among the controller's responsibilities is ensuring that read and write operations are performed accurately and efficiently.

There are two common hardware specifications used in modern servers. The first is called Integrated Device Electronics (IDE). IDE-based hard disks have been supported in PC-based computers for many years, although related specifications have evolved. IDE hard disk controllers (which are often integrated into the motherboards of modern servers) can support two IDE devices per controller channel. Most systems include two IDE controller channels to support up to four total devices. Common IDE devices include hard disk drives, CD-ROM drives, CD-recordable devices, DVD-ROM devices, DVD-recordable devices, and other removable storage solutions. Throughout the past several years, the performance of IDE devices has improved significantly while their costs have decreased, making IDE devices a reasonable choice for many server implementations.

The Small Computer System Interface (SCSI) standard, like IDE, has been around for quite a while. SCSI hard disks and hard disk controllers can offer improved performance over IDE devices for several reasons. First, each SCSI controller can support up to seven logical devices (including the controller itself). The benefit is obvious—servers can include many hard disk devices with a limited number of controllers. Next, SCSI hard disk devices tend to provide higher performance due to lower latency and higher rotation speeds. SCSI controllers can also efficiently manage multiple concurrent requests for storage resources more efficiently than can IDE controllers. Another advantage of SCSI technology is that modern implementations may allow for "hot-plugging" of hard disks. This means that, assuming that the hardware supports it, hard disks can be dynamically added or removed from a server while the machine is up and running. Of course, all of these advantages come at a price—the cost of SCSI solutions is generally far higher than the cost of IDE-based storage solutions (at least in the area of initial purchase cost).

It's important to note that this section covers what is the most common configuration for small- to medium-sized servers. There are, of course, other technologies that involve storage virtualization and the recording of data on disk arrays that are not physically connected to a machine. More information about these types of configurations is available from storage hardware and software vendors.

Regardless of the hardware technology used, hard disks must be partitioned to support volumes, partitions, and file systems. Now that you have a basic understanding of hard disk technology from the hardware side, let's take a look at how these resources can be configured in Windows Server 2003.

Since storage resource management is so important, new technologies such as network attached storage (NAS) and storage area networks (SANs) are becoming popular choices for medium- to large-sized organizations. Although you're unlikely to be asked questions related to these technologies, keep them in mind when you're working in the real world.

Choosing a File System

A file system specifies how data is actually stored on devices such as hard disks. All operating systems support at least one type of file system. Windows Server 2003 supports three different file systems for local volumes. The options are file allocation table (FAT), FAT32, and NTFS. Let's look at the purposes and functions of these different file systems.

FAT and FAT32

The FAT file system dates back to the days of Microsoft's MS-DOS product line. It was originally designed to provide a simple, easy-to-use system for storing files on a personal computer. FAT provides basic functionality for reading, writing, moving, and copying files. However, FAT has several limitations, including lack of support for long filenames and inefficient use of space on larger hard disks.

To overcome these limitations, Microsoft introduced the FAT32 file system with its Windows 95 operating system. The most significant new features in FAT32 included support for long filenames and improved efficiency in using larger hard disk partitions. In Windows Server 2003, the FAT and FAT32 file systems are supported for backward compatibility and are used mainly for dual-boot situations (for supporting access to earlier operating systems such as MS-DOS, and Windows 95/98/ME).

As you may have guessed, there are other limitations to using FAT-based partitions. First, since FAT and FAT32 file systems were originally designed to provide storage for basic personal computer applications, they do not provide for any file-system security. That is, one cannot set file system permissions on a FAT-based partition—all users will have access to all data on that system. The closest thing to file system protection is setting files to "read-only," but even with that, any user can simply change it back to read/write. Also, FAT partitions are limited in reliability features.

NTFS

To overcome many of the limitations of FAT-based file systems, Microsoft included the NTFS file system in its Windows NT operating system platform. The NTFS file system provides many features and advantages over other file systems, including the following:

- **File system security**   Files and folders stored on NTFS partitions include *access control lists (ACLs)* that can be used to specify which users and groups have access to files. Through the use of file system security, systems administrators can assign very granular permissions to users and groups. This feature is integral to a secure operating system and is the basis for controlling storage resource access.

- **Support for large volumes**   NTFS supports files and volumes of up to 16 exabytes (which is one *billion* gigabytes). This support overcomes the partition size limitations imposed by FAT file systems, and it makes more efficient use of disk space on larger devices.

- **Encryption**   The purpose of encryption is to encode data in a format that prevents it from being used, even if it is intercepted by unauthorized users. When working in networked environments, it's especially important to consider this level of security for sensitive data. Encrypted files will remain unintelligible even if they are read from outside the operating system. For example, if a hard disk is moved between Windows Server 2003 computers, users must have the encryption key in order to access encrypted files.

■ **Compression** NTFS supports the ability to compress files at the level of the file system redirector. The effect is that users and systems administrators can choose to quickly and easily enable compression, and all of the work is handled seamlessly behind the scenes.

exam
ⓦatch
A good rule of thumb is to use NTFS whenever you can and to use FAT or FAT32 partitions whenever you must. Keep this in mind when you're asked to select a file system for a Windows Server 2003 machine. Unless you have "special circumstances" (such as supporting multiboot configurations or older operating systems), the best choice is likely to be NTFS.

Whenever you format a new partition, you'll have to choose the file system that should be used. This can be specified during the installation of Windows Server 2003 (where you can choose to create new partitions or to convert them, as shown in Figure 5-1).

Or, you can use the various tools (which you'll look at later in this chapter) to change the file system on an existing volume. It's important to note that FAT and FAT32 partitions can be converted to NTFS, but NTFS partitions cannot be converted to FAT or FAT32 partitions

FIGURE 5-1 Selecting a file system type during installation

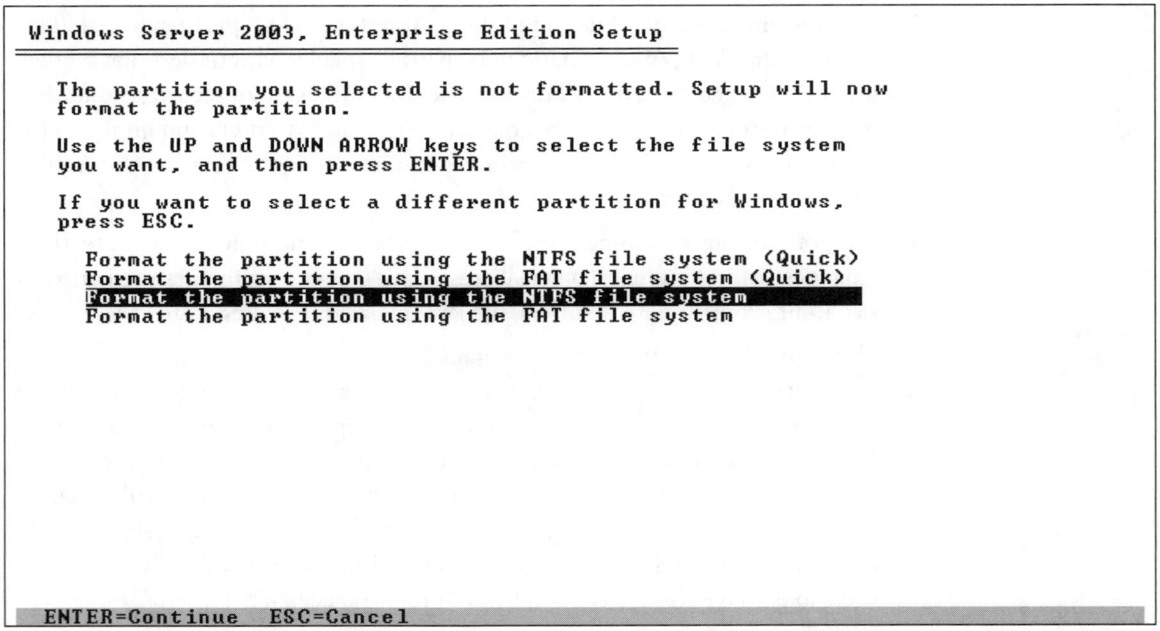

```
Windows Server 2003, Enterprise Edition Setup

    The partition you selected is not formatted. Setup will now
    format the partition.

    Use the UP and DOWN ARROW keys to select the file system
    you want, and then press ENTER.

    If you want to select a different partition for Windows,
    press ESC.

        Format the partition using the NTFS file system (Quick)
        Format the partition using the FAT file system (Quick)
        Format the partition using the NTFS file system
        Format the partition using the FAT file system

    ENTER=Continue   ESC=Cancel
```

(without a complete loss of data). You'll look at how partition types can be selected and converted later in this chapter. For now, however, keep in mind that the NTFS file system provides many benefits over the older and more limited FAT and FAT32 partition types.

Understanding Disk Types

In Windows Server 2003, two main types of disks can be configured—basic disks and dynamic disks. Again, the concern here is related to backward compatibility. Basic disks provide support for older operating systems, whereas dynamic disks provide many advantages. Let's take a look at the details of each.

Basic Disks

If you've worked with earlier versions of Windows, you're probably familiar with what Microsoft refers to as "basic disks" in Windows Server 2003. *Basic disks* are compatible with operating systems ranging from MS-DOS up through current Windows operating systems.

A basic disk can consist of multiple partitions. Two types of partitions are possible:

- **Primary partitions** A primary partition can be used to boot an operating system. You can configure up to four primary partitions on a single physical disk. Or, you can configure up to three primary partitions and one extended partition. Primary partitions can be marked as "Active," indicating that they can be used to boot computers using many different types of operating systems.

- **Extended partition** A physical disk can consist of up to one extended partition. Extended partitions are not bootable, but each can hold multiple

SCENARIO & SOLUTION	
You want to implement a file system that allows for the use of long filenames.	Implement either FAT32 or NTFS.
You are setting up a test machine that will allow booting from Windows ME, Windows NT 4.0, and Windows 2003 Server.	You must configure at least one partition with the FAT or FAT32 file system in order to support this configuration.
You need to implement a secure Windows 2003 Server system that will host a sensitive database.	Implement NTFS for all partitions.

logical partitions. For example, a single extended partition might include the logical "E:", "F:", and "G:" partitions.

This may sound a bit confusing, so let's take a look at some examples of basic disk configurations. Figure 5-2 provides an example of some basic disk configurations.

Basic disks are recommended primarily for use on portable computers, and on machines in which multiple boot configurations are required. For example, if you are dual-booting Windows Server 2003 and Windows ME, you must keep at least one disk configured as a basic disk. However, this compatibility comes at a price, as basic disks cannot be used in advanced disk configurations.

Dynamic Disks

Although basic disks will meet simple storage needs for many systems, Windows Server 2003 supports many additional features through *dynamic disks*. Dynamic disks provide several advantages over basic disks. First, dynamic disks can be added to and removed from a system while the operating system is still running (assuming that the hardware platform supports this). Dynamic disks can be configured to provide for fault tolerance, and to take advantage of several different disk configurations that span multiple disks. When you create a dynamic disk, Windows Server 2003 writes information that uniquely describes the disk. This information can be used when disks are moved between server machines, or when volumes need to be reconfigured.

A dynamic disk can contain one or more *dynamic volumes*. Windows Server 2003 supports several different configurations of dynamic volumes, including the following:

- Simple volumes
- Spanned volumes

FIGURE 5-2

Various partition schemes for basic disks

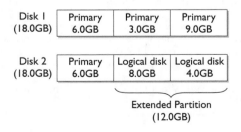

- Striped volumes
- Mirrored volumes
- RAID-5 volumes

Each has various benefits related to disk management, disk performance, and fault tolerance. You'll look at each of these volume configurations in detail, later in this section.

Support for Itanium-Based Servers

Windows Server 2003 provides support for Intel-based 64-bit platforms in various editions (Intel's 64-bit processor is known as the Itanium). Although the majority of the content that I'll present in this chapter pertains equally to 32- and 64-bit systems, there are some differences. The 32-bit computer systems use a disk configuration based on a *master boot record (MBR)*. In contrast, Itanium-based computers use a partition type known as a *GUID partition table (GPT)*. While most of this is handled behind the scenes, you should be aware of the difference.

The boot process for Itanium-based servers differs from that of MBR systems in that an Extensible Firmware Interface (EFI) partition is used to store code that is used to start up the system. For more details related to EFI, see the Windows Server 2003 Help and Support Center and your server's documentation. If you're running Windows Server 2003 on an Itanium-based server, you can convert an MBR disk to a GPT disk.

Both basic disks and dynamic disks are supported on GPT-based systems. Therefore, the same disk configurations covered throughout this chapter are supported on both MBR- and GPT-based systems.

Dynamic Disk Configurations and RAID

You already know that dynamic disks are designed to provide greater reliability, flexibility, and fault tolerance when compared to basic disks. As any experienced systems administrator can attest, it's a simple fact that hardware can and will fail. Unfortunately, we can't predict when events like hard disk crashes will occur. However, we can reasonably protect against them to minimize the likelihood and potential damage from these failures. In this section, you'll look at the details of how dynamic disk configurations can help mitigate some of these risks.

A mature IT industry standard known as *RAID (redundant array of independent disks)* technology provides higher levels of fault tolerance and, in some cases, improved disk performance. Microsoft has provided multiple levels of RAID functionality within Windows Server 2003, although the terminology used is slightly different. In this section, you'll take a look at how various configurations of dynamic disks provide improved disk manageability.

on the job

You may still come across literature that explains the RAID acronym as standing for "redundant array of inexpensive disks." Originally, the acronym was based on a comparison of the type of storage found in mainframe and high-end computer storage (which tended to be highly reliable, but also very expensive), and other available disk technologies. The thinking was that several smaller, less reliable, storage devices could be combined to equal the reliability of the then much more expensive storage units. Times have changed, however, and the term Independent is much more meaningful in current computing environments.

Spanned Volumes

One of the most commonly experienced problems for systems administrators is running out of disk space. It seems that no matter how much disk space is available, users will want more! Using only basic disk configurations, this can present problems. For example, there's no way for me to simply "add" additional disk space to my D: partition, even after I install a new hard disk in my server. Instead, I'd have to create a new volume and somehow allocate the new space to users (using a new file share or different drive mappings). Fortunately, for anyone that's ever wished that they could add two volumes together to appear as one, there's a good solution. A *spanned volume* is a single logical volume that consists of space from two or more regions of unallocated space on dynamic disks. Spanned volumes are designed to consolidate space from multiple volumes into a single logical device. Figure 5-3 provides an example of a spanned volume. In this configuration, users access the entire volume using the logical volume letter of "G:". The actual data that is stored on the volume is spread across the various partitions that make up the spanned volume. Note that a spanned volume can contain multiple partitions located on the same physical disk, or on different physical disks.

Another big management benefit of dealing with spanned volumes is that they can be extended after they're originally created. So, if you need to add more disk space to your "E:" drive to support additional users, you can simply add a new hard disk (or use unallocated space from an existing one) to the existing spanned device. As a systems administrator, you won't have to move any of the data between partitions, and your users won't even notice the change (except for the fact that there is now more storage space on that volume). Unfortunately, once a partition is added to a spanned volume, it cannot be removed without deleting and re-creating the entire logical volume.

A spanned
volume: The "G:"
device actually
contains space
from multiple
partitions.

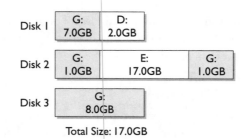

That means that you'll lose all of the data on all of the volumes in the spanned set if
you want to change the configuration of the spanned volume.

When data is written to a spanned volume, it is written to the various partitions
that make up the volume in sequence. That is, information will first be written to
the first physical storage space in the spanned volume. When this partition is filled,
subsequent data will be written to the next physical partition. Figure 5-4 provides
an example of how data is written to a spanned volume. The performance effects of
using a spanned volume are generally negligible—that is, performance is not significantly
increased nor decreased when comparing the speed of a spanned volume with that of
multiple logical partitions configured on the same disks.

Spanned volumes offer convenience in administration by allowing you to access
free space on multiple disks using a single logical drive letter or path. However, there
are drawbacks to using spanned volumes. First and foremost, it's important to understand
that spanned volumes are *not* fault-tolerant. In fact, the implementation of spanned
volumes can *increase* the number of potential points of failure for a dynamic disk.
That is, if one of the drives in the spanned volume set fails, the entire volume will

How data is
written to a
spanned volume

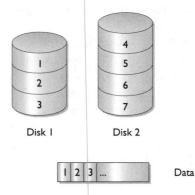

be compromised, and you will lose all of the data stored on the entire logical spanned volume. This is an important trade-off to consider in the real world, since it can put your data at risk.

Striped Volumes

A *striped volume* is very similar in purpose and concept to a spanned volume. A striped volume consists of multiple physical partitions that are combined into one logical volume. Striped volumes differ from spanned volumes in the way that data is written to (and, consequently, read from) the disk. In a striped volume, data is written to the various partitions that are part of the volume in small chunks. If you're writing a large file to a striped volume that consists of four physical partitions, approximately 25 percent of the file will be stored on each of the four partitions.

Figure 5-5 provides an example of how data is written to a striped volume. Note that data is written to all of the physical partitions concurrently. This can result in faster read and write performance, since the method of "striping" data allows multiple physical hard disks to work on reading or writing files concurrently. By reducing the bottleneck of the disk subsystem waiting for data to be read by a single hard disk device, multiple drives can be working concurrently. Striped volumes can also improve scalability for file servers and other server-side applications, since it allows multiple concurrent requests to be serviced much more efficiently than would be possible using a single hard disk.

on the
①ob

It's important to keep in mind that the expected performance improvements stated for various disk configurations are based on the technical mechanisms by which they work. In the real world, you will need to test your hardware to determine the actual noticeable effects of these techniques. You might find that some effects are negligible.

You cannot extend a striped volume, nor can you remove partitions from the striped volume once it has been created. For this reason, striped volumes are a little less manageable than spanned volumes (which allow you to add available disk space without re-creating the volume).

Striped volumes present the same vulnerability as spanned volumes: If one of the physical volumes in the striped volume fails, you will lose all of the data stored on the entire logical volume. You should always keep this in mind when deciding whether or not to implement disk striping.

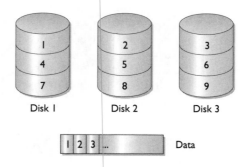

FIGURE 5-5

How data is
written to striped
volumes

Disk 1   Disk 2   Disk 3

Data

on the

ob

Perhaps the lack of fault tolerance is one reason that striped volumes are also known as RAID-0 (or "disk striping")—they don't meet the "redundancy" requirement for RAID.

Mirrored Volumes

The concept of *mirrored volumes* is rather simple: As the term suggests, a mirrored volume consists of two disks, each of which is an exact copy of the other. Whenever data is written to one volume in a mirror, the data is also written to the other volume. When data is being read, it can be read from either volume. In order to create a mirrored volume, you must have two partitions of equal size (although the total space on the devices may be different). It is recommended that you use two entire physical drives that are of the same size (and, preferably, from the same manufacturer) when you create a mirrored volume. Figure 5-6 provides a depiction of a mirrored volume. Notice that 50 percent of the total available disk space will be unusable for stored data. That is, if you have two 18GB hard disks (36.0GB of total disk space) configured in a mirrored volume, you will be able to store a total of only 18GB of data on the volume.

A mirrored volume can have effects on performance. First, the bad news: Since data must be written to two physical disks instead of one, there will likely be a performance decrease for write operations. However, this performance impact may be minimal, since the two disks can be written to independently, and most modern disk controllers can send write commands to multiple devices at the same time. Now, some good news: Since data can be read from one of two physical hard disks, mirrored volumes can benefit from increased read performance. The only other performance effect to be considered is that disk I/O will be slowed down when a mirror is being created (and when a mirror needs to be regenerated in the event of a failure).

FIGURE 5-6

A mirrored
volume
configuration

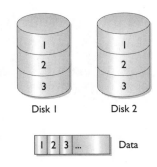

Disk 1   Disk 2

| 1 | 2 | 3 | ... | Data

on the job   ***Disk mirroring is also known as RAID Level 1 (defined as "disk mirroring").***

The fundamental purpose of disk mirroring is to provide fault tolerance—that is, the ability of a machine to continue to operate in the event that a hard disk fails. Disk mirroring is also the only fault-tolerant technology that's supported for Windows Server 2003 boot and system partitions.

Disk Duplexing

Although disk mirroring provides a certain level of fault tolerance (that is, it prevents data loss and downtime when one of the mirrored disks fails), it does not prevent the failure of a single disk controller from making the drives unavailable. *Disk duplexing* is designed to get around this by using separate disk controllers for each of the two drives in the mirrored volume (see Figure 5-7). Physically, this may be implemented through the use of multiple SCSI adapters, or multiple IDE controllers. Disk duplexing also provides the additional benefit of increasing disk write performance (although the overall effect with mirroring might still be a decrease in performance).

Since the storage on a mirrored volume is fault-tolerant, a mirrored volume can be "broken" in order to allow full use of both disks in the mirrored volume.

exam

watch   ***Disk duplexing is a purely physical solution—there's no way to "configure" disk duplexing in Windows Server 2003 (other than being sure to create mirror copies on disks that are attached to different physical controllers).***

RAID-5 Volumes

If you've been thinking ahead about various disk configurations, you're probably interested in finding a solution that provides the performance benefits of disk striping with fault tolerance. Well, look no further! RAID-5 volumes are

Using disk
duplexing to
remove the disk
controller as a
point of failure

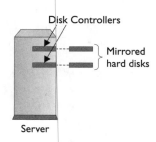

Disk Controllers

Mirrored
hard disks

Server

similar in design to striped volumes with one important difference: RAID-5 volumes store parity information that can be used to regenerate data in the event of the failure of one of the members in the logical volume. They are, therefore, fault-tolerant. The concept is that, if a disk should fail, the information stored on the other disks in the volume can be used to rebuild the lost data. Figure 5-8 provides a depiction of how data is written to a RAID-5 volume (also known as a "stripe set with parity").

At least three (but not more than 32) physical devices are required in order to build a RAID-5 volume. When data is written to a RAID-5 volume, parity information is calculated, and the data and parity are written in stripes across the disks. For example, in a three-disk RAID-5 configuration, stripes of data and parity are stored on each of the disks. The end result is that the amount of usable space in the volume will be decreased by the size of one of the disks in the volume. For example, if you have a RAID-5 volume that is made up of four 18GB hard disks (a total of 72.0GB of physical disk space), you will be able to use only 54.0GB for storing data.

on the

Job

It is incorrect to think that, in a RAID-5 volume, one drive is used for storing the parity information while the other two devices store actual data. Actually, all of the disks contain data and parity information. That specific configuration is actually called a RAID-4 volume (also known as a "volume set with parity"). Since disk striping provides benefits over volume striping, RAID-4 is rarely used in production environments.

The main benefit of RAID-5 volumes is that they provide fault tolerance. As with the other dynamic volume configurations, there are performance impacts. This time, let's start with the good news: Read operations are faster when you use RAID-5. This is because, as with striped volumes, multiple physical disks can be used to read data. The drawback is in the area of writing to the volume. Since parity information must be calculated and written to disk for all data that is being stored, write performance can be considerably slower (especially for software-based RAID

FIGURE 5-8

How data is
written to a
RAID-5 volume

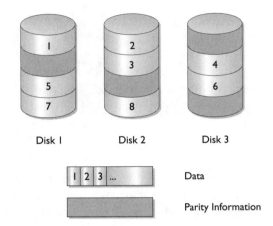

solutions). This is because approximately three times as much memory (as well as the associated CPU overhead) must be used, and the disk controllers and hard disks must write more data to the disks. Furthermore, although the disk array is fault-tolerant, performance will be decreased in the event of a failure of one of the disks in the volume.

Recovering from a RAID-5 Disk Failure   Recovering from the failure of one of the disks in a RAID-5 array is a fairly simple process. Using the Disk Management tool (which you'll read about later in this chapter), you can simply choose to reactivate or repair the failed portion of the array. This process will use the parity information and data stored on the other portions of the logical volume to recalculate the information that was stored on the failed volume. It's important to note that you will experience increased CPU utilization and a decrease in overall disk performance until the failure is repaired, since every read request will require data to be recalculated. Similarly, the process of rebuilding the failed portion of the volume will put a load on the computer's CPU, disk controllers, and hard disks. Keep this in mind when you are deciding when you want to replace the failed partition (some administrators may choose to do this during off-hours, while others may choose to "bite the bullet" and do it as quickly as possible).

Remember that if more than one disk in the RAID-5 volume fails, you will lose all of the data on the entire logical volume. In that case, you'll need to delete all of the volumes that are part of the RAID-5 configuration and re-create the volume from scratch.

on the
job

I've often heard systems administrators (and, especially, misinformed vendors) claim that adding additional disks to a RAID-5 volume will improve reliability. Actually, the exact opposite is true. Remember, the more disks that you have in a system, the greater the chance is of two drives failing before you can repair one.

Summary of Dynamic Disk Technologies

So far, you've looked at several different types of dynamic volume configurations that are support by Windows Server 2003. Let's summarize the strengths and weaknesses of these configurations before we move on. Table 5-1 provides a comparison of the different configurations that are possible for dynamic disk configurations, along with their strengths and weaknesses.

Upgrading from a Windows NT 4.0 Multidisk Configuration

Microsoft made changes to the disk storage architecture (including the addition of the dynamic volumes feature) starting with the Windows 2000 platform. Table 5-2 matches up the disk configurations available in Windows NT 4.0 with those that are available in Windows Server 2003.

If you are upgrading directly from Windows NT 4.0 to Windows Server 2003, preexisting volume sets and stripe sets can be preserved as part of the upgrade. After

| **TABLE 5-1** | Comparing Features of Multiple Types of Different Dynamic Volumes |

Technology	Minimum # of Disks	Unusable Space	Types of Partitions	Fault-Tolerant	Read Performance	Write Performance
Spanned volumes	2	None	System and boot partitions cannot participate	No	Negligible	Negligible
Striped volumes	2	None	System and boot partitions cannot participate	No	Increased	Increased
Mirrored volumes	2	50%	Any (including system or boot partitions)	Yes	Increased	Decreased
RAID-5 volumes	3	Equal to the size of one of the members in the volume	System and boot partitions cannot participate	Yes	Increased	Decreased

TABLE 5-2	Windows NT 4.0 Disk Configuration	Windows Server 2003 Disk Configuration
Comparing Windows NT 4.0 and Windows Server 2003 Disk Configurations	Volume set	Spanned volume
	Stripe set	Striped volume
	Mirror set	Mirrored volume
	Striped set with parity	RAID-5 volume

the upgrade process, you will be bound by Windows Server 2003's rules—specifically, that means that you must convert disks to dynamic disks before you can create new multidisk configurations. An alternative for upgrading (and your only choice if you're performing a new installation), is to back up all of your Windows NT 4.0 disks and then restore the data to newly created Windows Server 2003 disk configurations.

Using Hardware RAID Solutions

Windows Server 2003 includes technology only for implementing software-based RAID. That is, the overhead related to creating and managing dynamic volumes such as striped sets, disk mirroring, and RAID-5 volumes is managed by the operating system. As you

SCENARIO & SOLUTION

You want to implement fault tolerance for a system or boot partition.	Implement mirrored volumes.
You want to combine space from four physical hard disks into one logical volume. You want to make sure that the resulting volume is fault-tolerant.	Implement a RAID-5 volume.
You want to combine space from multiple physical hard disks into one logical volume. You want to make the most efficient use of disk space.	Implement a spanned or striped volume. Both methods will meet the requirements, although the striped volume may result in better performance.
You want to create a single volume that contains space from two different physical hard disks. You want to be able to easily extend this volume when you add new hard disks.	Implement a spanned volume. This method will allow you to extend the volume when you need to.

Although you could memorize the performance effects of various types of dynamic volume configurations, you'll probably find it to be far easier (and more useful) to truly understand where the performance effects come from. For example, read performance for large files can be

dramatically improved in a striped volume, as it allows multiple physical hard disks to service requests, and write performance on RAID-5 volumes is decreased, since parity information must be calculated and written. There's less of a chance that you'll forget the benefits of each type of dynamic volume if you think this way on the exam.

have seen, RAID technologies can cause disk performance overhead by using CPU, memory, and other system resources. Fortunately, you have an alternative.

Hardware-based RAID solutions can increase performance while minimizing the impacts of the overhead that RAID technology can incur. Hardware-based RAID solutions are generally implemented on a RAID-capable disk controller that handles all of the operations that are required to maintain disk striping, disk spanning, and/or parity operations. Table 5-3 provides information about various RAID levels and their Windows Server 2003 counterparts. Note that in advanced configurations, RAID levels can be combined together to provide varying levels of performance and redundancy.

Hardware RAID solutions are available for both IDE and SCSI hard disks. Although SCSI implementations are more commonly used, some IDE solutions can provide

TABLE 5-3	RAID Level	RAID Description	Windows Server 2003 Technology	Notes
A Listing of Common RAID Levels	0	Disk striping	Striped volumes	
	1	Disk mirroring	Mirrored volumes	
	5	Disk striping with parity	RAID-5 volumes	
	0 + 1 (or "10")	Mirrored stripe sets	Not supported	Used where high performance is required; solution can be costly because of 100% redundancy

INSIDE THE EXAM

Choosing a Disk Implementation Strategy

Microsoft knows that you can figure out how to use the intuitive Disk Management interface (which you'll read about later in this chapter) to perform disk management tasks. What the company really wants you to understand is how to choose the best disk strategy, given a set of requirements and circumstances. And given this information, you should know how to best implement your solution. In order to do well on these types of exam questions, you should begin with a solid understanding of the concepts that we've covered thus far.

The best way to approach questions related to managing storage is to start with the requirements. If, for example, you must provide fault tolerance for a volume, you know that you have two options: mirrored volumes or RAID-5 volumes. Now, suppose you have to provide fault tolerance for the system partition. That leaves just one option: disk mirroring. Or, suppose you have only one extra hard disk with available space. Again, disk mirroring would be the only available option.

More complicated questions may involve multiple situations on a single server. For example, suppose you need to provide fault tolerance for two different volumes (one of which is the system partition). And, you have only four physical devices. In this case, you may have to configure mirroring for both volumes (leaving an additional disk available for another use). Also, watch out for phrases like "you want to make the most efficient use of disk space." Remember that disk mirroring will result in a loss of 50 percent of usable disk space, and RAID-5 volumes will result in a loss of usable space equal to that of one disk in the volume. Finally, keep the basics in mind—the only way to implement fault tolerance in Windows Server 2003 (without using a hardware-based solution) is to use disk mirroring or RAID-5 volumes.

If you learn to think critically about the strengths and weakness of the various dynamic volume configurations that are possible in Windows Server 2003, it will be difficult for Microsoft to throw something unexpected your way!

similar performance for a much lower cost. SCSI-based hardware RAID controllers can also support "hot-swapping," which allows you to add and remove hard disks to and from a system while the machine is running.

When you use a hardware-based RAID solution, all of the setup and administration of disk arrays is handled through software that is specifically designed to interact with the disk controller. This software may run from within Windows Server 2003. Or, you can use the built-in BIOS chip on the controller (which usually must be accessed during system startup).

Although it's good advice for any hardware, you should be especially sure that a specific hardware-based RAID solution fully supports Windows Server 2003. If it doesn't, you could end up with data corruption issues, boot failures, or intermittent system lockups!

When you implement RAID at the hardware level, Windows Server 2003 will not recognize that RAID has been implemented, and the entire logical volume will appear as a single physical disk in the Windows Disk Management tools. For example, if you have created a RAID-5 volume that consists of four 19.0GB hard disks at the hardware level, Windows Server 2003 will see the array as a single physical disk that can store 57.0GB.

Overall, using hardware RAID solutions can greatly improve disk performance and can reduce the burden placed on your computer's other resources. Consider hardware-based solutions for your busiest and most critical servers.

CERTIFICATION OBJECTIVE 5.02

Configuring, Managing, and Troubleshooting Disks Using the Disk Management Tool

Thus far, you've examined a great deal of information about physical disks, partition types, volume types, and dynamic disk configurations. Now, it's time to drill down into exactly *how* storage resources can be managed in your server operating systems.

Since it's such an important part of system administration, Windows Server 2003 includes several methods that you can use to easily administer your disk storage.

In this section, you'll take a look at a GUI-based tool that's probably familiar to you already, as well as a few new ways to get things done in Windows Server 2003.

Often, when you're responsible for administering multiple machines, you'll want to take a quick look at the disk configuration for a system. You may also want to make some changes to the partitioning of the disks. You can access Disk Management tools through the Computer Management administrative tool, or by creating your own MMC console that includes the Disk Management snap-in. When you access the Disk Management information, you'll see a display that looks like the one shown in Figure 5-9.

FIGURE 5-9	Viewing disk configuration information with the Disk Management snap-in

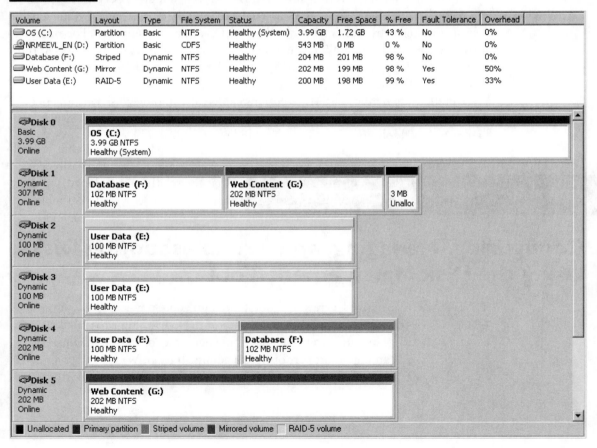

on the
Ⓞob

You may be wondering how I was able to set up a machine with so many small, different hard drives. Rest assured, this wasn't done by robbing a computer museum. Instead, I used the VMWare Workstation virtual machine software from VMWare, Inc. This software application allows you to create "virtual machines" in which operating systems can be installed. After an operating system is installed, you can quickly and easily add or remove virtual disk devices. This is a great way to implement and test dynamic volume configuration. For more information, see www.vmware.com.

The top portion of the display shows detailed statistics related to the logical volumes that are available on your system. Included are details about

- The type of partition that is configured on each volume
- The file system
- The status of each disk
- Disk space usage statistics, including the capacity of the volume, and the amount and percentage of disk space used
- Whether or not the volume is fault-tolerant

The bottom portion of the display provides a graphical view of the details related to the logical layout of local disks. With this view, you can quickly and easily see how each disk is physically partitioned. Note that the relative visual lengths of the bars that represent volumes may not be consistent between devices. To get more detailed information about a single volume, simply right-click the volume and choose Properties. You'll see information similar to that shown in Figure 5-10.

As its name implies, the Disk Management tool doesn't limit you to just viewing information. It also allows you to create and delete partitions, reformat partitions, and configure dynamic disks. Furthermore, the tool is very useful for systems administration, since it allows you to connect to a remote computer to view disk configuration over the network. Let's drill-down into the methods that are available for managing disks.

exam
ⓦatch
In order to perform the disk-related functions presented in this section, you must have appropriate permissions. By default, members of the Administrators and Backup Operators groups have sufficient permissions to initialize disks and create and format volumes.

FIGURE 5-10

Viewing detailed
properties for a
logical volume

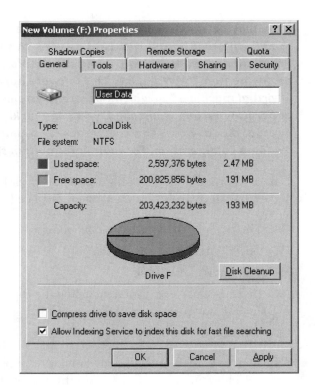

Initializing Disks

Once a new disk is installed in a Windows Server 2003 computer, it will be shown in
the Disk Management tool as "Not initialized." Before you can use a new disk, it must
be initialized for use. By default, the process of initializing a disk makes it a basic volume.
In some cases (for example, if you're using a hardware disk controller that allows for
hot-plugging hard drives), the Disk Management tool may not automatically recognize
the newly added disk. In this case, you may need to choose "Rescan Disks" from the
Action menu.

To initialize a disk, you can use the Initialize Disk Wizard. The wizard can be
launched by right-clicking a disk and choosing "Initialize Disk." As shown in the
second screen here, you'll be given the opportunity to initialize one or more of the
uninitialized disks on the machine.

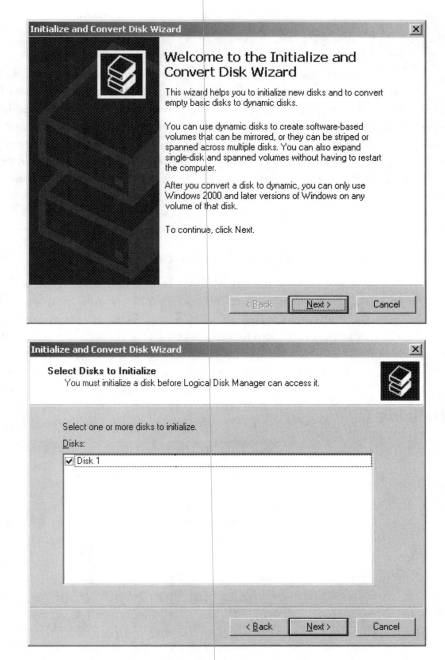

Once the initialization process is complete, you can choose whether you want to start creating partitions or you want to convert the disk to a dynamic disk.

Since the various operations in this section can require you to have up to several free hard disks in a server, it may be difficult for you to walk through all of the steps. Ideally, you'd have access to a server that contains many physical devices that can be reconfigured without causing problems to users. However, that's probably unrealistic in many environments. To make things a little easier, I've been sure to add as many screenshots as possible to help you learn what to expect when managing basic and dynamic disks. And, be sure to check out the content on the accompanying CD-ROM for demonstrations of these techniques (see Appendix A for details).

Creating Partitions and Volumes on Basic Disks

Creating partitions on basic disks is a fairly straightforward process. To begin, simply right-click an initialized basic volume and select New Partition. As you might have expected, this will launch the New Partition Wizard. As was covered earlier in this chapter, there are two types of partitions that you can create on a basic disk: primary partitions and extended partitions. Extended partitions can contain multiple logical drives.

When you launch the wizard, the first decision you'll have to make is regarding what type of partition you want to create. Assuming you're starting with a blank basic disk, you'll have only two options—primary partition or extended partition. If you already have an extended partition, you can also choose to add a logical drive.

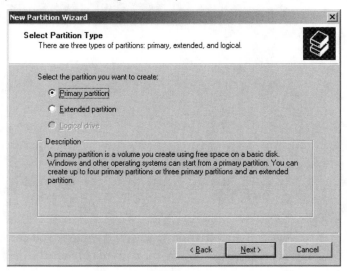

Once you've chosen the partition type, you'll have to specify the size of the partition.

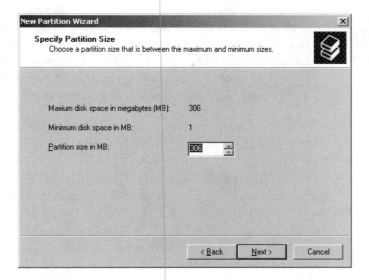

Next, you'll be able to specify whether you want to assign a drive letter or path to the newly created partition. The drop-down list for assigning a drive letter will include all of the unused drive letters for the system (see the following illustration). Instead of assigning a drive letter to the new partition, you can mount it on any empty folder in your file system. We'll cover the details of volume mount points later in this chapter. For now, however, just know that this feature allows you to map an existing physical path (for example, "C:\UserData") to a new partition or volume. If you're unsure about the drive letter or path assignment, you can choose not to assign either. You can later assign drive letters and/or paths to the partition using the Disk Administrator.

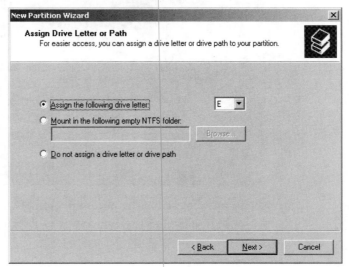

Although the Disk Administrator tool makes it fairly easy to change drive letters, you should use caution when doing so. Many applications may rely on specific paths in order to function correctly. Since changing a drive letter will change these paths, you should perform this operation only if you're fairly sure that it won't have adverse effects on your system.

Finally, the New Partition Wizard will prompt you for information about how you want to format the new partition (see the next illustration). You can choose not to format the partition (although you'll have to do it later, before you can use it). Or, you can choose the file system (FAT, FAT32, or NTFS), the allocation unit size, and the volume label (the name of the disk). In most cases, you will want to stay with the default allocation unit size. This option can be used to improve performance for certain applications that take advantage of low-level disk reading and writing mechanisms (such as some database servers or special hard disk–related applications). In general, you will want to leave the allocation unit size as "default." Two other options are available for performing a quick format (which is generally safe if you know that a disk does not have any errors) and for enabling file and folder compression for all data on the volume.

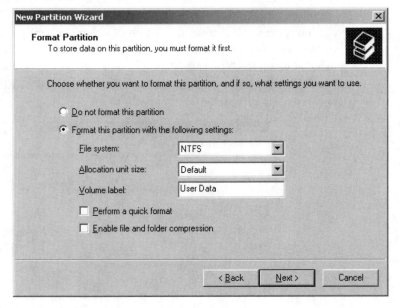

Once you've answered all of the necessary prompts, the New Partition Wizard will summarize your selections (as shown in the following illustration). It may be helpful to copy and paste this text into a log file so that you remember which options you have chosen to perform. When you're ready to create the partition, simply click Finish, and the wizard will perform the selected operations. The end result (depending on the options you chose) will be a new partition that is ready for meeting your users' needs. You can walk through the New Partition Wizard again to create any additional partitions.

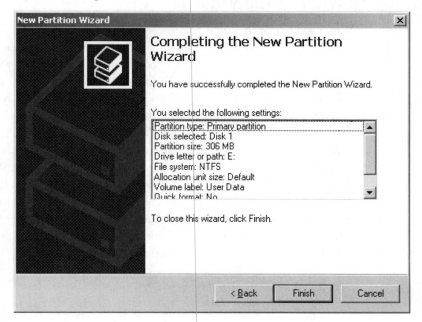

Converting a Basic Disk to a Dynamic Disk

As you learned earlier in this chapter, there are many benefits to using dynamic disks. If you don't have a need to support basic disks, a good first step after initialization is to convert the new disk to a dynamic disk. This process can easily be done by right-clicking a basic disk and selecting Convert To Dynamic Disk. You'll be given the option to select one or more of the basic disks that are configured on the system for conversion. Depending on the current configuration of the basic disk, the volume may have to be "unmounted" in order for the operation to complete. For a disk that is hosting the operating system, this will mean that the system must be rebooted. For other disks, it will mean that the disk will be unavailable for use for a short period of time while the conversion is being performed.

You also have the option of converting a dynamic disk to a basic disk, but you can do this only if the basic disk does not contain any partitions. That means that, if you are already storing data on that disk, you will have to back up all of the data and delete the volume before you can perform the disk conversion.

Creating New Dynamic Volumes

When you're creating new dynamic volumes, depending on your disk configuration, you may be able to choose from many different dynamic volume configurations. Fortunately, the New Volume Wizard can make it make it easy to configure your disks according to your requirements. To launch the wizard, simple right-click any dynamic volume that has available space. You'll see the introduction screen first, as is usual.

The first step in the wizard will be to select the type of volume that you want to create. As shown in the following illustration, you may have many different options. The New Volume Wizard is smart enough to determine which disk configurations are possible given the current disk configuration. For example, if you have only a single dynamic volume available, your only option may be to select the Simple volume type. If you have multiple volumes, you'll have additional options. As we covered the details of all of the different dynamic volume types earlier in this chapter, the following descriptions will assume that you have a sufficient number of physical disks with unallocated space to create a new RAID-5 volume.

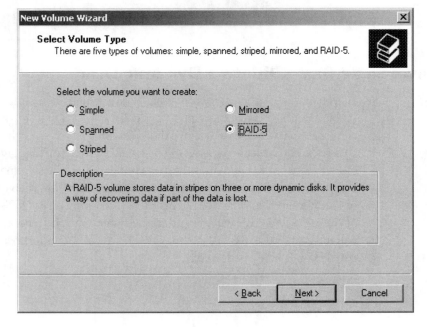

The next step of the wizard will prompt you for information about which disk(s) you want to configure. If you chose a Simple volume, you'll be able to specify only a single disk. Otherwise, you can specify multiple disks to be part of the new volume (shown here). For volumes that include multiple disks, the wizard will automatically calculate the total volume size and the maximum available space.

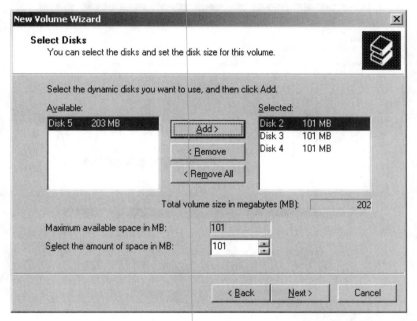

As with the creation of other types of partitions, you can choose to provide a drive letter and/or a mount point for the new volume. Then, you can choose from among the available formatting options for the volume. Note that your options may be limited (specifically, you may be forced to choose NTFS for certain dynamic volume configurations). Once you're done, you'll see a final screen confirming the options you've selected.

When you click Finish, the wizard will begin creating the dynamic volume (see Figure 5-11).

Exercise 5-1 walks you through the process of setting up a new disk in Windows Server 2003.

| FIGURE 5-11 | Creating a new dynamic RAID-5 volume |

Disk 0		
Basic 3.99 GB Online	**OS (C:)** 3.99 GB NTFS Healthy (System)	

Disk 1		
Basic 306 MB Online	**User Data (E:)** 306 MB NTFS Healthy	

Disk 2		
Dynamic 100 MB Online	**(F:)** 100 MB Formatting : (30%)	

Disk 3		
Dynamic 100 MB Online	**(F:)** 100 MB Formatting : (30%)	

Disk 4		
Dynamic 203 MB Online	**(F:)** 100 MB Formatting : (30%)	103 MB Unallocated

Disk 5		
Dynamic 203 MB Online	203 MB Unallocated	

■ Unallocated ■ Primary partition ☐ RAID-5 volume

EXERCISE 5-1

CertCam & MasterSim 5-1 ON THE CD

Setting Up a New Disk

This exercise assumes that you have a hard disk that does not contain any useful data installed in a Windows Server 2003 machine. It also assumes that the disk has been initialized as a basic disk, and that it has not been formatted.

1. Log on to the computer as an Administrator and open the Disk Management tool by clicking the System Control Panel applet and then clicking Disk Management. You will see a list of all of the disks that are physically installed in the computer.

2. Be sure that you have backed up or copied any useful data from this volume before continuing. Right-click the disk that you want to configure and select Convert To Dynamic Disk. You will have the option to choose one or more disks to convert to dynamic disks. Make sure that only the volume that you

selected is configured and then click OK. The disk will be converted to a dynamic disk.

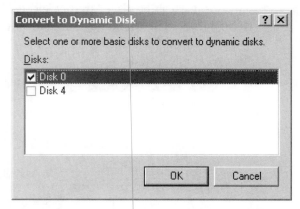

3. Now that you have a new dynamic disk configured, it's time to create a new volume. Right-click the Unallocated Space for the new drive and select New Volume. This will launch the New Volume Wizard. Click Next to begin.

4. For the sake of this exercise, you will create a new Simple volume using all of the space on this disk. Select Simple for the type of volume and then click Next.

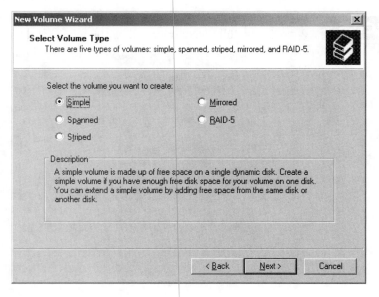

5. In the Select Disks screen, you may see other available disks in the Available selection box. However, since you have chosen to create a simple volume, only one disk can be placed in the Selected box. Ensure that the proper disk is listed there. The wizard has automatically calculated and defaulted to the maximum available space for the partition. Leave this information as-is and click Next to continue.

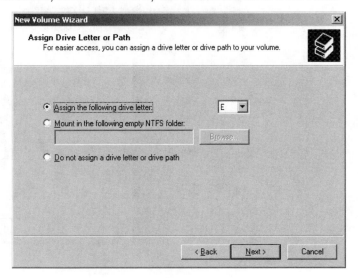

6. In the Assign Drive Letter Or Path step, select the drive letter that is automatically recommended by the wizard and then click Next.

7. In the Format Volume step, provide a name (such as "User Data") for the new volume. Leave all of the other settings at their defaults and click Next to continue.

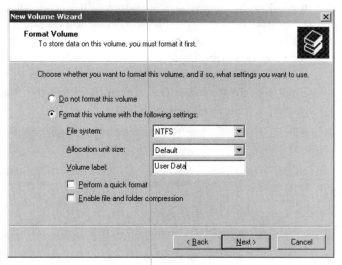

8. You'll be provided with a summary of the operation and options you have selected for the new volume. Ensure that the information is correct and then click Finish to have the wizard create the partition. In the Disk Management screen, you'll see that the disk is being formatted. The time it takes to format the disk will be based on the speed of your hardware and the size of the disk. Once the formatting is complete, the disk will be ready to use through the drive letter that you specified in step 6. When finished, close the Disk Management console.

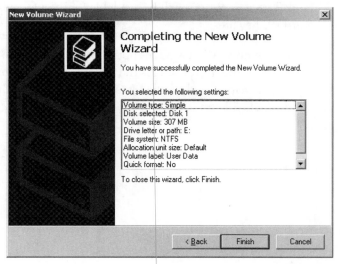

Managing Mirrored Volumes

In addition to using the New Volume Wizard, you can create a mirrored volume by right-clicking an existing simple volume and choosing Add Mirror. This option will be available only as long as you have at least one available disk with sufficient disk space to create the mirror. Using the Add Mirror dialog box (shown in the following illustration), you can choose on which disk you want to create the mirror. Since the size of the mirror must be the same as the size of the volume you are mirroring, no further information is required.

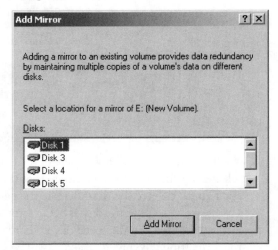

Once a mirror has been created, you can manage it using the Disk Management tool. Two new options will be available for the volumes that are participating in the mirror. They are

- **Remove Mirror**   This option will allow you to remove one of the two disks from the mirror set. As the dialog box states, you will still have one copy of the data stored on the remaining volume, but the volume will no longer be fault-tolerant.

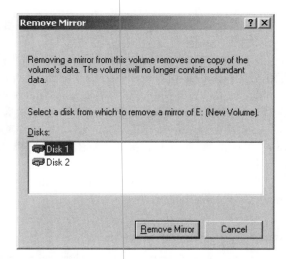

■ **Break Mirrored Volume**   Instead of removing a mirror (which results in the loss of one copy of the data), you can choose to break the mirrored volume. This operation will leave you with two copies of the data—one stored on each volume that was previously in the mirror set. Since, originally, the mirror set was referred to by a single drive letter, you will now have a new drive letter. Remember that volumes are no longer fault-tolerant, and that changes made to one volume will not be made to another. The following illustration shows you the confirmation dialog box that you'll see when breaking a mirrored volume.

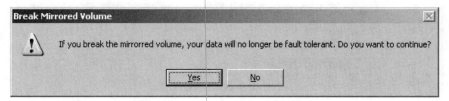

In the event that one of the volumes in the mirror fails (for example, through the failure of a physical hard disk), you should replace the failed disk. In order to rebuild a failed mirror set, you'll have two options. The first is to "Reactivate" the mirror. This operation rebuilds the mirror set using the newly replaced drive. Or if you are unable to quickly replace the device, you can create a new mirror copy on another device. This option is labeled "Repair Volume." When you choose this option, you'll be prompted for information about which disk you want to use to replace the failed one. Of course, you must have at least one eligible dynamic disk available before you can perform this operation.

This will re-create the mirror and reestablish fault tolerance. Figure 5-12 shows a mirrored volume being reactivated.

FIGURE 5-12   Reactivating a failed mirrored volume

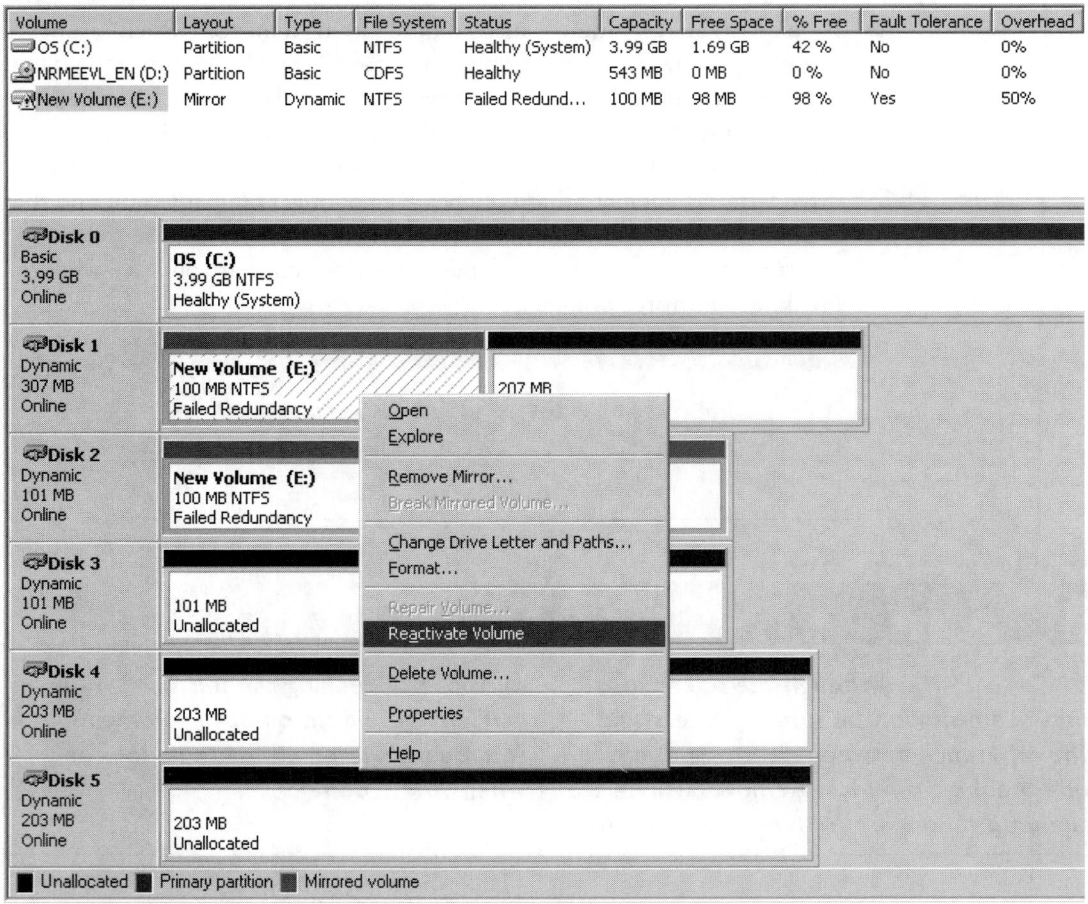

Volume	Layout	Type	File System	Status	Capacity	Free Space	% Free	Fault Tolerance	Overhead
OS (C:)	Partition	Basic	NTFS	Healthy (System)	3.99 GB	1.69 GB	42 %	No	0%
NRMEEVL_EN (D:)	Partition	Basic	CDFS	Healthy	543 MB	0 MB	0 %	No	0%
New Volume (E:)	Mirror	Dynamic	NTFS	Failed Redund...	100 MB	98 MB	98 %	Yes	50%

Disk 0
Basic
3.99 GB
Online

OS (C:)
3.99 GB NTFS
Healthy (System)

Disk 1
Dynamic
307 MB
Online

New Volume (E:)
100 MB NTFS
Failed Redundancy

207 MB

Open
Explore

Disk 2
Dynamic
101 MB
Online

New Volume (E:)
100 MB NTFS
Failed Redundancy

Remove Mirror...
Break Mirrored Volume...

Disk 3
Dynamic
101 MB
Online

101 MB
Unallocated

Change Drive Letter and Paths...
Format...

Repair Volume...
Reactivate Volume

Disk 4
Dynamic
203 MB
Online

203 MB
Unallocated

Delete Volume...

Properties

Help

Disk 5
Dynamic
203 MB
Online

203 MB
Unallocated

■ Unallocated ■ Primary partition ■ Mirrored volume

Moving Disks to Another Computer

Server upgrades, server consolidation, or just general business changes may require you to move one or more hard disks from one server to another. For example, business reorganization might require you to move entire disks full of user data to other servers. Fortunately, Windows Server 2003 provides you with a mechanism for moving disks to another computer.

Before you begin this process, be sure that the Disk Manager reports the status of all of your hard disks as "healthy." The process for moving disks to another computer involves the following steps:

1. In the Device Manager, under the "Disk Drives" branch, right-click the disk(s) you want to move and select Uninstall. Once you confirm the removal of the disk, the device will be removed from the Device Manager. For more information on using the Device Manager, see Chapter 2.

2. If you're moving one or more dynamic disks, open the Disk Manager. Right-click the disk(s) you want to move and choose Remove Disk (see Figure 5-13). The disk will disappear from the Disk Manager user interface.

3. Physically move the hard disk devices to the new computer. If you're using hardware that supports it, you may be able to do this while the machine is still running. If not, you'll need to physically remove the disks while the source and destination machines are powered down.

4. Boot the destination server (the one that contains the disks you just moved). When you boot the computer, you may see the Add New Hardware Wizard. Follow the prompts to install the new hardware.

5. On the destination server, open the Disk Manager tool. From the Action menu, choose Rescan Disks. The moved disks should now appear within the Disk Manager user interface. The disks will be marked as "Foreign" disks. To complete the move process, right-click these disks and select Import Foreign Disks (see Figure 5-14). You'll now be able to walk through the process of making these disks available for use in the new server.

As long as you follow the proper procedure, moving disks between systems can be a painless process. And, it can save you many hours in copying and reconfiguring the data manually!

FIGURE 5-13 Removing a hard disk in order to move it to another server

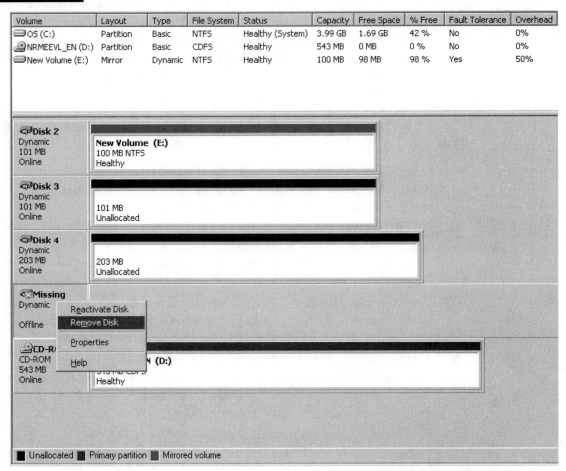

Volume	Layout	Type	File System	Status	Capacity	Free Space	% Free	Fault Tolerance	Overhead
OS (C:)	Partition	Basic	NTFS	Healthy (System)	3.99 GB	1.69 GB	42 %	No	0%
NRMEEVL_EN (D:)	Partition	Basic	CDFS	Healthy	543 MB	0 MB	0 %	No	0%
New Volume (E:)	Mirror	Dynamic	NTFS	Healthy	100 MB	98 MB	98 %	Yes	50%

Disk 2
Dynamic
101 MB
Online

New Volume (E:)
100 MB NTFS
Healthy

Disk 3
Dynamic
101 MB
Online

101 MB
Unallocated

Disk 4
Dynamic
203 MB
Online

203 MB
Unallocated

Missing
Dynamic

Offline

| Reactivate Disk |
| Remove Disk |
| Properties |
| Help |

CD-R
CD-ROM
543 MB
Online

N (D:)

Healthy

■ Unallocated ■ Primary partition ■ Mirrored volume

Managing RAID-5 Volumes

Earlier in this section, you learned how RAID-5 volumes can be created using the New Volume Wizard. Since multiple disks are involved in the configuration process, the wizard is the only way to create this type of dynamic volume. In general, RAID-5 volumes are administered in the same way as other dynamic volume types. Although they cannot be extended (as simple or spanned volumes can), they do offer fault

FIGURE 5-14 Importing a foreign disk

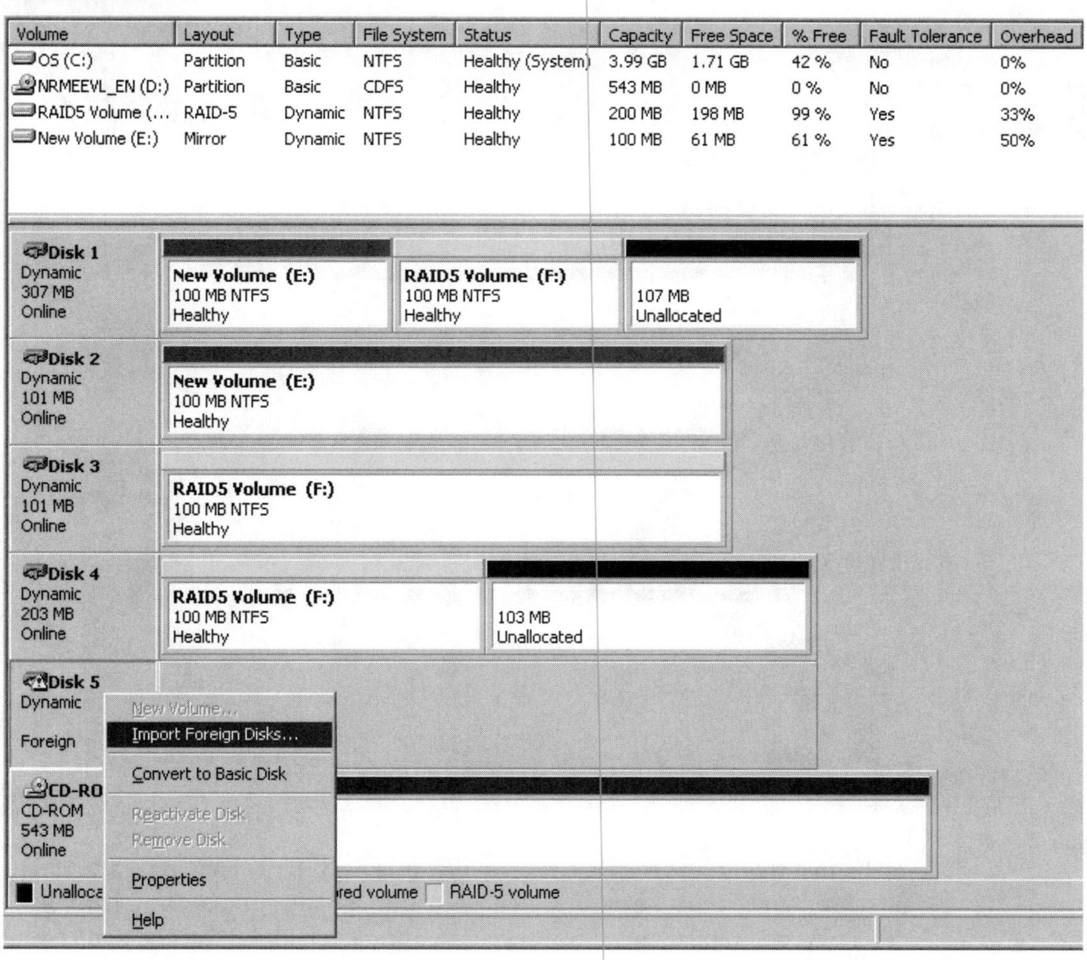

Volume	Layout	Type	File System	Status	Capacity	Free Space	% Free	Fault Tolerance	Overhead
OS (C:)	Partition	Basic	NTFS	Healthy (System)	3.99 GB	1.71 GB	42 %	No	0%
NRMEEVL_EN (D:)	Partition	Basic	CDFS	Healthy	543 MB	0 MB	0 %	No	0%
RAID5 Volume (...	RAID-5	Dynamic	NTFS	Healthy	200 MB	198 MB	99 %	Yes	33%
New Volume (E:)	Mirror	Dynamic	NTFS	Healthy	100 MB	61 MB	61 %	Yes	50%

Disk 1
Dynamic
307 MB
Online

New Volume (E:)
100 MB NTFS
Healthy

RAID5 Volume (F:)
100 MB NTFS
Healthy

107 MB
Unallocated

Disk 2
Dynamic
101 MB
Online

New Volume (E:)
100 MB NTFS
Healthy

Disk 3
Dynamic
101 MB
Online

RAID5 Volume (F:)
100 MB NTFS
Healthy

Disk 4
Dynamic
203 MB
Online

RAID5 Volume (F:)
100 MB NTFS
Healthy

103 MB
Unallocated

Disk 5
Dynamic

Foreign

New Volume...
Import Foreign Disks...
Convert to Basic Disk
Reactivate Disk
Remove Disk
Properties
Help

CD-RO
CD-ROM
543 MB
Online

Unalloca   red volume   RAID-5 volume

tolerance (like mirrored volumes). If a disk in a RAID-5 volume becomes unavailable (through a hardware failure or disk corruption), the volume will no longer be fault-tolerant. And although the data will still be available, performance will be degraded, since Windows Server 2003 must manually re-create the lost information in memory for every read request. Figure 5-15 shows what you might see in the Disk Manager after a disk failure occurs within a RAID-5 volume. Obviously, this is a situation you would want to resolve quickly.

FIGURE 5-15   Viewing disk failure information in the Disk Manager

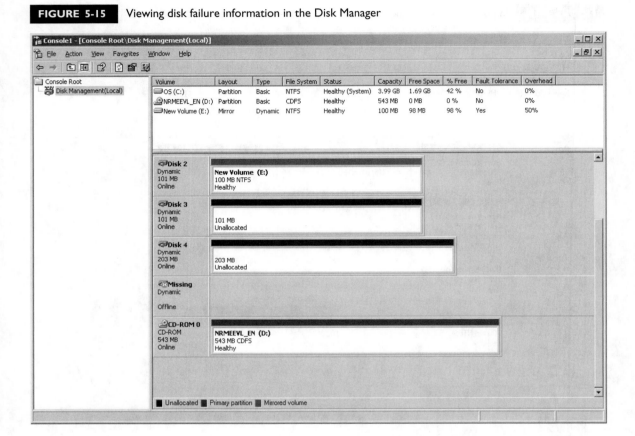

The first step in recovering from a failure in a RAID-5 volume is to replace the failed hardware, if that's possible. Generally, this will mean replacing a hard disk with a new one (and, depending on your hardware, rebooting the computer). Once the drive has been replaced, you can open the Disk Manager and choose Reactivate Volume to rebuild the information that was lost. Alternatively, you can choose the Repair Volume option. This operation allows you to select another available dynamic disk to replace the failed one. Often, systems administrators will configure critical servers with a "spare" disk, kept available just for this purpose. Figure 5-16 shows a RAID-5 volume that has a "failed redundancy status," and Figure 5-17 shows the volume being repaired.

FIGURE 5-16	Viewing failed redundancy information in the Disk Manager

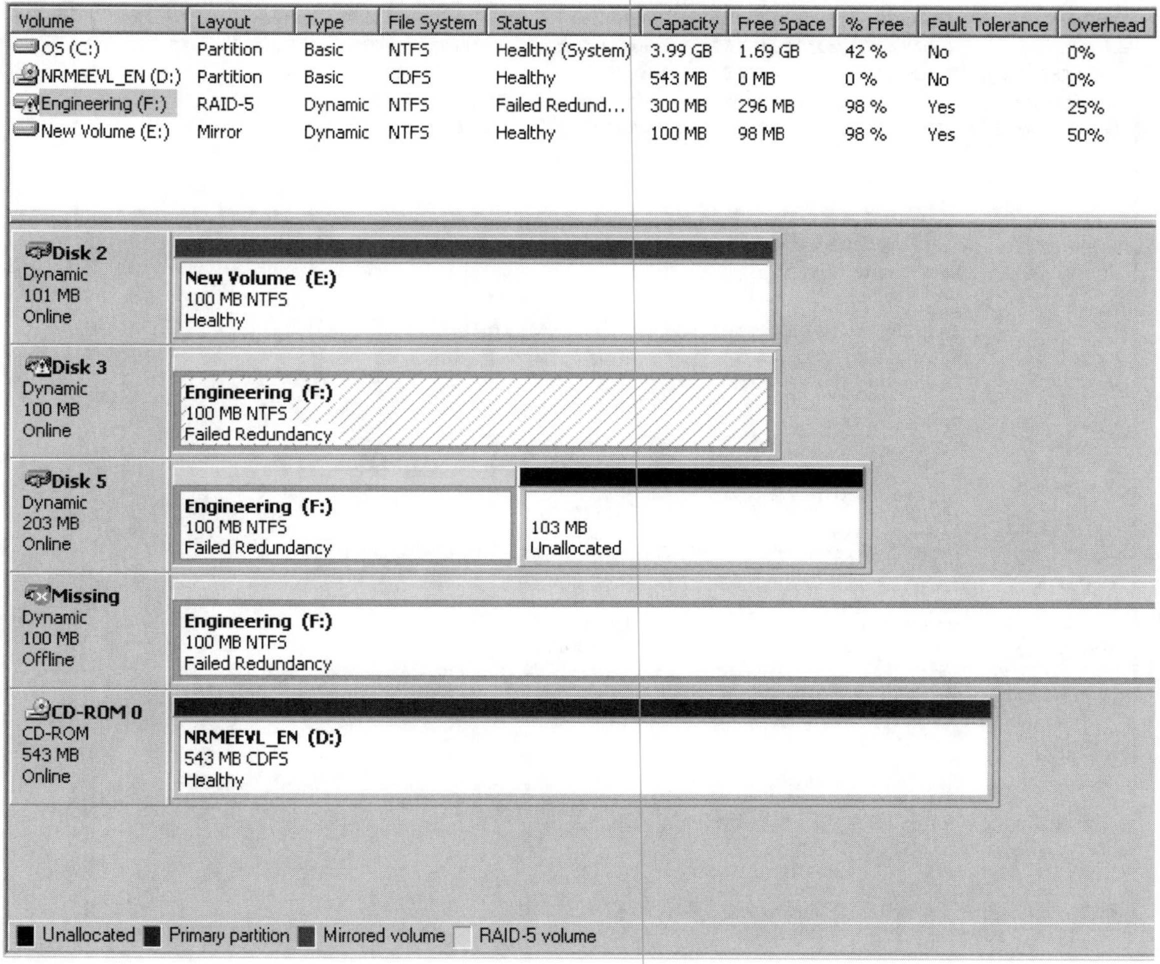

Volume	Layout	Type	File System	Status	Capacity	Free Space	% Free	Fault Tolerance	Overhead
OS (C:)	Partition	Basic	NTFS	Healthy (System)	3.99 GB	1.69 GB	42 %	No	0%
NRMEEVL_EN (D:)	Partition	Basic	CDFS	Healthy	543 MB	0 MB	0 %	No	0%
Engineering (F:)	RAID-5	Dynamic	NTFS	Failed Redund...	300 MB	296 MB	98 %	Yes	25%
New Volume (E:)	Mirror	Dynamic	NTFS	Healthy	100 MB	98 MB	98 %	Yes	50%

Disk 2
Dynamic
101 MB
Online

New Volume (E:)
100 MB NTFS
Healthy

Disk 3
Dynamic
100 MB
Online

Engineering (F:)
100 MB NTFS
Failed Redundancy

Disk 5
Dynamic
203 MB
Online

Engineering (F:)
100 MB NTFS
Failed Redundancy

103 MB
Unallocated

Missing
Dynamic
100 MB
Offline

Engineering (F:)
100 MB NTFS
Failed Redundancy

CD-ROM 0
CD-ROM
543 MB
Online

NRMEEVL_EN (D:)
543 MB CDFS
Healthy

■ Unallocated ■ Primary partition ■ Mirrored volume ☐ RAID-5 volume

It's important to note that, since many calculations will be required to rebuild the information, this process can use significant CPU time and disk subsystem resources. Once the volume has been repaired, performance should be back to normal, and the dynamic volume will be fault-tolerant again.

Exercise 5-2 walks you through the process of implementing a RAID-5 volume.

| FIGURE 5-17 | Repairing a RAID-5 volume after fixing a disk failure |

Volume	Layout	Type	File System	Status	Capacity	Free Space	% Free	Fault Tolerance	Overhead
▭OS (C:)	Partition	Basic	NTFS	Healthy (System)	3.99 GB	1.69 GB	42 %	No	0%
▭NRMEEVL_EN (D:)	Partition	Basic	CDFS	Healthy	543 MB	0 MB	0 %	No	0%
▭Engineering (F:)	RAID-5	Dynamic	NTFS	Resynching : (...	300 MB	296 MB	98 %	Yes	25%
▭New Volume (E:)	Mirror	Dynamic	NTFS	Healthy	100 MB	98 MB	98 %	Yes	50%

Disk 2
Dynamic
101 MB
Online

New Volume (E:)
100 MB NTFS
Healthy

Disk 3
Dynamic
100 MB
Online

Engineering (F:)
100 MB NTFS
Resynching : (25%)

Disk 4
Dynamic
203 MB
Online

Engineering (F:)
100 MB NTFS
Resynching : (25%)

103 MB
Unallocated

Disk 5
Dynamic
203 MB
Online

Engineering (F:)
100 MB NTFS
Resynching : (25%)

103 MB
Unallocated

CD-ROM 0
CD-ROM
543 MB
Online

NRMEEVL_EN (D:)
543 MB CDFS
Healthy

■ Unallocated ■ Primary partition ■ Mirrored volume ☐ RAID-5 volume

---

EXERCISE 5-2

MasterSim 5-2 ON THE CD

Implementing a RAID-5 Dynamic Volume

In order to successfully complete this exercise, you must be running an installation of
Windows Server 2003 that has at least three separate physical disks available for use.
It is assumed that these disks are formatted, are configured as dynamic disks, and do
not contain any volumes.

1. Log on to the computer as an Administrator. Open the Disk Management tool by clicking the System Control Panel applet and then clicking Disk Management. You should see at least three physical disks that are configured as dynamic disks. All three disks should show a status of "Online," and all of their space should be marked as "Unallocated."

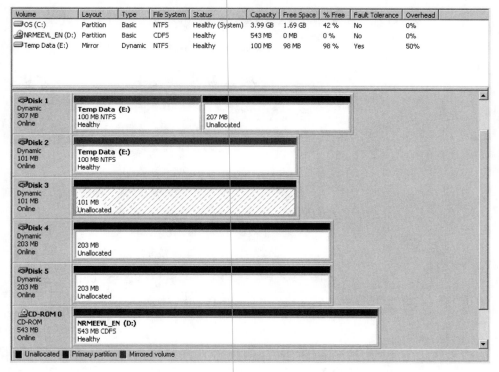

2. In order to begin the creation of a new RAID-5 volume, right-click the unallocated space for the first of the three drives you want to configure and select New Volume. This will launch the New Volume Wizard. Click Next to begin.

3. On the Select Volume Type step, choose RAID-5 and then click Next.

4. On the Select Disks step, you'll need to have at least three disks to the "Selected" side of the user interface. Note that the Next button will be disabled until you do this. Select two additional disks from the available column and click Add to move them to the Selected column. The wizard will automatically calculate the maximum available space for the volume.

Note that this amount will be equal to the smallest of the selected disks (since each participant in a RAID-5 volume must be of equal size). Also, if you choose to reduce the amount of space used on one of the disks, the value will be changed for all of the disks. Select the maximum available size and then click Next to continue.

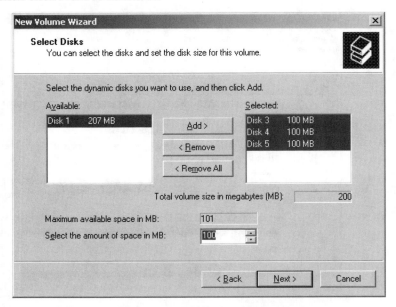

5. In the Assign Drive Letter Or Path step, select the drive letter that is automatically recommended by the wizard and then click Next.

6. In the Format Volume step, provide a name (such as "Public Data") for the new volume. Leave all of the other settings at their defaults and click Next to continue.

7. You'll be provided with a summary of the operation and options you have selected for the new volume (shown in the following illustration). Ensure that the information is correct and then click Finish to have the wizard create the new RAID-5 volume.

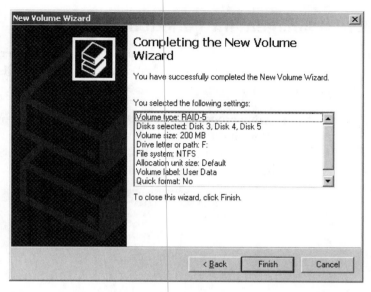

8. In the Disk Management screen, you'll see that the disk is being formatted. Once the formatting is complete, the disk will be ready to use through the drive letter that you specified in step 5. When finished, close the Disk Management console.

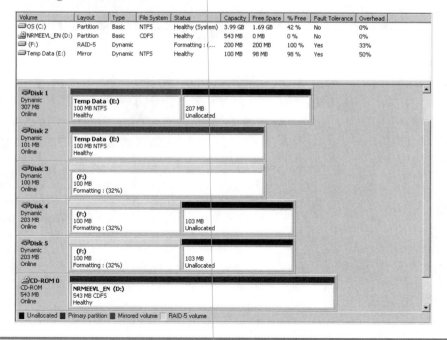

Other Disk Management Functions

In addition to the basic disk creation and management operations that you've looked at thus far, you can perform several other tasks using the Disk Management tool. Here are some of those operations:

- **Viewing properties** The Disk Management user interface can provide a lot of information about disks. If you want to view additional details for a particular volume, you can simply right-click it and select Properties. Similarly, you can right-click a disk to see details about the disk itself.

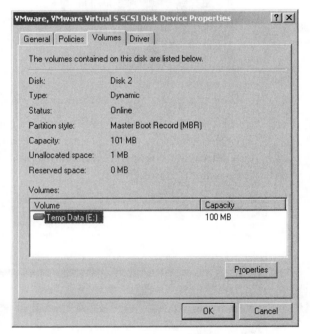

- **Formatting** Once a volume has been created, you can format or reformat it by right-clicking the volume and choosing Format. As shown in the following illustration, you'll have the option to specify the file system, the allocation unit size, and the name of the new volume. You can also specify whether you want to enable compression and whether you want to perform a quick format operation.

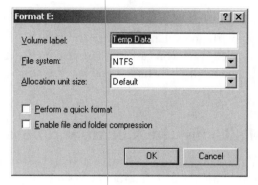

- **Changing drive letter and paths** Windows Server 2003 lets you assign a single drive letter to a volume. In addition, you can have zero or more mounted volume paths for the selected volume. This feature provides a great deal of flexibility in making additional disk space easy to access. You'll learn more details related to volume mount points later in this chapter.

- **Extending a simple or spanned volume** This operation is simply done by right-clicking the dynamic volume that you want to extend and choosing Extend Volume. This will launch the Extend Volume Wizard, which will prompt you to select to which disk(s) the partition should be extended.

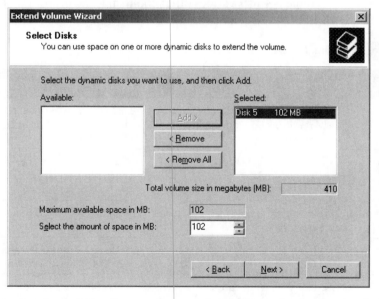

- **Reactivating a disk** In some cases, a hard disk may not completely fail, but errors in reading from, or writing to, the disk may occur. In such a case, the disk may become inactivated (which is shown in the Disk Management tool with an exclamation mark on the name of the disk). In order to recover from this issue, you can try to reactivate the disk. However, if that operation fails, you will likely have to replace the disk and rebuild any dynamic volume that it is part of.

Managing Disks Using the Command Line

You'll probably use Disk Management as your first choice for administering disks. The graphical interface of that tool makes it easy to perform even the most complicated actions. However, there are limitations to GUI tools. For example, suppose you want to script some modification so that you can apply it to many different servers. Or, what if you want to schedule an operation to occur at a later time? These things can't be done via the GUI interface. Fortunately, there are alternatives to using the Disk Manager.

As is the case in many other areas of Windows Server 2003, you can perform some powerful tasks through a command-line interface. Command-line utilities can be useful when you're trying to automate some processes (in a batch file that runs during logon, for example), or when you know exactly what you want to do and don't need the assistance provided by GUI tools.

Table 5-4 lists various other command-line utilities that can be used for managing disks from the command line.

TABLE 5-4   Disk Management Command-Line Utilities

Utility	Purpose	Notes
Chkdsk	Command-line utility for checking disks for errors and, optionally, repairing those errors	Disks can also be checked through the GUI; some checking and repair operations may require a reboot of the system.
Convert	Converts a FAT or FAT32 file system to NTFS	The conversion is one-way (that is, NTFS partitions cannot be converted to FAT or FAT32); converting the boot or system volume will require a reboot.
DiskPart	Performs disk management for basic and dynamic disks	Scripts can be used to automate common functions.
Format	Formats a partition	Systems administrators can choose the file system to use for the new partition.
FSUtil	Used for managing various NTFS file system features, such as configuring disk quotas	This command provides for a lot of control over the file system, and some functions should be used only by experienced systems administrators.

TABLE 5-4	Disk Management Command-Line Utilities *(continued)*	

Utility	Purpose	Notes
Mountvol	Used for mounting or unmounting a volume at an NTFS mounting point	Can be used to provide information about volume GUIDs.
VSSAdmin	Used for administering Volume Shadow Storage features	

Now that you have a basic idea of which command-line tools are available, let's look at some in detail (for more information on all of the tools, see the Windows Server 2003 Help and Support tool).

Using the DiskPart Tool

Since it's of particular use for performing the commands covered in this chapter, let's take a look at the DiskPart tool. Through the use of the various commands supported by this utility, you can create scripts that automate the process of creating and formatting partitions on various disks. This could be useful, for example, in a situation where you want to make similar changes on multiple machines. The list of available commands includes "add disk," "convert dynamic," "create partition primary," and "detail volume." A complete list of the syntax and commands available for the DiskPart utility is available in the Help and Support Center.

There are two main ways in which you can use the DiskPart utility. The first is in interactive mode. To enter interactive mode, simply type **DiskPart** at the command line. You'll see a DiskPart> prompt. Here, you can enter commands to perform your administration and management tasks. You'll probably want to start by viewing a list of available commands. You can do this by simply typing **Help** at the DiskPart prompt. You'll see the commands shown in Figure 5-18. Many of the commands in DiskPart require "context" information. What this means is that you'll need to select a disk, volume, or partition before performing certain commands.

Although the interactive mode is useful for one-off operations, you may want to script the use of DiskPart. To do this, you must first create a text file that includes the commands that you want the utility to carry out. For example, you might create a text file including the following commands:

```
select disk=0
select partition=1
detail disk
detail volume
```

FIGURE 5-18   Viewing help for the DiskPart utility

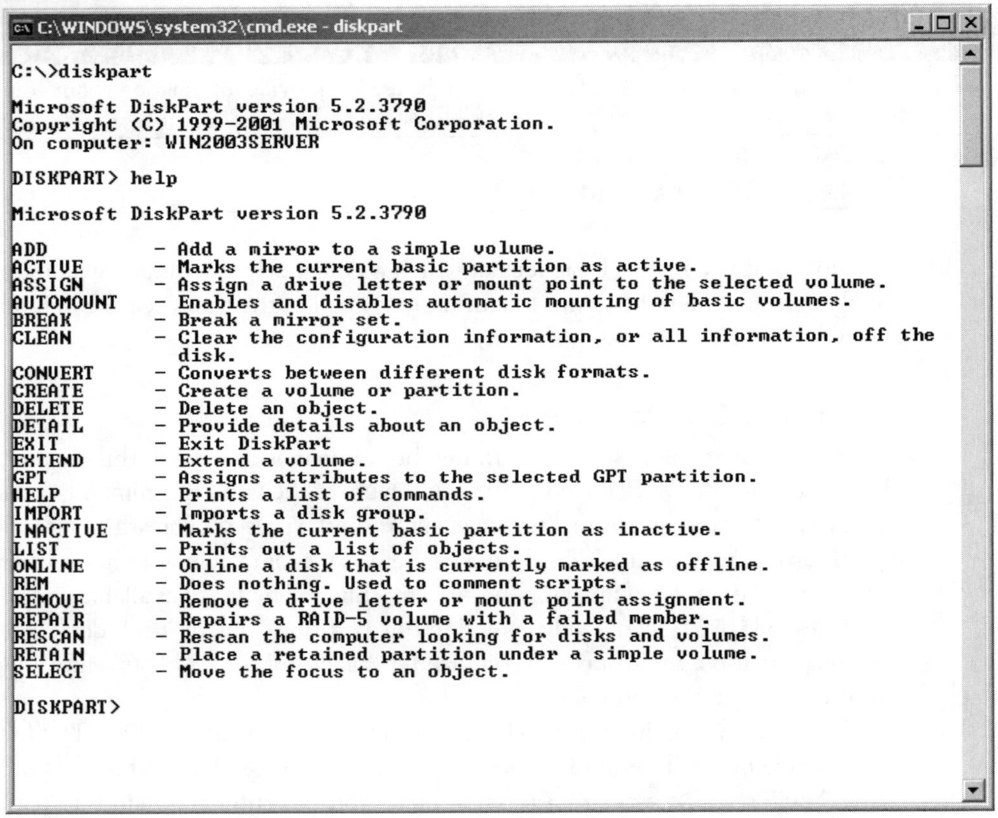

```
C:\WINDOWS\system32\cmd.exe - diskpart

C:\>diskpart

Microsoft DiskPart version 5.2.3790
Copyright (C) 1999-2001 Microsoft Corporation.
On computer: WIN2003SERVER

DISKPART> help

Microsoft DiskPart version 5.2.3790

ADD         - Add a mirror to a simple volume.
ACTIVE      - Marks the current basic partition as active.
ASSIGN      - Assign a drive letter or mount point to the selected volume.
AUTOMOUNT   - Enables and disables automatic mounting of basic volumes.
BREAK       - Break a mirror set.
CLEAN       - Clear the configuration information, or all information, off the
              disk.
CONVERT     - Converts between different disk formats.
CREATE      - Create a volume or partition.
DELETE      - Delete an object.
DETAIL      - Provide details about an object.
EXIT        - Exit DiskPart
EXTEND      - Extend a volume.
GPT         - Assigns attributes to the selected GPT partition.
HELP        - Prints a list of commands.
IMPORT      - Imports a disk group.
INACTIVE    - Marks the current basic partition as inactive.
LIST        - Prints out a list of objects.
ONLINE      - Online a disk that is currently marked as offline.
REM         - Does nothing. Used to comment scripts.
REMOVE      - Remove a drive letter or mount point assignment.
REPAIR      - Repairs a RAID-5 volume with a failed member.
RESCAN      - Rescan the computer looking for disks and volumes.
RETAIN      - Place a retained partition under a simple volume.
SELECT      - Move the focus to an object.

DISKPART>
```

These commands will cause DiskPart to return information about the first partition on the first physical disk located on your machine. You can call the DiskPart utility with a command similar to the following:

```
DiskPart /s "C:\MyScripts\View Disk Information.script"
```

Figure 5-19 shows the results.

on the
job

A rather annoying "feature" of the numbering of disks, partitions, and volumes is that some of them are zero-based and some are one-based (that is, the first disk is labeled "0," whereas the first partition is labeled "1"). Since you can create a lot of problems by incorrectly using the DiskPart tool, be sure you select the appropriate object before carrying out an action!

FIGURE 5-19   Viewing the results of running a DiskPart script

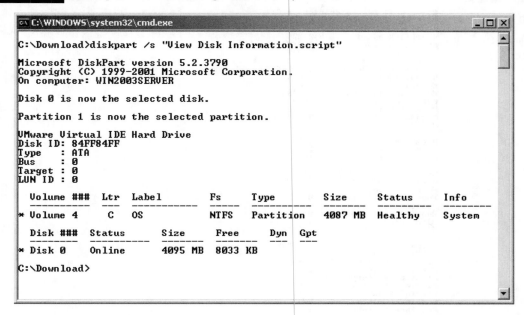

```
C:\Download>diskpart /s "View Disk Information.script"

Microsoft DiskPart version 5.2.3790
Copyright (C) 1999-2001 Microsoft Corporation.
On computer: WIN2003SERVER

Disk 0 is now the selected disk.

Partition 1 is now the selected partition.

VMware Virtual IDE Hard Drive
Disk ID: 84FF84FF
Type    : ATA
Bus     : 0
Target  : 0
LUN ID  : 0

  Volume ###  Ltr  Label        Fs     Type        Size     Status     Info
  ----------  ---  ----------   -----  ----------  -------  ---------  --------
* Volume 4     C   OS           NTFS   Partition   4087 MB  Healthy    System

  Disk ###  Status      Size     Free     Dyn  Gpt
  --------  ----------  -------  -------   ---  ---
* Disk 0    Online      4095 MB  8033 KB

C:\Download>
```

Using the FSUtil tool

The File System Utility (FSUtil) tool is useful for viewing detailed information about the file systems that are in use on your servers. Unlike the DiskPart tool, the FSUtil tool does not run interactively. Instead, you must pass it the entire command that you want to execute on a single line. For example, the following command will return basic statistics related to the C: volume on a server (the results are shown in Figure 5-20).

```
fsutil fsinfo statistics C:
```

Overall, the command-line disk management utilities provide you with a powerful method for quickly and easily viewing and modifying disk configurations.

Troubleshooting Disk Issues

When managing basic and dynamic disks using the Disk Manager tool or command-line utilities, you may find that your disks and volumes have various statuses. In previous sections, you've looked at the various ways in which disks can be managed to resolve problems. For example, you looked at how disks can be repaired or reactivated in the case of failure. In this section, you'll take a brief look at the possible statuses for disks and volumes, along with their meanings.

FIGURE 5-20

Using FSUtil to
view file system
statistics

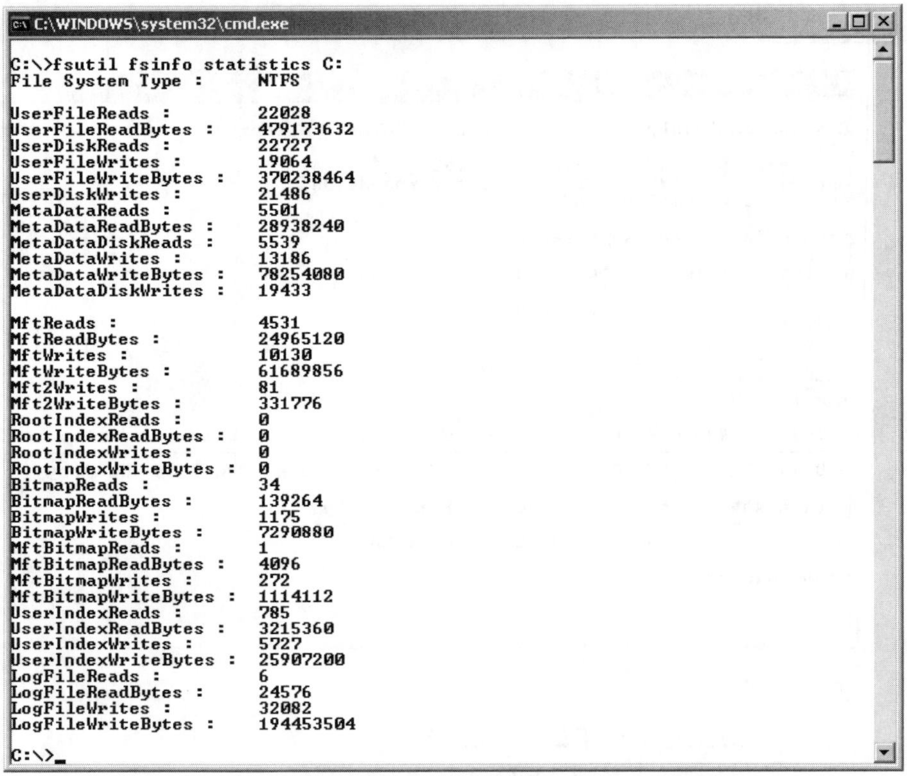

```
C:\>fsutil fsinfo statistics C:
File System Type :     NTFS

UserFileReads :        22028
UserFileReadBytes :    479173632
UserDiskReads :        22727
UserFileWrites :       19064
UserFileWriteBytes :   370238464
UserDiskWrites :       21486
MetaDataReads :        5501
MetaDataReadBytes :    28938240
MetaDataDiskReads :    5539
MetaDataWrites :       13186
MetaDataWriteBytes :   78254080
MetaDataDiskWrites :   19433

MftReads :             4531
MftReadBytes :         24965120
MftWrites :            10130
MftWriteBytes :        61689856
Mft2Writes :           81
Mft2WriteBytes :       331776
RootIndexReads :       0
RootIndexReadBytes :   0
RootIndexWrites :      0
RootIndexWriteBytes :  0
BitmapReads :          34
BitmapReadBytes :      139264
BitmapWrites :         1175
BitmapWriteBytes :     7290880
MftBitmapReads :       1
MftBitmapReadBytes :   4096
MftBitmapWrites :      272
MftBitmapWriteBytes :  1114112
UserIndexReads :       785
UserIndexReadBytes :   3215360
UserIndexWrites :      5727
UserIndexWriteBytes :  25907200
LogFileReads :         6
LogFileReadBytes :     24576
LogFileWrites :        32082
LogFileWriteBytes :    194453504

C:\>
```

Disk Status Information

Disks within the Disk Manager tool can have several different statuses that specify
how a disk is functioning. Table 5-5 provides a listing of various disk statuses, along
with the basic meaning of each.

TABLE 5-5

Disk Statuses and
Their Meanings

Disk Status	Meaning
Audio CD	The disk is an audio compact disc.
Foreign	A dynamic disk is recognized as belonging to another machine (perhaps because you're moving it from another server). The disk can be imported so that it can be used in this machine.
Initializing	The disk is being converted from a basic disk to a dynamic disk. This process is generally relatively fast.
Missing	A dynamic disk is unavailable (perhaps due to failure or having been removed from the server). When the disk is replaced, you can reactivate it to make it available for use again.

	Disk Status	Meaning
TABLE 5-5 Disk Statuses and Their Meanings *(continued)*	No Media	A removable media drive (e.g., a CD-ROM or DVD-ROM device) does not currently contain any media.
	Not Initialized	This status may appear on a disk that has been newly added to a server system. Before a disk can be used, it must be initialized.
	Online	This is the normal status for a disk that is available and is working properly.
	Online (Errors)	If a server encounters errors when reading and writing to a dynamic disk, the disk will be noted as being Online, but with errors. You can attempt to reactivate the disk (to place it back in Online status), but if the problem occurs again, it's possible that there is a physical problem with the device.
	Offline	If a dynamic disk is not accessible, it will be marked as Offline. If the problem has been corrected, you can try to reactivate the disk to place it Online. If that fails, the hardware may need to be verified and/or replaced.
	Unreadable	This status may occur if bad media are placed in a removable drive, or if a device has failed. You should verify and/or replace the hardware to try to resolve the issue. You may need to use the Rescan Disks option to retest the device after a change is made.

Volume Status Information

Volumes can have various statuses, depending on their current state and any operations that might be in process. Table 5-6 provides a listing of various volume statuses, along with common troubleshooting steps (if appropriate).

By being prepared ahead of time for the various failure and error messages and statuses that are possible, you'll be set for common disk-related troubleshooting steps.

e x a m

ⓦatch

The information in these tables may seem overwhelming, especially if you're trying to memorize all of the possible statuses. A better approach would be to gain a solid understanding of the disk configurations that are supported and various events that might occur with them. If you need to, review the information presented earlier in this chapter.

TABLE 5-6	Volume Statuses, Their Meanings, and Troubleshooting Steps	

Volume Status	Description	Troubleshooting
Failed	The disk is not functioning properly.	Attempt to reactivate the disk. If unsuccessful, replace the disk.
Failed Redundancy	One of the volumes in a fault-tolerant set (mirrored or RAID-5 volumes) has failed.	Repair or replace the failed device. Then, reactivate the volume to reenable the fault tolerance. Alternatively, you can use the repair option to use another disk to rebuild the redundancy.
Formatting	The disk is currently being formatted.	N/A
Healthy	The disk is available and is working properly. Various substatuses can provide more information about the volume.	N/A
Regenerating	A disk in a RAID-5 volume is being rebuilt.	N/A
Resynching	A disk in a mirrored volume is being resynchronized to ensure that both disks contain the same information.	N/A
Unknown	May specify foreign disks or other error conditions.	Foreign disks may be imported. If problems with redundancy information are encountered, the volume may have to be re-created.
Data Incomplete	One or more disks for a multidisk volume is not present. For example, only two disks out of a three-disk spanned volume are present.	Move the other disk(s) to the new computer. If this is not possible, you may have to re-create the entire volume.
Data Not Redundant	A disk is in a mirrored or RAID-5 configuration, but the data is not redundant.	Fix the problem with the redundant volume set by reactivating or repairing the volume.
Stale Data	Information stored on one or more disks in a volume may not be up-to-date.	Try to reactivate the volume set. Verify the hardware.

More Storage Management Techniques

Now that you have a good, solid understanding of Windows Server 2003's disk architecture and how it can be managed, let's look at some more features that enable you to better administer disk resources. The goal is to make data easily accessible and manageable for systems administrators and end users alike.

Thus far, we've limited our discussion to the basic operations that every systems administrator should be familiar with, regardless of the operating system or platform on which they're running. The features in Windows Server 2003 go far beyond those basic requirements, however. In this section, you'll take a look at some advanced file system and storage management features that can save time and improve operations.

Understanding Volume Mount Points

Volume mount points enable you to make a volume available through a point in an existing file system. For example, you can add a new dynamic volume to your hard disk. Then, you can mount this volume to a path called C:\Storage. When users access the C:\Storage folder, they'll actually be reading and writing data to and from the separate volume.

Volume mount points allow you to easily administer storage resources without copying large amounts of data between file systems. For example, suppose your D:\Users\Public folder is running low on space. To solve the problem, you want to add another hard disk to your machine to provide additional storage space. You have several ways to do this. Perhaps the most obvious is to create another volume (for example, "E:"), and then instruct your users to store data in the new location. Using volume mount points, however, you could back up the data stored in this folder, mount a dynamic volume to the path D:\Users\Public, and then restore the data. Figure 5-21 shows another possible example of how volume mount points might be implemented. In this way, users would not have to make any changes, and they'll be able to take advantage of the new storage space without any reconfiguration.

You can easily create and manage volume mount points by using the Disk Management MMC utility or the mountvol command-line utility. For example, in Disk Management, you can right-click a volume, choose Change Drive Letter and Paths" and then click "Add" to create a new volume mount point (shown in the following illustration). Or, you can run the command `mountvol /L` to view a list of shadow copies on the local system.

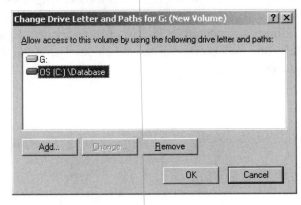

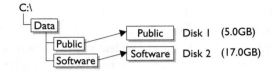

FIGURE 5-21

A logical overview
of volume mount
points

Using NTFS Compression

NTFS compression functions at the level of the file system redirector (the components
of the operating system that are required for reading and writing data to disks). A common
concern among systems administrators is that enabling compression can create significant
overhead, causing a decrease in overall performance. While this is certainly true, modern
computers are able to perform these operations so quickly that the performance hit
may be undetectable on all but the busiest of servers. Note that in some cases, using
NTFS compression can actually *increase* performance by reducing the number of
physical read operations that must be performed in order to pull data from disk.

on the
job

*NTFS compression's main strength is that it is easy to configure and that
file compression and decompression operations are transparent to users.
However, in the interest of performance and manageability, it does not
perform the highest levels of compression. If you want greater
compression, look for third-party tools and utilities that can be used to
compress files.*

NTFS compression can be enabled for an entire volume, or for specific folders
(or files). To enable compression, you can simply access the properties of a volume, a
folder, or a file. For example, by viewing the properties of a local drive, you can place
a check mark in the Compress Drive To Save Disk Space option (see Figure 5-22).

When you enable this option, you can choose to apply changes only to the selected
item (which specifies that future files will be compressed), or you can choose to apply
the compression setting to all of the underlying folders. By default, Windows Explorer
will show compressed folders in an alternate color. Also, files that are compressed
using NTFS compression cannot be encrypted. In all other ways, however, using
files and folders on compressed volumes is done in the same way as managing
uncompressed files.

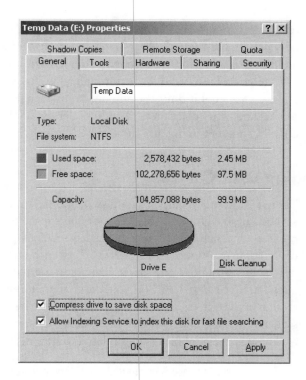

FIGURE 5-22

Enabling
compression
for the contents
of an entire
hard disk

CERTIFICATION OBJECTIVE 5.03

Managing and Monitoring Disk Quotas

At the beginning of this chapter, I mentioned that one of the common problems that face IT systems administrators is that no amount of storage space seems to be enough for users. It seems that there's always another application or file that wants to use up every last byte of available space on your file servers. In some cases, these requirements are legitimate—in order to support more users, you'll definitely need more drive space. But in other cases, a lot of space is wasted due to poor management by end users.

Often, users don't realize that disk space is limited and that it can be very expensive to purchase, maintain, and back up large file servers. Therefore, many users will look at network shares (such as their home directories) as virtually bottomless pits that can hold all of their files forever. The end result is that file shares tend to be filled with outdated information, unnecessary copies of the same data, and generally, things that really don't need to be stored. Sometimes, it takes only one or a few users to hog so much space on a server that you need to add additional hard disks just to support them. So how can you manage this problem?

One possible solution for better managing disk space is through the use of disk quotas. Disk quotas limit the amount of disk space that users can occupy on file servers and other computers. Windows Server 2003 provides basic support for enabling and enforcing disk quotas. Let's start by taking a look at how quotas work.

Understanding Disk Quotas

There are two main purposes for disk quotas in Windows Server 2003. The first is to set and enforce limits on the amount of disk space that users can use. The other is to provide a mechanism for monitoring disk space usage. Quotas are defined at the level of a volume in Windows Server 2003. That means that you can set up and configure disk usage restrictions only per volume (and not to specific folders or shares). Also, quotas can be created only on volumes that are formatted with the NTFS file system. Quotas apply to local users (users that log on to the computer on which the quotas are set), and to remote users (users that access your server over the network).

There are several other rules related to how disk quotas work:

- *Disk space usage is calculated according to file ownership.* This is a very important point to keep in mind. Since disk quotas are defined at the level of the volume, all files that a user owns (regardless of its location within the volume) will count toward the disk quota limit. This also means that if one user takes ownership of a file or folder, that user's disk usage will increase, and the former owner's disk usage will decrease.

- *Quotas can be used to track disk usage and/or to restrict excessive disk usage.* When quotas are configured for a volume, an Administrator can choose whether she wants to track disk usage. This will allow for reporting on disk usage for specific users, but it will not deny disk space to users that exceed their limits. Alternatively, the disk quota can be enforced, and users that exceed their limits will not be able to store additional files on a volume until they lower their disk usage.

- *Quotas do not apply to Administrators.* If a user is a member of the Administrators group on a computer, he or she will not be limited by disk quotas.

- *You can set quotas on remote file systems.* This is possible as long as you are an administrator of the remote machine, and the root volume of the remote volume is shared. This is useful for when you want to administer disk quotas over the network.

■ *NTFS compression has no bearing on quota-related disk usage calculations.* So, far example, if a systems administrator or a user enables NTFS compression for a folder on which quotas are based, the uncompressed file sizes will still be used to determine users' disk space usage.

■ *Quota events can be logged.* When disk quota warning levels or limits are reached, an event can be written to the event log. These events can be periodically reviewed by systems administrators to check for excessive disk usage or to notify users of pending disk usage limits.

Now that you have looked at the basic rules and concepts related to how disk quotas work, let's look at how disk quotas can be configured.

Enabling and Configuring Disk Quotas

By default, when you install Windows Server 2003, disk quotas are not enabled for any volumes. The first step in implementing disk quotas for tracking or restricting disk usage is to enable this feature. This process is fairly simple. To view quota settings, right-click a volume (using Windows Explorer or the My Computer icon) and select the quota tab. Figure 5-23 shows the options that are available.

Using these configuration settings, you can see the current status of quotas for the volume (whether they are enabled or disabled). Then, you can choose whether you want to enable quota management. Note that this will not automatically deny disk space to users—that's the purpose of the next option, labeled Deny Disk Space To Users Exceeding Limit. If you choose to deny disk space to users, you have two options for the default settings for new users. First, you can choose not to deny disk space. This setting specifies that disk space will not be limited for users that don't have specific quota entries. The other option is to define a default disk space limit and a warning level. Finally, you can choose logging options for disk quota functionality. You can choose to log events when a user exceeds his or her warning levels or disk limit levels. As you'll see later in this section, you will be able to use the Event Viewer to view log entries related to disk quotas.

FIGURE 5-23

Viewing quota
settings for a
volume

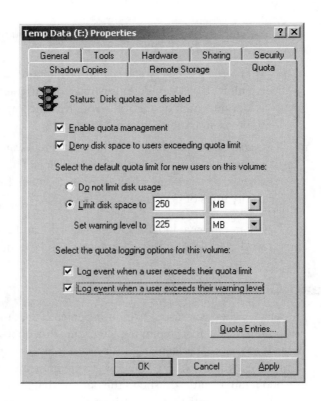

To enable disk quotas for this volume, you can click either Apply or OK. You will see a dialog box that notifies you that the current disk will need to be scanned for existing usage statistics and that this may take several minutes.

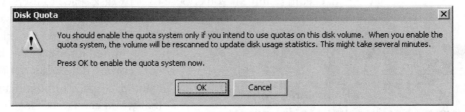

You can also enable default disk quota settings when you configure your computer with the File Server role. This method is covered in Chapter 4.

Managing Quota Entries

Quota entries define to which users quotas will apply, and what that user's disk usage limits are. By clicking the Quota Entries button on the Disk Quota tab, you can specify disk usage limits and warning level settings for individual users of this volume (see Figure 5-24).

To add new quotas, click New Entry. You will be given the choice to select a user (which can be a local user or a domain user). Then, you can specify whether you want to enable limits for this user and, if so, what those limits should be.

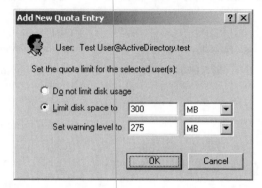

In order to delete a quota entry, the user whose entry you delete must not own any files on the volume. Therefore, you must either take ownership of any files owned by the user, or you must move those files to another volume.

Using the Quota Entries dialog box, you can also choose to export quota entry information to a file (which has no default name or extension). You can then import these quota settings on other volumes to save time and avoid errors.

Monitoring Disk Quota Usage

Once you have enabled disk quotas, it's important to monitor them to determine which users are at or near their limits, and to view overall disk space usage information. In this section, you'll look at ways in which you can monitor disk quota information.

FIGURE 5-24 Viewing quota entry information

Quota Entries for OS (C:)

Quota   Edit   View   Help

Status	Name	Logon Name	Amount Used	Quota Limit	Warning Level	Percent Used
OK	Test User4	TestUser4@ActiveDirectory.test	0 bytes	50 MB	45 MB	0
OK	Test User3	TestUser3@ActiveDirectory.test	0 bytes	100 MB	75 MB	0
OK	Test User2	TestUser@ActiveDirectory.test	0 bytes	50 MB	45 MB	0
OK	Test User1	TestUser1@ActiveDirectory.test	0 bytes	100 MB	75 MB	0
OK		NT AUTHORITY\LOCAL SERVICE	219 KB	No Limit	No Limit	N/A
OK		NT AUTHORITY\NETWORK SERVICE	246 KB	No Limit	No Limit	N/A
OK		BUILTIN\Administrators	2.41 GB	No Limit	No Limit	N/A

SCENARIO & SOLUTION

You want to track disk usage for specific users of a volume, but you do not want to deny disk space to any users.	Enable disk quotas for the volume, but do not enable the Deny Disk Space To Users Exceeding Quota Limit option.
You want to set separate disk quotas for various folders located on the same volume.	This is not possible using Windows Server 2003's disk quota system.
You want to provide different quota limits for different groups of users.	Use the Quota Entries screen to specify quota settings for each user individually. Windows Server 2003 does not permit setting quotas on groups, but you can use the Quota Entries dialog to change settings for multiple users at a time.
You want to copy quota settings from a volume named "UserData" to a volume named "FileShare1."	Export the quota entries from the UserData volume to a file. Then, import the file on the FileShare1 volume.

Using Quota Entries to Monitor Quotas

The Quota Entries dialog box that you looked at in the preceding section provides a good way to view disk quota–related information. The Percent Used column shows the percentage of the disk quota that is used by all of the users that have entries. By clicking this column, you can sort the list to view which users are at, or near, their disk usage limits. For convenience, you can also reorder the columns by dragging them.

When viewing quota entries, the information you're viewing may be cached. Therefore, you might want to select View | Refresh to refresh the list of names to account for any changes that may have occurred since the last time you used the utility.

Viewing Quota Information with the Event Viewer

Earlier, you saw how you could configure disk quota settings to generate log entries based on warnings or when disk limits are exceeded. In order to view the logged events, you can use the Event Viewer application. Disk quota–related logging events are stored in the System event log. When you want to restrict the view to only quota-related events, you can set the filter to show only events that are coming from the "ntfs" event source. Figure 5-25 shows some disk quota–related events. Figure 5-26 shows the details of a quota limit message. For more information on using the Event Viewer, see Chapter 8.

FIGURE 5-25   Viewing quota-related events using the Event Viewer

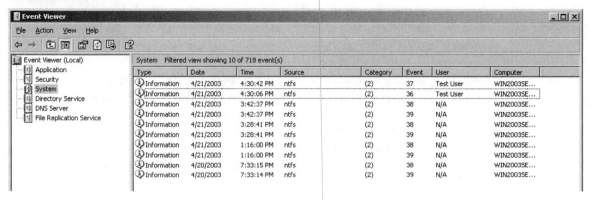

In addition to using the Quota Entries graphical tool for examining disk quota information, you can also use a command-line utility to get the same information. Let's look at that next.

FIGURE 5-26

Viewing details about a quota log entry

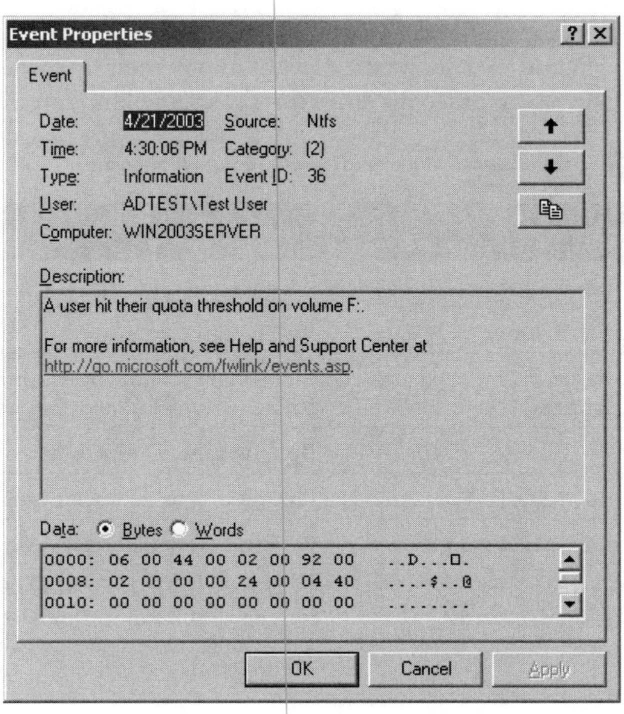

Using FSUtil to Monitor Quotas

You covered the basics of the FSUtil command earlier in this chapter. One very useful feature of the FSUtil command is in managing disk quota settings and reporting disk quota usage. Table 5-7 provides a list of useful quota-related commands that are supported by the FSUtil command.

When working with most of these commands, you'll be required to provide volume information. This information can be provided in several different ways:

- **Volume drive letter**   The letter of a drive, followed by a colon (e.g., "C:").
- **Volume mount point path**   You can specify the path of a volume mount point. For example, "C:\UserData" (assuming that it is a valid mount point) can be set.
- **Volume name**   This method (which is by far the most complicated) uses the volume's globally unique identifier (GUID). The name is in the format \\?\Volume{*GUID*}. You will need to replace "{GUID}" with the value for an existing disk. You can obtain the GUID for a volume by using the `mountvol /L` command.

For example, you can enter the command `fsutil quota query C:`. Figure 5-27 shows the types of information that would be returned. Note that the values returned for query thresholds and limits are in bytes.

TABLE 5-7   Quota-Related Commands for the FSUtil Command

FSUtil Command	Purpose
`fsutil quota disable` *Volume*	Disables disk quotas on the specified volume.
`fsutil quota enforce` *Volume*	Enables disk quota enforcement on the specified volume.
`fsutil quota modify` *Volume* *Threshold Limit* [*UserName*]	Modifies an existing quota entry, or creates a new one using the provided threshold and volume information.
`fsutil quota query` *Volume*	Returns a list of existing quota entries and settings.
`fsutil quota track` *Volume*	Enables disk usage tracking on the specified volume.
`fsutil quota violations`	Returns a list of users that have met or exceeded their quota limits.
`fsutil behavior set quotanotify` *Frequency*	By default, quota log entries are updated every hour. If you want log entries to be made more frequently, you can specify a lower value (note: the Frequency value is in seconds, so the default setting is "3600").

FIGURE 5-27   Viewing the results of running an FSUtil command

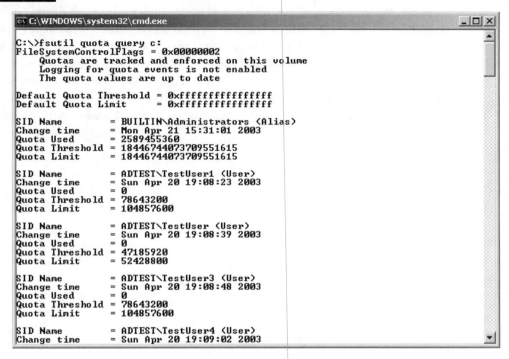

```
C:\>fsutil quota query c:
FileSystemControlFlags = 0x00000002
    Quotas are tracked and enforced on this volume
    Logging for quota events is not enabled
    The quota values are up to date

Default Quota Threshold = 0xffffffffffffffff
Default Quota Limit     = 0xffffffffffffffff

SID Name        = BUILTIN\Administrators (Alias)
Change time     = Mon Apr 21 15:31:01 2003
Quota Used      = 2589455360
Quota Threshold = 18446744073709551615
Quota Limit     = 18446744073709551615

SID Name        = ADTEST\TestUser1 (User)
Change time     = Sun Apr 20 19:08:23 2003
Quota Used      = 0
Quota Threshold = 78643200
Quota Limit     = 104857600

SID Name        = ADTEST\TestUser (User)
Change time     = Sun Apr 20 19:08:39 2003
Quota Used      = 0
Quota Threshold = 47185920
Quota Limit     = 52428800

SID Name        = ADTEST\TestUser3 (User)
Change time     = Sun Apr 20 19:08:48 2003
Quota Used      = 0
Quota Threshold = 78643200
Quota Limit     = 104857600

SID Name        = ADTEST\TestUser4 (User)
Change time     = Sun Apr 20 19:09:02 2003
```

Similarly, you can view information about quota violations by using the command `fsutil quota query C:`. For more details related to syntax and other options of the FSUtil command, see the Windows Help and Support Center.

CERTIFICATION SUMMARY

In this chapter, you covered a lot of information related to how systems administrators can manage storage resources in Windows Server 2003. You started by growing familiar with some important disk concepts, including partitions, basic disks, dynamic disks, and dynamic volume configurations. With the ability to create simple, striped, spanned, mirrored, and RAID-5 volumes, systems administrators can configure their systems to meet a wide range of requirements.

Drawing on these concepts, you drilled down into the actual *how* of managing disk storage. The primary tool that most of us will use to view and configure disk resources is the Disk Management snap-in. Using this tool, you saw how new volumes could be created. You also looked at several useful command-line utilities. Finally, you looked into disk quotas as a method for tracking and managing disk usage. Setting up disk quotas is a simple process, but systems administrators must be sure to closely monitor disk usage to identify trends and impending problems.

Using all of the techniques covered in this chapter, you should be well prepared for managing storage resources in Windows Server 2003. And, you'll be ready to tackle any storage-related questions that Microsoft might throw your way on the exam.

TWO-MINUTE DRILL

Understand and Select Server Disk Configurations Options

❑ The FAT and FAT32 file systems are designed primarily for backward compatibility and lack many of the features of NTFS.

❑ The NTFS file system provides many advantages over FAT-based file systems, including support for file system security, compression, encryption, and efficient use of space on large disks.

❑ Basic disks are designed primarily for backward compatibility with older versions of Windows and other operating systems.

❑ Basic disks can contain primary partitions (which can be used for booting operating systems) and extended partitions (which can contain multiple logical devices).

❑ Dynamic disks support advanced disk configurations, including spanned, striped, mirrored, and RAID-5 volumes.

❑ Basic disks and dynamic disks can be managed using the Disk Manager graphical tool, or through various command-line utilities such as DiskPart.

Configure, Manage, and Troubleshoot Server Disks Using the Disk Management Tool

❑ A simple dynamic volume can be created on a dynamic disk. This type of volume can be extended to include additional space on the same disks or on others.

❑ Spanned volumes can include the space from multiple physical disks and from noncontiguous portions of single disks.

❑ Striped volumes are like spanned volumes, except that they cannot be extended and can offer improved performance.

❑ Mirrored volumes offer fault tolerance for any partition, including the system or boot partition. The cost is a 50-percent decrease in the amount of available disk space.

❑ RAID-5 volumes combine the performance benefits of striped volumes with fault tolerance.

❑ A RAID-5 volume must include space from at least three different disks. The usable space in the volume will be decreased by the size of one of the members of the volume.

Manage and Monitor Disk Quotas

❑ Disk quotas are established on a per-volume basis and are designed to track and, optionally, limit the disk space available to users.

❑ When disk quotas are enabled, systems administrators can choose whether events are logged.

❑ The Quota Entries screen provides a quick and easy way to view disk quota usage information.

❑ Logged events can be viewed in the System log using the Event Viewer application.

❑ The FSUtil command-line utility can be used to manage quota settings and view quota information.

SELF TEST

The following questions will help you measure your understanding of the material presented in this chapter. Read all the choices carefully because there may be more than one correct answer. Choose all correct answers for each question.

Understand and Select Server Disk Configurations Options

1. You are a systems administrator for a Windows Server 2003 machine that has been configured with a dynamic disk. The dynamic disk contains two simple dynamic volumes. How can you convert the disk to a basic disk without losing any data?

   A. Perform the conversion directly using the Disk Manager tool.

   B. Perform the conversion directly using the DiskPart command-line utility.

   C. Perform the conversion directly using the FSUtil command-line utility.

   D. Back up the data on the simple volumes and then delete them. Perform the conversion to a basic disk and create any required volume(s). Once the conversion is complete, copy the data back to the new basic disk.

   E. None of the above.

2. During which of the following times can you select or change the file system of a Windows Server 2003 partition? (Choose all that apply.)

   A. After the operating system has been installed

   B. When formatting a new disk

   C. During the text-based portion of the setup process

   D. During the graphical portion of the setup process

3. Monica is a systems administrator who is configuring a new computer for a test lab. She needs the system to be able to boot between multiple operating systems, including Windows 98, Windows ME, and Windows Server 2003. The server contains multiple physical disks, and she wants to use the same Windows Server 2003 disk configuration for all of them. Which of the following disk configurations will meet these requirements?

   A. Dynamic disks configured with NTFS

   B. Dynamic disks configured with FAT32

   C. Basic disks configured with NTFS

   D. Basic disks configured with FAT32

   E. None of the above

4. Carlos is a systems administrator of a Windows Server 2003 machine. He has just added a new disk to the server and has configured it as a basic disk. He wants to configure the device to have three local drive letters. How can he do this? (Choose all that apply.)

   A. Create a single primary partition on the disk and then assign three drive letters to the partition.

   B. Convert the disk to a dynamic disk and then create three simple volumes, each with one of the drive letters.

   C. Create three separate primary partitions on the basic disk and assign a drive letter to each.

   D. Create a single extended partition. Within the extended partition, create three logical drives, each with its own drive letter.

   E. Convert the disk to a dynamic disk and then create a new spanned volume. Assign three drive letters to the spanned volume.

Configure, Manage, and Troubleshoot Server Disks Using the Disk Management Tool

5. Which of the following types of dynamic volumes can be used to provide fault tolerance for the boot partition of a Windows Server 2003 machine?

   A. Striped

   B. Mirrored

   C. RAID-5

   D. Spanned

   E. Simple

6. Tran is a systems administrator who is in charge of a very busy file server that experiences frequent write operations. After doing some performance monitoring on the server, she has decided that implementing a RAID solution will increase performance. The solution must also provide fault tolerance. However, the server is an older machine, and the CPU and memory utilization on the server is very high already. Which of the following methods will likely provide the best overall performance?

   A. Adding several new dynamic volumes

   B. Creating a new RAID-5 volume and copying all files to the new volume

   C. Implementing a hardware-based RAID solution

   D. Combining all of the data onto a single, large physical disk

7. Which of the following types of dynamic volumes will provide the best write performance?

    A. Simple

    B. Spanned

    C. Striped

    D. RAID-5

    E. Mirrored

8. After a reorganization of your department, you are moving several disks (all configured as dynamic disks) from one Windows Server 2003 machine to another. The data must be preserved during the move. You have already performed the necessary operations on the source server, and you have installed the disks on the destination server. The disks are visible in the Disk Manager. Which of these steps must you take before you can use the new disks?

    A. Reinitialize the new disks so that they can be used by the new server.

    B. Right-click the transferred disks and select Import Foreign Disk.

    C. Reactivate the new disks so that they can be used by the destination server.

    D. Format the new disks using NTFS to ensure that they are ready for use in the new machine.

    E. None of the above.

9. Several months ago, Chris implemented a RAID-5 volume on a Windows Server 2003 machine that he is responsible for. The volume includes four physical disks. Recently, users have complained of decreased performance. Upon examining the disk configuration, Chris found that the Disk Manager shows the status of the volume as "Failed redundancy." The Disk Manager also shows the disks in the volume as "Failed." Which of the following steps should he take to resolve the problem? (Choose all that apply; each answer is part of the solution.)

    A. Break the RAID-5 volume.

    B. Reduce the number of disks in the RAID-5 volume.

    C. Reactivate the RAID-5 volume.

    D. Replace the failed hard disk with a new one.

    E. Do nothing—the failure will be automatically resolved.

10. Which of the following types of dynamic volumes can be extended after they have been created? (Choose all that apply.)

    A. Spanned

    B. Mirrored

    C. RAID-5

    D. Simple

    E. Striped

Manage and Monitor Disk Quotas

11. You have enabled disk quotas and logging of quota-related events. In which of the following logs shown in the Event Viewer will these events be displayed?

A. System

B. Active Directory

C. File System

D. NTFS

E. Security

12. Helene wants to write a batch file that will display disk quota usage information. Which of the following commands will display this information?

A. `fsutil quota violations`

B. `diskquota /status`

C. `fsutil quota query C:`

D. `fsutil fsinfo volumeinfo C:\`

E. None of the above

13. Raj is a systems administrator for several Windows Server 2003 file servers that are part of the same domain. On one of these machines, he has configured disk quotas for users throughout his organization. He now wants to apply these same settings to a volume on a new server that has been added to the domain. How can he do this with the least administrative effort?

A. Copy all of the contents of the source volume to the new volume. Reset the file system permissions.

B. Manually re-create the quota entries on the new volume.

C. Use the Copy From command from the Quota Entries window and specify the source volume.

D. Export the quota entries from the source volume to a file. Then, import the quota entries on the new volume.

LAB QUESTION

You are a systems administrator for the Accounting department of a large organization. Recently, you have been tasked with implementing a new server to manage the increased needs of the Accounting department. This new server must meet several requirements. First, there must be at least 50GB of usable disk space for storing user files. Second, the system must be able to survive the failure of any single hard disk. Finally, performance is an important concern for all of the users.

You have purchased a new server that will be used to meet these requirements. Your budget did not allow for the inclusion of a hardware-based RAID solution. The server shipped with six physical SCSI hard disks, each of which is 18GB in capacity. All of the disks are attached to a single SCSI controller. The disk shipped with no operating system, and you have installed Windows Server 2003 to an NTFS partition that spans the entire first 18GB disk.

How should you configure this server to meet the Accounting department's requirements?

SELF TEST ANSWERS

Understand and Select Server Disk Configurations Options

1. ☑ **D.** If a dynamic disk contains volumes, it cannot be directly converted to a basic disk. Instead, you must first delete any volumes on the dynamic disk. Therefore, you must manually back up all of the data on the volumes, perform the conversion, and then copy the data back.
   ☒ A, B, C are incorrect because it is not possible to directly perform a conversion from a dynamic disk that contains volumes to a basic disk.

2. ☑ **A, B, C.** You can choose whether you want the partition to be formatted with a FAT-based file system or NTFS during any of these times.
   ☒ D is incorrect because, after the text-based portion of the setup process is complete, it is too late to make any changes to the file system that is used by any partition.

3. ☑ **D.** Only basic disks configured with the FAT32 file system will support Windows 98, Windows ME, and Windows Server 2003.
   ☒ A, B, and C are incorrect because of the fact that Windows 98 and Windows ME do not recognize NTFS partitions or dynamic disks. Since Monica wants to configure all of the disks in the same way, only a basic disk configured with FAT32 will work.

4. ☑ **B, C, D.** Each of these options will allow Carlos to configure the new device to use multiple device letters. Since this is a new disk, it will be easy either to create primary and extended partitions (in the case of a basic disk) or to create simple volumes (following the conversion to a dynamic disk). These choices highlight the flexibility of Windows Server 2003's disk architecture.
   ☒ A is incorrect because a partition can have only one logical drive letter assigned to it. E is incorrect because a spanned volume is still considered a single volume, and it can have only one logical drive letter.

Configure, Manage, and Troubleshoot Server Disks Using the Disk Management Tool

5. ☑ **B.** The only fault-tolerant configuration that offers support for system and boot partitions is disk mirroring.
   ☒ A, D, and E are incorrect because these types of dynamic volumes do not provide fault tolerance. C is incorrect because RAID-5 volumes cannot contain a system or boot partition.

6. ☑ **C.** Since the server is already using much of its CPU and memory resources, a hardware-based solution is the best choice. Hardware-based RAID controllers offload a

significant amount of CPU overhead from the server itself, while still providing for fault tolerance and increased performance.

☒ A is incorrect because the addition of dynamic volumes, by itself, will not have any impact on performance. B is incorrect because the creation of a new RAID-5 volume in Windows Server 2003 will likely add significant CPU overhead (since the server performs many write operations). D is incorrect because, in general, multiple smaller disks can provide increased performance over a single large disk.

7. ☑ **C.** In striped volumes, data is written to multiple physical devices simultaneously. This can noticeably improve performance for large read operations, since multiple physical disks can be read from simultaneously.

☒ A, B, D, and E are incorrect, since these dynamic disk configurations either have no impact on write performance or may exhibit decreased write performance.

8. ☑ **B.** Following the transfer of the disks into a new machine, they will be marked as "Foreign" (indicating the disks were created on another machine). Before they can be used on the destination server, you must choose Import Foreign Disk. This will make the disks available for use.

☒ A and D are incorrect because they would result in the loss of all data on the transferred disks. C is incorrect, since reactivation is possible only for fault-tolerant volumes and for disks that are already accessible on the server.

9. ☑ **C** and **D.** The first step in resolving this problem is to correct the hardware failure that occurred. In this case, the safest solution would be to replace the failed hard disk with a new one. Once the new hardware is ready for use, the RAID-5 volume can be reactivated to regenerate the lost information.

☒ A is incorrect because this would result in the loss of all data on the volume. B is incorrect because RAID-5 volumes, once they have been created, cannot be resized. E is incorrect because this problem will not correct itself—the hardware failure must be resolved, and the RAID-5 volume must be reactivated.

10. ☑ **A** and **D.** Both simple and spanned volumes can be extended to include additional space on the same or on different physical disks.

☒ B, C, and E are incorrect because these dynamic volume types cannot be extended after their creation.

Manage and Monitor Disk Quotas

11. ☑ **A.** Disk quota–related events are stored in the System log.

☒ B, C, D, and E are incorrect since quota-related events are stored in the System log.

12. ☑ **C.** This command will provide information about all of the users for which Quota Entries exist, along with information about disk usage.
    ☒ A is incorrect, since it will display information only about users that have exceeded their quotas. B is not a valid command. D will not provide information related to quotas.

13. ☑ **D.** The Quota Entries utility allows you to export quota information to a file. This file can then be imported using the Quota Entries utility on the new volume. This method ensures quick and accurate copying of the quota settings.
    ☒ A is incorrect, since this would not result in the copying of quota settings. B would work, but this process is certainly not as efficient as using the export/import process. C is incorrect because there is no such option in the Quota Entries utility.

LAB ANSWER

The most important thing to keep in mind when designing disk storage solutions is that there can be multiple solutions that meet the requirements. Often, your job is to find the best one (or *ones*, if multiple options are equally good). Let's start by taking a look at what we have to work with. We have six 18GB hard disks for a total of 108GB of usable disk space (I'm ignoring overhead and slack for the sake of simplicity). Our requirements are to provide at least 50GB of usable disk space for user files, and to ensure that all of the disks are fault tolerant.

You know that implementing fault tolerance involves redundancy. And, redundancy involves a loss of usable disk space. Let's start with protecting the operating system. Since a hardware-based RAID solution was not purchased, that leaves only one option—software-based disk mirroring. If it's configured as a basic disk currently, you'll need to convert the first disk to a dynamic disk. Once that's done, you can simply create a mirror of the first disk on the second 18GB disk. So far, you've lost 18GB of usable disk space.

Now, let's look at the remaining four physical disks. You have only two options for providing fault tolerance. You can create two mirrored disks, or you can create a RAID-5 volume involving all of them. If you implement disk mirroring, you'll lose 50 percent of the available disk space, leaving only 32GB of the original 64GB available for use. That won't meet the requirement of 50GB of usable disk space.

So, that leaves the second option—to create a single RAID-5 volume containing all four disks. In this case, you'll lose the space of one of the disks to redundancy, but that would leave 54GB (3 × 18GB) of usable disk space. You have met the requirements with a little bit of extra breathing room. Regarding performance, mirroring would probably have been better, but it would not have met the space requirements. Note that if you had an additional disk (five total), you could have used a combination of mirroring (perhaps for the most frequently used files) and RAID-5 (for the remaining three disks).

How could this solution be improved upon? Well, for one thing, there still exists a single point of failure: the disk controller. Similar to putting all of one's eggs in a single basket, the failure of the disk controller would result in a total loss of access to the server (at least until the control was replaced). The same is true for many other critical system components, including the CPU, memory, and network cards. Fortunately, disk controller failures are relatively rare. When the budget allows for it, the purchase of an additional controller could improve performance and increase reliability.

As you have seen, there are several potential "right" answers to this lab question. Be sure to keep this in mind when you're taking the exam, and when you're working on storage management in the real world!

MICROSOFT® CERTIFIED SYSTEMS ENGINEER
& MICROSOFT® CERTIFIED SYSTEMS ADMINISTRATOR

6

Managing and Implementing Disaster Recovery

CERTIFICATION OBJECTIVES

Modern organizations depend on information in order to meet business and technical goals. They therefore depend on the availability of their computers, and the data that they manage. Perhaps one of the most important functions for IT professionals today is the protection of data. In addition to managing performance, security, and other functions, you need to make sure that the information that's stored on your organization's client and server computer systems is protected from hardware failures and other problems that could result in the loss of irreplaceable information.

Realizing this, Microsoft expects you to have a solid understanding of how to implement and schedule backup jobs. Drawing on this understanding, you should know how to recover from various types of failures or problems—ranging from the loss of a few user files to the failure of an entire server. Fortunately, as you'll see in this chapter, Microsoft has provided many different methods for enhancing reliability and data protection in Windows Server 2003. It's up to you—the systems administrator—to put these features to good use!

In this chapter, you'll start by looking at the concepts upon which Windows Server 2003's backup technology is based. You'll then look at ways in which the Windows Backup utility can be used to protect the various types of information that exist on your server installations. Then, we'll change the focus to the other (and at least as important) aspect of data protection—recovery. You'll look at how you can recover data and operating system information in the event that certain types of failure occur. There's a lot to cover, so let's get started!

on the **Job**

It seems that occasionally, the IT industry will start a huge push emphasizing the importance of disaster recovery, business continuity planning, and a host of other data protection methods. Resist the urge to follow the fashions and trends related to backups and data protection. The best long-term solution is to make overall data protection an integral part of your systems administration efforts. Whenever you are planning for adding a new server, plan for its backup and recovery, as well. And, budget time and hardware costs for performing these backups. In the real world, backup and recovery concerns should be a part of just about any IT implementation.

Understanding Backup Concepts, Procedures, and Operations

There are several reasons for backing up data. Some are obvious, and some may not be the ones that you think of first when asked about why you need to back up data. First and foremost, the fundamental purpose of performing backups is to allow for recovery. All too often, it seems that systems administrators design and implement backup solutions. They even spend time periodically verifying that backups were performed correctly. These operations are important, but you should always keep the end goal in mind—recovering data. In many cases, it's simply not good enough just to be able to retrieve information after it's lost. As a systems administrator, you must make sure that recovery operations can be performed quickly and accurately, and that they meet the needs of your organization.

With all that said, start by looking at what types of problems you're trying to protect against. Reasons for investing time, effort, and resources in implementing backup and recovery techniques include

- **Protecting against hardware failures**   A simple fact for almost all technology is that it will eventually fail. Pessimists would say that there's some supernatural force that seems to wait for the worst possible time for a failure to occur before it rears its ugly head. Computer hardware devices have finite lifetimes, and almost any systems administrator can probably tell stories about failed hard disks or a CPU fan that failed, causing intermittent server lockups during periods of activity. Some types of failures, such as the failure of a noncritical server, can be minor annoyances. Others, such as corrupted hard disks, can result in significant data loss. In any case, hardware failures do occur, and the creation of backups is necessary to manage the negative impact of these events.

- **Protecting against accidental data loss**   If you ask a systems administrator about why he or she performs backups, they're likely to mention the threat of hardware failures first. However, although the threat of hardware failures is very real, in most environments, simple human error is a much more likely cause of problems. For example, a mistake in modifying or deleting a Microsoft Word document can cause a lot of damage from which you can't easily recover (as I typed that, by the way, I just made another copy of the manuscript for this chapter!). For example, suppose a systems administrator accidentally deletes a large number of users. Without the necessary backups, it would probably be impossible to recover the lost information. And, the "user-friendliness" of modern operating systems and applications makes it simple to make mistakes that can result in data loss.

■ **Recording and maintaining historical data**   Certain types of information exhibit a very strange characteristic: You know it's important, but you never really know exactly which data you'll need when. An important function for many IT organizations is to keep an archive of old data, in case it's ever needed again. For example, suppose that a lawsuit is filed against your organization and that a court order requires that certain memos be made available as evidence. Or, perhaps your company has decided to reenter a marketplace that it exited several years ago. Without a good historical record of data, you may never be able to get this information (for better or for worse). For many organizations, knowledge is one of the most important assets that the company "owns." And, the financial services and medical industries also have mandatory legal requirements to keep specific types of information for extended periods of time. By keeping backups over time, you can recover information from older data when necessary.

■ **Protection against malicious users**   Even in the most secure environments, it is conceivable that unauthorized users (or authorized ones with malicious intent!) could delete or modify valuable information. In such cases, the loss of data might require valid backups from which to restore critical information. Without adequate backups, the damage that can be caused by intentional actions can be permanent and irreversible.

Now that you have a basic understanding of some of the reasons for performing backups, let's drill down into some important technical information about how backups can be performed.

Understanding Backup Operations

The art of making backups of important data is almost as old as modern computers themselves. An entire subset of the IT industry is devoted to providing backup and recovery hardware and software. Although the specific tools and features may vary between systems, some general backup-related concepts are often used. In this section, you'll take a look at different ways in which backup operations can be performed.

In an ideal world, storage would be so cheap that you'd never have to worry about running out of space to do backups. Storage itself would be so reliable, in fact, that backups would rarely be necessary. And, backup operations would complete instantly, not requiring any significant time or resources that could slow down servers during busy hours. Unfortunately, in the real world, the situation is quite different. In the simplest backup operation, you would choose to back up all of the files on your server very frequently. Real-world constraints, however, may prevent this. Some of the possible issues that your IT organization may face include

- **Hardware limitations**   Hardware devices and media are all limited by the laws of physics. In relation to performing backups, the main limitations are in regards to speed and capacity. Backup media can store only a limited amount of information (although these limits are being increased seemingly every day). And, it takes time to transfer data between different storage devices. Limitations of the storage hardware and any connections between them can severely limit how much information you can transfer in a given time.

- **Budget constraints**   Almost all organizations are limited by one important resource—money. As with many other areas of IT, systems administrators and IT decision-makers must choose the most cost-effective method for meeting their backup requirements. These constraints can further limit backup performance and capacity.

- **A limited "backup window"**   Performing backup operations can use valuable resources on busy servers. In some environments, the performance impact of performing backups makes it prohibitive during busy times. Therefore, many systems administrators have a limited amount of time (often referred to as the "backup window") in which their backup operations must complete.

- **Limited personnel**   In most IT environments, there simply isn't enough time or personnel to manually monitor all backup operations. Therefore, automated methods that are reliable (and periodically tested) are a must.

- **End-user issues**   Many users would like all of the data that they've ever created to be readily available in an instant. And, they'd like to be able to "undo" the deletion of a file that occurred several months ago. Because of the constraints of storage space, it's not practical to retain all of this data. Still, data must be made available for users to effectively do their jobs.

- **Backup retention**   For various reasons, businesses may require their IT departments to store back data for extended periods of time. This can place significant burdens on backup devices, since their storage capacities are limited. Generally, long-term backups are created on removable media, which are then stored off-site.

All of these constraints, when combined, can make the implementation of backup and recovery a major challenge. For example, you may not have enough storage to make a copy of all of the data on your server every day. And, even if you did, the operation might take far too long to be efficient. Or, the hardware required to make that happen would cost far more than your budget allows. To work within all of these limitations, you will likely need to decide what's important to back up, and when those backups should be made. That's why almost all backup utilities (including Windows Server 2003's Backup utility) support different backup types. It's time to take a look at the various options that are available.

Understanding the Archive Flag

One of the most important issues when dealing with backups is keeping track of which files have been backed up and which files need to be backed up. In Windows Server 2003, this is provided for within the supported file systems through an attribute known as the *Archive flag*. Generally, whenever a backup of a file is made, the Archive flag for the file is removed (specifying that the file has been backed up). And, whenever a new file is created or an existing one is modified, the archive flag is added (indicating that the current version of the file has not been backed up).

For the most part, you'll depend on your backup utilities and Windows Server 2003 to handle setting the Archive flag for you automatically. However, you can view the attributes of files or folders by right-clicking them and selecting Properties. By clicking Advanced, you will see the option File Is Ready For Archiving. The following illustration shows an example of the attributes for a file.

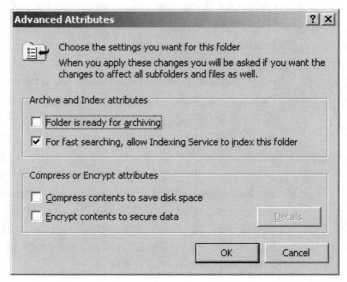

You can change the setting of the archive flag by simply placing or removing a check mark in this box. Note that, as with other attributes, you'll be given the opportunity to apply the change to the current object and, optionally, to any child objects (for example, to any files and folders located within a folder on which you set the archive attribute). Now that you understand the purpose of the archive flag and how it works, look at how this information is actually used to make the job of managing backups easier.

Normal Backups

In some scenarios, you might choose to always back up all of the files on your servers with every backup operation. In other cases, however, it is much more efficient and manageable to back up only files that have changed recently. There are several backup types that you can choose to work with when you use the Windows Backup utility. In this section, you'll look at several different types of backup operations. You'll also look at the details regarding how you can restore data from backups of that type.

A *normal* backup operation (also called a "full backup") will back up all of the selected files and then mark them as having been backed up. If time and resources permit, normal backups are the simplest way to store and recover data. Since all of the selected files are backed up, recovering from a normal backup requires access only to the medium on which the normal backup is stored.

Although it is simple to perform backup and recovery operations using normal backups, there are drawbacks to this method. First, since all of the selected data is being backed up, normal backups may require significantly more storage space (and time) than would other backup types. For example, consider the case of backing up a file server that holds 30GB of data. If you chose to implement full backups on a daily schedule (see Figure 6-1), you will generate 30GB of data in each backup (even if none or only a few of the files have changed).

Normal backups form the basis of many other types of backup operations. Let's take a look at those next.

FIGURE 6-1   Performing daily full backups

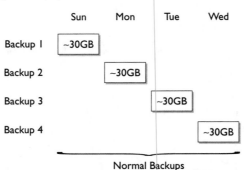

Incremental Backups

An *incremental* backup operation copies all selected files that are marked as ready for backup and then marks those files as having been backed up. The purpose of an incremental backup is to copy all files that have changed since the last full or incremental backup operation. When the next incremental backup is run, only the files that are not marked as having been backed up are stored.

Incremental backups are used in conjunction with normal backups. The general process is to make a full backup and then to make subsequent incremental backups. The benefit to this method is that only files that have changed since the last full or incremental backup will be stored. This can reduce backup times and disk or tape storage space requirements.

Common backup schedules involve a weekly full backup with incremental backups performed on every other day of the week. As an example, suppose that you are required to back up a busy file server nightly. You might start by making a full backup of the file server, and this backup might contain 30GB of data. Since your storage capacity is limited, you schedule an incremental backup operation to occur. This operation might result in a backup that is only a few gigabytes in size, because only the files that were changed since the last normal or incremental backup will be recorded. You can continue to make incremental backups on subsequent days (see Figure 6-2). Note that, if files change daily, the current version of those files will end up on each of the incremental backups.

There's an important issue that should be taken into account when performing incremental backups. When recovering information from an incremental backup operation a systems administrator will be required to first restore the normal (full) backup and then to restore *each* of the incremental backups taken up to the point of failure. Note that this means that you must have access to the original normal backup and access to *all* of the incremental backups intact in order to perform a complete restore.

For example, I might perform a normal backup on Sunday night. Then, I could choose to perform an incremental backup each night from Monday through Saturday.

| FIGURE 6-2 | Implementing incremental backups |

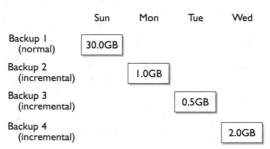

Each of the incremental backups would store only the files and folders that had been modified since the previous day. Suppose that on Thursday afternoon, a failure occurred on one of my servers and all of the data was lost. In order to restore the information, I'd have to first restore the full backup (from Sunday) and then restore (in order) backups from Monday, Tuesday, and Wednesday. That will recover my files up to the point of the backup on Wednesday evening.

Differential Backups

Differential backups are similar in purpose to incremental backups with one important exception: Differential backups copy all files that are marked for backup, but they do not mark the files as backed up. This makes differential backups "cumulative" (cumulative is another name for differential backups). The purpose of a differential backup is to store all of the files and folders that have changed since the last normal backup, regardless of whether or not any other differential backups have been made (see Figure 6-3).

When restoring files in a situation that uses normal and differential backups, you need to restore only the normal backup and the *latest* differential backup. Compared to incremental backups, the trade-off is that a differential backup can take longer to perform and can use up significantly more storage space (especially when the normal backups are far apart, and differential backups are frequent). However, the major advantage is that the restore operation is quicker, easier, and safer: You only need the latest differential backup, instead of a chain of all of the incremental ones.

Consider a simple example: Suppose I perform a full backup every Sunday evening, and then a differential backup every evening from Monday through Saturday. If a complete data loss event occurred on Thursday morning, I would first restore that data from the full backup on Sunday and then restore the data from Wednesday's differential backup. That would restore my files up to the time of the last differential backup.

FIGURE 6-3   Performing differential backups

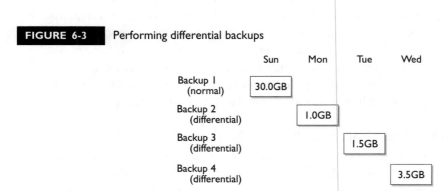

	Sun	Mon	Tue	Wed
Backup 1 (normal)	30.0GB			
Backup 2 (differential)		1.0GB		
Backup 3 (differential)			1.5GB	
Backup 4 (differential)				3.5GB

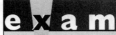

Copy Backups

Copy backups back up all of the selected files but do not mark them as backed up. That is, the operation is similar to a normal backup, except the archive flag is not changed. This is useful when you want to make additional backups of files for moving files off-site or to make multiple copies of the same data or save it for archival purposes. Since the archive flag is not changed, you can usually perform a copy backup at any time without having to worry about affecting the rest of your backup operations. Often, this is done by IT organizations that want to make a monthly "archival" copy of all of the data on their server.

Daily Backups

Daily backups record all files that have changed during the current day. This operation uses the file time/date stamps to determine which files should be backed up and does not mark the files as having been backed up. Only files that have been created or modified on the specified day will be stored. This option is useful if your specific environment wants to back up information based on dates.

Combining Backup Types

In more advanced backup and recovery scenarios, systems administrators may choose to combine normal, daily, incremental, and differential backup types as part of a single backup plan. In general, however, it is sufficient to use only one or two of these methods (for example, normal backups with incremental backups). If you require a combination of multiple backup types, be sure that you fully understand which types of files are being backed up. On very busy mission-critical servers that contain a large volume of data, systems administrators may choose to implement a combination of normal, differential, and incremental backups. Implementing such a method requires a solid understanding of the operations that will be required to recover data given various times of failure.

Summary of Backup Types

Since the various backup types are important, let's take one last look at a comparison between normal, incremental, and differential backup operations. Figure 6-4 provides an example of the differences between these operations and the data that they store.

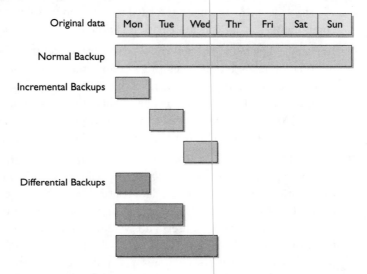

FIGURE 6-4   Understanding the differences between normal, incremental, and differential backups

Protecting System State Information

In addition to normal user data files, modern servers include various data that is required to run the operating system and to keep track of distributed databases (such as Active Directory). In many cases, these files cannot simply be backed up using basic backup and recovery methods.

When planning to back up information on your Windows Server 2003 machines, a very important component to keep in mind is the *System State* data. System State information includes the components that the operating system relies on for normal operations. The Windows Backup utility offers you the ability to back up the System State as part of your backup operations. Specifically, the System State information includes the following:

- **System files**   Windows Server 2003 relies on thousands of different files in order to operate properly. These files provide functionality that is depended upon by the operating system. Often, many of these files may be marked as "in use" and may not be accessible to a normal backup operation. Similarly, you cannot simply overwrite system files during a recovery operation. Using the System State option, you can back up and recover system files using Windows Backup or a compatible third-party backup product.

- **Boot files**   These are the files required for booting the Windows Server 2003 operating system and can be used in the case of boot file corruption.

- **COM+ Class Registration Database**   Applications that run on a Windows Server 2003 computer might require the registration of various shared code components. As part of the System State backup process, Windows Backup will store all of the information related to Component Object Model+ (COM+) components so that this information can be restored after a loss of data.

- **Registry** The Windows Server 2003 Registry is a central repository of information related to the operating system configuration (such as desktop and network settings), user settings, and application settings. The Registry and the information that it contains is absolutely vital to the proper functioning of Windows Server 2003 and should be one of your biggest priorities when you're backing up your servers. A System State backup includes the contents of the Registry.

- **Active Directory** If your server is functioning as an Active Directory domain controller, the Active Directory data store will be backed up. This information contains all of the data that is necessary to create and manage network resources such as users and computers. In most environments that use the Active Directory, users and systems administrators rely on the proper functioning of these services in order to do their jobs. Although all of the domain controllers within a domain contain a copy of the Active Directory database, it's very important to back up this information in case a restore is required because a change is inadvertently made.

on the
job

The process of restoring the Active Directory from a backup is an important one, but it's not covered on this exam. For more information, see the Windows Server 2003 Help and Support Center.

- **SysVol** The SysVol directory includes data and files that are shared between the domain controllers within an Active Directory domain. This information is relied upon by many operating system services for proper functioning, if your server is functioning as an Active Directory domain controller.

- **Clustering configuration** If you are running the clustering feature of Windows Server 2003 (a feature available in the Enterprise and Datacenter Editions of the product), clustering information will also be backed up as part of the system state. This information can be used during a recovery operation to automatically reconfigure a machine as part of a cluster.

- **Certificate Services Database** If your server is running Certificate Services, it's likely that your organization depends on these certificates to be available in order to access various resources. The System State data includes backups of all of the certificates that are hosted by the server.

- **Internet Information Services (IIS) metabase** A critical function for many servers is providing Internet functionality. Often, developers and systems administrators spend significant time in installing, configuring, and optimizing IIS for their purposes. The System State information includes the

IIS configuration, if an installation of Windows Server 2003 has this service enabled. For more details about IIS, see Chapter 7.

When you specify that you want to back up the "System State" in Windows Backup, all of the preceding files and data will be backed up. If you want to be able to perform a full system recovery, it's critical to include this option. Regardless of your permissions, you can back up system state information only for the local computer. The same is true for restoring System State—it can be done only on the local computer if you are using Windows Backup.

INSIDE THE EXAM

Creating a Backup Plan Based on Recovery Requirements

One of the best approaches to designing and implementing a backup plan is to start by considering the recovery requirements. After all, the purpose of performing backups is to ensure that you can get your data back, should something go wrong. When considering various options for implementing backup operations on the exam, be sure to keep in mind the detailed recovery requirements. Often, some seemingly irrelevant phrases can make all the difference. Let's look at some examples.

Suppose that your organization is required to perform backups of a file server nightly. You may have several different recovery requirements for this server. One requirement may be that, at most, up to one full day's worth of data can be lost. That should automatically get you to thinking that you'll need to perform at least one backup per day. Now, suppose that backup storage space is limited, and the file share contains a lot of data. In this case, you'll need to consider incorporating differential and/or incremental backups into your strategy. Other concerns might include allowing for

recovery in the shortest possible time. In that case, you may want to start with making frequent normal backups (since that would require restoring from only a single backup). Alternatively, if you want to perform *backups* in the shortest amount of time (for busy servers, perhaps), you will want to choose to implement incremental or differential backup types.

Suppose you need to ensure that you can recover your server from a failure of the operating system partition. In order to allow that, you'll need to make sure that you're backing up the System State data frequently.

There are also other pieces of information that can affect your backup strategy. For example, if you're trying to perform operations "in the shortest possible time," you may have to give up disk space to meet this requirement.

When you're trying to devise backup strategies on the exam, keep in mind the subtle (and not-so-subtle) hints that you're given in the exam questions. Remember, your task is to choose the *best* solution, based on various requirements.

Understanding Backups and Security

An important issue related to performing backups is security. In general, your organization will want to restrict access to sensitive data. For example, your CEO may not want systems administrators to be able to directly access company financial information. When it comes to performing backups, however, this can lead to a potential problem: How can systems administrators back up all of the data on their servers without having full access to it all? Fortunately, Windows Server 2003 provides a way to do this.

In order to back up data, Windows Server 2003 allows systems administrators and applications to be given the right to bypass standard security. However, this feature can be used only to backup and restore data—not to access it. If your computer is running a stand-alone server, users must be a member of the local Administrator or Backup Operators group in order to back up all data on the server. If your environment includes a domain, domain administrators and members of the Backup Operators built-in security group can perform backups.

If a user is not a member of the Administrator or Backup Operators group, she can back up only files of which she is the Owner, or any files on which she has at least Read permissions. For more information on configuring permissions, see Chapter 4.

Additionally, when you create a backup using the Windows Backup utility, you'll have the option to "Allow only the owner and the Administrator to access the backup data." This option specifies that only users with Administrator permissions, or the user that created the backup itself, will be able to access the contents of the backup.

on the
job

You should secure your backups at least as strongly as you secure your servers and their data. Remember that, unless you're using a solution that provides for encryption of backups, if someone has access to your backup media, they can take their time in attempting to extract sensitive information without having to connect to your servers. Keep this in mind when you consider how to manage and protect your backup media.

Understanding Shadow Copy

The overwhelming majority of modern business applications and servers depend greatly on storage resources. For example, database services rely on exclusive access to portions of the disk subsystem in order to manage the physical storage of data files. Although this usually leads to an efficient use of system resources, it can pose problems. For example, if a database server has marked specific files as being "in-use," they can't easily be backed up. The same is true for some operating system files, such as components of the System State information, device drivers, and other important software. And, for many of us, it seems that no matter how often we remind users to close applications and log out of machines before they leave the office, many important files will be left open. Of course, these types of data are extremely important to back up. So how is this done?

Windows Server 2003 includes a feature called "Shadow Copy." There are two main ways in which Shadow Copy can be used. In this section, you'll take a brief look at both.

Using Volume Shadow Copy for Backups

When Windows Backup performs its operations, the utility may need exclusive access to files in order to back them up. If a service or application is using the file at the time that the backup is being performed, the utility may be forced to skip the file altogether. Additionally, since applications and services will generally be required to remain running when a backup is occurring, it's possible that files could be updated during the backup operation. If the backup operation marks a file as being in use, this might result in an error in other applications.

An excellent solution for these potential problems is the Volume Shadow Copy feature included in the Windows Server 2003 platform. This technology works by making a copy of the data that is to be backed up, and then backing up the copy of the data. The copy is able to access files that would otherwise be inaccessible in order to make a copy. It also tracks any changes that might occur during the backup process. The result is that users, applications, and services can continue to work while systems administrators can be assured that the data will be backed up properly.

Best of all, it's easy to use the Volume Shadow Copy feature since, when you create backup operations, the Windows Backup utility can implement it whenever it's needed. This is one of the first steps that the Windows Backup utility performs. Although there will be some performance impact of the backup operation, you can be sure that your files are safely backed up using Volume Shadow Copy.

As long as you are not backing up the System State information, there is an advanced option that allows you to disable the Shadow Copy feature. Generally, you will only want to use this option for troubleshooting purposes.

Shadow Copies for Users

An important feature present in most modern operating systems is protection against accidental deletion of important information. In Windows, that takes the form of the Recycle Bin—when I choose to "delete" a file, it's actually moved to the Recycle Bin, where it's stored as long as there's sufficient space remaining on my hard drive. Eventually, the files will be permanently deleted. But, during the many times that I've accidentally deleted files, the recycle bin has been a life saver! Even more often, I've accidentally modified a file (through, for example, a poorly planned search-and-replace in a book chapter), and really needed an older version of the file.

Unfortunately, if I choose to delete a file on a remote server, the file is pretty much gone forever. No backup copy is made, and I can't change my mind a few seconds later (without restoring the file from a backup). With Shadow Copy, however, that is changed. Using Shadow Copy, systems administrators can configure Windows Server 2003 volumes and folders to retain multiple copies of files as they're modified. The benefit is that users can now choose to "undelete" files, and they can go back to previous revisions of files! Of course, the level of recoverability will be based on the frequency of Shadow Copies. Let's look at how all of this works (along with some limitations).

You can quickly and easily set up Shadow Copy functionality for a volume by right-clicking the volume in Explorer and choosing Properties. When you click the Shadow Copy tab, you'll see the options shown in Figure 6-5. By default, Shadow Copy is disabled, but you can click the Enable button to make it active. When you choose to Enable Shadow Copies, you'll see the warning shown in Figure 6-6.

Once you've enabled Shadow Copy, you'll probably want to review the settings. The important decision that you'll need to make concerns how much space you

FIGURE 6-5

Viewing Shadow
Copy options for
a volume

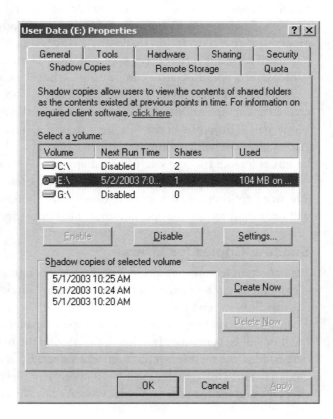

Confirming the
enabling of
Volume Shadow
copies

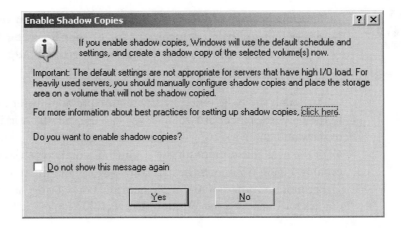

want to allow for Shadow Copies of the data stored on that volume. You can choose to use an unlimited amount of space, or you can specify a limit (see the following illustration). Finally, by clicking Schedule, you can specify exactly how often Shadow Copies are created. Keep in mind that more frequent copies will result in better data protection at the expense of disk space and, potentially, some decrease in performance. Overall, however, Shadow Copy can save many painful hours of work for systems administrators and users alike!

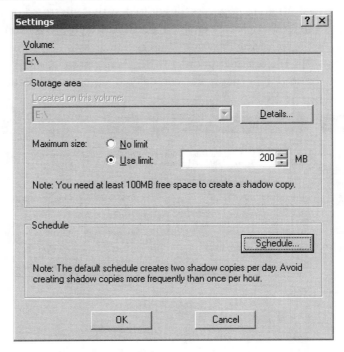

Shadow copies, the Recycle Bin, and other related technologies should never be used as a replacement for proper backups; instead, consider them a feature that can work in conjunction with backup operations to improve the user experience.

Although the basic functionality required to administer Shadow Copy is included in the properties sheet of a volume, you can use the VSSAdmin command-line utility to view and change settings from a command prompt or a batch file. To get a list of all of the available options for the command, simply type **vssadmin /?** at the command prompt. Figure 6-7 shows the available options and the results of running the utility.

For more information on implementing, configuring, and managing Shadow Copies for Users, see the Windows Server 2003 Help and Support Center.

Restoring Shadow Copy Data

In order for users to be able to access shadow copy information, they must have the appropriate client software installed. By default, this client is available within the SystemRoot directory of an installation of Windows Server 2003. Specifically, it's located within the \System32\Clients\twclient folder (with versions for x86 and both Intel and AMD 64-bit platforms). This will install the Previous Versions client software. Client computers may have to be rebooted before they can use this feature.

When users access files or folders that are stored on a shared folder in which shadow copies are enabled, they'll see multiple versions of those files. As shown in the following illustration, users can click the Previous Versions tab in the properties of a file or folder in order to access or restore earlier versions of the file. Similarly, to restore files that have been deleted, users can click the folder in which the files used

---

FIGURE 6-7

Viewing Shadow Copy information using the VSSAdmin tool

```
C:\WINDOWS\system32\cmd.exe                                          _ □ ×

C:\>vssadmin /?
vssadmin 1.1 - Volume Shadow Copy Service administrative command-line tool
(C) Copyright 2001 Microsoft Corp.

---- Commands Supported ----

Add ShadowStorage     - Add a new volume shadow copy storage association
Create Shadow         - Create a new volume shadow copy
Delete Shadows        - Delete volume shadow copies
Delete ShadowStorage  - Delete volume shadow copy storage associations
List Providers        - List registered volume shadow copy providers
List Shadows          - List existing volume shadow copies
List ShadowStorage    - List volume shadow copy storage associations
List Volumes          - List volumes eligible for shadow copies
List Writers          - List subscribed volume shadow copy writers
Resize ShadowStorage  - Resize a volume shadow copy storage association

C:\>
```

to reside. The Previous Versions tab will show files that have been moved or deleted from the selected folder.

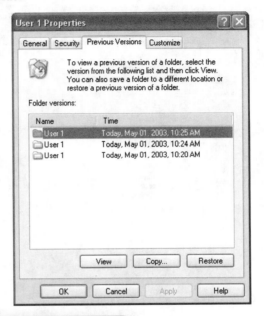

CERTIFICATION OBJECTIVE 6.02

Creating and Scheduling Backups Using Windows Backup

So far, you've looked at many important concepts that are related to the backup and recovery process. Now, it's time to put that information to use by learning how to implement backups using Windows Server 2003's Backup utility. This tool provides basic backup and recovery functionality, as well as some more advanced options such as scheduling backup jobs.

The Windows Backup utility is designed to provide functions that are commonly used in the backup and recovery process. Although large environments may choose to implement third-party backup solutions, Windows Backup can provide adequate functionality for many environments. In this section, you'll look at the details of how you can use the built-in tools in Windows Server 2003 to back up and recover data.

Windows Backup is installed, by default, with every installation of Windows Server 2003. To access the utility, choose Start | Programs | Accessories | System Tools | Backup. Figure 6-8 shows the main screen for the Windows Server 2003

FIGURE 6-8

The main screen
of the Windows
Server 2003
Backup utility

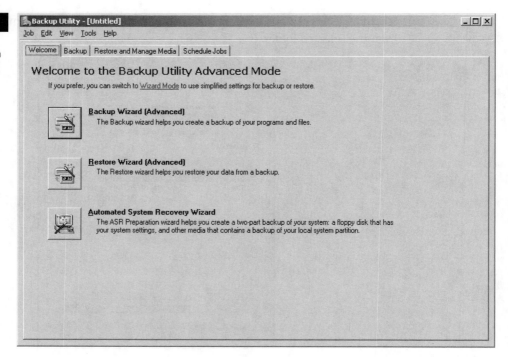

Backup utility. You can also quickly launch this utility by choosing Start | Run and typing **ntbackup**.

Next, let's take a look at how this tool is used.

Performing a Backup with the Backup or Restore Wizard

There are two main modes for the Windows Backup utility. The default mode is the Backup or Restore Wizard (see Figure 6-9). The wizard is designed to walk you through the basic steps that are required to create and set up a backup job, or to restore data from an existing backup file. The wizard provides an organized method for systems administrators to perform the most common operations.

Related to backups, you will be able to choose the following settings through the wizard.

Backup or Restore

The first decision you'll have to make (hopefully an easy one) is whether you want to back up or restore data. In this chapter, you'll start by looking at

FIGURE 6-9

Viewing the
Welcome page
for the Backup or
Restore Wizard

backup operations. Details related to recovery will be provided later in
the chapter.

What to Back Up

The first step in defining a backup operation is to choose which files need to be stored
(see Figure 6-10). The default option is to select All Information On This Computer.
This is definitely the simplest type of backup to make (and the most complete). As
the option name implies, this setting will back up all of the files on the local system
(including the operating system folders, System State information, the Program Files
folder, and all user data on all volumes). Also, when you select to back up all information
on the computer, the wizard can automatically create an Automated System Recovery
(ASR) diskette. You'll learn more about the ASR feature later in this chapter. If you
have adequate storage space to perform this type of backup, it's the best choice.

To have more control over the backup process, you can select Let Me Choose
What To Back Up. With this option, you'll be given the opportunity to choose
exactly which files and folders you want to back up. The dialog box (shown in the
following illustration) allows you to choose any level within your file system. For
example, you might choose to back up the entire C:\ volume, or you might specify
that you only want to store the C:\Data directory, including any subfolders of this

FIGURE 6-10

Specifying
whether all or
some files should
be backed up

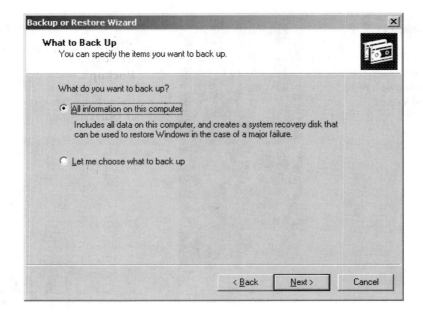

directory. Note that under the "My Computer" branch, there is a selection for "System State." You also have the ability to back up information that is stored on a remote computer on your network.

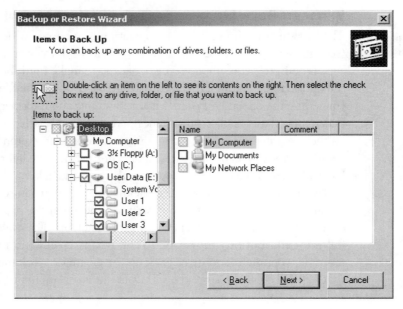

on the **J**ob

Personally, I find the fact that the Backup Wizard window cannot be resized to be really annoying. If you're having trouble using this small window to select which files you want to back up, you'll need to use the Advanced mode of the Windows Backup utility.

Backup Type, Destination, and Name

In this step of the wizard (shown in Figure 6-11), you can specify the type of backup that you want to create. On all systems, you'll have the option to back up to a file, but if you also have a local tape device (or other backup device) installed on the system, you'll have additional options to select from. Assuming you choose the File option, you'll need to specify the file system location and filename for the backup. You can enter in a local path, or the UNC path to a network share. Finally, you should type a descriptive name for the backup (for example, "Full System State Backup").

This is all of the information that is required in order to perform a simple backup operation. In many cases, however, you may want to choose more advanced options. To do this, you can click Advanced in the last step of the wizard. When you do this, another set of steps will be available (see Figure 6-12). Here, you'll be able to choose the following settings.

Type of Backup

Here, you'll be able to choose the type of backup that you want to perform. The options include Normal, Copy, Incremental, Differential, and Daily. Additionally, you

---

FIGURE 6-11

Specifying backup destination options

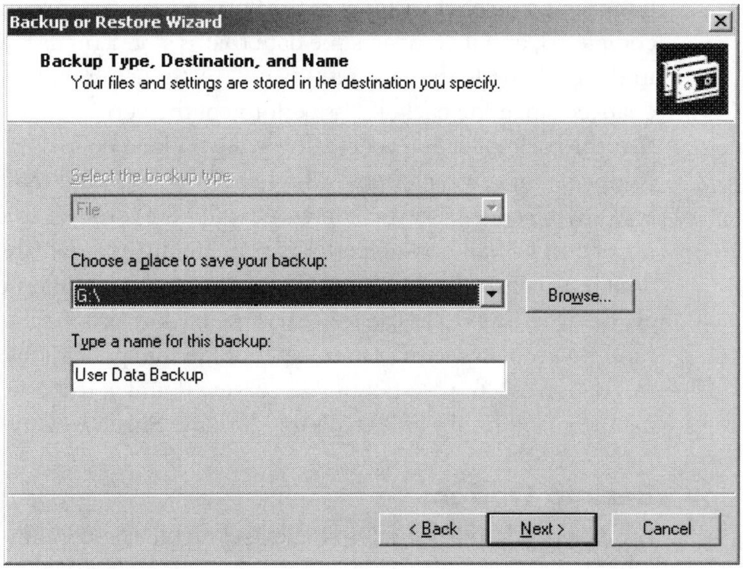

Backup or Restore Wizard	☒

Backup Type, Destination, and Name
Your files and settings are stored in the destination you specify.

Select the backup type:

File ▾

Choose a place to save your backup:

G:\ ▾   Browse...

Type a name for this backup:

User Data Backup

< Back   Next >   Cancel

FIGURE 6-12

Configuring
advanced options
in the Backup or
Restore Wizard

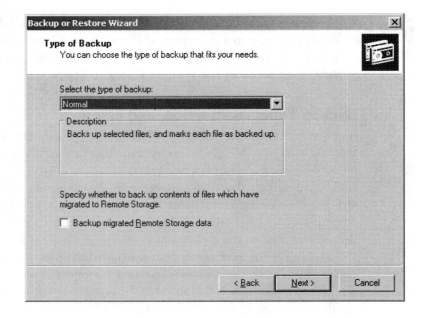

can choose whether you want to store data that has already been moved via remote
storage (you'll learn more about remote storage later in this chapter).

How to Back Up

Here, you can choose whether you want to perform a *verify* operation after a backup
has been completed (see Figure 6-13). The verify process runs after a backup job is
completed, and it compares the data that is stored on disk with the data that is located
in the backup file that was just created. Although some of the data on disk may have
changed since the backup was performed, the verification process will generally prove
that the backup file is readable. If you are backing up to a hardware device that supports
compression, you can choose whether or not you want to enable compression for this
backup. In general, using compression will help conserve storage space with a negligible
impact on overall backup performance. Finally, you can choose whether you want to
disable Volume Shadow Copy. This feature allows Windows Backup to copy files that
are being written to at the time that the backup process needs to access them. If you
run into problems with certain types of files or applications, you might want to disable
this option as a troubleshooting step. Note that if you choose to back up System State
data, you will not be able to disable Volume Shadow Copy.

Backup Options

For ease of administration, a single backup file can contain multiple backup sets. This
is helpful, for example, if you want to keep incremental backups together with their

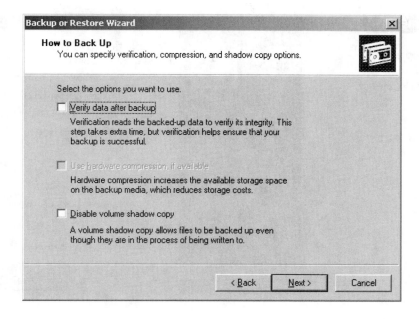

FIGURE 6-13

Viewing settings
in the How To
Back Up
advanced options

associated normal backups. In this dialog box, you'll be able to specify whether you want to overwrite all of the backups in the existing backup file, or if you want to append the backup to the ones that are already in the file. The same applies if you're storing data to a tape device or other hardware backup solution. For security, if you choose to replace the backups in the existing file, you can restrict access to the backup file to only the owner of the backup file or an Administrator (otherwise, the selection for this setting that was used when the file was created will be used).

When to Back Up

The default option for running a backup is to run it immediately (once you're finished with the Backup or Restore Wizard). However, you also have the option of choosing to schedule the job to run once or on a schedule that you define. In addition to the basic schedule, you can define various Settings options for the scheduled job. You'll learn more about scheduling options later in this section.

Once you've configured all of the settings that are needed, you're ready to start the backup operation. The last step of the wizard will confirm your selections (as shown in Figure 6-14), and clicking Finish will execute them. If you choose to perform the operation immediately, the backup will begin. Otherwise, the job will be scheduled.

During the progress of the backup, you'll see a lot of useful information. The following illustration provides a screenshot of the Backup Progress details provided during a System State backup operation. The progress window will attempt to estimate how long the backup will take, and will provide information about which

FIGURE 6-14

Completing the
Backup or
Restore Wizard

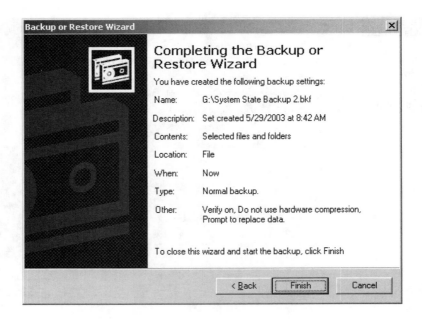

files are being backed up. The length of the operation will vary depending on your
selections and the amount of data that must be copied.

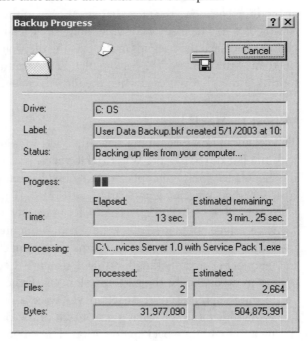

on the **Job**

Although Windows Backup will likely meet the basic needs of most systems administrators, it's important to know that the tool is limited (especially when used in large networking environments). Windows Backup is designed to make backups only on the local computer. Therefore, it doesn't include remote backup management functionality. And, there's no easy way to centrally administer Windows Backup. While this may be fine for a few servers, larger environments should consider investing in a third-party Enterprise-level backup solution.

Once the backup process is complete, you'll be able to view information in the Backup Progress summary dialog box (see the next illustration). To view additional details, you can also click the Report button. The results (shown in Figure 6-15) provide details about the operations that were performed, how long the operations took, and any errors that were encountered. If you want

FIGURE 6-15	

Viewing a backup report

```
backup05.log - Notepad                                          _ □ ×
File  Edit  Format  View  Help
Backup Status
Operation: Backup
Active backup destination: File
Media name: "User Data Backup.bkf created 5/1/2003 at 6:18 PM"

Backup (via shadow copy) of "E: User Data"
Backup set #2 on media #1
Backup description: "Set created 5/1/2003 at 6:18 PM"
Media name: "User Data Backup.bkf created 5/1/2003 at 10:32 AM"

Backup Type: Normal

Backup started on 5/1/2003 at 6:19 PM.
Backup completed on 5/1/2003 at 6:19 PM.
Directories: 4
Files: 10
Bytes: 1,664,443
Time:  2 seconds

----------------------
```

to retain this information, you can simply save the text file so that it can be accessed later.

```
┌─────────────────────────────────────────────────────────┐
│ Backup Progress                                   ? │ X │
├─────────────────────────────────────────────────────────┤
│                                                           │
│   The backup is complete.                   ┌─────────┐   │
│                                             │  Close  │   │
│                                             └─────────┘   │
│   To see detailed information, click Report. ┌────────┐   │
│                                              │Report..│   │
│                                              └────────┘   │
│                                                           │
│   Drive:      ┌──────────────────────────────────────┐   │
│               │ E: User Data                         │   │
│               └──────────────────────────────────────┘   │
│   Label:      ┌──────────────────────────────────────┐   │
│               │ User Data Backup.bkf created 5/1/2003 at 10:│
│               └──────────────────────────────────────┘   │
│   Status:     ┌──────────────────────────────────────┐   │
│               │ Completed                            │   │
│               └──────────────────────────────────────┘   │
│                                                           │
│               Elapsed:            Estimated remaining:    │
│   Time:       ┌──────────────┐    ┌──────────────────┐   │
│               │       1 sec. │    │                  │   │
│               └──────────────┘    └──────────────────┘   │
│                                                           │
│               Processed:          Estimated:             │
│   Files:      ┌──────────────┐    ┌──────────────────┐   │
│               │           10 │    │              10  │   │
│               └──────────────┘    └──────────────────┘   │
│   Bytes:      ┌──────────────┐    ┌──────────────────┐   │
│               │    1,664,443 │    │      1,664,443   │   │
│               └──────────────┘    └──────────────────┘   │
└─────────────────────────────────────────────────────────┘
```

Using Advanced Mode for Backups

Although the Backup or Restore Wizard walks you step-by-step through the basic options that are available for creating a backup job, many systems administrators will probably prefer the more advanced user interface of the Windows Backup utility. To access this interface, you can simply click the link labeled "Advanced" in the default Windows Backup welcome screen.

From here, you can launch the Backup Wizard, the Restore Wizard, or the Automated System Recovery Wizard (which we'll cover later in this chapter). To configure backup jobs and options, you can simply choose from the various tabs in the interface.

On the Backup tab (shown in Figure 6-16), you'll be able to choose which files you want to back up and the destination type and location for the backup operation. Using the options in the Job menu, you can save the settings for a backup job to disk. The default file extension for this file is *.bks. Using this interface, you can specify the same types of information that you were prompted for when using the wizard. For example, you can specify where files are going to be stored in the backup, and where the backup will be created (either to a file or disk).

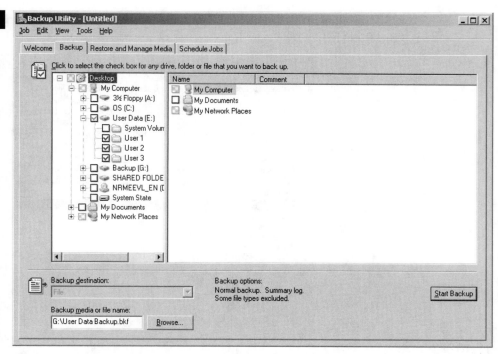

FIGURE 6-16

Viewing the
Backup tab in
the Windows
Backup utility

A useful option is the ability to save the selection of files that you want to back up. You might create a backup job that stores all user-related information, and save it with the name "User Data." Later, if you want to perform another backup of this information, you can simply load the list of files into Windows Backup. Note that the file itself is a simple text file that includes a single path per line. You can view this file using a utility such as Notepad.

Configuring Backup Options

An important set of configuration options are accessible by choosing Tools | Options (see the next illustration). Using this dialog box, you'll be able to set many different options that will govern how Windows Backup will perform various operations. Note that there are many more options available here than through the Advanced section of the Backup or Restore Wizard. For details about the available options, you can use the ToolTip help.

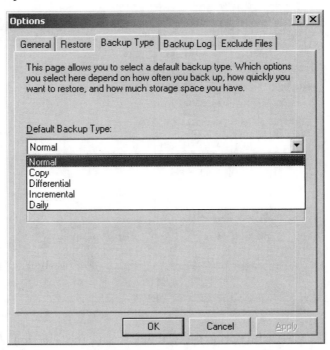

Once you have selected the operations that you want to perform, you can simply choose Job | Start. You'll be shown a prompt that allows you to specify details for the backup. You can also click Advanced to see further details about the type of backup operation that you want to perform (see the following two illustrations).

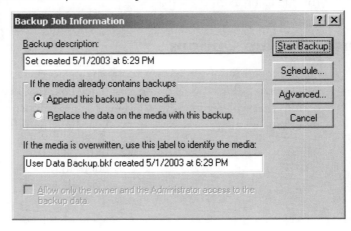

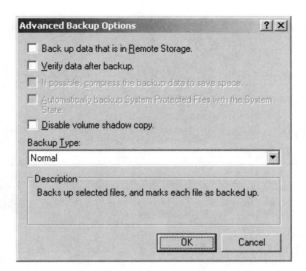

So far, you've looked at two methods for creating backup jobs. First, you looked at the simple Backup or Restore Wizard, and then you looked at the Advanced user interface in Windows Backup. Regardless of which method you choose, you should now know how to configure backups to meet your requirements. Now, let's move on to steps required to schedule a backup operation.

Scheduling Backups

Although you can easily use the Windows Backup utility interactively (that is, you can click through the various options and settings manually each time you want to perform a backup), you'll probably want to schedule backup operations to occur regularly. Apart from being easier, scheduled processes are far more reliable. You can ensure that scheduled jobs are executed accurately and consistently. Unlike you (hopefully!), the Windows Server 2003 scheduling services don't take evenings, weekends, and vacations off!

Another reason to schedule backups is that the act of backing up data can sometimes slow down your production servers. Therefore, you'll probably want to configure the backups to occur at night, during shift changes, or during other periods of relatively light system usage.

Windows Backup includes a built-in scheduling utility that can be used to quickly and easily schedule backup operations. There are two main ways for scheduling backup jobs. The first is to use the Advanced options in the Backup Wizard to specify a schedule for the job. The second is to use the Schedule functionality of the Advanced mode (see Figure 6-17).

This view provides you with a simple but useful calendar. You can use this interface to view any scheduled jobs. To create a new backup job, you can click the Add Job

FIGURE 6-17

Scheduling
backup
operations in the
Windows Server
2003 backup
utility

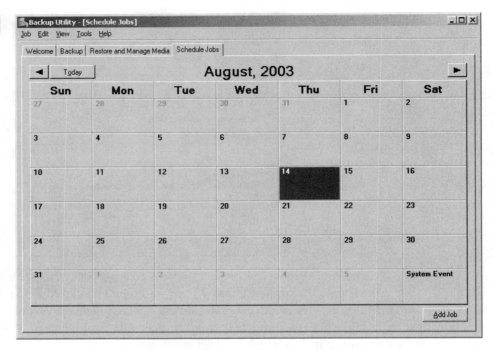

button. This will launch the Backup Wizard and will allow you to specify options for
the job. On the When To Back Up step of the wizard, you can click Schedule to
specify details regarding when the backup job will be executed. Figure 6-18 shows the
options that are available.

FIGURE 6-18

Viewing backup
job schedule
options

When you schedule a backup job, you can specify one of the following options for when the job should run:

- **Daily** The operation will be run at a certain time and every specific number of days.

- **Weekly** The job will run every specific number of weeks on the days and times that you specify.

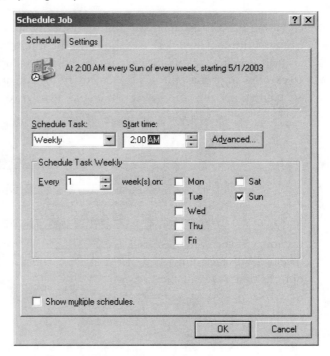

- **Monthly** The job can be scheduled to run on a monthly basis (for all months, or for scheduled months). You can specify on which day of the month the job will run.

- **Once** The job will run only once, at the date and time that you specify. This is a useful function if you want to have a single backup operation performed after work hours.

- **At System Startup** The backup job will automatically launch after the system is rebooted. Note that this can add significant load to your system during a restart.

- **At Logon** Whenever the user that created the specific backup job schedule logs on to the system, the backup job will be executed.

- **When Idle** Sometimes, it's difficult to be sure when your server will be least busy. You can use the option "when idle" to specify that the backup operation should start as soon as server resource usage has been low for a specified amount of time. Note that on very busy servers, there's no guarantee that the backup job will *ever* run.

Note that you also have the ability to specify multiple schedules by clicking the Show Multiple Schedules box (shown in the following illustration). This provides you with the most flexibility when scheduling backups. For example, you might want to execute an operation every Sunday morning, and also every evening. Each separate schedule is given a name, so it can be made easier to identify.

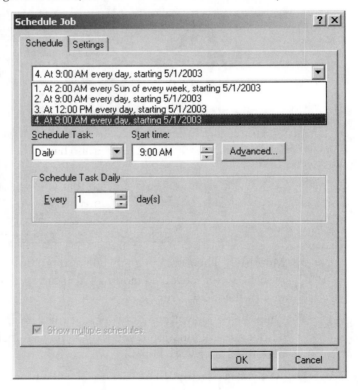

In addition to all of the scheduling options that you've seen so far, you can also click the Settings tab of the Schedule Job dialog box to specify additional details. As shown next, you can indicate options such as the maximum time that the job can run before it is automatically stopped.

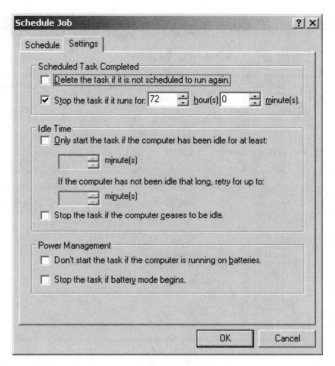

Although the graphical user interface of the Windows Backup utility is the easiest method for creating backup schedules, you also have other options. Later in this chapter, you'll look at how you can run the Windows Backup utility from the command line. Once you have determined the command that you want to run, there are two main ways in which you can schedule it to run. The first method is the Scheduled Tasks Control Panel applet. Using this interface, you can provide details about how and when the command should run.

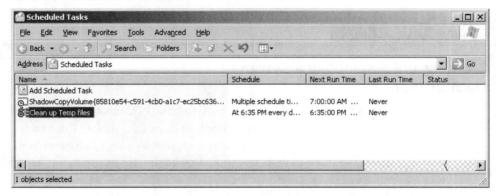

The other option for scheduling tasks is to use the `schtasks` command-line utility. Figure 6-19 shows the command-line help for this utility. For more

FIGURE 6-19

Viewing options
for the schtasks
command-line
utility

```
C:\WINDOWS\system32\cmd.exe                                          _ □ ×
C:\>schtasks /?

SCHTASKS /parameter [arguments]

Description:
    Enables an administrator to create, delete, query, change, run and
    end scheduled tasks on a local or remote system. Replaces AT.exe.

Parameter List:
    /Create         Creates a new scheduled task.

    /Delete         Deletes the scheduled task(s).

    /Query          Displays all scheduled tasks.

    /Change         Changes the properties of scheduled task.

    /Run            Runs the scheduled task immediately.

    /End            Stops the currently running scheduled task.

    /?              Displays this help message.

Examples:
    SCHTASKS
    SCHTASKS /?
    SCHTASKS /Run /?
    SCHTASKS /End /?
    SCHTASKS /Create /?
    SCHTASKS /Delete /?
    SCHTASKS /Query  /?
    SCHTASKS /Change /?

C:\>
```

information on scheduling tasks, see the Windows Server 2003 Help and
Support Center.

Now that you have learned about many of the operations that are possible using
Windows Backup, let's apply that information. Exercise 6-1 walks you through the
process of creating a backup of your server's System State using the Windows Backup
utility's Advanced mode.

EXERCISE 6-1

CertCam & MasterSim 6-1 ON THE CD

Creating and Scheduling a System State Backup

In this exercise, you'll create a System State backup on a Windows Server 2003
computer using the Backup Wizard. In order to complete this exercise, you must have
enough storage space on the local computer to store the System State Data. Although
the size of this will vary, you should make sure that you have at least 500MB of free
space available.

1. Log on to the server as an Administrator and then choose Start | Programs | Accessories | System Tools | Backup. By default, this will launch the Backup or Restore Wizard. Click the Advanced link to open the Advanced mode of the Windows Backup utility.

2. On the Tools menu, select Backup Wizard. Click Next to begin using the wizard.

3. The first selection you'll have to make is what to back up. On the What To Back Up step, select Only Back Up The System State Data and then click Next to continue.

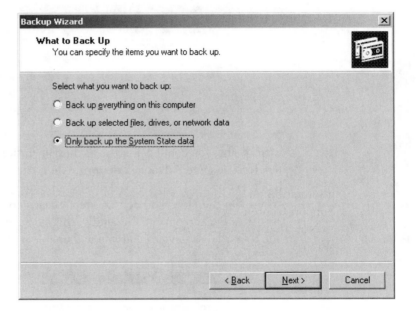

4. On this step, you'll be able to specify where you want the backup to be created. If the local computer has a tape backup or other removable media device installed, you'll be able to choose it in the first drop-down menu. If this is the case, select File for the type of backup to perform. Otherwise, the menu will be grayed out and File will be automatically selected. Next, specify the location and name for the backup file. Note that you can click Browse to navigate to available resources. For the sake of this exercise, choose a local directory that has sufficient free space to store the System State information (at least 500MB free). Also, make a

note of the location of this file, as you will be using it in Exercise 6-2. Click Next to continue.

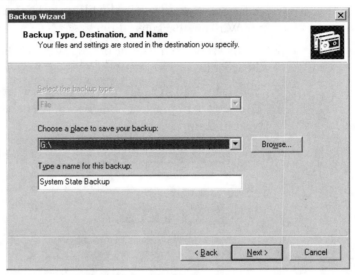

5. At this point, you could begin the backup operation. But first, let's take a quick look at some Advanced options. Click Advanced to access the options. Click Next on the Type Of Backup step in order to continue with the default settings. On the How To Back Up step, place a check mark in the Verify Data After Backup option. Generally, this step is not required for backups made to hard disk devices, but you will enable it for the sake of this exercise. Click Next to continue.

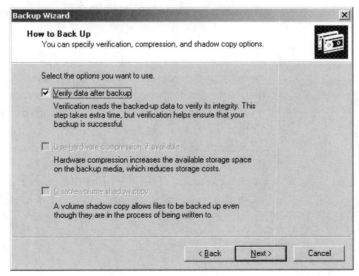

6. On the Backup Options step, choose to Replace The Existing Backups. This option will make sure that, if the file that you specified in step 4 already exists, all backup data in the file will be replaced by the contents of this backup. It will also allow you to select a backup security option—to restrict access to the backup set to only the Administrator and the creator of the backup set. Enable this option, then click Next.

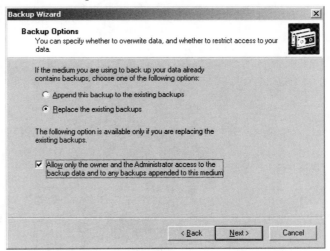

7. On the When To Back Up step, you can specify when you want the backup operation to be performed. The default option is to create the backup immediately ("Now"). In the exercise, you want to schedule the backup operation to occur at a specific time. Select Later and then enter **Single System State Backup** for the job name.

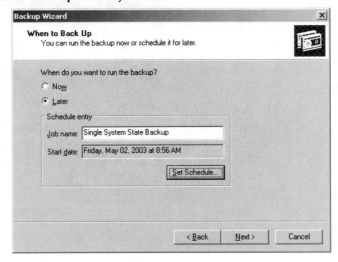

8. Click the Set Schedule button to access the schedule settings. Specify that the task should run "Once." Choose a time that is approximately ten minutes in the future and ensure that the current date is selected. Click OK to set the schedule. You'll be prompted to provide logon information for a user account that has permissions to perform the backup operation. Enter the username and password of a member of the Administrators or Backup Operators group and then click OK. This security information will be used when the scheduled job is launched. Click Next to continue the Backup Wizard.

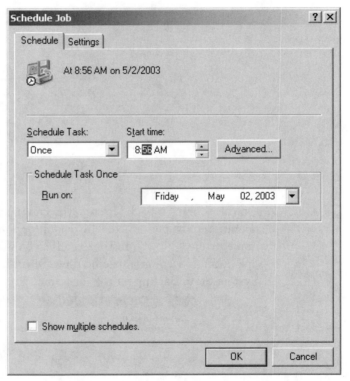

9. Once you have completed the Advanced option selections, you'll be presented with a final confirmation of your selections. If you had specified that the backup should begin immediately, this would start the backup operation. Since you have chosen to schedule the job for a future time, the job will be created and scheduled. Click Finish to continue.

10. To verify that the backup job has been scheduled, click the Schedule Jobs item in the Windows Backup utility. You should see an item scheduled for the current day. You can click the item to view additional information about the schedule and details for the backup job.

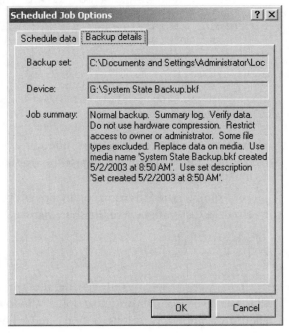

11. When the time that you set in step 8 arrives, the backup job should begin automatically. The job will run whether or not the Windows Backup utility is open, and whether or not a user is logged on to the system. When you are finished, close the Windows Backup utility.

on the Job

Unlike many commercial backup software and hardware solutions, Windows Backup does not provide any support for compression of data. However, the backup files that are created with Windows Backup are highly compressible with NTFS compression or other utilities. Depending on the type of data that you're backing up, you can save a lot of disk space by compressing backup files with utilities such as WinZip (www.winzip.com) or ZipMagic (www.ontrack.com/zipmagic/).

Automating Backups from the Command Line

In addition to using the GUI tools that are available for creating and managing backup jobs, you may want to automate backups through the use of batch files. The `ntbackup` command-line interface allows you to do this. The syntax of this command is as follows:

```
ntbackup backup [systemstate] "@FileName.bks" /J {"JobName"}
    [/P {"PoolName"}] [/G {"GUIDName"}] [/T { "TapeName"}]
    [/N {"MediaName"}] [/F {"FileName"}] [/D {"SetDescription"}]
    [/DS {"ServerName"}] [/IS {"ServerName"}] [/A]
    [/V:{yes | no}] [/R:{yes | no}] [/L:{f | s | n}]
    [/M {BackupType}] [/RS:{yes | no}] [/HC:{on | off}]
    [/SNAP:{on | off}]
```

As you can see, there are many different options available. In fact, all of the operations that are possible through the graphical Windows Backup utility are available from the command line.

For example, the following command will perform a normal backup of all of the files on the C:\ volume to a file share named "Backups" on the machine Server1.

```
ntbackup backup c:\ /j "Test Backup" /f
    "\\Server1\Backups\TestBackup.bkf" /m Normal
```

If you want to specify only specific files to back up, you can use a selected list that was saved from within the graphic Windows Backup utility. For more details about the various operations, options, and other arguments that are available, type **ntbackup /?** at the command prompt, or search for "ntbackup" in the Windows Server 2003 Help and Support Center (see Figure 6-20).

FIGURE 6-20

Viewing parameters and usage information for the ntbackup command-line utility

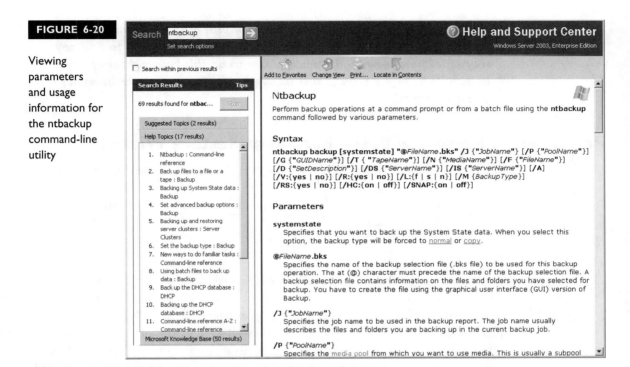

CERTIFICATION OBJECTIVE 6.03

Restoring Data and Managing Backup Media with Windows Backup

Thus far, you've looked at various ways in which you can use the Windows Backup utility to create backups of important system information and user data. The next logical step is to take a look at how that data can be restored. Fortunately, the methods are just as straightforward as those related to backup operations. Let's take a look at several methods for restoring data.

on the **job**

Although many IT professionals spend plenty of time in creating backups (as they should), few seem to allocate sufficient time for testing restore processes. It's extremely important to do this for several reasons. First and foremost, by testing, you'll be able to ensure that you can restore data, should the need arise. Second, you'll get a good idea of how long it will take you to restore data (this can be very valuable during an emergency

*situation, since it can help others make appropriate decisions). Finally,
you'll be able to identify any flaws in your backup plan and to find any
room for improvement. It's much better to do this before disaster strikes.
Be sure to take the time to test recovery operations and processes before
you need them!*

Performing a Restore with the Backup or Restore Wizard

As was the case with backup operations, the quickest and easiest way to perform a restore operation is to use the Backup or Restore Wizard. When you start the wizard, you should choose the Restore Files And Settings option. The wizard will walk you through the following steps.

What to Restore

The first step in the restore process is to determine which drives, files, and/or folders you want to restore (see Figure 6-21). You start by pointing the Backup or Restore Wizard to a valid backup file. You can do this by clicking Browse. Once you select the appropriate backup file, Windows Backup will read the contents of the backup and will display a list of the various options that are available for restore. When you make a selection at one level (for example, a folder), all of the lower-level items are selected by default. You can override these default selections by checking and unchecking items at any level. Select the appropriate files and then continue.

FIGURE 6-21

Choosing what to
restore in the
Backup or
Restore Wizard

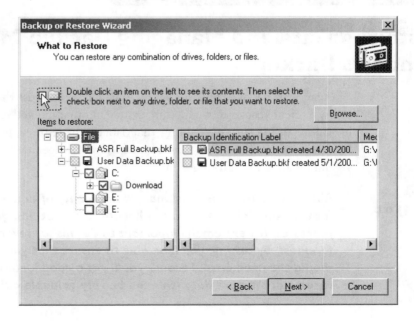

Note that the restore operation, by default, will restore files to their original locations and that the operation will leave any existing files as they are.

Although the selection of what to restore is the only required option, you should also be aware of the various other settings that are available. By clicking Advanced, you can choose the following settings.

Where to Restore

An important option that you should consider is where you want files to be restored. The default option is to restore files to their original location. This is useful if you've experienced a loss of data, and you want to choose the quickest method for replacing it. You can also choose to restore the files to an alternate location (see Figure 6-22). This option allows you to specify another folder into which the selected contents of the restore operation will be placed. This is a useful option if you want to access the data that was stored in the backup file without affecting any of the existing files on your system. Finally, you can choose to restore the selected file(s) to a single directory. This option will restore all of the files to a single folder on your system (that is, the path information for the original files is discarded).

How to Restore

When you restore files, the default setting is for any existing files to be left alone (see Figure 6-23). For example, if you have a file called "MyStuff.doc" in the same

FIGURE 6-22

Choosing where restored files will be saved

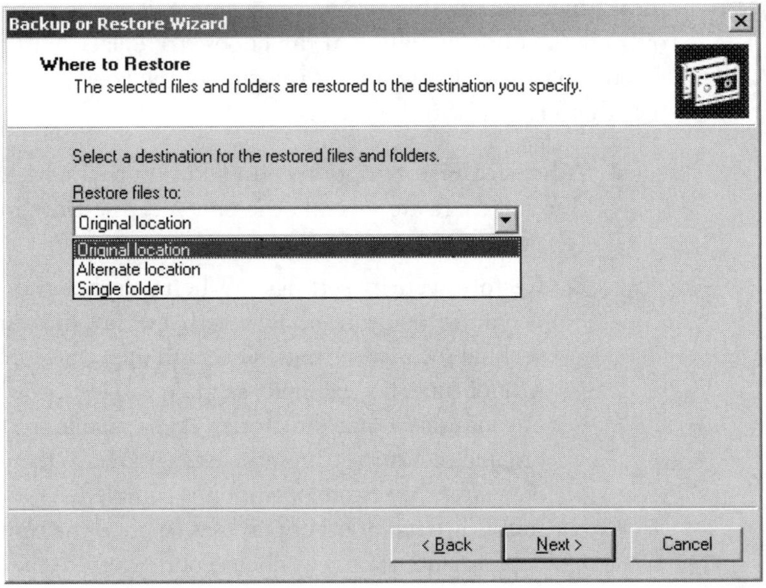

FIGURE 6-23

Selecting options for "How To Restore"

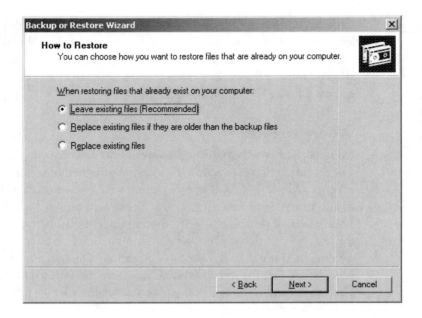

location within the backup file and in the file system, the restore operation will leave the existing file alone (regardless of whether or not it has been modified since the backup). This is, by far, the safest option, since it ensures that no existing files are replaced or changed in any way.

The second option is to replace existing files if they are older than the backup files. You would use this option, for example, if you're restoring a newer set of data over an older one. Finally, you can choose to replace existing files. This is often used when you're sure that you want the data in the backup file to overwrite any other files that may exist in the file system

■ **Advanced restore options** In addition to the basic options we've discussed thus far, there are several other advanced settings for restore operations (shown in Figure 6-24). These include

■ **Restore security settings** When you choose to perform a restore operation, you can specify whether or not the restored files will retain their original security settings. This is an important option, since it can save you a lot of time. For example, suppose you lost the volume that contains all of your users' home directories. If you enable the option to restore the original security settings, the users will have the proper permissions to their data after the restore operation is completed. On the other hand, if you're restoring data for other purposes (such as the transfer of some data between departments), you may choose not to restore the security settings.

FIGURE 6-24

Specifying
advanced restore
options

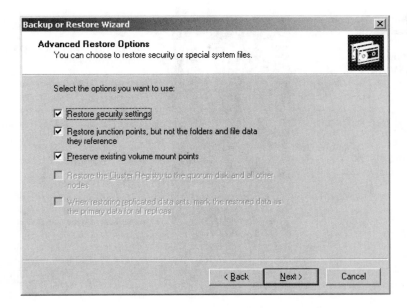

- **Restore junction points, but not the folders and file data that they reference** Junction points are logical pointers to other storage resources (for details on junction points, see the Windows Server 2003 Help and Support Center). When you enable this option, the junction points will be restored, but the files and folders that the junction points refer to will not.

- **Preserve existing volume points** When you perform a restore operation, this option specifies that any existing volume points will remain unchanged. This is an important setting if volume points have changed since the backup was created. (For more information on volume points, see Chapter 5).

- **Restore the Cluster Registry to the quorum disk and all other nodes** This option applies only if you're running the Enterprise or DataCenter edition of Windows Server 2003 and if the information that you're restoring is handled by clustered nodes. Clustering is outside the scope of this book (and the MS exam that it covers), but you can get more information in the Windows Server 2003 Resource Kit.

- **When restoring replicated data sets, mark the restored data as the primary for all replicas** As with the previous option, this option applies only to clustered systems. When this option is enabled, the restored data will be designated as the authoritative information, and all replicas will be updated with the data from the backup.

Once you're finished with the options that you want for the restore process, you're ready to begin the restore. Figure 6-25 shows the summary screen that

provides information about the options you selected. After you click Finish, the
operation will begin.

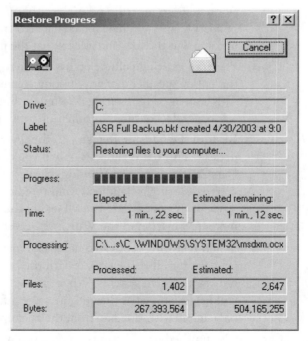

Finally, as with the backup operation, you'll see a summary dialog box. And,
you'll have the option of viewing a text file report of the details of the operation.

Using Advanced Mode for Restores

You can use the Advanced mode of the Windows Backup utility to perform additional restore operations. To access this mode, simply click the Advanced Mode link when the wizard is launched. Figure 6-26 shows the options that are available with the Restore And Manage Media tab of the interface. Windows Server 2003 automatically keeps track of any backups that were made using the local Windows Backup utility. Through this interface, you can view a list of all of the backups that were performed on the local machine, along with data about the contents of these backups.

If information about the backup file that you want to restore from does not appear in the list, you should choose the Tools | Catalog A Backup File option. This will allow you to point Windows Backup to a backup file. When the file is found, the contents of the file will be cataloged, and (as long as the file is intact) the details will be available on the Restore And Manage Media tab. The other options that are available are the same ones that were covered earlier in this chapter.

Restoring System State Information

Earlier in this chapter, we looked at the importance of System State data. Various types of failures can cause problems that require you to restore the System State on

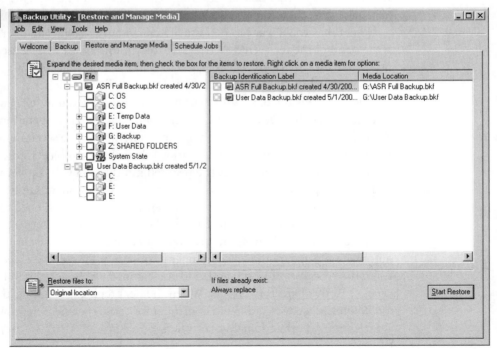

FIGURE 6-26

Viewing the Restore And Manage Media interface in Windows Backup your server. For example, you may have made an accidental modification to information stored in the Active Directory data store. Or, a hard disk failure might have resulted in the loss of data. If operating system files were located on this hard disk, it will be necessary to restore the system state information.

The actual steps involved when restoring System State information are based on the details of what has caused the data loss and what effects this data loss has had on the system. In the best case (relatively speaking, of course), the System State information is corrupt or inaccurate, but the operating system can still boot. If this is the case, all that must be done is to boot the operating system and restore the System State information. This operation will replace the current System State information with that from the backup. Therefore, any changes that have been made since the last backup will be completely lost and must be redone. Note that restoring System State can be done only on the local server.

Restoring System State on a Domain Controller

A special consideration must be taken into account when performing a System State restore on an Active Directory domain controller. The System State information normally includes data stored in the Active Directory database. If you were to perform a simple restore of this information, it will be overwritten by more updated information that is stored on other domain controllers in your environment. This is known as a *nonauthoritative restore*.

Sometimes you'll want to perform an *authoritative restore*—an operation in which some or all of the recovered Active Directory information will be used to update other domain controllers. All objects within the Active Directory have serial numbers that specify when they were last updated. Generally, the higher the serial number, the more current the data. Information with a higher serial number will overwrite information with a lower serial number. Following a restore operation, many of the Active Directory objects on a domain controller may have serial numbers that are lower (which indicates older information) than those of objects stored on other domain controllers. Therefore, the restored information will be overwritten.

If you are performing a recovery operation to "undo" an accidental update (such as the deletion of an account or even an entire OU), you will need to prevent this by using the authoritative restore mode. The way the authoritative restore works is that, immediately following the recovery of Active Directory information, you automatically update the serial number information for specific objects. This is done using the ntdsutil command, and you can update the serial numbers of many types of Active Directory objects. When the next replication occurs, the information stored on the recovered domain controller for those specific objects will overwrite information on other domain controllers.

Generally, on a domain controller, the Active Directory database is always marked as in use. Since so many functions depend on the data stored in the Active Directory database, you cannot simply overwrite the existing files during a restore operation. When performing a System State recovery that includes Active Directory data on a domain controller, you must reboot the computer in the Active Directory Services Restore Mode. This is done by pressing F8 during the boot process and choosing this option.

When you log on to the computer after selecting this option, you'll see the option to boot into "Directory Services Restore Mode" (you'll further study all of the available boot options later in this chapter). Note that this mode is designed only for you to perform special operations related to the Active Directory (such as performing an authoritative or nonauthoritative restore operation). Once you have finished the restore operation (and any `ntdsutil` operations that might be required), you should reboot the computer to restart the Active Directory services.

Exercise 6-2 walks through the process of restoring data from a backup that you created in a previous exercise.

EXERCISE 6-2

CertCam & MasterSim 6-2 ON THE CD

Restoring System State Data Using the Windows Backup Utility

In order to successfully complete the steps in this exercise, you must first have created a backup according to the steps in Exercise 6-1. To prevent issues with overwriting configuration information (including the Active Directory database), you will choose to restore the System State information to an alternate location.

1. Log on to the server as a member of the Administrators group and open the Windows Backup utility by choosing Start | Programs | Accessories | System Tools | Backup. If the Backup or Restore Wizard is launched, click the Advanced link. Select the Restore And Manage Media tab.

2. You should see the backup that you created in Exercise 6-1 listed in the Restore And Manage Media window. If, for some reason, the file does not show up, choose Tools | Catalog A Backup File and specify the location of the file. In the left side of the user interface, expand the branch for this backup set. Then, place a check mark next to the System State option.

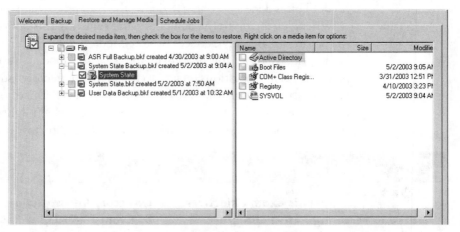

3. Next, you want to ensure that the system state information will be replaced by the restore operation. Choose Tools | Options and then click the Restore tab. Select the option to Always Replace The File On My Computer and then click OK.

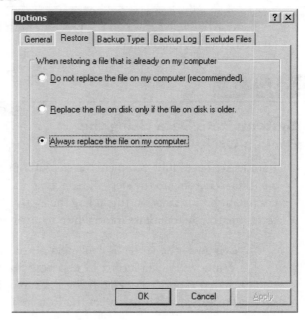

4. In order to avoid any problems that might be caused by restoring the System State information on this server, you will choose to restore the data to an alternate location. Select Alternate Location for the Restore Files To option. Then, specify a folder on the local file system into which the restored information will be saved (you should have at least 500MB of free space in that location). If you wanted to perform an actual restore of the System State, you would choose the option of Original Location.

Restore files to:	If files already exist:	
Alternate location	Always replace	Start Restore
Alternate location:		
G:\Restore	Browse...	

5. Finally, to begin the operation, click Start Restore. A warning will appear stating that not all of the contents of the backup will be restored. Click OK to continue. You'll now see a Confirm Restore dialog box.

Confirm Restore   ? ✕

To set advanced options for restoring your data, click Advanced.

To start restoring your data now, click OK.

OK   Cancel   Advanced...

6. Click OK to begin the restore operation. The files will be extracted from the backup set and stored in the location that you specified in step 4.

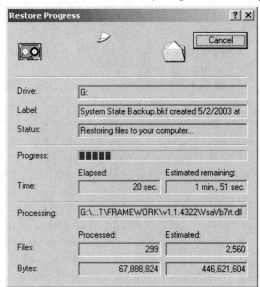

Restore Progress	? ✕
	Cancel
Drive:	G:
Label:	System State Backup.bkf created 5/2/2003 at
Status:	Restoring files to your computer...
Progress:	■■■■■
	Elapsed: / Estimated remaining:
Time:	20 sec. / 1 min., 51 sec.
Processing:	G:\...T\FRAMEWORK\v1.1.4322\VsaVb7rt.dll
	Processed: / Estimated:
Files:	299 / 2,560
Bytes:	67,888,824 / 446,621,604

7. Once the backup operation is complete, click the Report button to view the details of the restore. Then, close the Report and the Restore dialog box. Exit the Windows Backup utility. To view the files that were restored, you can use Windows Explorer to access the folder that you specified in step 4.

Managing Backup Media

When dealing with systems administration, it seems that you can never have enough storage space to meet the needs of your users. Although the costs of disk-based storage resources are constantly spiraling downward, many organizations are outpacing this trend by producing and depending on larger quantities of data. One potential solution for mass data storage is through the use of removable media devices, such as tape drives. In many cases, tape-based backup units can provide lower costs per data volume. Furthermore, the removable media can be backed up and moved to other systems, as needed. However, this comes at a cost: Accessing data from tapes can be a slow, cumbersome, and tedious process.

As organizations are required to back up increasing amounts of data, hardware solutions are attempting to keep the pace. Fundamental concerns include overcoming the storage capacity limitations of removable media storage devices and making the associated storage media easier to manage. One method of accomplishing these goals is through the use of media autoloaders or "jukeboxes." These devices are used to automatically manage and switch storage media to ensure that the proper medium is available for certain operations. The benefit is that, once these systems are set up, limited human interaction is required to manually change tapes. Physically, an autoloader consists of one or more backup devices (such as a tape backup unit), and a robotic system that is used for inserting and removing media for these devices.

The generic term "media" can refer to many different types of storage, including optical (such as writable and rewritable CDs and DVDs) and magnetic (including a wide array of different tape-based storage options). As you can imagine, in even the smallest environments, it can become difficult to keep track of which tapes belong to which backup sets or applications. One way of doing this is to use traditional labels that are physically attached to tapes. This can become problematic if media are reused, however. Another method for tracking media is to use a bar-code system. Organizations do this by purchasing a bar code system that allows for creating special labels that, when read by a bar-code scanner, can provide details about the purpose of the media. Additionally, many types of media include on-disc or on-tape identifiers which can be used to store some basic description information about the contents of the media. For example, AIT (Advanced Intelligent Tape) tapes have a built-in memory chip for storing identification and catalog information.

In the following section, you'll look at how media can be managed in Windows Server 2003 in particular.

Managing Media in Windows Backup

Many common functions are required when using removable storage to back up data on your servers. Fortunately, the Windows Backup utility provides support for these basic functions. If your server has an installed tape backup device, you'll be able to perform the following operations from the Tools | Media Tools menu of Windows Backup:

- **Format** Before a tape can be used to store data, it must be formatted. This operation will format the tape so that Windows Backup can store information on it. Note that formatting a tape will remove all data on the media. Generally, after you purchase new media, this is the first step that you'll need to perform.

- **Retension** As tapes are constantly wound and rewound in the course of normal operations, the tape itself can become loosely wrapped around the spindles of the medium. A retension operation can resolve this. Note that not all media require retensioning, so consult your hardware documentation before using this feature.

- **Mark tape as free** Often, you may want to reuse removable media that have been used for previous backup operations. In order to do this, you can mark a tape as being available for use. Note that marking a tape as free does not delete any of the data on the tape, and the data may still be accessible until it is overwritten.

If you select a backup set in the Restore And Manage Media tab, and then select the Tools | Media Tools, you'll see the following options (see Figure 6-27):

- **Catalog** This option will read the information about the contents of the selected backup set. Depending on the type of media and hardware you're using, this operation may take up to a few minutes (loading catalogs from disk-based backups generally takes only a few seconds).

- **Delete Catalog** This option will delete information about the backup catalog from the system, but it will not delete the backup itself. This option is useful if you know that you will not want to restore from a backup set that is shown in the user interface.

- **Delete Catalog from System** This option will delete information about a backup catalog *and* will delete the backup set itself from the system. You should use this option only when you are sure that you will never want to restore from this backup set.

Viewing Media
Tools options in
the Windows
Backup utility

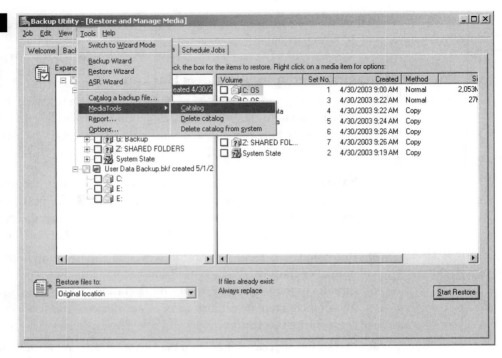

Now that you know how to perform basic media management, let's look at how to handle more complex configurations.

Using Removable Storage

It can be difficult enough for systems administrators to keep track of storage media for a few servers, and the problem is worsened when dealing with autoloaders. Windows Server 2003 includes a tool called "Removable Storage" that is designed to make the management of backup media simpler and easier. This feature allows different applications to access the media stored in a media library with minimal administrative effort. The Removable Storage tool can be found in the Administrative Tools program group. When you launch it, you'll see a screen similar to the one shown in Figure 6-28.

When it comes to setting up the removable storage feature, you must start by installing your media hardware. The instructions for doing this will accompany the solution that you purchased. Let's take a look at some features and concepts related to removable media.

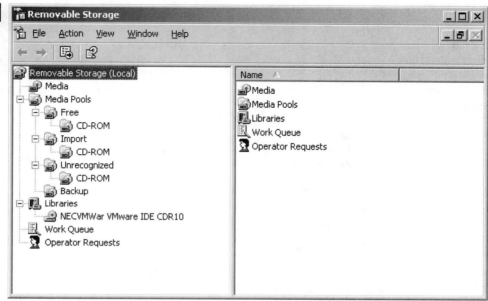

FIGURE 6-28

Viewing information in the Removable Storage tool

Removable Storage Concepts

Now that you have a basic idea of the purpose of removable storage management, let's take a look at some terms and concepts that are designed to simplify media management. The first term you'll need to be familiar with is *media libraries*. A library is a collection of media, along with the device(s) that can read these media. The simplest example of a library is a CD-ROM. The library would include the CD-ROM device, as well as any CDs that you intend to make available to this machine. Automated media changers, such as tape autoloaders or CD-ROM jukeboxes, are also media libraries. Removable Storage can keep track of media (whether installed in the media library or not), and it provides a standard way for applications to request media. You can keep track of media libraries using the Removable Storage tool (see Figure 6-29).

FIGURE 6-29

Viewing
information about
media pools using
the Removable
Storage tool

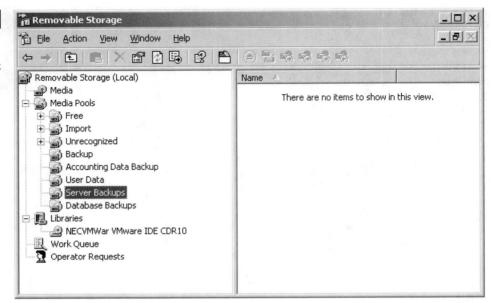

Removable Storage also uses a concept of *media pools* to organize removable storage media. A media pool can contain some or all of the storage media that are present in an autochanger device. Generally, systems administrators will configure multiple media pools, each of which is used for storing a specific type of information. For example, I might create three separate media pools labeled "User Data," "Server Backups," and "Database Backups." Each of these media pools can contain multiple pieces of media (for example, several tapes).

You have many advanced features available when creating media pools. For example, you can build a hierarchy of media pools, based on your organization's requirements. There are several different types of media pools in the Removable Storage tool. These are

■ **Free**   Media that are located in the "free" media pool are designated as being ready for use. This means that the media in this pool do not contain any useful information that must be retained. If an application needs to store data, it can request media from the free media pool.

■ **Import**   When media are moved between Windows Server 2003 installations, they are marked as imported. This means that the media have been configured in another Removable Storage system (one other than the local system). Imported media can be added to other media pools, if you wish to use them on the local system.

- **Unrecognized** When new media are introduced into a system, they are first categorized as "unrecognized." Generally, you'll want to make this new media available for use by assigning it to other media pools. Note that, unless the media are assigned to a media pool, it will not be tracked by the Removable Storage feature.

- **Application** Applications can create their own media pools that appear in the Removable Storage user interface. One such familiar application is the Windows Backup utility. This utility creates an application media tool called "Backup."

To create a new media pool in the Removal Storage tool, right-click Media Pools and select Create. As shown in Figure 6-30, you can provide a name and description for the new pool. Then, you must specify which types of media you want to manage. You build a hierarchy by creating a media pool that contains other media pools, or you can specify the type of media that should be included in the pool. The "allocation/ dellocation policy" settings allow you to specify if and how media from this pool can be used by applications.

FIGURE 6-30

Creating a new media pool in the Removable Storage tool

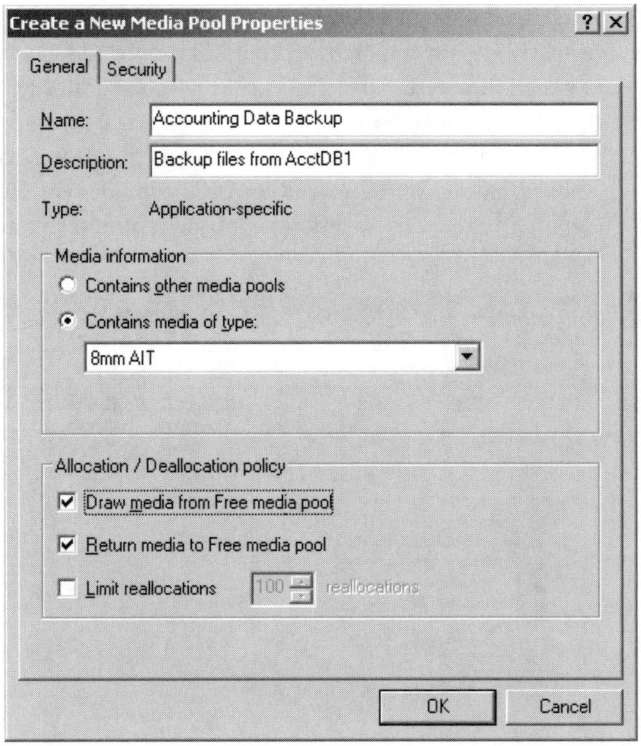

In addition to allowing you to configure media libraries and media pools for use by applications, the Removable Storage tool can provide you with information about how current media and devices are being used (see Figure 6-31). Additionally, it can notify systems administrators (called "operators") when manual intervention is required. For example, media that are not currently installed in a library might be requested, and an administrator may need to provide those media.

on the **Job**

The Removable Storage feature can also be managed using the `rsm` *command-line utility. For more information, see the Windows Server 2003 Help and Support Center.*

Now that you have a solid understanding of how you can manage backup media with Removable Storage, let's take a look at a related feature.

Understanding Remote Storage

You already looked at one tool that makes use of removable backup media—Windows Backup. However, if you want to move your least-used files to tape using only this utility, you'll need to devote significant time to the process. Not only would you need to regularly identify which files should be moved to tape, but you'd also have to keep track of which files were moved and on which media they're stored. Then, when you receive the inevitable request to restore the data, you'll have to load up the appropriate media and perform the restore operation. Clearly this process could use some improvement!

Fortunately, Windows Server 2003 provides the Remote Storage feature, which can greatly reduce the amount of time required to offload data to cheaper media.

FIGURE 6-31

Viewing operation information in the Removable Storage tool

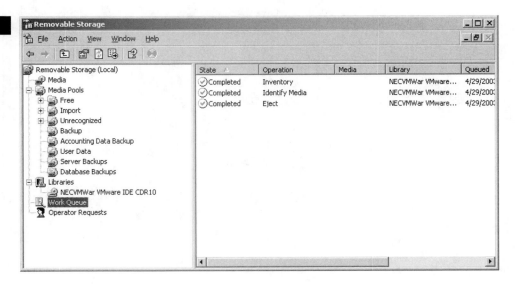

on the **Job**

The Remote Storage feature is available only on the Enterprise Edition and Datacenter Edition of Windows Server 2003. The Remote Storage feature has specific requirements for the hardware configurations that it supports. When evaluating hardware solutions, be sure to ask vendors whether their solution offers native support for Windows Server 2003.

Remote Storage is a technology in Windows Server 2003 that takes advantage of the operating system's support for Removable Storage devices. As you saw earlier in this chapter, removable storage devices can include many different types of media, such as tape backups, optical backup systems, and virtually any other device for which the vendor has created the appropriate drivers. Remote storage works by automatically identifying seldom-accessed files (based on criteria determined by the systems administrator) and then automatically copying this data to a Removable Storage device. But wait, there's more! The files that are automatically "moved" don't disappear from the various volumes on which they're stored. Instead, their icons are changed to signify that they're stored on another device. When users attempt to access the files, they are automatically accessed from the removable storage device (if the media are available) and copied back to the disk for use.

It doesn't take much imagination to see how these features can save many hours of time and effort for systems administrators.

on the **Job**

You should not use Remote Storage as a replacement for backup operations. Although Remote Storage copies files to tape, it does not ensure that all files will ever be copied. It also does not keep a proper archive of data. For the best data protection and accessibility, use Remote Storage with your normal backup operations—not instead of them.

In order to implement remote storage, you'll first need to configure your removable storage device. Once you have the devices appropriately configured, you'll need to specify which volumes will be affected by remote storage. These volumes are known as *managed volumes*.

You can use the Remote Storage Administrative Tool to create managed volumes and to configure the settings for the Remote Storage services. When you first run the tool, you'll be prompted to work with the Remote Storage Setup Wizard. This process will ensure that your machine meets the requirements for Remote Storage and then will walk you through the basic configuration. For more information about the Remote Storage tool, see the Windows Server 2003 Help and Support Center.

on the **Job**

Although the 70-290 Exam Objectives do not mention Remote Storage, this can be a very powerful and useful tool to use when implementing and managing storage resources in the real world.

CERTIFICATION OBJECTIVE 6.04

Performing System Recovery for a Server

So far, you have looked at restoring System State data on the local server using the Windows Backup utility. If your server cannot boot, however, using the Windows Backup utility is not an option. Fortunately, there are features in Windows Server 2003 that can be used to resolve this more serious issue.

Generally, if you have lost critical information on your server installations, it's necessary to reinstall the operating system. The problem with this method, however, is that a lot of configuration must be done. And if you don't do this correctly, you could end up with some pretty big problems. For example, suppose that the non-fault-tolerant system partition on one of your database servers fails due to a hard disk crash. In this case, the operating system will become unavailable, and you will not be able to boot the system. The basic process of recovering from this issue involves replacing the failed hardware and then reinstalling Windows Server 2003. During the installation process, you should try to re-create the original disk, operating system, and application configuration of the server before failure. Then, once the operating system is installed, you can start to restore the system from backup.

As you can tell, this is a lot of work. Worse yet, there's room for error, especially if you haven't completely documented your server's configuration. Fortunately, Windows Server 2003 provides an easier and safer way to rebuild a failed system. The Automated System Recovery (ASR) feature allows you to create a special floppy disk that can be used to provide the installation process with enough information to start the recovery process. It then allows you to start restoring data from the storage medium on which a complete system backup was stored. This method allows you to avoid the time-consuming step of reinstalling Windows Server 2003 just so that you can start a restore operation. Let's take a look at how you can prepare your system to use ASR.

On several occasions, I've worked with systems administrators that seem to want to "forget troubleshooting and reinstall," even when minor problems occur. You should really resist the urge to do this! Although it may be more difficult in the short run, it's probably much better to figure out what went wrong. The information you learn could help you prevent the problem or, at least, more quickly solve it in the future. And, it will help grow your troubleshooting skills. When it comes to solving server-related issues, curing the disease by killing the patient is generally not a good approach!

Recovering from a Hardware Failure

In a worst-case scenario, all of the information on a server has been lost or a hardware failure is preventing the machine from properly booting. Since this means that you cannot simply run Windows Backup to restore from a recent backup, you must use other techniques. In the case of a nonbooting server, there are several steps that you must take in order to recover the system. These steps include the following:

1. Fix any hardware problem that may prevent the computer from booting (for example, replace any failed hard disks). Depending on the type of failure, this might involve reconfiguring hard disks so that they match the original configuration.

2. Reinstall the operating system. This should be performed like a regular installation on a new system. For more information on installing Windows Server 2003, see Chapter 1.

3. Establish access to the backup media. This may involve reinstalling any device drivers that may be required by your backup device. If you backed up information to the file system, this will not apply. If the backup is stored on a network device, you must be sure that you have network access to the backup.

4. Restore the System State information using the Windows Backup utility. Optionally, you may choose to restore other files, such as user data or program files.

This general process is required to recover from most types of hardware faults and will work with most operating systems. However, when downtime is critical, the process can be time-consuming. Fortunately, Windows Server 2003 provides a better way of restoring a system to its previous status after a hardware failure has been resolved. Let's move on to that, next.

Preparing for Automated System Recovery

In order to use ASR, you must first use the Windows Backup utility to create an ASR floppy disk and the necessary backups. There are two ways to do this. First, if you're using the Backup or Restore Wizard, you can select the All Information On This Computer option on the What To Backup step. When you select this option, the wizard will automatically select all necessary system files and data to be backed up. It will then begin the backup process for your data. You'll need to make sure that the media that you're backing up to (whether disk, tape, or optical) have enough storage space to retain a backup of this size. Upon completion of the backup process, you'll be prompted to insert a floppy disk into the server (see the following illustration). This disk will contain the information that is necessary for the ASR feature to do its job, including disk configuration and device driver information.

If you've worked with earlier versions of the Windows platform, you're probably familiar with Emergency Repair Disks (ERDs). ASR replaces this functionality.

The other method for creating an ASR backup is to use the Advanced mode of the Windows Backup Tool. You can click the Automated System Recovery Wizard option either from the Welcome page or from the Tools menu. This will launch the Automated System Recovery Preparation Wizard (shown in Figure 6-32).

Using this wizard is very simple. In fact, since you must back up all system-related files, the only choice that you have is to choose the backup location. Once you've made this selection, you'll see the final confirmation shown in Figure 6-33. When you click Finish, the backup process will continue just as it does when you use the Backup or Restore Wizard.

FIGURE 6-32

Launching the ASR Preparation Wizard

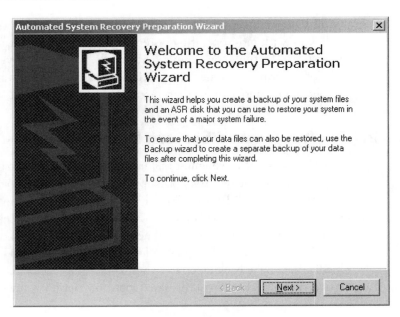

FIGURE 6-33

Completing the
ASR Preparation
Wizard

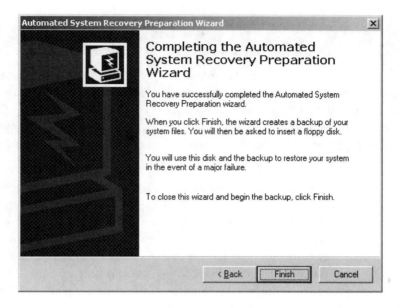

So far, you've looked at how you can create an ASR disk and backup. That process is simple enough. The real "magic" is in the recovery process. Let's move on to that, next.

Whenever you make changes to your system configuration (such as disk reconfiguration, the installation of a new mission-critical application, or the installation of new hardware or device drivers), you should also update your ASR backup. This will ensure that the ASR process can rebuild your server configuration correctly.

Restoring a Server with Automated System Recovery

As mentioned earlier, the Automated System Recovery process is designed to be used when your system won't boot (due, for example, to a loss of a disk array or the failure of a physical disk), and you need to reinstall and rebuild the entire system. As far as system recovery goes, using ASR should generally be considered a "last step." That is, you should use ASR only when all other methods of troubleshooting fail.

In order to perform an Automated System Recovery, you will need to have the following available:

- An Automated System Recovery disk
- Access to a full system backup on a local device (including disk, tape, or another local storage device)
- A copy of the Windows Server 2003 installation media

exam

ⓦatch   *If you're asked to recover from a server failure on the exam, be sure to consider the simplest and easiest way to troubleshoot a problem. If the issue is minor, using ASR may resolve it. However,*   *it's likely that ASR is not the best solution for resolving minor issues. Remember, you're not just looking for a solution that works—you're looking for the solution that is quickest, easiest, and safest!*

Now, let's look at the process that's required to perform an Automated System Recovery. First, boot your system using the Windows Server 2003 CD-ROM. This is usually done by simply inserting the CD-ROM into the CD-ROM drive and rebooting the computer (for more information on the setup process, see Chapter 1). Note that some computers may require changes to the BIOS configuration in order to boot from media other than the hard disk (consult your hardware owner's manual for details, if you're not sure how to enter the BIOS and configure settings).

When setup starts, press F2 as soon as the text-mode portion of the installation process begins. This option will specify that you want to perform the Automated System Recovery process, and you'll be prompted to insert your ASR floppy disk:

```
Windows Setup




                    Please insert the disk labeled:

              Windows Automated System Recovery Disk

                        into the floppy drive.


                      Press any key when ready.
```

At this point, the ASR process will use the information stored on the disk to determine how your system should be configured. The first step will be to format your operating system disk. This will completely erase all data on that disk (something that can be quite scary if you're not sure what to expect). The ASR process will then continue to install Windows Server 2003 in what will look like a normal setup process. The major difference is that the ASR setup process will not require any information from you—all of the configuration options and details were stored on the ASR floppy.

```
Windows Server 2003, Enterprise Edition Setup


              Please wait while Setup formats the partition
                      \Device\Harddisk0\Partition1
          on 4095 MB Disk 0 at Id 0 on bus 0 on atapi [MBR].






        Setup is formatting...
                                        68%
        [███████████████████████████        ]
```

If the ASR process is unable to find your backup set, the ASR Wizard may be launched to ask you to provide the location of the backup that you created. You should be able to choose from files on the local server, or from a local tape device (if one is installed in the system).

Once the Automated System Recovery process is complete, your operating system will be reinstalled, and the data that was present in the system backup file will have been restored. If you've ever had to restore an entire server before manually, you'll see that this process can save a significant amount of time.

Using the Recovery Console

In older versions of Windows, including Windows 3.1, Windows 95, Windows 98, and Windows ME, systems administrators could boot their computers using a floppy disk. This technique was useful for resolving issues in which the primary operating system on the computer failed to start. For example, by booting with an MS-DOS floppy disk, you could move, copy, or delete files, and you could perform some basic configuration tasks. With Windows Server 2003, however, security features and the NTFS file system make it impossible to simply boot with an old MS-DOS disk (assuming you can still find one!). However, when your server systems will not boot, you need to have some way to be able to perform basic configuration and file system tasks. Fortunately, there's a solution: the Recovery Console.

There are two main ways to access the Recovery Console. The first method is always available to systems administrators. You can begin by booting your computer using the Windows Server 2003 installation CD-ROM. When prompted, you can choose to enter the Recovery Console. Now, let's look at another way of accessing the Recovery Console.

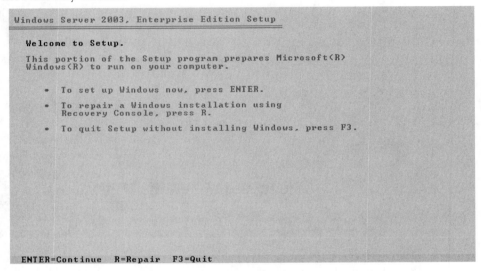

Adding the Recovery Console as a Startup Option

Although you can always access the Recovery Console using the Windows Server 2003 installation media, when a serious problem occurs, you may not feel like rummaging around for the installation disc. Fortunately, you can copy the contents of the Recovery Console to your system and make the console available as a startup option. To do this, you will need the Windows Server 2003 installation media. Simply enter the following command from within the I386 directory of the installation media:

```
winnt32.exe /cmdcons
```

Although the command does not provide any output on the command line, you will see this graphical dialog box:

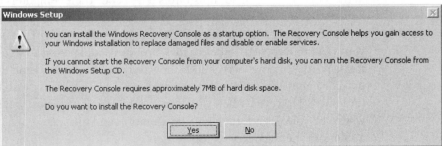

When you click Yes to continue, the Recovery Console installation process will check for updated files over the Internet (assuming you have an Internet connection). This is shown in Figure 6-34.

Finally, once the installation is complete, you'll be notified that the Console can be accessed from the Startup Menu.

If, for some reason, you want to remove the Recovery Console after it has been created, you can simply delete the hidden folder named "cmdcons" (which will be located in the root of the boot partition). Then, you can manually modify the boot.ini file or use the Startup And Recovery Options dialog box to remove the Recovery Console option from the Startup Menu.

However, just about any system should be able to spare the 7MB of disk space that is required for the console files, and having this option available can be very handy in a pinch!

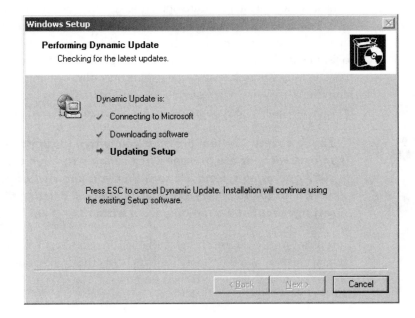

Using the Recovery Console

When you first launch the Recovery Console (either through setup or through a Startup Menu option), you'll be prompted to choose the installation of Windows that you want to log on to. If your computer has multiple installations of Windows 2000 Server or Windows Server 2003, you'll be shown a list of the known installations. Once you select the appropriate installation, you'll be prompted to provide the Administrator password for the computer. Note that, whether or not the computer is functioning as a domain controller, you will need to provide the password for the local Administrator account. This process is shown here.

```
Microsoft Windows(R) Recovery Console.

The Recovery Console provides system repair and recovery functionality.

Type EXIT to quit the Recovery Console and restart the computer.


1: C:\WINDOWS

Which Windows installation would you like to log onto
<To cancel, press ENTER)? 1
Type the Administrator password: *************
```

After you have logged on to the Recovery Console, you'll have access to the file system and can use various commands to work with the operating system configuration.

Recovery Console Commands

Although at first it may resemble a standard Windows command prompt, the Recovery Console is actually a miniature operating system that can be used to perform simple tasks. First, you can navigate through the various file systems on your server. You will have access to various commands such as cd to change the current directory and dir to list files in the file system. In addition, you will be able to run many different functions that can help you isolate and repair some operating system problems. There are limitations, however. For example, you will be unable to launch program files or utilities, and advanced command-line utilities are not available.

on the **j o b**

The Recovery Console provides you with a lot of power without the safeguards that are present when running through the Windows Server 2003 operating system. Be sure that you know what you're doing when you work with the Recovery Console. In general, deleting files and reconfiguring settings should be done only from within the "real" operating system.

You can retrieve a list of the available Recovery Console commands by typing **Help** at the command prompt. Table 6-1 lists the commands available through the recovery console, along with their purposes.

| TABLE 6-1 | Recovery Console Commands and Their Purposes |

Recovery Console Command	Purpose
Attrib	Changes file or directory attributes (such as "read-only").
Batch	Executes a batch file. The batch file can be any text file that contains Recovery Console commands.
BootCfg	Allows for the modification of the boot.ini file. The boot.ini file controls which options are available at system startup.
ChDir (cd)	Changes the current directory. When used without an argument, it displays the path of the current directory.
ChkDsk	Performs a check of the disk. Included are tests of the file system, security descriptors, and other data. The /F switch can be used to instruct the utility to fix any problems that it may find (otherwise, no changes are made to the file system).
Cls	Clears the screen.
Copy	Makes a copy of a file.
Delete (Del)	Deletes a file.
Dir	Displays all of the files in the current directory or, if an argument is provided, in the specified directory.
Disable	Disables a system service or device driver. For a list of services and device drivers, run the `listsvc` command. When an item is disabled, it will not be automatically started the next time the system is booted.
DiskPart	Used to manage file system partitions. DiskPart can be used to create and delete partitions, as needed.
Enable	Enables or starts a system service or device driver. For a list of services and device drivers, run the `listsvc` command. When an item is "enabled," it will be started when the system is next booted.
Exit	Exits the Recovery Console and reboots the computer.
Expand	Extracts data from a compression file. Data must be compressed in CABinet file format.
FixBoot	Writes a new master boot record (MBR) on a bootable partition. This command is useful if, for some reason, the boot sector of a hard drive has become corrupted or modified (such as in the case of the installation of another operating system).
FixMBR	Repairs the master boot record (MBR) on a bootable partition.
Format	Formats an existing partition.

| TABLE 6-1 | Recovery Console Commands and Their Purposes *(continued)* |

Recovery Console Command	Purpose
Help	Displays a list of commands that are available from within the Recovery Console.
ListSvc	Lists the services and drivers that are available on the selected installation of Windows. These items can be configured using the Enable and Disable commands.
Logon	Can be used to log on to an installation of Windows Server 2003 on the same machine. This command is useful if you have multiple Windows installations on the same machine.
Map	Displays a list of drive letter mappings.
MkDir (md)	Creates a new directory on an existing file system.
More (Type)	Used to display the contents of a text file to the screen.
Rename (ren)	Renames a file.
RmDir (rd)	Deletes a directory.
Set	With no arguments, this command displays a list of environment variables. It can also be used to set environment variables that will be used on the next startup.
SystemRoot	Changes the current active directory to the System directory of the Windows Server 2003 installation that you're logged in to.

on the Job

As with most other Windows Server 2003 command-line functions, the Recovery Console is case-insensitive. I have used mixed-case in this section only to provide for readability.

All of these commands can be useful in one way or another. For example, suppose that you've installed a new service on your Windows Server 2003 machine, and now you are having problems that are preventing your system from starting up. You can use the Recovery Console to disable the service. First, start by using the ListSvc command to return a list of the drivers and services that are installed and configured on the machine. Once you have found the name of the service you want to disable, you can use the Disable command to specify that it should not start up the next time Windows Server 2003 is booted.

```
Abiosdsk          Disabled

ACPI              Boot
    Microsoft ACPI Driver
ACPIEC            Disabled

adpu160m          Disabled

adpu320           Disabled

afcnt             Disabled

AFD               Auto
    AFD Networking Support Environment
agp440            Boot
    Intel AGP Bus Filter
Aha154x           Disabled

aic78u2           Disabled

aic78xx           Disabled

Alerter           Disabled
    Alerter
ALG               Manual
    Application Layer Gateway Service
AliIde            Disabled

AppMgmt           Manual
    Application Management
AsyncMac          Manual
    RAS Asynchronous Media Driver
More:   ENTER=Scroll (Line)    SPACE=Scroll (Page)    ESC=Stop
```

Overall, the Recovery Console provides a lot of basic functionality that can be
used to troubleshoot Windows startup and configuration problems.

Using Windows Startup Options

In general, systems administrators depend on the tools and features present in the
operating system in order to diagnose and troubleshoot problems. For example, we
may install or remove device drivers, configure and disable services, or make video
configuration changes. Sometimes, however, we need to troubleshoot problems that
prevent the operating system from booting properly. For example, the installation of
a poorly written device driver may cause Windows Server 2003 to fail to boot at all.
Since we can't use the operating system to troubleshoot the problem, we need other
approaches for fixing the problem.

Windows Server 2003 includes many different startup options that can be used for
troubleshooting whenever the operating system will not properly start up. You can
access these operations during the boot process by pressing F8 when you see the boot
menu. The following illustration shows the various startup options that are available.

To select one of the special boot options, simply use the cursor keys and hit ENTER to make a selection.

```
Windows Advanced Options Menu
Please select an option:

     Safe Mode
     Safe Mode with Networking
     Safe Mode with Command Prompt

     Enable Boot Logging
     Enable VGA Mode
     Last Known Good Configuration (your most recent settings that worked)
     Directory Services Restore Mode (Windows domain controllers only)
     Debugging Mode

     Start Windows Normally
     Reboot
     Return to OS Choices Menu

Use the up and down arrow keys to move the highlight to your choice.
```

In this section, you'll take a brief look at the various startup modes that are available.

exam

Ⓦatch   *An important aspect of troubleshooting a server using various startup options is the ability to actually resolve*   *hardware-related problems once the system is started. For more information on that topic, refer to Chapter 2.*

Using Safe Mode

A common source of problems that could prevent Windows Server 2003 from booting or operating properly is the installation drivers or services that run on startup. When starting up Windows Server 2003 in safe mode, only the bare essentials will be loaded during the boot process. This includes the following:

- Mouse drivers
- Keyboard support
- Basic video support
- Hard disk storage drivers
- Necessary system services

Figure 6-35 shows the warning that you'll see when you enter safe mode.

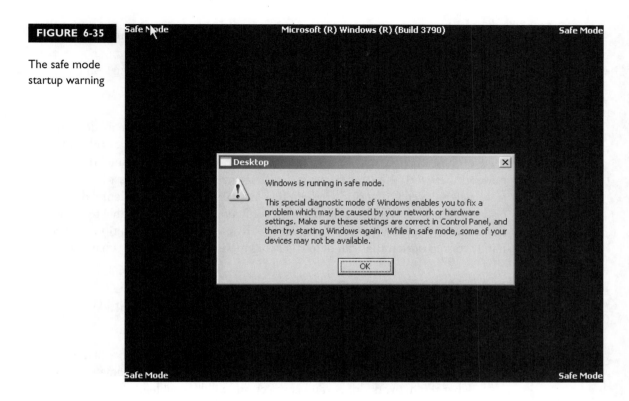

FIGURE 6-35

The safe mode
startup warning

Note that advanced drivers for certain types of devices, as well as networking options, are not loaded when booting in safe mode. If the problem is driver- or service-related, it's likely that you will be able boot the system in this mode. Then, you can perform basic configuration tasks using the operating system's features (such as the Control Panel System utility). When you are finished troubleshooting, you should reboot your computer and try to boot in the normal mode again.

Understanding the Last Known Good Configuration

If you're like me, you've run into problems with server driver configurations and you've found yourself wishing that there was some simple way to turn back the clock and pretend that the installation never happened. Windows Server 2003 makes this possible by giving you the ability to boot to the last configuration of the system that is known to have worked properly. The way this feature works is that, whenever users log on locally to a system, a record of the system's configuration is made. If, the next time the server is rebooted, it fails to start up properly, this configuration information is not recorded.

Therefore, if you have a startup problem, you can revert the system to the state that it was in during the last successful startup. Specifically, what is going on behind the scenes is that the following Registry key (and all subkeys) is being restored:

```
HKEY_LOCAL_MACHINE\System\CurrentControlSet
```

This feature comes with one big limitation, however—if you have made certain types of systems changes (like driver installations) since the last successful startup, some of these changes may be lost. For example, if you replace existing drivers with newer drivers with the same name, you will not be able to use the Last Known Good feature to recover. Or if critical system files are missing (due to accidental deletion or uninstallation), the Last Known Good configuration will not be able to recover those files automatically. Still, using the Last Known Good configuration is a very handy startup option that can help you avoid more significant server changes.

Using Other Startup Options

In addition to the startup options you've seen already, there are several additional options available via the boot menu. These include

- **Safe Mode With Networking**   Like safe mode, this option boots the system with a minimal configuration. The major difference, as the name implies, is that the network drivers and connections will be enabled. This mode is useful if you want to copy data to and from network resources, or if you want to perform troubleshooting using remote tools.

- **Safe Mode With Command Prompt**   Again, this operation works much like safe mode in that a minimal set of drivers is loaded. The difference is that, once you log on to Windows Server 2003, the standard Windows Explorer and desktop shells are not loaded. Instead, a Command Prompt window is opened. Since the operating system is running (although in a limited mode), you have access to all of the command-line utilities that you would be able to use while running after a normal startup. When you are finished using the command prompt, you can type the **Exit** command and then reboot the computer. Or, you can press CTRL-ALT-DEL to access the Task Manager to perform other tasks (such as a system shutdown).

- **Enable Boot Logging**   Sometimes it's helpful to see exactly what's going on behind the scenes while Windows is booting up. When you choose to enable boot logging, a new text file called ntbtlog.txt will be created within your Windows system root directory. You can view this information using a standard text editor, such as Notepad (see Figure 6-36). The drawback to selecting this

FIGURE 6-36

Viewing a portion of the boot log

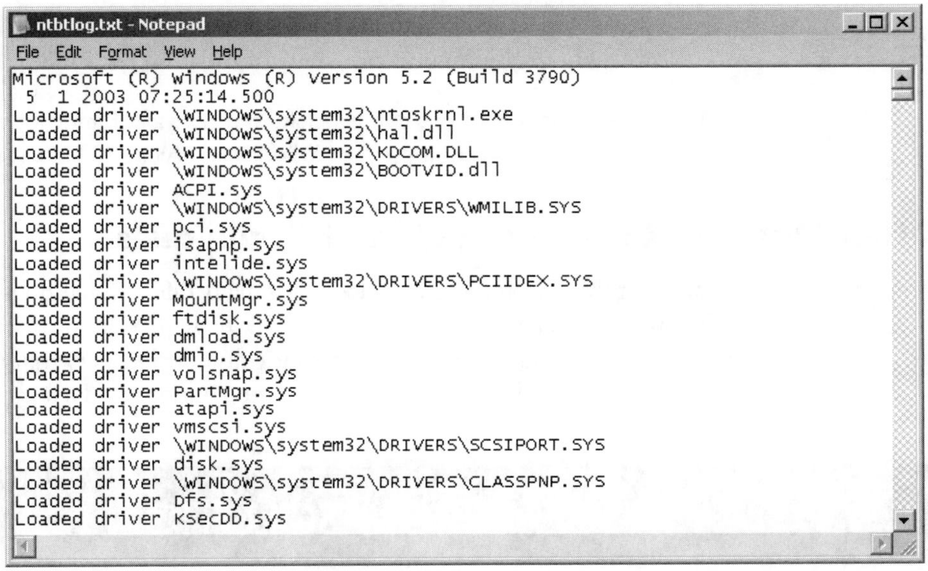

```
ntbtlog.txt - Notepad
File  Edit  Format  View  Help
Microsoft (R) Windows (R) Version 5.2 (Build 3790)
5  1 2003 07:25:14.500
Loaded driver \WINDOWS\system32\ntoskrnl.exe
Loaded driver \WINDOWS\system32\hal.dll
Loaded driver \WINDOWS\system32\KDCOM.DLL
Loaded driver \WINDOWS\system32\BOOTVID.dll
Loaded driver ACPI.sys
Loaded driver \WINDOWS\system32\DRIVERS\WMILIB.SYS
Loaded driver pci.sys
Loaded driver isapnp.sys
Loaded driver intelide.sys
Loaded driver \WINDOWS\system32\DRIVERS\PCIIDEX.SYS
Loaded driver MountMgr.sys
Loaded driver ftdisk.sys
Loaded driver dmload.sys
Loaded driver dmio.sys
Loaded driver volsnap.sys
Loaded driver PartMgr.sys
Loaded driver atapi.sys
Loaded driver vmscsi.sys
Loaded driver \WINDOWS\system32\DRIVERS\SCSIPORT.SYS
Loaded driver disk.sys
Loaded driver \WINDOWS\system32\DRIVERS\CLASSPNP.SYS
Loaded driver Dfs.sys
Loaded driver KSecDD.sys
```

option is that system startup will be a little slower. Note that the boot log is also automatically created when you boot to any of the safe mode options.

■ **Enable VGA Mode** There are several situations in which you may need to troubleshoot video issues. First, if you installed an incorrect video driver that is preventing the display from coming up, you may want to start with the basic Windows VGA driver. Or, suppose you've hooked your server up to an old monitor that was just lying around in the server room. Perhaps this old monitor doesn't support the higher resolutions and refresh rates that your system is configured to use. In either case, you can choose the Enable VGA Mode option to boot using a minimal video driver. Note that VGA mode drivers are automatically loaded whenever you choose a safe mode startup option, as well.

■ **Directory Services Restore Mode** This option is available only on Windows Server 2003 installations that are configured as domain controllers. In order to restore Active Directory information, the various services related to the Active Directory must be disabled upon startup. That's the purpose of the Directory Services Restore mode. After you log on to the system, you'll be able to restore the Active Directory database using the Windows Backup utility.

■ **Debugging Mode** This option specifies that Windows should send startup information through the serial port on the computer. This method of reporting startup data is particularly useful for "headless" servers (machines that are not connected to standard output devices such as a monitor), and for software developers that are creating or debugging drivers. Using a serial cable, another computer can view information reported by the boot process.

All of these startup options can be useful in one way or another when you're trying to troubleshoot problems that prevent Windows Server 2003 from starting up properly.

Other Disaster Recovery Tools and Techniques

Throughout this chapter, you have looked at many different methods for troubleshooting problems that you may experience when working with Windows Server 2003. There are a few other features related to performing disaster recovery that we should cover. In this section, we'll look at how you can set startup options, and a few other useful features.

SCENARIO & SOLUTION	
You have installed a new driver and the system fails to reboot.	Your first troubleshooting step should be to try the Last Known Good configuration option. This should boot the computer into the last configuration that was known to work properly.
You are experiencing a system startup failure, and the Last Known Good startup option doesn't work.	In this case, you can try booting the system to safe mode. This startup mode will load only a minimal set of drivers and services and will (hopefully) allow you to solve any configuration issues that might have occurred. Also, once the system has been booted, Device Driver Rollback functionality (described in Chapter 2), can be used to troubleshoot problems caused by driver installations.
The system will not start normally, and it will not load in safe mode. Also, the Last Known Good configuration does not seem to work.	Okay, now we're moving down the list of available options for troubleshooting. If the easier troubleshooting steps don't work, you'll need to move on to more advanced ones. If you suspect that the problem is due to a missing operating system file, a service that isn't loading properly, or some other error that you think you could repair if you could just get into the system, it may be time to try the Recovery Console. Various Recovery Console commands can be used to enable or disable drivers and services.
You have connected your server to an older monitor that does not support the video settings that you've configured.	Your first choice should be to use the Enable VGA Mode option, since this will perform a normal boot on the server, except for the loading of your video driver. Choosing one of the various safe mode options will also work.

Specifying Startup and Recovery Options

As you might expect, the Windows Server 2003 startup process is configurable. Additionally, you can specify what should happen whenever a system error occurs. These options are set using the Startup and Recovery options. You can access these settings through the Control Panel System utility (or by right-clicking the My Computer icon and selecting Properties). On the Advanced tab, click Settings in the Startup And Recovery section. You'll see the dialog box shown in Figure 6-37.

The first portion of the screen provides options related to system startup. Specifically, you'll be able to choose which operating system choice should be the default, and how long the menu should be displayed before the default is chosen. You'll see multiple options here if the local system is configured with multiple operating systems, or if you have installed the Recovery Console (a feature that you learned about earlier in this chapter). There's also a setting that specifies how long the recovery options menu should be shown. This pertains to the menu of startup options that is displayed after an abnormal shutdown of the server. After the specified amount of time, the boot process will automatically choose the default option. These changes are actually recorded in the boot.ini file, which is located in the

FIGURE 6-37

Viewing Startup and Recovery options

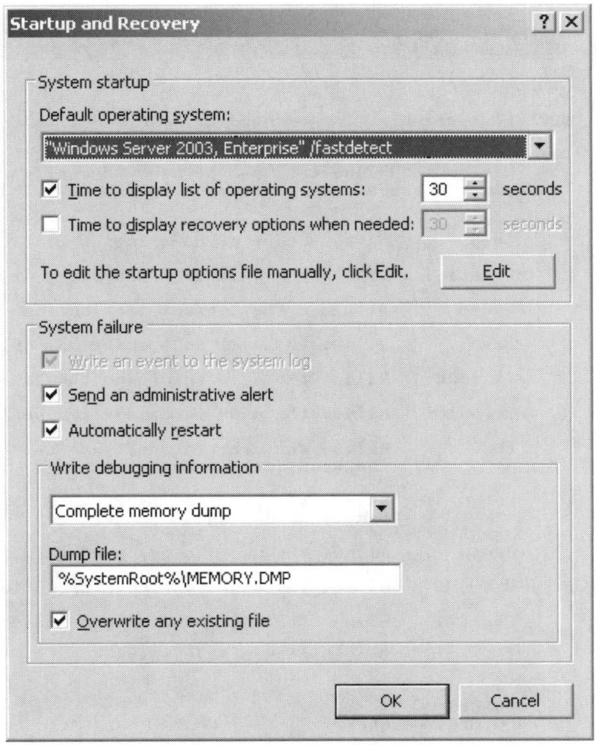

root directory of the boot partition. You can click the Edit menu to modify the file manually, if you wish. Alternatively, you can use the bootcfg.exe command-line utility to make boot changes (see Figure 6-38).

The second portion of the dialog box provides options for actions that will automatically be taken when a system failure is encountered. A system failure is generally caused by the failure of hardware, by poorly written device drivers, or through the failure of low-level system software. Here, you can specify whether an administrative alert should be sent (via a simple network message) and whether the system should be automatically restarted after an error occurs. Generally, you will want your servers to automatically restart, unless you specifically want to view crash information on the screen. Finally, you can specify what type of debugging information will be recorded. The default is to perform a "complete memory dump." This means that all of the contents of the server's memory will be written to disk after the crash occurs. This file (which will equal the total size of all of the physical memory installed in the server) can be used by Microsoft's product support engineers, or other experts, to determine the root cause of failures. Finally, you can specify the location to which the memory dump file will be written. This is useful, for example, if your system partition is fairly full and you have a large amount of memory installed in the machine.

FIGURE 6-38

Viewing options for the bootcfg.exe utility

```
C:\WINDOWS\system32\cmd.exe                                          _ □ ×

C:\>bootcfg /?

BOOTCFG /parameter [arguments]

Description:
    This command line tool can be used to configure, query, change or
    delete the boot entry settings in the BOOT.INI file.

Parameter List:
    /Copy      Makes a copy of an existing boot entry.

    /Delete    Deletes an existing boot entry from the BOOT.INI file.

    /Query     Displays the current boot entries and their settings.

    /Raw       Allows the user to specify any switch to be added.

    /Timeout   Allows the user to change the Timeout value.

    /Default   Allows the user to change the Default boot entry.

    /EMS       Allows the user to configure the /redirect switch
               for headless support.

    /Debug     Allows the user to specify the port and baudrate for
               remote debugging.

    /Addsw     Allows the user to add predefined switches.

    /Rmsw      Allows the user to remove predefined switches.

    /Dbg1394   Allows the user to configure 1394 port for debugging.

    /?         Displays this help message.

Examples:
    BOOTCFG /Copy /?
    BOOTCFG /Delete /?
```

Overall, the Startup and Recovery options provide you with some added control over how your Windows Server 2003 installation will behave on startup and how it will handle system failures.

Using the Shutdown Event Tracker

All but the smallest environments that are running Windows Server 2003 will have multiple systems administrators. When working in such an environment, communications and organized processes are extremely important. One piece of information that may not always be readily available is the reason for server shutdowns or reboots. For example, another systems administrator might be in the habit of rebooting a server every time any software is installed (something that is really not necessary for many applications running on Windows 2000 or later). If you later need to troubleshoot downtime issues with this server, you may not know why so many reboots have been performed. The issue may be hardware reliability issues (in which case, you may choose to replace the server altogether), or it could simply be planned reboots for administrative tasks.

In order to keep track of this information, Windows Server 2003 includes the Shutdown Event Tracker. As shown in Figure 6-39, the Shutdown Event Tracker forces you to specify a reason for the shutdown or restart of a server. Microsoft has enabled the Shutdown Event Tracker, by default, as it is a recommended practice to

Specifying information in the Shutdown Event Tracker

track this information. Additionally, the Shutdown Event Tracker will be automatically launched upon the next logon to the machine, if a server goes down unexpectedly. Again, you'll have the option of entering in any information that you know regarding the reason for the crash.

on the
job

An unsupported command-line utility called uptime is included in the Windows Server 2003 Resource Kit. This utility can show you detailed information about how long the server has been running, and it can provide a list of times that the server was shut down or restarted.

You can use the event IDs shown in Table 6-2 in Event Viewer for viewing information about shutdowns. The items are logged to the System event log. For more information on finding specific items using Event Viewer, see Chapter 8.

Shutdown Event Categories In order to make the information that the Shutdown Event Tracker collects as useful as possible, you should take a little bit of time to create conventions for how the various categories that are provided will be used, and to offer some uniformity for the descriptions that are entered. For example, if you want to track a lot of details, you can have systems administrators enter a URL to an intranet page or document ID that relates to IT documentation to which they can refer for more information about the restart. Although it takes a little bit of time and effort to track shutdown and restart events, the information can be priceless when you're troubleshooting downtime issues.

You can also specify whether the shutdown was planned or unplanned (this setting will slightly change the options that are available in the drop-down box). The default categories that are included within the Shutdown Event Tracker include the following:

- Planned Categories:
  - Other
  - Hardware: Maintenance
  - Hardware: Installation

TABLE 6-2	Event ID	Description
Shutdown Event Tracker-Related Event IDs	1073	An attempt to shut down the computer was aborted.
	1074	Provides a user-supplied reason for an expected shutdown or restart.
	1075	An attempt to shut down the computer was aborted.
	1076	Provides a user-supplied reason for the last unexpected shutdown.
	6008	Error: The previous shutdown was unexpected.

- Operating System: Reconfiguration
- Application: Maintenance
- Application: Installation
- Unplanned Categories:
  - Other
  - Hardware: Maintenance
  - Hardware: Installation
  - Operating System: Reconfiguration
  - Application: Maintenance
  - Application: Installation
  - Application: Unresponsive
  - Application: Unstable

Although it's not recommended, you can disable the Shutdown Event Tracker. This can be done through Group Policy settings (a topic that is covered in Chapter 4). If you want to make a change for the local machine, the specific policy setting is located in Local Computer Policy | Computer Configuration | Administrative Templates | Display Shutdown Event Tracker. The options are shown in Figure 6-40.

FIGURE 6-40

Configuring the Shutdown Event Tracker

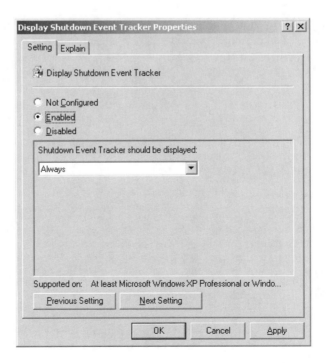

CERTIFICATION SUMMARY

Managing server uptime and reliability is often something that systems administrators (and their management) take for granted. However, having systems that are truly safe requires a solid understanding of backup and recovery procedures. In this chapter, you began by looking at an overview of the types of backup operations that can be performed. Based on this information, you saw how Windows Server 2003's Backup utility can be used to implement basic backup procedures.

The next logical step was to look at how these backups can be used in the process of disaster recovery. Depending on the types of problems or failures that have occurred, there are many different methods for restoring your server to normal operating status. The first and most obvious is simply recovering data (including system state information) from recent backups. However, Windows Server 2003 offers many additional features, including Automated System Recovery, the ability to efficiently manage storage media, the Recovery Console, and many different startup options.

All of these features can be used to help protect your data and your server configurations. With this knowledge, you won't panic when things go wrong (or when you're asked on the exam about what to do given a certain situation). Be sure that you understand all Windows Server 2003's disaster recovery features *before* you need them in the real world or on the exam!

TWO-MINUTE DRILL

Understand Backup Concepts, Procedures, and Operations

❑ When designing and implementing backup methods, be sure to keep in mind your recovery requirements.

❑ The Windows Backup utility enables you to perform normal, differential, incremental, copy, and daily backup operations.

❑ Backups can be created to local disks, to network locations or to locally attached mass storage devices (including tape and optical storage).

❑ The Volume Shadow Copy feature of Windows Server 2003 allows you to back up files that are in use without affecting other applications that are running on the system.

Create and Schedule Backups Using Windows Backup

❑ The Windows Backup utility provides you with the ability to schedule backup jobs using one or multiple schedules.

❑ Backup jobs can be scheduled using the `ntbackup` command-line utility, combined with task scheduling features of Windows Server 2003.

Restore Data and Manage Backup Media Using Windows Backup

❑ The Windows Backup utility provides several options for restoring backed up data, including replacement of system state information.

❑ The Removable Storage and Remote Storage features in Windows Server 2003 help you manage storage media and organize backups.

Perform System Recovery for a Server

❑ The Recovery Console is designed to provide a method for troubleshooting problems with Windows Server 2003 when the operating system will not properly start up.

❑ If other troubleshooting options fail, you can rebuild your Windows Server 2003 machine using Automated System Recovery (ASR).

❑ The first step in system recovery is to repair or replace the hardware that has failed.

❑ If you are experiencing problems that are preventing the proper startup of Windows Server 2003, you should look into using safe mode, boot logging, or various other startup options.

SELF TEST

The following questions will help you measure your understanding of the material presented in this chapter. Read all the choices carefully because there may be more than one correct answer. Choose all correct answers for each question.

Understand Backup Concepts, Procedures, and Operations

1. Maria is a systems administrator who is responsible for managing several Windows Server 2003 installations. She has configured backup jobs that include normal and incremental backup operations. Recently, her manager asked her to create an additional backup of all of the data on the server for archival purposes. Which of the following backup operations should Maria choose in order to avoid creating problems with the current backup procedure? (Choose all that apply.)

    A. Normal

    B. Incremental

    C. Copy

    D. Daily

    E. Differential

2. You are responsible for backing up data on a large file server on which data does not change frequently. You must backup the data nightly, but you have limited storage space. Which of the following backup operations would provide a complete backup plan that minimizes backup storage space?

    A. Normal only

    B. Incremental only

    C. Differential only

    D. Normal and incremental

    E. Normal and differential

    F. None of the above meets the requirements

3. Which of the following backup operations stores data by timestamps? (Choose all that apply.)

    A. Copy

    B. Normal

    C. Incremental

    D. Differential

    E. Daily

4. Your backup schedule involves the use of incremental backups, which are done nightly. You want to ensure that specific files are included in tonight's incremental backup operation. How can you do this without affecting other backup operations?

A. Perform a normal backup tonight and cancel the incremental backup.

B. Perform a differential backup tonight, following the completion of the incremental backup.

C. Perform a copy backup before the incremental backup is run.

D. Perform a daily backup before the incremental backup is run.

E. Manually ensure that the archive flag is enabled for the specific files that you want to back up.

5. Which of the following is/are true regarding the creation of a System State backup? (Choose all that apply.)

A. The backup will include all of the files stored on the local server.

B. The backup will include Registry information.

C. The backup will include user settings information.

D. The backup will copy only files that have changed since the last System State backup.

E. You will not be able to disable the Volume Shadow Copy feature for the backup operation.

Create and Schedule Backups Using Windows Backup

6. Michael has created a batch file that uses the `ntbackup` command to execute a backup operation. Which of the following methods can he use to schedule the backup job to execute nightly?

A. The `schtasks` command-line utility

B. The Windows Backup utility

C. The Scheduled Tasks Control Panel applet

D. None of the above

7. Jennie wants to create a batch file that uses the `ntbackup` command. She wants to store only specific files, located in particular folders throughout the file system. How can she most easily create a list of the files to be backed up?

A. Use the Backup or Restore Wizard to create a list of selected files.

B. Select the files using the Backup tab of the Advanced Windows Backup user interface and then choose Job | Save Selections As.

C. Create a new text file that contains a list of all of the files and folders that are to be backed up.

D. Include the list of files and folders that are to be backed up as a parameter for the `ntbackup` command.

E. None of the above.

8. You want to schedule a single backup job to run at 3:00 P.M. every weekday and at 11:00 A.M. on Sunday. What is the minimum number of backup schedules that you must configure?

 A. 1

 B. 2

 C. 3

 D. 7

Restore Data and Manage Backup Media Using Windows Backup

9. You are attempting to restore files using the Advanced mode of the Windows Backup utility, but the Restore And Manage Media tab does not show information about the backup you created. How can you most easily resolve this problem?

 A. Create a new backup with the exact same settings as the old one and then use that backup to restore the files.

 B. Copy the backup over an existing *.bkf file that does appear in the Restore And Manage Media tab.

 C. Choose View | All Backups in the Advanced mode of the Windows Backup utility.

 D. Select Tools | Catalog A Backup File and specify the location of the backup.

10. Last week, Raj created a System State backup of an installation of Windows Server 2003. He now wants to view some of the files that were part of the System State backup, but he does not want to actually replace the System State information on the local server. How can he most easily do this?

 A. Manually open the System State backup using a text editor to view its contents.

 B. Restore the System State files to an alternate location.

 C. Restore the System State information on another installation of Windows Server 2003.

 D. None of the above.

11. You are attempting to restore some user data files from a full backup that you created the previous day. You perform the restore with the default options. You find that files that had been previously deleted have been properly restored, but files that had been modified since the backup were not restored. Which of the following recovery options must you choose in order to replace the modified files?

 A. Do not replace the file on my computer.

 B. Replace the file on disk only if the file on disk is older.

 C. Always replace the file on my computer.

 D. Verify data after the backup completes.

 E. None of the above.

Perform System Recovery for a Server

12. You are the systems administrator for several Windows Server 2003 computers. Recently, you have noticed that other systems administrators have rebooted several of these servers. How can you most easily ensure that other systems administrators will provide information about the reason for a server reboot?

A. Make sure that the Shutdown Event Tracker is enabled and use the Event Viewer to view shutdown-related events.

B. Do nothing—detailed system shutdown information is always recorded.

C. Enable auditing of system startup and shutdown events.

D. Use Group Policy to send an administrative alert whenever the server is rebooted.

E. None of the above.

13. Which of the following is/are required in order to perform Automated System Recovery? (Choose all that apply.)

A. Access to the Windows Server 2003 installation media

B. An Automated System Recovery diskette

C. A locally attached tape backup device

D. Access to a locally available full backup file

E. A network interface card

14. Three days ago, you used the Windows Backup utility to create a backup of all of the files on your computer (using the Backup or Restore Wizard). Recently, the hard disk that contains the system partition on your Windows Server 2003 computer failed. You have replaced the hardware, but you need to restore the operating system to its previous state. Which of the following methods will perform this most quickly and easily?

A. Reinstall the Windows Server 2003 operating system and use the Last Known Good configuration boot option to return the system to its previous state.

B. Reconfigure the new hard disk with the same settings as were used when you first installed the server. Reinstall Windows Server 2003 and then use the Windows Backup utility to restore the System State.

C. Start the setup process from the Windows Server 2003 installation media and then choose to perform an Automated System Recovery.

D. Set up another server with Windows Server 2003 and then restore the System State information on that server. Rebuild the failed server and then copy the configuration information from the other server.

15. Following the installation of an updated SCSI disk controller driver, Andrew has found that his Windows Server 2003 operating system no longer completes the boot process. Which of the following startup options might allow him to repair the error with the least amount of effort?

    A. Safe Mode

    B. Safe Mode With Networking

    C. Safe Mode With Command Prompt

    D. Rebooting normally

    E. Last Known Good Configuration

LAB QUESTION

You are a systems administrator for a large organization. Your company has experienced dramatic growth in the last six months, and many new servers are being deployed. The existing servers in your environment have also been burdened with more users and data. For example, your most important servers are accessed from users around the world, and they're in use almost 24 hours per day. In order to accommodate the additional needs of users, you have been adding storage to current servers (most of which have plenty of room for expandability). Although this addresses the immediate concern—the need for more storage space—it raises other challenges. One of these is the important issue of performing backups.

Up until now, you have chosen to perform full backups of all of the data on your servers every night. However, the volume of data has grown greatly, and so, too, has the time required to perform the backups. It's clear that you cannot afford to perform full backups every night due to performance and storage considerations. Nevertheless, your business depends heavily on its IT resources, and any loss of data is unacceptable. You're tasked with coming up with a backup methodology. There's one catch, though: Due to budget limitations, you can't purchase larger, faster backup solutions (at least not in the short term). You've got to work with what you already have. How can you come up with methods to back up more data using limited storage resources?

At first, this might seem like a problem: How can you back up a much larger amount of data in the same (or even less) time? There are two main constraints: First, the "backup window" (the times during which your production servers can sustain the performance impacts of performing backup operations) is limited by the increased usage of the servers. Second, your backup hardware can store only a limited amount of data per piece of media, and you're not always available to swap tapes in the middle of the night should the backup operation require more space.

SELF TEST ANSWERS

Understand Backup Concepts, Procedures, and Operations

1. ☑ **C.** Only a copy backup will meet the requirements without affecting the other backup operations. Copy operations will store all of the selected files without affecting their archive bits.

   ☒ **A, B, D,** and **E** are all incorrect because they would either result in changes to the archive bits for files (such as normal and incremental backups), or they would not include all of the files (such as daily and differential backups).

2. ☑ **D.** Only a normal backup, combined with incremental backups, will ensure that all of the data is properly backed up and that minimal backup storage space will be used.

   ☒ **A** is incorrect because nightly normal backups would result in the need for a lot of storage space. **B** and **C** are incorrect because incremental and differential backups, by themselves, cannot be used for full recovery. Finally, **E** would meet the requirements, but differential backups would be larger than incremental backups.

3. ☑ **E.** Daily backup operations are designed to copy all of the files that were created or modified on a specific date.

   ☒ **A, B, C,** and **D** are all incorrect because they do not rely on timestamp information.

4. ☑ **E.** Only this method will ensure that specific files will be included in the next incremental backup operation.

   ☒ **A, B, C,** and **D** are all incorrect because they would either interfere with the current backup schedule (by resetting archive attributes), or they would not result in the selected data being stored as part of the scheduled incremental backup operation.

5. ☑ **B, C,** and **E.** All of these facts are true about System State backups.

   ☒ **A** is incorrect because a System State backup, by itself, will not necessarily include all of the files on a server. **D** is incorrect because the System State backup will always include all of the information that is part of the System State.

Create and Schedule Backups Using Windows Backup

6. ☑ **A** and **C.** Both of these methods can be used to schedule the execution of a batch file.

   ☒ **B** is incorrect because the Windows Backup utility allows only the scheduling of backup jobs (not actual batch files).

7. ☑ **B.** The easiest way to create the file selection list is through the use of the Advanced mode of the Windows Backup utility. The save operation will create a text file that can be used with the **ntbackup** command to back up only the specified files.

   ☒ **A** is incorrect because the wizard will not allow for the creation of a file selection list.

C would work, but it is a tedious and error-prone process. D is not supported by the ntbackup utility for complex file selections.

8. ☑ **B.** In order to create this schedule, you must create at least one backup job to handle the backup for Sunday, and another that will run at 3:00 P.M. on selected days.
☒ None of the other options would meet the requirements with the least number of different schedules.

Restore Data and Manage Backup Media Using Windows Backup

9. ☑ **D.** In order to see information about a backup that does not appear in the window, you must first catalog the backup file.
☒ A is incorrect because this would result in the creation of a new backup that might not include all of the required files. B is incorrect because it is not an efficient way to access a backup file. C is not an option in the Windows Backup utility.

10. ☑ **B.** In order to view the contents of the backup without affecting the current system, Raj must restore the System State information to another location. He can then examine the contents of the backup.
☒ A is incorrect because backup files use a binary format that cannot be deciphered using a text editor. C is a possibility, but it would certainly require more effort than option A.

11. ☑ **C.** The files that had been modified since the backup was performed were not restored because either option A or B was selected. In order to ensure that the newer files are overwritten, you must choose to always replace the files.
☒ A and B are incorrect because they would not result in modified files being replaced by the restore operation. D has no effect on the restore operation.

Perform System Recovery for a Server

12. ☑ **A.** The purpose of the Shutdown Event Tracker is to enforce the collection of information about why a server was restarted. Of course, it is also up to the other systems administrators to provide accurate and complete information.
☒ B is incorrect because reasons for a shutdown are not automatically recorded unless the Shutdown Event Tracker is enabled. C is incorrect because auditing would track *when* reboots were occurring (and who performed them), but not *why* they occurred. Finally, D is not an available option related to server reboots.

13. ☑ **A, B,** and **D.** These are all requirements for performing an Automated System Recovery.
☒ C is incorrect because the backup may be stored on a local disk (as long as that disk is still accessible). E is incorrect because a network interface card is not required for performing the ASR process.

14. ☑ **C.** This scenario is a good example of where the Automated System Recovery feature can be used to rebuild the system with minimal effort.

☒ **A** is incorrect because the Last Known Good configuration is valid only if the operating system data is still accessible. After the failure of the hard disk, this would not work. Both B and D are possible, but these methods would require far more effort than A.

15. ☑ **E.** Since Andrew knows that it is likely that the installation of the new driver is causing the problem, the Last Known Good configuration will require the least effort to reboot the system into a usable state. If that does not work, he may have to resort to using safe mode or other recovery methods.

☒ **A, B,** and **C** are incorrect because the safe mode options—although they might work—would require Andrew to perform additional troubleshooting after the server is rebooted. They will clearly require more effort than option E. D is incorrect because, as the problem states, the server will not boot normally after the installation of the new driver.

LAB ANSWER

Although this may seem like a difficult problem, you should be able to reduce backup times and storage requirements by using multiple backup types. An efficient design would take advantage of full, differential, and incremental backup types. You can use full backups as the basis of your strategy. Then, you can selectively choose to perform differential and/or incremental backups (instead of full backups) nightly. By examining your business requirements, you decide to implement the following weekly schedule:

- **Full backups** (est. 8 hours)   Sunday afternoons
- **Differential backups** (est. 2 hours)   Tuesday and Thursday nights
- **Incremental backups** (est. 0.5–1 hour)   Monday, Wednesday, Friday, and Saturday nights

By using these backup types, you can significantly reduce the amount of time backup operations will take. For example, during the week, you will be backing up only a relatively small subset of all of the data stored on your servers. Therefore, the backups will also use up less space on your backup media (read: fewer required media changes during the week!).

The use of multiple types of backup operations does come at a price, however. One potential issue is that, should you need to restore files, you may need to load data from multiple backup sets. This can be a time-consuming and risky (in the case of the loss or failure of a tape) process. Also, when you restore data, you must understand how to recover from failures at various times during the week. Overall, though, this solution gives you a good method for continuing to protect your organization's data. And, it gives you an opportunity to use ingenuity to stay within budget!

In the real world, coming up with backup plans that meet real-world constraints can be a challenge. Fortunately, you're not alone in this type of problem, and there are many potential solutions. Before you think about investing in larger and faster storage solutions, consider using a combination of backup types to fit within your requirements (and budget). A little bit of planning can save costly upgrades while still providing the data protection your business requires.

7

Managing and Maintaining a Server Environment

O f the many different challenges that IT systems administrators must face, routine management and maintenance functions are among the most important. The purpose of these tasks is to ensure that your environment is running properly. Although routine maintenance may not be a glamorous job, it's vital to ensure that the computers in your environment are kept up-to-date. Fortunately, Microsoft has included many features to help you accomplish this task in Windows Server 2003.

Throughout this book, you've looked at many different ways to implement various features of Windows Server 2003. In this chapter, you'll look at ways to manage your servers, once they're properly up and running. You'll begin by looking at ways in which you can manage the task of keeping your clients and servers up-to-date. Then, you'll look at the management of software licensing, which will allow you to ensure that your environment is compliant. Perhaps one of the most useful technologies provided in Windows Server 2003 is Terminal Services. By enabling you to remotely view a server console, Terminal Services can make administering multiple servers quick and efficient (and, you'll be able to avoid sitting around in a cold and noisy server room!). Finally, you'll look at the details of setting up and managing a web server using Internet Information Services (IIS). Let's get started!

CERTIFICATION OBJECTIVE 7.01

Understanding and Managing Software Licensing

As computer users, we often take the availability of software for granted. It's extremely easy to just access a network share and install copies of applications and other software, often in just a few minutes. For systems administrators, however, it's very important to ensure that their organizations are in compliance with software licensing agreements. That is, before software is installed, you must be sure that you have purchased the appropriate license. You must remember—just because you have the *ability* to install a thousand copies of Microsoft Office XP, that doesn't mean that you have the *right* to do so!

Keeping track of software licenses can be a challenging problem. After all, the same CD can be used to install thousands of copies of an operating system or software product. Worse yet, it's difficult for IT staff to completely prevent users from installing unapproved or unlicensed software on their company machines (especially when installation packages may be easily accessible on the network). Nevertheless, in most organizations, it is up to the IT department to keep track of software licenses. The most important part of ensuring compliance with license agreements is to have an organized process for purchasing and keeping track of software and where it's being used. Also, a good understanding of the often complex and convoluted licensing schemes used by various vendors is a must. Even with these processes in place, however, a little assistance from some operating system tools might be just what you need.

Effectively tracking and managing licensing starts with understanding the various ways in which Windows Server 2003 can be purchased.

Choosing a Licensing Mode

In order to legally install a production version of Windows Server 2003, you must start by purchasing a license for the server product itself. As mentioned in Chapter 1, there are several different editions of Windows Server 2003, including:

- Web Edition
- Standard Edition
- Enterprise Edition
- DataCenter Edition

Each of these products comes with different features and prices. Purchasing one of these operating system editions allows you to install the product on one server machine.

on the **Job**

Microsoft has changed its licensing and pricing options many times throughout the years. In addition to several volume licensing programs, upgrade paths and other issues must be considered. The information in this chapter is designed to provide you with a basic background of Windows Server 2003 licensing issues. For complete, up-to-date information, see the "Microsoft Licensing" web page at http://www.microsoft.com/licensing. Often, a little bit of research into the various options can save your organization a lot of money!

In addition to purchasing a license to run Windows Server 2003 (a "Server" license), your organization must also purchase Client Access Licenses (CALs). CALs grant client computers the right to access Windows Server 2003 machines. When you purchase a Server license, you may also receive a certain number of CALs as part of the purchase. However, all but the smallest environments will need to determine how to purchase additional CALs to allow client computers to access and use resources on Windows Server 2003.

The licensing model that you choose determines how many users can connect to your server installation. You have two options for the licensing model during the installation of Windows Server 2003. They are

- **Per-server mode**   Per-server licensing is based on the number of concurrent connections that will be supported on a system. For example, if you configure your server to have 15 CALs, only 15 users can simultaneously access file and print services on that machine. Figure 7-1 shows an example of per-server licensing. When additional users attempt to connect, they will be given an error message that states that there are not enough licenses to allow the connection. The Per-server option is a good choice for very small environments that have one or only a few servers, or for specialized installations of Windows Server 2003.

- **Per-device or per-user mode**   In this mode, every client computer that accesses your Windows Server 2003 must have a separate license. However, once a client has a license, he or she can access any number of Windows servers. For example, if I have 50 workstations on my network, I would need to buy 50 per-user CALs for them. Even if I have dozens of servers, each of these computers could access any of the servers at any time. (Figure 7-2 illustrates the use of per-user licensing.) Therefore, this option is generally a good choice for environments that have more than a few servers.

FIGURE 7-1

An example of the per-server licensing mode

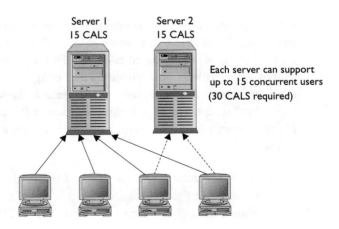

Server 1
15 CALS

Server 2
15 CALS

Each server can support
up to 15 concurrent users
(30 CALS required)

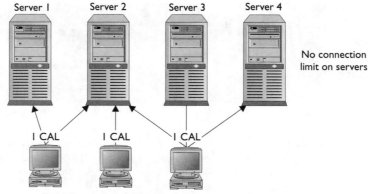

FIGURE 7-2

An example of the per-device or per-user licensing mode

Server 1   Server 2   Server 3   Server 4

No connection limit on servers

1 CAL   1 CAL   1 CAL

Each client can access any number of servers (1 CAL per client)

Per-user CALs are a new type of license that Microsoft has introduced with Windows Server 2003. Per-user CALs allow organizations to purchase licenses for specific users. Each licensed user can access Windows Server 2003 using any device. This is useful in situations where a single user might access multiple devices (such as workstations, portable computers, or personal digital assistants).

on the job

There are additional situations that you should keep in mind when purchasing CALs. First, only client computers that actually authenticate on Windows Server 2003 require CALs. Therefore, you do not need CALs for nonauthenticated Internet users (such as those that are accessing a public web server that is running Windows Server 2003). Second, if you're planning to deploy Terminal Services running in application mode, you'll need to look into additional Terminal Services CALs. The most current information on licensing can be found on the Microsoft Windows Server 2003 web site at http://www.microsoft.com/windowsserver2003.

An important point to keep in mind is that you are allowed to convert from per-server licensing to per-user licensing, although you are not allowed to convert from per-user licensing to per-server licensing. This is useful for growing environments, for example, that start with a few servers but then grow to host many servers. Because of your ability to perform a conversion of licensing models, Microsoft suggests that, when in doubt, you should choose the per-server mode. Figure 7-3 shows you the dialog box that will prompt you to choose a licensing model when you install Windows Server 2003.

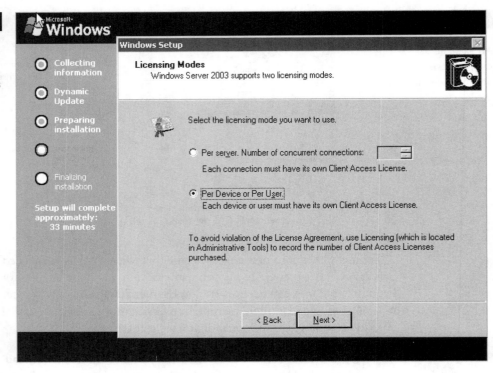

FIGURE 7-3

Viewing licensing options during the setup process

Licensing can be a very complicated topic in all but the simplest of environments. Therefore, be sure to check out the Microsoft Licensing web site at http://www.microsoft .com/licensing/ for more information on selecting a licensing model.

on the **Job**

As long as you support more than a couple of servers, there's a good chance that you can benefit from Microsoft's volume licensing programs. For more information, see http://www.microsoft.com/licensing/.

About Product Activation

Software piracy is a big issue for many software developers, and Microsoft is no exception. Although the stated numbers vary widely, it's clear that software developers lose considerable revenue through the practice of illegally copying and distributing their software. In an effort to reduce the amount of piracy, Microsoft has included a new "feature" called product activation in its newer products and operating systems. The product activation process requires users and systems administrators to "activate" their copy of the product within a set amount of time after the product is installed. The activation can be performed automatically over the Internet, or through a phone call to Microsoft's product activation hotline.

on the **j**ob

Production activation and product registration are completely separate actions (although you can choose to do them at the same time). In order to activate your copy of Windows, you are not required to send any personal information or information about your business to Microsoft.

Details about product activation options will be available while you walk through the process using the Activation Wizard (see Figure 7-4). You will need to perform product activation within a certain amount of time after the operating system is installed. If you fail to do so, you will no longer be able to use the operating system. For further information about product activation, see the Windows Server 2003 Help and Support Center.

FIGURE 7-4

Walking through the product activation process

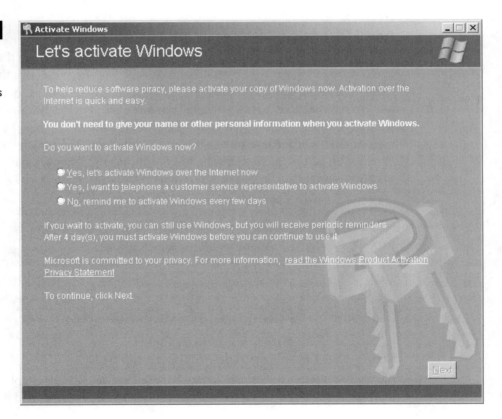

Once you have activated your copy of Windows Server 2003, that copy of the product will be licensed only to this machine. The product activation process creates a signature based on the hardware configuration of your machine. If you need to reinstall Windows Server 2003 using the same media on another computer (or, if you replace significant portions of the current machine), you may need to reactivate the product.

License Administration

Now that you have a good basic understanding of licensing options for Windows Server 2003, let's look at some ways in which license administration can be simplified. As mentioned before, during the installation of Windows Server 2003, you'll be prompted to select whether you want to use per-server or per-user licensing. Additionally, you can manage licensing after the operating system is installed. Windows Server 2003 includes two different utilities that can be used for managing licensing.

Local Licensing Settings

You can change the licensing options for the local machine by using the Licensing Control Panel applet. The options that are available correspond with the ones that were presented during the installation process. Basically, you can choose whether you want to run the server in per-server or "per-user or per-device" licensing mode. If you selected the "per-server" option, you will have the ability to change the number of licenses when you purchase more of them. The other available option is the Replication button. This allows you to choose how frequently license information is communicated to a Licensing server. Let's look at that next.

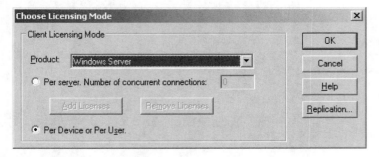

Using the Licensing Administrative Tool

Managing licensing for a single or just a few servers can be fairly simple. However, this task can become difficult to manage as the number of clients and servers in an environment grows. Microsoft has included a Licensing application that can be used to help make this job a little easier (at least for Microsoft products). Using this utility, you can view information about server licenses throughout your organization. In order for this to work properly, you must have the License Logging service enabled on at least one server machine in the environment. After you install Windows Server 2003, you can access the utility by going to Start | Programs | Administrative Tools | Licensing. This will open the Licensing utility.

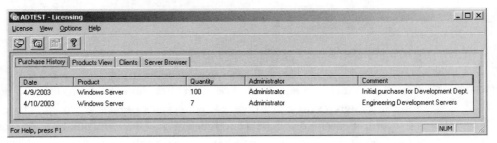

The Purchase History tab shows a listing of licenses that have been purchased. To add new licenses, click the New License button. As shown next, you'll have the option to specify the product for which the licenses were purchased, the number of licenses, and a descriptive comment. Note that this information is used only to help in keeping track of purchases; it does not affect the number of licenses available for configuration.

The Products view tab (shown in in the following illustration) can be used to provide a basic summary of the number of licenses that you have for each of the supported products in your environment. You can also use features in the Options menu to create new groups of licenses for other types of products. Finally, you can use the Clients tab to see which users are currently connected to a server and to view their license status information.

III 7-4

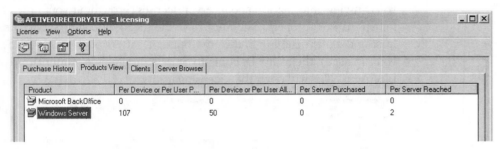

You'll notice that you can use this simple utility to keep track of the licenses that you've purchased, and how many licenses of each product you have available. Although it's no substitute for keeping track of licenses and purchase orders on your own, it can help you get a good idea of how many installations or users you can support. For more details on working with the Licensing tool, select Help | Help Topics from within the utility.

on the job

Although many IT administrators may fear that performing a software audit on the machines that they support will lead to huge, unexpected costs, there is one potential benefit to knowing exactly what software you have in your environment. Other than knowing that your organization is in compliance with licensing agreements, you may be able to negotiate volume purchasing agreements with vendors. For example, suppose you find that you actually have 510 copies of Microsoft Office XP installed on your machines (vs. the 475 that you thought you had initially). This might qualify you to obtain licenses at a discounted price, thus saving money overall!

CERTIFICATION OBJECTIVE 7.02

Managing Windows Operating System Updates

Modern server software is complex. As systems administrators, we expect our operating systems to handle many different types of tasks, and to do them well. However, it's a simple fact of life that software will have bugs, security issues, and other problems. These applications and operating systems are designed by human beings, and we all make mistakes. Some of these will be relatively minor issues that affect only a few users or systems. Others will be large breaches in the security systems that we all rely upon. In any case, a very important practice for avoiding these problems is to keep systems up-to-date with the latest patches, security updates, and related information.

on the job

At the time of this writing, implementing and managing security is definitely a hot topic. It's difficult to read any trade publication without encountering huge headlines about security issues (and solutions). When you hear about a security problem, be sure to read the information critically. Often, publishers will hastily claim that an operating system has been completely compromised and that no system is safe. Although it might make for exciting journalism, be critical of the details—determine if you're affected and what the impacts are. Then, develop your own plan to resolve the issue.

In general, it's difficult to ensure that all of your organization's computers are kept up-to-date with the latest patches, drivers, and other software. Often, it seems that as soon as you've fully deployed one set of fixes, another is made available! Or, you may realize that one or more servers may have been overlooked in the last set of updates. It's important to keep track of which updates are installed on which servers.

A major problem that prevents systems from being updated in many network environments is the systems administrator. When you consider all of the other challenges of the job, it's very difficult to visit client computers every time a new patch of update is made available. And, even if you could, it's easy to miss some machines (imagine the difficulty in updating a laptop for a salesperson who travels 100 percent of the time). Especially for servers, where uptime is critical, patches should be easy to detect and install. Fortunately, Windows Server 2003 includes several features that allow the operating systems and their various components to be automatically updated with the latest patches and updates.

In this section, you'll look at the various tools, technologies, and methods that you can use to ensure that your important systems are kept up-to-date.

Configuring Automatic Updates

The automatic updates feature in Windows Server 2003 can be configured to automatically download and install updates of the operating system without requiring user intervention. The types of updates that will be available include critical patches and security-related patches. To administer automatic updates for a Windows Server 2003 machine, open the System applet in the Control Panel. On the Automatic Updates tab (see Figure 7-5),

FIGURE 7-5

Viewing
Windows Server
2003's Automatic
Update settings

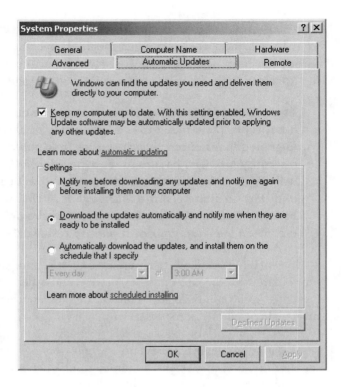

you must first choose whether or not you want to enable this feature. If you choose to
enable it, you can select from several settings:

- **Notify me before downloading any updates and notify me again before
  installing them on my computer**   This option gives you more control over
  when Windows Server 2003 will search for, and download, updates. If you
  are using a costly Internet connection, or if you have limited bandwidth,
  you may want to select this option.

- **Download the updates automatically and notify me when they are ready to
  be installed**   This option will allow Windows Server 2003 to regularly check
  for updates and to automatically download them, if they are available.
  Through the use of a system tray icon and a balloon, you'll be notified when
  updates are ready to be installed.

- **Automatically download the updates, and install them on the schedule
  that I specify**   This option is the most hands-off, automated method of the
  three selections. When this option is chosen, Windows Server 2003 will
  automatically download updates when they're available. It will then install

them at the specified time, without requiring any user intervention. If a patch requires a reboot of the server, this reboot will occur automatically. It is extremely important to keep this in mind, since users accessing the computer locally or over the network may be affected. Therefore, it's recommended that you select this option only if you're fairly certain that the server will not be in use at the scheduled time.

on the Job

It's important to test changes before you implement them on mission-critical production servers. In some cases, the installation of a patch may change the behavior of an important application, or it may make unexpected operating system changes. To protect against this type of issue, be sure to test updates on another machine before you install them on your important machines.

When you are prompted about updates that have been downloaded, you'll have the option of choosing which updates to install. If you chose not to install a specific update, but then you later change your mind, you can view a list of "Declined Updates" in the Automatic Updates settings.

Using the Windows Update Site

Although the Automatic Update feature can provide for automatically downloading and applying critical files, sometimes you may want to install optional updates on your system. The Windows Update site allows users and systems administrators to download updates for the Windows Server 2003 operating system from a single place. Updates include security enhancements, patches, driver updates, and other component updates. The easiest way to perform updates for a single Windows Server 2003 machine is to access the Windows Update site through your web browser. To do this, simply choose Start | Windows Update, or choose Tools | Windows Updates from within Internet Explorer. This will direct Internet Explorer to connect to the Windows Update site. From here, you can choose which components you want to update or install (see Figure 7-6).

When you visit the Windows Update site, the site will check to see if you have the latest version of the Windows Update ActiveX control installed. If you do not, you will be prompted to install or update the version before you can continue on to the site. You must click Yes on the security box (which allows the web control to be installed on your machine) in order to use the Windows Update site. Generally, the download is fairly quick, and it requires no additional configuration. However, some updates may require the restart of certain services, or rebooting the entire machine. Be sure to apply updates during a time when it will be least disruptive to users.

FIGURE 7-6   Using the Windows Update site in Windows Server 2003

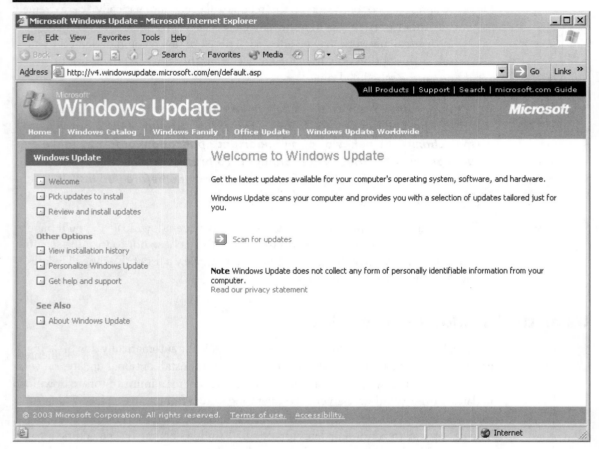

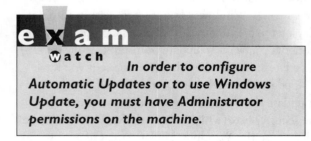

w a t c h   **In order to configure Automatic Updates or to use Windows Update, you must have Administrator permissions on the machine.**

Using Software Update Services

The Windows Update system can save a lot of time and effort in many network environments. However, there are some important limitations to this tool, especially when working in medium-to large-sized organizations. The first is that the Windows Update feature relies on connectivity to the Internet and, in many cases, will require significant bandwidth in order to download the many available patches and features that are available. For many businesses, this can place a significant load on Internet connections.

Second, Windows Update places the burden of obtaining and installing updates on end users (or systems administrators that must visit each machine). This can make it difficult to test, deploy, and manage patches when working with many different machines. It would just be too easy to forget about a single workstation or server when making the update rounds. Finally, it would be very helpful if systems administrators could test and approve updates before they're deployed to client machines.

In an Enterprise environment, you will probably want an easier and more powerful method to administer the update process. For example, you may not want all of your clients downloading large updates over your Internet connection. Instead, it would be much more efficient if they installed the updates over the LAN. Also, you don't want to have to visit each of these machines individually to apply the updates. Rather, you'd like to push the updates over the network, once you have properly tested them. Fortunately, there is just such a solution available.

Microsoft has made an update called Software Update Services (SUS) for its customers. This tool is designed for IT staff to view and download updates that may be required for the machines that they support. You can access the Microsoft Software Update Services web site at http://www.microsoft.com/windows2000/windowsupdate/sus/default.asp (note that this URL is part of the Windows 2000 Server site; rest assured, the latest versions of the download support Windows Server 2003). On this site, you will also find detailed information about the steps that are required to implement a Software Update Services infrastructure in your network environment. Software Update Services is based on the same software technology that is implemented by Microsoft for its own Windows Update web site.

on the
()ob

Microsoft Software Update Services (SUS) is an evolving technology. At the time of this writing, Microsoft is planning to add significant new features to this tool. For the latest information, be sure to check out the Microsoft SUS web site.

Let's take a brief look at what exactly you'll need to do in order to set up Software Update Services:

1. Download and install the latest version of the Microsoft Software Update Services server-side installation. This download package is available at the following link: http://www.microsoft.com/windows2000/windowsupdate/sus/default.asp. SUS can be installed on a Windows 2000 Server or Windows Server 2003 computer that is functioning in any role (including domain controllers). The SUS add-on is provided free to licensed users of Windows Server 2003 and Windows 2000 Server operating systems. For a complete list of requirements, see the information on the SUS web site.

2. Launch the Software Update Services administrative tool by clicking the newly created Microsoft Software Update Services icon located in the Administrative Tools program group. Since administration for SUS is managed through a web browser, this will launch your default browser and take you to the local SUS administration web page. You can also navigate to this page by using the URL http://ServerName/SUSAdmin.

3. Synchronize your SUS server to download the latest available updates. Notice that this process can take a significant amount of time, since it will connect to Microsoft's servers and obtain all of the patches that have been made available for the supported operating systems. For example, for my initial server synchronization, the server had to download almost 2500 files (many of which were several megabytes in size)! Figure 7-7 shows an example of the synchronization process in progress. Note that you can also schedule automatic synchronization. This is a recommended option, since it will ensure that your SUS servers stay up-to-date with the latest patches.

4. Approve various updates so that they can be made available to client computers. Generally, you will want to install and test various updates in a test environment to ensure their compatibility with your network and applications. Once you have determined that a patch is ready for deployment, you can approve it. Some updates might require a system reboot, or might have dependencies on other updates. This information will be provided when you look at the list of available updates.

5. Configure Automatic Update settings for clients using Group Policy. Specifically, the settings that you'll need to modify can be found within Computer Configuration | Administrative Templates | Windows Components | Windows Update. You will be able to control if and when the Automatic Updates feature will download and install updates. You will also be able to configure your clients to a URL of an SUS server that is located on your own network (for example, "http://UpdateServer1/SUS").

6. Next, you need to add support for SUS on the client side. SUS supports the following client-side operating systems: Windows 2000 Professional, Windows XP (Home or Professional), Windows 2000 Server (Standard and Advanced Editions with SP2 or later), and the Windows Server 2003 platform.

SUS also supports more advanced configurations. For example, you can configure a single SUS server as a distribution server for other SUS servers. Using this capability, you can have only one server in your environment download updates over the Internet. This server can then send updates to other SUS servers in your environment.

FIGURE 7-7   Synchronizing a Software Update Services server

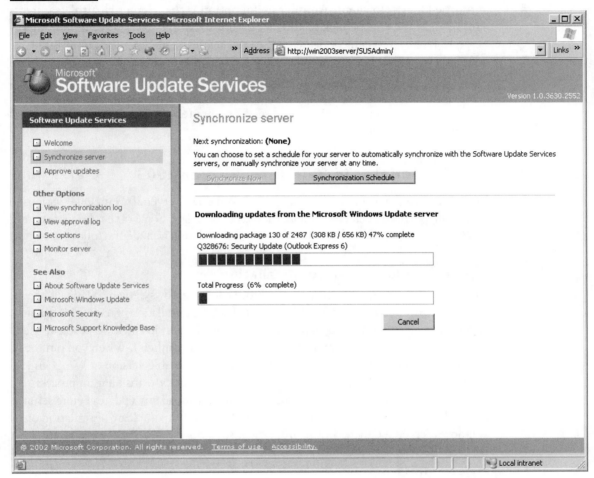

SUS servers can also redirect client computers that are requesting updates to other SUS servers. You can also use Windows Server 2003's Network Load Balancing feature to evenly distribute load across your SUS servers. The end result is efficient utilization of network bandwidth. For more details on setting up these features, see the Deployment Guide, available on the Software Update Services web site.

In addition to the features and functionality that you covered in the preceding steps, the SUS Administrator web pages provide additional capabilities. For example, you can view synchronization logs that will show when updated patches were downloaded from Microsoft, and whether or not the operation was successful.

You can also view an approval log, which keeps track of which updates you have authorized for deployment. Another useful option is the "Server Health" feature. This monitor provides a quick method for ensuring that your SUS server is performing properly. Finally, you can configure SUS to automatically send systems administrators an e-mail message whenever new updates are ready for testing and approval.

By using all of these features, an otherwise difficult task—keeping track of operating system updates in a networked environment—can be dramatically simplified. When managing more than a few client and server computers, be sure to make SUS an important tool in your bag of tricks.

Other Automatic Updates in Windows Server 2003

In addition to core operating system updates, Windows Server 2003 includes various other components that can be automatically kept up-to-date. Some of the various features of Windows Server 2003 that support automatic updating include the following.

Dynamic Update Before Installation

During the beginning of the installation process for Windows Server 2003, you'll be prompted to download any updates that might affect the installation process. This feature allows Microsoft to provide updates and fixes to any known installation problems (for example, problems caused by a lack of drivers or driver conflicts). When you run the Windows Server 2003 setup process from within a compatible version of Windows (such as Windows NT 4 Server or Windows 2000 Server), the installation process will provide you with the ability to automatically download any updates before setup begins. Note that this feature is not available if you perform a "clean" installation of Windows Server 2003 (by booting from the installation CD-ROM, for example).

Driver Updates

When you install a new hardware device into your computer, Windows Server 2003 will search for a suitable driver for the device. You can choose from among several different places to search for the driver, including the Windows Update site. As long as hardware vendors and Microsoft make the latest drivers available via this service, the necessity of finding, download, and installing drivers from various vendor web sites is avoided with a few simple mouse clicks. The same applies when you want to update a driver (which you can easily do by right-clicking a device in Device Manager and selecting Update Driver). For more information on working with hardware devices, see Chapter 2.

Managing System Patches and Security Updates

Since security issues can be discovered and addressed very often, keeping up with security can be a significant challenge. If you're responsible for security in your environment, be sure to bookmark the Microsoft Security web site: www.microsoft.com/security. Along with access to information about the latest security issues (and downloads for the fixes), the site includes a wealth of information for systems administrators that need to manage security (see Figure 7-8). Additionally, on this site, you can subscribe to Microsoft's security update information newsletters and alerts (which are sent by e-mail).

FIGURE 7-8   The main page of the Microsoft Security web page

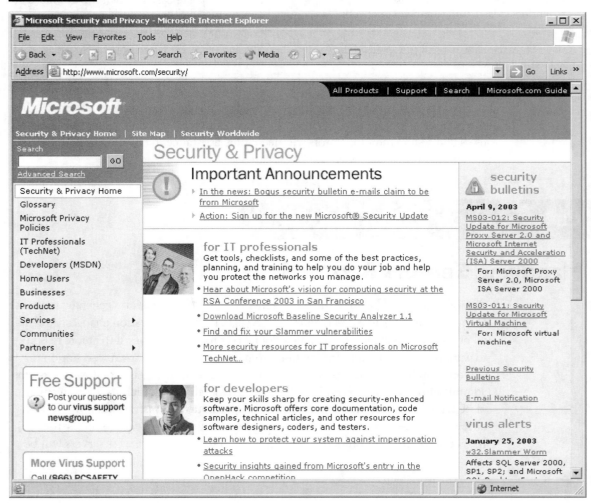

SCENARIO & SOLUTION

You want to view a list of available updates for one of your servers.	Access the Windows Update site to see which updates are available for the local machine. After you choose to scan for updates, you'll have the option of choosing which ones you want to install.
You want to ensure that patches are automatically installed on certain servers.	Enable the option to automatically download and install updates within the Automatic Updates configuration tab of the System Control Panel applet.
You want to set up a service for installing and distributing updates throughout your network.	Use Software Update Services (SUS) to download updates and to make them available to client computers on your network.
You want to manually control the application of patches on your servers.	Disable Automatic Updates using the System Control Panel applet.

If you're managing one or a few systems, it might be reasonable to just check this site periodically to view information about various updates and issues. However, most users and systems administrators will need some assistance in ensuring that all of their systems are up-to-date with the latest patches.

CERTIFICATION OBJECTIVE 7.03

Managing Servers Remotely

Although we've all heard of the many benefits of regular exercise, it's generally not much fun to have to walk to a dozen different servers to make configuration changes. And, if all of your servers are located in an icy cold server room, you have all the more reason to want to perform administration tasks from the comfort of your own workstation.

Fortunately, Windows Server 2003 includes several methods for allowing systems administrators to perform administrative tasks remotely. In addition to the convenience of being able to work from a remote console, remote administration allows you to efficiently access multiple servers, and to reduce physical access to server rooms. In fact, in many environments, the only reason to physically access servers will be for hardware maintenance and upgrades. Let's look at the features in Windows Server 2003 that make this a reality.

Using Remote Assistance

Almost every technical professional that's worked on a help desk or in end-user support has been in a situation that ends with, "Okay, I'll stop by your office to check out the problem." In small environments, this might be an efficient way to solve some problems. However, in distributed environments, visiting users' desktops might require the purchase of a plane ticket! Fortunately, there's a better way to reach out and "take over" someone's computer in order to troubleshoot problems.

Windows Server 2003 provides a feature known as Remote Assistance. The idea behind Remote Assistance is that it provides a method for someone to request assistance with their computer. The person that is providing assistance can view and/or control the requester's computer (with his or her permission, of course). The connection can be made over a local area network (LAN), or even over the Internet. Remote Assistance is available only on Windows XP and Windows Server 2003 computers.

on the *job*

Microsoft first provided a multiuser Windows NT kernel in Windows NT 4.0, Terminal Server Edition. Beginning with the Windows 2000 platform, all versions of Windows 2000, Windows XP, and Windows Server 2003 use the same multiuser kernel (although the various features that are available differ). Microsoft originally licensed this technology from Citrix, Inc. (www.citrix.com), and Citrix still makes add-on products that can increase the functionality of terminal services.

An "invitation" for Remote Assistance can be sent by a user through e-mail, Windows Messenger, or saving the invitation to a file. An important concern for this type of functionality is security—you don't want to allow just any user to be able to take over someone's desktop. Therefore, there are several ways in which systems administrators and users can prevent unauthorized users from accessing their systems. Let's look at these methods.

First, in order to enable Remote Assistance on a Windows Server 2003 computer, you must click the Remote tab in the System Control Panel applet. As shown in Figure 7-9, there is a setting labeled "Turn on remote assistance and allow invitations to be sent from this computer."

FIGURE 7-9

Setting Remote
access permissions

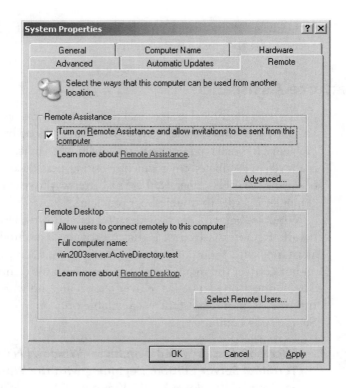

Furthermore, when you click Advanced, you can view details about how long an invitation is valid. Systems administrators can also restrict which users are able to create Remote Assistance requests. For more information about setting Group Policy options, see Chapters 3 and 4.

Exercise 7-1 walks through the process of enabling and accessing a computer via Remote Assistance.

EXERCISE 7-1

Using Remote Assistance

1. In order to access a machine via Remote Assistance, you first need to enable this feature. Choose Start | Settings | Control Panel | System. In the Remote tab, place a check mark next to the first option in the dialog box. Click OK to save the setting.

2. Now that Remote Assistance is enabled, you're going to send an invitation to provide assistance over the network. First, choose Start | Help and Support. Under Support Tasks, click Remote Assistance.

Ill 7-5

3. Select the option Invite Someone To Help You. Notice that you'll have several different options for sending the invitation (although some may be disabled due to your server's configuration).

Ill 7-6

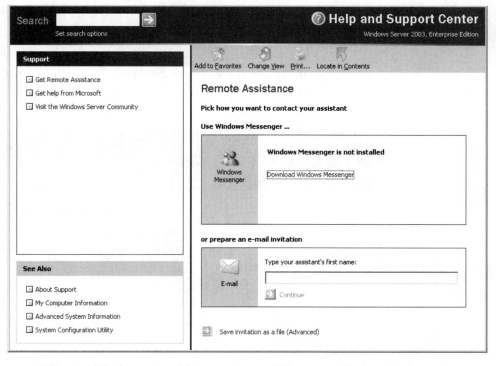

4. To simplify the steps of this exercise, you'll create a file-based invitation. Click Save Invitation As A File to continue. Leave the settings as their

defaults. Notice that you can change the amount of time that an invitation remains valid. Click Continue.

III 7-7

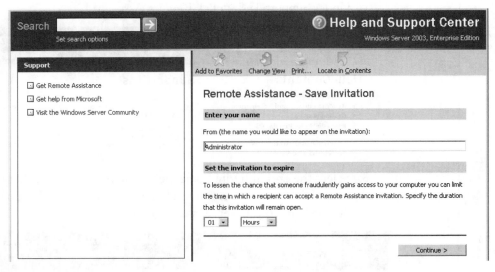

5. Type and confirm a password that will be part of this invitation. In order to use the invitation, the assistant must know this password. Finally, click Save Invitation to create the file. The file will be named "RAInvitation.msrcincident" by default.

III 7-8

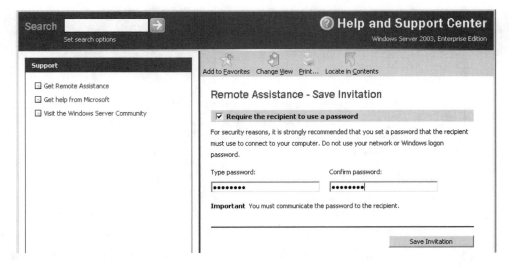

6. Once the file is saved, you'll be returned to the main Invitation screen. To see the status of the send invitation, click View Invitation Status. You'll see a screen similar to the one in the following illustration. By clicking Details, you can view more information about the invitation.

III 7-9

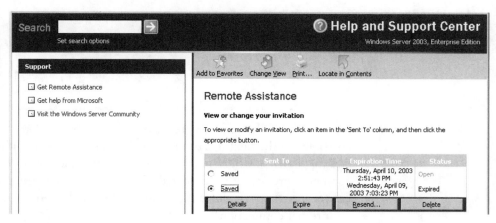

7. Next, copy the file to another computer. This other computer must be running either Windows XP or Windows 2003 Server, and you must have the Remote Desktop Client installed (for information on installing and using the Remote Desktop Client, see your operating system's help file). On the remote computer, double-click the file that you copied to this machine. This will prompt you for information about creating a connection. Enter the password and click Yes to start the session.

III 7-10

8. On the server computer, you should see a prompt that asks you whether you want to accept the remote connection. Click Yes to continue.

III 7-11

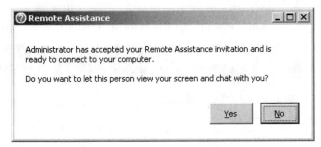

9. Now, switch back to the remote client (the one that initiated the connection). As shown in the next illustration, you'll be able to see the other computer's desktop, and you will be able to interact via text messages, or voice (if both computers are properly configured). You also have the option to send files between the two computers (a feature that's very helpful, especially across an Internet connection).

III 7-12

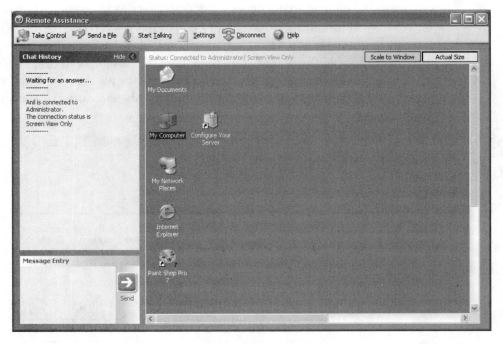

On the server side, you'll be able to chat with the remote computer and perform many of the same functions.

III 7-13

10. Once you are finished experimenting with this feature, you can click Disconnect on either the client or server side. This will end the session, and the Remote Assistance functionality will stop.

As you can see from the exercise, setting up a Remote Assistance connection can be quick and easy (especially compared to the alternative of having to visit the user's desktop). The process is even simpler if you have the Simple Mail Transport Service (SMTP) configured on the server so that the invitation can be sent via e-mail. Also, end users might choose to send the request via Windows Messenger.

Using Remote Assistance generally works fine in a LAN environment. When communicating over the Internet, however, there may be an additional challenge. It's important to remember that, in order for Remote Assistance to function across a firewall, communications between the computers must be allowed on TCP port 3389. If you're troubleshooting a situation in which Remote Assistance works fine over the LAN, but not over the Internet, this is probably a good first thing to check.

Using Remote Desktop for Administration

As its name implies, Remote Desktop for Administration allows you to create a remote connection to a Windows Server 2003 computer for the purpose of performing tasks that you would normally perform from the console. That is, it sends the video and audio output of the server to your console and allows you to use your mouse and keyboard to interact with the server. In most ways, accessing a server through Remote Desktop for Administration is identical to being seated in front of the machine itself.

Up to two simultaneous remote connections are allowed to connect to a Windows Server 2003 machine (in addition to one local connection using the server console). As with the Remote Assistance feature, there are several security settings that govern who can connect to a server remotely (or whether connections are accepted at all). In order to enable Remote Desktop for Administration, you must access the Remote tab of the System Control Panel applet. The second check box on this page allows you to enable the "master switch" for allowing remote administration (see Figure 7-10). You can also use the Select Remote Users button to specify which user(s) have access to remotely connect to the machine. By default, members of the Administrators group will automatically have access. Also, when you enable Remote Desktop you'll be alerted to the fact that accounts cannot have blank passwords if they need to create a remote connection.

You can also allow access by placing users in the Remote Desktop Users local group on a Windows 2003 member server. Administering Terminal Services is also fairly simple, thanks to a few administrative tools. You can view a list of the current remote connections to a Terminal Services server by using the Terminal Service Manager administrative tool (see Figure 7-11). By right-clicking the name of a user and clicking Send Message, you can send a brief message to the connected user (the message will pop up in

exam watch

With the release version of Windows Server 2003, Microsoft has named this feature "Remote Desktop for Administration." However, you might still see references to "Terminal Services Remote Server Administration mode." Keep in mind that both terms refer to the same feature.

exam watch

Be careful not to confuse Terminal Services for Administration mode with Terminal Services Applications mode. Terminal Services for Administration is designed to allow systems administrators to log on to a Windows Server 2003 computer for the purpose of performing administrative functions. In Application mode, Terminal Services is designed to allow end users to run productivity applications (such as Microsoft Office) remotely on the server. Application mode involves separate licensing and specific steps to be enabled. For more information, see the Windows Server 2003 Help and Support Center.

FIGURE 7-10

Enabling Remote
Desktop

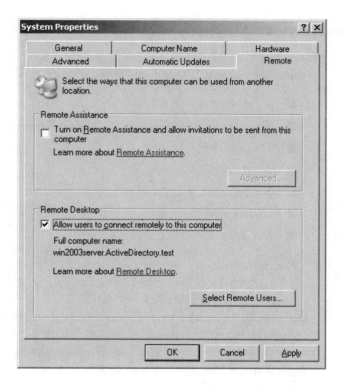

a modal message box on that user's screen). You can also choose to forcefully
disconnect or log off a user that is connected.

FIGURE 7-11

Using the
Terminal Services
Manager

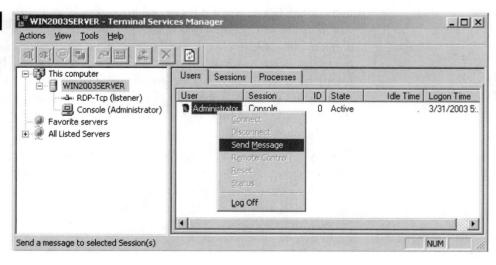

Using the Remote Desktop Client

Once you've enabled Remote Desktop on the server side, you can connect to it from a variety of different Windows operating systems, including:

- Windows 95
- Windows 98 and Windows 98 Second Edition
- Windows ME
- Windows NT 4.0
- Windows 2000
- Windows XP
- Windows Server 2003

The only client-side requirement is that that Remote Desktop client software must be installed locally on the computer. A copy of the client is also available on the Windows Server 2003 CD-ROM. The file is named MSRDPCLI.exe. You can place this file on a share that is accessible to your users for installation. Or, you can download the client from the following URL: http://www.microsoft.com/windowsxp/pro/downloads/rdclientdl.asp. On a Windows Server 2003 computer, you can also use the Remote Desktops administrative tool to quickly connect to multiple machines.

The Remote Desktop client software provides many different options for configuring the connection to the remote server. These options include

- **General** On this tab (shown in Figure 7-12), you can specify the computer name, the DNS name (if it is resolvable), or the IP address of the server to which you want to connect. You may also specify a username, password, and domain name. Generally, this will be the same information that you would use to log on to the server if you were located at the console. If you leave this information blank (or if it is incorrect), you'll be prompted to log on using the standard Windows logon dialog box. You can also choose to save connection information to *.rdp files so that you can use them on other computers (or to back them up on the same computer).

- **Display** You have several options regarding the size and resolution of the remote window. For example, you might want to run the window at a resolution that is lower than that of your client machine so that you can easily switch between windows. Similarly, you can modify the color depth to reduce bandwidth usage over the connection (see Figure 7-13).

Viewing General
settings in the
Remote Desktop
Client

Viewing Display
settings in the
Remote Desktop
Client

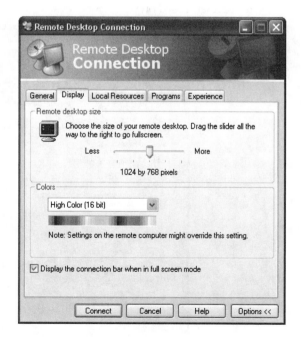

- **Local Resources**   Often, when working on a remote computer, you might want to have access to your local disk drives, printers, and serial devices. For example, if I want to copy a file from my machine to the remote machine, or if I want to print a document to my own printer (instead of the ones configured for the server), it would be useful to have them available. The options on this tab (shown in Figure 7-14) allow you to set options for making local devices available on the remote machine. For example, when Disk Drives is enabled, you'll see items such as "C on Workstation1" in the Explorer. This allows you to quickly and easily copy files between your client and the remote host. Other options on this tab allow you to specify behavior for the ALT-TAB keyboard combination and how sound should be managed.

- **Programs**   On this tab, you can specify a program that you want to start immediately after you connect to the remote server. This might be useful if you often use the same administrative tools or programs.

- **Experience**   Newer Windows platform operating systems offer many graphical enhancements that improve the look and feel of the Windows user interface. While they are generally welcome options, when you are connecting to a remote computer over a slow or unreliable connection, you might want to disable options such as the desktop background, animations, and other features. You can choose from presets based on your bandwidth, or you can choose Custom and specify which options you want to enable or disable (see Figure 7-15).

FIGURE 7-14

Viewing Local
Resources
settings in
the Remote
Desktop Client

FIGURE 7-15

Viewing
Experience
settings in
the Remote
Desktop Client

Exercise 7-2 walks through the process of enabling Remote Desktop for
Administration and connecting to a remote Windows Server 2003 computer.

EXERCISE 7-2

MasterSim 7-2 ON THE CD

Installing and Using Remote Desktop for Administration

1. To enable Remote Desktop for Administration, you should start by enabling
   this feature on the server side. To do this, choose Start | Settings | Control
   Panel | System. In the Remote tab, place a check mark next to the second
   option in the dialog box. Optionally, you can choose the Select Remote
   Users button to specify additional users that should have access to connect
   to this machine. Click OK to save the setting.

2. Next, from a computer that has the Remote Desktop Client software installed,
   launch the client program. This other computer may be running any version
   of Windows that is supported by the Remote Desktop Client.

3. On the General tab of the Remote Desktop Client, type the computer name or the IP address of the Windows Server 2003 computer that you enabled in step 1. This is the bare minimum information that's required to connect to a remote server. Next, click Options and enter a user name, a password, and the domain of the remote machine (if the server is a member of a domain). Optionally, you can leave this information blank to be prompted to authenticate once the connection has been made.

III 7-14

4. Click through the other tabs (the details of which are covered in the text) and set any other options as desired. Once you've chosen the appropriate options for this connection, click Connect button. You will then be connected to the remote computer.

III 7-15

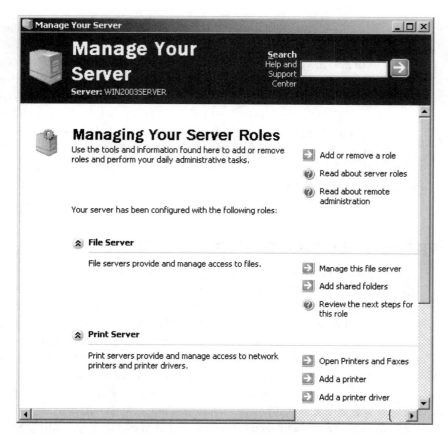

5. Once you're connected to the remote machine, you can use any of the administrative tools or software, just as if you were at the console. Once you're finished with your session, choose Start | Shut Down and then choose to Log Off of the computer. This will disconnect you from the server computer. If it is still open, close the Remote Desktop Client.

When you are done with your remote connection, you can choose to either Log Off of the remote system (which will close all of your programs and disconnect your client), or you can choose to just Disconnect. When you choose the option to Disconnect, your applications remain open, but your client is disconnected. The next time you log on to this machine, you will connect back to the same session, and you'll be able to continue where you left off. While this feature might seem very handy, there's a drawback: Remember that Windows Server 2003 supports only two concurrent remote connections when running Remote Desktop for Administration. If you're working in an environment with many systems administrators, leaving your session open on the server when you don't need it is a good way to annoy your coworkers!

Using Remote Desktop Web Connection

Although the Remote Desktop Client will work fine for many users, it is sometimes also convenient to allow users to use the Remote Desktop from within a web browser. To make the process of finding and connecting to a Terminal Services installation even easier, Microsoft has included the ability to connect to servers using a standard web browser. Through the use of a Terminal Services plug-in, users and systems administrators can quickly and easily create a terminal services connection without manually installing or configuring any additional software.

You can implement the Remote Desktop Web Connection functionality on the server side by using the Windows Components Wizard (accessible via the Add/Remove Programs Control Panel applet). Specifically, you'll need to enable the following item: Application Server | Internet Information Services (IIS) | World Wide Web Service | Remote Desktop Web Connection. This illustration shows a remote desktop creation created from within Internet Explorer:

III 7-16

For details on configuring and securing this option, see the Windows Server 2003 Help and Support Center. More information on configuring IIS is presented later in this chapter.

Other Windows Server 2003 Management Tools

In addition to the tools and techniques covered so far, there are several other remote management features in Windows Server 2003. In this section, you'll look at some really handy tools for working with your server machines from the comfort of your own workstation.

Using the Configure Your Server Wizard

In previous versions of Windows Server products, Microsoft installed the product with most of the advanced features enabled, by default. In general, this was done to improve usability—all of the major functionality that systems administrators might need would be readily available. For example, Internet Information Services (IIS) were enabled, by default. The problem with this is that often, a lot of functionality that is not needed on a server is left running. In some cases, this functionality can open avenues for security breaches.

In response to users' concerns about this, Microsoft has made a fairly dramatic switch with Windows Server 2003. Now, almost all of the optional components of the server operating are *disabled,* by default. It's now up to the systems administrator to explicitly enable any functionality that's required. Most systems administrators are used to configuring several options following the installation of the operating system. When many of the needed services are disabled by default, this can add a lot of work (and potential for leaving something out). Fortunately, Microsoft has included the Configure Your Server Wizard in Windows Server 2003 to help alleviate some of this burden.

If you've installed Windows Server 2003, you've already seen the Configure Your Server Wizard. As shown in Figure 7-16, this wizard is presented to you automatically when you first log on to the operating system, after installation.

The Configure Your Server Wizard is designed to define which "roles" are enabled for this computer. The list of available roles includes the following:

- File Server
- Print Server
- Application Server (IIS, ASP.NET)
- Mail Server (POP3, SMTP)

■ Terminal Server

■ Remote Access / VPN Server

■ Domain Controller (Active Directory)

■ DNS Server

■ DHCP Server

■ Streaming Media Server

■ WINS Server

Details related to these roles (and how to configure them) are covered throughout this book, but if you want additional information, you can simply click the "Read about" link in the right side of the user interface. Enabling or disabling basic functionality involves simply highlighting the appropriate item and then clicking Next. In some cases, the wizard will require additional information (as shown in Figure 7-17). In others, the configuration will be performed automatically. Overall, the Configure Your Server Wizard can help you enable only the services that you need on a specific installation of Windows Server 2003, thereby increasing security.

FIGURE 7-16	
Viewing options in the Configure Your Server Wizard	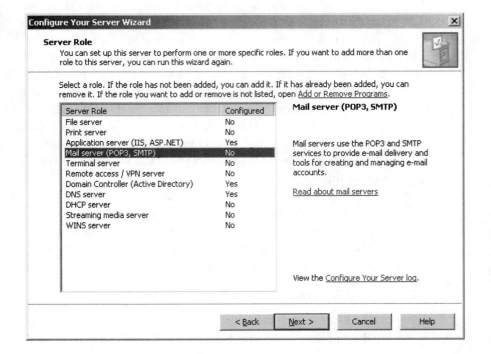

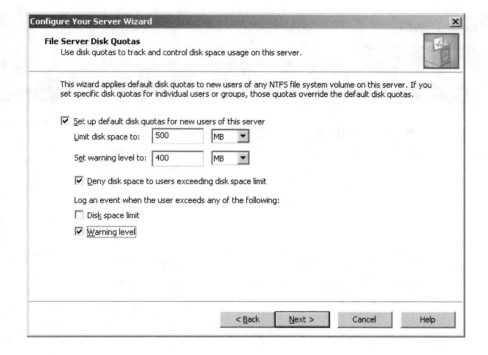

FIGURE 7-17

Options for enabling file services using the Configure Your Server Wizard

Once you've enabled the appropriate functionality using the Configure Your Server Wizard, you can use the Manage Your Server (see Figure 7-18) administrative tool to make changes to settings. For most server roles, you'll be given the option to launch various other administrative tools, and you'll have an option "Review the next steps for this role." For example, if you promote a server to a domain controller, you'll see the following links:

- Manage users and computers in Active Directory
- Manage domains and trusts
- Manage sites and services
- Review the next steps for this role

Especially if you're relatively new to Windows Server 2003 administration, the Manage Your Server Wizard can help you ensure that you haven't forgotten an important step or setting.

FIGURE 7-18 Administration using the Manage Your Server tool

Remote Administration Through Administrative Tools

Often, we overlook some of the most useful features available in Administrative Tools. When it comes to remote management of Windows Server 2003, many of the utilities that ship with the product allow for managing remote machines. For example, the Active Directory Users and Computers tool (which we examine more closely in Chapter 3), allows you to connect to other forests or domain controllers (see Figure 7-19).

Other tools, such as the DNS and DHCP snap-ins, also allow you to connect to other servers in your environment. Although the exact method for connecting to remote computers might vary, the ability to manage one server from another computer can save a lot of time and effort.

FIGURE 7-19

Remote
administration
using Active
Directory Users
and Computers

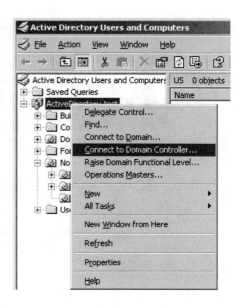

Using the Windows Server 2003 Administration Tools Pack

In the preceding section, you learned of the use of remote administration features in
Windows Server 2003's administrative tools. This is useful if you're logged into a Windows
Server 2003 computer and you want to administer another server. But, what if you're
sitting at a Windows XP machine? By default, you won't have the same administrative
tools that are available on your server machines.

To solve this problem, Microsoft has made available the Windows Server 2003
Administration Tools Pack. This pack of tools is available for installation from the
Windows Server 2003 distribution media. Although the exact location of the file
may differ on various CDs, the name of the file is adminpak.msi. It can be installed
on any Windows XP computer running Service Pack 1 or later.

on the
job

*You may be wondering why you would want to install these tools on another
Windows Server 2003 computer. There is a good reason: Suppose that you
want to administer a domain controller from a machine that is a member
server. In that case, you won't have automatically created shortcuts for tools
such as Active Directory Users and Computers. By installing the Administration
Tools Pack, you can easily access all of the tools you need.*

Once you install these tools, you'll have full access to the administration
applications that are included with Windows 2003 Server. There are also some
additional consoles that provide useful functions, such as the Active Directory
Management tool (see Figure 7-20).

FIGURE 7-20 Using the Active Directory Management administrative tool

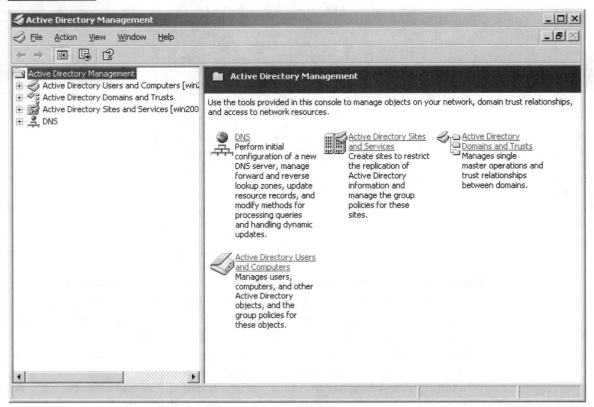

Using the Web Interface for Remote Administration

It has become increasingly common for systems and network administrators to configure and manage devices using a simple web browser. In fact, even most home-based networking devices (such as cable modem routers) offer a web-based configuration interface. There are many benefits to using such a system. Perhaps the best aspect is not having to manually install client-side tools in order to perform simple functions.

Windows Server 2003 includes a new feature called the Web Interface for Remote Administration. This feature allows you to perform many of the most common operations on your servers by simply using a web browser (see Figure 7-21).

By default, the Web Interface for Remote Administration is disabled on all editions of Windows 2003 Server, except for the Web Edition. Therefore, the first step that you'll need to take before you can use this interface is to enable it. Exercise 7-3 walks you through the process of installing, configuring, and using the Web Interface for Remote Administration.

FIGURE 7-21   Using the Web Interface for Remote Administration

EXERCISE 7-3

Installing and Using the Web Interface for Remote Administration

This exercise will automatically enable and activate the World Wide Web functionality of Internet Information Services (IIS). Detailed information about configuring and securing IIS is presented later in this chapter.

1. In order to use the Web Interface for Remote Administration, you must first enable it using the Windows Components Wizard. Open the Add / Remove Programs Control Panel applet and click Add / Remove Windows Components.

2. Double-click Application Server and then Internet Information Services (IIS). Place a check mark in the item labeled Remote Administration (HTML). Notice that other items may automatically be checked (depending on the current configuration of your servers). These are the items that must also be installed and configured in order for the Remote Administration functionality to be enabled.

III 7-17

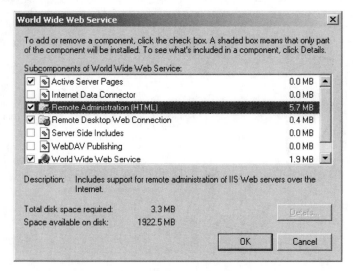

3. To accept the configuration, click OK three times and then click Next to continue the installation process. The Windows Components Wizard will install and configure the appropriate components to enable the Web Interface for Remote Administration. When the process is complete, click Finish.

4. Now that web-based administration is enabled, it's time to test this feature. On another computer, open a web browser and browse to the URL `https://ServerName:8098` (replace "ServerName" with the name of the computer on which you installed the Web Interface for Remote Administration).

5. When prompted for authentication information, type in the username and password for a user that is a member of the Administrators group on the server. Click OK to log in.

III 7-18

6. Once you have logged in, you will have the ability to access many different administration functions on the server. If you need additional help using this interface, click the Take A Tour option in the top-left area of the screen.

7. To view some useful functionality, click Users in the top navigation bar, and then click Local Groups. You should see a screen displaying all of the local groups on the server, similar to the one shown in the next illustration. Note that you can view group properties, add new groups, or delete existing ones.

III 7-19

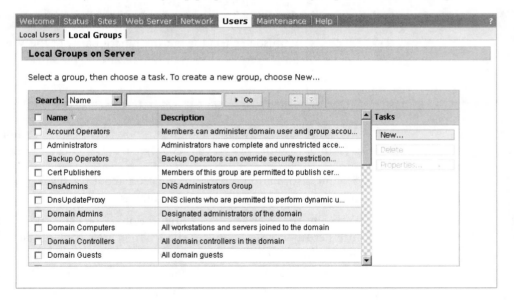

8. Next, let's take a quick look at one of the server logs. To do this, choose Maintenance | Logs | System log. As shown next, you'll see the same events that could be accessed using the Event Viewer administrative tool. You also have the ability to download a copy of the log file or to view details about log entries.

III 7-20

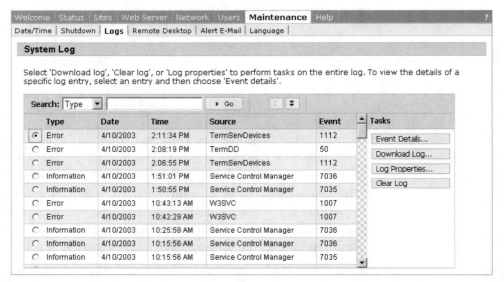

9. Once you're finished checking out the functionality of the Web Interface for Remote Administration, close your web browser. This will end your web-based remote administration session.

The Web Interface for Remote Administration offers a way to administer many different features of Windows Server 2003. Some of these features include

- **System Information** Basic information about the operating system version and hardware configuration of the computer.

- **Web Site and Web Server Configuration** You can configure settings for Internet Information Services (IIS), which are covered in more detail later in this chapter, through the web-based interface. You can configure services such as WWW and FTP, and you can set permissions on various web sites.

- **Network-related settings** Here you can view detailed information about the configuration of network adapters and network settings for the computer. You can also make changes to TCP/IP and other settings.

- **Users and Groups**   You can access all of the basic functionality of the Users and Groups snap-in that's available through the Computer Management administrative tool. Functionality allows you to view information about, create, and delete users and groups.

- **Shut down the server**   This option will specify the shutdown of the server. You can specify whether you want the shutdown operation to begin immediately, or that you want to schedule it to occur at a later time.

- **Launch a remote desktop connection**   This option will create a new Remote Desktop connection within the web browser window. It is helpful for performing tasks that are not supported by the web-based interface (for example, you can install software and access command-line utilities using the Remote Desktop connection).

- **Configure e-mail-based alerts for the server**   This option allows you to specify a standard e-mail address to which alerts will be sent. This is a good way to be notified of any server issues that might require your attention.

- **View server log files**   Using this feature, you can view the same event log files that are available through the standard Event Viewer administrative tool. Although the user interface is somewhat different, you can still drill-down on important event items to get details and other information.

All of these features allow you to quickly and easily access some of the most common administrative functions simply by launching a web browser and logging in. In many cases, when you just want to make some quick and simple administrative changes on a server, the Web Interface for Remote Administration is the best tool for the job!

Be sure to check out the corresponding scenarios and their solutions.

ex**a**m

w**a t c h**   *Keep in mind that the Web Interface for Remote Administration is not a complete replacement for Windows Server 2003's other remote tools. For example, you can't use it to perform management of the Active Directory, management of storage resources, or for installation of applications. In this case, it's just as important to know about a tool's limitations as it is to know about its features.*

Using Help and Support

The phrase "RTM" ("Read the Manual!") is a common cry heard from Help Desk and other IT staff. However, despite being technical people, many of us will resort to all kinds of trail-and-error steps to avoid having to read a product's documentation. In the past, there was good reason for this—many products included documentation that provided extremely unhelpful text such as, "To add a new user, click the Add User button."

SCENARIO & SOLUTION

You want to interactively execute an application on a remote server.	Use Remote Desktop for Administration or the Remote Desktop Web Connection. These features will allow you to interact with the remote server as if you were sitting at the console.
You want to quickly add a user to a group on a Windows 2003 Server domain controller from a Linux machine.	Use the Web Interface for Remote Administration. Since this tool allows you to use a web browser to administer Windows Server 2003, you won't need to install anything additional on the client computer.
You want to be able to create a Remote Desktop connection without manually installing the Remote Desktop Client.	Set up the Remote Desktop Web Connection functionality on the server side. Then, use Internet Explorer to connect to the appropriate web connection site. This will allow you to automatically download and install the necessary components to create a Remote Desktop connection.

Fortunately, that has largely changed in Windows Server 2003. The Help and Support Center (which can be conveniently accessed from the top level of the Start menu) provides a wealth of useful information about the product's hundreds of different features. Some of the types of content included are the following:

on the **job**

There are many advantages to the new user interface of the Help and Support Center. However, if you'd prefer to use the older-style help, you can access the "classic" version of the Windows Help system by clicking Start | Run and typing hh windows.chm.

- **Concepts** For many systems administrators (and especially for those with several years of experience), it's easy enough to figure out how to use the Windows user interface. However, sometimes you might need to get an overview of how some feature of the operating system works. This is where the "Concepts" sections of the help file fit in (see Figure 7-22). These sections dispense with procedural step-by-step information in favor of giving you the big picture of what you're trying to do.

- **"How-To" information** Often, you'll know exactly what you want to do, but you need instructions on how to do it. That's where "how-to" information fits in. As an example, suppose you're interested in finding out how you can disable the Shutdown Event Tracker. The respective portion in the documentation will walk you through the steps that you must follow.

FIGURE 7-22 Viewing concept information in the Help and Support Center

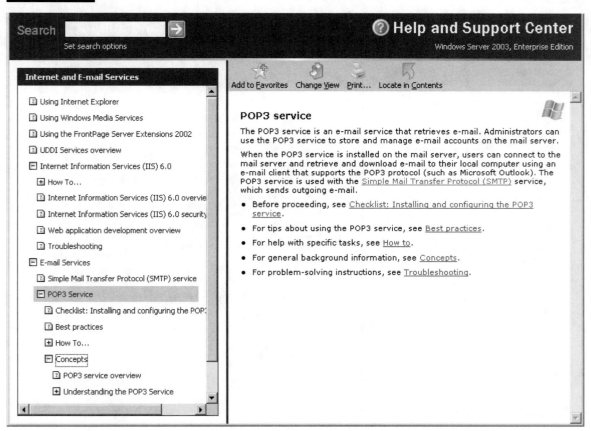

- **Best practices** As IT professionals, it's important that we understand how to best use a technology to meet business goals. That's the focus of "best practices." For example, instead of telling you what tools to use to implement DHCP, a best practice might describe how you can build redundancy into a routed DHCP environment.

- **Checklists** Regardless of how well some features are designed, it's often up to the systems administrator to ensure that all of the prerequisites for a task are carried out. It's very easy to forget to enable some options when setting up a new domain controller, for example. Checklists provide detailed information about what you need to know and what you need to do to successfully implement some feature (see Figure 7-23).

FIGURE 7-23   Viewing checklists in the Help and Support Center

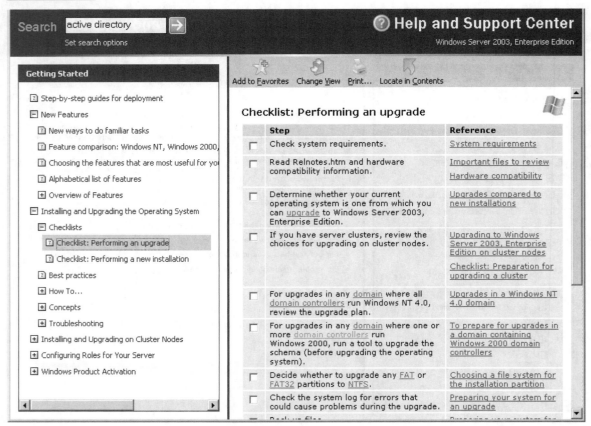

- **Troubleshooting and diagnostic utilities**   When you're faced with troubleshooting a specific problem, you'll want to follow a systematic, step-by-step approach. And along the way, you'll want to collect information that might lead you to the cause of the problem. The Help and Support Center can automate a lot of this otherwise manual work for you by performing a search of system configuration options and testing common areas in which problems might occur. The details shown in Figure 7-24 of working with the troubleshooting and diagnostic features of the Help and Support Center are covered in the next section.

- **Common issues**   Wouldn't it be great if you could find out the types of problems and issues that other systems administrators throughout the world are having? Even if you haven't encountered the same issue, it might be worthwhile to keep this information in mind for future reference. Microsoft

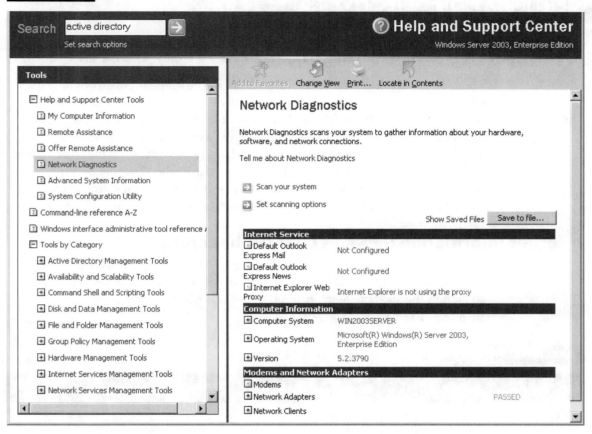

FIGURE 7-24   Using the Help and Support Center's diagnostic utilities

has made that type of functionality available in the Help and Support Center. As long as you have a connection to the Internet, you can view a list of the "Top Issues" that have been reported to Microsoft.

on the **job**

In many products, it seems that vendors include a Help system just to say that they have one. Often, you'll find such gems of wisdom as "To create a new document, select Create from the Document menu." The result is that many of us completely ignore documentation and use it only as a last resort (when we're thoroughly fed up with fumbling around, trying to find the answer). Don't make that mistake with the Help and Support Center included with Windows Server 2003! The online help that's included with the operating system is truly a valuable resource for finding information about the product and how to work with many of its features. Be sure to take advantage of the Help and Support Center when you need more information.

CERTIFICATION OBJECTIVE 7.04

Configuring and Managing an IIS Web Server

Throughout the last several years, the tremendous rise in the popularity of (and our reliance upon) the Internet has changed many things for IT. In the world of the Windows Server platform, Microsoft has continued to make updates in each new edition of its Internet Information Services (IIS) service. IIS is the service that allows Windows Servers to act as web, FTP, mail, and news servers. IIS 6.0 is the latest version of these services, and they are included as a basic part of the Windows Server 2003 platform. In this section, you'll look at the details related to understanding, configuring, and managing IIS. Let's start by taking a look at the basic architecture of IIS.

Internet Information Services (IIS) Architecture

Internet Information Services in Windows Server 2003 is really a collection of different services. At their most basic level, these services respond to specific types of user requests and return the appropriate information to users. The services that are included in IIS are listed in Table 7-1.

TABLE 7-1   A Listing of the Services Supported by IIS

IIS Service	Protocol	Purpose	Notes
Web Service	Hypertext Transfer Protocol (HTTP)	Allows users to access web sites (consisting of HTML pages) and web applications (consisting of "active" web pages)	Users can use a web browser to access a web server.
FTP Service	File Transfer Protocol (FTP)	Provides a simple mechanism for transferring files between users and computers	Users can use command-line utilities, graphical FTP applications, or FTP-enabled web browsers to access an FTP site.
SMTP Service	Simple Mail Transport Protocol (SMTP)	Sending e-mail messages to other servers	Internet-enabled e-mail software can communicate with SMTP servers; messages are relayed between SMTP servers using a "store-and-forward" mechanism.
NNTP Service	Network News Transport Protocol (NNTP)	Accessing newsgroups (threaded discussions based on specific topics)	Users need a news-enabled application (such as Microsoft's Outlook Express) in order to connect to newsgroups.

Note that, although the names of these services include the term "Internet," many of these services can be just as useful (or even more so) in a LAN or intranet environment. Today, web services such as Intranet servers and FTP sites are available throughout modern organizations.

Each of these protocols provides specific information to users that request it. In Windows Server 2003, all of these services can be managed through the Internet Information Services administrative tool (shown in Figure 7-25).

FIGURE 7-25   Viewing information about the local server in the IIS administrative tool

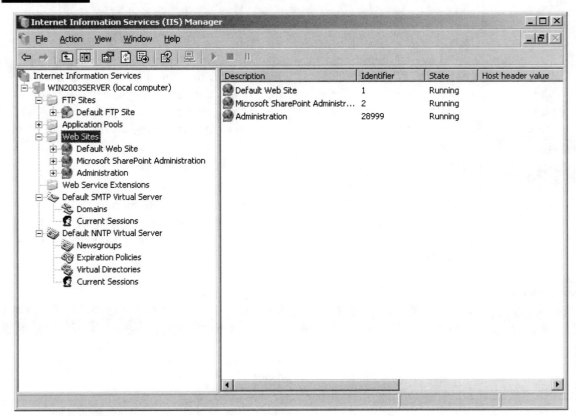

IIS Service	Windows Server 2003 Service Name
Web Service (HTTP)	World Wide Web Publishing
FTP Service	FTP Publishing
SMTP Service	Simple Mail Transfer Protocol (SMTP)
NNTP Service	Network News Transfer Protocol (NNTP)

The various services can also be started, stopped, paused, or restarted through the use of the Services administrative tool. Table 7-2 lists the various services and their names.

exam

ⓦatch   *Limited versions of Internet Information Services are available on Windows client-side operating systems, although they may be known by different names. The focus of this book and chapter (and the Microsoft exams it covers),* *however, is on the services included in Windows Server 2003. Know, though, that some of this functionality is also available for use in your desktop operating system (something that's very helpful for developers and traveling users).*

IIS Ports

Each of the services that's included with IIS uses one or more specific TCP ports. Table 7-3 provides a list of the default ports for the various services that are included with IIS. If you're configuring firewalls or other network devices, it's helpful to know which ports are used for which services.

TABLE 7-3 Protocols and Default Ports for IIS Services

Service Type	Site	Protocol	Port Number	Notes
IIS	Default Web Site	HTTP	80 443 for Secure Sockets Layer (SSL)	This is the default site to which clients will connect when they use the HTTP protocol without a port number.
IIS	Windows Media Administration Web site	HTTP	8080	Available only if Windows Media Services are installed and configured.

| TABLE 7-3 | Protocols and Default Ports for IIS Services *(continued)* |

Service Type	Site	Protocol	Port Number	Notes
IIS	Administration	HTTP	8099 8098 for SSL	Used for performing remote administration of a server.
IIS	Microsoft SharePoint Administartion	HTTP	4715	Used for web-based administration of Microsoft's SharePoint Services (if they're installed).
FTP	Default FTP Site	FTP	21	
SMTP	Default SMTP Virtual Server	SMTP	25	
NNTP	Default NNTP Virtual Server	NNTP	119 563 for SSL	

One method for increasing security is to change port settings to use nonstandard ports. Note, however, that this security method (sometimes referred to as "security through obscurity") is rarely the best method for securing network services, and it can sometimes cause applications that rely on standard ports to fail to work properly.

IIS Versions

Microsoft has included IIS in many of its operating systems. The version of IIS is somewhat independent of the version of the operating system on which it is supported. Table 7-4 provides a list of these different versions of IIS. Note that each Windows operating system supports only one version of IIS (you can't, for example, install IIS 4.0 on Windows Server 2003). However, Microsoft has worked hard to make sure those applications and major configuration settings are compatible across versions of IIS.

| TABLE 7-4 | Various Versions of IIS |

IIS Version	Operating System	Notes
IIS 1.0, 2.0, 3.0, and 4.0	Windows NT 4.0	IIS versions on Windows NT 4.0 can be upgraded through the application of Service Packs and/or Option Packs.
IIS 5.0	Windows 2000 Server	
IIS 5.0	Windows 2000 Professional	Limited version of IIS 5.0 for desktop users.
IIS 5.1	Windows XP Professional	Limited version of IIS for desktop users.
IIS 6.0	Windows Server 2003	

New Features in Windows Server 2003 and IIS 6.0

Many surveys of thousands of web sites prove that Microsoft's IIS is a popular choice for hosting web services on the Internet. There are many reasons for this, including ease of administration and advanced support for scripting languages. In IIS 6.0, Microsoft has made several architectural changes and improvements in IIS 6.0. The list of advances includes

- **More secure default configuration** In previous versions of IIS, Microsoft used default settings that loaded many of the available options of IIS. Although this improved usability, it left a large proportion of systems open to security flaws in services that administrators may not have even known were running. IIS 6.0 takes a different approach: it starts in a "locked down" configuration, and systems administrators must explicitly enable certain features before they will be available for use. You'll look at the details later in this chapter.

- **Built-in support for Microsoft's ASP.NET** ASP.NET is a completely new version of Microsoft's popular Active Server Pages (ASP) web development language. Based on Microsoft's .NET Framework, ASP.NET provides many performance and usability enhancements.

- **Failure protection and stability** A potential problem with complex web applications is that one or more poorly designed applications can sometimes inadvertently bring down an entire web server. IIS 6.0 offers several methods for isolating various processes in their own memory address space to prevent this from happening.

- **Enhanced security** IIS 6.0 includes support for many different authentication mechanisms. Systems administrators can choose the ones that best meet their needs and the needs of their users.

- **Unicode support** The latest version of IIS supports reading HTTP variables in the Unicode character set. This allows developers to write applications that can be made available to users throughout the world.

- **Enhanced resource management** Administrators can control what proportion of the available system resources IIS can consume. They can also specify maximum limits for the number of users and bandwidth usage.

- **Improved performance** Although this is always a goal for server platforms, IIS 6.0 has been designed to improve the performance of web services. At the time of this writing, however, specific benchmarks were not available.

- ■ **Increased uptime** Often, developers and web site administrators may have had to restart IIS in order to update components. In IIS 6.0, service restarts can be scheduled, and many operations no longer require the service to be restarted. The result is increased uptime and reliability.

- ■ **Improved administration** The administrative tools included with IIS 6.0 allows administrators to quickly and easily manage multiple web servers from a single console. Additionally, command-line tools and scripts are included for automating and programming tasks related to IIS services.

Overall, the goal was simply to make IIS 6.0 better than previous versions. Throughout the remainder of this chapter, you'll look at the tools and features that make IIS 6.0 a powerful Internet server platform.

The IIS Metabase

All versions of IIS store configuration information in a file called a "metabase". This file includes all of the configuration options that systems administrators might select for each of the services, sites, and virtual directories. Previous versions of IIS stored their configuration information in binary files that were not easily readable. IIS 6.0, the version of IIS that's supported on Windows Server 2003, stores information in two XML files. The files, named Metabase.xml and MBSchema.xml, are located within the *%SystemRoot%\System32\InetSrv* folder. These files can be loaded in any application that allows the viewing and/or editing of XML files. For example, you can open the XML files in Internet Explorer (which provides color-coding and formatting, as shown in Figure 7-26), or you can edit the files with Notepad.

on the
Ú o b

Just because you can manually modify the IIS metabase files, that doesn't mean you should. In order to successfully make changes, you must have a thorough understanding of the structure of the file. In general, manual modification of the metabase is probably best left to application developers and hard-core IIS administrators (for example, those that might manage hundreds of IIS servers).

There is also a subfolder called History that keeps track of prior configurations. Information stored in the History folder can be very useful for troubleshooting IIS problems and for keeping track of changes in the configuration. Systems administrators could, for example, compare versions of the history files with the current configuration to pinpoint changes. XML information is human-readable, and experienced systems administration can copy configurations and compare settings on different web servers.

| FIGURE 7-26 | Viewing the Metabase.xml file in Internet Explorer |

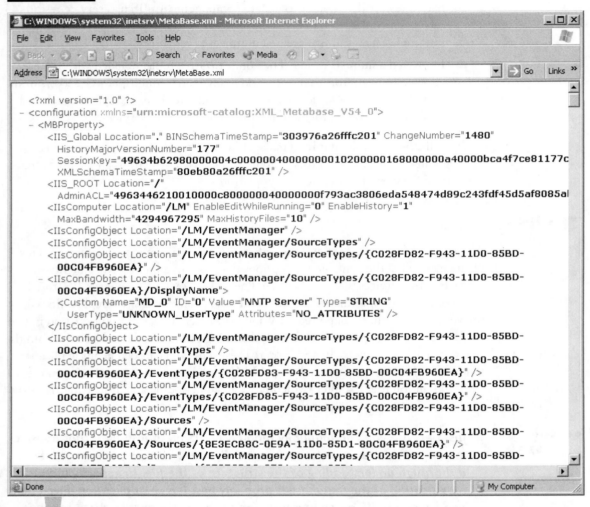

on the
Öob
You should be forewarned—do not manually edit the IIS metabase configuration files unless you're absolutely sure about what you're doing. For general administration, stick to the much-more-intuitive (and user-friendly) IIS administrative tool.

Sites and Virtual Directories

To allow for simplified administration, IIS supports the concepts of sites and virtual directories. It's important to understand the purpose and function of each of these aspects before you configure your server.

A *site* is a web server service that responds to a specific TCP/IP address and port number. For example, if the TCP/IP address of your machine is 168.5.24.3, IIS may respond to all requests that go to that IP address on TCP port 80 (the default port for HTTP communications). Usually, this is noted with a colon separating the IP address and the port (for example, "168.5.24.3:80"). Since you're using the default port, users could connect to this site by using the URL "http://168.5.24.3"). A single IIS server might host the following sites (note that these names are case-insensitive):

- www.MyCompany.com
- Partners.MyCompany.com
- Server1.Support.MyCompany.com
- www.CoolProducts.com
- 192.168.0.1

Each of these sites would respond to a different IP address and could have completely different configurations. Traditionally, there can be only one site that responds to a particular IP address and port. Multihomed computers (machines that have multiple network addresses bound to a single physical adapter, or machines that have multiple physical network adapters) can serve multiple sites. Each site will have a home directory—a physical path in which the files for the web site are stored.

In many cases, however, you will want to have several different web sites configured for the same IP address. This can be done through the use of HTTP host headers. You can specify what values IIS should look for in the client request when you are creating a new site. In addition to the IP address and port information, you can also specify a "host header value." IIS will use this information to determine to which sites users will be directed. One limitation of using HTTP host headers is that they do not readily support secure (HTTPS) connections. For more information on HTTP host headers, see the help file that accompanies the Internet Services Manager.

Virtual directories are just pointers to files located in other locations. For example, the www.mycompany.com site might respond to the following URL requests:

- www.mycompany.com
- www.mycompany.com/products
- www.mycompany.com/info/contactinfo

A site can contain many virtual directories. A web administrator could create a virtual directory called Public that points to the C:\WebSite\Public folder. Then, a user can obtain that information using a URL such as http://WebServer1/Public. Virtual directories provide a lot of flexibility in site design, since they don't require that all of your web content exist in one directory tree.

You'll look at the details related to working with sites and virtual directories later in this chapter. For now, Figure 7-27 provides an example of the relationship between sites and virtual directories.

Configuring IIS

Security is a key concern in almost all networked environments. This is especially true when it comes to servers and resources that will be accessible over the Internet. That's why it's extremely important for systems administrators to ensure that their IIS services are configured according to business requirements. In this section, you'll take a look at the ways in which you can configure your IIS server.

Enabling IIS

As has been mentioned several times, by default, IIS is disabled following the installation of Windows Server 2003. Therefore, the first step in working with IIS is to enable it.

There are two different ways to enable IIS on a Windows Server 2003 machine. The first is to use the Windows Components Wizard (available via the Add/Remove Programs Control Panel applet). Using this wizard (shown next), you can choose to install some, or all, IIS functionality. When you enable certain options, note that

FIGURE 7-27	
Comparing sites and virtual directories in IIS	

other options might automatically be selected. You can drill down into an item by double-clicking it or selecting it and then clicking Details. Once you're finished, click Next to enable the selected services. By using the Windows Component Wizard, you can select exactly which services you wish to enable.

III 7-21

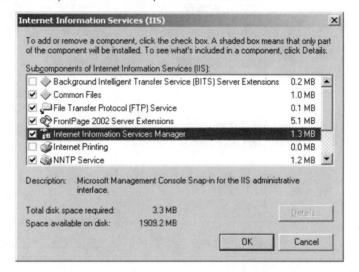

The other method for enabling IIS is through the use of the Configure Your Server Wizard. This method performs the basic operations required to enable IIS, along with its most commonly selected options. Specifically, you can choose to enable or disable the server role called Application Server (IIS, ASP.NET). Figure 7-28 shows the screen that prompts you with two available options.

Configuring IIS Server Properties

Once you've enabled IIS on Windows Server 2003, it's time to configure it to do what you want. Depending on the various options that you might have selected, it's possible that several web sites are already configured and ready for use. For example, if you selected the Remote Administration (HTML) option (which is covered earlier in this chapter), the server should already have the appropriate site configured and enabled.

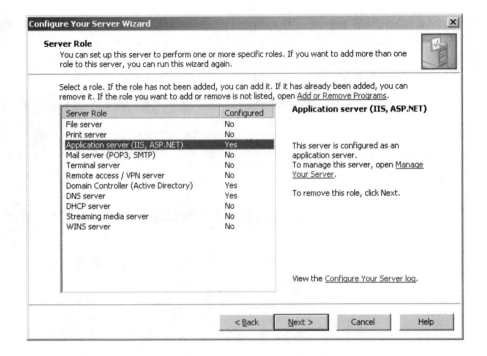

FIGURE 7-28

Enabling IIS with
the Configure
Your Server
Wizard

The main method for administering IIS is the Internet Information Services (IIS) Manager administrative tool. After you've enabled IIS, you'll see a screen in IIS Manager similar to the one shown earlier in Figure 7-25.

Through the interface of the IIS administrative tool, you can quickly and easily make changes to the IIS configuration. We'll walk through the many configuration options later in this chapter, but let's begin with the first steps.

Configuring Server Extensions

Although the basic concepts behind web servers are fairly simple, many modern web servers have evolved to include far more than just basic functionality. For example, Microsoft's IIS supports server-side scripting through its Active Server Pages (ASP) and ASP.NET languages. It can host components written in a variety of programming languages, including Visual Basic, Visual C#, and Visual C++. And, IIS also includes an Indexing Service that can be used by web site administrators to make their sites and documents searchable. Although these features can add valuable functionality to the web server (especially if you're able to take advantage of them), they can pose potential security risks. Therefore, most of the features of these tools are disabled even after you've enabled IIS. That increases security, but it puts the burden on the systems administrator to manually configure the options that he or she needs.

Fortunately, the process of enabling services and performing basic configuration settings in IIS is fairly straightforward. Using the IIS Manager tool, you can simply click the Web Service Extensions folder. Using this interface (shown in Figure 7-29), you can specify which types of extensions and server-side features you'd like to support.

on the
ö o b

Security is a very important topic for many organizations. However, when security problems are found, popular technical (and, increasingly, nontechnical) media sources tend to act as if these problems can cause you to immediately lose all of your data and to make you completely susceptible to hackers. Although security issues are serious, it's important for you, as an IT professional, to be able to separate the facts from the hype. Be sure to read the technical information (not just the commentary) about viruses, worms, security breaches, and other information that's presented in popular media.

When you select an item in the Web Services Extensions list, you can choose to Allow or Prohibit its use. This will control whether or not this feature is available. For example, if you have a web site that contains ASP files and "Active Server Pages" is set to "prohibited," these files will not be processed or returned to users. In addition to allowing or prohibiting certain features, you can view their properties. On the General tab (shown in Figure 7-30), you'll see which options depend upon the selected extension. On the Required Files tab, you'll be able to see which file(s) are being used to process IIS requests.

FIGURE 7-29   Using the IIS Manager to configure web service extensions

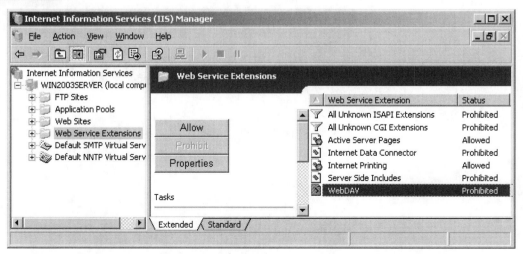

III 7-22

FIGURE 7-30

Viewing General
information for
Active Server
Pages extensions

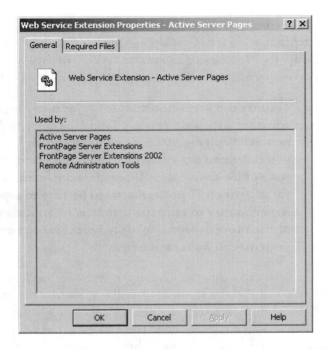

Finally, you have the ability to Add a new extension to the list of Web Service
Extensions. This is an advanced function that's designed for those organizations that
wish to create their own IIS request handlers (or, for cases in which an application
server extensions does not automatically register itself with IIS). All that's required
to implement a new extension is a list of the types of files that are handled, and a
path to the actual handler.

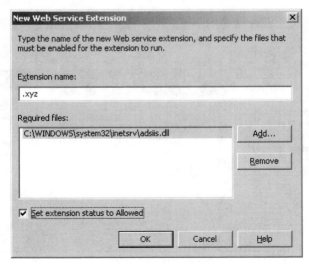

Creating and Managing Sites and Virtual Directories

Once you've performed that basic configuration of IIS, you'll want review the configuration to make sure that it meets the need of web developers and users. That's the topic of this section. First, for ease of management, IIS configuration settings can be configured at two main levels:

■ **Site level**　These settings control specific details related to a single site or service. For example, you might want to set custom authentication settings for an intranet site and different authentication settings for a public web site.

■ **Virtual directory level**　A site can consist of many virtual directories. For example, the www.mycompany.com site might include virtual directories for product information, downloadable files, and a customer support page. Each of these virtual directories can be provided with different security settings and configuration options.

These levels form a hierarchy that can be used to simplify administration. For example, you might choose to implement default settings for all sites at the server level. When you choose to apply the settings, you'll be prompted to choose which child objects you want the settings to apply to. In some cases, some settings can only be set at a specific level. But for the most part, the configuration settings are hierarchical.

Through the use of sites and virtual directories, you can configure your web server to provide content in several different ways. To create a new web site, you can simply right-click the Web Sites folder in the IIS administrative tool and select New | Web Site. You'll be given the chance to assign several different properties for this service (we'll cover the details later in this chapter).

The process for creating a new virtual directory is just as easy: Simply right-click an existing web site, click New and then select Virtual Directory. You'll be given the option to specify the location of the content that should be made available through that virtual directory.

Now that you have the basics out of the way, let's look at the various options that are available for web sites and virtual directories.

Configuring Web Site Properties

Many configuration options are available for web sites. In some cases, the default settings that are implemented by IIS might be sufficient for your environment. In most cases, however, you'll probably want to make some changes to meet your requirements. In this section, you'll get a high-level view of the types of options that are available for configuring web services that are hosted by IIS. You should start by right-clicking the name of a web site and choosing Properties.

Web Site Configuration

The Web Site tab (shown in Figure 7-31) presents the basic configuration options that are available for the specific site. These settings are very important because they determine how the site will respond to user HTTP requests. For example, you can specify on which IP address(es) and port(s) the site will respond. This setting is useful in multihomed servers (servers that have more than one network interface) because it can limit the network interfaces on which users can connect. Additionally, you can specify the TCP port(s) on which this server will respond to both standard HTTP requests and secure connection requests (via HTTPS, which uses the Secure Sockets Layer [SSL] for encrypting communications).

For example, you might want to use a URL of http://192.168.7.5:8937/MyWebSite to connect to the site. In that case, you'll want to configure the Web Site to respond to the IP address of 192.168.7.5 (which must already be an IP address that is assigned to this computer), and to respond on TCP port 8937. It's important to note that no two web services can be assigned to the same IP address and port number.

In the Connections portion of this property page, you can specify how long an HTTP connection will be kept open and whether or not HTTP Keep-Alives will be enabled. These settings can improve performance on busy servers if the optimal

Viewing the Web Site configuration property sheet of a web site in IIS settings are determined by someone that is familiar with the purpose and functionality of the web site.

Finally, you can specify logging settings in the General tab. These settings control what types of information will be recorded by IIS, and where the information will be stored. The first option is to choose the log format. Your options include

- W3C Extended Log File Format (the default setting)
- Microsoft IIS Logging
- NCSA Common Log File Format
- ODBC Logging

In some cases, you might want to change the log file format in order to provide compatibility with third-party log file analysis tools, or for compatibility with other web servers. You can configure additional settings for the log file format by clicking Properties (see Figure 7-32). This will allow you to specify the location of the log files, how often new log files are created, and what information is recorded to the log files. It's important to note that certain types of logging can cause a decrease in overall web server performance. For example, logging to an ODBC data source can use up significantly more resources than logging to a file. And, recording all of the available properties can make the log files take up considerable space within the file system (making the files harder to manage and analyze). Overall, be sure to collect only the information that is useful to you.

on the job

Whether you're running a mission-critical public server, or a company intranet web server, there's a potential goldmine of information sitting in your log files. The key to unlocking the information is to use a log file reporting tool such as products from WebTrends (www.webtrends.com) or Quest Software's Funnel Web Analyzer product (www.quest.com). The information that you collect can really help you in making better configuration decisions and in adjusting the content of the site.

Performance   On the Performance tab (shown in Figure 7-33), you can specify the total bandwidth that can be used by this site or service. For example, your company web site may have several sections, including a section for downloading technical papers. You may choose to limit the amount of bandwidth that can be used for downloading files to 300 KBps so that performance of the entire site doesn't suffer when a few users are trying to download multiple files.

FIGURE 7-32

Viewing log file
property settings

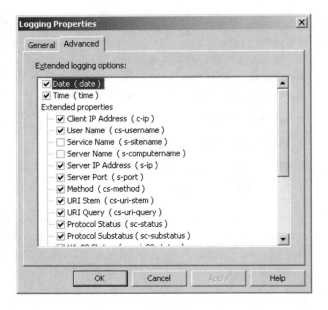

FIGURE 7-33

Viewing the
Performance
configuration
property sheet of
a web site in IIS

You can also configure the total number of connections that will be allowed to this site. This setting can improve performance, since a very large number of users connecting to a single site can slow down overall server performance. If the number of users exceeds the setting, the additional connection attempts will receive an error message stating that the server is unable to accept any new connections.

ISAPI Filters   Internet Server Application Programming Interface (ISAPI) filters can be used by IIS for handling special types of files. These pieces of code are used for processing HTTP requests. For example, a developer might write a DLL that automatically processes all files that have the ".superhtml" extension before the files are sent to users. Additionally, certain third-party application servers that work with IIS automatically add themselves as ISAPI filters.

Home Directory   The Home Directory tab is an important configuration section within the properties of a web site. This tab (shown in Figure 7-34) contains information about which files will be provided to users when they access the site. The first set of options includes the following:

- **A directory located on this computer**   This selection specifies that the content that should be sent to users is located within the local file system.
- **A share located on another computer**   This selection allows you to specify a network location for the files that should be available to users of this web site.
- **A redirection to a URL**   This option will automatically send a response to users, redirecting them to another web site. This is useful if you need to rename a site, or if content is moved. For example, you might automatically redirect all requests to http://www.OldCompanyName.com to http://www.NewCompanyName.com.

If you choose either of the first two options, you must specify the location of the files (either on the local computer or on a network share). Then, you must set the types of operations that are allowed for this content (for details, see the Help file). Finally, you can specify the name of the application (which can provide information for use by reporting tools), script permissions, and the application pool to which this site is assigned.

Documents   When a user requests a page from a site with a URL that does not include a specific document name (such as http://www.MyCompany.com/Products), IIS must know which file should be sent to the user. As shown in Figure 7-35, you can

FIGURE 7-34

Viewing the
Home Directory
configuration
property sheet of
a web site in IIS

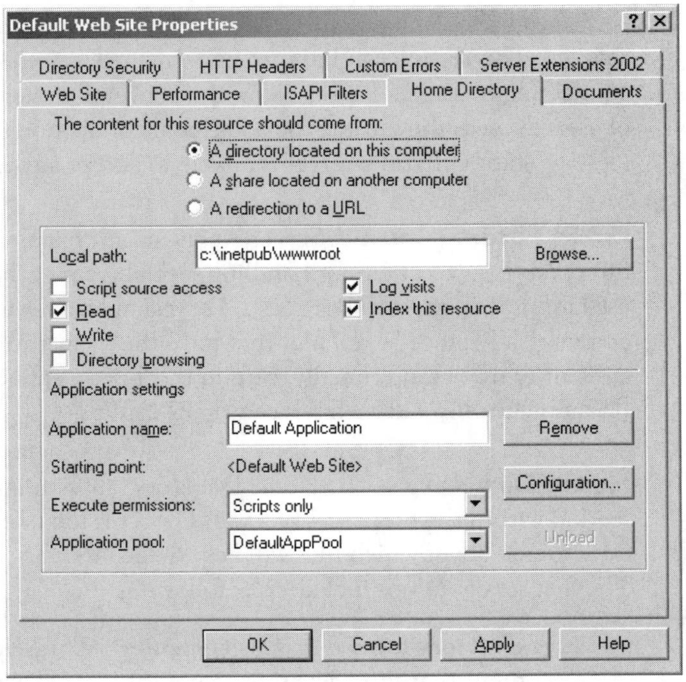

FIGURE 7-35

Viewing the
Documents
configuration
property sheet of
a web site in IIS

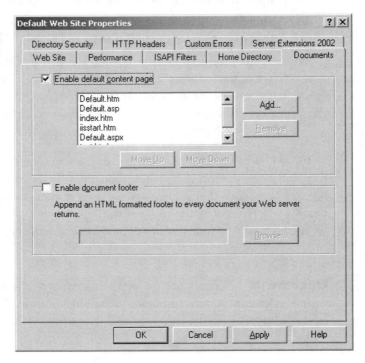

specify a list of default documents (in order). Additionally, you can enable a document footer. A *document footer* is a file that is automatically added to the end of every page request. This functionality might be useful, for example, if you have a standard file that will be used to send copyright information at the bottom of every page.

Directory Security   The Directory Security tab is important for determining how users must authenticate with this web site before they can access resources. Figure 7-36 shows the main options that are available. You'll notice that you can set different types of security.

By clicking Edit in the Anonymous Access And Authentication Controls section, you'll be given the dialog box shown in Figure 7-37. Your first option specifies whether you want to allow anonymous access to this site. If the site is for public use, you will probably want to enable this option. For example, when users visit a site such as www.MyCompany.com, I wouldn't require them to provide any authentication mechanism.

When a user connects to IIS in this way (assuming that you have enabled anonymous access), IIS will allow them to impersonate a specific account. The default account is IUSR_*MachineName*. Whenever a user attempts to access a file on this web site, IIS will test the permissions of this account. If the IUSR_*MachineName* account has

FIGURE 7-36

Viewing the main Directory Security configuration property sheet of a web site in IIS

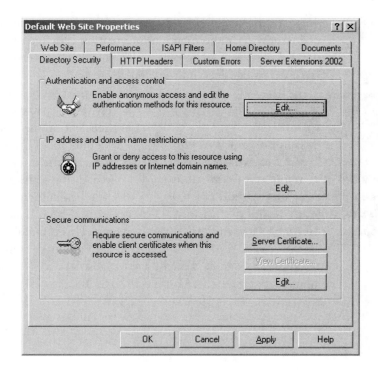

FIGURE 7-37

Viewing
authentication
methods settings

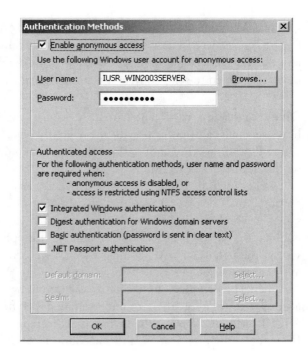

permissions to the file, then the user will be given the file; if not, the user will be forced to provide authentication information. The recommended option is for IIS to control the password automatically, but you can override this setting if you want IIS to use a special account that you've created.

The next set of options is for authenticated access. Here, you can control which authentication mechanisms may be used. For details about the various authentication options, see the online help.

In addition to restricting access to your web site through authentication, you can restrict access to certain IP addresses and/or domain names. This is useful if you want to allow or prevent groups of computers from accessing a web site. For example, I might want to restrict access to an intranet site to only computers that are located on the 192.168.100.x subnet.

exam
ⓦatch
It is important that you provide the IUSR_MachineName account with only the bare minimum permissions that are required for anonymous users on the web site. Any additional permissions could lead to potential security holes!

III 7-23

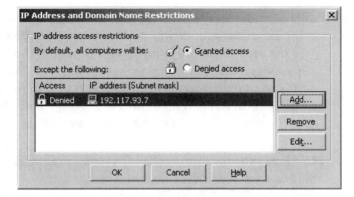

Finally, to provide for the encryption of data that is being sent between your server and clients, you can install and configure server certificates. Server certificates can be obtained from third-party security providers (such as VeriSign at www.verisign.com). The certificates are used to prove the identity of the web server and to create a secure communications link with your user. These settings are particularly important for sites that transmit data that must remain secure (for example, for web sites that accept credit card information). When you click the Server Certificate button, you'll be able to use the Web Server Certificate Wizard. This wizard will walk you through the steps that are required to install a certificate for use by this web site.

III 7-24

You can also make changes regarding whether or not SSL is required and client certificates are handled using the Edit button (see Figure 7-38).

on the
job

Remember that technology is only one portion of a true security solution. For example, you might have configured Windows Server 2003 to use all of the recommended security best practices that you've found. However, if your systems administrators are using weak passwords (or, worse yet, if they're sharing passwords), you might have a far greater security issue on your hands. Keep in mind that technology and operating system configuration is only one part of an overall security solution.

HTTP Headers Part of the HTTP specification allows the sending of custom information that describes properties of the page. This information is located in the header of an HTTP packet. You can configure the information that will be sent to clients through the use of the HTTP Headers tab (see Figure 7-39). For example, you can enable content expiration based on specific time settings. Content expiration information is used by the browser on the client side to determine whether a page can be loaded from cache (providing improved performance, but with the risk of getting outdated content), or if the server must be checked for an updated copy of the page. This commonly occurs when a user hits the Back button on their browser or when they view a page that they have visited recently. In addition to content expiration options, you can also add additional information to the headers of all files.

FIGURE 7-38

Editing SSL
Options in IIS
Manager

FIGURE 7-39

Viewing the
HTTP Headers
configuration
property sheet of
a web site in IIS

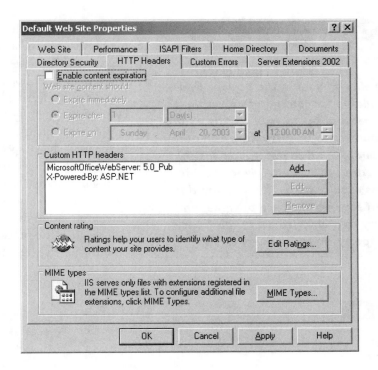

The HTTP Headers properties also allow you to input content rating information for the content provided on the web site. For example, if the site is not intended for use by children, you can specify that the site contains sensitive language and violence in the Ratings settings. When you click Edit Ratings, you'll also be given the option to view information and a questionnaire on the web. This will help you determine what types of content settings you want to specify. Users of your web site can choose which types of content are acceptable to them. Generally, this is configured in a third-party application or in compatible web browsers. If a site's ratings do not meet the requirements of the browser, the web page will not be shown (or a warning message will appear).

Custom Errors Perhaps the only thing worse than receiving an unexpected error on a web site is receiving an error message that gives you misleading or incomplete information. By default, IIS includes information for commonly encountered errors (for example, the 404 error, which specifies that the requested page could not be found, or a 500 error in the event of a serious internal server problem). In the Custom Errors tab, you can specify custom pages that can be returned to users in the event of an error. For example, on a public web site, you might want to send a friendlier version of the "Server busy" message that includes information about when peak hours of activity are for the site. To edit a setting, simply click the Edit Properties button (see Figure 7-40). You'll be given the option to specify the file that should be returned to the user when a specific error occurs.

As you have seen, there are many different configuration options that are available for working with IIS web sites. To bring a lot of this information together, Exercise 7-4 walks you through the process of enabling IIS and creating a new web site.

FIGURE 7-40

Viewing the Custom Errors configuration property sheet of a web site in IIS

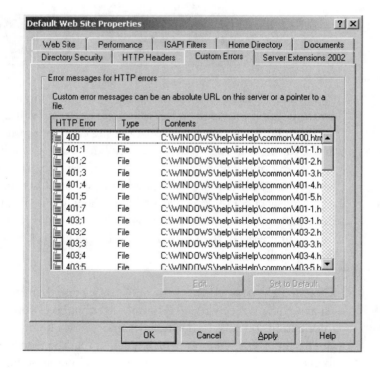

EXERCISE 7-4

Enabling and Configuring Internet Information Services (IIS)

This exercise assumes that you have not yet enabled IIS on your Windows Server 2003 machine. If IIS is already enabled, you may want to start by disabling it (using the last step of this exercise).

1. Open the Configure Your Server administrative tool. Click Next twice to view the Server Roles page. Select Application Server (IIS, ASP.NET) and then click Next.

2. On the Application Server Options page, you'll be able to select whether you want to enable FrontPage Server Extensions and/or whether you want to enable ASP.NET. For the sake of this exercise, leave both boxes unchecked and then click Next.

III 7-25

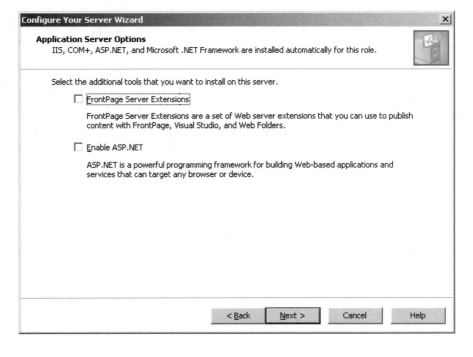

3. Here, you'll see a summary of your choices. To perform the installation and configuration, click Next. When the installation is complete, click Finish.

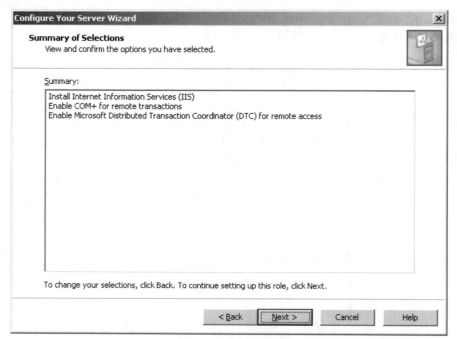

4. Next, let's create a web directory and a simple web page. Start by using Windows Explorer to create a folder named "WebTest" within the c:\Inetpub\wwwroot folder. Then, create a new file called TestPage.htm (you can use Notepad to do this). Place the following HTML code in the file and then save it:

```
<HTML>
<Title>IIS 6.0 Test Page</Title>
<Body>
<H1>IIS Test Page</H1><br>
This is a simple HTML page used for testing a new IIS web site.
</Body>
</HTML>
```

5. Test the page by double-clicking it. The page should open in Internet Explorer and look similar the one shown in the following illustration:

III 7-27

6. Now that IIS is enabled and you've created a simple test page, it's time to configure it to host a new web site. Start by opening the Internet Information Services (IIS) Manager administrative tool. Expand the branch for the local server. Then, right-click Web Sites and select New | Web Site. This will launch the Web Site Creation Wizard. Click Next to begin.

III 7-28

7. For the description of the site, enter **Test Web Site** and click Next. On the IP Address And Port Assignments step, leave the IP Address option at its

default setting "(All Unassigned)." For the TCP port, enter **8111**. Leave the host header field blank, then click Next.

III 7-29

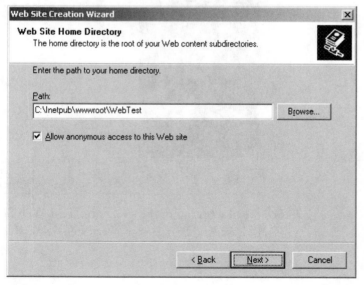

8. On the Web Site Home Directory, click Browse and find the folder that you created in step 4 (this should be "c:\inetpub\wwwroot\WebTest"). Leave the anonymous access option checked and click Next.

III 7-30

9. Leave the Web Site Access permissions at their default settings and then click Next. Finally, click Finish to create the new web site.

10. Now that the new site has been created, it's time to test it. You can do this from within the IIS Manager by selecting the "Test Web Site" object. In the right pane, right-click the TestPage.htm file and then click Browse. You should see the page that you created in step 5. Alternatively, you can open a web browser and navigate to the URL http://servername:8111/TestPage.htm.

III 7-31

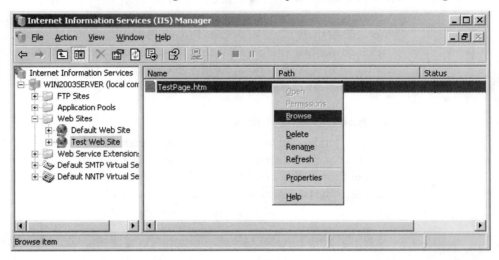

11. Once you've verified that the new web site works, close your browser and close the IIS Manager. Now that you're finished working with IIS, you'll disable it (to return the system to its original configuration). To do this, launch the Configure Your Server Wizard administrative tool and choose to remove the Application Server (IIS, ASP.NET) server role. This will disable IIS.

III 7-32

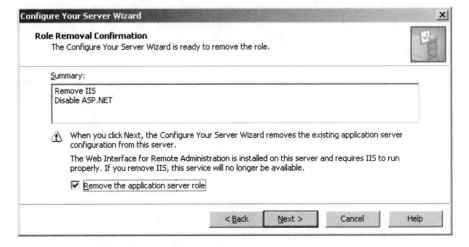

Now that you've taken a good look at all of the options that are available for configuring a web site, let's examine some other IIS features.

Configuring Virtual Directories

The process for configuring virtual directories is very similar to the process for configuration web sites. In fact, many of the options are exactly the same. It's important to note that the settings that you make at the virtual directory level will override any settings that are made at a higher level. Of course, if you change the settings for a web site that contains virtual directories, you'll be given the option of applying the same settings to child virtual directories.

IIS Backup and Recovery

For more production web servers, the configuration of IIS is very important. And, it can take a significant amount of time and effort just to set up the services the way you want them. You may be tempted to walk through all of the property sheets and document the configuration, but there's a much easier way. By right-clicking a server name and selecting All Tasks, you'll see several options:

- **Backup / Restore Configuration** This option allows you to create a backup of the current IIS configuration. As shown in Figure 7-40, you can specify a name for the backup. Optionally, you can force the configuration information to be encrypted and to be accessible only with the password that you provide. Note that IIS automatically makes backups of the configuration whenever changes occur. You can also restore the configuration to the point of a backup by clicking Restore. This will replace all web site and virtual directory settings to their state at the time of the backup.

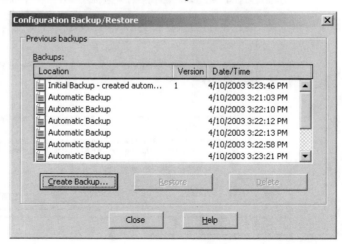

■ **Restart IIS** Although this isn't strictly related to backup and recovery, you can quickly stop, start, or restart the IIS service using this option (see Figure 7-41). You can also use this option to reboot the server (a handy option if you're administering a machine remotely).

■ **Save Configuration To Disk** As its name implies, this option will update the IIS metabase information on disk. This is helpful when you've just made changes that you want to have reflected in the metabase.

In addition to the options available at the server level, you can also save the configuration of a web site to the local server disk. To do this, right-click the name of a site and go to All Tasks | Save Configuration To Disk. You'll be prompted for the name and location of the saved file and, optionally, for password information.

This setting can be very useful when you're creating new web sites, since you have the ability to use the New | Web Site From File option. When you create a new web site this way, you'll automatically receive all of the options that were present in the original web site. This can save a lot of configuration time and, more important, prevent configuration errors!

FIGURE 7-41 Restarting the IIS service

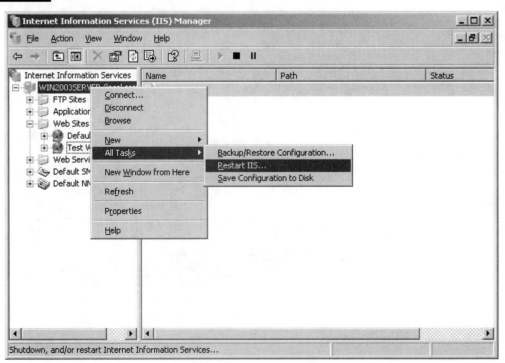

Configuring Application Pools

New in IIS 6.0 is the ability to support multiple "application pools." This is an advanced option for web developers and systems administrators that support multiple applications on the same server. Application pools allow administrators to specify options related to CPU, memory, and other resources on the server. As shown in Figure 7-42, you can view or set thresholds that are related to performance in the Performance tab of the properties of an application pool. Then, you can create or modify your web sites and virtual directories to run in various application pools.

Figure 7-43 shows options available in the Health tab. These settings can help detect and automatically resolve the failure of a web service running within the pool.

When you enable IIS 6.0 for the first time, only the "DefaultAppPool" will be available. Therefore, all of the sites and virtual directories will run in this pool.

FIGURE 7-42

Viewing application pool Performance properties

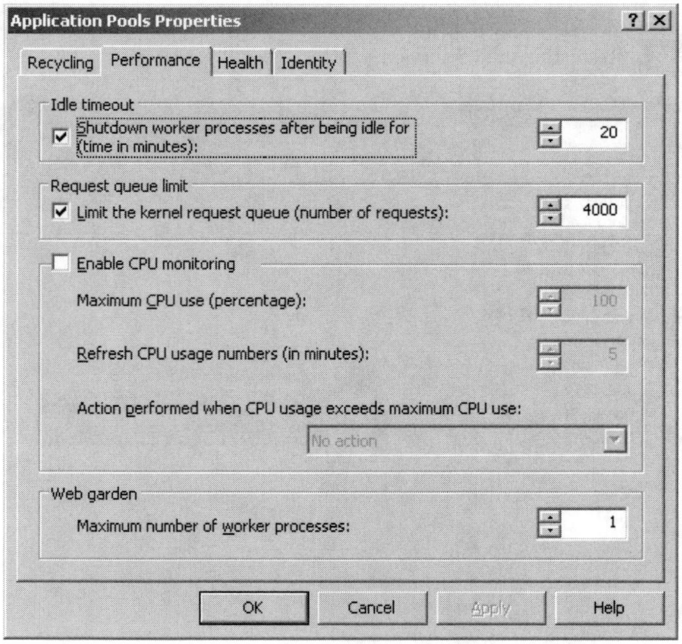

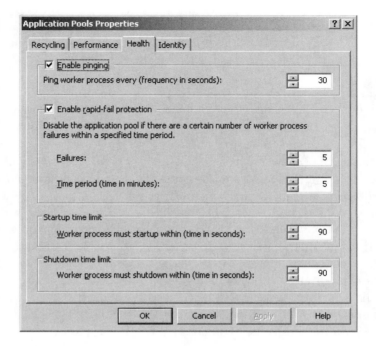

FIGURE 7-43

Viewing
application pool
Health properties

INSIDE THE EXAM

Managing IIS in the Real World

When Microsoft first made the initial versions of IIS available in Windows NT 4.0, companies were first starting to deploy web sites. The majority of sites were static, and most were primarily text-based. A web site was something that was "nice to have." Well, times have changed. Now, almost every organization, regardless of size, has some sort of web presence. And, sites provide much more than the name, address, and phone number of the company. Existing and potential customers rely on up-to-date news information, downloads, and other resources. This makes it essential for systems administrations in the current IT world to understand how web sites should be configured.

When answering questions related to web services on the exam, be sure to keep in mind the overall requirements of the site, and how it should be implemented in IIS. Generally, the top level of a site (such as www.MyCompany.com) would be configured

INSIDE THE EXAM

as an IIS site. Web pages, graphics, and other related files may reside under the root folder (the one that is configured for the site). Or, you can use virtual directories to point users to content located elsewhere. For example, if a user browses to "www.mycompany.com/support," she could be accessing content that is local to your server. Or, she may be returned content stored elsewhere on your network, or redirected to another web site altogether. When managing web services, this provides systems administrators with a lot of flexibility. If you choose to move some frequently accessed content to another site or server, you can easily redirect users to the new content.

Another important aspect of working with IIS is security. Security works in a hierarchical fashion that is similar to many other features of Windows Server 2003 (think about Active Directory domain and OU structures, and NTFS permissions). Your general approach to configuring IIS security should be to provide the minimal permissions that are required. This can help prevent unauthorized or accidental changes to your company's sites (both of which can be very costly and embarrassing). Keep in mind that security settings at lower levels (virtual directories, for instance) will override settings at higher levels.

Finally, when answering questions related to troubleshooting IIS-related issues on the exam, assume that services are disabled, unless you're told otherwise! For example, if a developer has placed a file called *.aspx (an ASP.NET page) into a virtual directory and it does not display properly, a good troubleshooting step would be to verify that ASP.NET is enabled. Since Windows Server 2003 ships with most services disabled, a common troubleshooting step for exam questions (and in the real world) will be to ensure that you've enabled the services and features that you need.

Understanding FTP Services

So far we have focused on how you can configure what is, by far, the most-used feature of IIS: web services. As mentioned earlier, however, IIS also supports other Internet services. In this section, you'll look at the basics of working with the File Transfer Protocol (FTP) service. Since many of the configuration options are similar to the ones that we covered for web sites, I'll provide basic information.

In order to enable FTP services, you must use the Windows Components Wizard (covered earlier in this chapter). The specific option that you'll need to enable is located in the following path: Application Server | Internet Information Services (IIS) | File Transfer Protocol (FTP Service).

Like the web service, the FTP service allows administrators to configure sites and virtual directories. Sites respond to a specific TCP/IP address and port combination, and virtual directories are simply pointers to other physical locations that contain files that can be accessed by remote users.

On the client side, users can use either a graphical FTP program or a command-line FTP utility to connect to a web site. All current versions of Windows include a built-in FTP client called, as you might have guessed, FTP. In either case, they can use the utility to transfer files to and from an FTP site over the Internet (provided, of course, that they have the appropriate permissions).

Configuring FTP Sites

You can use the Internet Information Services administrative tool to view and modify the configuration of your FTP sites. The configuration tabs that are available within the properties of an FTP site include

- **FTP Site** In this tab (shown in Figure 7-44), you can specify the primary settings for the FTP site, including the TCP/IP address and the port to which the site responds. The default port used by FTP sites is port 21. Since FTP servers may become very active (in terms of the number and type of files that are shared), you can limit the number of concurrent users and the total amount of bandwidth that's available for all of the clients. Finally, as with web sites, you can configure logging for all interactions with your FTP service. It's a good idea to enable this option so that you can see which users are transferring which files.

- **Security Accounts** The Security Accounts tab (see Figure 7-45) is designed to allow you to specify which users are able to make changes to the configuration of the FTP site. By default, only members of the Administrators group will be listed. Next, you can choose the name of the Windows Server 2003 user account that anonymous users will impersonate. Anyone who logs on to the FTP server using anonymous credentials will have the permissions assigned to this user.

- **Messages** Since FTP sites tend to look very cold and impersonal (compared to web sites, which can use graphics and other methods to engage the user), you might want to display some information to users as they log in. Most organizations will also want to specify details about the purpose of the site and a note that forbids unauthorized use. The Banner and Welcome messages are shown upon login. You can also specify a message that is sent just before a user disconnects from the FTP server, as well as one that is displayed whenever the maximum number of connections for the site is exceeded.

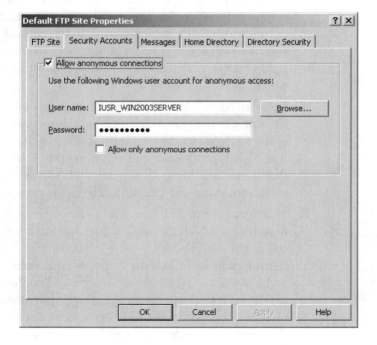

■ **Home Directory** The home directory is the file system folder that serves as the root for the web site. This is where users will connect, by default, when they log on. Alternatively, you can choose to specify the path to a share located on another machine. As shown in Figure 7-46, your options are to allow read (download) and/or write (upload) privileges to users, as well as deciding whether or not you want to log the users' interactions with the FTP server. You can also choose whether you want files displayed in Unix (four-digit years) format or MS-DOS (two-digit years) format.

■ **Directory Security** A simple fact of operating on the Internet is that there will likely be users or groups of users that you want to prevent from using your FTP site. On the Directory Security tab, you can specify which users will have access to connect to your system by IP address or DNS name. Although it's not exactly the ultimate in security, it does prevent casual unauthorized users from using your server resources.

Through the use of all of these options, you can make the FTP service behave the way your organization wants.

FIGURE 7-46

Setting home directory options for an FTP site

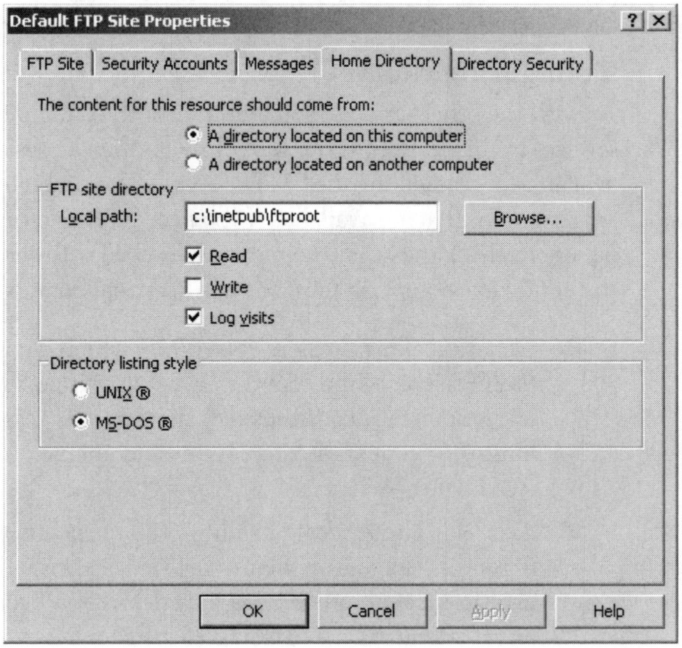

Understanding SMTP Services

The Simple Mail Transport Protocol (SMTP) is used for sending messages between systems. SMTP is also the default method for transferring e-mail messages over the Internet. SMTP is a connectionless mechanism by which computers can exchange information using the TCP/IP. That is, it does not require an active connection between two machines in order for messages to be stored. Instead, SMTP uses a "store-and-forward" method. If I want to send a message to someone@microsoft.com, for example, it really doesn't matter whether or not their mail server is running at the time (or if all of the network connections between my mail server and their mail server are working properly). By default, I'll send the message to my mail server, and it will be responsible for delivering the message. If the server is unavailable, the SMTP service can retry sending the e-mail multiple times (for example, every few hours for a period of two days). This built-in support for nonreliable connections is one of SMTP's greatest strengths.

IIS includes a built-in SMTP server and is configured with a single, default SMTP service, appropriately called the "Default SMTP Virtual Server." As with the other services in IIS, SMTP is disabled by default. In order to enable FTP services, you must use the Windows Components Wizard (covered earlier in this chapter). The specific option that you'll need to enable is located in the following path: Application Server | Internet Information Services (IIS) | SMTP Service.

Configuring the SMTP Service

As with the other services, you might want to configure various settings for the SMTP service. In this section, you'll walk through the various configuration options that are available for configuring the SMTP service. The goal is to give you a high-level overview of the options that are available. If you need further information about specific options, be sure to check the online help that is installed with IIS. Let's start by walking through the configuration option tabs for SMTP Virtual Servers in the IIS Manager:

- **General** This is where you specify which TCP/IP addresses(s) and ports this SMTP server will respond to. The default port for SMTP traffic is 25, and many applications will expect the server to respond to that port. You can limit the number of connections and enable or disable logging on this tab (see Figure 7-47).

- **Access** The Access tab allows you to specify who can use this SMTP site to send messages (see Figure 7-48). This is an important feature in the real world, since e-mail abuse is so widespread. If you don't secure your SMTP server adequately, a person could use your server to send thousands of unsolicited e-mail messages (affectionately called "spam" by Internet users).

FIGURE 7-47

The General tab
of the properties
of an SMTP site

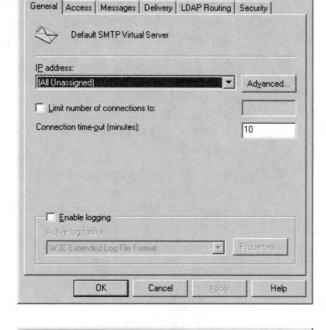

FIGURE 7-48

The Access tab of
the properties of
an SMTP site

Worse yet, many of the recipients of these messages might blame you, since your server information will show up in the headers of their messages. For these reasons, it's important to require authentication (wherever possible), and to prohibit SMTP relaying from unknown hosts.

- **Messages** On this tab, you can specify rules for the messages that are sent through the SMTP service. You can specify a maximum message size, and you can limit the number of recipients per message (both of these options help control Internet traffic). You can also choose to have nondeliverable mail notifications automatically sent via e-mail to an address that you specify.

- **Delivery** The options on the Delivery tab (see Figure 7-49) allow you to specify how many attempts the SMTP service will make before it considers a message as unsendable. You can also specify more advanced options, for example, authentication for other mail servers, and the use of a smart SMTP host (a host to which all messages are automatically forwarded for delivery).

FIGURE 7-49

Setting delivery options for the SMTP service

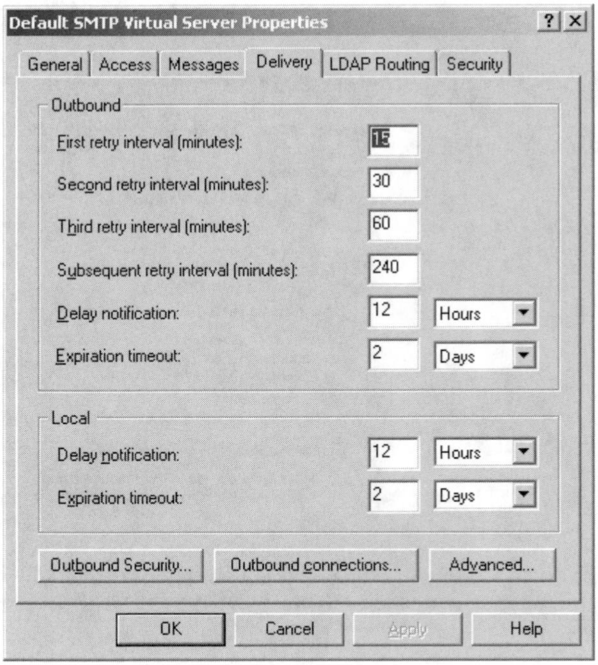

■ **LDAP Routing**   Lightweight Directory Access Protocol (LDAP) routing may be useful for organizations that have deployed directory services (such as the Active Directory) through their organization. LDAP information can be used for routing messages when this option is enabled and the proper information is provided.

■ **Security**   The Security tab specifies which users will have permissions to modify the properties of the SMTP service.

Also, using the IIS Manager, you can use the New SMTP Domain Wizard to add new domains for which the SMTP server will respond. This is useful if your organization wants to set up special e-mail domains. Finally, you can use the Current Sessions object in IIS Manager to view any current SMTP transfers that might be occurring.

SMTP can be a very useful protocol in many different ways. As we've all come to rely on our e-mail for important information, the SMTP service can serve as a relay between other users, applications, and services.

Understanding NNTP Services

The Network News Transport Protocol (NNTP) was designed to allow users to communicate in public and private forums over the Internet. Although it's not nearly as popular as the HTTP protocol, many millions of messages are transferred through NNTP every year. Usenet is by far the largest public set of newsgroups.

In order to access NNTP servers, users must use an NNTP-compatible news client. Outlook Express meets these requirements, and Figure 7-50 shows some of the information that can be obtained through Microsoft's public news servers. You'll notice that there are hundreds of available newsgroups, each of which focuses on a specific topic. Although most forums are unmoderated (and are therefore susceptible to spam and off-topic messages), much useful information can be found on these groups.

on the **Job**

You can access and search through a large portion of all of the messages ever posted to Usenet for free through the Google Groups web site at http://groups.google.com/.

FIGURE 7-50	Accessing Microsoft's public news server through Outlook Express

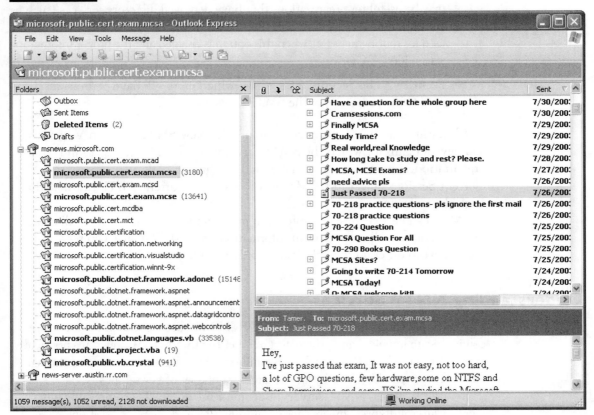

Configuring the NNTP Service

The NNTP virtual server is designed to host and replicate information from other news servers. Let's take a quick look at the available options (details are available in the IIS help file):

- **General** As with the other services, you can specify which IP addresses and port numbers the service will respond on. You can also choose whether you want to enable logging.

- **Access** On the Access tab (see Figure 7-51), you can specify whether users must authenticate before they connect to your server. You can also specify which other computers can access this NNTP server.

FIGURE 7-51

Viewing options
on the Access tab
of the NNTP
server properties

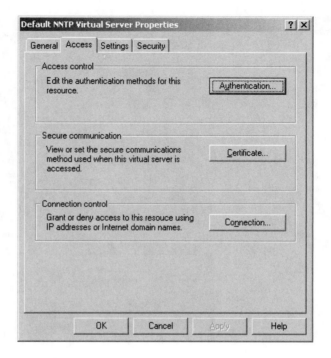

- **Settings** The Settings tab, shown in Figure 7-52, provides some important options that govern how the NNTP server will deal with messages and which operations are allowed. For example, you can limit the maximum size of a post. This is useful because, on many newsgroups (most of which have "binaries" in their names), users transfer gigabytes of files.
- **Security** The Security tab allows you to specify which users have access to change the settings of the NNTP service.

Although it's not as well known as HTTP, the NNTP protocol (with its global Usenet service) provides extremely useful resources for unmoderated information and discussions.

Administering IIS from the Command Line

So far, we've focused on the primary method of implementing and configuring the many services that are provided by IIS. The Internet Information Services administrative tool provides a lot of functionality for working with sites and virtual directories.

The Settings tab
for the NNTP
server

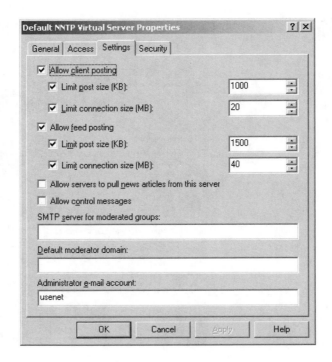

In addition, several VBScript commands are available for administering IIS from the command line. Table 7-5 provides a list of the commands, along with their methods (the operations that they allow). Since VBScript files can be executed directly, they work just like batch files or executables. That is, you can call them either from scripts or directly from the command line.

Figure 7-53 shows the results of running the **iisweb.vbs /query** command on Windows Server 2003 with IIS installed. These tools can also be helpful for documenting the configuration of IIS. For more information about the usage of each of these scripts, see the Help and Support Center.

on the job

One of the best ways to learn how to write scripts and code is to view examples. Fortunately, VBScript files can be viewed and edited in any text editor. If you're trying to write your own VBScript administration scripts, be sure to use the source code of the various IIS administration scripts as a valuable reference!

TABLE 7-5	Script Purpose	Script Name	Supported Methods
Command-Line Scripts for Administering IIS	Web sites	Iisweb.vbs	Create, delete, start, stop, pause, query
	FTP sites	Iisftp.vbs	Create, delete, start, stop, pause
	Web virtual directories	Iisvdir.vbs	Create, delete, query
	FTP virtual directories	Iisftpdr.vbs	Create, delete, query
	Back up/restore IIS configuration	Iisback.vbs	Backup, restore, delete list
	Import/export IIS configuration	Iiscnfg.vbs	Import, export

Monitoring IIS

Since the services provided by IIS can be mission-critical for many organizations, it's important to monitor the performance of your IIS servers. You can use the Windows Server 2003 Performance tool to track and collect performance information related to IIS (for details on measuring and optimizing performance, see Chapter 8). Specifically, you may want to collect some or all information from the objects listed in Table 7-6.

Note that the respective services must be configured and running in order for the performance counters to be available. For more information on using System Monitor and Performance Logs and Alerts to track performance, see Chapter 8.

FIGURE 7-53   Querying a web site from the command line using iisweb.vbs

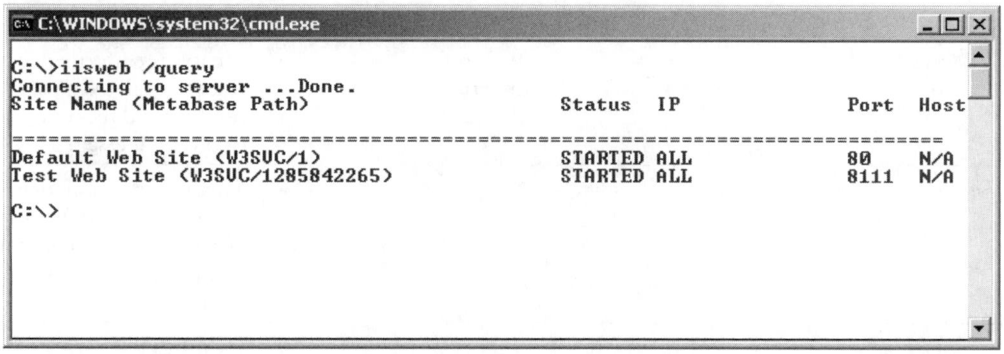

TABLE 7-6 Useful IIS-Related Performance Monitor Counters

Performance Object	Sample Counters	Description
Active Server Pages	—Errors/sec —Transactions/sec	Measures statistics related to the processing of ASP pages.
ASP.NET	—Request execution time —Request wait time —Requests rejected	Measures statistics related to the processing of ASP.NET pages.
ASP.NET Applications	—Anonymous requests —Cache total hit ratio —Requests / sec —Requests timed out	Measures statistics related to specific ASP.NET applications.
FTP Service	—Bytes Total / sec —Current connections	Measures the performance of the FTP service.
Internet Information Services Global	—File Cache Hits % —Total URIs Cached	Measures information related to all services within IIS.
NNTP Commands	—Group Commands —Article Commands —List Commands	Collects information related to the usage of the NNTP service.
NNTP Server	—Bytes Total / sec —Article Sent / sec	Measures performance statistics for the NNTP Server service.
SMTP NTFS Store Driver	—Messages in the queue directory —Messages deleted	Collects information related to SMTP messages stored within the file system.
SMTP Server	—Bytes Sent Total —Total connection errors	Measures performance statistics related to the sending and receiving of SMTP messages.
Web Service	—Bytes Total / sec —Get Requests / sec —Total Not Found errors	Measures performance statistics for the World Wide Web Service. Statistics can be limited per site for detailed analysis.
Web Service Cache	—File Cache Hits —Total Files Cached	Indicates the performance of IIS caching; low values might indicate a lack of memory.

CERTIFICATION SUMMARY

There are many tasks that systems administrators of any network operating system are expected to perform. Fortunately for those working on Windows Server 2003 machines, there are many different ways in which the server can be remotely administered. In this chapter, you have seen several different tools, utilities, and techniques for managing Windows Server 2003. All of these methods can save time and greatly increase the efficiency of server management.

We also covered details related to managing licenses and software updates within a network environment. We looked at licensing issues, and tools for keeping track of licenses. With an increased reliance on the security and reliability of computer systems, organizations are finding that it's extremely important to keep clients, servers, and applications up-to-date with the latest patches. We looked at Automatic Update, Windows Update, and other Windows Server 2003 features that can help you keep your environment up-to-date.

Finally, we examined a powerful and popular feature of Windows Server 2003—Internet Information Server. IIS provides an excellent solution for organizations that want to transfer data using popular Internet protocols. We began by looking at the architecture of IIS, including how TCP/IP addresses and ports map to sites. Then we looked at how virtual directories can provide significant configuration flexibility. Drawing on this, we looked at details related to web, FTP, SMTP, and NNTP services. Finally, we looked at additional methods for monitoring and managing IIS.

All of this information is important to systems administrators in the real world, and it will be worthwhile to learn it as you prepare for Microsoft's certification exams!

✓ TWO-MINUTE DRILL

Understand and Manage Software Licensing

❑ Windows Server 2003 requires the purchasing of Client Access Licenses (CALs) for machines or users that connect to the server.

❑ The Licensing Control Panel applet allows you to specify whether you are using per-server or per-user licensing. If you choose per-server, you must specify how many concurrent connections will be allowed.

❑ The Licensing administrative tool allows systems administrators to keep track of their purchase history for Windows Server 2003 and other Microsoft products.

Manage Windows Operating System Updates

❑ The Automatic Updates feature in Windows Server 2003 can be configured to automatically download critical updates and patches and to install them according to a schedule.

❑ The Windows Update option allows systems administrators to view and download updates that are available to keep the operating system up-to-date.

❑ Software Update Services can be used by systems administrators to set up and distribute selected patches and updates to client computers throughout their environment.

Manage Servers Remotely

❑ By using Remote Assistance, users can create "invitations" that can be sent to other users. These invitations can allow other users to remotely control their computers for troubleshooting or mentoring purposes.

❑ Remote Desktop for Administration allows up to two remote users to connect to a Windows Server 2003 machine for the purpose of remote administration.

❑ Several of the Windows Server 2003 administrative tools allow you to connect to and configure other Windows Server 2003 machines.

❑ The Web Interface for Remote Administration allows you to perform common administrative tasks using a web browser.

Configure and Manage an IIS Web Server

❑ Sites can be configured for one or more IP addresses and are generally used with individual domain names.

❑ Virtual directories are paths that can point to many different local and network locations. They are used to organize content under a site.

❑ IIS configuration is stored in XML files and can be backed up and restored using the Internet Services Manager utility.

❑ IIS also includes support for FTP, SMTP, and NNTP services.

SELF TEST

The following questions will help you measure your understanding of the material presented in this chapter. Read all the choices carefully because there might be more than one correct answer. Choose all correct answers for each question.

Understand and Manage Software Licensing

1. Your Manager has recently decided to deploy Windows Server 2003 in your network environment. You have determined that you want to license the product in per-server mode. Which of the following types of licenses must you purchase? (Choose all that apply.)

   A. A Windows Server 2003 license

   B. A Windows XP Professional license for each user that will access the server

   C. Enough Windows Server 2003 Client Access Licenses to support the maximum number of concurrent server connections you plan to have

   D. One Windows Server 2003 Client Access License for each potential user of the server

   E. None of the above

2. Carlos has moved the system hard disk from a Windows Server 2003 machine to another one with an identical hardware configuration. Which of the following steps will he likely need to take in order to continue to use Windows Server 2003 on the new machine?

   A. Reinstall the operating system using the Windows Server 2003 installation media.

   B. Perform Product Activation.

   C. Load the Recovery Console and type **FIXMBR**.

   D. Use Automated System Recovery on the new machine to recognize the new hardware.

   E. None of the above.

3. Jennifer is in charge of maintaining Microsoft software licenses for her entire organization. Which of the following tools should she use to keep track of Windows Server 2003 licenses in her company?

   A. The Licensing Control Panel applet

   B. The Manage Licenses administrative tool

   C. The LicenceMgr.exe command-line utility

   D. The Licensing administrative tool

   E. None of the above

4. Your organization has experienced significant growth recently, and 20 new users have been added to the Marketing department. A single Windows Server 2003 installation supports the users of this department. Recently, users have reported error messages stating that they cannot access resources on the server during the busiest times of the day. You have purchased additional licenses for the new users. Which of the following can you use to configure the new licenses on your server? (Choose all that apply.)

A. The Licensing Control Panel applet on any Windows Server 2003 machine in the environment

B. The Licensing Control Panel applet on the Marketing Windows Server 2003 machine

C. The Licensing administrative tool on any Windows Server 2003 machine in the environment

D. The Licensing administrative tool on the Marketing Windows Server 2003 machine

Manage Windows Operating System Updates

5. You are a systems administrator for a branch office of a small organization. One of your tasks is to ensure that all of the computers in the environment are kept up-to-date. Currently, however, your branch office has limited Internet connection bandwidth. You would like to download all applicable updates to a local server and then specify which computers should install the updates. You want to avoid having users directly download the updates over the Internet. How can you most easily do this?

A. Configure Automatic Updates to download updates only during the night.

B. Configure Automatic Updates on the client computers to download data from a local server.

C. Configure Windows Update on the client computers to download data from a local server.

D. Use Software Update Services.

E. None of the above.

6. You are a desktop administrator for a large organization. You want to ensure that the computers that you support are automatically updated with the latest patches, as soon as they become available. Which of the following Automatic Updates options will allow you to configure client computers so that no user intervention is required in order to apply updates?

A. Automatically download the updates, and install them on the schedule that I specify.

B. Notify me before downloading any updates and notify me again before installing them on my computer.

C. Download the updates automatically and notify me when they are ready to be installed.

D. Perform an unattended installation of any available updates.

E. None of the above.

7. You are troubleshooting a video-related problem on a client machine. You suspect that the drivers may be out-of-date, and you want to download the latest available drivers. Which of the following options can you use? (Choose all that apply.)

   A. Use options in the Device Manager to find updated drivers.

   B. Use the video card manufacturer's web site to download the latest drivers.

   C. Use the Automatic Updates feature to download the latest drivers.

   D. Use the Windows Update site to download the latest drivers.

Manage Servers Remotely

8. Which of the following remote administration features in Windows Server 2003 allows you to perform administrative tasks using a web browser? (Choose all that apply.)

   A. Remote Assistance

   B. The Windows Server 2003 Administration Tools Pack

   C. Web Interface for Remote Administration

   D. Remote Administration using standard Windows Server 2003 Administrative Tools

   E. Remote Desktop Web Connection

9. You have just set up a new installation of Windows Server 2003 that will function as a domain controller for a new domain. You also want to configure the server to provide file and print services and to work as an intranet web server. Which of the following will allow you to most easily enable these services? (Choose one.)

   A. The Manage Your Server Wizard

   B. The Windows Server 2003 Setup Process

   C. The Add/Remove Programs Control Panel applet

   D. The Configure Your Server Wizard

   E. None of the above

10. Nina has logged on to a Windows Server 2003 computer using the Remote Desktop Client. She is using Terminal Services in Remote Administration Mode. She has started a long-running backup operation under her own user process. She wants to terminate her connection with the server, but she wants the backup operation to continue. Which of the following options in the remote sessions should she choose?

   A. Shut down

   B. Log off

C. Disconnect

D. Pause Connection

E. None of the above

11. Which of the following operations *cannot* be performed using the Web Interface for Remote Administration? (Choose all that apply.)

A. Restarting the server

B. Changing the name of a server

C. Creating a new IIS web site

D. Promoting a domain controller

E. Installing new applications

F. Configuring Performance Monitor

G. Changing the Administrator password

H. Viewing server log files

Configure and Manage an IIS Web Server

12. Based on the requirements of your organization, you are configuring a new installation of IIS. Specifically, you want to be able to support the following URLs:

- www.ACMETools.com
- www.ACMETools.com/Products
- www.ACMETools.com/ContactInfo
- www.ACMESupport.com/Downloads

Which of the following is the simplest configuration that will allow you to support all of these URLs?

A. Four sites

B. Four sites and three virtual directories

C. Two sites and one virtual directory

D. One site and four virtual directories

E. None of the above

13. You are setting up a new IIS site for a web developer at your organization. The web developer has provided you with all of the content for the site, and you have configured a new site for use by the application. When you navigate to the new default URL (www.MyCompany.com/Products),

you receive an error stating that "The Page Cannot Be Found." However, when you enter a URL such as www.MyCompany.com/Products/Product1.html, the page loads properly. Which of the following changes to the properties of the IIS web site would most likely solve the problem?

A.   Change security settings in the Directory Security tab

B.   Change the location of the local path in the Home Directory tab

C.   Change the default content page in the General tab

D.   Change the default content page in the Documents tab

E.   Change the default content page in the Web Site tab

14.   Scott has recently been notified by his organization's development team that a new application will require an installation of IIS running on Windows Server 2003. This installation of IIS must support the Web Distributed Authoring and Versioning feature (WebDAV). Scott begins by installing IIS, and choosing the default options for all settings. Which of the following sections in the IIS Manager tool should Scott access in order to enable support for WebDAV?

A.   Web Service Extensions

B.   Protocols

C.   Features

D.   Web Sites

E.   Default Web Site

F.   Application Pools

G.   Default Application Pool

H.   Properties for the local server

15.   You are the systems administrator that is responsible for managing a software company's public web site. Following a recent product release, you find that a large amount of bandwidth is being consumed by people who are downloading demo versions of your latest product, and response times on the entire site is slow. Management has decided that they would like to restrict bandwidth available for users accessing the /Downloads virtual directory. Bandwidth limits for other portions of the site should not change. Currently, /Downloads is configured as a virtual directory that is part of your company's main IIS web site. On which of the following tabs can you limit the amount of bandwidth that is available for just the /Downloads virtual directory?

A.   HTTP headers

B.   Bandwidth

C.   General

D.   Performance

E.   None of the above

LAB QUESTION

You are a systems administrator for a medium-sized computer hardware manufacturer. Recently, due to the introduction of numerous successful products, your company has grown significantly. In the last several months, you have added 20 new Windows Server 2003 servers, and you now manage a group of ten full-time systems administrators. In the past, you performed the majority of systems administration tasks in the server room. You were able to log on to the appropriate machine and perform your tasks fairly quickly and easily.

However, now that the organization has many more servers and systems administrators, it is becoming difficult for everyone to work in the server room. You have delegated various administrative tasks to specific individuals. For example, one systems administrator is primarily responsible for ensuring that all of your servers are properly backed up. Another is responsible for managing file and print servers. You also have systems administrators that specialize in implementing and managing web services, and others that are responsible for monitoring and optimizing performance. Finally, you have a systems administrator that is primarily responsible for maintaining Active Directory and Group Policy information.

In general, the server environment is running very well. However, you often see that systems administrators have to wait "in line" to directly access specific machines in the server room. Furthermore, you have seen that the door to the server room is frequently left unlocked or open, since administrators are so often entering and leaving the room. You need to come up with a better solution.

Your goals are to provide more efficient means of administration, and to ensure the security of these servers. How can you best meet these goals?

SELF TEST ANSWERS

Understand and Manage Software Licensing

1. ☑ **A and C.** In order to install and run Windows Server 2003, you must first purchase a license for the server product. Then, you must choose which licensing mode you plan to use. Since you have determined that you want to use per-server licensing, you must purchase one CAL for each concurrent connection that you plan to support.

   ☒ **B** is incorrect because there is no requirement to purchase a Windows client operating system. **D** is incorrect because this would be required only if you will be running in per-seat mode.

2. ☑ **B.** After Carlos transfers the hard disk to another machine, it is likely that Windows Server 2003 will detect that a significant hardware change has been detected. He will be prompted to reactive his copy of Windows Server 2003 in order to continue using the product.

   ☒ **A and D** are incorrect because, although these steps are possible, they are not necessary, because the hardware configure of the new system is similar to that of the old one. **C** is incorrect because this step should not be necessary.

3. ☑ **D.** The Licensing administrative tool is designed to be used for tracking the purchase and allocation of licenses across an organization.

   ☒ **A** is incorrect because the Licensing administrative tool applies only to the local server. **B and C** are incorrect because they are not features of Windows Server 2003.

4. ☑ **B.** Based on the information in the question, it is evident that the server is running in per-server licensing mode. Users are reaching the concurrent access limit when accessing resources on the Marketing server. To increase this limit, you must use the Licensing tool on the local Windows Server 2003 machine.

   ☒ **A** is incorrect because the Licensing Control Panel utility is designed to work only on the local machine. **C and D** are incorrect because the Licensing administrative tool cannot be used to change the concurrent connections limit—it is designed only to keep track of license purchases.

Manage Windows Operating System Updates

5. ☑ **D.** Software Update Services is designed to allow systems administrators to download, test, and deploy patches to specific computers. The patches themselves can be hosted on a local server to save bandwidth.

   ☒ **A and B** are incorrect because these configuration options are not available for Automatic Updates functionality. **C** is incorrect because the Windows Update web site is available only on the Internet.

6. ☑ **A.** This option will automatically download updates when they become available and will then install them at the specified time. No user interaction is required.
   ☒ B and C are incorrect because both of those options would require user intervention. D is incorrect because it is not one of the available options for Automatic Updates.

7. ☑ **A, B,** and **D.** All of these options are possibilities for finding and downloading the latest drivers for a video card. It is generally recommended that you attempt to use the Windows Update site first, because this is generally the easiest method to locate, download, and install drivers.
   ☒ C is incorrect because the Automatic Updates feature applies only to critical updates such as security patches. It cannot be used to download and install updated drivers for a video card.

Manage Servers Remotely

8. ☑ **C** and **E.** Both of these features allow you to remotely administer Windows Server 2003 using a web browser.
   ☒ A, B, and D are incorrect because these methods do not allow you to administer Windows Server 2003 using a web browser.

9. ☑ **D.** The purpose of the Configure Your Server Wizard is to allow systems administrators to quickly enable and set up the various roles that the server will perform.
   ☒ A is incorrect because the Manage Your Server Wizard allows you to perform common administrative tasks *after* a server role is enabled. B is incorrect because you cannot choose these types of configuration options during the Setup process. C is incorrect because Add/Remove programs will allow you to install and uninstall features, but it cannot be used to enable the required features.

10. ☑ **C.** When she disconnects from a Remote Administration session, Nina's user process (and any operations that are being performed at the time) will continue to run. When she logs on to the system again, she will be able to view the same processes and applications that were running before the disconnection.
    ☒ A and B are incorrect because these operations would result in the termination of Nina's user process (and the backup operation would be terminated, as well). D is not an available option.

11. ☑ **D, E,** and **F.** These operations cannot be performed using the HTML-based Web Interface for Remote Administration. In general, the web interface is designed to provide access to the most commonly used administrative functions for a server.
    ☒ A, B, C, G, and H are all incorrect because these operations can be performed using the Web Interface for Remote Administration.

Configure and Manage an IIS Web Server

12. ☑ **E.** Based on the requirements, you should configure two separate IIS sites (one for www.ACMETools.com and one for www.ACMESupport.com). You should configure a total of three virtual directories (one for /Products, one for /ContactInfo, and one for /Downloads).

☒ **A, B, C, and D** are incorrect because they do not meet the requirements of supporting all of the URLs. Other configurations that meet these requirements (including those that involve the use of host headers) are possible, but the simplest option is to configure two sites and three virtual directories.

13. ☑ **D.** Since content can be retrieved by specifying a web page, you know that the web site is, in general, configured properly. However, it is likely that the default document that the developer created is not listed in the list of default content pages. This setting can be configured in the Documents tab.

☒ **A** is incorrect because the error message does not mention an issue with security. **B** is incorrect because the local path appears to be correct, since content can be accessed with a complete URL. Finally, **C and E** are incorrect because the default content page setting can be found only on the Documents tab.

14. ☑ **A.** By default, none of the advanced features are enabled (for security reasons). The Web Service Extensions section of the IIS Manager tool shows which features of IIS are enabled.

☒ **B and C** are incorrect because they are not sections in the IIS Manager tool. **D, E, F, G, and H** are possible options in the IIS Manager tool, but they cannot be used to enable or disable features of IIS.

15. ☑ **E.** Bandwidth limitations can be placed only on IIS sites and not on virtual directories. Therefore, none of the options would allow you to change the bandwidth throttling settings for just the /Downloads virtual directory. One option to reach this goal would be to create a new web site to host the content of the /Downloads virtual directory and enable bandwidth throttling on that site.

☒ **A, B, C, and D** are incorrect because none of these configuring settings can be used to effect bandwidth throttling for a virtual directory.

LAB ANSWER

The picture that is painted by this scenario begs for the use Windows Server 2003's remote administration features. Determining that is the easy part! The more challenging issue is in figuring which methods of remote administration would be best. The short answer, however, is likely to be "all of them." Let's look at some specific tasks, and the best tools for those jobs.

You might begin by identifying which types of tasks will require physical access to the server room. Of the job roles mentioned for systems administrations, only one really requires physical access to the server room. That role has to do with backups. This is because, generally, some human intervention will be required to change tapes or manage other types of media. Additionally, if you need to maintain server hardware, repair failed devices, or set up new servers, you will likely need physical access to the server room.

Next, let's look at some of the other specific tasks. Administrators that are responsible for working with the Active Directory will probably want to install the Windows Server 2003 Administration Tools Pack on their client computers. By using familiar utilities, such as the Active Directory Users and Computers administrative tools, they'll be able to connect to remote domain controllers and perform the most common tasks. Similarly, for performance monitoring, authorized users can use a local copy of the Performance administrative tool to monitor remote servers. It can take only a few minutes to create some simple "dashboards" that might show all of the most important information on a single graph. For example, you could easily monitor CPU utilization for five of your busiest servers on a single chart.

Administrators that manage file and print services might find it very easy to use the Web Interface for Remote Administration. Since it requires the use of only a standard web browser, authorized users can perform the most common operations (such as creating or modifying shares) from any computer. More complex operations (such as setting specific NTFS permissions) might require the use of Windows Explorer to remotely access the security settings for remote files and folders. The same tools would be equally viable for web administrators.

Regardless of their job requirements, all users can take advantage of the Remote Desktop for Administration feature (which they can access simply by installing the Remote Desktop Client and setting the appropriate server-side permissions). This feature makes the experience of interacting with the server almost identical to sitting at the console (except for the coldness and noise of the server room, of course). The only issue to keep in mind is that only two remote connections are supported per server, so it's important that systems administrators log off as soon as their tasks are complete.

Finally, by restricting physical access to the server room, you will have greatly helped overall security. A fundamental aspect of keeping your servers (and the data that they contain) safe is to limit the ability of people to directly access them. As you can see, through the use of many of Windows Server 2003's remote management features, you can greatly simplify administrative operations!

8

Performance Monitoring and Optimization

CERTIFICATION OBJECTIVES

I   t seems that computer systems can never be fast enough. Even with the newest technology, many IT environments are finding that users demand more: more bandwidth, increased application performance, and better overall response times. On the server side, as organizations grow and change, new demands are placed on existing resources. For example, that database server that supported only 25 users a few months ago may now support over 100 users, each of which depends on the server to get their job done. Worse yet, the amount of data on the machine may have increased dramatically. With this increase in demand, it might come as no surprise that users are now complaining that performance isn't as good as it used to be. Best of all, it's the job of the systems administrator (which is probably you) to improve performance. Although meeting those demands can be difficult, it's extremely important for the overall health of a well-managed IT environment. That's why performance monitoring and optimization are critical functions.

CERTIFICATION OBJECTIVE 8.01

Overview

In regards to Exam 70-290, Microsoft wants to make sure that you understand how to monitor performance using the built-in tools and features in Windows Server 2003. You can see that clearly in the several different exam objectives that cover performance monitoring. But that's not all! Although the tools themselves are user-friendly and easy to configure, it's most important that you understand *how* and *what* to monitor. In this chapter, you'll look at ways you can use the features in Windows Server 2003 to track and optimize performance of your server computers.

Let's begin by taking a look at the methods that you should use for monitoring and optimizing performance.

Performance Monitoring

Before you look at the specific tools and techniques that are available for monitoring performance in Windows Server 2003, you should start by putting together an organized process for performance monitoring and optimization. By taking the time to properly plan for performance optimization, you will be more likely to achieve the types of results you're looking for. And, you can avoid depending on "luck" (that is, making a few configuration changes at random, and hoping that they make things better). Let's start by looking at information about performance monitoring methodology.

Performance Monitoring Methodology

A vital first step in performance monitoring and optimization is to create a clear process that is to be followed. All too often, we're tempted to simply click a few buttons and see if the overall performance "feels" faster. However, this approach can sometimes lead to less-than-optimal results. And, it would be difficult to figure out whether you made the *best* possible change, and how much that change helped. This is one reason that using an organized methodology is extremely important.

The overall process of performance monitoring usually involves the following steps:

1. Establish a baseline of current performance.
2. Identify the bottleneck(s).
3. Plan for, and implement, changes.
4. Measure the effects of the changes.
5. Repeat the process (if necessary).

With this in mind, take a more detailed look at the steps in the process.

Establishing a Baseline

The first step in any performance optimization strategy is to be able to accurately and consistently measure performance. The insight that you'll gain from monitoring factors such as network utilization will be extremely useful in measuring the effects of any changes. The purpose of a baseline measurement is to create the "before" picture of performance. After you make changes, you'll revisit this information so that you can be sure that the changes had a positive impact.

When you think there may be some performance problems in your environment, you can start by doing some simple monitoring. As you'll see later in this chapter, the process can be quick and easy. Keep the following techniques in mind when you establish a baseline:

■ **Maintain a history of performance** You should always consider the performance optimization cycle as a continuous improvement process. Most IT environments tend to be very dynamic. That is, IT often makes changes and improvements to meet the changing needs of users that it supports. Since many changes can be made over time, it is important to keep track of the changes that have been made and the results you experienced. Having this knowledge documented will prevent the age-old question, "What did I do to solve this problem last time?" And, you can get a better picture of whether performance really has decreased, or if your users are just complaining because they're stressed out about other work-related issues such as deadlines.

■ **Plan for the impacts of monitoring**   In some cases, the simple act of monitoring performance can decrease performance. For example, suppose I chose to view every available performance statistic for my machine and then to save the information to a database. Furthermore, I chose to take samples of these statistics every second. Clearly, this would increase the load on the machine that I was monitoring and could therefore impact performance. Keep this in mind, as it may influence your results (although, if done consistently, the impact should be roughly equal between tests). Also, be sure that you're not significantly slowing down overall production performance through the implementation of monitoring (although, if this is inevitable, it may be worth the inconvenience to your users in the long run).

Isolating Bottlenecks

Once you have started collecting performance information, you're well on your way toward solving the problem. The next step is to take the information that you've collected and attempt to find the slowest steps in the process. A "bottleneck," simply defined, can be thought of as the slowest point in a given process (visualize water flowing out of the narrow neck of a bottle). For example, you might have found out that the network throughput for one of your print servers is far lower than that for other servers in the environment. As a result, you think that upgrading the network adapter or changing some network driver settings might have a positive effect.

When isolating bottlenecks, be sure to keep the following in mind:

■ **Carefully research your suggested changes**   The GUI used in Windows operating systems is designed to be easy to use. Even the most complicated options are often presented in Windows Server 2003 as simple check boxes. Although this can make administration much more efficient, it's too easy to just remove a check mark here or there without fully understanding the effects of what you're doing. You should resist the urge to make random changes, since some changes can cause large decreases in performance or can have an impact on functionality. Instead, take the time to learn about, plan for, and test what you're planning to do.

Once you have figured out what changes might help, it's time to move on to implementing the changes.

Making Changes

Once you've found a potential target for performance optimization, it's time to make changes. For example, you might find that a file server could really benefit from a memory upgrade. Or, you might notice that one of your servers is receiving far more activity than another and that moving resources between servers could improve overall response times. The types of changes that you make will vary widely according to the nature of the problem, but there are several things to keep in mind:

- ■ **Make only one change at a time** When it comes time to implement changes in your configuration, be sure to make only one change at a time (assuming, of course, that this is possible). For example, if you suspect that a server needs a hardware upgrade, you might want to try to upgrade the amount of physical memory first. If that resolves the issue (which you'll know by retesting), you're all set. If not, then you should move on to other changes. One of the problems with making multiple system changes is that, although you may have improved performance overall, it's hard to determine exactly which change had the positive effects. It's also possible, for example, that changing one parameter increased performance greatly while changing another decreased it slightly. While the overall result was an increase in performance, the second performance-reducing option should be identified so that the same mistake is not made again. To reduce chances of misleading results, always try to make only one change at a time.

- ■ **Set up a test environment** Making changes in a production environment can be risky and can have huge negative impacts on the users you support. These problems will likely outweigh any benefits you could receive from making performance tweaks. Therefore, to reduce the risks of negative impacts on users, attempt to make as many changes as possible within a test environment. Sometimes, the test environment might consist of just a single machine that is set up on its own network. When this isn't possible, be sure to make changes during off-peak hours or when the impact of an unexpected problem would be minimal.

Measure the Effects of the Change

Once you have made a change to your system configuration, it's time to figure out what effects the change had (if any). To do this, you should go back to the methods that you used to establish a performance baseline. If the problem that you were trying to solve was high CPU utilization, then you should again measure CPU utilization under similar conditions.

- **Be sure to take consistent measurements**   Consistency in monitoring performance is extremely important. You should strive toward having repeatable and accurate measurements. Controlling variables such as system load at various times during the day can help. For example, let's assume that I wanted to measure the number of transactions that I could simulate on the accounting database server within an hour. The results would be widely different if I ran the test during month-end accounting operations than if I ran the test on a Sunday morning. By running the same tests when the server was under a relatively static amount of load, I would be able to get more accurate and useful measurements.

- **Watch out for unexpected changes**   In some cases, you might have increased the performance of one area of the system (probably the area that you're focusing on), but the change might have caused problems in other areas. The best way to avoid this potential problem is to be sure that you're monitoring all of the important statistics for your machine.

- **Record the effects of your changes**   When you're retesting performance, you might find that a certain setting had no effect on performance. Although your first reaction might be to change the setting back to its original value, be sure to record this information. It might be valuable in the future to know what did and did not work when you tried to solve similar performance issues in the past.

Summary

At first glance, all of the information that you've covered thus far might seem like a bit much. For example, if you have a hunch that your server is running low on memory, wouldn't it be cheaper and quicker to just add more RAM to the server? Well, in some cases, this might be an acceptable solution. However, without having first established a baseline, you may not be able to easily determine whether performance is better, overall. You certainly don't want to wait until your users complain again to come back and upgrade the server once more.

Overall, through the use of proper performance optimization methodology, you should be able to find and move bottlenecks in your environment. With that in mind, let's look at some specific ways in which you can optimize performance in Windows Server 2003.

INSIDE THE EXAM

Performance Optimization: The Never-Ending Cycle

In the past, I've given several presentations on performance monitoring and optimization. Often, during the presentations, I'll ask users, "When is the performance optimization cycle complete?" Responses will range from "Never!" (which may certainly be true in some environments) to "Whenever I run out of time." The point is that you could always work toward optimizing performance further. However, you need to base your efforts on the potential value of your work. It's important to keep this in mind when you're looking at potential performance optimization efforts on the exam. Your goal should be to do what makes the most sense, in terms of the information you've been given.

For example, suppose users in the Marketing department complain that, during busy work hours, it can often take several minutes to open a large spreadsheet that is stored on a network server. You do some research and, sure enough, you find a network-level bottleneck. You also see that the server is running low on memory and that the CPUs on the machine are often pegged at 100 percent for minutes at a time. After you establish a baseline for the current performance, you might start optimizing performance by adding resources (such as RAM or an additional CPU, if the machine supports it) to your file server. When making changes (especially ones that will cost you time and money), it's important to go for the solution that provides the best performance increase. For example, adding a CPU to a server that is low on memory resources may not provide an overall performance increase, since the major bottleneck will be the lack of memory. Then, after making the changes, you should retest performance. You will probably have improved performance, at least a little.

But, the main question is, "Is it enough?" Perhaps the best answer will come from the users that originally complained about performance. If they're happy, should you continue to look at other areas for improvement? For example, perhaps adding or reconfiguring a switch on the network could further increase performance.

You should base your answer to this question on balancing the potential value (that is, the performance improvement that is likely to occur) against the potential effort (how much time and what resources will be required to make the change). If you find the value to be high and the effort to be low, then it's probably worth pursuing (whether your users are complaining or not). On the other hand, if the value is low and the effort is high, you might want to put this task lower on your priority list. Of course, there's a good chance that this "small" performance problem will become a much larger one in the future. But, you can always address the problem when the time is right.

Remember how I began this scenario by talking about the different types of responses I'd get when I asked when performance optimization can be considered "complete"? Well, I do have a personal favorite answer: "Performance optimization is complete when your users stop complaining." It may sound a bit cynical, but I think it's really on-target. Remember, always base your technical solutions on the needs of your environment. If users find performance to be great, so should you!

CERTIFICATION OBJECTIVE 8.02

Monitoring System Performance Using the System Monitor

A major design goal for the entire Windows platform is manageability. Microsoft has gone to great lengths to ensure that the tools that are necessary for maintaining and optimizing systems are included and are easily accessible. In this section, you'll take a look at the important Performance tool and how it can be used to measure and resolve performance issues.

Keep in mind that although Microsoft's terminology related to performance monitoring is not always consistent, I'll be using the term "System Monitor" to collectively refer to all of the functionality available within the Performance administrative tool.

The Windows Server 2003 System Monitor tool is designed to help you monitor, record, and analyze many different aspects of overall system performance. The actual tool can be most easily accessed through the Performance icon in the Administration Tools program group. When you click this icon, an MMC will open up, showing a snap-in that includes the System Monitor tool. The System Monitor itself is an ActiveX control that is designed to provide monitoring functionality. Although it is often used through the MMC as a snap-in, it can also be easily accessed by programmers through the use of Component Object Modeling (COM) technology. For example, you can embed an instance of the System Monitor within a web page (you'll look at an example in an exercise later in this chapter). Or, you could place a System Monitor control within a Microsoft Word document or in a custom Visual C application. This flexibility makes the System Monitor an extremely valuable tool for routine systems monitoring.

The System Monitor has several different modes of operation. For example, it can capture current activity for use in a graphical display. Or, it can perform long-term monitoring of system performance, storing data to a file or to a database for later analysis. Furthermore, you can set up performance-based alerts to notify you when certain performance events occur (for example, if a disk is running low on space, or CPU utilization has remained spiked at 100 percent for a period of time).

If you've had experience troubleshooting performance problems on the Windows platform, there's a good chance that you've used the built-in performance tools before. However, the System Monitor contains many powerful and advanced features that you may not have used. We'll cover those in this section.

Although the focus of this chapter is on ways to measure and optimize performance on Windows Server 2003, most of the same methodology and tools can be used on other Microsoft operating systems (clients and servers). The major difference is that you'll generally find many more performance objects and counters to monitor on Windows Server 2003.

Understanding Objects, Counters, and Instances

The System Monitor provides you with the ability to monitor a very large array of different aspects of system performance. The first step in monitoring performance is to decide what you want to monitor. In Windows Server 2003, the operating system and related services include hundreds of performance statistics that you can track. Of course, you'll generally want to monitor only specific items that you're interested in. To better organize all of the statistics that are available, the System Monitor provides the following levels of groupings:

- **Objects** An *object* within the System Monitor is the highest-level collection of various performance statistics that you can monitor. Objects are based on various areas of system resources. For example, there are objects called "Processor," "Memory," "Network Interface," and "Web Service." The exact list of objects that are available for monitoring will be based on your server's configuration. For example, if you have not installed the WINS service, the "WINS" object will not be available. Or if this machine has SQL Server 2000 installed, several "SQL Server" objects will be available. Each object contains one or more different counters that can be used to specify exactly what you wish to monitor.

- **Counters** *Counters* are the actual parameters that you can measure using the System Monitor. They are specific items that are grouped within objects. For example, within the Memory object, there is a counter for "Pages/sec." This counter measures how often Windows Server 2003 has to read data to/from disk instead of directly from physical memory (RAM).

- **Instances** Some counters will also have *instances*. An instance further identifies which performance parameter the counter is measuring. A simple example is on a server with two CPUs. If you decide that you want to monitor processor usage (the Processor object) and, specifically, that you're interested in utilization (the "%Processor Time" counter), you must still specify which CPU(s) you want to measure. In this example, you would have the choice of monitoring either of the two CPUs or a total value for both (using the "_Total" instance). Similarly, if you have multiple network adapters in your server, you can monitor each one individually.

Again, the exact items that you will be able to monitor will be based on your hardware and software configuration. For example, if you have not installed and configured the Internet Information Server (IIS) service, the options available within the Web Server objects will not be available. Or if you have multiple network adapters or CPUs in the server, you will have the option to view each instance separately or as part of the total value.

To add a counter to the System Monitor display, simply click the Add button on the toolbar (or right-click the System Monitor display and choose Add Counters). You'll see the dialog box shown in Figure 8-1. Note that you can choose to monitor counters from the local machine or from any other machine on your network. In order to monitor statistics from a remote machine, you must have the appropriate network permissions. A very useful feature of the Add Counters dialog box is the Explain button. When you click this button, you'll see a useful (although sometimes very brief) description of the purpose of the performance counter.

| FIGURE 8-1 | Adding a counter to the System Monitor view |

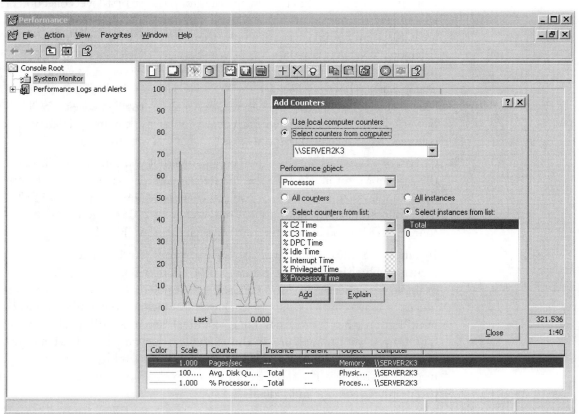

A very useful application of the System Monitor is to set up a central performance monitoring workstation. For example, you could create a single System Monitor graph that includes basic CPU, memory, and network statistics for several of your production servers. Then, IT staff could simply look at a single display to obtain the performance information that they need at any given time. With the System Monitor, you have everything you need to build a basic but powerful monitoring center!

Useful Objects and Counters

Now that you have an idea of how objects, counters, and instances are used to organize the hundreds of performance statistics that you can monitor, let's look at a list of some important statistics.

Have you ever felt intimidated by the sheer number of choices on a menu at a restaurant? Sure, you had some idea of what you wanted, but which of the 17 different types of pasta would be the best? One of the biggest challenges faced by many IT professionals lies in determining what to monitor in order to troubleshoot a specific problem. In the following sections, you'll look at the most important areas that systems administrators will want to monitor. In each section, I'll provide examples of some useful performance counters.

Monitoring server performance is an important aspect of the job of any IT professional. When monitoring Windows Server 2003 performance statistics, be sure that you measure only what's important to you. I'm willing to bet that you're already facing information overload, and the last thing you need is hundreds of pages and e-mails about performance alerts that you really don't care about. The end result will probably be that you'll begin ignoring all of the erroneous or meaningless pages that you receive. For example, if you're monitoring CPU utilization, the fact that one or more CPUs has reached a 100 percent utilization may not be all that important, since this indicates that your machine is being used. However, if the utilization remains at over 100 percent for a long period of time, this might indicate an important event. Choosing what to monitor (and what's important) can often be just as important as the act of monitoring itself.

Monitoring Memory Performance

For modern server machines, memory is a relatively cheap hardware subsystem to upgrade. But, how can you know if your server can benefit from additional memory? Fortunately, there are many different counters that you can monitor to find out how memory is being used on your servers (see Table 8-1).

TABLE 8-1   Useful Memory-Related Performance Statistics

Object	Counter	Purpose
Memory	Available MBytes	Displays the number of megabytes of physical memory (RAM) that is available for use by processes. If the number is low, the machine may benefit from additional RAM.
Memory	Pages/sec	Indicates the number of pages of memory that are being read from or written to disk per second. A high number may indicate that more memory is needed.
Paging File	% Usage	Indicates the amount of the Windows virtual memory file (paging file) that is in use. If this is a large number, the machine may benefit from a RAM upgrade.
Paging File	% Usage Peak	Returns information about the maximum usage of the paging file. If this amount is routinely high, the server may benefit from larger (or more) paging files.

Monitoring Network Performance

The fundamental purpose of most servers is to provide services and resources over the network. Therefore, it's important to monitor statistics related to the proper functioning of network communications to and from your servers. Overall performance in this area will be based on a combination of factors, including the quality and reliability of your network links and the amount of traffic on monitored network segments. Although there are many factors to consider, Table 8-2 lists the most important ones that are related to network performance.

TABLE 8-2   Useful Network-Related Performance Statistics

Object	Counter	Purpose
Network Interface	Bytes Total/ Second	Measures the total number of bytes sent to or received by the specified network interface card.
Network Interface	Output Queue Length	The number of operations that are awaiting network resources. If this value is routinely larger than around 2, it's likely that there is a network-related bottleneck.
Network Interface	Packets Received Errors	Specifies the number of received network packets that contained errors. A high number may indicate that there are problems with the network connection.
Network Interface	% Net Utilization	Specifies the percentage of total network resources being consumed. A high value may indicate network congestion. Note: You must have the Network Monitor agent installed on the local computer in order to view this counter.
Redirector	Bytes Received/sec Bytes Transmitted/sec	Measures the amount of information that is being sent to/from the server. Levels are generally high on file and print servers, whereas other applications may not require as much network interaction.

Monitoring Disk Performance

Applications such as database servers, messaging platforms, file and print services, and web servers can often require a significant amount of disk subsystem resources. And in many cases, the disk subsystem can be a major bottleneck. Windows Server 2003 includes these statistics in two main objects: Logical Disk (which allows monitoring of volumes and partitions) and Physical Disk (which allows monitoring performance of specific hard drives). Many counters are similar between the two objects. Important counters are listed in Table 8-3.

Monitoring Process Performance

Windows Server 2003 is capable of running many different processes on the same server. Complex configurations may have dozens of different processes that are competing for system resources. If you suspect that a particular application or service is causing a server to slow down, you'll probably want to look closely at information from the Process object. One way to get a quick snapshot of overall resource usage per process is to use the Task Manager (which we'll cover later in this chapter). However, the System Monitor can often provide much more detail. Table 8-4 provides a list of counters that are useful when you want to monitor processes.

Note that many different applications (such as SQL Server, Exchange Server, and Internet Information Server) provide their own statistics. In general, if specific statistics are available, it's a good idea to use those to drill down on performance details.

TABLE 8-3   Important Disk Performance Statistics

Object	Counter	Purpose
Physical Disk	Disk Reads/sec Disk Writes/sec	Indicates the amount of disk activity on the server.
Physical Disk	Avg. Disk Queue Length	Indicates the number of disk read or write requests that are waiting in order to access the disk. If this value is high, disk I/O could potentially be a bottleneck.
Physical Disk	% Disk Time	The percentage of time that the selected disk was busy. High values indicate that disk performance may be a bottleneck.
Logical Disk	Current Disk Queue Length	The number of operations that are awaiting disk subsystem resources. When this level is high, it indicates that the disk subsystem is a bottleneck.
Logical Disk	Free Megabytes	Monitors that amount of free space on any logical volume. This statistic is valuable when used with alerts.

TABLE 8-4 Process-Related System Monitor Statistics

Object	Counter	Purpose
Objects	Processes	A count of the number of processes running on the system at a given time.
Process	% Processor Time	Shows the amount of processor time used by a specific process. This statistic is useful for showing which process(es) are placing the most CPU load on the server.
Process	Elapsed Time	Indicates the total amount of time that a specific process has been running.
Process	Page Faults/sec	Indicates how many page faults are occurring for the process. A large number can indicate that a process may need more memory to operate efficiently.
Web Service	Bytes Total/sec	Indicates the number of bytes of data that have been transmitted to or from the local web service. This option is available only if Internet Information Server (IIS) is installed and the web server is running.

Monitoring Server Hardware

Often, when performance is slow, systems administrators tend to suspect the hardware. Perhaps there's too much load on the machine, or it's just not configured to operate efficiently. There are many different aspects of server hardware that can be monitored. You looked at several, including memory, network, and disk resources, already. Table 8-5 lists some hardware-specific statistics that you might want to monitor to ensure that your servers are running smoothly.

TABLE 8-5 Useful Hardware-Related System Monitor Counters and Their Purposes

Object	Counter	Purpose
Server	Bytes Total/sec	Specifies the number of bytes sent by the Server service on the local machine. A high value usually indicates that the server is responsible for fulfilling many outbound data requests (such as a file/print server).
Server	Server Sessions	Indicates the number of users that may be accessing the server.
Processor	% Processor Time	Indicates overall CPU performance. If the value is consistently high, the server may benefit from a CPU upgrade.
Processor	Interrupts/sec	Shows the amount of activity that is generated by system devices (such as the mouse or keyboard). If the value is extremely high, it's possible that a hardware device on the system may have failed.
System	Processor Queue Length	Specifies the number of threads that are awaiting CPU time. A high number might indicate that a reduction in available CPU resources is creating a potential bottleneck.
System	Processes	Indicates the number of processes currently running on the system.

SCENARIO & SOLUTION

You suspect that a particular process or application is using the majority of CPU time. You want to verify this.	You can track performance statistics for a single process using the counters in the Process object. This should help isolate the cause of the excessive CPU usage.
Other systems administrators have suggested that the performance of a file server would increase with the addition of more physical memory. You want to verify this before you purchase and install additional memory.	The counters that are included within the Memory object (specifically "pages/sec") can give you a good idea of whether the server would really benefit from a memory upgrade.
On a particular database server, you suspect that performance problems are being caused by the disk subsystem. You want to confirm this.	By monitoring various counters that are included in the Logical Disk and Physical Disk objects, you can get a good idea of how the disk subsystem is performing.
You want to determine whether CPU spikes are correlated with periods of high activity of the web service.	Monitor counters of both the Processor object and the Web Service object to find correlations between web service activity and CPU spikes.

System Monitor Views

Now that you know *what* to monitor, let's look at how this can be done. When you're monitoring performance statistics, you may have different goals. In order to allow you to view similar information in different ways, the System Monitor can provide output in multiple views. The different views that are available include

- **Graph view** The Graph view is the default display that is presented when you first access the Windows Server 2003 System Monitor. The chart displays values using the vertical axis and time using the horizontal axis. The vertical axis is actually a logarithmic scale that can be adjusted to suit the values that you're monitoring. The Graph view is useful for visually seeing the changes in values that you're interested in over a relatively brief time period. Each of the points that is plotted on the graph is based on an average value calculated during the sample interval for the measurement being made. For example, you may notice overall CPU utilization starting at a low value at the beginning of the chart and then becoming much higher during later measurements. This would indicate that the server has become busier. Figure 8-2 provides an example of the Graph view.

FIGURE 8-2   Viewing information in the System Monitor Graph view

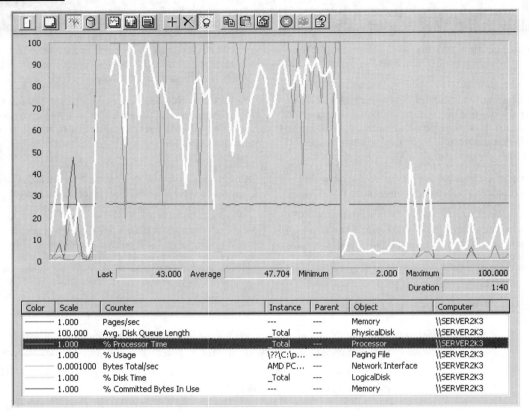

Color	Scale	Counter	Instance	Parent	Object	Computer	
	1.000	Pages/sec	---	---	Memory	\\SERVER2K3	
	100.000	Avg. Disk Queue Length	_Total	---	PhysicalDisk	\\SERVER2K3	
	1.000	% Processor Time	_Total	---	Processor	\\SERVER2K3	
	1.000	% Usage	\??\C:\p...	---	Paging File	\\SERVER2K3	
	0.0001000	Bytes Total/sec	AMD PC...	---	Network Interface	\\SERVER2K3	
	1.000	% Disk Time	_Total	---	LogicalDisk	\\SERVER2K3	
	1.000	% Committed Bytes In Use	---	---	Memory	\\SERVER2K3	

■ **Histogram view**   The Histogram view shows performance statistics and information using a set of relative bar charts. The histogram is useful for viewing a snapshot of the latest value for a given counter. For example, I might choose to monitor the amount of CPU time that was being used during the last collection interval. The length of each of the bars in the display would give me a visual representation of each value. It would also allow me to visually compare each measurement with the others. You can also set the histogram to display an average measurement as well as minimum and maximum thresholds. Figure 8-3 shows an example of data being displayed in the Histogram view.

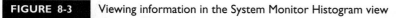

FIGURE 8-3   Viewing information in the System Monitor Histogram view

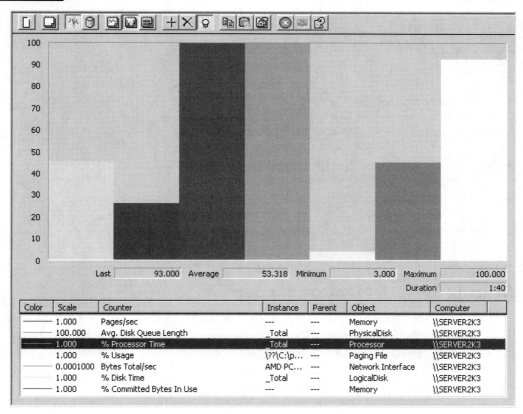

- **Report view**   Like the Histogram view, the Report view shows performance statistics based on the latest measurement, or displays an average measurement as well as minimum and maximum thresholds. It is most useful for determining exact values, since it provides information in numeric terms, unlike the Chart and Histogram views, which provide information graphically. Figure 8-4 provides an example of the type of information you'll see in the Report view.

As you can see, the different System Monitor output methods can be used to view information in the way that you want it. Although the System Monitor views are an excellent tool for creating a window into the immediate performance of your servers, you might also want to collect data over longer intervals and save it for later analysis. Let's look at how you can do that, next.

FIGURE 8-4   Viewing information in the System Monitor Report view

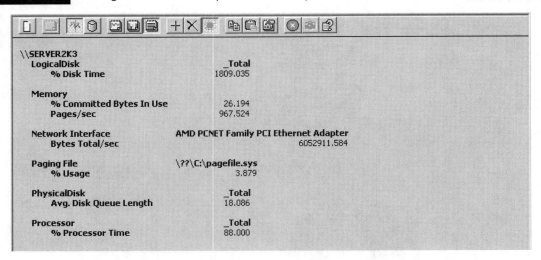

Configuring System Monitor Properties

In addition to the view options that are available, the System Monitor provides you with a large number of options for customizing the collection and display of data in accordance with your needs. To access these settings, you can simply right-click the System Monitor display and choose Properties. Let's take a look at the settings available on the various tabs of the interface:

- **General**   This tab, shown in Figure 8-5, is used for specifying the System Monitor view that you want to use to display data. You can also choose which types of information you want to display (for example, a legend describing the values that are being collected). There is also a section that allows you to choose what type of numerical data you want to use for the report and histogram views. An important setting that's available on this tab is the option to specify how often samples should be collected. The default setting is "every 1 second." This setting is useful for monitoring immediate system performance, but it allows you to view only a few minutes of data on the graph view. If you want to measure performance over a larger period of time, you can increase this value.

FIGURE 8-5

Viewing the
General settings
in the System
Monitor

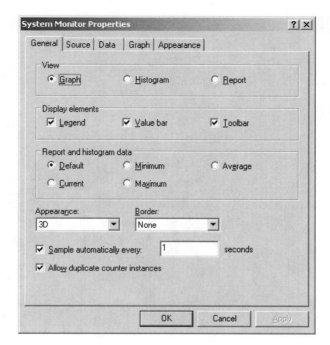

■ **Source** The default source for information that is displayed in the System
Monitor is "Current Activity." This means that the data that you're seeing
in the various graph views is based on the latest statistics collected by the
operating system. However, you can also choose to view information that has
been stored to a file or database by the System Monitor (see Figure 8-6). If you
choose either Log Files or Database, you can also specify the range of time that
will be displayed in the System Monitor. These options are extremely useful for
analyzing performance statistics that have been collected over a period of time.

■ **Data** The Data tab (shown in Figure 8-7) provides you with a list of the
current performance counters that have been added to the System Monitor
display. In addition to adding and removing counters, you can also change
the color, width, and style appearance properties. The Scale option allows
you to choose the multiplier for the Y-axis scale. For example, if you are
measuring the Memory | Pages/sec object, you might want to change the
scale to range from "0 to 10" or from "0 to 100," depending on the actual
statistics that you're monitoring.

FIGURE 8-6

Viewing the
Source settings
in the System
Monitor

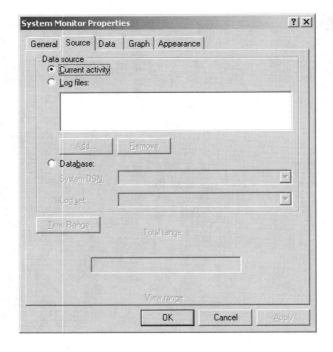

FIGURE 8-7

Viewing the Data
settings in the
System Monitor

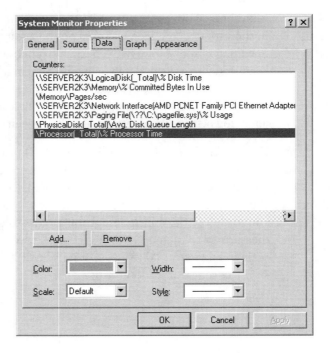

- **Graph** In the Graph tab, you can specify some additional options for output that apply only to the Graph view in the System Monitor. For example, you can provide a title for the System Monitor graph, a label for the vertical axis, and grid lines.

- **Appearance** The Appearance tab allows you to further fine-tune the output of the System Monitor. Specifically, you can change the Color and Font settings for the output. These settings can be useful for improving the readability of graphs, especially when you're collecting and analyzing a large quantity of information.

As you have seen, several options are available for modifying the output of the System Monitor display. Now that you have a good overview of the types of options available in the System Monitor, let's move on to actually using the System Monitor to collect and analyze useful information.

System Monitor and Security

In most environments, you wouldn't want just anyone monitoring critical server functions. Therefore, in order to be able to monitor performance objects, you must have the appropriate permissions. To simplify the administration of performance monitoring security, Windows Server 2003 includes two special groups for this purpose. They are

- **Performance Monitor Users** Members of this group have permissions to monitor performance statistics on the local computer. This means that they can launch the Performance tool locally to view statistics, or that they can collect performance statistics for this computer from another machine on the network.

- **Performance Log Users** Members of this group can configure and execute the tasks necessary to implement performance counters, logs, and alerts (all three of which we'll cover later in this chapter).

By managing the membership of these groups, you can avoid having to give people Administrator privileges just so that they can monitor performance on your machines.

Using System Monitor

In this section, you'll use the features of the System Monitor to set up a realistic collection of objects, counters, and instances that you want to monitor. You can use this process as a real-world template when you need to monitor or troubleshoot your own servers. Exercise 8-1 walks you through the necessary steps.

You will notice that since the System Monitor is an ActiveX control, it operates a little differently from other MMC snap-ins. For example, the only way to access help for the System Monitor is to use the Help icon (the yellow question mark symbol) on the System Monitor toolbar.

EXERCISE 8-1

CertCam & MasterSim 8-1 ON THE CD

Monitoring CPU, Memory, and Network Performance Using the System Monitor

1. Open the Performance tool by choosing Start | Programs | Administrative Tools | Performance. You'll see the System Monitor view, including the three default counters. Note that the system is already monitoring performance statistics for these three counters.

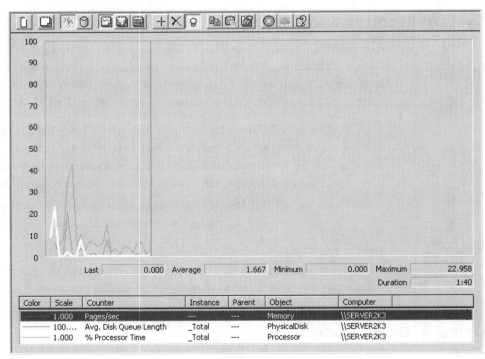

2. Click the Add button in the toolbar (or right-click the System Monitor display and select Add Counters. For the purpose of this exercise, you'll monitor only counters on the local computer, so select the first option, Use Local Computer Counters.

3. Next, you'll add some additional counters to the System Monitor display. Add the following counters:

Object	Counter	Instance
Logical Disk	% Disk Time	_Total
Logical Disk	% Free Space	_Total
Memory	Available Mbytes	
Network Interface	Bytes Total/sec	Choose an active network adapter for your system
Objects	Processes	
Paging File	% Usage	_Total
Server	Bytes Total/sec	
Server	Files Open	
Server	Logon Total	

When you are finished, click Close to return to the Graph view.

If you're performing this exercise on a busy machine, it's likely that you'll see lots of useful statistics already. If not, you might want to try generating some "load" on the machine. For example, try copying a large file over the network to see which statistics are affected. Or, launch Internet Explorer and browse to some web sites. This will help you see how that machine's various subsystems (such as CPU, memory, and networking) work under different types of load.

4. Notice that the system is currently collecting and displaying statistics for the counters that you selected. To view the information in the Histogram view,

click the Histogram button in the toolbar. Note that the latest performance statistics are shown in a bar format.

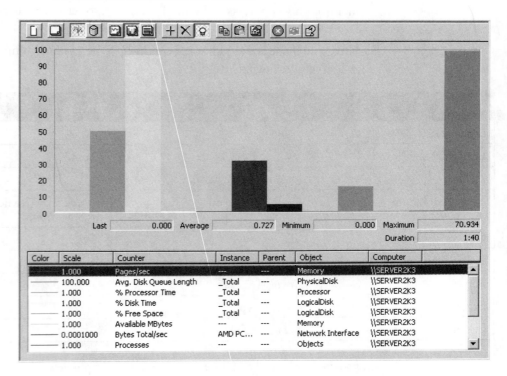

5. To view the information in Report view, click the Report button in the toolbar. Note that the information is now displayed as numerical statistics. When you're finished, click the Graph button to return to the default view.

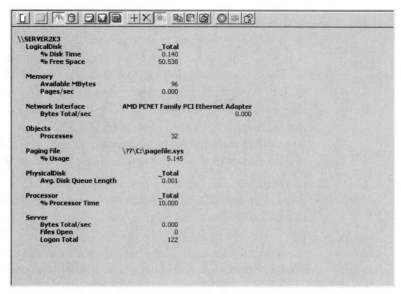

6. Assuming you're particularly interested in the "% Processor Time"
   counter, make the line easier to see. To do this, right-click Graph in the
   System Monitor and choose Properties. Click the Data tab and highlight the
   "\Processor(_Total)\%Processor Time" item. Then, select a wider line from the
   Width drop-down box. You can also change the color and style of the line to
   something more aesthetically pleasing. When finished, click OK. Notice that the
   line for this specific counter is now wider than the rest (making it easier to see).

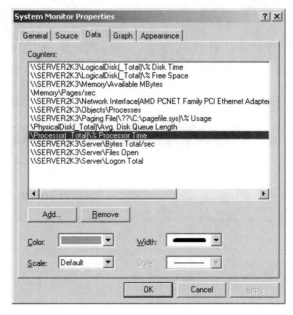

7. In this step, you're going to save the list of counters and objects (as well as other settings) that you've specified for the System Monitor. To do this, right-click the main System Monitor display and choose Save As. Name the file **Basic Server Monitoring.htm** and save the file to a location on your local file system, making a note of the location (you'll be using this file in later exercises). Notice that the default file extension for the file is .htm (an HTML file). This is because the actual settings are stored in an HTML format that includes ActiveX component parameters (you can view the file in Notepad or in your web browser to see the exact details).

8. In your file system, find the System Monitor file that you created and double-click it. The file should open in your default browser. Note that the display shows you the data that was collected thus far in a System Monitor control on the page. To view live data, simply click the Freeze Display button (the symbol that looks like a red sign with an X in it). This will unfreeze the display and will start displaying live captured information.

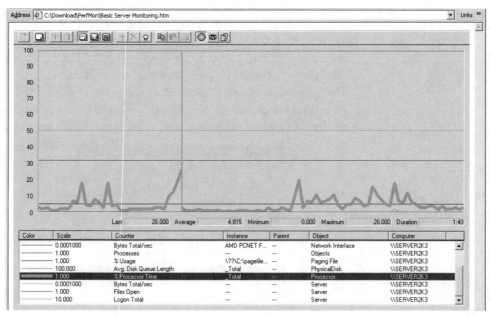

9. When finished, close your browser and the Performance console.

There's almost always some performance impact when you're monitoring a system. In many cases, however, the performance impact will be a justifiable "investment," since the information that you collect can ultimately be used to improve performance. When working with the System Monitor, there may appear to be gaps in the collection of statistics on very busy servers. For example, in the Graph view, you might see gaps in the lines when sufficient system resources for data collection were unavailable. If this is happening frequently, be sure to adjust the amount and frequency of performance data collection accordingly. Another helpful technique is to monitor the server remotely (using an instance of the System Monitor running on a workstation, for example).

CERTIFICATION OBJECTIVE 8.03

Tracking Performance Using Performance Logs and Alerts

In addition to viewing System Monitor information graphically, you also have the option of logging data to a file or database. This option is very useful for logging performance data over extended periods of time. For example, if you suspect that some of your servers are having CPU performance issues during certain times of the week, you can track CPU performance every 15 minutes for the next several weeks. This information could be logged to a file or to a database. Then, when you feel that you've collected enough information, you can load the data back into the System Monitor (or into a different tool that can read this information) for analysis.

To better collect data from machines over a long period of time (and to collect information from remote machines), the Performance Logs and Alerts functionality runs as a service. This means that you can start a performance log and then log off your computer, and the data collection will still continue. And, as long as the account under which the Performance Logs and Alerts service is running has the necessary permissions, you can record performance statistics from remote machines.

Now that you have a good idea of the purpose and function of Performance Logs and Alerts, let's drill down into the three available options.

on the **! job**

When you are working on deciding what to monitor, try to make reasonable settings for the amount of data that you're collecting and the sample frequency. For example, if you want to measure the number of open files on a server, it might be sufficient to measure this value every five minutes (instead of every few seconds). Or if you're interested in memory statistics, it might make sense to start with just a few of the counters within the Memory object (instead of all of the counters and instances). This will help minimize the impact of performance monitoring, but you'll still be able to get enough useful information to make decisions.

Counter Logs

Counter logs are designed for recording performance statistics over extended periods of time. When you create a counter log, you can choose to use an existing, saved collection of counters (which you create by clicking Save As in the System Monitor dialog box), or you can create a new set of counters from scratch (as shown in Figure 8-8). Note that, unlike in the basic System Monitor display, you can choose to monitor entire objects (although you still have the option to monitor individual counters). Next, you can choose how often the data will be sampled.

on the **! job**

The default sampling setting is every 15 seconds for counter logs (by contrast with the System Monitor default, which is every one second). This longer sampling interval is more appropriate for longer-term monitoring, since it results in the production of less data. Be sure that you have adequate storage space when you choose to implement counter logs for a large number of objects or for a short sampling interval.

Also on the General tab is an option for specifying the user under which the performance collection will be performed. This is particularly important if you plan to remotely monitor several machines, since the account that you specify must have permissions to monitor all of the machines specified.

Figure 8-9 shows the Log Files tab for the counter log settings. On this tab, you can specify where the data that is collected will be stored. Options include the following:

- **Text File (Comma Delimited)** Saves the results to a text file. The values are separated by commas. This format is useful for analyzing in Microsoft Excel or through other applications that can read standard text files.

- **Text File (Tab Delimited)** Similar to the comma-delimited text file, except a tab character is used to separate values, instead of a comma.

FIGURE 8-8

Creating a new
counter log

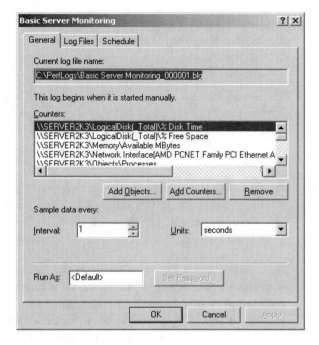

FIGURE 8-9

Viewing the Log
Files settings for a
counter log

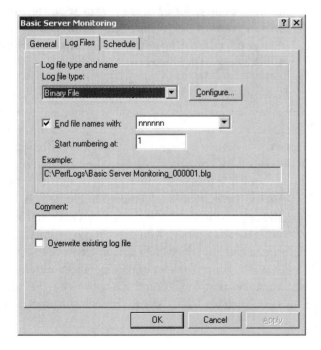

- **Binary File** Stores data to a binary file format that can be read by the System Monitor. This option can result in smaller file sizes and allows you to use the file as a source for performance information with the System Monitor or other compatible tools.

- **Binary Circular File** Specifies that binary files should be used in a circular fashion. For example, a binary file can be configured to be up to 10MB in size. Once the file has been filled, portions of it may be overwritten to accommodate additional data storage. Like standard binary files, binary circular files can also be viewed through the System Monitor.

- **SQL Database** This option allows you to store information to a standard ODBC-compliant data source (such as a Microsoft Access database or a SQL Server database). The data can then be read and reported on using standard database tools, or it can be read into the System Monitor for analysis.

on the **job**

Remember when I mentioned that the act of monitoring performance can sometimes decrease performance on a machine? This might be particularly true when you're logging to a database server (especially when the sample interval is small). Remember that relational database servers are designed to provide a lot of functionality, such as concurrency, security, and manageability. All of these features cause overhead that may translate into decreased performance in some cases. It's always a good practice to test your monitoring setup on a nonproduction machine before you start monitoring critical servers.

Based on the type of logging that you choose, you can click the Configure button to specify any additional details. For example, if you choose to store data in a SQL database, you'll need to specify connection information for the database. You also have the option of configuring a filename suffix for the files (or database tables) that will be created. Later, you can load the captured information (whether it's stored in one or multiple files) into the System Monitor for further reporting and analysis.

Finally, the Schedule tab (shown in Figure 8-10) allows you to specify when the logging of performance information will start and stop. You can choose to specify times for these events, or you can choose to start and stop the collection of information manually, using the Performance tool.

That may seem like a lot of configuration options for running a counter log, but I'm willing to bet that you'll find these options easy enough to use once you've had some practice! Exercise 8-2 walks you through the process of creating a new counter log.

FIGURE 8-10

Viewing the
Schedule settings
for a counter log

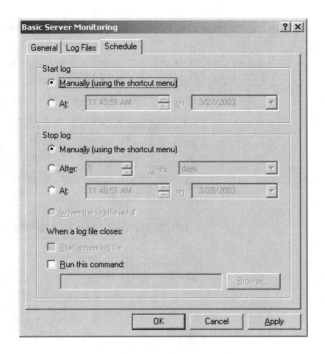

EXERCISE 8-2

CertCam & MasterSim 8-2 ON THE CD

Collecting and Analyzing Counter Log Data

This exercise assumes that you have completed Exercise 8-1, as you'll be using the
Basic Server Monitoring.htm file that you created.

1. Open the Performance tool by choosing Start | Programs | Administrative
   Tools | Performance.

2. Expand the Performance Logs and Alerts tool. Right-click Counter Logs and
   select New Settings From. In this exercise, you're going to use an existing set
   of counters (saved from a System Monitor view). In the Open dialog box,
   find the Basic Server Monitoring.htm file that you created previously. You'll
   receive a warning telling you that some settings may not be imported into the
   counter log. Click OK to continue.

3. In the New Log Settings dialog box, type **Basic Server Monitor** for the name and click OK. Note that the General tab of the Counter Log properties shows the list of objects, counters, and instances that you created previously. Using this interface, you could add or remove counters (or entire objects). Change the option to sample data every 5 seconds.

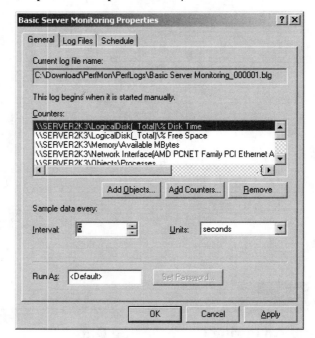

4. Once you've decided what to monitor (and how often to measure these statistics), you need to specify where the actual logged data will be stored. To do this, select the Log Files tab. In this exercise, you're going to stay with the default option: to log to a binary file.

5. To specify the location to which the log files will be stored, click Configure. Provide a path to a folder on your system (if it doesn't yet exist, a dialog box will prompt you to create it). Specify a limit of 10MB for the size of the file. This will tell the System Monitor to stop logging data to the file when this threshold is reached. Click OK.

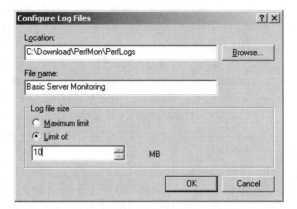

6. Leave the other settings in the Log Files dialog at their default. Finally, it's time to schedule the job. For the sake of this exercise, specify that you want to start and stop the log capture manually. Click OK to save the definition of the counter log.

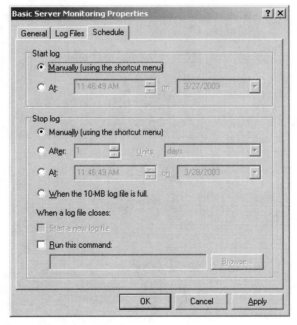

7. Now that you've defined the Basic Server Monitoring counter log, click it in the Performance Logs and Alerts interface and then click the Start button in the toolbar. This will cause the counter log to start collecting data (as indicated by the fact that the icon is now green). Since you set up the counter log to collect data every 5 seconds, wait at least two minutes before continuing to the next step.

8. To stop the collection of data, click the Stop button in the Performance Logs and Alerts tool.

9. Now that you've collected some data, it's time to analyze it. To do this, select the System Monitor item in the Performance tool. You'll see that the System Monitor is collecting live data. Since you want to read data from the log file that you created, right-click the graph, choose Properties, and then click the Source tab (alternatively, you can click the View Log Data icon in the toolbar).

10. In the Source tab, choose Log Files For The Data Source setting. Click Add and then find the file to which the logged data was saved (it will be in the location that you specified in step 5). Note that a new feature in Windows Server 2003 allows you to load multiple files for analysis. To view the time range that the log file covers, click Time Range. Notice that it includes the range of date/time values that are stored in the log file. You could further restrict which data is shown (to, for example, zoom in to activity at a certain time). However, for the sake of this exercise, you'll view all of the collected samples. Click OK to continue.

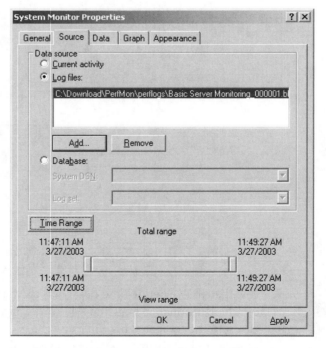

11. Notice that the System Monitor is no longer collecting new data. Instead, it's displaying the information that was stored in the counter log file. You can

click the Add or Remove button just as you would with a "live" trace, but you can choose to add a counter only if it was recorded in this data file.

12. When you're finished, close the Performance tool.

Trace Logs

Trace logs work in a way similar to counter logs, but they're used to record activity corresponding to events. Whereas counter logs will periodically poll and record system statistics, trace logs can record certain types of events as they occur. By default, several different providers are included with Windows Server 2003. As shown in Figure 8-11, the list includes the following:

- Process creations/deletions
- Thread creations/deletions
- Disk input/output
- Network TCP/IP
- Page faults
- File details

The General tab of the Trace Logs properties, showing the available system providers

As is the case with all types of performance monitoring, you should be sure that the information that you collect will be reasonably helpful to you. This is especially true for monitoring the "page faults" and "file details" items in a trace log. As you will be warned, collecting this type of information could result in a huge log file.

Third-party software developers can add additional providers to allow systems administrators to collect application-specific information. For example, Microsoft has a provider that is available for monitoring events related to the Active Directory. Microsoft products such as SQL Server and Exchange Server, and third-party vendors, such as Sybase and Oracle, provide their own application-specific counters, as well.

In the Log Files tab (see Figure 8-12), you can specify options for how the information will be stored. You have only two options: Sequential Trace File (which creates as many new trace files as needed) and Circular Trace File (which reuses trace files once they have been filled). The other options are similar to those seen for counter logs.

The Schedule tab allows you to specify when and how you want the trace file data collection to start and stop. Finally, the Advanced tab (shown in Figure 8-13) allows you to fine-tune the details related to how performance statistics will be collected.

FIGURE 8-12

The Log Files
settings for
trace logs

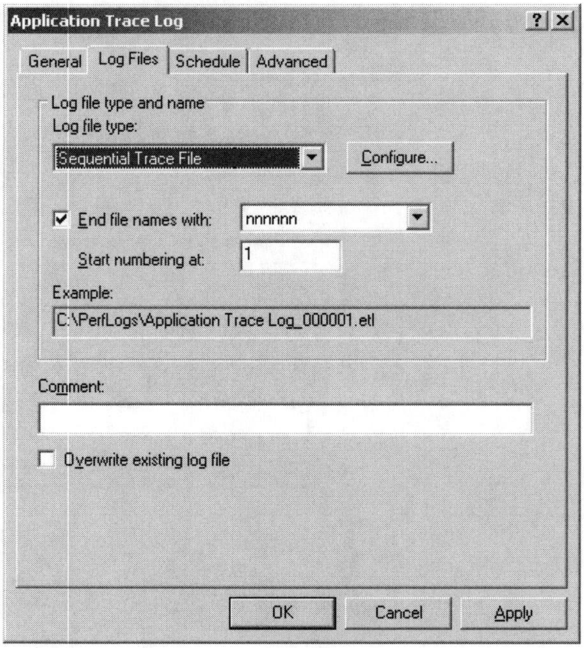

Application Trace Log	? ✕
General **Log Files** Schedule Advanced	

Log file type and name
Log file type:

Sequential Trace File ▼   Configure...

☑ End file names with: nnnnnn ▼

Start numbering at: 1

Example:
C:\PerfLogs\Application Trace Log_000001.etl

Comment:

☐ Overwrite existing log file

OK   Cancel   Apply

FIGURE 8-13

Viewing the
Advanced
properties
of a trace file

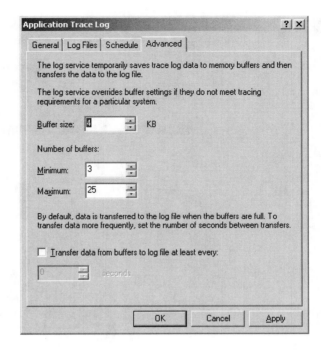

The default buffer settings should be fine for most types of data collection, but you may want to change them in case you are measuring activity such as application or system crashes.

Alerts

Although the basic System Monitor views provide a lot of information, they don't interrupt you when something interesting happens. You would have to get a coworker (ideally one that you don't like very much) to watch a monitor and tap you on the shoulder whenever certain events occurred, in order to get this functionality. Fortunately (for you, and for your coworkers), the alerts functionality can do this for you automatically. Alerts can be configured to trigger events whenever certain performance thresholds are reached. For example, if CPU usage exceeds 75 percent for a period of 30 seconds, you might want to be notified. Alerts can also take specific actions whenever an event is triggered.

Figure 8-14 shows the General tab of an alert. Note that you can specify which counters you want to configure, and you can specify the thresholds for these objects. Thresholds are configured as limits, and you can specify that an alert will fire when a value is either over or under a number that you specify.

FIGURE 8-14

Viewing General
properties for
an alert

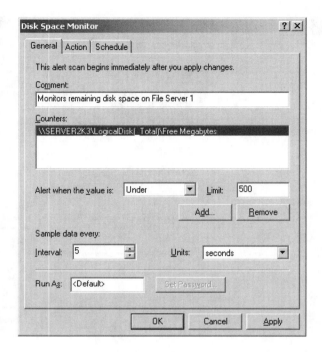

Next, you can decide what happens when an alert is fired. To do this, click the Action tab. As shown in Figure 8-15, you can choose one or more of the following options:

- **Log an entry in the application event log**   This option will write a new event to the application event log whenever the alert occurs. To view the log entries, you can simply access the Event Viewer application.

- **Send a network message to**   When the alert fires, a network message (using a broadcast) will be sent to a specific computer. If the Alerter service is running on both computers, the user on that machine will see a pop-up message indicating the details about the alert. Although you want to use this option judiciously (no one wants to receive hundreds of pop-up boxes while they're working!), it can be very useful in some monitoring environments.

- **Start performance data log**   When an alert is fired, you might want to trigger the collection of performance data. For example, I might want to start recording the number of users that are connected to my server when the CPU utilization exceeds 75 percent. This option allows you to do just that, once you have defined an appropriate counter log that specifies what information you want to record.

- **Run this program**   You can choose to run a program (such as a batch file or a script) in response to an alert. For example, you could write a batch file that clears out files in temporary directories whenever disk space is running low.

FIGURE 8-15

FIGURE 8-15

Viewing Alert
Action options

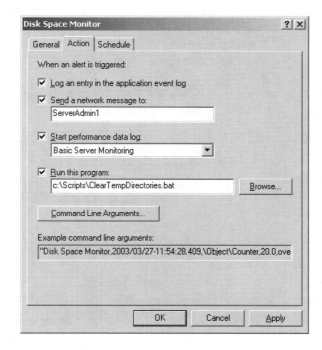

Finally, the Schedule tab allows you to specify when the alert will be started. The process for creating and enabling an alert is quite simple, as you'll see when you walk through Exercise 8-3.

EXERCISE 8-3

Creating a CPU Performance Alert Using the System Monitor

1. Open the Performance tool by choosing Start | Programs | Administrative Tools | Performance.

2. Expand the Performance Logs and Alerts tool. Right-click Alerts and select New Alert Settings. Name the alert **CPU Spikes** and click OK.

3. In the General tab of the interface, enter the following comment: **This alert is fired when CPU utilization is high**. Click Add and add the "_Total" instance of the (Processor | % Processor time counter). Choose to alert when

the value is over 25. Change the interval to sample data every 1 second. Note that you're setting that value very low for the purpose of this exercise (to make sure that the alert fires).

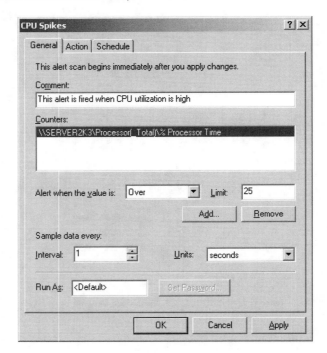

4. To specify what should happen when the alert fires, click the Action tab. Leave the default option checked to ensure that an item is written to the application event log.

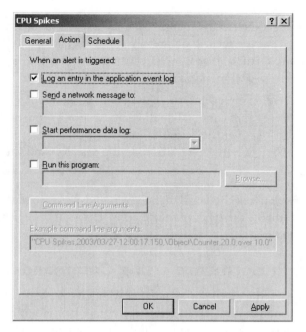

5. Click the Schedule tab. In this exercise, you'll choose to start and stop the alert manually (this is especially important because the alert threshold is set so low). Click OK to complete the definition of the alert.

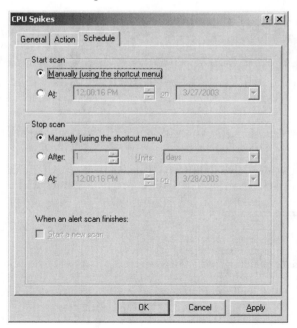

6. Notice that the alert is started automatically. Now, perform some actions on the local computer that should cause the CPU to spike for a brief period of time (for example, open up a few browser instances, or open a large Word document). This will ensure that the alert is fired.

7. To view information about the alert, you can use the Event Viewer application. The illustration shows some information about the event. We'll cover the details of working with the Event Viewer later in this chapter. When you're finished, stop the alert and then close the Performance tool.

Each of the Performance Logs and Alerts modes has its specific advantages in terms of the types of information you want to collect, and how you want the information to be used.

Monitoring Performance Using Command-Line Utilities

As is the case in other areas of Windows Server 2003, Microsoft has included several command-line utilities that can be used for monitoring performance. Although the much more user-friendly GUI of the System Monitor is great for ad-hoc monitoring, these tools make it easy to script the collection of statistics. For example, you can have a batch file run when an alert fires. This batch file might perform several custom

SCENARIO & SOLUTION

You want to view real-time information about CPU performance on an eight-CPU server.	Use the Graph view in the System Monitor, and various counters and instances from the Processor object.
You want to view exact numerical statistics for several performance monitor counters.	Use the Report view of the System Monitor. This will provide information in statistical format.
You are experiencing rare, intermittent periods in which your server takes a very long time to respond to network requests. You want to track CPU and memory performance over time to troubleshoot this issue.	Create and start a new counter log that monitors the statistics of interest, and store the results to a file. Periodically, analyze the files using the System Monitor, and look for correlations between the problem and CPU/memory usage.
An application developer is concerned that a service that he wrote might be taking up significant server resources during periods of high load. You want to find out how often the application process exceeds 80 percent CPU utilization.	Configure a new performance-based alert, and set a threshold for the % CPU Utilization value for the process. Every time the process uses more than 80 percent of CPU time, an event will be written to the System event log.

operations that collect and analyze performance information using the performance-related command-line utilities.

In this section, you'll look at four command-line utilities that are related to performance monitoring. In order to run any of these commands, simply open a command prompt and type the name of the command. For information about the exact syntax for a command, just type the name of the command followed by /?. Keep all of these utilities in mind when you want to work with captured performance data, or you want to automate the collection of performance information.

Using Logman to Collect Performance Information

The logman utility can be used to perform the same functions that are available in the Performance Logs and Alerts GUI utility. For example, you can use the following command to start the collection of CPU performance data:

```
logman create counter perf_log -c "\Processor(_Total)\%
Processor Time"
```

This will create a new performance log that collects information for the "% Processor Time" command. Note that you must know the full name of any counters that you wish to monitor. In case you don't have them all memorized (and who does?), you can use the typeperf utility to get their names. Let's cover that next.

on the job

The performance-monitoring command-line utilities can take many different arguments. If you need to use a lot of them, this could lead to a very long command line that is hard to read and troubleshoot. Fortunately, most of the command-line utilities that are included with Windows Server 2003 allow you to read the switches from a separate configuration file. This is very helpful when you're initially writing the command, and for maintainability of the configuration (since you can troubleshoot each line separately). For more information on using separate configuration files, see the respective help screens for each of the tools.

Using typePerf to Monitor Performance Statistics

typeperf works similarly to the **logman** command in that it monitors the performance data that you tell it to. If **logman** is the command-line analog of Performance Logs and Alerts, then typeperf is the command-line analog of the System Monitor. That is, it's used more for the live collection of data when the command is run (instead of the longer-term collection of data to a file). As in the System Monitor, you can choose to output the data to the screen (although, in this case, the output will go to the command window instead of to a graphical display). To get a list of all of the performance monitoring counters that are available on your system, you can simply run the command `typeperf -q "Memory"`. Note that, as shown in Figure 8-16, the list of counters can sometimes be very long, so you may want to save it to a text file.

Once you've decided what you want to monitor, you can specify the counter(s) on the command line. For example, if you want to display information about the amount of memory paging that is occurring on the system, you can use the following simple command:

```
typeperf "Memory\pages/sec"
```

on the job

It's important to pay attention to the backslash and forward slash characters in `typeperf` commands. The backslash separates counters, objects, and instances. The forward slash character may be used within the name of a counter, object, or instance.

FIGURE 8-16

Viewing counter information using typeperf

```
C:\WINDOWS\system32\cmd.exe                                    _ □ ×

C:\>typeperf -q "Memory"
\Memory\Page Faults/sec
\Memory\Available Bytes
\Memory\Committed Bytes
\Memory\Commit Limit
\Memory\Write Copies/sec
\Memory\Transition Faults/sec
\Memory\Cache Faults/sec
\Memory\Demand Zero Faults/sec
\Memory\Pages/sec
\Memory\Pages Input/sec
\Memory\Page Reads/sec
\Memory\Pages Output/sec
\Memory\Pool Paged Bytes
\Memory\Pool Nonpaged Bytes
\Memory\Page Writes/sec
\Memory\Pool Paged Allocs
\Memory\Pool Nonpaged Allocs
\Memory\Free System Page Table Entries
\Memory\Cache Bytes
\Memory\Cache Bytes Peak
\Memory\Pool Paged Resident Bytes
\Memory\System Code Total Bytes
\Memory\System Code Resident Bytes
\Memory\System Driver Total Bytes
\Memory\System Driver Resident Bytes
\Memory\System Cache Resident Bytes
\Memory\% Committed Bytes In Use
\Memory\Available KBytes
\Memory\Available MBytes
\Memory\Transition Pages RePurposed/sec

The command completed successfully.

C:\>_
```

FIGURE 8-17

Sample output of memory performance information with the typeperf utility

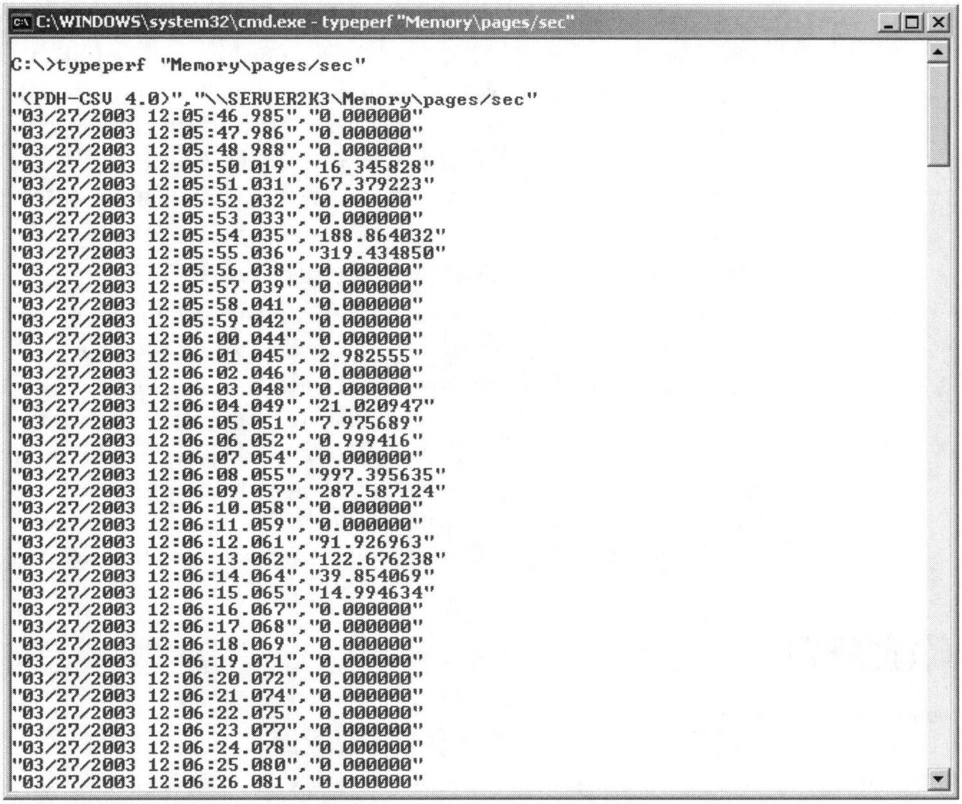

```
C:\WINDOWS\system32\cmd.exe - typeperf "Memory\pages/sec"

C:\>typeperf "Memory\pages/sec"

"(PDH-CSV 4.0)","\\SERVER2K3\Memory\pages/sec"
"03/27/2003 12:05:46.985","0.000000"
"03/27/2003 12:05:47.986","0.000000"
"03/27/2003 12:05:48.988","0.000000"
"03/27/2003 12:05:50.019","16.345828"
"03/27/2003 12:05:51.031","67.379223"
"03/27/2003 12:05:52.032","0.000000"
"03/27/2003 12:05:53.033","0.000000"
"03/27/2003 12:05:54.035","188.864032"
"03/27/2003 12:05:55.036","319.434850"
"03/27/2003 12:05:56.038","0.000000"
"03/27/2003 12:05:57.039","0.000000"
"03/27/2003 12:05:58.041","0.000000"
"03/27/2003 12:05:59.042","0.000000"
"03/27/2003 12:06:00.044","0.000000"
"03/27/2003 12:06:01.045","2.982555"
"03/27/2003 12:06:02.046","0.000000"
"03/27/2003 12:06:03.048","0.000000"
"03/27/2003 12:06:04.049","21.020947"
"03/27/2003 12:06:05.051","7.975689"
"03/27/2003 12:06:06.052","0.999416"
"03/27/2003 12:06:07.054","0.000000"
"03/27/2003 12:06:08.055","997.395635"
"03/27/2003 12:06:09.057","287.587124"
"03/27/2003 12:06:10.058","0.000000"
"03/27/2003 12:06:11.059","0.000000"
"03/27/2003 12:06:12.061","91.926963"
"03/27/2003 12:06:13.062","122.676238"
"03/27/2003 12:06:14.064","39.854069"
"03/27/2003 12:06:15.065","14.994634"
"03/27/2003 12:06:16.067","0.000000"
"03/27/2003 12:06:17.068","0.000000"
"03/27/2003 12:06:18.069","0.000000"
"03/27/2003 12:06:19.071","0.000000"
"03/27/2003 12:06:20.072","0.000000"
"03/27/2003 12:06:21.074","0.000000"
"03/27/2003 12:06:22.075","0.000000"
"03/27/2003 12:06:23.077","0.000000"
"03/27/2003 12:06:24.078","0.000000"
"03/27/2003 12:06:25.080","0.000000"
"03/27/2003 12:06:26.081","0.000000"
```

Sample output from the command is shown in Figure 8-17. To stop the display of information, you can simply press CTRL-C. Of course, the `typeperf` utility has many different command-line options that allow you to output the data to a file or to a relational database.

Using Relog to Manage Captured Performance Information

One of the decisions that you have to make when choosing to monitor performance is where and how the data is collected and stored. For example, you might choose to record CPU and memory statistics every five seconds and then store the results in a single binary file. What if you later decide that you really only needed to collect information every 30 seconds, that you're only interested in CPU performance (and not memory), and the size of the file is too large? Or, what if you really wanted to store the information to a tab-separated value (TSV) file, instead of to a binary file? The `relog` utility is used to perform just those types of tasks. `Relog` can take an existing log file (stored in any format supported by the Performance tool) and output it to any other supported format. Additionally, you can choose to limit the type and amount of data that is copied. For example, you might choose to copy only statistics that are related to memory counters and to copy only every fifth sample of information. Of course, you must have recorded at least this much information in the source file that you're using. For more information, see the help information for the `relog` utility.

Using tracerpt to Analyze Trace Events

Although you can collect a great deal of event-related information using the trace logs functionality in the Performance Logs and Alerts tool, the GUI version of the Performance tool does not provide you with a way to analyze these files. Although third-party tools and utilities can be used to analyze the resulting files, Windows Server 2003 includes the **tracerpt** command-line utility for this purpose. The syntax for the **tracerpt** command (shown in Figure 8-18) takes an existing event trace file as input and then writes the results to an output text file. The text file can then be viewed in Notepad or other utilities in order to find the events of interest.

FIGURE 8-18	
Viewing help for the tracerpt command	

```
C:\>tracerpt -?

Microsoft r TraceRpt.Exe (5.2.3757.0)
c Microsoft Corporation. All rights reserved.

Tracerpt processes binary Event Trace Session log files or real-time streams
from instrumented Event Trace providers and creates a report or a text (CSV)
file describing the events generated.

Usage:
tracerpt { <filename [filename ...]> | -rt <session_name [session_name ...]>
                                } [options]

Parameters:
  <filename [filename ...]>      Event Trace log file to process.

Options:
  -?                             Displays context sensitive help.
  -o [filename]                  Text (CSV) output file. Default is
                                 dumpfile.csv.
  -summary [filename]            Summary report text file (CSV) file. Default
                                 is summary.txt.
  -report [filename]             Text output report file. Default is
                                 workload.txt.
  -rt <session_name [session_name ...]>   Real-time Event Trace Session data
                                 source.
  -config <filename>             Settings file containing command options.
  -y                             Answer yes to all questions without prompting.
  -f <XML|TXT|HTML>              Report format.

Examples:
  tracerpt logfile1.etl logfile2.etl -o -report
  tracerpt logfile.etl -o logdmp.csv -summary logdmp.txt -report logrpt.txt
  tracerpt -rt EVENT_SESSION_1 EVENT_SESSION_2 -o logfile.csv

C:\>
```

Adding and Removing Performance Counters with Lodctr and Unlodctr

As I mentioned earlier in this chapter, the list of available performance objects, counters, and instances on a Windows Server 2003 is not fixed. Various applications and services (for example, Microsoft's Exchange Server) can add performance counters to the list of available statistics. Certain performance counters can be marked by application developers as "extensible." To change settings for these counters (or to add or remove them entirely), you can use the Lodctr and Unlodctr utilities.

In order to create new performance counters, you must write the appropriate logic and information into a dynamic link library (DLL) file. This task, which must be done by programmers, can be performed in various languages such as Microsoft's Visual Basic or Visual C++. Once the DLL has been written (according to specifications available from Microsoft), you can use the Lodctr utility to add to the list of performance statistics that are available for monitoring. You can also use Lodctr to make changes to the explanatory text that defines what the specific counter does.

Similarly, if you need to remove a reference to a performance counter that you added to a system, you can use the Unlodctr utility. This will not delete the DLL that implements the performance monitoring functionality, but it will remove the statistics from the list of available counters to monitor. You can also use these command-line tools to back up and restore a list of all of the performance counters that are available on your computer. Lodctr and Unlodctr are advanced utilities that are designed for use by experienced developers and systems administrators who want to extend the functionality of Windows Server 2003's built-in Performance tools.

Other Performance Monitoring and Optimization Tools

In addition to the System Monitor, Windows Server 2003 comes with several other tools that can be used for monitoring and optimizing performance. In this section, you'll take a look at the Task Manager, Event Viewer, and Network Monitor tools.

The Task Manager

The Windows Task Manager is designed to provide you with a quick snapshot of overall system performance, along with a list of the running applications and processes on the machine. Although you could get the same information using the System Monitor, the Task Manager is often much more easily accessible. To get to the Task Manager, you can right-click the taskbar and select Task Manager. Or, you can access it by pressing CTRL-ALT-DEL (assuming you're logged on to the machine). Finally, you can use the CTRL-SHIFT-ESC keyboard shortcut. There are five tabs in the Task Manager interface, including:

- **Applications**   The Applications tab shows a list of the applications that are currently running on the system (see Figure 8-19). Note that each task is also accompanied by a "status." Should an application "hang," you'll see the status of "Not Responding." In that case, you can simply click the name of the task and select End Task to end the process. You can also use the Windows menu to rearrange the program windows on your desktop.
- **Processes**   The Processes tab (see Figure 8-20) shows a list of all of the processes that are currently running on the local system. This includes tasks launched by user applications, as well as any services or other threads of execution that are running. You can end a process by right-clicking it and selecting End Process. If the process has spawned other processes, you can close them all by selecting End Process Tree.

One feature that is useful in the Task Manager is the ability to change the priority of a running process. For example, if you have an application that takes up a significant amount of processing time, but you're trying to perform some other tasks on that machine, you can lower the priority of that process. There are several built-in priority classes for processes running in Windows Server 2003. They are (in order of highest priority to lowest):

- Realtime
- High
- Above Normal
- Normal
- Below Normal
- Low

FIGURE 8-19

Viewing the
Applications tab
in the Task
Manager

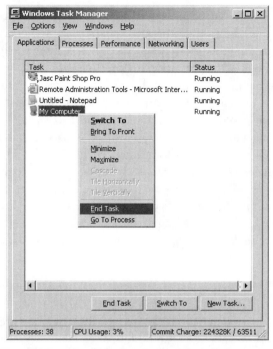

FIGURE 8-20

Viewing the
Processes tab in
the Task Manager

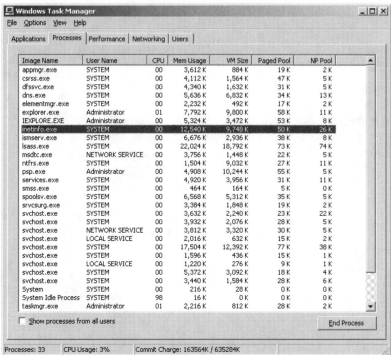

In order to set an application to "high" or "realtime" priority, you must have local Administrator permissions. Note, however, as the Task Manager will warn you, changing the priority of a process may cause problems with certain applications. And, changing an application to "realtime" priority can cause your system to appear to hang, as that process will be able to use up all system resources until it lets go of them. You can also launch applications at different priority levels using the **start** command from a command prompt (type **start /?** to get the syntax for the command). If you're using a machine that has multiple CPUs, you can use the Set Affinity option within the Processes tab to force a process to use one CPU (which can increase overall efficiency by minimizing the overhead related to multiprocessing).

By selecting the View | Select Columns option, you'll be able to select which columns of information you want to see in the Processes tab (see Figure 8-21). You can click any heading to automatically sort the list by that value. For example, you can click the Mem Usage column to sort the list of processes by the amount of memory they're using.

- **Performance** This tab is designed to give you a quick snapshot of overall CPU and memory usage statistics. It is useful for finding out exactly how much of your system's critical resources are in use. Figure 8-22 shows an example of the Performance tab.

FIGURE 8-21

A list of columns that are available for viewing in the Processes tab of the Task Manager

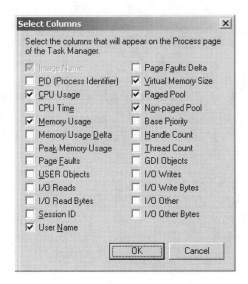

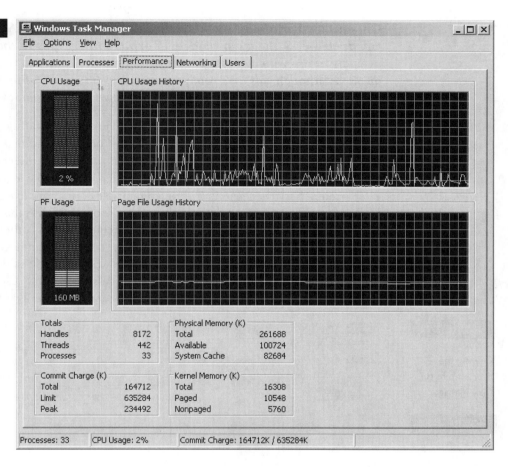

FIGURE 8-22

Viewing the
Performance
tab in the Task
Manager

on the **Job**

If you haven't done so already, you should get used to referring to the Task Manager regularly when you're using your system, as it will give you a good idea of how busy the machine is. To me, not using the Task Manager is like driving without looking out the window!

■ **Networking**   Since networking functionality is such an integral part of all modern operating systems, the Task Manager includes a listing of the network adapters that are currently active on the local system, along with performance information about the network utilization for those adapters. Like the Performance tab, this tab gives you a quick snapshot about the network utilization on the local machine.

on the **Job**

On both the Performance and Networking tabs in the Task Manager, you can double-click the main window to expand the graphs so that they take over the entire window. Just double-click again to revert to the default display. Although this isn't really a standard Windows GUI feature, it is useful if you want to save screen real estate within the window.

■ **Users** As Windows Server 2003 is a true multiuser operating system (that is, multiple users and processes can be logged onto the system at the same time), the Users tab in the Task Manager shows all of the users that are currently logged on to the machine. Note that users can be logged on via a Terminal Services session, or through multiple concurrent logons on the local machine. Figure 8-23 shows an example of the Users tab in the Task Manager. Note that there are options to interact with any other users that are logged on to the machine. For example, you can Disconnect the user (which forcibly disconnects the user, possibly resulting in lost data), Log Off the user (which performs a logoff of the process), and Send A Message to the user (which causes a pop-up message to appear on the user's desktop).

FIGURE 8-23

Viewing the
Users tab in the
Task Manager

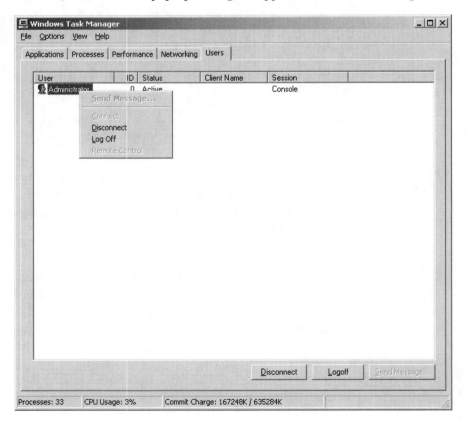

Overall, the Task Manager is a very handy tool for looking at exactly what processes are currently executing on your system, and how your system is doing with regards to resources. If you get used to taking advantage of these features, you'll find yourself spending less time wondering what your machine is "thinking about."

The Event Viewer

Many different applications and processes that run on Windows Server 2003 might need to log information in some way. For example, you might have a backup utility that wants to notify you of the successful completion of a backup job. Or, a service such as the SMTP service might log an error that occurred when attempting to send a message. Rather than have all of these different processes use their own method for recording these messages, the Windows platform includes event log functionality. Through the use of event logs, systems administrators can conveniently look in one place for information about their system.

Figure 8-24 shows a sample view of information displayed in the Event Viewer. Messages that are recorded within the Event Viewer are of three major types:

- **Information**   Log events that are used primarily to inform the administrator of events. For example, a database server might write an Information event when a new database is created.

- **Warning**   Messages that describe a problem that may have occurred in an application. Usually, details about the error are included in the text of the warning.

- **Error**   Specifies that the message is the result of an error that occurred in a process or application. Usually, more details about the specific error are included in the text of the warning.

Several different event logs are available from within Windows. The exact logs that are available are dependent on the exact services that are installed on the system. For example, if the machine is configured as a DNS server, the DNS item will be available. A partial list of event logs includes the following:

- **Application**   The Application event log holds messages that have been generated by applications (programs or services) that are running on the machine. For example, if your Windows Server 2003 is running the Microsoft Fax service, this program can log messages to the application log. Third-party programs may also use the Application log to store event information.

- **Security**   Security-related events (such as auditing information) are stored in the Security log. In order for events to be recorded here, you must first enable auditing, and then you must select which objects and actions should be audited. These topics are covered in detail in Chapter 4.

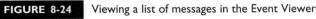

FIGURE 8-24 Viewing a list of messages in the Event Viewer

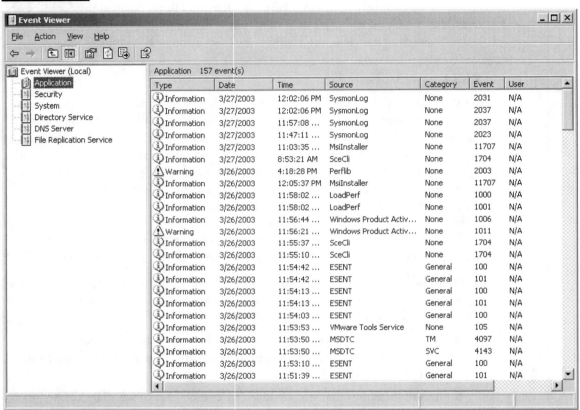

■ **System** The System event log stores information that comes from operating system processes. For example, the Service Control Manager might log a message related to the start of a service. Or, the DHCP service might log an error if it is running out of IP addresses to issue to clients.

■ **Directory Service** If the machine you're examining is a Windows 2000 or Windows 2003 server running as an Active Directory domain controller, you'll see the Directory Service log. This log contains information related to Active Directory replication and other actions that might be of interest to you.

You can view details about any of the events in any of the logs by simply double-clicking the event item. You'll see a dialog box similar to the one shown in Figure 8-25. Note that the descriptive text includes details about the error that occurred, and that it even includes a URL that can be accessed for more information about the error.

FIGURE 8-25

Viewing details
about an item
in the System
event log

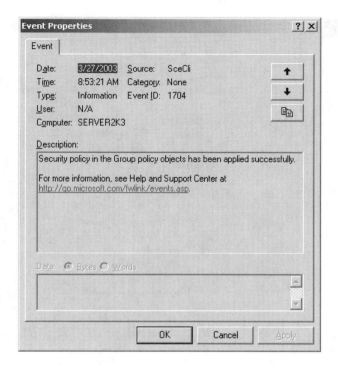

Several configuration options are available for the event logs on a Windows Server 2003 machine. To access the configuration options, simply right-click a specific event log item in the Event Viewer and select Properties. The General tab of the event log properties allows you to change several settings related to the log (see Figure 8-26). The settings in the Log Size section of the dialog box are important, as they govern how much information the log files can store. Here, you can specify the maximum log size (in kilobytes) and the behavior of what should happen when this size is reached. The options are

■ **Overwrite events as needed** This setting will use a "first in, first out" method. That is, when the log is full, the oldest events will automatically be deleted to make room for the newest events. This is a useful option if you want to make sure that you don't miss any new events due to the log file growing too large. However, note that old events will be permanently lost.

■ **Overwrite events older than ___ days** This option specifies that, when the maximum log file size is reached, events older than the specified number of days may be deleted. Note that with this option selected, the log file may still become completely filled and prevent the writing of new events. If that happens, the server will totally stop. Therefore, it's important that the size of the event log is sufficient to hold at least this number of days worth of information.

FIGURE 8-26

Viewing the
properties of an
event log in the
Event Viewer

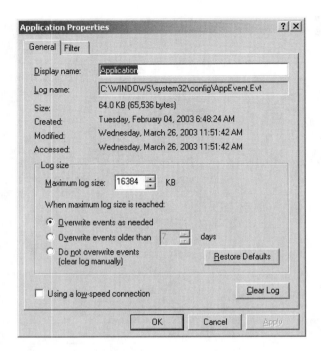

- **Do not overwrite events** This option specifies that events should not be overwritten, even if the log file is full. Use this option only if you require this level of protection for items in the event log, since it depends on the administrator to manually clear out the log periodically.

The second tab in the properties of an event log is the Filter tab (shown in Figure 8-27. This tab can be used to specify which information will be shown in the Event Viewer display. We'll cover the details of working with filters later in this section. For now, however, note that filters to not remove information from the event logs; they only restrict what is shown in the display. Rest assured, if you want to see other information, you can always change the filter settings.

Additionally, you can right-click the name of any event log file and save the contents to a file (in either a binary *.evt format or a comma- or tab-delimited text file). This is useful in case you want to save the events on a server for later analysis.

Since so much important information can be stored in the event logs, it's a good practice to regularly review event information. This is especially true if you suspect that problems are occurring on the server. However, one potential problem with the event logs is that they may contain thousands of items that you're not interested in. Fortunately, the Event Viewer application provides an easy way to filter the data to only what you want to see. Exercise 8-4 walks you through the process of finding specific event information using the Event Viewer.

FIGURE 8-27

Viewing Filter
options properties
of an event log

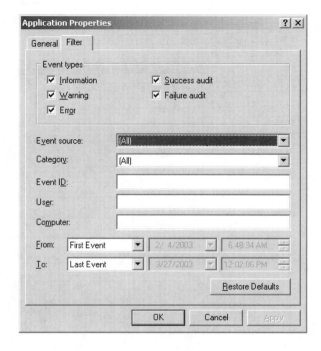

The display of the Event Viewer does not automatically refresh when new events are recorded. Therefore, you should periodically refresh the display using the F5 key, or by selecting Refresh from the Action menu.

EXERCISE 8-4

Finding Event Information Using the Event Viewer

In this exercise, assume that you want to view information about errors that have been logged on the machine.

1. Open the Event Viewer by choosing Start | Programs | Administrative Tools | Event Viewer.

2. Click the System item to view information about all of the log entries in the System log. You will likely have many information messages.

3. In order to narrow down the number of messages that you're looking at, let's filter the display to show only Warnings. To do this, right-click the System item and select Properties. Then, on the Filter tab, uncheck all of the event

types except for Warning (leave all other settings at their defaults). Click OK to apply the settings.

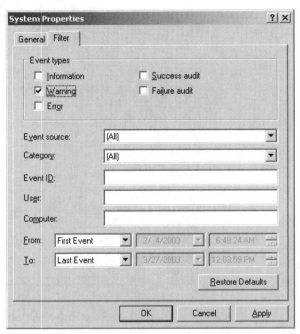

4. You will now see only the Warning messages that have been entered into the System log. To view details about a specific item, simply double-click it. To move between the items, you can use the up and down arrows. Click OK once you're finished viewing the details.

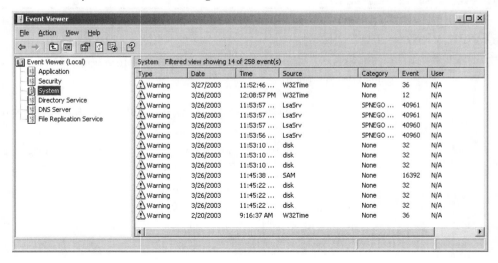

5. To disable the filter of the System log, right-click the System item, select View, and then click All Records. You will now see all of the items in the System log. When you're finished, close the Event Viewer.

Network Monitor

Often, when you're troubleshooting performance-related issues, you'll need to examine information from the network level. For example, a user might complain that access to a specific server is slow during certain times of the day. You might use the System Monitor to check out the server and find that it's performing fine and that the system resources aren't being fully used. The next step might be to take a look at the network.

Windows Server 2003 includes the Network Monitor utility for capturing and analyzing packets that are being transferred on your network. To access Network Monitor, simply click the Network Monitor icon in the Administrative Tools program group (if it's not installed, you can add Network Monitor by selecting the Windows Components option in the Add/Remove Programs Control Panel applet). In order for the Network Monitor to work properly, you must also have the Network Monitor Driver installed in the properties of the network connection(s) that you want to work with. To install the driver, access the properties of the network adapter(s) on which you want to enable the driver, and then click Install | Protocol | Add | Network Monitor Driver.

If your machine has multiple network adapters, you'll first be prompted to choose which network you wish to monitor (if you don't recognize the MAC addresses that are provided, you can map them to network connections by running **IPConfig /All** from the command line). You can start a basic network capture by simply selecting Start from the Capture menu. Network Monitor will then start to record packets that are being transferred on this network interface, along with important network statistics (see Figure 8-28).

on the **Job**

The version of Network Monitor that is included with Windows Server 2003 is the "lite" version. This version is limited to monitoring network traffic that moves to or from the local server. The complete version of Network Monitor is available from Microsoft as a part of the Systems Management Server product (for more information, see http://www.microsoft.com/servers/sms). The major difference in the complete version is that it allows you to monitor traffic that is destined for machines other than the local computer (that is, it puts your network adapter in "promiscuous" mode).

FIGURE 8-28   Capturing network packet information using Network Monitor

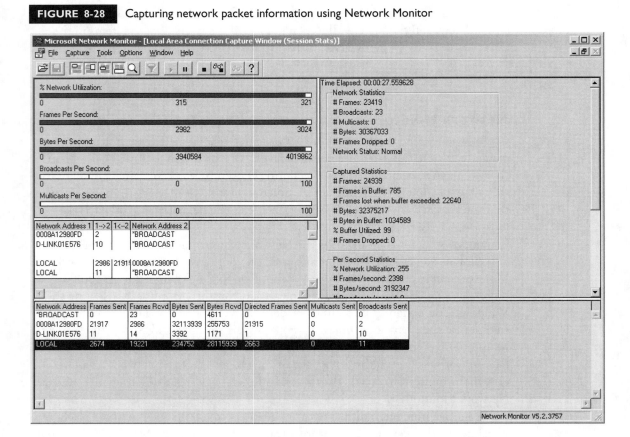

If you're working on a busy network, there's a good chance that you'll experience a lot of traffic that is captured. Fortunately, Network Monitor supports filtering. Filtering can be performed at different levels. First, you can filter the traffic that is to be collected during the capture process. For example, you might want to record only information about TCP/IP packets. Second, you can filter information based on the packets that are collected (after the capture has been stopped). This allows you to further drill down into the types of packets that you're interested in. As shown in Figure 8-29, you can display a great deal of detailed information about every packet that has been collected.

It is beyond the scope of this book to dive into the many details that are related to capturing and analyzing network packets (also called "network sniffing"). However, for the sake of the exam (and for troubleshooting network-related issues), be aware that the Network Monitor is an extremely powerful tool that's at your disposal.

FIGURE 8-29   Viewing detailed information about captured packets

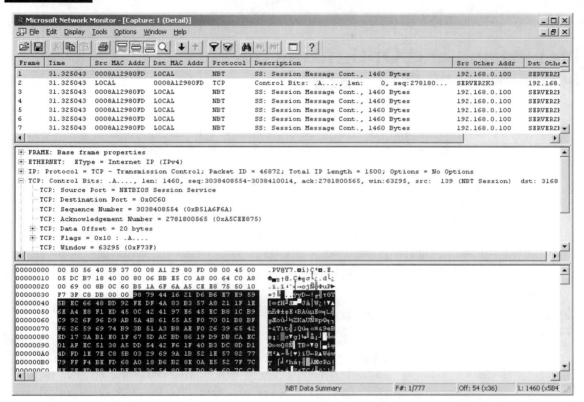

SCENARIO & SOLUTION

You want to measure the overall performance of your server, including CPU and memory utilization.	Use Performance Monitor and add the appropriate objects and counters. You can also create logs of performance activity for longer-term analysis.
You are having performance issues with a few of your servers during certain times of the week. You want to collect more information about the problem.	Create a performance log to collect information about your servers and to save them to disk (or a database). After you have collected sufficient information, use the System Monitor to analyze the saved data.
You want to get a quick snapshot of current CPU and memory utilization.	Use the Task Manager to provide basic information about system resource usage.
Users are complaining about slow performance when logging on in the morning.	Use the System Monitor to track various statistics on your domain controllers. You may want to measure network, CPU, process, and memory statistics to isolate the cause of the problem.

Monitoring and Optimizing Server Hardware Performance

Thus far, you've focused primarily on ways that you can identify and isolate bottlenecks on your machine. For example, you looked at ways for monitoring CPU and memory performance statistics. In this section, you'll look at some ways to apply that information. Specifically, I'll describe some techniques for optimizing system resource usage. It's helpful to note that Microsoft has designed Windows Server 2003 to be a largely "self-tuning" system. That is, the operating system is designed to monitor its own performance and to make adjustments automatically. The result is that, for the most part, your systems will manage their own resources. With that said, however, there are several settings that can improve performance for the systems in your environment. Let's start by taking a look at ways to optimize CPU performance.

Optimizing CPU Performance

CPU resources can often be a bottleneck on very busy servers (especially those that often run processing-intensive operations such as Microsoft's SQL Server 2000). If your CPUs are consistently running at a high percentage of utilization (for example, above 100 percent utilization for several hours at a time), you may have a CPU bottleneck. To a large extent, the performance of the CPU in your servers is managed automatically.

on the job

Every once in a while, I'll run into systems administrators that panic when they see their servers spike the CPU at a 100 percent utilization for short periods of time. However, this is perfectly normal—various processes and services that are requested by users can cause the CPUs to become very active for a brief period of time. In fact, CPU spikes can be a good thing. This is because, if the CPU utilization is at 100 percent, it shows that there are no other bottlenecks on the system. Overall, be realistic with what you monitor, and be sure to interpret the information you collect objectively.

If you find that your machine is consistently starved for processing resources, you have a few options. First, if your server hardware supports it, you may be able to add additional CPUs (or upgrade existing ones). Adding additional processors can improve performance dramatically for certain types of applications. For example, Microsoft's SQL Server 2000 is designed to take advantage of multiple CPUs, and busy SQL Server installations can often benefit from additional processors. Other applications and services may not be able to take full advantage of multiple CPUs. Regardless of the application, however, you should know that the speed increases that come from adding CPUs to most machines are not linear. That is, a system that has a single processor running at 1.5 GHz will often outperform a system that has two 750 MHz chips. This is due to the overhead associated with distributing threads and processing cycles between processors (and, to some extent, the lack of Windows software that is truly designed to take advantage of multiprocessor hardware).

Another option to improve CPU performance is to upgrade the processor(s) that is/are in your machine. Since CPU prices fall quickly after their introduction, you might find a CPU upgrade to be very cost-effective. However, be sure to find out which CPU upgrades are supported by the server hardware manufacturer, and ask how performing the upgrade might affect your warranty. In addition to the clock speed of the CPU, be sure to consider how much Level 2 (L2) cache the chip has, as this can have a dramatic effect on performance. Overall, there are ways to improve CPU performance, but the largest gains will be made through hardware upgrades.

Optimizing Disk Performance

An important resource on most busy servers is disk I/O. Many operations require the system to read and write data to/from the hard disk. Accessing data from hard disk is far slower than accessing data from other forms of memory (such as the CPU cache or physical RAM). Therefore, disk I/O can often be a bottleneck, and optimizing it can be very useful in troubleshooting performance problems. You can detect disk I/O performance problems by examining various counters within the Physical Disk and Logical Disk objects. For example, if the "% Disk Time" value is consistently high, you may have a performance issue related to disk I/O. Or, the server may be spending significant time performing virtual memory paging.

One option for resolving disk performance issues is to upgrade the disk subsystem. Although the upgrade can be costly, it can often greatly improve overall server performance. For example, you might consider upgrading an IDE-based hard disk system to one that uses SCSI disks (SCSI disks usually offer lowered data access times, and SCSI controllers can efficiently handle many physical devices on the same bus). SCSI controllers also provide the added benefit of offloading most of the CPU overhead to the disk controller. Or, you might want to upgrade to a hardware-based RAID storage system (see Chapter 5 for more information about the performance of RAID).

Simple maintenance can also improve disk performance. You may have noticed that, over time, disk performance can sometimes decrease. This is caused by the fact that files and file systems tend to get fragmented. All data on a hard disk is stored in sectors. Ideally, files will be stored in contiguous sectors on the hard disk. When this is the case, the hard disk can read the data in a quick operation, without having to move around to different areas of the disk. However, in the real world, files get fragmented through the creation and deletion of portions of data that are different in size. The end result is that the hard disk must do additional work in order to obtain the data it needs from the disk.

Fortunately, there's a simple solution: disk defragmentation. Windows Server 2003 includes a basic, built-in defragmentation tool that can reorganize the physical storage of data to improve performance. The changes that are made through the defragmentation process are completely invisible to users, applications, and processes that are running on the machine.

on the
Job

Although the version of the defragmentation tool that is included with Windows Server 2003 does a reasonably good job, it leaves several features to be desired. For example, you can't defragment a disk that's located on a remote computer. And, you can't schedule defragmentation to work automatically, in the background. Third-party utilities can file in some of these gaps and can perform additional functions such as decrementing the paging file and the Master File Table (MFT). For more information, see the Executive Software web site at http://www.executivesoftware.com, the Winternals web site (http://www.winternals.com), and the Raxco Software web site at http://www.perfectdisk.com.

EXERCISE 8-5

Using the Disk Defragmenter Tool

1. Open the Computer Management snap-in by choosing Start | Programs | Administrative Tools | Computer Management. Alternatively, you can click the My Computer icon on your desktop (if it's present), and select Manage.

2. Under the System Tools node, click Disk Defragmenter. You'll see a list of all of the local hard disks on your system.

3. To check the defragmentation level of one of the partitions, select a partition from the top list. Then, click Analyze. The dialog box will return a recommendation about the level of fragmentation of this partition. To view details, click View Report. When finished, close the report window.

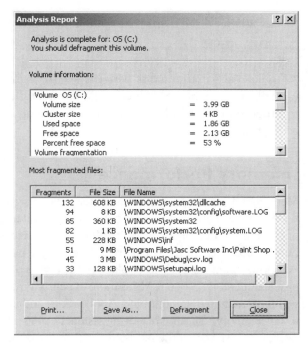

4. To defragment the disk, simply click Defragment. The graphical display will show the progress of the operation. Note that defragmenting a hard disk can be resource-intensive (especially with respect to disk I/O and CPU utilization), so be sure to perform this operation on a nonproduction machine or during a time of little activity.

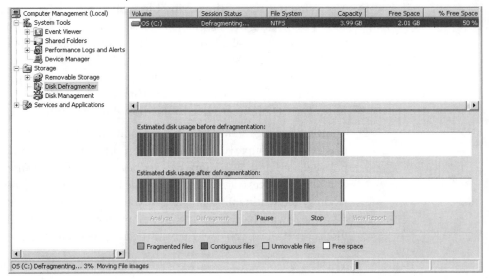

> 5. When finished, close the Computer Management tool.

You can also optimize disk performance through the use of RAID technology (described in Chapter 5), which can allow multiple physical hard disks to work together to increase disk efficiency throughout and to reduce contention and data access times.

Optimizing Memory Performance

Memory is a very important resource for server systems, and Windows Server 2003 is no exception. Fortunately, a lot of the memory management that's required by the operating system is done automatically. For example, upon installation, Windows Server 2003 determines a default location for the paging file. The paging file is used by Windows operating systems to place certain types of data on the hard disk instead of in physical memory. Since RAM is more expensive than hard disk space, most servers will have a limited amount of it. Applications and processes know only that they're using "memory," and the operating system decides whether that memory physically resides in RAM or on the hard disk (within the paging file). To put things in perspective, accessing data from memory can be hundreds of thousands of times faster than accessing data from a hard disk.

There are a few ways to optimize performance settings related to memory. These include

- **Verifying the size of the paging file** Microsoft recommends that the total size of the paging file should be at least 1.5 times the amount of physical memory that's installed in the machine. For example, if your Windows Server 2003 contains 512MB (approximately 0.5GB) of physical memory, you'll want to make sure that the total size of the paging file is approximately 750MB (0.75GB). This will ensure that Windows will have sufficient space in the paging file to provide for memory-hungry applications.

- **Splitting the paging file** If you have multiple physical disks on your system, you may be able to improve performance by splitting the paging file across multiple physical hard disks. This improves performance by allowing multiple physical hard disks to access data at the same time (thereby reducing the average seeking, reading, and writing time). Note that you should split the paging file only across multiple *physical* hard disks. If you attempt to split the paging file across logical disks or partitions, you could actually decrease performance considerably.

- **Monitoring memory usage**   As you saw earlier in this chapter, the System Monitor provides you with several counters and objects that can be used to monitor memory performance. Specific objects of interest include the Memory object and the Paging File object, both of which can give you an idea of how well your system is using memory and if an upgrade might help.

You can easily make changes to Paging File settings by accessing the System icon in the Control Panel (or by right-clicking the My Computer icon and selecting Properties). The settings can be accessed by clicking the Advanced tab, and then on Settings in the Performance section (see Figure 8-30). Note that you can optimize memory usage for background services (the default for servers), or for applications. You can also specify whether memory usage should favor Programs (the default setting for servers), or the system cache.

Finally, by clicking Change in the Virtual Memory section, you can change paging file options. Figure 8-31 shows the options that include the minimum and maximum paging file sizes for each partition on the local machine. You can manually configure a size, allow the operating system to set the size, or choose to disable the paging file entirely. The latter option is highly discouraged and should be used only for very specific situations.

FIGURE 8-30

Viewing advanced systems settings

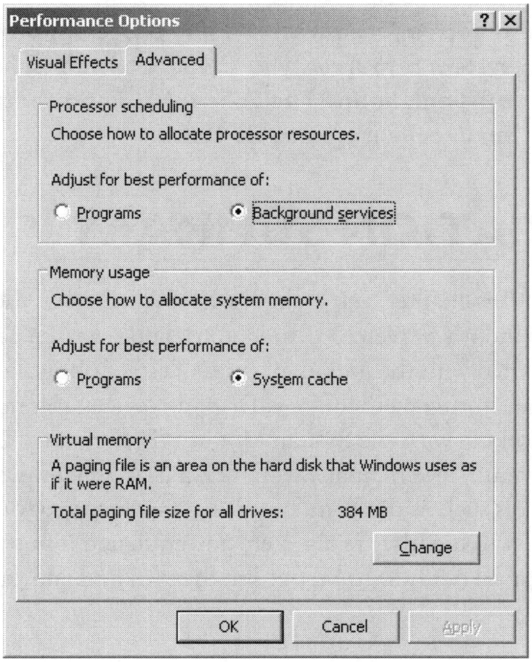

FIGURE 8-31

Viewing paging
file settings

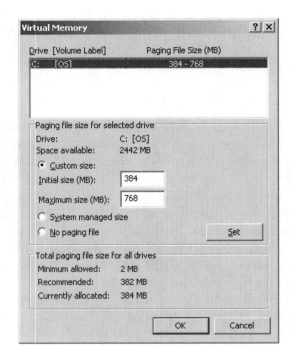

If you're faced with running processes or applications that use significant system resources, you should consider scheduling them to run during off-peak hours. The Scheduled Tasks feature in Windows Server 2003 is an excellent way to do this.

CERTIFICATION SUMMARY

In this chapter, you looked at how you can use the tools and utilities included with Windows Server 2003 to monitor and optimize performance of your servers. You started with the important topic of establishing and following an organized performance monitoring methodology. Drawing on that information, you looked at techniques for working with the System Monitor, Performance Logs and Alerts, Task Manager, and Event Viewer. Finally, you took a look at a few ways to improve performance using tools such as the Windows disk defragmenter. Although all of these tools are fairly easy to use, they're also very powerful, and it's up to you, the systems administrator, to find out how to best utilize them to find and troubleshoot performance issues.

✓ TWO-MINUTE DRILL

Monitor System Performance Using the System Monitor

❑ A good performance monitoring and optimization methodology involves establishing a performance baseline, identifying bottlenecks, and making one change at a time.

❑ The System Monitor allows you to monitor performance statistics that are organized into objects, counters, and instances.

❑ The System Monitor includes several views that can be used for capturing and analyzing information, including graph, histogram, and report views.

Track Performance Using Performance Logs and Alerts

❑ You can configure alerts to fire at performance thresholds that you specify.

❑ Alert information can be written to the System event log, and information can be read using the Event Viewer administrative tool.

❑ The Task Manager can provide a quick snapshot of system performance, including data about running applications, memory usage, and CPU utilization.

❑ The `LogMan`, `TypePerf`, `Relog`, and `TraceRpt` command-line utilities can be used to implement and manage performance monitoring from a command prompt.

Monitor and Optimize Server Hardware Performance

❑ Performance Logs and Alerts can be used to track performance statistics over time, and the resulting log files can be analyzed with the System Monitor.

❑ You can monitor important server subsystems using the Network, Memory, Process, Logical Disk, and Physical Disk objects.

❑ Application developers can add their own performance monitoring objects to Windows Server 2003.

❑ You can use Network Monitor to view performance statistics at the network level.

❑ By configuring Windows Server 2003's CPU, memory, and paging file settings, you can improve overall system performance.

SELF TEST

The following questions will help you measure your understanding of the material presented in this chapter. Read all the choices carefully because there might be more than one correct answer. Choose all correct answers for each question, unless stated otherwise.

Monitor System Performance Using the System Monitor

1. Based on past performance monitoring information, it appears that your server is experiencing excessive network utilization. The server has multiple network adapters, and you want to determine which one is receiving the most traffic. Which of the following types of System Monitor statistics allows you to specify which network adapter you want to monitor?

   A. Objects
   B. Counters
   C. Instances
   D. Logs
   E. None of the above

2. Newman wants to create a console in which he can monitor memory-related performance statistics in real time for three different Windows Server 2003 computers. How can he do this with the least effort?

   A. Open the System Monitor on each computer and add the appropriate counters to track.
   B. Open the Performance Logs and Alerts tool on each computer and add the appropriate counters to track.
   C. Open the System Monitor on one server and add counters from all three servers to this view.
   D. Open multiple instances of the Task Manager on one server and configure each to monitor one of the servers.
   E. Open instances of the Task Manager on each server and use the Remote Desktop for Administration feature to monitor the servers.

Track Performance Using Performance Logs and Alerts

3. Sharon is a systems administrator who is responsible for managing several file servers for her organization. Recently, users have complained that, during peak periods of activity, it can take a long time to retrieve documents from two of these servers. Sharon suspects that the problem is due to intermittent periods of high disk throughout. Which of the following Windows Server

2003 features can she use to write event log information whenever a certain level of disk throughput is exceeded?

A. Event Viewer

B. Alerts

C. Trace logs

D. Counter logs

E. None of the above

4. You have recently defined eight different performance-based alerts on a particular Windows Server 2003 machine. The alerts have been active for several days. When you use the Event Viewer to examine the server log files, you find that there are thousands of items in the log files. Which of the following methods will allow you to view only performance-based alert events?

A. Select the Application event log and delete events that do not have a source of "Performance Events."

B. Select the System event log and delete events that do not have a source of "Performance Events."

C. Select the Application event log and use filtering options to view only the event IDs of interest.

D. Select the System event log and use filtering options to view only the event IDs of interest.

E. None of the above.

5. After monitoring a production Windows Server 2003 database server over a period of two weeks, you see that frequently, the CPU utilization for all four processors on the server will remain at, or above, 95 percent for several hours at a time. Upon closer monitoring, you find that the average number of memory pages/sec over the two-week interval is less than 1. You also notice that network utilization is rarely over 10 percent and that the %Disk Time levels are low. Based on this information, which of the following types of upgrades will most likely result in the greatest performance increase?

A. Upgrade the CPU(s).

B. Add additional memory.

C. Add a network card.

D. Upgrade to a newer version of the database server software.

E. Improve the disk I/O subsystem.

6. Which of the following tasks can be directly performed using performance-based alerts? (Choose all that apply.)

A. Automatically running a batch file that reboots the server when the CPU utilization exceeds 90 percent.

    B. Automatically running an executable file that deletes temporary files when there is less than 5 percent of free disk space on a logical volume.

    C. Writing an event to the System log when paging file usage exceeds 85 percent.

    D. Writing an event to the Application log when a specific process uses more than 10 percent of total CPU time.

    E. Send an e-mail message to a group of systems administrators whenever an alert fires.

    F. Automatically starting the System Monitor whenever bytes sent/sec over a specific network adapter exceeds 2.0 megabytes per second.

    G. Firing performance-based alerts only during normal working hours.

7. Kramer has recently noticed that there is a large amount of disk activity on one of the physical hard disks on a Windows Server 2003 file server computer. The particular hard disk contains multiple logical volumes. Kramer wants to determine which of the logical volumes is receiving the most disk activity. Which of the following System Monitor statistics will allow him to track the information that he needs to isolate this problem? (Choose all that apply.)

    A. Physical Disk | % Disk Time

    B. Physical Disk | % Disk Write Time

    C. Logical Disk | % Disk Time

    D. Logical Disk | % Disk Read Time

    E. Logical Disk | Disk Bytes/sec

8. Elaine wants to track CPU utilization over a period of five minutes. Which of the following System Monitor views will allow her to do this?

    A. Chart

    B. Histogram

    C. Report

    D. Current Activity

    E. None of the above

9. Recently, users have complained that during particular times of the month, server performance is very slow. Jerry suspects that the problem is due to excessive swapping of information from memory to disk, so he decides to track information about the Memory | Pages/sec counter over time. However, the problem occurs very rarely. Which of the following methods should Jerry implement to track down the problem?

    A. System Monitor | Graph View

    B. System Monitor | Reports View

    C. Performance Logs and Alerts | Alerts

D. Performance Logs and Alerts | Trace Logs

E. Performance Logs and Alerts | Counter Logs

10. Hunter was running an application on a Windows Server 2003 machine, and now it doesn't appear to respond to any keyboard or mouse input. Additionally, the display is not being refreshed. The application has remained in this state for almost five minutes. Also, the CPU utilization on the server has remained at 100 percent for the entire time that the application has not been responding. The application appears to be using a large portion of overall processing time. Which of these actions should Hunter take to resolve the issue without affecting other applications on the server?

A. Wait until the application begins responding again.

B. Restart the server.

C. Use System Monitor to end the process.

D. Use the Task Manager to end the process.

E. Do nothing; Windows Server 2003 will automatically end the application.

F. Log off the computer.

Monitor and Optimize Server Hardware Performance

11. Recently, your environment has been seeing excessive network traffic from various client computers. Your manager has asked you to determine from which computers the excessive traffic is originating, and to determine what type of packets are being sent. Which of the following tools would allow you to most easily do this?

A. Network Monitor

B. Task Manager

C. System Monitor

D. Performance Logs and Alerts

E. Event Viewer

F. None of the above

12. You are attempting to monitor performance statistics using the System Monitor. On the local computer, you are able to add several counters that are related to SQL Server. You now want to monitor performance on a remote machine. Both computers are running Windows Server 2003. From the local machine, when you try to add SQL Server–related performance counters from the remote computer, the SQL Server–related objects do not appear in the drop-down list (although many other objects do appear). What is the most likely reason for this?

A. You do not have the appropriate Windows Server 2003 permissions on the local computer.

B. You do not have the appropriate Windows Server 2003 permissions on the remote computer.

   C.   You do not have the appropriate SQL Server permissions on the local computer.

   D.   You do not have the appropriate SQL Server permissions on the remote computer.

   E.   The network connection between the two computers is not functioning.

   F.   SQL Server is not installed on the remote computer.

   G.   None of the above.

LAB QUESTION

You are a systems administrator for a medium-sized company. You're responsible for managing everything from network design and implementation to the daily administration of file servers for the Marketing department. During the past year, the organization has been growing very quickly, and many new employees are added every month. Overall, things have been working properly. However, recently, you've started to receive complaints about overall performance.

   You decide to start talking to various users about the specific problems that they're experiencing. Specific complaints include the following:

- ■ "Logging on to the network on Monday mornings can take several minutes. Also, on days following a Holiday, the network seems to be extremely slow."

- ■ "When I try to access files stored on the Marketing07 server, performance is pretty good. However, when I try to get even the smallest files from Marketing03, I have to wait a long time. This seems to be the case, even when I'm working on weekends."

- ■ "At various times during the day, I get 'page not found' errors in my browser. However, I know that my system is working properly since reloading the page often solves the problem. The issues seem to be random."

Other users seem to have similar complaints about overall performance when connecting to your company's file servers. Drawing on this information, describe the process and tools in Windows Server 2003 that you can use to troubleshoot the problem.

SELF TEST ANSWERS

Monitor System Performance Using the System Monitor

1. ☑ **C.** Instances are subsets of certain counters, and they allow you to specify for which item you want to monitor statistics. In this case, you could monitor instances for each of the network adapters separately, or you could choose the "_Total" instance to view overall performance information for all network adapters in the server.

   ☒ A and B are incorrect because they would not allow the monitoring of specific network adapters. D is incorrect because this is not a type of performance statistic.

2. ☑ **C.** The easiest way to monitor performance information for multiple servers is to use the System Monitor's ability to get statistics from remote computers. This will allow Newman to view all of the information that he needs from a single console.

   ☒ A and E are incorrect because, although they do meet the requirements, they also require significant effort to implement and manage. B is incorrect because this will not provide a way to monitor statistics in real time. D is incorrect because the Task Manager can be used only to view information about the local computer.

Track Performance Using Performance Logs and Alerts

3. ☑ **B.** Through the use of performance-based alerts, Sharon can configure a threshold for the one or more disk utilization counters. Whenever the threshold is exceeded, an entry will be written to the System event log.

   ☒ A is incorrect because the Event Viewer cannot be used to write events to the log. C and D are incorrect because they do not create events in the server log.

4. ☑ **D.** Performance-based alert information is stored in the System event log. To make the information in this log more manageable, you can filter the events to view only the event IDs that are of interest.

   ☒ A and C are incorrect because alert information is written only to the System event log. A and B are both incorrect because the Event Viewer does not allow you to delete events.

5. ☑ **A.** Since the CPU utilization is the only parameter that is high, it's likely that the server could benefit from CPU upgrades (if the hardware platform supports this). Note that having all four CPUs spike to 100 percent for short periods of time is not necessarily a problem. However, in this case, the complete CPU utilization lasted for long periods of time.

   ☒ B, C, and E are unlikely to help, because the performance information indicates that these subsystems are not bottlenecks. D may help in some cases, but without further information, it cannot be considered the most likely to result in a performance increase.

6. ☑ **A, B, C, F,** and **G.** All of these are features or actions that can be performed using performance-based alerts. For example, you can run a batch file based on an alert (as in options A and B), you can specify that a log entry should be written to the System log (as in option C), you can automatically start a System Monitor trace (as in option F), and you can specify a schedule for when alerts should run (as in option G).

   ☒ D is incorrect because performance-based alerts are always written to the System log. E is incorrect because, through the use of performance-based alerts, you cannot automatically send e-mail messages to a group of systems administrators. You can, however, create a batch file or a script file that performs this function and then specify that it should run whenever the alert is fired.

7. ☑ **C, D,** and **E.** By monitoring various counters and instances of the Logical Disk object, Kramer can determine which of the logical volumes is experiencing the most activity.

   ☒ A and B are incorrect because the physical disk counters provide instances only for physical disks. Since Kramer is already aware of which physical disk is experiencing the most activity, this will not help isolate the problem.

8. ☑ **A.** Only the Chart view in the System Monitor will graph the data over time.

   ☒ B and C are incorrect because these options would not provide the information to view the statistics over time. D is incorrect because this is not a System Monitor view.

9. ☑ **E.** The counter logs feature of the Performance Logs and Alerts functionality will allow Jerry to track and record data over time. He can then use the System Monitor to analyze the captured information and isolate periods of excessive swapping.

   ☒ A and B are incorrect because the System Monitor would not easily allow Jerry to collect information over the period of a month. Although the sampling interval could be reduced, this would likely result in the loss of important statistics. C and D are incorrect because they do not allow for tracking the appropriate counter over time.

10. ☑ **D.** Since the process is using significant CPU resources, and it hasn't responded, the best approach would be for Hunter to use the End Process command on the Processes tab of the Task Manager. Generally, this will not affect other applications that are running on the server.

   ☒ A is incorrect because it does not appear that the application will return control to the user. Even if it did do so eventually, the current CPU burden must be significantly decreasing overall performance. The same is true for option E, since Windows Server 2003 may never automatically shut down the application. Options B and F are incorrect because they could affect other applications on the computer. Finally, C is incorrect because the System Monitor cannot be used to stop processes.

Monitor and Optimize Server Hardware Performance

11. ☑ **A.** By using Network Monitor, you can determine the source of various types of network traffic. You can also drill down into the details of network packets to see exactly what types of information are being transmitted. Note, however, that with the version of Network Monitor that is included with Windows Server 2003, you can monitor only broadcasts and traffic that is destined to the server on which you are performing monitoring.

☒ **B, C, and D** are incorrect because, while these tools will provide basic network performance information, they do not provide the level of detail required in the scenario. E is incorrect because the Event Viewer does not allow for tracking network packet information.

12. ☑ **F.** If SQL Server is not installed on a computer, the SQL Server performance monitor counters will not be available. This is the most likely reason that you can access other performance statistics, but not those related to SQL Server.

☒ **A, B, C, and D** are all incorrect because neither Windows Server 2003 nor SQL Server permissions would allow you to view some performance objects and not others. Similarly, E is incorrect because you are able to access some performance objects on the remote computer. If the network connection was down, you would not be able to connect to that machine at all.

LAB ANSWER

Overall, the information that is provided by your users isn't conclusive. There are many factors that could be causing the problems that they're complaining about.
More likely, there are several *different* problems that must be solved to address their concerns. However, when using Windows Server 2003, you have several tools and techniques for determining the performance issues.

So what's the "correct" answer to this question? The single most important aspect of troubleshooting any performance-related problem is to take an organized and methodical approach toward isolating the issues. Through an effective process of elimination, you should be able to pinpoint the problem (or at the very least, determine what the problem is not). Based on that information, you can focus your efforts on the more likely causes.

In this specific scenario, it seems like performance issues are occurring at the network level and on at least some of the Marketing file servers. Since one user mentioned that the Marketing03 server is consistently slow, you can start there. To get a quick snapshot of the server's performance, take a look at the Task Manager. You'll be able to check the immediate CPU utilization and memory usage. It's likely that you'll need more details, so a good place to start collecting information is the System Monitor. Perhaps by monitoring CPU, disk I/O, memory, and network statistics, you can get a good picture of why the server is slow. Since the user mentioned that Marketing07 seems to be performing well, you can compare the statistics collected from both servers. It's likely that you'll find that a hardware upgrade would help. Or, you might find that all of the most frequently used files are stored on Marketing03, and that moving these files to another machine could dramatically improve performance.

In the area of network issues, there are some indications that you might be experiencing some packet loss (based on the comments from the user who mentioned that she would intermittently receive "page not found" errors). Through the use of Network Monitor, you can capture statistics for several hours throughout the day. Specifically, you might want to look for any dropped or corrupted packets that may show up from time to time.

Should the problem prove to be more elusive, you'll probably need to revisit the System Monitor and start collecting data over time (for example, days or weeks) to spot any trends in performance. When you have a good guess about how to improve performance, be sure to implement one change at a time and then to retest performance. This process will help ensure that you're making progress in your efforts.

Through an organized approach, you can take a seemingly chaotic situation and determine how to isolate and fix the issue. If all goes well, you'll quickly and easily resolve the issue. In the worst case, you can rest assured that you're taking an organized approach to eliminating potential causes of the issue.

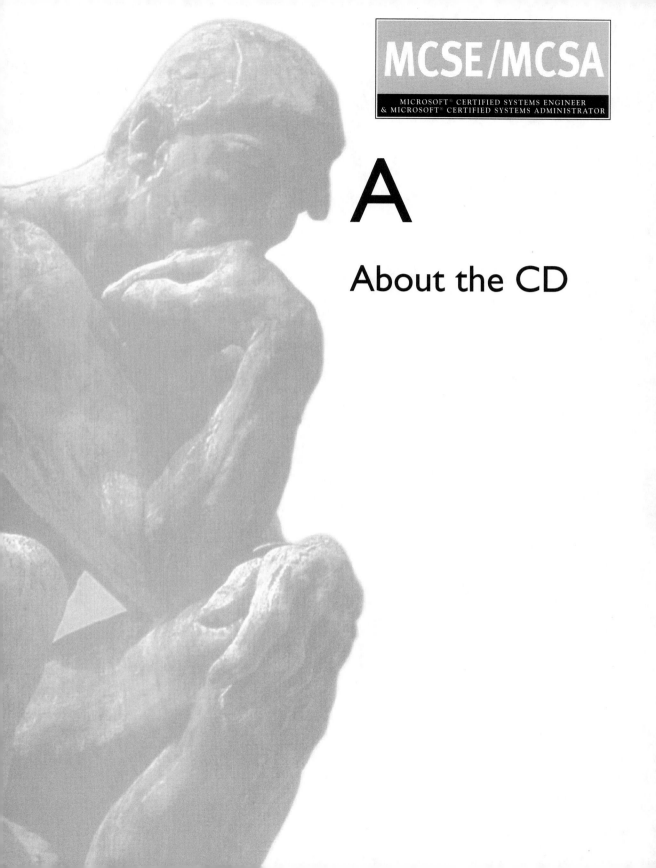

A

About the CD

The CD-ROM included with this book comes complete with MasterExam, MasterSim, CertCam movie clips, the electronic version of the book, and Session #1 of LearnKey's on-line training. The software is easy to install on any Windows 98/NT/2000/XP computer and must be installed to access the MasterExam and MasterSim features. You may, however, browse the electronic book and CertCams directly from the CD without installation. To register for LearnKey's online training and a second bonus MasterExam, simply click the Online Training link on the Main Page and follow the directions to the free online registration.

System Requirements

Software requires Windows 98 or higher and Internet Explorer 5.0 or above and 20 MB of hard disk space for full installation. The Electronic book requires Adobe Acrobat Reader. To access the Online Training from LearnKey you must have RealPlayer Basic 8 or RealOne Plugin, which will be automatically installed when you launch the on-line training.

LearnKey Online Training

The **LearnKey Online Training** link will allow you to access online training from Osborne.Onlineexpert .com. The first session of this course is provided at no charge. Additional Session for this course and other courses may be purchased directly from www.LearnKey.com or by calling 800 865-0165.

The first time that you run the Training, you will required to Register with the online product. Follow the instructions for a first time user. Please make sure to use a valid e-mail address.

Prior to running the Online Training you will need to add the Real Plugin and the RealCBT plugin to your system. This will automatically be facilitated to your system when you run the training the first time.

Installing and Running MasterExam and MasterSim

If your computer CD-ROM drive is configured to auto run, the CD-ROM will automatically start up upon inserting the disk. From the opening screen you may install MasterExam or MasterSim by pressing the *MasterExam* or *MasterSim* buttons. This will begin the installation process and create a program group named "LearnKey." To run MasterExam or MasterSim use START | PROGRAMS | LEARNKEY. If the auto run feature did not launch your CD, browse to the CD and Click on the LaunchTraining.exe icon.

MasterExam

MasterExam provides you with a simulation of the actual exam. The number of questions, the type of questions, and the time allowed are intended to be an accurate representation of the exam environment. You have the option to take an open book exam, including hints, references, and answers, a closed book exam, or the timed MasterExam simulation.

When you launch MasterExam, a digital clock display will appear in the upper left-hand corner of your screen. The clock will continue to count down to zero unless you choose to end the exam before the time expires.

MasterSim

The MasterSim is a set of interactive labs that will provide you with a wide variety of tasks to allow the user to experience the software environment even if the software is not installed. Once you have installed the MasterSim you may access it quickly through this CD launch page or you may also access it through START | PROGRAMS | LEARNKEY.

Electronic Book

The entire contents of the Study Guide are provided in PDF. Adobe's Acrobat Reader has been included on the CD.

CertCam

CertCam .AVI clips provide detailed examples of key certification objectives. These clips walk you step-by-step through various system configurations. You can access the clips directly from the CertCam table of contents by pressing the CertCam button on the Main Page.

The CertCam .AVI clips are recorded and produced using TechSmith's Camtasia Producer. Since .AVI clips can be very large, ExamSim uses TechSmith's special AVI Codec to compress the clips. The file named tsccvid.dll is copied to your Windows\System folder during the first auto run. If the .AVI clip runs with audio but no video, you may need to re-install the file from the CD-ROM. Browse to the PROGRAMS | CERTCAMS folder, and run TSCC.

Help

A help file is provided through the help button on the main page in the lower left hand corner. Individual help features are also available through MasterExam, MasterSim, and LearnKey's Online Training.

Removing Installation(s)

MasterExam and MasterSim are installed to your hard drive. For BEST results for removal of programs use the START | PROGRAMS | LEARNKEY | UNINSTALL options to remove MasterExam or MasterSim.

If you desire to remove the Real Player use the Add/Remove Programs Icon from your Control Panel. You may also remove the LearnKey training program from this location.

Technical Support

For questions regarding the technical content of the electronic book, MasterExam, or CertCams, please visit www.osborne.com or email customer.service@mcgraw-hill.com. For customers outside the 50 United States, email: international_cs@mcgraw-hill.com.

LearnKey Technical Suport

For technical problems with the software (installation, operation, removing installations), and for questions regarding LearnKey Online Training and MasterSim content, please visit www.learnkey.com or email techsupport@learnkey.com.

INDEX

K

L

M

N

P

T

INTERNATIONAL CONTACT INFORMATION

AUSTRALIA
McGraw-Hill Book Company
Australia Pty. Ltd.
TEL +61-2-9900-1800
FAX +61-2-9878-8881
http://www.mcgraw-hill.com.au
books-it_sydney@mcgraw-hill.com

CANADA
McGraw-Hill Ryerson Ltd.
TEL +905-430-5000
FAX +905-430-5020
http://www.mcgraw-hill.ca

**GREECE, MIDDLE EAST, & AFRICA
(Excluding South Africa)**
McGraw-Hill Hellas
TEL +30-210-6560-990
TEL +30-210-6560-993
TEL +30-210-6560-994
FAX +30-210-6545-525

MEXICO (Also serving Latin America)
McGraw-Hill Interamericana Editores
S.A. de C.V.
TEL +525-1500-5108
FAX +525-117-1589
http://www.mcgraw-hill.com.mx
carlos_ruiz@mcgraw-hill.com

SINGAPORE (Serving Asia)
McGraw-Hill Book Company
TEL +65-6863-1580
FAX +65-6862-3354
http://www.mcgraw-hill.com.sg
mghasia@mcgraw-hill.com

SOUTH AFRICA
McGraw-Hill South Africa
TEL +27-11-622-7512
FAX +27-11-622-9045
robyn_swanepoel@mcgraw-hill.com

SPAIN
McGraw-Hill/
Interamericana de España, S.A.U.
TEL +34-91-180-3000
FAX +34-91-372-8513
http://www.mcgraw-hill.es
professional@mcgraw-hill.es

**UNITED KINGDOM, NORTHERN,
EASTERN, & CENTRAL EUROPE**
McGraw-Hill Education Europe
TEL +44-1-628-502500
FAX +44-1-628-770224
http://www.mcgraw-hill.co.uk
emea_queries@mcgraw-hill.com

ALL OTHER INQUIRIES Contact:
McGraw-Hill/Osborne
TEL +1-510-420-7700
FAX +1-510-420-7703
http://www.osborne.com
omg_international@mcgraw-hill.com

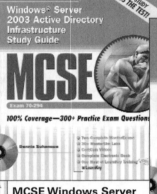